WORKS OF
RICHARD SIBBES

Works of
RICHARD SIBBES

Volume 2

*

EDITED BY
Alexander B. Grosart

THE BANNER OF TRUTH TRUST

THE BANNER OF TRUTH TRUST
3 Murrayfield Road, Edinburgh EH12 6EL
P. O. Box 621, Carlisle, Pennsylvania 17013, U.S.A.

*

The Complete Works of Richard Sibbes first published in
7 volumes 1862–64
This second reprint of volume 2 first published by the Banner of
Truth Trust 1983
Reprinted 2001
ISBN 0 85151 370 0

*

Printed and bound in Great Britain at the
University Press, Cambridge

CONTENTS.

BOWELS OPENED;
OR, EXPOSITORY SERMONS ON CANTICLES IV. 16, V. VI.

THE SPOUSE, HER EARNEST DESIRE AFTER CHRIST.

A BREATHING AFTER GOD.

THE RETURNING BACKSLIDER;

OR, A COMMENTARY UPON HOSEA XIV.

THE GLORIOUS FEAST OF THE GOSPEL.

PREFATORY NOTE.

HAVING embraced in Volume I. the whole of the works of Sibbes published by himself, together with related portions restored to their proper places (*e. g.*, 'The Description of Christ,' and 'The Sword of the Wicked'), the present volume contains his larger Treatises from the Old Testament, together with lesser kindred 'Sermons,' which will be followed by his Commentaries on portions of the New Testament.

A. B. G.

BOWELS OPENED,

BEING EXPOSITORY SERMONS ON CANT. IV. 16, V., VI.

The **expository** sermons which compose the treatise, entitled, in the quaint phrase-ology of the age, 'Bowels Opened,' (no doubt derived from the Hebraic idea of the seat of the affections being in the 'bowels,' Cant. v. 4 ; and compare 1 John iii. 17) passed through three editions, as follows :—

(a) 1st edition, 4to, 1639.

(b) 2d edition, 4to, 1641. There is no intimation of its being a '2d edition ;' but it really was so. The pagination is wholly different from a.

(c) 3d edition, 4to, 1648. This *is* designated '3d edition,' and the pagination differs from a and b. Prefixed to it is a portrait of Sibbes, *ætat* 58. Underneath it **are** these lines, without signature or initial :

'Thy learning, meekness, wisedome, heavenly minde,
    Soe full of love, soe zealous, soe discreete,
    Thy works, ye Church, yea Heaven, where they doe finde
    A crowne—declare, for earth they were not meete.
    Whoe, slighting thee, himselfe preferrs before,
    Let him gett to thee,—he shall then know more.'

Our text follows a, with comparison of b and c for correction of misprints. Its title-page is given below.* **G.**

* Original title page :—

**BOWELS
O P E N E D,**
OR
A DISCOVERY OF THE
Neere and deere Love, Union and
Communion betwixt Christ and the
Church, and consequently betwixt
Him and every beleeving soul.
Delivered in divers Sermons on the Fourth **Fifth**
and Sixt Chapters of the CANTICLES
By that Reverend and Faithfull Minister of the
Word, DOCTOR SIBS, late Preacher unto
the Honourable Societie of *Grayes Inne,* and Master
of Katharine Hall in Cambridge.
Being in part finished by his owne pen in his life
time, and the rest of them perused and corrected
by those whom he intrusted with the
publishing of his works.
CANT.4.10.
Thou hast ravished my heart, my Sister, my Spouse : thou hast ravished my heart with one of thine eyes, and with one chaine of thy necke.

LONDON.
Printed by *G. M.* for *George Edwards* in the Old Baily in
Greene-Arbour at the signe of the Angell, MDCXXXIX.†

† It may be noted that Obadiah Sedgwick's famous folio on 'The Covenants,' (1661) is entitled, 'The Bowels of Tender Mercy Sealed in the Everlasting Covenant.' Thomas Willocks and Faithful Teat have similarly quaintly-titled treatises on 'Canticles.' This book seems to have had a special attraction for the Puritan Divines.

G.

* For full and interesting notices of this great historic name, consult Burke, and any of the 'Peerages;' also the recently issued family papers at Kimbolton, by the present Duke of Manchester. He was the patron and beloved friend of John Howe.—G.

† The celebrated Dr Thomas Goodwin, who discharged the office of 'prefacer' or editor for many of his Puritan contemporaries, e.g., besides Sibbes, Burroughes, and Hooker. Cf. Memoir by Dr Halley.—G.

‡ Philip Nye was one of the foremost men in the great Puritan struggle. He died in 1672. Cf. 'Nonconf. Memorial,' i. 95, 96; and Hanburg's 'Historical Memorials relating to the Independents,' throughout the work.—G.

TO THE CHRISTIAN READER.

THE perusal of this book being committed unto me by an ancient and a faithful friend of mine, I found it, I confess, so full of heavenly treasure, and such lively expressions of the invaluable riches of the love of Christ towards all his poor servants that sue and seek unto him, that I sent unto the godly and learned author, earnestly entreating him to publish the same, judging it altogether unmeet that so precious matter should be concealed from public use: when he excused himself, by undervaluing his own meditations; but withal signified his desire of the church's good, if by anything in his works it might never so little be promoted. I could not but declare myself in recommending this treatise as a very profitable and excellent help both to the understanding of that dark and most divine Scripture, and also to kindle in the heart all heavenly affections unto Jesus Christ.

It is well known how backward I am and ever have been to cumber the press, but yet I would not be guilty in depriving the dear children of God of the spiritual and sweet consolations which are here very plentifully offered unto them.

And the whole frame of all these sermons is carried with such wisdom, gravity, piety, judgment, and experience, that it commends itself unto all that are godly wise; and I doubt not but that they shall find their temptations answered, their fainting spirits revived, their understandings enlightened, and their graces confirmed, so as they shall have cause to praise God for the worthy author's godly and painful labours. And thus desiring the Father of all mercies and the God of all comfort to bless this work to the consolation and edification of those that seek his favour and desire to fear his holy name, I rest

Thine in Jesus Christ,

J[OHN] DOD.*

---

* John Dod is one of the most venerable of Puritan 'worthies.' He lived to a 'great age.' Born in 1549, he died in 1645. Consult Brook ('Lives of the Puritans,' vol. iii. pp. 1–6); also Clark ('Lives of Thirty-two English Divines,' folio, 1677, pp. 168–178).—G.

BOWELS OPENED.

I am come into my garden, my sister, my spouse: I have eaten my honey-comb with my honey; I have drunk my wine with my milk: eat, O friends; drink, yea, drink abundantly, O beloved.—CANT. V. 1.

OTHER books of Solomon lie more obvious and open to common under-standing; but, as none entered into the holy of holies but the high priest, Lev. xvi. 2, *seq.*, and Heb. ix. 7, so none can enter into the mystery of this Song of songs, but such as have more near communion with Christ. Songs, and specially marriage songs, serve to express men's own joys, and others' praises. So this book contains *the mutual joys and mutual praises betwixt Christ and his church.*

And as Christ and his church are the greatest persons that partake of human nature, so whatsoever is excellent in the whole world is borrowed to set out the excellencies of these two great lovers.

It is called 'Solomon's Song,' who, next unto Christ, was the greatest son of wisdom that ever the church bred, whose understanding, as it was 'large as the sand of the sea,' 1 Kings iv. 29, so his affections, especially that of love, were as large, as we may see by his many wives, and by the delight he sought to take in whatsoever nature could afford. Which affec-tion of love, in him misplaced, had been his undoing, but that he was one beloved of God, who by his Spirit raised his soul to lovely objects of a higher nature. Here in this argument there is no danger for the deepest wit, or the largest affection, yea, of a Solomon, to overreach. For the knowledge of the love of Christ to his church is above all knowledge, Eph. iii. 19. The angels themselves may admire it, though they cannot com-prehend it. It may well, therefore, be called the 'Song of Solomon;' the most excellent song of a man of the highest conceit* and deepest appre-hension, and of the highest matters, *the intercourse betwixt Christ, the highest Lord of lords, and his best beloved contracted spouse.*

There are divers things in this song that a corrupt heart, unto which all things are defiled, may take offence; but 'to the pure all things are pure,' Titus i. 15. Such a sinful abuse of this heavenly book is far from the inten-tion of the Holy Ghost in it, which is by stooping low to us, to take

* That is, 'imagination.'—G.

advantage to raise us higher unto him, that by taking advantage of the sweetest passage of our life, *marriage*, and the most delightful affection, *love*, in the sweetest manner of expression, *by a song*, he might carry up the soul to things of a heavenly nature. We see in summer that one heat weakens another; and a great light being near a little one, draws away and obscures the flame of the other. So it is when the affections are taken up higher to their fit object; they die unto all earthly things, whilst that heavenly flame consumes and wastes all base affections and earthly desires. Amongst other ways of mortification, there be two remarkable—

1. *By embittering all earthly things unto us, whereby the affections are deaded* to them.*

2. *By shewing more noble, excellent, and fit objects*, that the soul, issuing more largely and strongly into them, may be diverted, and so by degrees die unto other things. The Holy Spirit hath chosen this way in this song, by elevating and raising our affections and love, to take it off from other things, that so it might run in its right channel. It is pity that a sweet stream should not rather run into a garden than into a puddle. What a shame is it that man, having in him such excellent affections as love, joy, delight, should cleave to dirty, base things, that are worse than himself, so becoming debased like them! Therefore the Spirit of God, out of mercy and pity to man, would raise up his affections, by taking comparison from earthly things, leading to higher matters, that only deserve love, joy, delight, and admiration. Let God's stooping to us occasion our rising up unto him. For here the greatest things, the 'mystery of mysteries,' the communion betwixt Christ and his church, is set out in the familiar comparison of a marriage, that so we might the better see it in the glass of comparison, which we cannot so directly conceive of; as we may see the sun in water, whose beams we cannot so directly look upon. Only our care must be not to look so much on the colours as the picture, and not so much on the picture as on the person itself represented; that we look not so much to the resemblance as to the person resembled.†

Some would have Solomon, by a spirit of prophecy, to take a view here of all the time, from his age to the second coming of Christ, and in this song, as in an abridgment, to set down the several passages and periods of the church in several ages, as containing divers things which are more correspondent to one age of the church than another (*a*). But howsoever this song may contain, we deny not, a story of the church in several ages, yet this hinders not, but that most passages of it agree to the spiritual estate of the church in every age, as most interpreters have thought. In this song there is,

1. A strong desire of the church of nearer communion with Christ; and then,

2. Some declining again in affection.

3. After this we have her recovery and regaining again of love; after which,

4. The church falls again into a declining of affection; whereupon follows a further strangeness of Christ to her than before, which continues until,

5. That the church, perceiving of Christ's constant affection unto her, notwithstanding her unkind dealing, recovers, and cleaves faster to Christ than ever   , chap. iii.

These passages agree to the experience of the best Christians in the state of their own lives. This observation must carry strength through this whole song, that *there is the same regard of the whole church, and of every particular member, in regard of the chiefest privileges and graces that accompany salvation.* There is the same reason of every drop of water as of the

* That is, ' deadened.'—G.   † That is, ' represented.'—G.

whole ocean, all is water; and of every spark of fire as of the whole element
of fire, all is fire. Of those homogeneal bodies, as we call them, there is
the same respect of the part and of the whole. And therefore, as the whole
church is the spouse of Christ, so is every particular Christian; and as the
whole church desires still nearer communion with Christ, so doth every particular member. But to come to the words, ' I am come into my garden,' &c.

This chapter is not so well broken and divided from the former as it
might have been, for it were better and more consequent* that the last verse
of the former chapter were added to the beginning of this.

' *Awake, O north wind; and come, thou south; blow upon my garden, that
the spices thereof may flow out. Let my beloved come into his garden, and eat
his pleasant fruits,*' Cant. iv. 16.

And therefore, by reason of connection of this chapter with the former
verse, we will first speak somewhat of it briefly, only to make way for that
which follows. The words contain—

1. *A turning of Christ's speech to the winds to blow upon his garden, with
the end why,* ' that the spices thereof may flow out.'

2. *We have an invitation of Christ, by the church, to come into his garden,*
with the end, ' to eat his pleasant fruits.'

Quest. It may be a question whether this command be the words of
Christ or the desire of his spouse ?

Ans. The words are spoken by Christ, because he calls it ' *my* garden,'
and the church after invites him to eat of ' *his* pleasant fruits,' not of hers.
Yet the words may be likewise an answer to a former secret desire of the
church, whereof the order is this : The church being sensible of some deadness of spirit, secretly desires some further quickening. Christ then answers
those desires by commanding the winds to blow upon her. For ordinarily
Christ first stirs up desires, and then answers the desires of his own Spirit
by further increase, as here, ' Awake, thou north wind; and come, thou
south; and blow upon my garden,' &c.

1. For the first point named, we see here that Christ *sends forth his
Spirit, with command to all means,* under the name of ' north and south
wind,' to further the fruitfulness of his church. The wind is nature's fan.
What winds are to the garden, that the Spirit of Christ, in the use of
means, is to the soul. From comparison fetched from Christ's commanding the winds, we may in general observe, that *all creatures stand in obedience
to Christ, as ready at a word, whensoever he speaks to them.* They are all, as
it were, asleep until he awakes them. He can call for the wind out of his
treasures when he pleases : he holds them in his fist, Prov. xxx. 4.

Use. Which may comfort all those that are Christ's, that they are under
one that hath all creatures at his beck under him to do them service, and
at his check to do them no harm. This drew the disciples in admiration
to say, ' What manner of man is this, that even the winds and the seas
obey him ?' Mat. viii. 27. And cannot the same power still the winds and
waves of the churches and states, and cause a sudden calm, if, as the disciples, we awake him with our prayers.

2. Secondly, we see here that Christ speaks to *winds contrary one to
another,* both in regard of the coasts from whence they blow, and in their
quality; but both agree in this, that both are necessary for the garden :
where we see that *the courses that Christ takes, and the means that he uses
with his church, may seem contrary; but by a wise ordering, all agree in the
wholesome issue.* A prosperous and an afflicted condition are contrary : a

* That is, ' in sequence.'—G.

mild and a sharp course may seem to cross one another; yet sweetly they agree in this, that as the church needeth both, so Christ useth both for the church's good. The north is a nipping wind, and the south a cherishing wind; therefore the south wind is the welcomer and sweeter after the north wind hath blown. But howsoever, all things are ours: 'Paul, Apollos, Cephas, things present and to come, life, death,' &c., 1 Cor. iii. 21, 22; 'all things work together for good to us, being in Christ,' Rom. viii. 28.

Use 1. Hence it is that the manifold wisdom of Christ *maketh use of such variety of conditions;* and hence it is that the Spirit of Christ is mild in some men's ministries, and sharp in others : nay, in the very same minister, as the state of the soul they have to deal withal requires.

Use 2. Sometimes, again, *the people of God need purging, and sometimes refreshing.* Whereupon the Spirit of God carries itself suitably to both conditions; and the Spirit in the godly themselves draws good out of every condition, sure [as] they are that all winds blow them good, and [that] were it not for their good, no winds should blow upon them. But in regard that these times of ours, by long peace and plenty, grow cold, heavy, and secure, we need therefore all kinds of winds to blow upon us, and all little enough. Time was when we were more quick and lively, but now the heat of our spirits is* abated. We must therefore take heed of it, and ' quicken those things that are ready to die,' Rev. iii. 2; or else, instead of the north and south wind, God will send an east wind that shall dry up all, as it is, Hos. xiii. 15.

Use 3. Again, if Christ can raise or lay, bind up or let loose, all kind of winds at his pleasure, then if means be wanting or fruitless, it is he that says to the clouds, Drop not, and to the winds, Blow not. Therefore, *we must acknowledge him in want or plenty of means.* The Spirit of Christ in the use of means is a free agent, sometimes blows strongly, sometimes more mildly, sometimes not at all. No creature hath these winds in a bag at command, and therefore it is wisdom to yield to the gales of the Spirit. Though in some other things, as Solomon observes, it may hinder to observe the winds, Eccles. xi. 4, yet here it is necessary and profitable to observe the winds of the Spirit.

Now, for the clear understanding of what we are to speak of, let us first observe—

1. Why the Spirit of God, in the use of the means, is compared to wind. And then,

2. Why the church is compared to a garden; which shall be handled in the proper place.

But first for the wind.

1. 'The wind bloweth where it listeth,' as it is John iii. 8. So the Spirit of God blows freely, and openeth the heart of some, and poureth grace plentifully in them.

2. The wind, especially the north wind, *hath a cleansing force.* So the Spirit of God purgeth our hearts ' from dead works to serve the living God, making us partakers of the divine nature,' 2 Pet. i. 4.

3. The wind *disperseth and scattereth clouds, and makes a serenity in the air.* So doth the Spirit disperse such clouds as corruption and Satan raise up in the soul, that we may clearly see the face of God in Jesus Christ.

---

* It is printed ' are.' But such inaccuracy is not uncommon in Sibbes and his contemporaries. If the nearer noun be plural, it, and not the nominative proper, regulates the use of the verb. This remark is made once for all, that apparent misprints may not be placed to oversight.—G.

4. The wind hath *a cooling and a tempering quality, and tempers the distemper of nature*. As in some hot countries there be yearly anniversary winds, which blow at certain times in summer, tempering the heat; so the Spirit of God allayeth the unnatural heats of the soul in fiery temptations, and bringeth it into a good temper.

5. The wind being subtle, *searcheth into every corner and cranny*. So the Spirit likewise is of a searching nature, and discerneth betwixt the joints and the marrow, betwixt the flesh and the Spirit, &c., searching those hidden corruptions, that nature could never have found out.

6. The wind hath *a cherishing and a fructifying force*. So the Spirit is a quickening and a cherishing Spirit, and maketh the heart, which is as a barren wilderness, to be fruitful.

7. The wind hath *a power of conveying sweet smells in the air, to carry them from one to another*. So the Spirit in the word conveyeth the seeds of grace and comfort from one to another. It draws out what sweetness is in the spirits of men, and makes them fragrant and delightful to others.

8. The wind, again, *bears down all before it, beats down houses, and trees, like the cedars in Lebanon*, turns them up by the roots, and lays all flat. So the Spirit is mighty in operation. There is no standing before it. It brings down mountains, and every high thing that exalts itself, and lays them level; nay, the Roman and those other mighty empires could not stand before it.

For these respects and the like, the ' blowing of the Spirit' is compared to wind. For which end Christ here commands the wind to ' blow upon his garden.'

1. *To blow*, &c. See here the order, linking, and concatenation of things one under another. To the prospering of a poor flower or plant in a garden, not only soil is needful, but air and wind also, and the influence of heaven; and God commanding all, as here the winds to blow upon his garden. To this end, as a wonderful mercy to his people, it is said, ' And it shall come to pass in that day, I will hear, saith the Lord : I will hear the heavens, and they shall hear the earth; and the earth shall hear the corn, the wine, and the oil; and they shall hear Jezreel,' Hos. ii. 21, 22. As the creatures are from God, so the order and dependence of creatures one from another, to teach us not only what to pray for, but also what to pray fitly for; not only to pray for the dew of heaven, but also for seasonable and cherishing winds. It is not the soil, but the season, that makes fruitful, *Non ager sed annus facit fructus*, and that from seasonable winds and influences. So in spiritual things there is a chain of causes and effects : prayer comes from faith, Rom. x. 14 ; faith from the hearing of the word ; hearing from a preacher, by whom God by his Spirit blows upon the heart; and a preacher from God's sending. If the God of nature should but hinder and take away one link of nature's chain, the whole frame would be disturbed. Well, that which Christ commands here, is for the winds to ' blow upon his garden.'

And we need blowing : our spirits will be becalmed else, and stand at a stay ; and Satan will be sure by himself, and such as are his bellows, to blow up the seeds of sinful lusts in us. For there are two spirits in the church, the one always blowing against the other. Therefore, the best had need to be stirred up ; otherwise, with Moses, Exod. xvii. 12, their hands will be ready to fall down, and abate in their affection. Therefore we need blowing—

1. In regard of our natural inability.

2. In regard of our dulness and heaviness, cleaving to nature occasionally.

3. In regard of contrary winds from without.

Satan hath his bellows filled with his spirit, that hinders the work of grace all they can; so that we need not only Christ's blowing, but also his stopping other contrary winds, that they blow not, Rev. vii. 1.

4. In regard of the estate and condition of the new Covenant, wherein all beginning, growth, and ending, is from grace, and nothing but grace.

5. Because old grace, without a fresh supply, will not hold against new crosses and temptations.

Use. Therefore when Christ draws, let us run after him ; when he blows, let us open unto him. It may be the last blast that ever we shall have from him. And let us set upon duties with this encouragement, that Christ will blow upon us, not only to prevent us, but also to maintain his own graces in us. But O! where is this stirring up of ourselves, and one another, upon these grounds!

Quest. But, *why is the church compared to a garden ?*

Ans. Christ herein takes all manner of terms to express himself and the state of the church, as it is to him, to shew us that wheresoever we are, we may have occasion of heavenly thoughts, to raise up our thoughts to higher matters. His church is his 'temple,' when we are in the temple ; it is a 'field' when we are there; a 'garden,' if we walk in a garden. It is also a 'spouse' and a 'sister,' &c. But more particularly the church is resembled to a garden.

1. *Because a garden is taken out of the common waste ground, to be appropriated to a more particular use.* So the church of Christ is taken out of the wilderness of this waste world, to a particular use. It is in respect of the rest, as Goshen to Egypt, Exod. ix. 26, wherein light was, when all else was in darkness. And indeed wherein doth the church differ from other grounds, but that Christ hath taken it in? It is the same soil as other grounds are ; but, he dresseth and fits it to bear spices and herbs.

2. *In a garden nothing comes up naturally of itself,* but as it is planted and set. So nothing is good in the heart, but as it is planted and set by the heavenly husbandman, John xv. 4 ; and Mat. xv. 3. We need not sow the wilderness, for the seeds of weeds prosper naturally. The earth is a mother to weeds, but a stepmother to herbs. So weeds and passions grow too rank naturally, but nothing grows in the church of itself, but as it is set by the hand of Christ, who is the author, dresser, and pruner of his garden.

3. Again, *in a garden nothing uses to be planted but what is useful and delightful.* So there is no grace in the heart of a Christian, but it is useful, as occasion serves, both to God and man.

4. Further, *in a garden there are variety of flowers and spices,* especially in those hot countries. So in a Christian, there is somewhat of every grace. As some cannot hear of a curious flower, but they will have it in their garden, so a Christian cannot hear of any grace but he labours to obtain it. They labour for graces for all seasons, and occasions. They have for prosperity, temperance and sobriety ; for adversity, patience and hope to sustain them. For those that are above them, they have respect and obedience; and for those under them, suitable usage in all conditions of Christianity. For the Spirit of God in them is a seminary of spiritual good things. As in the corruption of nature, before the Spirit of God came to us, there was the seminary of all ill weeds in us, so when there is a new quality and new principles put in us, therewith comes the seeds of all graces.

5. Again, *of all other places, we most delight in our gardens to walk there and take our pleasure*, and take care thereof, for fencing, weeding, watering, and planting. So Christ's chief care and delight is for his church. He walks in the midst of the 'seven golden candlesticks,' Rev. ii. 1; and if he defend and protect States, it is that they may be a harbour to his church.

6. And then again, as in gardens there had wont to have *fountains and streams which run through their gardens*, (as paradise had four streams which ran through it); so the church is Christ's paradise; and his Spirit is a spring in the midst of it, to refresh the souls of his upon all their faintings, and so the soul of a Christian becomes as a watered garden.

7. So also, 'their fountains were sealed up,' Cant. iv. 12; so the joys of the church and particular Christians are, as it were, sealed up. A stranger, it is said, 'shall not meddle with this joy of the church,' Prov. xiv. 10.

8. Lastly, *a garden stands always in need of weeding and dressing*. Continual labour and cost must be bestowed upon it; sometimes planting, pruning, and weeding, &c. So in the church and hearts of Christians, Christ hath always somewhat to do. We would else soon be overgrown and turn wild. In all which, and the like respects, Christ calleth upon the winds 'to blow upon his garden.'

Use 1. If then the church be a severed portion, then *we should walk as men of a severed condition from the world*, not as men of the world, but as Christians; to make good that we are so, by feeling the graces of God's Spirit in some comfortable measure, that so Christ may have something in us, that he may delight to dwell with us, so to be subject to his pruning and dressing. For, it is so far from being an ill sign, that Christ is at cost* with us, in following us with afflictions, that it is rather a sure sign of his love. For, the care of this blessed husbandman is to prune us, so as to make us fruitful. Men care not for heath and wilderness, whereupon they bestow no cost. So when God prunes us by crosses and afflictions, and sows good seed in us, it is a sign he means to dwell with us, and delight in us.

2. And then also, we should not strive so much for *common liberties* of the world that common people delight in, but for *peculiar graces*, that God may delight in us as his garden.

3. And then, let us learn hence, *not to despise any nation or person*, seeing God can take out of the waste wilderness whom he will, and make the desert an Eden.

4. Again, *let us bless God for ourselves*, that our lot hath fallen into such a pleasant place, to be planted in the church, the place of God's delight.

5. And this also should move us *to be fruitful*. For men will endure a fruitless tree in the waste wilderness, but in their garden who will endure it? Dignity should mind us of duty. It is strange to be fruitless and barren in this place that we live in, being watered with the dew of heaven, under the sweet influence of the means. This fruitless estate being often watered from heaven, how fearfully is it threatened by the Holy Ghost, that 'it is near unto cursing and burning,' Heb. vi. 8. For in this case, visible churches, if they prosper not, God will remove the hedge, and lay them waste, having a garden elsewhere. Sometimes God's plants prosper better in Babylon, than in Judea. It is to be feared God may complain of us, as he doth of his people, 'I have planted thee a noble vine; how art thou then come to be degenerated?' Jer. ii. 21. If in this case we regard iniquity in our heart, the Lord will not regard the best thing that comes from us, as our prayers, Heb. xii. 17.

* That is, 'expense.'—G.

We must then learn of himself, how and wherein to please him. Obedience from a broken heart is the best sacrifice. Mark in [the] Scriptures what he abhors, what he delights in. We use to say of our friends, Would God I knew how to please them. Christ teacheth us, that 'without faith it is impossible to please him,' Heb. xi. 6. Let us then strive and labour to be fruitful in our places and callings. For it is the greatest honour in this world, for God to dignify us with such a condition, as to make us fruitful. ' We must not bring forth fruit to ourselves,' as God complains of Ephraim, [Israel], Hos. x. 1. Honour, riches, and the like, are but secondary things, arbitrary at God's pleasure to cast in ; but, to have an active heart fruitful from this ground, that God hath planted us for this purpose, that we may do good to mankind, this is an excellent consideration not to profane our calling. The blessed man is said to be, ' a tree planted by the water side, that brings forth fruit in due season,' Ps. i. 3. But it is not every fruit ; not that fruit which Moses complains of, Deut. xxxii. 32, the wine of dragons, and the gall of asps : but good fruit, as John speaks ; ' Every tree that bringeth not forth good fruit, is hewn down, and cast into the fire,' Mat. iii. 10.

6. Lastly, in that the church is called Christ's garden, this may *strengthen our faith in God's care and protection.* The church may seem to lie open to all incursions, but it hath an invisible hedge about it, a wall without it, and a well within it, Zech. ii. 5. God himself is a wall of fire about it, and his Spirit a well of living waters running through it to refresh and comfort it. As it was said of Canaan, so it may be said of the church, ' The eye of the Lord is upon it all the year long,' Deut. xi. 12, and he waters it continually. From which especial care of God over it, this is a good plea for us to God, ' I am thine, save me ;' I am a plant of thine own setting ; nothing is in me but what is thine, therefore cherish what is thine. So, for the whole church the plea is good : ' The church is thine ; fence it, water it, defend it, keep the wild boar out of it.' Therefore the enemies thereof shall one day know what it is to make a breach upon God's vineyard. In the mean time, let us labour to keep our hearts as a garden, that nothing that defileth may enter. In which respects the church is compared to a garden, upon which Christ commands the north and south wind, all the means of grace, to blow.

But to what end must these winds blow upon the garden ?

' That the spices thereof may flow out.'

The end of this blowing is, you see, ' that the spices thereof may flow out.' Good things in us lie dead and bound up, unless the Spirit let them out. We ebb and flow, open and shut, as the Spirit blows upon us; without blowing, no flowing. There were gracious good things in the church, but they wanted blowing up and further spreading, whence we may observe, that,

Obs. 1. *We need not only grace to put life into us at the first, but likewise grace to quicken and draw forth that grace that we have.* This is the difference betwixt man's blowing and the Spirit's. Man, when he blows, if grace be not there before, spends all his labour upon a dead coal, which he cannot make take fire. But the Spirit first kindles a holy fire, and then increases the flame. Christ had in the use of means wrought on the church before, and now further promoteth his own work. We must first take in, and then send out; first be cisterns to contain, and then conduits to convey. The wind first blows, and then the spices of the church flow out. We are first sweet in ourselves, and then sweet to others.

Obs. 2. Whence we see further, that *it is not enough to be good in our-*

selves, but our goodness must flow out ; that is, grow more strong, useful to continue and stream forth for the good of others. We must labour to be, as was said of John, burning and shining Christians, John v. 35. For Christ is not like a box of ointment shut up and not opened, but like that box of ointment that Mary poured out, which perfumes all the whole house with the sweetness thereof. For the Spirit is herein like wind; it carries the sweet savour of grace to others. A Christian, so soon as he finds any rooting in God, is of a spreading disposition, and makes the places he lives in the better for him. The whole body is the better for every good member, as we see in Onesimus, Phil. 11. The meanest persons, when they become good, are useful and profitable ; of briars, become flowers. The very naming of a good man casts a sweet savour, as presenting some grace to the heart of the hearer. For then we have what we have to purpose, when others have occasion to bless God for us, for conveying comfort to them by us. And for our furtherance herein, therefore, the winds are called upon to awake and blow upon Christ's garden, ' that the spices thereof may flow out.'

Obs. 3. Hence we see, also, that *where once God begins, he goes on, and delights to add encouragement to encouragement, to maintain new setters up in religion,* and doth not only give them a stock of grace at the beginning, but also helps them to trade. He is not only Alpha, but Omega, unto them, the beginning and the ending, Rev. i. 8. He doth not only plant graces, but also watereth and cherisheth them. Where the Spirit of Christ is, it is an encouraging Spirit; for not only it infuseth grace, but also stirs it up, that we may be ready prepared for every good work, otherwise we cannot do that which we are able to do. The Spirit must bring all into exercise, else the habits of grace will lie asleep. We need a present Spirit to do every good; not only the power to will, but the will itself; and not only the will, but the deed, is from the Spirit, which should stir us up to go to Christ, that he may stir up his own graces in us, that they may flow out.

Use. Let us labour, then, in ourselves to be full of goodness, that so we may be fitted to do good to all. As God is good, and does good to all, so must we strive to be as like him as may be ; in which case, for others' sakes, we must pray that God would make the winds to blow out fully upon us, ' that our spices may flow out' for their good. For a Christian in his right temper thinks that he hath nothing good to purpose, but that which does good to others.

Thus far of Christ's command to the north and south wind to awake and blow upon his garden, that the spices thereof may flow out. In the next place we have—

II. Christ's invitation by the church to come into his garden, with the end thereof,' to eat his pleasant fruits.'

Which words shew *the church's further desire of Christ's presence to delight in the graces of his own Spirit in her.* She invites him to come and take delight in the graces of his own Spirit; and she calls him ' Beloved,' because all her love is, or should be, imparted and spent on Christ, who gave himself to a cursed death for her. Our love should run in strength no other way, therefore the church calls Christ her ' Beloved.' Christ was there before, but she desires a further presence of him, whence we may observe, that

Wheresoever grace is truly begun and stirred up, there is still a further desire of Christ's presence ; and approaching daily more and more near to the soul, the church thinks him never near enough to her until she be in heaven with him. The true spouse and the bride always, unless in desertion and temptation, crieth, ' Come, Lord Jesus, come quickly,' Rev. xxii. 20. Now, these degrees of Christ's approaches to the soul, until his second coming, are, that he may manifest himself more and more in defending, comforting, and enabling his church with grace. Every further manifestation of his presence is a further coming.

Quest. But why is the church thus earnest?

Reason 1. First, because *grace helps to see our need of Christ,* and so helps us to prize him the more ; which high esteem breeds a hungering, earnest desire after him, and a desire of further likeness and suitableness to him.

Secondly, because the church well knows that when Christ comes to the soul *he comes not alone, but with his Spirit, and his Spirit with abundance of peace and comfort.* This she knows, what need she hath of his presence, that without him there is no comfortable living; for wheresoever he is, he makes the soul a kind of heaven, and all conditions of life comfortable.

Use. Hence we may see that those that do not desire the presence of Christ in his ordinances are, it is to be feared, such as the wind of the Holy Ghost never blew upon. There are some of such a disposition as they cannot endure the presence of Christ, such as antichrist and his limbs,* whom the presence of Christ in his ordinances blasts and consumes. Such are not only profane and worldly persons, but proud hypocrites, who glory in something of their own ; and therefore their hearts rise against Christ and his ordinances, as laying open and shaming their emptiness and carnalness. The Spirit in the spouse is always saying to Christ, ' Come.' It hath never enough of him. He was now in a sort present; but the church, after it is once blown upon, is not satisfied without a further presence. It is from the Spirit that we desire more of the Spirit, and from the presence of Christ that we desire a further presence and communion with him. Now,

The end and reason why Christ is desired by the Church to come into his garden is ' to eat his pleasant fruits ;' that is, to give him contentment. And is it not fit that Christ should eat the fruit of his own vine? have comfort of his own garden? to taste of his own fruits ? The only delight Christ hath in the world is in his garden, and that he might take the more delight in it, he makes it fruitful; and those fruits are precious fruits, as growing from plants set by his own hand, relishing of his own Spirit, and so fitted for his taste. Now, the church, knowing what fitted Christ's taste best, and knowing the fruits of grace in her heart, desireth that Christ would delight in his own graces in her, and kindly accept of what she presented him with. Whence we see that

A gracious heart is privy to its own grace and sincerity when it is in a right temper, and so far as it is privy is bold with Christ in a sweet and reverend†manner. So much sincerity, so much confidence. If our heart condemn us not of unsincerity, we may in a reverend† manner speak boldly to Christ. It is not fit there should be strangeness betwixt Christ and his spouse; neither, indeed, will there be, when Christ hath blown upon her, and when she is on the growing hand. But mark the order.

First, Christ blows, and then the church says, ' Come.' Christ begins in love, then love draws love. Christ draws the church, and she runs after him, Cant. i. 4. The fire of love melts more than the fire of affliction.

Again, we may see here in the church a carefulness to please Christ. As it is the duty, so it is the disposition, of the church of Christ, to please her husband.

---

* That is, ' members,' = adherents.—G.   † That is, ' reverent.'—ED.

1. The reason is, first, our happiness stands in his contentment, and all cannot but be well in that house where the husband and the wife delight in, and make much of, each other.

2. And again, after that the church hath denied herself and the vanities of the world, entering into a way and course of mortification, whom else hath she to give herself to, or receive contentment from? Our manner is to study to please men whom we hope to rise by, being careful that all we do may be well taken of them. As for Christ, we put him off with anything. If he likes it, so it is; if not, it is the best that he is like to have.

Uses. 1. Oh! let us take the apostle's counsel, 'To labour to walk worthy of the Lord, &c., unto all well-pleasing, increasing in knowledge, and fruitfulness in every good work,' Col. i. 9, 10. And this knowledge must not only be a general wisdom in knowing truths, but a special understanding of his good-will to us, and our special duties again to him.

2. Again, that we may please Christ the better, labour to be cleansed from that which is offensive to him: let the spring be clean. Therefore the psalmist, desiring that the words of his mouth and the meditations of his heart might be acceptable before God, first begs 'cleansing from his secret sins,' Ps. xix. 12.

3. And still we must remember that he himself must work in us whatsoever is well-pleasing in his sight, that so we may be perfect in every good thing to do his will, having grace whereby we may serve him acceptably. And one prevailing argument with him is, that we desire to be such as he may take delight in: 'the upright are his delight.' It cannot but please him when we desire grace for this end that we may please him. If we study to please men in whom there is but little good, should we not much more study to please Christ, the fountain of goodness? Labour therefore to be spiritual; for 'to be carnally minded is death,' Rom. viii. 6, and 'those that are in the flesh cannot please God.'

The church desires Christ to come into his garden, 'to eat his pleasant fruits,' where we see, *the church gives all to Christ*. The garden is his, the fruit his, the pleasantness and preciousness of the fruit is his. And as the fruits please him, so the humble acknowledgment that they come from him doth exceedingly please him. It is enough for us to have the comfort, let him have the glory. It came from a good spirit in David when he said, 'Of thine own, Lord, I give thee,' &c., 1 Chron. xxix. 14. God accounts the works and fruits that come from us to be ours, because the judgment and resolution of will, whereby we do them, is ours. This he doth to encourage us; but because the grace whereby we judge and will aright, comes from God, it is our duty to ascribe whatsoever is good in us, or comes from us, unto him; so God shall lose no praise, and we lose no encouragement. The imperfections in well-doing are only ours, and those Christ will pardon, as knowing how to bear with the infirmities of his spouse, being 'the weaker vessel,' 1 Pet. iii. 7.

Use. This therefore should cheer up our spirits in the wants and blemishes of our performances. They are notwithstanding precious fruits in Christ's acceptance, so that we desire to please him above all things, and to have nearer communion with him. *Fruitfulness unto pleasingness may stand with imperfections*, so that we be sensible of them, and ashamed for them. Although the fruit be little, yet it is precious, there is a blessing in it. Imperfections help us against temptations to pride, not to be matter of discouragement, which Satan aims at. And as Christ commands the north and south wind to blow for cherishing, so Satan labours to stir up an east pinching wind, to take either from endeavour, or to make us heartless in endeavour. Why should we think basely of that which Christ thinks precious? Why should we think that offensive which he counts as incense? We must not give false witness of the work of grace in our hearts, but bless God that he will work anything in such polluted hearts as ours. What though, as they come from us, they have a relish of the old man, seeing he takes them from us, 'perfumes them with his own sweet odours,' Rev. viii. 3, and so presents them unto God. He is our High Priest which makes all acceptable, both persons, prayers, and performances, sprinkling them all with his blood, Heb. ix. 14.

To conclude this point, let it be our study to be in such a condition wherein we may please Christ; and whereas we are daily prone to offend him, let us daily renew our covenant with him, and in him: and fetch encouragements of well-doing from this, that what we do is not only well-pleasing unto him, but rewarded of him. And to this end desire him, that he would give command to north and south, to all sort of means, to be effectual for making us more fruitful, that he may delight in us as his pleasant gardens. And then what is in the world that we need much care for or fear?

Now, upon the church's invitation for Christ to come into his garden, follows his gracious answer unto the church's desire, in the first verse of this fifth chapter:

'I am come into my garden, my sister, my spouse: I have gathered my myrrh with my spice; I have eaten my honeycomb with my honey; I have drunk my wine with my milk: eat, O friends; drink, yea, drink abundantly, O beloved,' Cant. v. 1.

Which words contain in them *an answer to the desire of the church in the latter part of the verse formerly handled:* 'Awake, thou north wind; and come, thou south,' &c.

Then, ver. 2, is set forth *the secure estate of the church at this time,* 'I sleep, but my heart waketh;' in setting down whereof the Holy Ghost here by Solomon shews likewise,

The loving intercourse betwixt Christ and the church one with another.

Now Christ, upon the secure estate and condition of the church, desires her 'to open unto him,' ver 2; which desire and waiting of Christ is put off and slighted with poor and slender excuses: ver. 3, 'I have put off my coat; how shall I put it on?' &c.

The success* of which excuses is, that Christ seems to go away from her (and indeed to her sight and sense departs): ver. 6, 'I opened to my beloved; but my beloved had withdrawn himself,' &c.; whereupon she lays about her, is restless, and inquires after Christ from the watchmen, who misuse, 'wound her, and take away her veil from her,' ver. 7.

Another intercourse in this chapter here is, that *the church for all this gives not over searching after Christ,* but asks the daughters of Jerusalem what was become of her beloved, ver. 8; and withal, in a few words, but full of large expression, she relates her case unto them, that 'she was sick of love,' and so 'chargeth them to tell her beloved,' 'if they find him.' Whereupon a question moved by them, touching her beloved, ver. 9, 'What is thy beloved more than another beloved?' she takes occasion, being full of love, which is glad of all occasion to speak of the beloved, to

* That is, 'the result.'—G.

burst forth into his praises, by many elegant expressions, verses 10, 11, 12, &c.

1. In general, setting him at a large distance, beyond comparison from all others, to be ' the chiefest of ten thousand,' ver. 10.

2. In particulars, ver. 11, &c. : ' his head is as most fine gold,' &c.

The issue whereof was, that the 'daughters of Jerusalem' become like-wise enamoured with him, chap. vi. 1; and thereupon inquire also after him, ' Whither is thy beloved gone, O thou fairest among women?' &c. Unto which demand the church makes answer, chap. vi. 2; and so, ver. 3 of that chapter makes a confident, triumphant close unto all these grand passages forenamed, ' I am my beloved's, and my beloved is mine,' &c.; all of which will better appear in the particulars themselves.

The first thing then which offereth itself to our consideration is *Christ's answer to the church's invitation*, chap. iv. 16 :

' I am come into my garden, my sister, my spouse : I have gathered my myrrh with my spice; I have eaten my honeycomb with my honey; I have drunk my wine with my milk : eat, O friends; drink, yea, drink abundantly, O beloved.' In which verse we have,

I. Christ's answer to the church's petition, ' I am come into my garden.'

II. A compellation, or description of the church, ' My sister, my spouse.'

III. Christ's acceptation of what he had gotten there, ' I have gathered my myrrh with my spice; I have eaten my honeycomb with my honey.' There is,

IV. An invitation of all Christ's friends to a magnifique* abundant feast, ' Eat, O friends; drink, yea drink abundantly, O beloved.'

I. For the first, then, in that Christ makes such a real answer unto the church's invitation, ' I am come into my garden,' &c., we see, *that Christ comes into his garden.* 'Tis much that he that hath heaven to delight in, will delight to dwell among the sons of sinful men; but this he doth for us, and so takes notice of the church's petition.

' Let my beloved come into his garden, and eat his pleasant fruit.' The right speech of the church that gives all to Christ, who, when she hath made such a petition, hears it. The order is this—

First of all, God *makes his church lovely*, planteth good things therein, and then stirs up in her good desires : both fitness to pray from an inward gracious disposition, and holy desires; after which, Christ hearing the voice of his own Spirit in her, and regarding his own preparations, he answers them graciously. Whence, in the first place, we may observe, that,

God makes us good, stirs up holy desires in us, and then answers the desires of his holy Spirit in us.

A notable place for this we have, Ps. x. 17, which shews how God first prepares the heart to pray, and then hears these desires of the soul stirred up by his own Spirit, ' Lord, thou hast heard the desires of the humble.' None are fit to pray but the humble, such as discern their own wants : ' Thou wilt prepare their hearts, thou wilt make thine ear to hear.' So Rom. viii. 26, it is said, ' Likewise the Spirit also helpeth our infirmi-ties; for we know not what we should pray for as we ought : but the Spirit itself maketh intercession for us, with groanings which cannot be uttered.' Thus the Spirit not only stirs up our heart to pray, but also prepares our hearts unto it. Especially this is necessary for us, when our thoughts are confused with trouble, grief, and passions, not knowing what to pray. In

* That is, ' magnificent.'—G.

this case the Spirit dictates the words of prayer, or else, in a confusion of thoughts, sums up all in a volley of sighs and unexpressible groans. Thus it is true, that our hearts can neither be lifted up to prayer, nor rightly prepared for it, in any frame fitting, but by God's own Spirit. Nothing is accepted of God toward heaven and happiness, but that which is spiritual : all saving and sanctifying good comes from above. Therefore God must prepare the heart, stir up holy desires, dictate prayer ; must do all in all, being our ' Alpha and Omega,' Rev. i. 8.

1. Now God hears our prayers, First, *Because the materials of these holy desires are good in themselves, and from the person from whence they come, his beloved spouse,* as it is in Cant. ii. 14, where Christ, desiring to hear the voice of his church, saith, ' Let me see thy countenance, and let me hear thy voice ; for sweet is thy voice, and thy countenance is comely.' Thus the voice of the Spouse is sweet, because it is stirred up by his own Spirit, which burns the incense, and whence all comes which is savingly good. This offering up of our prayers in the name of Christ, is that which with his sweet odours perfumes all our sacrifices and prayers ; because, being in the covenant of grace, God respects whatsoever comes from us, as we do the desires of our near friends, Rev. viii. 3.

2. And then, again, God hears our prayers, *because he looks upon us as we are in election, and choice of God the Father, who hath given us to him.* Not only as in the near bond of marriage, husband and wife, but also as he hath given us to Christ ; which is his plea unto the Father, John xvii. 6, ' Thine they were, thou gavest them me,' &c. The desires of the church please him, because they are stirred up by his Spirit, and proceed from her that is his ; whose voice he delights to hear, and the prayers of others for his church are accepted, because they are for her that is his beloved.

To confirm this further, see Isa. lviii. 9. ' Thou then shalt cry, and the Lord shall answer ; thou shalt call, and presently he shall say, Here I am,' &c. . So as soon as Daniel had ended that excellent prayer, the angel telleth him, ' At the beginning of thy supplications the decree came forth,' &c., Dan. ix. 23. So because he knows what to put into our hearts, he knows our desires and thoughts, and therefore accepts of our prayers and hears us, because he loves the voice of his own Spirit in us. So it is said, ' He fulfils the desires of them that fear him ; and he is near to all that call upon him, to all that call upon him in truth,' Ps. cxlv. 18. And our Saviour, he saith, ' Ask and ye shall receive,' &c., Mat. vii. 7. So we have it, 1 John v. 14, ' And we know if we ask anything according to his will, he heareth us.'

Use 1. Let it therefore be a singular comfort to us, that in all wants, so in that of friends, when we have none to go to, yet we have God, to whom we may freely pour out our hearts. There being no place in the world that can restrain us from his presence, or his Spirit from us, he can hear us and help us in all places. What a blessed estate is this ! None can hinder us from driving this trade with Christ in heaven.

Use 2. And let us make another use of it likewise, to be a means to stir up our hearts to make use of our privileges. What a prerogative is it for a favourite to have the fare * of his prince ! him we account happy. Surely he is much more happy that hath God's care, him to be his father in the covenant of grace : him reconciled, upon all occasions, to pour out his heart before him, who is merciful and faithful, wise and most able to help us. ' Why are we discouraged, therefore ; and why are we cast down,' Ps.

* Qu. ' care ?' or ' fare ?'—ED.

xlii. 11, when we have such a powerful and such a gracious God to go to in all our extremities ? He that can pray can never be much uncomfortable.

Use 3. So likewise, it should stir us up to keep our peace with God, that so we may always have access unto him, and communion with him. What a pitiful case is it to lose other comforts, and therewith also to be in such a state, that we cannot go to God with any boldness ! It is the greatest loss of all when we have lost the spirit of prayer ; for, if we lose other things, we may recover them by prayer. But when we have lost this boldness to go to God, and are afraid to look him in the face, as malefactors the judge, this is a woful state.

Now there are diverse cases wherein the soul is not in a state fit for prayer. As that first, Ps. lxvi. 18, ' If I regard iniquity in my heart, the Lord will not regard my prayer.' If a man hath a naughty heart, that purposeth to live in any sin against God, he takes him for an enemy, and therefore will not regard his prayer. Therefore we must come with a resolute purpose to break off all sinful courses, and to give up ourselves to the guidance of God's Spirit. And this will be a forcible reason to move us thereunto, because so long as we live in any known sin unrepented of, God neither regards us nor our prayers. What a fearful estate is this, that when we have such need of God's favour in all estates ; in sickness, the hour of death, and in spiritual temptation, to be in such a condition as that we dare not go to God ! Though our lives be civil,* yet if we have false hearts that feed themselves with evil imaginations, and with a purpose of sinning, though we act it not, the Lord will not regard the prayers of such a one ; they are abominable. The very ' sacrifice of the wicked is abominable,' Prov. xv. 8.

2. Another case is, when we will not forgive others. We know it is directly set down in the Lord's prayer, ' Forgive us our trespasses, as we forgive them that trespass against us,' Mat. vi. 14 ; and there is further added, ver. 15, ' If you forgive not men their trespasses, neither will your heavenly Father forgive you.' If our hearts tell us we have no disposition to pardon, be at peace and agreement, then we do but take God's name in vain when we ask him to forgive our sins, and we continue in envy and malice. In this case God will not regard our prayers, as it is said, ' I care not for your prayers, or for any service you perform to me,' Isa. i. 15. Why ? ' For your hands are full of blood,' Isa. lxvi. 1. You are unmerciful, of a cruel, fierce disposition, which cannot appear before God rightly, nor humble itself in prayer. If it doth, its own bloody and cruel disposition will be objected against the prayers, which are not mingled with faith and love, but with wrath and bitterness. Shall I look for mercy, that have no merciful heart myself ? Can I hope to find that of God, that others cannot find from me ? An unbroken disposition, which counts ' pride an ornament,' Ps. lxxiii. 6, that is cruel and fierce, it cannot go to God in prayer. For, whosoever would prevail with God in prayer must be humble ; for our supplications must come from a loving, peaceable disposition, where there is a resolution against all sin, Ps. lxxiii. 1. Neither is it sufficient to avoid grudging and malice against these, but we must look that others have not cause to grudge against us, as it is commanded : ' If thou bring thy gifts to the altar, and there rememberest that thy brother hath ought against thee ; leave there thy gift before the altar, and go thy way ; first be reconciled to thy brother, and then come and offer thy gift,' Mat. v. 23. So that if

* That is, ' moral.'—G

we do not seek reconciliation with men unto whom we have done wrong, God will not be reconciled to us, nor accept any service from us.

If then we would have our prayers and our persons accepted or respected, let us make conscience of that which hath been said, and not lose such a blessed privilege as this is, that God may regard our prayers. But here may be asked—

Quest. How shall I know whether God regard my prayers or not?

Ans. 1. First, *When he grants the thing prayed for, or enlargeth our hearts to pray still.* It is a greater gift than the thing itself we beg, to have a spirit of prayer with a heart enlarged; for, as long as the heart is enlarged to prayer, it is a sign that God hath a special regard of us, and will grant our petition in the best and fittest time.

2. When *he answers us in a better and higher kind*, as Paul when he prayed for the taking away of the prick of the flesh, had promises of sufficient grace, 2 Cor. xii. 7–9.

3. When, again, *he gives us inward peace, though he gives not the thing*, as Phil. iv. 6, ' In nothing be careful, but in all things let your requests be made to God with prayer and thanksgiving.'

Obj. But sometimes he doth not answer our requests.

Ans. It is true he doth not, but ' the peace of God which passeth all understanding guards our hearts and minds in the knowledge and love of God,' Philip. iv. 7. So though he answers not our prayers in particular, yet he vouchsafes inward peace unto us, assuring us that it shall go well with us, though not in that particular we beg. And thus in not hearing their prayers, yet they have their hearts' desire when God's will is made known. Is not this sufficient for a Christian, either to have the thing, or to have inward peace, with assurance that it shall go better with them than if they had it; with a spirit enlarged to pray, till they have the thing prayed for. If any of these be, God respects our prayers.

Again, in that Christ is thus ready to come into his garden upon the church's invitation, we may further observe, that

Christ vouchsafes his gracious presence to his children upon their desire of it.

The point is clear. From the beginning of the world, the church hath had the presence of Christ alway; for either he hath been present in sacrifices, or in some other things, signs of his presence, as in the ' bush,' Exod. iii. 2, or some more glorious manifestation of his presence, the ark, Exod. xxv. 22, and in the cloud and pillar of fire, Exod. xiii. 21, and after that more gloriously in the temple. He hath ever been present with his church in some sign or evidence of his presence; he delighted to be with the children of men. Sometimes before that he assumed a body, and afterward laid it down again, until he came, indeed, to take our nature upon him, never to leave it again. But here is meant a spiritual presence most of all, which the church in some sort ever had, now desires, and he offers, as being a God ' hearing prayer,' Ps. lxv. 2. And to instance in one place for all, to see how ready Christ hath always been to shew his presence to the church upon their desire. What else is the burden of the 107th Psalm but a repetition of God's readiness to shew his presence in the church, upon their seeking unto him, and unfeigned desire of it, notwithstanding all their manifold provocations of him to anger? which is well summed up, Ps. cvi. 43, ' Many times did he deliver them, but they provoked him with their counsel, and were brought low for their iniquity. Nevertheless, he regarded their affliction when he heard their cry.'

It doth not content the church to have a kind of spiritual presence of

Christ, but it is carried from desire to desire, till the whole desire be accomplished; for as there are gradual presences of Christ, so there are suitable desires in the church which rise by degrees. Christ was present, 1, by his gracious spirit; and then, 2, more graciously present in his incarnation, the sweetest time that ever the church had from the beginning of the world until then. It being 'the desire of nations,' Hag. ii. 7, for the description of those who lived before his coming is from 'the waiting for the consolation of Israel,' that is, for the first coming of Christ. And then there is a 3d and more glorious presence of Christ, that all of us wait for, whereby we are described to be such 'as wait for the coming of Christ,' Mark xv. 43. For the soul of a Christian is never satisfied until it enjoy the highest desire of Christ's presence, which the church knew well enough must follow in time. Therefore, she especially desires this spiritual presence in a larger and fuller measure, which she in some measure already had. So, then, Christ is graciously present in his church by his Holy Spirit. 'I will be with you,' saith he, 'unto the end of the world,' Mat. xxviii. 20. It is his promise. When I am gone myself, 'I will not leave you comfortless,' John xiv. 18, but leave with you my vicar-general, the Holy Spirit, the Comforter, who shall be alway with you. But—

Quest. How shall we know that Christ is present in us?

Ans. To know this, we shall not need to pull him from heaven. We may know it in the word and sacraments, and in the communion of saints; for these are the conveyances whereby he manifests himself, together with the work of his own gracious Spirit in us; for, as we need not take the sun from heaven to know whether or not it be up, or be day, which may be known by the light, heat, and fruitfulness of the creature; and as in the spring we need not look to the heaven to see whether the sun be come near us or not, for looking on the earth we may see all green, fresh, lively, strong, and vigorous; so it is with the presence of Christ. We may know he is present by that light which is in the soul, convincing us of better courses to be taken, of a spiritual life, to know heavenly things, and the difference of them from earthly, and to set a price upon them. When there is, together with light, a heat above nature, the affections are kindled to love the best things, and to joy in them; and when, together with heat, there is strength and vigour to carry us to spiritual duties, framing us to a holy communion with God, and one with another; and likewise when there is every way cheerfulness and enlargement of spirit, as it is with the creature when the sun approacheth. For these causes the church desires Christ, that she may have more light, life, heat, vigour, strength, and that she may be more cheerful and fruitful in duties. The soul, when it is once made spiritual, doth still desire a further and further presence of Christ, to be made better and better.

What a comfort is this to Christians, that they have the presence of Christ so far forth as shall make them happy, and as the earth will afford. Nothing but heaven, or rather Christ in heaven itself, will content the child of God. In the mean time, his presence in the congregation makes their souls, as it were, heaven. If the king's presence, who carries the court with him, makes all places where he is a court, so Christ he carries a kind of heaven with him. Wheresoever he is, his presence hath with it life, light, comfort, strength, and all; for one beam of his countenance will scatter all the clouds of grief whatsoever. It is no matter where we be, so Christ be with us. If with the three children in a fiery furnace, it is no matter, if 'a fourth be there also,' Dan. iii. 25. So if Christ be with us, the flames nor nothing shall hurt us. If in a dungeon, as Paul and Silas were, Acts xvi. 24, if Christ's presence be there, by his Spirit to enlarge our souls, all is comfortable whatsoever. It changeth the nature of all things, sweeteneth everything, besides that sweetness which it brings unto the soul, by the presence of the Spirit; as we see in the Acts, when they had received the Holy Ghost more abundantly, they cared not what they suffered, regarded not whipping; nay, were glad 'that they were accounted worthy to suffer anything for Christ,' Acts v. 41. Whence came this fortitude ? From the presence of Christ, and the Comforter which he had formerly promised.

So let us have the Spirit of Christ that comes from him; then it is no matter what our condition be in the world. Upon this ground let us fear nothing that shall befall us in God's cause, whatsoever it is. We shall have a spirit of prayer at the worst. God never takes away the spirit of suppli-cation from his children, but leaves them that, until at length he possess them fully of their desires. In all Christ's delays, let us look unto the cause, and to our carriage therein; renew our repentance, that we may be in a fit state to go to God, and God to come to us. Desire him to fit us for prayer and holy communion with him, that we may never doubt of his presence.

THE SECOND SERMON.

I am come into my garden, my sister, my spouse: I have gathered my myrrh with my spice; I have gathered my honeycomb with my honey; I have drunk my wine with my milk: eat, O friends; drink, yea, drink abun-dantly, O beloved.'—CANT. V. 1.

THIS song is a mirror of Christ's love, a discovery of which we have in part in this verse; wherein Christ accepts of the invitation of the church, and comes into his garden; and he entertains her with the terms of sister and spouse. Herein observe *the description of the church, and the sweet compellation,* 'my sister, my spouse;' where there is both affinity and consanguinity, all the bonds that may tie us to Christ, and Christ to us.

1. His sister, by blood.
2. His spouse, by marriage.

Christ is our brother, *and the church, and every particular true member thereof, is his sister.* ' I go,' saith Christ, 'to my Father and to your Father, to my God and to your God,' John xx. 17. ' Go,' saith he, ' and tell my brethren.' This was after his resurrection. His advancement did not change his disposition. Go, tell my brethren that left me so un-kindly; go, tell Peter that was most unkind of all, and most cast down with the sense of it. He became our brother by incarnation, for all our union is from the first union of two natures in one person. Christ be-came bone of our bone and flesh of our flesh, to make us spiritually bone of his bone and flesh of his flesh.

Therefore let us labour to be like to him, who for that purpose be-came like to us, Immanuel, God with us, Isa. vii. 14; that we might be like him, and 'partake of the divine nature,' 2 Pet. i. 4. Whom should we rather desire to be like than one so great, so gracious, so loving ?

Again, ' Christ was not ashamed to call us brethren,' Heb. ii. 11, nor ' abhorred the virgin's womb,' to be shut up in those dark cells and straits; but took our base nature, when it was at the worst, and not only our nature, but our miserable condition and curse due unto us. Was he not ashamed of us? and shall we be ashamed to own him and his cause? Against this cowardice it is a thunderbolt which our Saviour Christ pronounceth, ' He that is ashamed of me before men, him will I be ashamed of before my Father, and all the holy angels,' Mark viii. 38. It argues a base disposition, either for frown or favour to desert a good cause in evil times.

Again, *It is a point of comfort to know that we have a brother who is a favourite in heaven;* who, though he abased himself for us, is yet Lord over all. Unless he had been our brother, he could not have been our husband; for husband and wife should be of one nature. That he might marry us, therefore, he came and took our nature, so to be fitted to fulfil the work of our redemption. But now he is in heaven, set down at the right hand of God: the true Joseph, the high steward of heaven; he hath all power committed unto him; he rules all. What a comfort is this to a poor soul that hath no friends in the world, that yet he hath a friend in heaven that will own him for his brother, in and through whom he may go to the throne of grace boldly and pour out his soul, Heb. iv. 15, 16. What a comfort was it to Joseph's brethren that their brother was the second person in the kingdom.

Again, *It should be a motive to have good Christians in high estimation, and to take heed how we wrong them,* for their brother will take their part. ' Saul, Saul, why persecutest thou me?' Acts ix. 4, saith the Head in heaven, when his members were trodden on upon earth. It is more to wrong a Christian than the world takes it for, for Christ takes it as done to himself. Absalom was a man wicked and unnatural, yet he could not endure the wrong that was done to his sister Tamar, 2 Sam. xiii. 1. Jacob's sons took it as a high indignity that their sister should be so abused, Gen. xxxiv. Hath Christ no affections, now he is in heaven, to her that is so near him as the church is? Howsoever he suffer men to tyrannise over her for a while, yet it will appear ere long that he will take the church's part, for he is her brother.

' My sister, my spouse.'

The church is the daughter of a King, begotten of God; the sister and spouse of a King, because she is the sister and spouse of Christ, and the mother of all that are spiritual kings. The church of Christ is every way royal. Therefore we are kings because we are Christians. Hence the Holy Ghost doth add here to sister, spouse. Indeed, taking the advantage of such relations as are most comfortable, to set out the excellent and transcendant relation that is between Christ and his church; all other are not what they are termed, so much as glasses to see better things. Riches, beauty, marriage, nobility, &c., are scarce worthy of their names. These are but titles and empty things. Though our base nature make great matters of them, yet the reality and substance of all these are in heavenly things. True riches are the heavenly graces; true nobility is to be born of God, to be the sister and spouse of Christ; true pleasures are those of the Spirit, which endure for ever, and will stand by us when all outward comforts will vanish. That mystical union and sweet communion is set down with such variety of expressions, to shew *that whatsoever is scattered in the creature severally is in him entirely.* He is both a friend and a brother, a head and a husband, to us; therefore he takes the names of all. Whence we may observe further,

That *the church is the spouse of Christ.* It springs out of him; even as

Eve taken out of Adam's rib, so the spouse of Christ was taken out of his side. When it was pierced, the church rose out of his blood and death; for he redeemed it, by satisfying divine justice; we being in such a condition that Christ must redeem us before he would wed us. First, he must be *incarnate in our nature* before he could be a fit husband; and then, because we were in bondage and captivity, we must be redeemed before he could marry us: 'he purchased his church with his own blood,' Acts xx. 28. Christ hath right to us, he bought us dearly.

Again, another foundation of this marriage between Christ and us, is *consent*. He works us by his Spirit to yield to him. There must be consent on our part, which is not in us by nature, but wrought by his Spirit, &c. We yield to take him upon his own terms; that is, that we shall leave our father's house, all our former carnal acquaintance, when he hath wrought our consent. Then the marriage between him and us is struck up.

Some few resemblances will make the consideration of this the more comfortable.

1. The husband takes his wife under his own name. She, losing her own name, is called by his. So we are called Christians, of Christ.

2. The wife is taken with all her debt, and made partaker of the honours and riches of her husband. Whatsoever he hath is hers, and he stands answerable for all her debts. So it is here : we have not only the name of Christ upon us, but we partake his honours, and are kings, priests, and heirs with him, Rev. i. 5, 6. Whatsoever he hath, he hath taken us into the fellowship of it ; so that his riches are ours, and likewise, whatsoever is ours that is ill, he hath taken it upon him, even the wrath due to us. For he came between that and us, when he was made sin and a curse for us, 2 Cor. v. 21 ; so there is a blessed change between Christ and us. His honours and riches are ours. We have nothing to bestow on him, but our beggary, sins and miseries, which he took upon him.

3. Those that bring together these two different parties, are the friends of the bride ; that is, the ministers, as it is, John iii. 23. They are the *paranymphi*, the friends of the bride, that learn of Christ what to report to his spouse, and so they woo for Christ, and open the riches, beauty, honour, and all that is lovely in him, which is indeed the especial duty of ministers—to lay open his unsearchable riches, that the church may know what a husband she is like to have, if she cleave to him ; and what an one she leaves, if she forsake him. It was well said in the council of Basil, out of Bernard, ' *Nemo committit sponsam suam Vicario; nemo enim Ecclesiæ sponsus est,*'—None commits his wife to a vicar, for none is the husband of the church. To be husband of the church is one of the incommunicable titles of Christ, yet usurped by the pope. Innocent the Third was the first that wronged Christ's bed by challenging the title of Sponsus, husband of the church. Bernard forbids his scholar Eugenius this title (Epist. ccxxxvii. ad Eugenium). It is enough for ministers to be friends of the Bride. Let us yield him to be husband of the church, that hath given himself to sanctify it with washing of water and blood, Eph. v. 26. We are a wife of blood to him.

In this sweet conjunction we must know, that by nature we are clean otherways than spouses ; for what was Solomon's wife, Pharaoh's daughter ? A heathen, till she came to be Solomon's spouse. And as we read in Moses, the strange woman must have her hair cut off, and her nails pared, Deut. xxi. 12. Before she should be taken into the church, there must be an alteration ; so before the church, which is not heathenish, but indeed

hellish by nature, and led by the spirit of the world, be fit to be the spouse
of Christ, there must be an alteration and a change of nature, Is. xi. 6–8 ;
John iii. 3.   Christ must alter, renew, purge, and fit us for himself.   The
apostle saith, Eph. v. 24, it was the end of his death, not only to take us
to heaven, but to sanctify us on earth, and prepare us that we might be fit
spouses for himself.

Use 1. *Let us oft think of this nearness between Christ and us,* if we have
once given our names to him, and not be discouraged for any sin or unworthiness in us. Who sues a wife for debt, when she is married ? *Uxori
lis non intenditur.* Therefore answer all accusations thus :—' Go to Christ.'
If you have anything to say to me, go to my husband.   God is just, but
he will not have his justice twice satisfied, seeing whatsoever is due thereunto is satisfied by Christ our husband.   What a comfort is this to a
distressed conscience !   If sin cannot dismay us, which is the ill of ills
and cause of all evil, what other ill can dismay us ?   He that exhorts us
to bear with the infirmities one of another, and hath enjoined the husband
to bear with the wife, as the weaker vessel, 1 Pet. iii. 7, will not he bear
with his church as the weaker vessel, performing the duty of an husband
in all our infirmities ?

⊢ *Use* 2. Again, his desire is to make her better, and not to cast her away
for that which is amiss.   And for outward ills, they are but to refine, and
make us more conformable to Christ our husband, to fit us for heaven, the
same way that he went.   They have a blessing in them all, for he takes
away all that is hurtful, he pities and keeps us ' as the apple of his eye,'
Zech. ii. 8.   Therefore, let us often think of this, since he hath vouchsafed to take us so near to himself.   Let us not lose the comfort that this
meditation will yield us.   We love for goodness, beauty, riches ; but
Christ loves us to make us so, and then loves us because we are so, in all
estates whatsoever.

Use 3. And if Christ be so near us, *let us labour for chaste judgments,*
that we do not defile them with errors, seeing the whole soul is espoused to
Christ.   Truth is the spouse of our understandings.   *Veritas est sponsa
intellectus.*   It is left * to us to be wanton in opinions, to take up what conceit we will of things.   So we ought to have chaste affections, not cleaving
to base things.   It hath been ofttimes seen, that one husband hath many
wives, but never from the beginning of the world, that one wife hath had
many husbands.   God promiseth to betroth his church to him in righteousness and faithfulness, that is, as he will be faithful to her, so she shall by
his grace be faithful to him ; faithfulness shall be mutual ; the church shall
not be false to Christ.   So there is no Christian soul must think to have
many husbands ; for Christ in this case is a jealous husband.   Take heed
therefore of spiritual harlotry of heart, for our affections are for Christ, and
cannot be better bestowed.   In other things we lose our love, and the things
loved ; but here we lose not our love, but this is a perfecting love, which
draws us to love that which is better than ourselves.   We are, as we affect ; †
our affections are, as their objects be.   If they be set upon better things
than ourselves, they are bettered by it.   They are never rightly bestowed,
but when they are set upon Christ ; and upon other things as they answer
and stand with the love of Christ.   For the prime love, when it is rightly
bestowed, it orders and regulates all other loves whatsoever.   No man
knows how to use earthly things, but a Christian, that hath first pitched
his love on Christ.   Then seeing all things in him, and in all them, a beam

* Qu. ' not left ? '—Ed.   † That is, ' choose.'—G.

of that love of his, intending happiness to him, so he knows how to use everything in order. Therefore let us keep our communion with Christ, and esteem nothing more than his love, because he esteems nothing more than ours.

Quest. But how shall we know, whether we be espoused to Christ or not?

Ans. 1. Our hearts can tell us, *whether we yield consent to him or not.* In particular, whether we have received him, as he will be received, as a right husband, that is, *whether we receive him to be ruled by him,* to make him our head. For the wife, when she yields to be married, therewith also surrenders up her own will, to be ruled by her husband. So far she hath denied her own will; she hath no will of her own. . Christ hath wisdom enough for us, and himself too, whose wisdom and will must be ours. To be led by divine truths so far as they are discovered unto us, and to submit ourselves thereunto, is a sign of a gracious heart, that is married to Christ.

Ans. 2. Again, *a willingness to follow Christ in all conditions as he is discovered in the word.* To suffer Christ to have the sovereignty in our affections, above all other things and persons in the world ; this is the right disposition of a true spouse. For as it was at the first institution, there must be a leaving of father, and mother, and all, to cleave to our husband* : so here, when anything and Christ cannot stand together, or else we shall never have the comfort of his sweet name. Many men will be glad to own Christ to be great by him, but as St Austin complains in his time, Christ Jesus is not loved for Jesus his own sake. *Vix diligitur Jesus propter Jesum,* but for other things, that he brings with him, peace, plenty, &c.—as far as it stands with these contentments. If Christ and the world part once, it will be known which we followed. In times of peace this is hardly† discerned. If he will pay men's debts, so as they may have the credit and glory of the name to be called Christians, if he will redeem them from the danger of sin, all is well ; but only such have the comfort of this communion, as love him for himself. Let us not so much trouble ourselves about signs as be careful to do our duty to Christ, and then will Christ discover his love clearly unto us.

Use 4. Now, they that are not brought so near to this happy condition by Christ, may yet have this encouragement, there is yet place of grace for them. Let them therefore consider but these three things.

1. The excellency of Christ, and of the state of the church, when it is so near him.

2. The necessity of this, to be so near him.

3. That there is hope of it.

There is in Christ whatsoever may commend a husband ; birth, comeliness, riches, friends, wisdom, authority, &c.

1. The excellency of this condition to be one with Christ, is, *that all things are ours.* For he is the King, and the church the Queen of all. All things are serviceable to us. It is a wondrous nearness, to be nearer to Christ than the angels, who are not his body, but servants that attend upon the church. The bride is nearer to him than the angels, for, ' he is the head and husband thereof, and not of the angels,' Heb. ii. 16. What an excellent condition is this for poor flesh and blood, that creeps up and down the earth here despised !

2. But especially, if we consider *the necessity of it.* We are all indebted for more than we are worth. To divine justice we owe a debt of obedience,

* See Gen. ii. 24 and Mat. xix. 5; Mark x. 7, but it is ' wife,' not ' husband.'—G.

† That is with ' difficulty.'—G.

and in want of that we owe a debt of punishment, and we cannot answer one for a thousand. What will become of us if we have not a husband to discharge all our debts, but to be imprisoned for ever?

A person that is a stranger to Christ, though he were an Ahithophel for his brain, a Judas for his profession, a Saul for his place, yet if his sins be set before him, he will be swallowed up of despair, fearing to be shut up eternally under God's wrath. Therefore, if nothing else move, yet let necessity compel us to take Christ.

3. Consider not only how suitable and how necessary he is unto us, but what *hope there is to have him*, whenas he sueth to us by his messengers, and wooeth us, whenas we should rather seek to him; and with other messengers sendeth a privy messenger, his Holy Spirit, to incline our hearts. Let us therefore, as we love our souls, suffer ourselves to be won. But more of this in another place. The next branch is,

III. *Christ's acceptation.* 'I have gathered my myrrh with my spice,' &c. So that, together with Christ's presence, here is a gracious acceptance of the provision of the church, with a delight in it, and withal, a bringing of more with him. The church had a double desire, 1, That Christ would come to accept of what she had for him of his own grace, which he had wrought in her soul; and 2, She was also verily persuaded that he would not come empty handed, only to accept of what was there, but also would bring abundance of grace and comfort with him. Therefore she desires acceptation and increase; both which desires he answers. He comes to his garden, shews his acceptation, and withal he brings more. 'I have gathered my myrrh with my spice. I have eaten my honeycomb with my honey; I have drunk my wine with my milk,' &c. Whence we observe,

That God accepts of the graces of his children, and delights in them.

First, Because *they are the fruits that come from his children, his spouse, his friend.* Love of the person wins acceptance of that which is presented from the person. What comes from love is lovingly taken.

Second, They are the graces of his Spirit. If we have anything that is good, all comes from the Spirit, which is first in Christ our husband, and then in us. As the ointment was first poured on Aaron's head, Ps. cxxxiii. 2, and then ran down upon his rich garments, so all comes from Christ to us. St Paul calls the wife ' the glory of her husband,' 1 Cor. xi. 7, because, as in a glass, she resembleth the graces of her husband, who may see his own graces in her. So it is with Christ and the church. Face answereth to face, as Solomon saith in another case, Prov. xxvii. 19. Christ sees his own face, beauty, glory, in his church; she reflects his beams; he looks in love upon her, and always with his looks conveys grace and comfort; and the church doth reflect back again his grace. Therefore Christ loves but the reflection of his own graces in his children, and therefore accepts them.

Third, His kindness is such *as he takes all in good part.* Christ is love and kindness itself. Why doth he give unto her the name of spouse and sister, but that he would be kind and loving, and that we should conceive so of him? We see, then, the graces of Christ accepting of us and what we do in his strength. Both we ourselves are sacrifices, and what we offer is a sacrifice acceptable to God, through him that offered himself as a sacrifice of sweet smelling savour, from which God smells a savour of rest. God accepts of Christ first, and then of us, and what comes from us in him. We may boldly pray, as Ps. xx. 3, 'Lord, remember all our offerings, and accept all our sacrifices.' The blessed apostle St Paul doth will us ' to offer up ourselves,' Rom. xii. 1, a holy and acceptable sacrifice to God, when we are once in Christ. In the Old Testament we have divers manifestations of this acceptation. He accepted the sacrifice of Abel, as it is thought, by fire from heaven, and so Elijah's sacrifice, and Solomon's, by fire, 1 Kings xviii. 38; 1 Chron, xxi. 26. So in the New Testament he shewed his acceptation of the disciples meeting together, by a mighty wind, and then filling them with the Holy Ghost, Acts ii. 3. But now the declaration of the acceptation of our persons, graces, and sacrifice that we offer to him, is most in peace of conscience and joy in the Holy Ghost, and from a holy fire of love kindled by the Spirit, whereby our sacrifices are burned. In the incense of prayer, how many sweet spices are burned together by this fire of faith working by love; as humility and patience in submitting to God's will, hope of a gracious answer, holiness, love to others, &c.

Use 1. If so be that God accepts the performances and graces, especially the prayers of his children, let it be an argument to encourage us *to be much in all holy duties*. It would dead the heart of any man to perform service where it should not be accepted, and the eye turned aside, not vouchsafing a gracious look upon it. This would be a killing of all comfortable endeavours. But when all that is good is accepted, and what is amiss is pardoned, when a broken desire, a cup of cold water shall not go unrespected, nay, unrewarded, Mat. x. 42, what can we desire more? It is infidelity which is dishonourable to God and uncomfortable to ourselves, that makes us so barren and cold in duties.

Use 2. Only let our care be to *approve our hearts unto Christ*. When our hearts are right, we cannot but think comfortably of Christ. Those that have offended some great persons are afraid, when they hear from them, because they think they are in a state displeasing to them. So a soul that is under the guilt of any sin is so far from thinking that God accepts of it, that it looks to hear nothing from him but some message of anger and displeasure. But one that preserves acquaintance, due distance, and respect to a great person, hears from him with comfort. Before he breaks open a letter, or sees anything, he supposes it comes from a friend, one that loves him. So, as we would desire to hear nothing but good news from heaven, and acceptation of all that we do, let us be careful to preserve ourselves in a good estate, or else our souls will tremble upon any discovery of God's wrath. The guilty conscience argues, what can God shew to me, being such a wretch? The heart of such an one cannot but misgive, as, where peace is made, it will speak comfort. It is said of Daniel that he was a man of God's desires, Dan. ix. 23; x. 11, 19; and of St John, that Christ so loved him that he leaned on his breast, John xxi. 20. Every one cannot be a Daniel, nor one that leans on Christ's bosom. There are degrees of favour and love; but there is no child of God but he is beloved and accepted of him in some degree. But something of this before in the former chapter.

'I have gathered my myrrh with my spice; I have eaten my honeycomb with my honey,' &c.

That is, I have taken contentment in thy graces, together with acceptation. There is a delight, and God not only accepts, but he delights in the graces of his children. 'All my delight,' saith David, 'is in those that are excellent,' Ps. xvi. 3. But this is not all, Christ comes with an enlargement of what he finds.

Christ comes, and comes not empty whensoever he comes, but with abundance of grace.   If St Paul, who was but Christ's instrument, could tell the Romans, ' I hope to come to you in abundance of grace and comfort,' Rom. xv. 29, because he was a blessed instrument to convey good from Christ to the people of God, as a conduit-pipe, how much more shall Christ himself, where he is present, come with graces and comfort! Those that have communion with Christ, therefore, have a comfortable communion, being sure to have it enlarged, for ' to him that hath shall be given,' Mat. xxv. 29. It is not only true of his last coming, when he shall come to judge the quick and the dead, ' I come, and my reward is with me,' Rev. xxii. 12, but also of all his intermediate comings that are between.   When he comes to the soul, he comes not only to accept what is there, but still with his reward with him, the increase of grace, to recompense all that is good with the increase thereof.   This made his presence so desired in the gospel with those that had gracious hearts.   They knew all was the better for Christ, the company the better, for he never left any house or table where he was, but there was an increase of comfort, and of grace.   And as it was in his personal, so it is in his spiritual presence.   ·He never comes, but he increases grace and comfort.

Therefore, let us be stirred up to have communion with Christ, by this motive, that thus we shall have an increase of a further measure of grace. Let us labour to be such as Christ may delight in, for our graces are honey and spices to him, and where he tastes sweetness he will bring more with him.   To him that overcometh he promiseth ' the hidden manna,' Rev. ii. 17.   They had manna before, but he means they shall have more abundant communion with me, who am ' the hidden manna.'   There is abundance in him to be had, as the soul is capable of abundance.   Therefore we may most fruitfully and comfortably be conversant in holy exercises and communion with Christ, because our souls are fit to be enlarged more and more, till they have their fulness in heaven ; and still there is more grace and comfort to be had in Christ, the more we have to deal with him.

But to come to shew what is meant by honey and wine, &c.   Not to take uncertain grounds from these words, but that which may be a foundation for us to build comfort and instruction on, we will not shew in particular what is meant by wine and honey (for that is not intended by the Holy Ghost), but shew in general how acceptable the graces of the Spirit of Christ are to him, that they feed him and delight him, as wine and honey do us, because in the covenant of grace he filleth us by his Spirit of grace, to have comfort in us as we have in him.   For, except there be a mutual joy in one another, there is not communion.   Therefore Christ furnisheth his church with so much grace as is necessary for a state of absence here, that may fit her for communion with him for ever in heaven.   As Isaac sent Rebecca, before the marriage, jewels and ornaments to wear, Gen. xxiv. 22, that she might be more lovely when they met, so our blessed Saviour, he sends to his spouse from heaven jewels and ornaments, that is, graces, wherewith adorned, he may delight in her more and more till the marriage be fulfilled.   Therefore in this book the church is brought in, delighting in Christ, and he in the church.   ' Thy love,' saith the church to him, ' is sweeter than wine,' Cant. i. 2.   Christ saith to the church again, ' Thy love is sweeter than wine.'   Whatsoever Christ saith to the church, the church saith back again to Christ, and he back again to the church. So there is a mutual contentment and joy one in another.   ' Eat, O friends, drink,' &c.

Here is an invitation.   When he comes stored with more grace and comfort, he stirs them up; both the church, others, and all that bear good-will to his people, that they would delight in the graces and comforts of his church.   Whence observe, that

Obs. We ought to rejoice in the comforts and graces of others, and of ourselves.

He stirreth up the church here, as well as others; for he speaks to all, both to the church and the friends of it.   He had need to stir her up to enjoy the comfort of her own grace; for they are two distinct benefits, to have grace, and to know that we have it, though one Spirit work both, 1 Cor. ii. 12.   The Spirit works grace, and shews us the things that God hath given us, yet sometimes it doth the one, and not the other.   In the time of desertion and of temptation, we have grace, but we know it not; right to comfort, but we feel it not.   There is no comfort of a secret, un-known treasure; but so it is with the church, she doth not always take notice of her own graces, and the right she hath to comfort.

We have need to have Christ's Spirit to help us to know what good is in us. And indeed a Christian should not only examine his heart for the evil that is in him, to be humbled; but what good there is, that he may joy and be thankful.   And since Christ accepts the very first fruits, the earnest, and delights in them, we should know what he delights in, that we may go boldly to him; considering that it is not of ourselves, but of Christ, whatso-ever is graciously good.   Therefore we ought to know our own graces; for Christ, when he will have us comfortable indeed, will discover to us what cause we have to rejoice, and shew us what is the work of his own Spirit, and our right to all comfort.

And so, for others, we should not only joy in ourselves, and in our own condition and lot; but also in the happy condition of every good Christian. There is joy in heaven at the conversion of one sinner, Luke xv. 10.   God the Father joys to have a new son; God the Son to see the fruit of his own redemption, that one is pulled out of the state of damnation; and God the Holy Ghost, that he hath a new temple to dwell in; the angels, that they have a new charge to look to, that they had not before, to join with them to praise God.   So there is joy in heaven; the Father, Son, and Holy Ghost, with the angels, joy at it; and all true-hearted Christians joy in the graces one of another.

Reasons.   For, 1. God, Christ, and the Holy Ghost have glory by it; and 2, the church hath comfort by the increase of a saint.   3. The prayer of a Christian adds new strength to the church.   What a happy condition is it when God's glory, the church's comfort and strength, and our own joy, meet together.   So that we should all take notice of the grace of God in others.

We ought to take notice of the works of God in creation and providence, when we see plants, stars, and such like, or else we dishonour God. What then should we do for his gifts and graces in his children, that are above these in dignity? should we not take notice of what is graciously good, and praise God for it?   Thus they did for Paul's conversion, 'they glorified God.'   For when they saw that Paul of a wolf was become not only a sheep, but a shepherd and leader of God's flock, they glorified God, Gal. i. 24.

So the believing Jews, when the Gentiles were converted, 'they glorified God, that he had taken the Gentiles to be his garden and people,' Acts xi. 18. When Paul and others had planted the gospel, and God gave the increase, the godly Jews rejoiced at that good.   So, we that are Gentiles, should re-joice to hear of the conversion of the Jews, and pray for it; for then there will be a general joy when that is.   Want of joy shews want of grace.

There is not a surer character of a Satanical and Cainish disposition, than
to look on the graces of God's children with a malignant eye : as Cain,
who hated his brother, because his works were better than his, 1 John iii. 12.
Those that deprave * the graces of God in others, and cloud them with disgraces, that they may not shine, and will not have the sweet ointment of
their good names to spread, but cast dead flies into it, shew that they are
of his disposition that is the accuser of the brethren. It is a sign of the
child of the devil. All that have grace in them, are of Christ's and of the
angels' disposition. They joy at the conversion and growth of any Christians. Here, such as they, are styled friends and beloved ; and indeed
none but friends and beloved can love as Christ loves, and delight as Christ
delights.

THE THIRD SERMON.

I am come into my garden, my sister, my spouse: I have gathered my myrrh
with my spice; I have eaten my honeycomb with my honey; I have drunk
my wine with my milk; eat O friends; drink, yea, drink abundantly,
*O beloved! I sleep, but my heart waketh, &c.—*CANT. v. 1, 2.

IT hath been shewed how Christ and the church were feasting together.
She entreated his company ' to come into his garden and eat his pleasant
fruits.' He, according to her desire, was come ; and not only feasted on
the church's provision, but also brought more with him. Christ taking
walks in his garden, that is, his church, and every particular soul, which is
as a sweet paradise for him to delight in, is much refreshed ; and in witness
of acceptance brings increase. What greater encouragement can we wish,
than that we, being by nature as the earth, since the fall, accursed, should
be the soil of Christ's delight, planted and watered by him ; and that what
we yield should be so well taken of him. We are under so gracious a
covenant that all our services are accepted ; not only our honey, but honeycomb ; not only our wine, but our milk ; our weak services as well as our
strong ; because the Spirit which we have from him sweeteneth all. As in
nature there is one common influence from heaven, but yet variety of
flowers, violets, roses, gilliflowers, spices, all sweet in their several kind,
with a different kind of sweetness : so all graces have their beginning from
the common influence of Christ's Spirit, though they differ one from another ; and are all accepted of the ' Father of lights,' from whence they
come, James i. 17. Christ wonders at his own grace, ' O woman, great is
thy faith,' Matt. xv. 28 ; and Cant. iii. 6, ' Who is this that cometh out
of the wilderness like pillars of smoke, perfumed with myrrh and frankincense, with all powders of the merchant ?'

Let not the weakest of all others be discouraged. Christ looks not to
what he brings, so much as out of what store ; that which is least in quantity may be most in proportion, as the widow's mite was more in acceptance than richer offerings, Luke xxi. 3, ' A pair of turtle doves,' Levit.
v. 7, was accepted in the law, and those that brought but goats' hair to
the building of the tabernacle, Exod. xxxv. 6.

The particulars here specified that Christ took delight in, and inviteth
others to a further degree of delight in, are

Myrrh and spice, honey and honeycomb, milk.

* That is, 'speak evil of.'—G.

Which shew, 1. The sweetness of grace and spiritual comfort. 2. The variety. 3. The use.

Myrrh and spices, 1, refresh the spirits, and 2, preserve from putrefaction ; which are therefore used in embalming. If the soul be not embalmed with grace, it is a noisome, carrion soul ; and as it is in itself, so whatsoever cometh from it is abominable.

Milk and honey nourish and strengthen; and *wine* increaseth spirits; and thereupon encourageth and allayeth sorrow and cares. ' Give wine to him that is ready to die,' Prov. xxxi. 6. The sense of the love of Christ is sweeter than wine ; it banisheth fears, and sorrow, and care.

From this mutual delight between Christ and his spouse we observe next, that

There is a mutual feasting betwixt Christ and his church. The church bringeth what she hath of his Spirit; and Christ comes with more plenty.

For there being so near a covenant between him and us, we are by his grace to perform all offices on our part. We invite him, and he inviteth us. There is not the meanest Christian in whom there is not somewhat to welcome Christ withal; but Christ sends his provision before, and comes, as we say, to his own cost. He sends a spirit of faith, a spirit of love, a spirit of obedience. 1. Some are content to invite others, but are loth to go to others, as if it were against state. They would have wherewith to entertain Christ, but are unwilling to be beholden to Christ. 2. Some are content to have benefit by Christ, as his righteousness to cover them, &c., but they desire not grace to entertain Christ ; but a heart truly gracious desireth both to delight in Christ, and that Christ may delight in it. It desireth grace together with mercy, holiness with happiness. Christ could not delight in his love to us, if we by his grace had not a love planted in our hearts to him. But to come to speak of this feast.

We see it pleaseth Christ to veil heavenly matters with comparisons fetched from earthly things, that so he may enter into our souls the better by our senses.

1. Christ maketh us a *feast, a marriage feast, a marriage feast with the King's Son*, of all feasts the most magnificent. A feast, first, in regard of the choice rarities we have in Christ. We have the best, and the best of the best. ' Fat things, and the marrow of fatness ; wine, and wine on the lees,' Isa. xxv. 6, refined, that preserveth the strength. The comforts we have from Christ, are the best comforts ; the peace, the best peace ; the privileges, the highest privileges. ' His flesh,' crucified for us, to satisfy divine justice, ' is meat indeed; his blood, shed for us, is drink indeed,' John vi. 55; that is, the only meat and drink to refresh our souls; because these feed our souls, and that to eternal life. The love of God the Father in giving Christ to death ; and Christ's love in giving himself, together with full contentment to divine justice ; this gift it is that the soul especially feeds on. What could Christ give, better than himself to feed on? He thought nothing else worthy for the soul to feed on ; and this it daily feeds on, as daily guilt riseth from the breakings out of the remainder of corruption. Other dainties are from this ; from hence we have the Spirit, and graces of the Spirit. If he giveth himself, will he not give all things with himself?

2. As Christ maketh a feast of choice things for his elect and choice spouse, *so there is variety*, as in a feast. ' Christ is made to us of God, wisdom, righteousness, sanctification, and redemption,' 1 Cor. i. 30, that we should not be too much cast down with thought of our own folly, guilt, unholiness, and misery. There is that in Christ which answereth to all our wants, and

an all-sufficiency for all degrees of happiness. Therefore, he hath terms
from whatsoever is glorious and comfortable in heaven and earth. Christ
is all marrow, all sweetness. All the several graces and comforts we have,
and the several promises whereby they are made over and conveyed unto
us, are but Christ dished out in several manner, as the need of every
Christian shall require. Christ himself is the ocean, issuing into several
streams, to refresh the city of God. We can be in no condition, but we
have a promise to feed on, and ' all promises are yea and amen,' 2 Cor. i.
20,' made to us ' in Christ,' and performed to us ' for Christ.'

3. Therefore, as we have in Christ a feast for variety, so for *sufficiency of
all good*. No man goeth hungry from a feast. It was never heard for any
to famish at a feast. In Christ there is not only abundance, but redun-
dance, a diffusive and a spreading goodness; as in breasts to give milk,
in clouds to drop down showers, in the sun to send forth beams. As
Christ is full of grace and truth, so he fully dischargeth all his offices.
There is an overflowing of all that is good for our good. He that could
multiply bread for the body, he can multiply grace for our soul. If he
giveth life, he giveth it in abundance, John x. 10. If he giveth water of
life, he giveth rivers, not small streams, John vii. 38. If he giveth peace
and joy, he giveth it in abundance; his scope is to fill up our joy to the
full. As he is able, so ' is he willing to do for us far more abundantly than
we are able to think or speak,' Eph. iii. 20. Where Christ is present, he
bringeth plenty with him. If wine be wanting at the first, he will rather
turn water into wine, than there should be a fail.

4. In a feast there is variety of *friendly company;* so here friends are
stirred up to refresh themselves with us. We have the blessed Trinity, the
angels, and all our fellow-members in Christ to come with us.

There is no envy in spiritual things, wherein whatsoever the one hath,
the other hath not the less.

5. In a feast, because it is intended for rejoicing, *there is music;* and
what music like to the sweet harmony between God, reconciled in Christ,
and the soul, and between the soul and itself, in inward peace and joy of
the Holy Ghost, shedding the love of Christ in the soul. We do not only
joy, but glory, under hope of glory, and in afflictions, and in God now as
ours, in whom now by Christ we have an interest, Rom. vi. 2–10. When
we come sorrowful to this feast, we depart cheerful. This, as David's harp,
stills all passions and distempers of spirit.

The founder and master of the feast is Christ himself; and withal is
both guest, and banquet, and all. All graces and comforts are the fruits
of his Spirit; and he alone that infused the soul, can satisfy the soul. He
that is above the conscience can only quiet the conscience. He is that
wisdom that ' sends forth maids,' Prov. ix. 3, his ministers, to invite to his
feast. It is he that cheereth up his guests, as here. Those that invited
others, brought ointment, and poured it out upon them, to shew their welcome, and to cheer them up, as may appear by our Saviour's speech to the
Pharisee that invited him, Luke vii. 44. So we have from Christ both the
oil of grace and oil of gladness. ' He creates the fruits of the lips to be
peace,' Isa. lvii. 19, speaking that peace and joy to the heart that others
do to the ear. ' He raiseth pastors according to his own heart, to feed his
sheep,' Jer. iii. 15.

The vessels wherein Christ conveyeth his dainties are the ministry of the
word and sacraments. By the word and sacraments we come to enjoy
Christ and his comforts and graces; and by this feast of grace we come at

length to the feast of feasts, that feast of glory, when we shall be satisfied
with the image of God, and enjoy fulness of pleasures for evermore; and,
which adds to the fulness, we shall fully know that it shall be a never-
interrupted joy.

We see, then, that we cannot please Christ better than in shewing ourselves welcome, by cheerful taking part of his rich provision. It is an
honour to his bounty to fall to; and it is the temper of spirit that a Christian aims at, to 'rejoice always in the Lord,' Phil. iv. 4, and that from
enjoying our privileges in him. We are not bidden to mourn always, but
to 'rejoice always,' and that upon good advisement; 'Rejoice,' and 'I say
again,' saith St Paul, 'rejoice.' Indeed, we have causes of mourning, but it
is that the seed of joy should be sown in mourning; and we can never be in so
forlorn a condition, wherein, if we understand Christ and ourselves, we have
not cause of joy. 'In me,' saith Christ, 'ye shall have peace,' John xvi. 33.
The world will feed us with 'bread of affliction,' Hos. ix. 4. If the world
can help it, we shall have sorrow enough; and Christ knows that well
enough, and stirs us up to a cheerful feeding on that he hath procured for
us. He hath both will, and skill, and power, and authority to feed us to
everlasting life, for the Father sent him forth, and sealed him to that purpose. All the springs of our joy are from him, Ps. lxxxvii. 7.

Our duty is to accept of Christ's inviting of us. What will we do for him,
if we will not feast with him? We will not suffer with him, if we will not
feast with him; we will not suffer with him, if we will not joy with him,
and in him. Happy are they that come, though compelled by crosses and
other sharp ways. If we rudely and churlishly refuse his feast here, we
are like never to taste of his feast hereafter. Nothing provokes so deeply
as kindness despised. It was the cause of the Jews' rejection. 'How
shall we escape,' not if we persecute, but 'if we do but neglect so great
salvation?' Heb. ii. 3.

That which we should labour to bring with us is a taste of these dainties,
and an appetite to them. The soul hath a taste of its own, and as all
creatures that have life have a taste to relish and distinguish of that which
is good for them, from that which is offensive, so wheresoever spiritual life
is, there is likewise a taste suitable to the sweet relish that is in spiritual
things. God should lose the glory of many excellent creatures if there were
not several senses to discern of several goodness in them. So if there were
not a taste in the soul, we could never delight in God, and his rich goodness in Christ.

Taste is the most necessary sense for the preservation of the creature,
because there is nearest application in taste; and that we should not be
deceived in taste, we hear, see, and smell before, and if these senses give
a good report of the object, then we taste of it and digest it, and turn it
into fit nourishment. *Omnis vita gustu ducitur.* So the spirit of man, after
judgment of the fitness of what is presented, tastes of it, delights in it, and
is nourished by it. There is an attractive, drawing power in the soul,
whereby every member sucks that out of the food that is convenient for it.
So the soul draws out what is well digested by judgment, and makes it its
own for several uses.

The chief thing that Christ requireth is a good stomach to these dainties.

1. The means to procure an appetite. We are first *to be sensible of
spiritual wants and misery.* The passover lamb was eaten with sour herbs;
so Christ crucified, relisheth best to a soul affected with bitterness of sin.
Whilst men are rich in their conceit, they go empty away. The duties and

performances they trust to, are but husks, windy, empty chaff. Swelling is not kind nourishment.

2. *That which hinders the sharpness of the stomach are, cold defluxions, that dull and flat the edge of it.* So upon plodding upon the world, cold distillations drop upon the soul, and take away the savour and desire of heavenly things. These things fill not. There is both a vanity of emptiness, and a vanity of short continuance in them. ' Why should we lay out our money,' Isa. lv. 2, spend our time, our wits, our endeavour so much about them? This makes so many starvelings in religion.

Besides, there be other noisome affections to be purged, as 1 Pet. ii. 1, ['Wherefore laying aside all malice, and all guile, and hypocrisies, and envies, and all evil speakings,' which breed a distaste and disaffection to spiritual things;] as malice and guile, &c. How can Christ be sweet to that soul unto which revenge is sweet!

3. *Exercise quickens appetite.* Those that exercise themselves unto godliness, see a need of spiritual strength to maintain duty. A dull formalist keeps his round, and is many years after where he was before; sees no need of further growth or strength. A Christian life, managed as it should be indeed, as it hath much going out, so it must have much coming in. It will not else be kept up. Those that have a journey to go, will refresh themselves for afterward, lest they faint by the way.

4. *Company likewise* of such as ' labour for that blessed food that endureth to life eternal,' John vi. 27, provoketh to fall too as the rest do, especially if they be equal or go beyond us in parts. For we will reason with ourselves, Have not I as much need as they? If these things be good for them, then they are good for me.

Thus St Paul foretelleth, that the example of the Gentiles should provoke the Jews to come in, and taste of the banquet Christ hath provided for both, Rom. xi. 25, 26. Especially this should stir us up earnestly to take our part in that Christ hath provided, because we know not how soon the table may be taken away. When men see the dishes in removing, though before they have discoursed away much time of their supper, yet then they will fall fresh to it. We know not how long wisdom will be inviting of us. It will be our wisdom to take our time, lest we put off so long, as wisdom herself laughs at our destruction; and a famine be sent, of all famines the most miserable, a famine of the word, and then we may pine away eternally without comfort. Christ will not always stand inviting of us. If we will none of his cheer, others will, and shall, when we shall starve.

Let this draw us on, that we see here Christ's hearty and free welcome, the gracious look that we are like to have from him. He counts it an honour, since he hath made such rich provision, for us to take part, and for our part, shew our unwillingness, that such free kindness should be refused. We cannot honour his bounty more than to feed liberally of that he liberally sets before us. We are glad to perceive our friends upon invitation to think themselves welcome. Let us open our mouth wide, since Christ is so ready to fill it. We are not straitened in his love, but in our own hearts. The widow's oil failed not till her vessels failed, 2 Kings iv. 6. We are bidden to delight in the Lord, and in whom should we delight, but where all fulness is to be had to delight in? Our spirits are not so large as those blessed comforts are which we are called to the enjoyment of. If the capacity of our souls were a thousand times larger, yet there is so large a sea of comfort in Christ, as they are not able to comprehend it. A taste of these good things breeds ' joy unspeakable,' and ' peace that passeth all

understanding,' Philip. iv. 7. What will the fulness do? This taste we
feel in the ordinances will bring us to that fulness hereafter. Oh, let us
keep our appetites for these things which are so delightful, so suitable to
the soul. How great is that goodness which he both lays up for hereafter,
and lays out for his, even here in this life !

In some ages of the church, the feasts that Christ hath made have been
more solemn and sumptuous than in other thereafter, as Christ hath been
more or less clearly and generally manifested. At Christ's first coming
there was a greater feast than before ; because the riches of God's love in
Christ were then laid open, and the pale of the church was enlarged by the
coming in of the Gentiles. So will there be a royal feast, when the Jews
shall be converted. ' Blessed then shall those be that shall be called to
the supper of the Lamb,' Rev. xix. 9. Suppers are in the end of the day,
and this supper shall be furnished towards the end of the world.

But then will be the true magnificent supper, when all that belong to
God's election shall meet together, and feed upon that heavenly manna for
ever. Then there will.be nothing but marrow itself, and wine without all
dregs. In all our contentments here, there is some mixture of the contrary;
then nothing but pure quintessence. In the mean time, he lets fall some
manna in this our wilderness, he lets us relish that now. It will not
putrefy as the other manna did, but endure, and make us endure for ever.
It's the true ' bread of life.'

Mark how Christ draws his spouse on to drink, and drink abundantly.
There is no danger of taking too much. Where the spring is infinite, we
can never draw these wells dry, never suck these breasts of consolation too
much ; and the more strong and cheerful we are, the better service we
shall perform, and the more accepted. Delight is as sugar, sweet in itself,
and it sweetens all things else. The joy of the Lord is our strength.
Duties come off more gracefully, and religion is made more lovely in the
eyes of all, when it comes forth in strength and cheerfulness. Christ's
housekeeping is credited hereby. In our Father's house is plenty enough,
Luke xv. 17. When the martyrs had drunk largely of this wine, it made
them forget friends, riches, honours, life itself. The joy stirred up by it,
carried them through all torments.

If any be hindered by conceit of unworthiness, if affected deeply with it,
let them consider what kind of men were compelled to the banquet, the
blind, the lame, Luke xiv. 21. See a lively picture of God's mercy in the
example of the prodigal. He fears sharp chiding, and the father provides
a rich banquet. He *goeth* to his father, but the father *runs* to meet him,
Luke xv. 20. Did Christ ever turn back any that came unto him, if they
came out of a true sense of their wants ?

' Eat, O friends.' Christ, out of the largeness of his affections, multiplieth
new titles and compellations—' beloved ' and ' friends.' Christ provides a
banquet, and invites his friends, not his enemies. Those good things that
neither ' eye hath seen, nor ear hath heard, that are above our conceit to
apprehend,' 1 Cor. ii. 9 ; these are provided for ' those that love him,'
not that hate him. He mingles another cup for them, ' a cup of wrath,'
and they are to ' drink up the very dregs of it,' Ps. lxxv. 8. Friendship
is the sweetness, intimateness, and strength of love. In our friends our
love dwells and rests itself. Conjugal friendship is the sweetest friendship.
All the kinds and degrees of friendship meet in Christ towards his spouse.
It is the friendship of a husband, of a brother ; and if there be any relation in
the world wherein friendship is, all is too little to express the love of Christ.

In friendship there is mutual consent, an union of judgment and affections. There is a mutual sympathy in the good and ill one of another, as if there were one soul in two bodies (b). There be mutual friends and mutual enemies. 'Do I not hate them,' saith David, 'that hate thee?' Ps. cxxxix. 21. There is mutual love of one another for their own sakes. In flattery, men love themselves most; in semblance, love others, but all is in reflection to themselves.

There is liberty which is the life of friendship; there is a free intercourse between friends, a free opening of secrets. So here Christ openeth his secrets to us, and we to him. We acquaint him with the most hidden thoughts of our hearts, and we lay open all our cares and desires before him. Thus Abraham was called God's friend, 2 Chron. xx. 7, and the disciples Christ's friends, John xv. 15. It is the office of the Spirit to reveal the secrets of Christ's heart to us, concerning our own salvation. He doth not reveal himself to the world.

In friendship, there is mutual solace and comfort one in another. Christ delighteth himself in his love to his church, and his church delighteth herself in her love to Christ. Christ's delight was to be with the sons of men, and ours is to be with him.

In friendship there is a mutual honour and respect one of another; but here is some difference in this friendship. For though Christ calls us friends, and therein in some sort brings himself down to us, yet we must remember that this is a friendship of unequals. Christ's honouring of us is his putting honour upon us. Our honouring of him is the giving him the 'honour due to his name,' 1 Chron. xvi. 29. This friendship must be maintained by due respect on our parts. As he is our friend, so he is our king, and knows how to correct us if we forget our distance. If he here seem to use us hardly, it is that he may use us the more kindly after. He suffers much for us, therefore we may well allow him the liberty of seasonable correcting of us.

He that inspireth friendship into others will undoubtedly keep the laws of friendship himself, will count our enemies his enemies. The enemies of the church shall one day know that the church is not friendless.

And as his friendship is sweet, so constant in all conditions. He useth not his friends as we do flowers, regard them only when they are fresh; but he breeds that in us that may make us such as he may still delight in us. If other friends fail, as friends may fail, yet this friend will never fail us. If we be not ashamed of him, he will never be ashamed of us. How comfortable would our life be if we could draw out the comfort that this title of *friend* affordeth! It is a comfortable, a fruitful, an eternal friendship.

'I sleep, but my heart waketh.' Here the church expresseth a changeable passage of her spiritual condition, after she had recovered herself out of a former desertion, expressed in the beginning of the third chapter; and enjoyed a comfortable intercourse with Christ. Now she falleth into a deeper desertion and temptation, from the remainder of corruption getting strength. The church now falleth asleep, then was awake in the night, and sought her beloved. Here is no present awaking, no seeking; there no misusage by the watchmen, as here. There she findeth him more speedily; here she falls sick with love before Christ discovereth himself.

Before we come to the words, observe in general,

Obs. 1. *That the state of the Church and every Christian is subject to spiritual alterations.* The church is always ' beloved,' a ' spouse,' a ' friend;' but in this one state there falleth out variety of changes. No creature sub-

ject to so many changes as man. From a state of innocency he fell into a
state of corruption. From that he, by grace, is restored to a state of grace,
and from grace to glory, where his condition shall be as Christ's now is, and
as heaven the place is, altogether unchangeable. And in that state of
grace, how many intercourses be there! the foundation of God's love to us,
and grace in us always remaining the same. Once beloved, for ever beloved.

We see here, after a feast, the church falleth asleep. See it in Abraham, sometimes 'strong in faith,' sometimes fearful. David sometimes
standing, sometimes falling, sometimes recovering himself and standing
faster, sometimes triumphing, 'The Lord is the light of my countenance,
whom shall I fear?' Ps. xxvii. 1; sometimes, again, 'I shall one day fall
by the hands of Saul,' 1 Sam. xxvii. 1. In the very same psalm he begins
with 'Rebuke me not in thy wrath,' and ends with 'Away, ye wicked,' Ps.
vi. 1, 10. Elias, though zealous, yet after flies for his life, 1 Kings xix.
So Job, Peter, sometimes resolute and valiant, other while sinks for fear,
Job vi.; Mat. xiv. 30.

The reason. The ground is, by reason of variety of outward occurrences
working upon the diversity of principles in us, nature and grace. Both
nature and grace are always active in us in some degree. When corruption gets strength, then we find a sick state creeping upon us, and lose our
former frame. It is with the soul as with the body. In a certain period
of time it gathereth ill humours, which break out into aguish distempers at
length; so the relics of a spiritual disease not carried away, will ripen and
gather to a head. This should teach us, when we are well, to study to keep
an even course, and to watch over the first stirrings, and likewise, if we see
some unevenness in our ways, not to censure ourselves or others over
harshly. Exact evenness is to be striven after here, but to be enjoyed in
another world.

Obs. 2. We see, by comparing the state of the church here with the
state of it in the third chapter, that *where corruption is not thoroughly purged,
and a careful watch kept over the soul, thereafter** *a recovery, will follow a more
dangerous distemper.* Corruption will not only strive for life, but for rule.
If there had been a thorough reformation in the church after her former
trouble, and a thorough closing with Christ, she would not thus have fallen
into a more dangerous condition. We see David, in his later times, falls
to 'numbering of the people,' 2 Sam. xxiv. 1, *seq.;* and Samson, after he had
done great services for the church, at length shamefully betrays his strength;
and he that had ruled others submits to be ruled by a base strumpet, Jud. xvi.
Jonah, for not thorough repenting for his running from his calling, falls
after to quarrel with God himself, Jonah iv. 9. It is the best, therefore, to
deal thoroughly with our hearts, else flesh unsubdued will owe us a greater
shame, and we shall dishonour our own beginnings. Yet this is the comfort, that this will occasion deeper humility and hatred of sin in those that
are God's, and a faster cleaving to God than ever before, as we see in the
church here. Afterwards grace will have the better at last.

Obs. 3. We may observe the *ingenuity*† *of the church in laying open her
own state.* It is the disposition of God's people to be ingenuous in opening their state to God, as in David, Nehemiah, Ezra, &c.

The reason is thus:—

(1.) By a free and full confession we give *God the honour of his wisdom
in knowing of our own condition, secret and open.* We give him the honour
of mercy that will not take advantage against us, the honour of power and

---

* Qu. 'there, after?'—ED.   † That is, 'ingenuousness.'—G.

authority over us, if he should shew his strength against us. We yield
unto him the glory of all his chief prerogatives; whereupon Joshua moveth
Achan to a free confession, ' My son, give glory to God,' Joshua vii. 19.

(2.) *We shame Satan*, who first takes away shame of sinning, and then
takes away shame for sin. He tempts us not to be ashamed to do that we
are ashamed to confess, so we, by silence, keep Satan's counsel against
our own souls. If we accuse ourselves, we put him out of office who is the
' accuser of the brethren,' Rev. xii. 10.

(3.) We *prevent, likewise, malicious imputations from the world.* Austin
answered roundly and well when he was upbraided with the sins of his former age : ' What thou,' saith he, ' findest fault with, I have condemned in
myself before.' *Quæ tu reprehendis, ego damnavi.*

(4.) This ingenuous dealing *easeth the soul*, giving vent to the grief of it.
Whiles the arrow's head sticks in the wound, it will not heal. Sin unconfessed is like a broken piece of rusty iron in the body, *ferrum in vulnere.*
It must be gotten out, else it will, by rankling and festering, cause more
danger. It is like poison in the stomach, if it be not presently cast up it
will infect the whole body. Is it not better to take shame to ourselves now,
than to be shamed hereafter before angels, devils, and men ? How careful
is God of us, by this private way to prevent future shame !

(5.) This faithful dealing with ourselves is oft a means of *present delivery
out of any trouble.* David, in Ps. xxxii. 4, was in a great distemper both
of body and spirit ; his moisture was turned into the drought of summer.
It is thought he made this psalm between the time of his sin and his pardon. What course taketh he ? ' I said,' saith he, that is, ' I resolved to
confess my sin, and thou forgavest the iniquity of my sin,' ver. 5. Upon
a free and full, a faithful and ingenuous confession, without all guile of
spirit, he found ease presently, both in soul and body. The cause of God's
severe dealing with us is, that we should deal severely with ourselves. The
best trial of religion in us is by those actions whereby we reflect on ourselves by judging and condemning of ourselves, for this argueth a spirit
without guile. Sin and shifting* came into the world together. The subtilty of proud nature, especially in eminency, is such that sins may pass
for virtues, because sin and Satan are alike in this, they cannot endure to
appear in their own colour and habit, and so those that oppose it shall be
accounted opposers of good. This guile of spirit hath no blessedness belonging to it. Take heed of it.

Obs. 4. Mark, further, one sign of a gracious soul, *to be abased for lesser
defects, sleepiness, and indisposition to good.* One would think drowsiness
were no such great matter. Oh, but the church had such sweet acquaintance with Christ, that every little indisposition that hindered any degree
of communion was grievous to her ! You shall have a Judas, a Saul, an
enormous offender confess great falls that gripe his conscience. All shall
be cast up, that the conscience, being disburdened, may feel a little ease ;
but how few have you humbled for dulness of spirit, want of love, of zeal,
and cheerfulness in duty ? This, accompanied with strife against it, argues
a good spirit indeed.

A carnal man is not more humbled for gross sins than a gracious Christian for wants in good actions, when it is not with him as it hath been,
and as he would. The reason is, where there is a clear and heavenly light,
there lesser motes are discernible ; and spiritual life is sensible of any obstruction and hindrance. This goeth in the world for unnecessary nicety (c).

* That is, ' evasions, expedients.'—G.

The world straineth not at these gnats. But those upon whose hearts the sun of righteousness hath shined have both a clear sight and a tender heart.

To come to the words, 'I sleep.' The church fetcheth a comparison from the body to express the state of the soul. It is one use of our body to help us in spiritual expressions. Whilst the soul dwelleth in the body, it dependeth much in the conceiving of things upon the phantasy,* and the phantasy upon the senses. We come to conceive of spiritual sleep by sleep of the body, which we are all well enough acquainted with.

The church, as she consists of a double principle, flesh and spirit mingled together in all parts, as darkness and light in the twilight and dawning of the day ; so here she expresseth her condition in regard of either part. So far as she was carnal, she slept; so far as she was spiritual, she was awake.

In this mixed condition the flesh for the present prevailed, yet so as the spirit had its working; ' she slept, but her heart waked.'

The words contain a confession, 'I sleep;' and a correction, 'but my heart waketh.' She hath a double aspect, one to the ill, 'her sleeping;' the other to the good, ' the heart in some degree awaked.' The Spirit of God is a discerning Spirit, it discovereth what is flesh and what is spirit.

So that we must not conceive this sleep to be that dead sleep all men are in by nature, nor to be that judicial sleep, that spirit of slumber, which is a further degree of that natural sleep to which God giveth up some, as a seal of their desperate condition ; but here is meant that sleep that ariseth out of the remainder of corruption unsubdued, and now, is here in the church, prevailing over the better part. Flesh and spirit have both their intercourse in us, as Moses and Amalek had. Unless we stand upon our guard, the flesh will get the upper ground, as we see here. The best are no further safe than they are watchful.

For the clear understanding of this, observe some correspondency in the resemblance; wherein too much curiosity is loathsome,† and postill-like (d); and calleth the mind too much from the kernel to the shell.

Bodily and spiritual sleep resemble each other in the causes, in the effects, and in the dangerous issue.

1. The sleep of the body cometh from the *obstruction and binding up of the senses by vapours which arise out of the stomach*. So there be spiritual fumes of worldly cares and desires that obstruct the senses of the soul. Therefore our blessed Saviour counts it a spiritual surfeiting, when the soul is oppressed with care about the world, Luke xxi. 34. Lusts bring the soul a-bed. Prosperity is a strong vapour. If it overcome not the brain, yet it weakeneth it, as strong waters do. See it in Solomon himself.

2. The disciples fell asleep in the garden when they were *oppressed with heaviness and sorrow*, Luke xxii. 45, which passions will have the like effect upon the soul.

3. Sleep ariseth oft from *weariness and want of spirits*. So there is a spiritual weariness arising from discouragements and too much expense ‡ of the strength of the soul upon other matters; upon impertinencies that concern not the best state of the soul.

4. Some are brought asleep by *music*. So many, by flattering enticements and insinuations of others, joining with their own flattering, deceitful heart, are cast into a spiritual sleep.

5. Sleep ariseth from *want of exercise*. When there is a cessation from spiritual exercise, about the proper object of it, there followeth a spiritual sleep. Exercise keeps waking.

* That is, 'fancy.'—G. † That is, ' offensive.'—G. ‡ That is, ' expenditure.'—G.

6. Sleep ariseth oft from *cold diseases, as lethargies*; from cold, gross humours. Cold, earthly, gross affections about the things here below, benumb the soul, and bring it into a heavy, drowsy, sleepy temper.

7. Sometimes sleep is caused by *some kind of poison*, especially the poison of asps, which kills in sleeping. And do not sinful delights do the like to the soul? Insensible evils are the most dangerous evils.

8. Otherwhile *slothful, yawning company* dispose to sleep. There is no more ordinary cause of spiritual sleep, than conversing with spiritual sluggards, that count it a high point of wisdom not to be forward in religion. These formal, proud persons, as they are cold themselves, so they labour to cast water upon the heat of others. Nay, those that are otherwise good, if declining in their first love, will incline others to a fellowship in the same secure temper, lest they should be upbraided by the vigilancy of others. They are like in the effects.

1. Men disposed to be asleep *desire to be alone*. Those likewise that are disposed to take a spiritual nap, will avoid company, especially of such as would awake them. They will hardly endure rousing means.

2. Men will *draw the curtains and shut out light*, when they mean to compose themselves to rest. So when men favour themselves in some ways not allowable, they are afraid to be disquieted by the light. Light both discovereth, awaketh, and stirs up to working. And men when they are loth to do what they know, are loth to know what they should do. 'They that sleep, sleep in the night,' 1 Thess. v. 7. Asa, otherwise a good king, shut up the prophet in prison for doing his duty, 2 Chron. xvi. 10. Much of the anger that men bear against the word laid open to them, is because it will not suffer them to sleep quietly in their sins. Such as will suffer them to live quietly in their sins,—they are quiet and honest men. There cannot be a worse sign than when men will not endure wholesome words. It is a sign they are in an ill league with that they should above all wage war against.

3. In sleep, *phantasy ruleth, and dreams in phantasy*. Men in sleep dream of false good, and forget true danger.

Many cherish golden dreams; dream of meat, and when they awake, their soul is empty, Isa. xxix. 8. Vain hopes are the dreams of waking men, as vain dreams are all the waking of sleeping and carnal men, whose life is but a dream.

In sleep, there is no exercise of senses or motion. As then, men are not sensible of good or ill, they move neither to good or ill. Motion followeth sensibleness. What good we are not sensible of, we move not unto. Hence sleep is of kin to death, for the time, depriving us of the use of all senses; and a secure professor in appearance differs little from a dead professor. Both of them are unactive in good; and what they do, they do it without delight, in an uncomely and unacceptable manner, unbeseeming the state of a Christian. It is all one to have no senses, and not to use them. We may say of men in this sleepy temper, as the Scripture speaks of idols, 'they have eyes and see not, ears and hear not,' &c., Ps. cxv. 5.

So likewise they are alike in danger. In sleep, the preciousest thing men carry about them is taken away without resistance; and they are ready to let loose what they held fast before, were it never so rich a jewel. And it is so in spiritual sleepiness. Men suffer the profession of the truth to be wrung from them, without much withstanding; and with letting fall their watch, let fall likewise, if not their grace, yet the exercise of their graces, and are in danger to be robbed of all.

There is no danger but a man in sleep is fair for, and exposed unto.
Sisera was slain asleep, Jud. v. 26, and Ishbosheth at noonday, 2 Sam. iv. 7;
and there is no temptation, no sin, no judgment, but a secure, drowsy
Christian is open for ; which is the ground of so oft enforcing watchfulness
by the Spirit of God in the Scriptures. As spiritual deadness of spirit is a
cause of other sin, so likewise it is a punishment of them. God poureth a
spirit of ' dead sleep upon men, and closeth up their eyes,' Isa. xxix. 10,
till some heavy judgment falleth upon them ; and how many carnal men
never awake in this world, till they awake in hell! No wonder therefore that Satan labours to cast men into a dead sleep all that he can ;
and deludes them, with dreams of a false good, that their estate is good,
and like so to continue ; that to-morrow shall be as to-day ; that no danger
is near, though God's wrath hangeth over their head, ready to be revealed
from heaven.

Thus we see how the resemblance holds. Some apply this to Constantine's time, about three hundred years after Christ, when the church upon
peace and plenty grew secure, and suffered ecclesiastical abuses to creep in.
Religion begat plenty, and the daughter devoured the mother. This made
the writers of the ecclesiastical stories, to question whether the church hath
more hurt by open persecution or peace, when one Christian undermineth
and rageth against another.* Human inventions were so multiplied, that
not long after, in Augustine's time, he complained that the condition of the
Jews was more tolerable than theirs ; † for though the Jews were under
burdens, yet they were such as were imposed by God himself, and not
human presumptions. But Gerson many hundred years after increaseth
his complaint.‡ If, O Augustine, thou saidst thus in thy time, what wouldst
thou have said if thou hadst lived now, when men, as a toy§ taketh them
in the head, will multiply burdens ? And he was not afraid to say, that
the number of human Constitutions was such, that if they were observed
in rigour, the greatest part of the church would be damned. Thus, whilst
the husbandmen slept, the envious man Satan slept not, but sew‖ his tares.
Thus popery grew up by degrees, till it overspread the church, whilst the
watchmen that should have kept others awake, fell asleep themselves. And
thus we answer the papists, when they quarrel with us about the beginning
of their errors. They ask of us, when such and such an heresy began ? We
answer, that those that should have observed them, were asleep. Popery
is a mystery that crept into the church by degrees, under glorious pretences.¶ Their errors had modest beginnings. Worshipping of images
arose from reserving the pictures of friends, and after that were brought
into the church. Invocation of saints arose from some of the fathers'
figurative turning of their speech to some that were dead. Transubstantiation had rise from some transcendent, unwary phrases of the fathers. The
papacy itself, from some titles of the Romish Church and bishop. Nothing
in popery so gross, but had some small beginnings, which being neglected
by those that should have watched over the church, grew at length unsuffer-
able. No wonder if the papists be cast into a dead sleep ; they have drunk
too deep of the whore's cup. They that worship images are, as the Scrip-

---

* Theodoret, lib 5.

† Augustine, Epist. ad Januar. cxix. Tolerabilior Judæorum conditio quam nostra.

‡ Si tuo tempore hæc dicebas (O sapiens Augustine) quid nostra tempestate
dixisses ? Si tenerentur in suo rigore, maxima pars Ecclesiæ damnaretur. Gerson
de vit. spiritual.   § That is, ' trifle.'—G.

‖ That is, ' sowed.'—G.   ¶ See Memoir of Sibbes, vol. i. p. lxv.

ture saith, ' like unto them, they have eyes and see not,' &c., Ps. cxv. 5. They cannot discern of their errors, though they be never so ridiculous and senseless, as prayer in an unknown tongue, and such like.

And upon this state of the church let us add this caution.

A Caution. If the best men be so prone to sleep, then we cannot safely at all times build upon their judgment. The fathers of the church were not always awake. There be few of them, but in some things we may appeal from themselves sleeping, to themselves waking. The best, having some darkness left in their understandings, and some lusts unsubdued in their affections, may write and speak sometimes out of the worst part and principle that is in them, as well as out of the best, when they keep not close to the rule.

When our adversaries press us with the authority of fathers, we appeal to them, where they speak advisedly and of purpose.* When they were not awaked by heretics, they speak sometimes unworthily, and give advantages to heretics that followed. It is the manner of our adversaries to make the unwarrantable practice of the ancienter time a rule of their practice, and the doubtful opinions of the ancients their own grand tenets ; wherein in both they deal unsafely for themselves, and injuriously towards us, when we upon grounds in some things dissent; which liberty (oft when they should not) they will take to themselves.

But howsoever this sleepy condition agreeth to the former times of the church, yet I wish there were not cause to apply it to ourselves, in this latter age of the church, wherein many of the ancient heresies are revived ; and besides, the evils that accompany long peace take hold of us, and will prevail too far, if we do not rouse up ourselves. The church is in the commonwealth, and usually they flourish and fall together. When there is a sleep of the church, for the most part there is a sleep of the state. A civil sleep is, when in grounds of danger there is no apprehension of danger ; and this sleep is a punishment of spiritual sleep, when with Ephraim a state hath ' grey hairs, and knoweth it not,' Hos. vii. 9 ; when judgments abroad will not awake men. When noise and pinching will not awake, the sleep must needs be deep. The whole world almost is in combustion round about us ; and many countries thought themselves as safe, a little before their troubles, as we now think ourselves. If fear of outward dangers will not awake, then spiritual dangers will not, as being more secret, and not obvious to sense. No wonder, then, if few will believe our report of the fearful condition of wicked men in the world to come. A man may be startled and awaked with outward dangers that is spiritually sottish, but he that is careless of outward danger, will be regardless of what we say in spiritual dangers. The fear of danger may be the greater, when, as it was amongst the Jews, those that should be watchful themselves, and awake others, instead of awaking, rock the cradle, and cry ' Peace, peace, the temple of the Lord, the temple of the Lord,' Jer. vii. 4. Yet we must never forget to be mindful, with thankfulness, for peace and the gospel of peace, which yet by God's blessing we enjoy, always suspecting the readiness of nature to grow secure under the abundance of favours, and so to bless ourselves in that condition.

Signs of a sleepy state. 1. Now we know that sleep is creeping upon us, by *comparing our present condition with our former,* when we were in a more wakeful frame, when the graces of God's Spirit were in exercise in us. If we differ from that we were, then all is not well.

---

* Patres in maximis sunt nostri, in multis varii, in minimis vestri.— *Wh*[*itaker*].

2. Compare ourselves again with that *state and frame that a Christian
should be in;* for sometimes a Christian goes under an uncomfortable
condition all the days of his life, so that he is not fit to make himself his
pattern. The true rule is, that description that is in the word, of a waking
and living Christian. What should a man be, take him at the best, the
varying from that is a sleepy estate. As, for instance, a Christian should
walk 'in the comfort of the Holy Ghost,' Acts ix. 31, live and walk by
faith; he should depend upon God, and resist temptations. Faith should
work by love, and love to ourselves should move us to honour ourselves as
members of Christ, to disdain to defile ourselves by sin. Our hope, if it
be waking, will purge us, and make us suitable to the condition we hope
for in heaven, and the company we hope to have fellowship with there.

3. Again, *look to the examples of others that are more gracious.* I have as
many encouragements to be thankful to God, and fruitful. They enjoy no
more means than I; and yet they abound in assurance, are comfortable in
all conditions. I am down in a little trouble, subject to passion, to barrenness, and distrust, as if there were no promises of God made to sowing in
righteousness. Thus a man may discern he is asleep, by comparing himself with others that are better than himself.

4. Again, it is evident that we are growing on to a sleepy condition by
this, when we find *a backwardness to spiritual duties,* as to prayer, thanksgiving, and spiritual conference. It should be the joy of a Christian, as it
is his prerogative, to come into the presence of Christ, and to be enabled to
do that, that is above himself. When what is spiritual in a duty will not
down with us, it is a sign our souls are in a sleepy temper. There is not
a proportion between the soul and the business in heavenly duties. Whom
do we speak to but God? whom do we .hear speak in the word but God?
what should be the temper of those that speak to God, and hear him speak
to them? It should be regardful, reverent, observant. Those that are
watchful to the eye of a prince, what observance they shew, when they are
to receive anything from him or to put up any request to him. 'Offer this
to thy king,' saith the Lord by Malachi, Mal i. 8. When a man comes
drowsily to God, to sacrifice, to hear, to pray, &c., offer this carriage to
man; will he take it at thy hands? Oh the mercy of our patient God, that
will endure such services as we most frequently perform! By this indisposedness to duty more or less, may we discover our sleepiness.

5. When the soul begins to *admire outward excellencies;* when it awakes
much to profits, pleasures, and honours; when men admire great men, rich
men, great places. The strength and fat of the soul are consumed by
feeding on these things; so that when it comes to spiritual things it must
needs be faint and drowsy. By these and the like signs, let us labour to
search the state of our souls.

Motives against sleepiness. 1. And to stir us up the more, *consider the
danger of a secure, sleepy estate.* There is no sin but a man is exposed unto
in a secure estate. Therefore the devil labours all he can to cast men into
this temper; which he must do before he can make him fall into any gross
sin. When he is asleep, he is in a fit frame for any ill action; he is in a
temper fit for the devil to work upon; to bring into any dream or error; to
inflame the fancies and conceits with outward excellencies. The devil hath
a faculty this way, to make outward things great that are nothing worth,
and to make such sins little as, if we were awake, would affright us. He
works strongest upon the fancy, when the soul is sleepy or a little drowsy.

There is no man that comes to gross sin suddenly. But he falls by little and little; first to slumber, and from slumber to sleep, and from sleep to security; and so from one degree to another. It is the inlet to all sins, and the beginning of all danger. Therefore the Lord takes a contrary course with his. When he would preserve a state or person, he plants in them first a spirit of faith, to believe that there is such a danger, or such a good to be apprehended, upon watching and going on in a course befitting that condition; and then faith, if it be a matter of threatening, stirs up fear, which waketh up care and diligence. This is God's method, when he intends the preservation of any.

2. A man in his sleep *is fit to lose all*. A sleepy hand lets anything go with ease. A man hath grace and comfort; he lets it go in his spiritual sleepiness,—grace in a great measure, and the sense and comfort of it altogether. A Christian hath always the divine nature in him, that works in some degree; yet notwithstanding in regard of his present temper and feeling, he may be in such a case, that he shall differ nothing from a reprobate, nay, he may come to feel more than any ordinary wicked man feels whiles he lives in the world, as divers good Christians do. And all this, through their carelessness,—that they suffer themselves to be robbed of first beginnings, by yielding to delights, company, and contentments. Feeding their conceits with carnal excellencies, so favouring corruptions, and flattering that that is naught in them, they lose the comfort of all that is good. Who would do this for the gaining of a little broken sleep; I say broken sleep, for the better a man is, the more unquietly shall he sleep in such a state. He shall feel startlings and frights in the midst of his carnal delights if he belong to God.

3, Besides, *God meets them with some crosses in this world*, that they shall gain nothing by it. There is none of God's children that ever gained by yielding to any corruption, or drowsiness, though God saved their souls. It is always true, a secure state is a sure forerunner of some great cross, or of some great sin. God cannot endure such a temper of soul; lifeless and unfeeling performances and sacrifices, to him that hath given us such encouragements. It must needs be distasteful to God, when we go drowsily and heavily about his work. ' Cursed is he that doth the work of the Lord negligently,' Jer. xlviii. 10. If it were to sheath his sword in the bowels of his enemy, to which man is exceedingly prone, yet if it be not done with diligence and an eye to God, a man is cursed in it.

4. And it is an *odious temper to God*. For doth not he deserve cheerful service at our hands? hath he been a 'wilderness' to us? doth he not deserve the marrow of our souls? doth not his greatness require it at our hands, that our senses be all waking? and doth not his mercy deserve, that our love should take all care, to serve him that is so gracious and good to us? Is it not the fruit of our redemption to serve him without fear, in holiness and righteousness all the days of our lives? Luke i. 14.

5. It is a state not only odious to God, but *irksome to our own spirits*. The conscience is never fully at peace in a drowsy state or in drowsy performances.

Likewise it is not graceful to others. It breeds not love in them to good things, but dislike. Carnal men, let them see a Christian not carry himself waking, as he should, though they be a thousand times worse themselves, yet notwithstanding they think it should not be so. Such a course doth not suit with so much knowledge and so much grace.

Let a man consider, wherefore God hath given the powers of the soul and the graces of the Spirit. Are they not given for exercise, and to be employed about their proper objects? A man is not a man, a Christian is

not a Christian, when he is not waking. He so far degenerates from himself, as he yields unto any unbeseeming carriage. Wherefore hath God
given us understanding, but to conceive the best things? Wherefore have
we judgment, but to judge aright between the things of heaven and
earth? Wherefore have we love planted in us, but to set it on lovely
objects? Wherefore faith, but to trust God over all? Wherefore hatred,
but to fly ill? Wherefore have we affections, but for spiritual things?
When therefore our affections are dull, and lose their edge to these
things, being quick only to earthly things, what a temper is this! How
doth a man answer his creation, the state of a new creature! Wherefore are all graces planted in the soul, as faith and love, and hope and
patience, but to be in exercise, and waking? To have these, and to let
them sleep and lie unexercised, so far a Christian forgets himself, and is
not himself. A Christian as a Christian, that is, in his right temper, should
be in the act and exercise of what is good in him, upon all occasions ; as
we say of God, he is a pure act, because he is always in working. The
Spirit of God is a pure act, in whom is no suffering but all action, about
that that is fit for so glorious a nature. So it is with the spirit of a man,
that hath the Spirit of God. He is in act, in exercise, in operation, as the
Spirit is more or less in him. So he is more or less in operation, more or
less fruitful. What a world of good might Christians do, if they were in a
right temper! What a deal of ill might they escape and avoid that they lie
in, if they would rouse up their souls to be as Christians should be, and as
their soul and conscience tells them they ought and might be, did they
rightly improve the means they have !

THE FOURTH SERMON.

I sleep, but my heart wakes, &c.—CANT. V. 2.

THE words, as it hath been shewed, contain a confession, ' I sleep,' and
a correction, ' my heart waketh.' The confession hath been handled, now
something of the correction or exception.

' My heart waketh.' The word heart, you know, includes the whole soul,
for the understanding is the heart, ' an understanding heart,' Job xxxviii. 36.
To ' lay things up in our hearts,' Luke ii. 51, there it is memory ; and to
cleave in heart is to cleave in will, Acts xi. 23. To ' rejoice in heart,' Isa.
xxx. 29, that is in the affection. So that all the powers of the soul, the
inward man, as Paul calleth it, 2 Cor. iv. 16, is the heart.

' I sleep, but my heart waketh.' Indeed the church might have said,
My heart sleepeth, but my heart waketh. For it is the same faculty, the
same power of the soul, both in the state of corruption, and of grace, in
which the soul is ; as in the twilight we cannot say, this is light and that is
darkness, because there is such a mixture. In all the powers of the soul
there is something good and something ill, something flesh and something
spirit. The heart was asleep, and likewise was awake. ' I sleep, but my
heart waketh.'

Obs. 1. You see here, then, first of all, in this correction, *that a Christian
hath two principles in him,* that which is good, and that which is evil, whence
issueth the weakness of his actions and affections. They are all mixed, as
are the principles from which they come forth.

Obs. 2. We may observe, further, *that a Christian man may know how it is with himself*. Though he be mixed of flesh and spirit, he hath a distinguishing knowledge and judgment whereby he knows both the good and evil in himself. In a dungeon where is nothing but darkness, both on the eye that should see and on that which should be seen, he can see nothing; but where there is a supernatural principle, where there is this mixture, there the light of the Spirit searcheth the dark corners of the heart. A man that hath the Spirit knoweth both; he knoweth himself and his own heart. The Spirit hath a light of its own, even as reason hath. How doth reason know what it doth? By a reflect act inbred in the soul. Shall a man that is natural reflect upon his state, and know what he knows, what he thinks, what he doth, and may not the soul that is raised to an higher estate know as much? Undoubtedly it may. Besides, we have the Spirit of God, which is light, and self-evidencing. It shews unto us where it is, and what it is. The work of the Spirit may sometimes be hindered, as in times of temptation. Then I confess a man may look wholly upon corruption, and so mistake himself in judging by that which he sees present in himself, and not by the other principle which is concealed for a time from him. But a Christian, when he is not in such a temptation, he knows his own estate, and can distinguish between the principles in him of the flesh and spirit, grace and nature.

Again, we see here in that the church saith, 'but my heart waketh,' that she doth acknowledge there is good as well as evil. As the church is ingenious* to confess that which is amiss, 'I sleep,' so she is as true in confessing that which is good in herself, 'but my heart waketh,' which yields us another observation.

Obs. 3. We should *as well acknowledge that which is good as that which is evil in our hearts*.

Because we must not bear false witness, as not against others, much less against ourselves. Many help Satan, the accuser, and plead his cause against the Spirit, their comforter, in refusing to see what God seeth in them. We must make conscience of this, to know the good as well as the evil, though it be never so little.

To come in particular, what is that good the church here confesseth, when she saith that 'her heart waketh?'

(1.) She in her sleepy estate, *first*, hath her *judgment sound in that which is truth, of persons, things, and courses*. Christians are not so benighted when they sleep, or given up to such a reprobate judgment, as that they discern not differences. They can discern that such are in a good way, and such are not; that such means are good, and such are not. A Christian ofttimes is forced to do work out of judgment, in case his affections are asleep or distracted; and such works are approved of God, as they come from a right judgment and conviction, though the evil of them be chastised.

(2.) But all is not in the judgment. The child of God asleep hath a *working in the will*. Choosing the better part, which he will cleave to, he hath a general purpose 'to please God in all things,' and no settled purpose in particular for to sleep. Thus answerable to his judgment, therefore, he chooseth the better part and side; he owns God and his cause, even in evil times, cleaving in resolution of heart to the best ways, though with weakness.

Take David in his sleepy time between his repentance and his foul sin. If one should have asked him what he thought of the ways of God and of

* That is, 'ingenuous.'—G.

the contrary, he would have given you an answer out of sound judgment thus and thus. If you should have asked him what course he would have followed in his choice, resolution, and purpose, he would have answered savourly.

(3.) Again, there remaineth *affection answerable to their judgment*, which, though they find, and feel it not for a time, it being perhaps scattered, yet there is a secret love to Christ, and to his cause and side, joined with joy in the welfare of the church and people of God; rejoicing in the prosperity of the righteous, with a secret grief for the contrary. The pulses will beat this way, and good affections will discover themselves. Take him in his sleepy estate, the judgment is sound in the main, the will, the affections, the joy, the delight, the sorrow. This is an evidence his heart is awake.

(4.) *The conscience likewise is awake.* The heart is taken ofttimes for the conscience in Scripture. A good conscience, called a merry heart, is ' a continual feast,' Prov. xv. 15. Now, the conscience of God's children is never so sleepy but it awaketh in some comfortable measure. Though perhaps it may be deaded * in a particular act, yet notwithstanding there is so much life in it, as upon speech or conference, &c., there will be an opening of it, and a yielding at the length to the strength of spiritual reason. His conscience is not seared. David was but a little roused by Nathan, yet you see how he presently confessed ingeniously † that he had sinned, 2 Sam. xii. 13. So, when he had numbered the people, his conscience presently smote him, 2 Sam. xxiv. 10; and when he resolved to kill Nabal and all his family, which was a wicked and carnal passion, in which there was nothing but flesh; yet when he was stopped by the advice and discreet counsel of Abigail, we see how presently he yielded, 1 Sam. xxv. 32, *seq.* There is a kind of perpetual tenderness of conscience in God's people. All the difference is of more or less.

(5.) And answerable to these inward powers is the *outward obedience of God's children.* In their sleepy estate they go on in a course of obedience. Though deadly and coldly, and not with that glory that may give others good example or yield themselves comfort, yet there is a course of good duties. His ordinary way is good, howsoever he may step aside. His fits may be sleepy when his estate is waking. We must distinguish between a state and a fit. A man may have an aguish fit in a sound body. The state of a Christian is a waking state in the inward man. The bye-courses he falleth into are but fits, out of which he recovers himself.

Use 1. Whence, for use, let us magnify the goodness of God, that will remain by his Spirit, and let it stay to preserve life in such hearts as ours are, so prone to security and sleepiness. Let it put us in mind of other like merciful and gracious doings of our God for us, that he gave his Spirit to us when we had nothing good in us, when it met with nothing but enmity, rebellion, and indisposedness. Nay, consider how he debased himself and became man, in being united to our frail flesh, after an admirable ‡ nearness, and all out of mercy to save us.

Use 2. If so be that Satan shall tempt us in such occasions, let us enter into our own souls, and search the truth of grace, our judgment, our wills, our constant course of obedience, and the inward principle whence it comes, that we may be able to stand in the time of temptation. What upheld the church but this reflect act, by the help of the Spirit, that she was able to judge of the good as well as of the ill? Thus David, ' The desires of our souls are towards thee,' Ps. xxxviii. 9; and though all this have befallen us,

* That is, 'deadened.'—G.   † That is, 'ingenuously.'—G.   ‡ That is, 'wonderful.'—G.

yet have we not forgotten thy name, Ps. xliv. 20. This will enable us to appeal to God, as Peter, 'Lord, thou knowest I love thee,' John xxi. 15. It is an evidence of a good estate.

Obs. 1. 'My heart waketh.' *God's children never totally fall from grace.* Though they sleep, yet their heart is awake. The prophet Isaiah, speaking of the church and children of God, Isa. vi. 13, saith, 'It shall be as a tree, as an oak whose substance is in them, when they cast their leaves.' Though you see neither fruit nor leaves, yet there is life in the root, 'the seed remains in them.' There is alway a seed remaining. It is an immortal seed that we are begotten by. Peter, when he denied his Master, was like an oak that was weather-beaten; yet there was life still in the root, 1 Pet. i. 3, Mat. xxvi. 32, *seq.* For, questionless, Peter loved Christ from his heart. Sometimes a Christian may be in such a poor case, as the spiritual life runneth all to the heart, and the outward man is left destitute; as in wars, when the enemy hath conquered the field, the people run into the city, and if they be beaten out of the city, they run into the castle. The grace of God sometimes fails in the outward action, in the field, when yet it retireth to the heart, in which fort it is impregnable. 'My heart waketh.'

When the outward man sleeps, and there are weak, dull performances, and perhaps actions amiss, too, yet notwithstanding 'the heart waketh.' As we see in a swoon or great scars, the blood, spirits, and life, though they leave the face and hands, &c., yet they are in the heart. It is said in the Scripture of Eutychus, 'His life is in him still,' though he seemed to be dead, Acts xx. 9. As Christ said of Lazarus, John xi. 4, so a man may say of a Christian in his worst state, His life is in him still; he is not dead, but sleeps; 'his heart waketh.'

Obs. 2. *This is a sound doctrine and comfortable, agreeable to Scripture and the experience of God's people.* We must not lose it, therefore, but make use of it against the time of temptation. There are some pulses that discover life in the sickest man, so are there some breathings and spiritual motions of heart that will comfort in such times. These two never fail on God's part, his love, which is unchangeable, and his grace, a fruit of his love; and two on our part, the impression of that love, and the gracious work of the new creature. 'Christ never dies,' saith the apostle, Heb. vii. 25. As he never dies in himself, after his resurrection, so he never dies in his children. There is always spiritual life.

Use for comfort. 'The heart waketh.' This is a secret of God's sanctuary, only belonging to God's people. Others have nothing to do with it. They shall ever love God, and God will ever love them. The apostle, 1 Cor. xiii. 8, saith, 'Love never fails.' Gifts, you know, shall be abolished, because the manner of knowing we now use shall cease. 'We see through a glass,' &c., 'but love abideth,' 1 Cor. xiii. 12. Doth our love to God abide for ever, and doth not his love to us, whence it cometh? Ours is but a reflection of God's love. Let us comfort ourselves, therefore, in this for the time to come, that in all the uncertainty of things in this life we have to-day and lose to-morrow, as we see in Job, there is somewhat a saint may build on that is constant and unmoveable. 'I am the Lord, I change not; therefore you sons of Jacob are not consumed,' Mal. iii. 6. God should deny himself, as it were, which he cannot do, and his own constant nature, if he should vary this way.

Obs. 3. *A Christian is what his heart and inward man is.* It is a true speech of divines, God and nature begin there. Art begins with the face and outward lineaments, as hypocrisy, outward painting and expressions;

but grace at the centre, and from thence goes to the circumference. And therefore the church values herself here by the disposition and temper of her heart. Thus I am for my outward carriage, &c. ' I sleep, but my heart, that waketh.'

Therefore, let us enter into our consciences and souls, for the trial of our estates, how it is with our judgments. Do we allow of the ways of God and of the law of the inward man? How is it with our affections and bent to good things? how with our hatred, our zeal? Is it not more for outward things than for inward? We know what Jehu said to Jonadab, when he would have him into his chariot, ' Is thine heart as mine? Then come to me,' 2 Kings x. 15. So saith Christ, Is thine heart as mine? then give me thy hand. But first God must have our hearts, and then our hands. A man otherwise is but a ghost in religion, which goes up and down, without a spirit of its own; but a picture that hath an outside, and is nothing within. Therefore, especially, let us look to our hearts. ' Oh, that there were such an heart in this people,' saith God to Moses, ' to fear me always, for their good,' Deut. v. 29. This is it that God's children desire, that their hearts may be aright set. ' Wash thy heart, O Jerusalem,' saith the prophet, ' from thy wickedness,' &c., Jer. iv. 14. Indeed, all the outward man depends upon this. Therefore, Satan, if he can get this fort, he is safe, and so Satan's vicar, Prov. iv. 23. It was a watchword that was in Gregory XIII. his time, in Queen Elizabeth's days, ' My son, give me thy heart. Dissemble, go to church, and do what you will; but, *da mihi cor,* be in heart a papist, and go where you will' (*e*). God is not content with the heart alone. The devil knows if he have the heart he hath all; but God, as he made all, both soul and body, he will have all. But yet in times of temptation the chief trial is in the heart.

And from hence we may have a main difference between one Christian and another. A sound Christian doth what he doth from the heart; he begins the work there. What good he doth he loves in his heart first, judgeth it to be good, and then he doeth it.

An hypocrite doth what he doth outwardly, and allows not inwardly of that good he doth. He would do ill, and not good, if it were in his choice. The good that he doth is for by-ends, for correspondence, or dependence upon others, or conformity with the times, to cover his designs under formality of religion, that he may not be known outwardly, as he is inwardly, an atheist and an hypocrite. So he hath false aims; his heart is not directed to a right mark. But it is otherwise with God's child. Whatsoever good he doth, it is in his heart first; whatsoever ill he abstains from, he doth it from his heart, judging it to be naught; therefore he hates it, and will not do it. Here is a main difference of the church from all others. It wakes in the heart, though the outward man sleeps. But other men's hearts sleep when they wake, as you know some men will walk and do many things in their sleep. An hypocrite is such a kind of man. He walks and goes up and down, but his heart is asleep. He knows not what he doth, nor doth he the thing out of judgment or love, but as one asleep, as it were. He hath no inward affection unto the things he doth. A Christian is the contrary; his heart is awake when he is asleep.

Another difference from the words you may have thus. A Christian, by the power of God's Spirit in him, is sensible of the contrarieties in him, complains, and is ashamed for the same. But an hypocrite is not so; he is not sensible of his sleepiness. ' I sleep,' saith the church. So much as the church saith she slept, so much she did not sleep; for a man that is asleep cannot say he is asleep, nor a dead man that he is dead. So far as he saith he is asleep, he is awake. Now, the church confesseth that she was asleep by that part that was awake in her. Other men do not complain, are not sensible of their sleepiness and slumbering, but compose themselves to slumber, and seek darkness, which is a friend of sleep. They would willingly be ignorant, to keep their conscience dull and dumb as much as they can, that it may not upbraid them. This is the disposition of a carnal man; he is not sensible of his estate as here the church is.

Obs. 4. *A waking state is a blessed state.* The church you see supports and comforts herself that she was waking in her inward man, that she was happy in that respect.

Quest. How shall we do to keep and preserve our souls in this waking condition, especially in these drowsy times?

Ans. 1. *Propound unto them waking considerations.* What causeth our sleeps but want of matters of more serious observation? None will sleep when a thing is presented of excellency more than ordinary. To see, and know, and think of what a state we are now advanced unto in Christ; what we shall be ere long, yet the fearful estate we should be in, if God leave us to ourselves! a state of astonishment, miserable and wretched, beyond speech, nay, beyond conceit!* Thus did the blessed souls in former times exercise their thoughts, raise, and stir them up by meditation, that so they might hold their souls in a high esteem of the best things, and not suffer them to sleep. We never fall to sleep in earthly and carnal delights, till the soul let its hold go of the best things, and ceaseth to think of, and to wonder at them. What made Moses to fall from the delights of Egypt? He saw the basest things in religion were greater than the greatest things in the court, yea, in the world. 'He esteemed the reproach of Christ better than the greatest treasures of Egypt,' Heb. xi. 26.

2. Make the *heart think of the shortness and vanity of this life*, with the uncertainty of the time of our death; and of what wondrous consequent† it is to be in the state of grace before we die. The uncertainty of the gales of grace, that there may be a good hour which, if we pass, we may never have the like again, Luke xix. 42, Mat. xxiii. 37; as the angel descended at a certain hour into the pool of Bethesda, John v. 4, when those that entered not immediately after, went away sick as they came. So there are certain good hours which let us not neglect. This will help to keep us waking.

3. *The necessity of grace,* and then the free dispensing of it in God's good time, and withal the terror of the Lord's-day, 'Remembering,' saith St Paul, 'the terror of the Lord, I labour to stir up all men,' &c., 2 Cor. v. 11. Indeed it should make us stir up our hearts when we consider the terror of the Lord; to think that ere long we shall be all drawn to an exact account, before a strict, precise judge. And shall our eyes then be sleeping and careless? These and such like considerations out of spiritual wisdom we should propound to ourselves, that so we might have waking souls, and preserve them in a right temper.

Ans. 2. *To keep faith waking.* The soul is as the object is that is presented to it, and as the certainty of the apprehension is of that object. It conduceth much therefore to the awakening of the soul to keep faith awake. It is not the greatness alone, but the presence of great things that stirs us. Now it is the nature of faith to make things powerfully present to the soul; for it sets things before us in the word of Jehovah, that made all things of

---

* That is 'conception.'—G.   † That is, 'consequence.'—G.

nothing, and is Lord of his word, to give a being to whatsoever he hath spoken, Heb. xi. 1. Faith is an awakening grace. Keep that awake, and it will keep all other graces waking.

When a man believes, that all these things shall be on fire ere long; that heaven and earth shall fall in pieces; that we shall be called to give an account, [and that] before that time we may be taken away—is it not a wonder we stand so long, when cities, stone walls fall, and kingdoms come to sudden periods? When faith apprehends, and sets this to the eye of the soul, it affects the same marvellously. Therefore let faith set before the soul some present thoughts according to its temper. Sometimes terrible things to awaken it out of its dulness; sometimes glorious things, promises and mercies, to waken it out of its sadness, &c. When we are in a prosperous estate let faith make present all the sins and temptations that usually accompany such an estate, as pride, security, self-applause, and the like. If in adversity, think also of what sins may beset us there. This will awaken up such graces in us, as are suitable to such an estate, for the preventing of such sins and temptations, and so keep our hearts in 'exercise to godliness,' 1 Tim. iv. 7; than which, nothing will more prevent sleeping.

Ans. 3. And withal, *labour for abundance of the Spirit of God.* For what makes men sleepy, and drowsy? The want of spirits. We are dull, and overloaden with gross humours, whereby the strength sinks and fails. Christians should know, that there is a necessity, if they will keep themselves waking, to keep themselves spiritual. Pray for the Spirit above all things. It is the life of our life, the soul of our soul. What is the body without the soul, or the soul without the Spirit of God? Even a dead lump. And let us keep ourselves in such good ways, as we may expect the presence of the Spirit to be about us, which will keep us awake.

Ans. 4. *We must keep ourselves in as much light as may be.* For all sleepiness comes with darkness. Let us keep our souls in a perpetual light. When any doubt or dark thought ariseth, upon yielding thereunto comes a sleepy temper. Sleepiness in the affections ariseth from darkness of judgment. The more we labour to increase our knowledge, and the more the spiritual light and beams of it shine in at our windows, the better it will be for us, and the more shall we be able to keep awake. What makes men in their corruptions to avoid the ministry of the word, or anything that may awake their consciences? It is the desire they have to sleep. They know, the more they know, the more they must practise, or else they must have a galled conscience. They see religion will not stand with their ends. Rich they must be, and great they will be; but if they suffer the light to grow upon them, that will tell them they must not rise, and be great, by these and such courses. A gracious heart will be desirous of spiritual knowledge especially, and not care how near the word comes; because they ingeniously* and freely desire to be spiritually better. They make all things in the world yield to the inward man. They desire to know their own corruptions and evils more and more. And therefore love the light 'as children of the light, and of the day,' 1 Thess. v. 5. Sleep is a work of darkness. Men therefore of dark and drowsy hearts desire darkness, for that very end that their consciences may sleep.

Ans. 5. *Labour to preserve the soul in the fear of God:* because fear is a waking affection, yea, one of the wakefullest. For, naturally we are more moved with dangers, than stirred with hopes. Therefore, that affection, that is most conversant about danger, is the most rousing and waking

* That is, 'ingenuously.'—G.

affection. Preserve therefore the fear of God by all means. It is one character of a Christian, who, when he hath lost almost all grace, to his feeling, yet the fear of God is always left with him. He fears sin, and the reward of it, and therefore God makes that awe the bond of the new covenant. ' I will put my fear into their hearts, that they shall never depart from me,' Jer. xxxii. 39. One Christian is better than another, by how much more he wakes, and fears more than another. Of all Christians, mark those are most gracious, spiritual, and heavenly, that are the most awful and careful of their speeches, courses, and demeanours ; tender even of offending God in little things. You shall not have light and common oaths come from them, nor unsavoury speeches. Sometimes a good Christian may in a state of sleepiness be faulty some way. But he grows in the knowledge of the greatness of God, and the experience of his own infirmities, as he grows in the sense of the love of God. He is afraid to lose that sweet communion any way, or to grieve the Spirit of God. Therefore, always as a man grows in grace, he grows in awfulness, and in jealousy of his own corruptions. Therefore let us preserve by all means this awful affection, the fear of God. Let us then often search the state of our own souls ; our going backward or forward ; how it is between God and our souls ; how fit we are to die, and to suffer ; how fit for the times that may befall us. Let us examine the state of our own souls, which will preserve us in a waking estate ; especially examine ourselves in regard of the sins of the place, and the times where we live ; of the sins of our own inclination, how we stand affected and biassed in all those respects, and see how jealous we are of dangers in this kind. Those that will keep waking souls, must consider the danger of the place where they live, and the times ; what sins reign, what sins such a company as they converse with, are subject unto, and their own weakness to be led away with such temptations. This jealousy is a branch of that fear that we spake of before, arising from the searching of our own hearts, and dispositions. It is a notable means to keep us awake, when we keep our hearts in fear of such sins as either by calling, custom, company, or the time we live in, or by our own disposition, we are most prone to.

There is no Christian, but he hath some special sin, to which he is more prone than to another, one way or other, either by course of life, or complexion. Here now is the care and watchfulness of a Christian spirit, that knowing by examination, and trial of his own heart, his weakness, he doth especially fence against that, which he is most inclined to ; and is able to speak most against that sin of all others, and to bring the strongest arguments to dishearten others from practice of it.

Ans. 6. In the last place it is a thing of no small consequence, *that we keep company with waking and faithful Christians*, such as neither sleep themselves or do willingly suffer any to sleep that are near them.

It is a report, and a true one, of the sweating sickness, that they that were kept awake by those that were with them, escaped ; but the sickness was deadly if they were suffered to sleep. It is one of the best fruits of the communion of saints, and of our spiritual good acquaintance, to keep one another awake. It is an unpleasing work on both sides. But we shall one day cry out against all them that have pleased themselves and us, in rocking us asleep, and thank those that have pulled us ' with fear,' Jude 23, out of the fire, though against our wills.

Let us labour upon our own hearts in the conscionable* use of all these means, in their several times and seasons, that we may keep our hearts

* That is, ' conscientious.'—G.

waking; and the more earnest ought we to be, from consideration of the present age and season in which we live.

Certainly a drowsy temper is the most ordinary temper in the world. For would men suffer idle words, yea, filthy and rotten talk to come from their mouths if they were awake? Would a waking man run into a pit? or upon a sword's point? A man that is asleep may do anything. What do men mean when they fear not to lie, dissemble, and rush upon the pikes of God's displeasure? When they say one thing and do another, are they not dead? or take them at the best, are they not asleep? Were they awake, would they ever do thus? Will not a fowl that hath wings, avoid the snare? or will a beast run into a pit when it sees it? There is a snare laid in your playhouses, gaming houses, common houses, that gentlemen frequent that generally profess religion, and take the communion. If the eye of their souls were awake, would they run into these snares, that their own conscience tells them are so? If there be any goodness in their souls, it is wondrous sleepy. There is no man, even the best, but may complain something, that they are overtaken in the contagion of these infectious times. They catch drowsy tempers, as our Saviour saith, of those latter times. 'For the abundance of iniquity, the love of many shall wax cold,' Mat. xxiv. 12. A chill temper grows ever from the coldness of the times that we live in, wherein the best may complain of coldness; but there is a great difference. The life of many, we see, is a continual sleep.

Let us especially watch over ourselves, in the use of liberty and such things as are in themselves lawful. It is a blessed state, when a Christian carries himself so in his liberty, that his heart condemns him not for the abuse of that which it alloweth, and justly in a moderate use. Recreations are lawful; who denies it? To refresh a man's self, is not only lawful, but necessary. God knew it well enough, therefore hath allotted time for sleep, and the like. But we must not turn recreation into a calling, to spend too much time in it.

Where there is least fear, there is most danger always. Now because in lawful things there is least fear, we are there in most danger. It is true for the most part, *licitis perimus omnes*, more men perish in the church of God by the abuse of lawful things, than by unlawful; more by meat, than by poison. Because every man takes heed of poison, being* he knows the venom of it, but how many men surfeit, and die by meat! So, many men die by lawful things. They eternally perish in the abuse of their liberties, more than in gross sins. Therefore let us keep awake, that we may carry ourselves so in our liberties, that we condemn not ourselves in the use of them. We will conclude this point with the meditation of the excellency of a waking Christian. When he is in his right temper, he is an excellent person, fit for all essays.† He is then impregnable. Satan hath nothing to do with him, for he, as it is said, is then a wise man, and 'hath his eyes in his head,' Eccles. iii. 4. He knows himself, his state, his enemies, and adversaries, the snares of prosperity and adversity, and of all conditions, &c. Therefore, he being awake, is not overcome of the evil of any condition, and is ready for the good of any estate. He that hath a waking soul, he sees all the advantages of good, and all the snares that might draw him to ill, Mark xiii. 37. What a blessed estate is this! In all things therefore watch; in all estates, in all times, and in all actions. There is a danger in everything without watchfulness. There is a scorpion under every stone,

* That is, 'seeing it is.'—G.

† That is, 'attempts.' Sibbes's spelling is 'assaies,'—Qu.' assaults?'—G.

as the proverb is, a snare under every blessing of God, and in every condition, which Satan useth as a weapon to hurt us ; adversity to discourage us, prosperity to puff us up : when, if a Christian hath not a waking soul, Satan hath him in his snare, in prosperity to be proud and secure ; in adversity to murmur, repine, be dejected, and call God's providence into question.   When a Christian hath a heart and grace to awake, then his love, his patience, his faith is awake, as it should be.   He is fit for all conditions, to do good in them, and to take good by them.

Let us therefore labour to preserve watchful and waking hearts continually, that so we may be fit to live, to die, and to appear before the judgment seat of God ; to do what we should do, and suffer what we should suffer, being squared for all estates whatsoever.

THE FIFTH SERMON.

It is the voice of my Beloved that knocketh, saying, Open to me, my sister, my love, my dove, my undefiled ; for my head is filled with dew, and my locks with the drops of the night.—CANT. V. 2.

HITHERTO, by God's assistance, we have heard largely both of the church's sleeping and heart-waking ; what this sleeping and heart-waking is ; how it comes ; the trials of these opposite dispositions ; of the danger of sleeping, and excellency of heart-waking ; and of the helps and means, both to shun the one and preserve the other.   Now, the church, having so freely and in-geniously* confessed what she could against herself, proceeds yet further to acquaint us with the particulars in her heart-waking disposition, which were twofold.   She heard and discerned ' the voice of her Beloved,' who, for all her sleep, was her Beloved still ; and more than that, she remembers all his sweet words and allurements, whereby he pressed her to open unto him, saying, ' Open to me, my love, my dove, my undefiled ; ' which is set out and amplified with a further moving argument of those inconveniences Christ had suffered in his waiting for entertainment in her heart, ' For my head is filled with dew, and my locks with the drops of the night,' all which aggravates her offence ; and his rare goodness and patience towards miserable sinners, so to wait from time to time for admission into our wretched souls, that he may rule and govern them by his Holy Spirit.   Therefore, we had great reason to shun this sleepy distemper of soul, which for the present so locks up ' the everlasting gates of our soul, that the King of glory cannot enter in,' Ps. xxiv. 7, and to strive for this blessed heart-waking disposition, which may help us at all times to see our dangers, and, by God's blessing, recover us out of them, as here the church doth at length, though first smarting and well beaten by the watchmen, in a world of perplexities ere she can recover the sense of her former union and communion with Christ.

And surely we find by experience what a woful thing it is for the soul which hath once tasted how gracious the Lord is, to be long without a sense of God's love ; for when it looks upon sin as the cause of this separation, this is for the time as so many deaths unto it.   Therefore, the church's experience must be our warning-piece to take heed how we grieve the Spirit, and so fall into this spiritual sleep.   Wherein yet this is a good sign, that yet we are not in a desperate dead sleep when we can with her say,

' It is the voice of my Beloved that knocks, saying, Open unto me,' &c.

* That is, ' ingenuously.'—G.

In which words you have,
1. The church's acknowledgment of Christ's voice.
2. Of his carriage towards her.
1. Her acknowledgment is set down here, ' It is the voice of my Beloved.'
2. His carriage, ' He knocks,' &c.   Wherein,
    (1.) His patience in suffering things unworthy and utterly unbeseeming
for him.   He doth not only ' knock,' but he continues knocking, till ' his
head was filled with dew, and his locks with the drops of the night.'
    (2.) His friendly compellation, ' Open to me, my love, my dove, my un-
defiled.'   Lo, here are sweet actions, sweet words, and all to melt the heart
of the spouse!
    First, *the church's acknowledgment* is to be considered, confessing, ' It is
the voice of her beloved.'   The first thing to be observed in this acknowledgment is, that the church, however sleepy and drowsy she was, yet notwithstanding, her heart was so far awake as to know the voice of her husband.   The point is this,
    *Obs. That a Christian soul doth know and may discern the voice of Christ,
yea, and that even in a lazy, sleepy estate, but much more when in a good and
lively frame.*   God's believers are Christ's sheep, John x. 3.   Now, ' My
sheep,' saith Christ, ' hear my voice,' verse 4.   It is the ear-mark, as
it were, of a Christian, one of the characters of the new man, ' to taste
words by the ear,' as Job saith, Job xii. 11.   He hath a spiritual taste, a
discerning relish in his ear, because he hath the Spirit of God, and therefore relisheth what is connatural, and suitable to the Spirit.   Now, the voice
of Christ without in the ministry, and the Spirit of Christ within in the
heart, are connatural, and suitable each to other.
    And surely so it is, *that this is one way to discern a true Christian from
another, even by a taste in hearing.*   For those that have a spiritual relish,
they can hear with some delight things that are most spiritual.   As the
heathen man said of a meadow, that some creatures come to eat one sort of
herbs, others another, all that which is fit for them; men to walk therein for
delight; all for ends suitable to their nature; so, in coming to hear the word
of God, some come to observe the elegancy of words and phrases, some to
catch advantage perhaps against the speaker, men of a devilish temper; and
some to conform themselves to the customs of the places they live in, or to
satisfy the clamours of a troubled conscience, that will have some divine
duty performed, else it goes on with much vexation.   But every true Christian comes and relisheth what is spiritual; and when outward things can
convey in similitudes spiritual things aptly to the mind, he relisheth this, not
as elegant and pleasing his fancy so much, as for conveying the voice of
Christ unto his soul, so that a man may much be helped to know his state
in grace and what he is, by his ear.   ' Itching ears,' 2 Tim. iv. 3, usually
are such as are ' led with lust,' as the apostle saith, and they must be clawed.
They are sick, and nothing will down with them.   They quarrel with everything that is wholesome, as they did with manna.   No sermons will please
them, no bread is fine and white enough; whereas, indeed, it is their own
distemper is in fault.   As those that go in a ship upon the sea, it is not the
tossing but the stomach that causeth a sickness, the choler within, and not
the waves without, so the disquiet of these men, that nothing will down with
them, is from their own distemper.   If Christ himself were here a-preach-
ing, they would be sure to cavil at something, as then men did when he
preached in his own person, because they labour of lusts, which they resolve
to feed and cherish.

And again, observe it against our adversaries. What say they? How shall we know that the word is the word of God? For this heretic saith thus, and this interprets it thus. This is the common objection of the great rabbis amongst them in their writings, how we can know the word to be God's, considering there are such heresies in the churches, and such contrariety of opinions concerning the Scriptures read in the churches.

Even thus to object and ask is an argument and testimony that these men have not the Spirit of Christ, for ' his sheep know his voice,' John x. 3, who, howsoever they cannot interpret all places of Scripture, yet they can discern in the Scripture what is suitable food for them, or in the unfolding of the Scriptures in preaching they can discern agreeable food for them, having a faculty to reject that which is not fit for nourishment, to let it go. As there is in nature passages fit for concoction and digestion and for rejection, so there is in the soul to work out of the word, even out of that which is hard, yet wholesome, what is fit for the soul and spirit. If it be cast down, it feeds upon the promises for direction and consolation; and what is not fit for nourishment, that it rejects, that is, if it be of a contrary nature, heterogeneal. Therefore, we answer them thus, that ' God's sheep hear his voice,' John x. 4; that his word left in the church, when it is unfolded, his Spirit goes together with it, breeding a relish of the word in the hearts of people, whereby they are able to taste and relish it, and it hath a supernatural power and majesty in it which carries its own evidence with it. How shall we know light to be light? It carries evidence in itself that it is light. How know we that the fire is hot? Because it carries evidence in itself that it is so. So if you ask how we know the word of God to be the word of God; it carries in itself inbred arguments and characters, that the soul can say none but this word can be the word of God; it hath such a majesty and power to cast down, and raise up, and to comfort, and to direct with such power and majesty, that it carries with it its own evidence, and it is argument enough for it, 1 Cor. xiv. 24, 25; 2 Cor. x. 4, 5. And thus we answer them, which they can answer no way but by cavils. ' God's sheep hear the voice of Christ.' He speaks, and the church understands him, ' and a stranger's voice they will not hear,' John x. 5.

And indeed, this is the only sure way of understanding the word to be of God, from an inbred principle of the majesty in the word, and a powerful work thereof on the soul itself; and an assent so grounded is that which makes a sound Christian. If we should ask, what is the reason there be so many that apostatize, fall away, grow profane, and are so unfruitful under the gospel, notwithstanding they hear so much as they do? The answer is, their souls were never founded and bottomed upon this, that it is the word of God, and divine truth, so as to be able to say, I have felt it by experience, that it is the voice of Christ. Therefore they so soon apostatize, let Jesuits, or seducers set upon them. They were never persuaded from inbred arguments, that the voice of Christ is the word of God. Others from strictness grow profane, because they were never convinced by the power and majesty of the truth in itself; and then in the end they despair, notwithstanding all the promises, because they were never convinced of the truth of them. They cannot say Amen to all the promises. But the church can say confidently, upon sound experience, ' It is the voice of my beloved,' &c.

Again, whereas the church saith here, It is the voice of my beloved, &c., and knows this voice of her beloved, we may note—

Obs. That the church of God, and every Christian, takes notice of the means that God useth for their salvation.

A Christian is sensible of all the blessed helps he hath to salvation. To a dead heart, it is all one whether they have means or no means ; but a Christian soul takes notice of all the means. 'It is the voice of my beloved that knocketh.' It seeth Christ in all.

And mark what the church saith, moreover, 'It is the voice of my beloved.' She acknowledgeth Christ to be beloved of her, though she were asleep. So then here is a distinction between the sleep of a Christian and the dead sleep of another natural man. The one when he sleeps, his heart doth not only wake, but it is awake to discern the voice of Christ. It can relish in reading what is spiritual and good, what is savoury, and what not. And likewise take a Christian at the worst : when he is asleep, he loves Christ, he will do nothing against him. 'I can do nothing,' saith Paul, 'against the truth, but for the truth,' 2 Cor. xiii. 8. He will do nothing against the cause of religion. There is a new nature in him, that he cannot do otherwise. He cannot but love ; he cannot sin with a full purpose, nor speak against a good cause, because he hath a new nature, that leads him another way. Christ is her beloved still though she sleep.

Obs. Take a Christian at the lowest, his heart yearns after Christ.

Acknowledging him to be his beloved, there is a conjugal chastity in the soul of a Christian. Holding firm to the covenant and marriage between Christ and it, he keeps that unviolable. Though he may be untoward, sleepy, and drowsy, yet there is always a conjugal, spouse-like affection. 'It is the voice of my beloved,' &c.

Now, leaving the church's notice of the voice of Christ, we come to Christ's carriage towards her.

1. 'He knocketh ;' and then we have—

2. His patience in that carriage. 'My head is filled with dew, and my locks with the drops of the night,' &c. Here is patience and mercy, to endure this indignity at the church's hand, to stand at her courtesy to come in ; besides, 3, the compellation, afterwards to be spoken of. The general observation from Christ's carriage is this—

Obs. That Christ still desires a further and further communion with his church.

Even as the true soul that is touched with the Spirit, desires nearer and nearer communion with Christ ; so he seeks nearer and nearer communion with his spouse, by all sanctified means. Christ hath never enough of the soul. He would have them more and more open to him. Our hearts are for Christ, who hath the heaven of heavens, and the soul of a believing Christian for himself to dwell in. He contents not himself to be in heaven alone, but he will have our hearts. He knocks here, waits, speaks friendly and lovingly, with such sweet words, 'My love, my dove,' &c. We had a blessed communion in the state of innocency, and shall have a glorious communion in heaven, when the marriage shall be consummated ; but now the time of this life is but as the time of the contract, during which there are yet many mutual passages of love between him and his spouse, a desire of mutual communion of either side. Christ desires further entertainment in his church's heart and affection, that he might lodge and dwell there. And likewise there is the like desire in the church, when she is in a right temper ; so that if any strangeness be between Christ and any man's soul, that hath tasted how good the Lord is, let him not blame Christ for it, for he delights not in strangeness. He that knocks and stands knocking, while his locks are bedewed with the drops of the night, doth he delight in strangeness, that makes all this love to a Christian's soul ? Certainly no. Therefore look for the cause of his strangeness at any time in thine own self. As, *whether we cast ourselves imprudently into company, that are not fit to be consulted withal*, in whom the Spirit is not, and who cannot do us any good, or they cast themselves to us. Evil company is a great damping, whereby a Christian loseth his comfort much, especially that intimate communion with God ; whence we may fall into security.

Again, *discontinuing of religious exercises doth wonderfully cause Christ to withdraw himself*. He makes no more love to our souls, when we neglect the means, and discontinue holy exercises, and religious company, when we stir not up the graces of God's Spirit. Being this way negligent, it is no wonder that Christ makes no more love to our souls, when we prize and value not the communion that should be between the soul and Christ, as we should. 'Whom have I in heaven but thee ?' Ps. lxxiii. 25. 'Thy lovingkindness is better than life,' saith the psalmist, Ps. lxiii. 3. When we prize not this, it is just with Christ to make himself strange. Where love is not valued and esteemed, it is estranged, and for a while hides itself. So that these, with other courses and failings, we may find to be the ground and reason of the strangeness between Christ and the soul, for certainly the cause is not in him. For we see here, he useth all means to be entertained by a Christian soul : ' he knocks.'

You know what he says to the church of Laodicea—' Behold, I stand at the door, and knock,' Rev. iii. 20 ; so here—' It is the voice of my beloved that knocketh.' Therefore, in such a case, search your own hearts, where, if there be deadness and desertion of spirit, lay the blame upon yourselves, and enter into a search of your own ways, and see what may be the cause.

Now, to come more particularly to Christ's carriage here, knocking at the heart of the sleepy church, we see that *Christ takes not the advantage and forfeiture of the sins of his church, to leave them altogether, but makes further and further love to them*. Though the church be sleepy, Christ continues knocking. The church of Laodicea was a lukewarm, proud, hypocritical church ; yet ' Behold,' saith Christ, ' I stand at the door, and knock,' Rev. iii. 20 ; and it was such a church as was vainglorious and conceited. ' I am rich, and want nothing, when she was poor, blind, and naked,' Rev. iii. 17. And here he doth not only stand knocking, but he withal suffereth indignities—' the dew' to fall upon him, which we shall speak more of hereafter. Christ, therefore, refuseth not weak sinners. He that commands, ' that we should receive him that is weak in the faith,' Rom. xiv. 1, and not cast him off from our fellowship and company, will he reject him that is weak and sleepy ? No. What father will pass by or neglect his child, for some failings and weaknesses ? Nature will move him to respect him as his child.

Now, Christ is merciful both by his office and by his nature. Our nature he took upon him, that he might be a merciful Redeemer, Heb. ii. 17. And then as God also, he is love, ' God is love,' 1 John iv. 16 : that is, whatsoever God shews himself to his church, he doth it in love. If he be angry in correcting, it is out of love ; if merciful, it is out of love ; if he be powerful in defending his church, and revenging himself on her enemies, all is love. ' God is love,' saith John, John iv. 8 : that is, he shews himself only in ways, expressions, and characters of love to his church. So Christ, as God, is all love to the church. And we see the Scriptures also to set out God as love, both in his essence and in his relations. 1. In relations of love to his church, he is a father : ' As a father pitieth his child, so the Lord pities them that fear him,' Ps. ciii. 13. And, 2. Also in those sweet attributes of love, which are his essence, as we see, Exod.

xxxiv. 6. When God describes himself to Moses, after his desire to know
him, in the former chapter, ' Thou canst not see me and live ; ' yet he
would make him know him, as was fit for him to be known—'Jehovah,
Jehovah, strong, merciful, gracious, long-suffering,' &c., Exod. xxxiv. 6.
Thus God will be known in these attributes of consolation. So Christ, as
God, is all love and mercy. Likewise Christ, as man, he was man for this
end, to be all love and mercy. Take him in his office as Jesus, to be a
Saviour ; he carrieth salvation in his wings, as it is in Mal. iv. 2, both by
office and by nature.

And here how excellently is the expression of Christ's mercy, love, and
patience set out ! He knocks, ' my beloved knocks,' &c., saying, ' Open.'
He knocks for further entrance, as was shewed before. Some he had
already, but he would have further. As you know we have divers rooms
and places in our houses. There is the court, the hall, the parlour, and
closet : the hall for common persons, the parlour for those of better
fashion, the closet for a man's self, and those that are intimate friends.
So a Christian hath room in his heart for worldly thoughts, but his closet,
his inmost affections, are kept for his inmost friend Christ, who is not content with the hall, but will come into the very closet. He knocks, that we
should open, and let him come into our hearts, into our more intimate
affections and love. Nothing will content him but intimateness, for he deserves it. As we shall see, he knocks for this end. But how doth he
knock ?

Every kind of way. 1. It is taken from the fashion of men in this kind,
God condescending to speak to us in our own language. Sometimes, you
know, there is a knocking or calling for entrance by voice, when a voice
may serve, and then there needs no further knocking.

Sometimes both by voice and knocking. If voice will not serve, knocking comes after. So it is here. Christ doth knock and speak, useth a
voice of his word, and knocks by his works, and both together sometimes,
whether by works of mercy or of judgment. He labours to enter into the
soul, to raise the sleepy soul that way. He begins with mercy usually.

(1.) By *mercies*. All the creatures and blessings of God carry in them,
as it were, a voice of God to the soul, that it would entertain his love.
There goes a voice of love with every blessing. And the love, the mercy,
and the goodness of God in the creature, is better than the creature itself.
As we say of gifts, the love of the giver is better than the gift itself. So
the love of God in all his sweet benefits is better than the thing itself.
And so in that we have. There is a voice, as it were, entreating us to
entertain God and Christ in all his mercies, yea, every creature, as one
saith, and benefit, speaks, as it were, thus to us : We serve thee, that thou
mayest serve him that made thee and us. There is a speech, as it were,
in every favour. Which mercies, if they cannot prevail, then,

(2.) Come *corrections*, which are the voice of God also. ' Hear the rod,
and him that smiteth,' Micah vi. 9.

2. But hath the rod a voice ? Yes, for what do corrections speak, but
amendment of the fault we are corrected for ? So we must hear the rod. All
corrections tend to this purpose. They are as knockings, that we should open
to God and Christ. And because corrections of themselves will not amend us,
God to this kind of knocking adds a voice. He teacheth and corrects together, ' Happy is that man that thou correctest, and teachest out of thy law,'
saith the psalmist, Ps. xciv. 12. Correction without teaching is to little purpose. Therefore God adds instruction to correction. He opens the conscience,

so that it tells us it is for this that you are corrected; and together with conscience, gives his Spirit to tell us it is for this or that you are corrected; you are to blame in this, this you have done that you should not have done. So that corrections are knockings, but then especially when they have instruction thus with them. They are messengers from God, both blessings and corrections, Lev. xxvi. 24, *seq.* They will not away, especially corrections, till they have an answer, for they are sent of God, who will add seven times more; and if the first be not answered, then he sends after them. He will be sure to have an answer, either in our conversion or confusion, when he begins once.

3. Many other ways he useth to knock at our hearts. *The examples of those we live among that are good, they call upon us,* Luke xiii. 2, 3; 1 Cor. x. 33. The patterns of their holy life, the examples of God's justice upon others, are speeches to us. God knocks at our door then. He intends our correction when he visits another, when, if we amend by that, he needs not take us in hand.

4. But besides all this, there is a more near knocking that Christ useth to the church, *his ministerial knocking.* When he was here in the days of his flesh, he was a preacher and prophet himself, and now he is ascended into heaven, he hath given gifts to men, and men to the church, Eph. iv. 11, *seq.,* whom he speaks by, to the end of the world. They are Christ's mouth, as we said of the penmen of holy Scripture. They were but the hand to write; Christ was the head to indite. So in preaching and unfolding the word they are but Christ's mouth and his voice, as it is said of John, Mat. iii. 3. Now he is in heaven, he speaks by them, ' He that heareth you heareth me, he that despiseth you despiseth me,' Luke x. 16. Christ is either received or rejected in his ministers, as it is said of Noah's time, ' The Spirit of Christ preached in the days of Noah to the souls now in prison,' &c., 1 Pet. iii. 19. Christ as God did preach, before he was incarnate, by Noah to the old world, which is now in prison, in hell, because they refused to hear Christ speak to them by Noah. Much more now, after the days of his flesh, that he is in heaven, he speaks and preacheth to us, which, if we regard not, we are like to be in prison, as those souls are now in prison for neglecting the preaching of Noah, 1 Pet iii. 19. So the ministers are Christ's mouth. When they speak, he speaks by them, and they are as ambassadors of Christ, whom they should imitate in mildness. ' We therefore, as ambassadors, beseech and entreat you, as if Christ by us should speak to you; so we entreat you to be reconciled unto God,' 2 Cor. v. 20. And you know what heart-breaking words the apostle useth in all his epistles, especially when he writes to Christians in a good state, as to the Philippians, ' If there be any bowels of mercy, if there be any consolation in Christ,' then regard what I say, ' be of one mind.' Phil. ii. 1. And among the Thessalonians he was as a nurse to them, 1 Thess. ii. 7. So Christ speaks by them, and puts his own affections into them, that as he is tender and full of bowels himself, so he hath put the same bowels into those that are his true ministers.

He speaks by them, and they use all kind of means that Christ may be entertained into their hearts. They move all stones, as it were, sometimes threatenings, sometimes entreaties, sometimes they come as ' sons of thunder,' Mark iii. 17; sometimes with the still voice of sweet promises. And because one man is not so fit as another for all varieties of conditions and spirits, therefore God gives variety of gifts to his ministers, that they may knock at the heart of every man by their several gifts. For some have more rousing, some more insinuating gifts; some more legal, some more evangelical spirits, yet all for the church's good. John Baptist, by a more thundering way of preaching, to make way for Christ to come, threateneth judgment. But Christ, then he comes with a 'Blessed are the poor in spirit,' 'blessed are they that hunger and thirst for righteousness,' &c., Mat v. 3. All kind of means have been used in the ministry from the beginning of the world.

5. And because of itself this ministry it is a dead letter; therefore he joins that with the word, which knocks at the heart together with the word, not severed from it, but is the life of it. *Oh! the Spirit is the life, and soul of the word;* and when the inward word, or voice of the Spirit, and the outward word or ministry go together, then Christ doth more effectually knock and stir up the heart.

Now this Spirit with sweet inspirations knocks, moves the heart, lightens the understanding, quickens the dull affections, and stirs them up to duty, as it is, Isa. xxx. 21, 'And thine ears shall hear a voice behind thee saying, This is the way, walk in it.' The Spirit moves us sweetly, agreeable to our own nature. It offers not violence to us; but so as in Hosea xi. 4, 'I drew them by the cords of a man.' That is, by reasons and motives befitting the nature of man, motives of love. So the Spirit, together with the word, works upon us, as we are men by rational motives, setting good before us, if we will let Christ in to govern and rule us; and by the danger on the contrary, so moving and stirring up our affections. These be 'the cords of a man.'

6. And besides his Spirit, God hath planted in us a *conscience* to call upon us, to be his vicar; a little god in us to do his office, to call upon us, direct us, check and condemn us, which in great mercy he hath placed in us.

Thus we see what means Christ useth here—his voice, works, and word; works of mercy and of correction; his word, together with his Spirit, and the conscience, that he hath planted, to be, as it were, a god in us; which together with his Spirit may move us to duty. This Austin speaks of when he says, *Deus in me,* &c. 'God spake in me oft, and I knew it not' (*f*). He means it of conscience, together with the Spirit, stirring up motives to leave his sinful courses. God knocked in me, and I considered it not. I cried, *modò* and *modò, sine modo.* I put off God, now I will, and now I will, but I had no moderation, I knew no limits. And whilst Christ thus knocketh, all the three persons may be said to do it. For as it is said elsewhere, that 'God was and is in Christ reconciling the world,' &c., 2 Cor. v. 19. For whatsoever Christ did, he did it as anointed, and by office. And therefore God doth it in Christ, and by Christ, and so in some sort God died in his human nature, when Christ died. So here the father beseecheth when Christ beseecheth, because he beseecheth, that is sent from him, and anointed of the Father. And God the Father stoops to us when Christ stoops, because he is sent of the Father, and doth all by his Father's command and commission, John v. 27. So besides his own bowels, there is the Father and the Spirit with Christ, who doth all by his Spirit, and from his Father, from whom he hath commission. Therefore God the Father, Son, and Holy Ghost knock at the heart. 'Open to me, my love, my dove, my undefiled;' but Christ especially by his Spirit, because it is his office.

Obj. But some may object, Christ can open to himself, why doth he not take the key and open, and make way for himself? Who will knock, when he hath the key himself? and who will knock, when there is none within to open ?   Christ can open to himself, and we have no free will, nor power to open.

Bellarmine makes this objection, and speaks very rudely, that he is an unwise man to knock, where there is no man within to open ; and that if Christ knock, and we cannot open, it is a delusion to exhort to open, and that therefore there must needs be free will in us to open (f*).

The answer is, *first*, Christ speaks to the spouse here, and so, many such exhortations are given to them that have the Spirit of God already, who could by the help thereof open.   For good and gracious men are moved first by the Spirit, and then they move ; they are *moti moventes*, and *acti agentes*.   They are acted first by the Spirit, and then they do act by it, not of themselves ; as the inferior orbs move not, but as they are moved by the superior.   The question is not of them in the state of grace, but at their first conversion, when especially we say that Christ speaks to them that he means to convert.   He knocks at their hearts, and opens together with his speech.   Then there goes a power that they shall open ; for his words are operative words.   As it was in the creation, ' Let there be light,' it was an operative word, ' and there was light,' Gen. i. 3.   Let there be such a creature, it was an operative working word, and there was such a creature presently.   So he opens together with that word.   With that invitation and command there goes an almighty power to enable the soul to open.   Were it not a wise reason to say, when Christ called to Lazarus to ' come forth,' John xi. 43, that we should reason he had life to yield to Christ, when he bade him come forth?   No, he was rotten, in his grave, almost ; but with Christ's speaking to Lazarus, there went an almighty power, that gave life to him, by which life he heard what Christ said, ' Arise, Lazarus.'   So Christ by his Spirit clothes his word in the ministry, when he speaks to people with a mighty power.   As the minister speaks to the ear, Christ speaks, opens, and unlocks the heart at the same time ; and gives it power to open, not from itself, but from Christ.   Paul speaks to Lydia's ear, Christ to her heart, and opened it, as the text says, Acts xvi. 13, whereby she believes ;* so Christ opens the heart.

Quest.   But why doth he thus work ?

Ans.   Because he will preserve nature, and the principles thereof; and so he deals with us, working accordingly.   The manner of working of the reasonable creature, is to work freely by a sweet inclination, not by violence.   Therefore when he works the work of conversion, he doth it in a sweet manner, though it be mighty for the efficaciousness of it.   He admonisheth us with entreaty and persuasion, as if we did it ourselves.   But though the manner be thus sweet, yet with this manner there goeth an almighty power.   Therefore he doth it strongly as coming from himself, and sweetly, as the speaking is to us, preserving our nature.   So the action is from him, which hath an almighty power with it.   As holy Bernard saith, ' Thou dealest sweetly with my soul in regard of myself;' that is, thou workest upon me, as a man with the words of love, yet strongly in regard of thyself.   For except he add strength with sweetness, the work will not follow ; but when there are both, an almighty work is wrought in the soul of a Christian; and so wrought, as the manner of man's working is preserved in a sweet and free manner, whilst he is changed from contrary to contrary.   And it is also with the greatest reason that can be, in that now he sees more reason to be good, than in the days of darkness he did to be naught, God works

---

* 'Lydia's Heart Opened,' is the title of one of Sibbes's most delightful minor books.—G

so sweetly. God speaks to us after the manner of men, but he works in us
as the great God. He speaks to us as a man in our own language, sweetly;
but he works in us almightily, after a powerful manner, as God. So we
must understand such phrases as these, 'I knock; open to me, my love, my
dove,' &c. We may take further notice,

Obs. That the heart of a Christian is the house and temple of Christ.

He hath but two houses to dwell in ; the heavens, and the heart of an
humble broken-hearted sinner, Isa. lvii. 15.

Quest. How can Christ come into the soul ?

Ans. He comes into the heart by his Spirit. It is a special entertainment that he looks for. Open thine ears that thou mayest hear my word ;
thy love, that thou mayest love me more; thy joy, that thou mayest delight
in me more; open thy whole soul that I may dwell in it. A Christian should
be God's house, and a true Christian is the true temple of God. He left the
other two temples therefore ; but his own body, and his church he never
leaves. For a house is for a man to solace himself in, and to rest in, and
to lay up whatsoever is precious to him. So with Christ. A man will repair his house, so Christ will repair our souls, and make them better, and make
them more holy, and spiritual, and every way fit for such a guest as he is.

Quest. How shall we know whether Christ dwells in our hearts or not ?

Ans. We may know *by the servants what master dwells in an house.* If
Christ be in the soul, there comes out of the house good speeches. And we
watch the senses, so as there comes nothing in to defile the soul, and disturb
Christ, and nothing goes out to offend God. When we hear men full of
gracious sweet speeches, it is a sign Christ dwells there. If we hear the
contrary, it shews Christ dwells not there. For Christ would move the
whole man to do that which might edify and comfort.

Again, where Christ comes, *assistance comes there.* When Christ was
born, all Jerusalem was in an uproar ; so, when Christ is born in the soul,
there is an uproar. Corruption arms itself against grace. There is a combat betwixt flesh and spirit. But Christ subdues the flesh by little and
little. God's image is stamped upon the soul where Christ is ; and if we
have opened unto the Lord of glory, he will make us glorious.

Christ hath never enough of us, nor we have never enough of him till we
be in heaven ; and, therefore, we pray, 'Thy kingdom come.' And till
Christ comes in his kingdom, he desires his kingdom should come to us.
Open, saith he, *stupenda dignatio,* &c., as he cries out. It is a stupendous
condescendence, when he that hath heaven to hold him, angels to attend
him, those glorious creatures ; he that hath the command of every creature,
that do yield presently homage when he commands, the frogs, and lice, and
all the host of heaven are ready to do his will ! for him to condescend and
to entreat us to be good to our own souls, and to beseech us to be reconciled to him, as if he had offended us, who have done the wrong and not
he, or as if that we had power and riches to do him good; here greatness
beseecheth meanness, riches poverty, all-sufficiency want, and life itself
comes to dead, drowsy souls. What a wondrous condescending is this !
Yet, notwithstanding, Christ vouchsafes to make the heart of a sinful,
sleepy man to be his house, his temple. He knocks, and knocks here,
saying, ' Open to me,' &c.

Use 1. This is useful many ways, as *first, cherish all the good conceits** we
can of Christ.* Time will come that the devil will set upon us with sharp
temptations, fiery darts, temptations to despair, and present Christ amiss,

* That is, ' conceptions.'—G.

as if Christ were not willing to receive us.   Whenas you see he knocks at
our hearts to open to him, useth mercies and judgments, the ministry of his
Spirit and conscience, and all.   Will not he then entertain us, when we
come to him, that seeks this entertainment at our hands ?   Certainly he
will.   Therefore, let us labour to cherish good conceits of Christ.   This is
the finisher and beginning of the conversion of a poor sinful soul, even to
consider the infinite love and condescendence of Christ Jesus for the good of
our souls.   We need not wonder at this his willingness to receive us, when
we first know that God became man, happiness became misery, and life
itself came to die, and to be ' a curse for us,' Gal. iii. 13.   He hath done
the greater, and will he not do the less ?   Therefore, think not strange that
he useth all these means, considering how low he descended into the womb
of the virgin for us, Ephes. iv. 9.

Now such considerations as these, being mixed with the Spirit and set
on by him, are effectual for the conversion of poor souls.   Is there such
love in God to become man, and to be a suitor to woo me for my love ?
Surely, thinks the soul then, he desires my salvation and conversion.   And
to what kind of persons doth he come ?   None can object unworthiness.
I am poor : 'He comes to the poor,' Isa. xiv. 32 and xxix. 19.   I am
laden and wretched : ' Come unto me, all ye that are weary and laden,'
Mat. xi. 28.   I have nothing : ' Come and buy honey, milk, and wine,
though you have nothing,' Isa. lv. 1.   He takes away all objections.   But
I am stung with the sense of my sins : ' Blessed are they that hunger and
thirst,' &c., Mat. v. 6.   But I am empty of all : ' Blessed are the poor in
spirit,' Mat. v. 3.   You can object nothing, but it is taken away by the
Holy Ghost, wisely preventing* all the objections of a sinful soul.   This is
the beginning of conversion, these very conceits.   And when we are converted, these thoughts, entertained with admiration of Christ's condescending, are effectual to give Christ further entrance into the soul, whereby a
more happy communion is wrought still more and more between Christ and
the soul of a Christian.

Use 2. *Oh, but take heed that these make not any secure.*   For, if we give
not entrance to Christ, all this will be a further aggravation of our damnation.   How will this justify the sentence upon us hereafter, when Christ
shall set us on the left hand, and say, ' Depart from me,' Mat. xxv. 41, for
I invited you to come to me, I knocked at the door of your hearts, and you
would give me no entrance.   Depart from us, said you ; therefore, now,
Depart you from me.   What do profane persons in the church but bid
Christ depart from them, especially in the motions of his Spirit ?   They
entertain him in the outward room, the brain ; they know a little of Christ,
but, in the heart, the secret room, he must not come there to rule.   Is it
not equal that he should bid us, ' Depart, ye cursed, I know you not' ? Mat.
xxv. 41 ; you would not give entrance to me, I will not now to you, as to the
foolish virgins he speaks, Mat. xxv. 12, and Prov. i. 28.   Wisdom knocks,
and hath no entrance ; therefore, in times of danger, they call upon her,
but she rejoiceth at their destruction.   Where God magnifies his mercy in
this kind, in sweet allurements, and inviting by judgments, mercies, ministry, and Spirit, he will magnify his judgment after.   Those that have
neglected heaven with the prerogatives and advantages in this kind, they
shall be cast into hell.   ' Woe to thee, Chorazin,' &c., Mat. xi. 21, as you
know in the gospel.   This is one thing that may humble us of this place
and nation, that Christ hath no further entrance, nor better entertainment

* That is, ' anticipating.'—G.

after so long knocking! for the entertaining of his word is the welcoming
of himself, as it is, Col. iii. 16. ' Let the word of God dwell plentifully in
you.' And, ' Let Christ dwell in your hearts by faith,' Eph. iii. 17. Compare those places; let the word dwell plenteously in you by wisdom, and
let Christ dwell in your hearts by faith. For then doth Christ dwell in the
heart, when the truth dwells in us. Therefore, what entertainment we give
to his truth, we give to himself. Now what means of knocking hath he not
used among us a long time? For works of all sorts, he hath drawn us by
the cords of a man, by all kind of favours. For mercies, how many deliverances have we had (no nation the like; we are a miracle of the Christian world) from foreign invasion, and domestical conspiracies at home?
How many mercies do we enjoy! Abundance, together with long peace and
plenty. Besides, if this would not do, God hath added corrections with all
these, in every element, in every manner. Infection in the air, judgments
in inundations. We have had rumours of wars, &c. Threatenings, shakings
of the rod only, but such as might have awaked us. And then he hath
knocked at our hearts by the example of other nations. By what he hath
done to them, he hath shewed us what he might justly have done to us.
We are no better than they.

As for his ministerial knocking: above threescore years we have lived
under the ministry of the gospel. This land hath been Goshen, a land of
light, when many other places are in darkness. Especially we that live in
this Goshen, this place, and such like, where the light shines in a more
abundant measure. Ministers have been sent, and variety of gifts. There
hath been piping and mourning, as Christ complains in his time, that they
were like froward children, that neither sweet piping nor doleful mourning
would move to be tractable to their fellows. ' They had John, who came
mourning,' Mat. xi. 17, and Christ comforting with blessing in his mouth.
All kind of means have been used.

And for the motions of his Spirit, who are there at this time, who thus
live in the church under the ministry, who cannot say that God thereby
hath smote their hearts, those hard rocks, again and again, and awaked
their consciences, partly with corrections public and personal, and partly
with benefits? Yet notwithstanding, what little way is given to Christ!
Many are indifferent, and lukewarm either way, but rather incline to the
worst.

Let us then consider of it. The greater means, the greater judgments
afterwards, if we be not won by them. Therefore let us labour to hold
Christ, to entertain him. Let him have the best room in our souls, to
dwell in our hearts. Let us give up the keys to him, and desire him to
rule our understandings, to know nothing but him, and what may stand
with his truth, not to yield to any error or corruption. Let us desire that
he would rule in our wills and affections; sway all, give all to him. For
that is his meaning, when he says, ' Open to me,' so that I may rule, as in
mine own house, as the husband rules in his family, and a king in his
kingdom. He will have all yielded up to him. And he comes to beat
down all, whatsoever is exalted against him; and that is the reason men
are so loth to open unto him. They know if they open to the Spirit of
God, he will turn them out of their fool's paradise, and make them resolve
upon other courses of life, which, because they will not turn unto, they
repel the sweet motions of the Spirit of Christ, and pull away his graces,
building bulwarks against Christ, as lusts, strange imaginations, and resolutions, 2 Cor. x. 3–5. Let the ministers say what they will, and the Spirit

move as he will, thus they live, and thus they will live. Let us take notice, therefore, of all the means that God useth to the State, and to us in particular, and every one labour to amend one. Every soul is the temple, the house, Christ should dwell in. Let every soul, therefore, among us, consider what means Christ useth to come into his soul to dwell with him, and to rule there.

And what shall we lose by it? Do we entertain Christ to our loss? Doth he come empty? No; he comes with all grace. His goodness is a communicative, diffusive goodness. He comes to spread his treasures, to enrich the heart with all grace and strength, to bear all afflictions, to encounter all dangers, to bring peace of conscience, and joy in the Holy Ghost. He comes, indeed, to make our hearts, as it were, a heaven. Do but consider this. He comes not for his own ends; but to empty his goodness into our hearts. As a breast that desires to empty itself when it is full; so this fountain hath the fulness of a fountain, which strives to empty his goodness into our souls. He comes out of love to us. Let these considerations melt our hearts for our unkindness, that we suffer him to stand so long at the door knocking, as it is said here.

If we find not our suits answered so soon as we would, remember, we have made him also wait for us. Perhaps to humble us, and after that to encourage us, he will make us wait; for we have made him wait. Let us not give over, for certainly he that desires us to open, that he may pour out his grace upon us, he will not reject us when we come to him, Mat. vii. 7; Hab. ii. 3. If he answers us not at first, yet he will at last. Let us go on and wait, seeing there is no one duty pressed more in Scripture than this. And we see it is equity, ' He waits for us,' Isa. xxx. 18. It is good reason we should wait for him. If we have not comfort presently when we desire it, let us attend upon Christ, as he hath attended upon us, for when he comes, he comes with advantage, Isa. lx. 16. So that when we wait, we lose nothing thereby, but are gainers by it, increasing our patience, Isa. lxiv. 4; James i. 4. The longer we wait, he comes with the more abundant grace and comfort in the end, and shews himself rich, and bountiful to them that wait upon him, Isa. xl. 1, *et seq.*

THE SIXTH SERMON.

It is the voice of my beloved that knocketh, saying, Open unto me, my love, my dove, my undefiled, &c.—CANT. V. 2.

IN the first part of this verse hath been handled the church's own condition, which she was in, after some blessed feelings that she had of the love of Christ.

Now, in the next words, the church sets down an acknowledgment of the carriage of Christ to her in this her sleepy condition. ' It is the voice of my beloved that knocks, saying, Open to me, my sister, my love, my dove,' &c. She acknowledgeth Christ's voice in her sleepy estate, and sets down his carriage thus, ' how he knocks', and then also speaks, ' Open to me,' and then sets down what he suffered for her, ' My head is filled with dew, and my locks with the drops of the night.' And that nothing might be wanting that might move her heart to respect this his carriage towards her, he useth sweet titles, a loving compellation, ' Open

to me,' saith he, 'my sister, my love, my dove, my undefiled,' as so many
cords of love to draw her. So here wants neither loving carriage, sweet
words, nor patience. 'It is the voice of my beloved that knocketh.'

The church, as she takes notice of the voice of Christ, so she doth
also of the means he useth, and seeth his love in them all. 'It is the
voice of my beloved that knocketh, saying, Open to me,' &c. Here is also
another distinguishing note of a sound Christian from an unsound. A
sanctified spirit sees Christ in the means. This is, says the heart, the
word of Christ, and this the mercy of Christ, to take such pains with my
soul, to send his ministers, to provide his ordinances, to give gifts to men,
and men to the church, Eph. iv. 11, 12. 'It is the voice of my beloved
that knocketh.'

But we must especially understand it of the ministerial voice, whereby
Christ doth chiefly make way for himself into the heart, and that by all
kind of ways dispensed therein : as gifts of all sorts, some rougher, some
milder, all kind of methods and ways in the ministry to make way for himself. First of all by the threatenings of the law, and by terrors. As John
was sent before Christ, and as the storm went before the still and calm
voice, wherein God came to Elias, 1 Kings xix. 12, so he useth all kinds of
courses in the ministry. And ministers, by the direction of the Spirit,
turn themselves, as it were, into all shapes and fashions, both of speech and
spirit, to win people to God, in so much, that God appeals to them, 'What
could I have done more for my church, that I have not done ?' Isa. v. 4.

Use. Therefore let us take notice of this voice of Christ in the word, and
not think as good Samuel thought, that Eli spake, when God spake, 1 Sam.
iii. 5. Let us think that God speaks to us in the ministry, that Christ
comes to woo us, and win us thereby.

And we ministers are the friends of the Bridegroom, who are to hear
what Christ saith and would have said to the church ; and we must pray to
him, that he would teach us what to teach others. We are to procure the
contract, and to perfect it till the marriage be in heaven. That is our work.

And you that are hearers, if you do not regard Christ's sweet voice in the
ministry, which God hath appointed for the government of the world, know
that there is a voice that you cannot shake off. That peremptory voice at
the day of judgment, when he will say, 'Go, ye cursed, into hell fire,' &c.,
Mat. xxv. 30. And that God who delights to be styled 'a God hearing
prayer,' Ps. lxv. 2, will not hear thee, but saith, 'Such a one as turns his
ear away from hearing the law, his prayer is abominable,' Prov. xxviii. 9.
It is a doleful thing, that he that made us, and allureth us in the ministry,
that follows us with all evidences of his love, and adds, together with the
ministry, many sweet motions of his Spirit, that he should delight in the
destruction of his creatures, and not endure the sight of them, 'Depart
away from me, ye cursed, into hell fire,' &c. There are scarce any in the
church, but Christ hath allured at one time or other to come in, and in
many he opens their understandings in a great measure, and knocks upon
their hearts, that they, as it were, half open unto Christ, like Agrippa, that
said to Paul, 'Thou almost persuadest me to be a Christian,' Acts xxvi. 28.
So Herod 'did many things, and he heard gladly,' Mark vi. 20. They are
half open, seem to open, but are not effectually converted. But at last
they see, that further yielding will not stand with that which they resolve
not to part with, their lusts, their present condition, that they make their
God, and their heaven. Whereupon they shut the door again. When they
have opened it a little to the motions of God's Spirit, they dare give no

further way, because they cannot learn the first lesson in Christ's school, to deny themselves and take up their cross.

This is an undoubted conclusion. Our blessed Saviour giveth such means and motions of his Spirit to the vilest persons in the church, that their own hearts tell them, they have more means and sweeter motions than they yield to, and that the sentence of condemnation is not pronounced upon them for merely not knowing of Christ, but upon some grounds of rebellion, in that they go not so far as they are provoked,* and put on† by the Spirit of God. They resist the Holy Spirit. There can be no resistance where there is not a going beyond the desire and will of him whom he resisteth, Acts vii. 51. A man doth not resist, when he gives way as far as he is moved. There is no wicked man in the church, that gives so much way as he is moved and stirred to by the Spirit and word of God.

Away then with these impudent, ungracious objections about God's decree for matter of election. Let us make it sure. And for any ill conceits that may rise in our hearts about that other of reprobation, let this damp them all, that in the church of God, he offers unto the vilest wretch so much means, with the motions of his Spirit, as he resisting, proves inexcusable ; his own rebellion therefore being the cause of his rejection. Let men cease from cavilling; God hath that in their own breast, in the heart of every carnal man, which will speak for God against him, and stop his mouth that he shall be silent and speechless at the day of judgment, Mat. xxii. 12.

Thus we see that Christ doth condescend so low as to account it almost a part of his happiness to have our souls for a temple to dwell in, to rule there. Therefore he makes all this earnest suit, with strong expressions what he suffereth.

And since Christ bears this great and large affection to his poor church, it may encourage us to pray heartily for the same, and to spread before God the state thereof. Why, Lord ? it is that part of the world that is thy sister, thy love, thy dove, thy undefiled ; the communion with whom thou lovest above all the world besides. It is a strong argument to prevail with God. Therefore let us commend the state of the church at this time, or at any time, with this confidence. Lord, it is the church that thou lovest. They thought they prevailed much with Christ when they laboured to bring him to Lazarus, saying, ' Lord, he whom thou lovest is sick,' John xi. 3. So say we, the church whom thou lovest, that is, thy only love, in whom thy love is concenterate,‡ as it were, and gathered to a head, as though thou hadst no other love in the world but thy church, this thy love is in this state and condition. It is good to think of prevailing arguments ; not to move God so much as our own hearts ; to strengthen our faith to prevail with God, which is much fortified with the consideration of Christ's wondrous loving expression to his poor church. Then come to Christ, offer thyself, and he will meet thee. Are not two loving well-wishers well met ? When thou offerest thyself to him, and he seeks thy love, will he reject thee when thou comest to him that seeks thy love, and seeketh it in this passionate, affectionate manner, as he doth ? Therefore, be of good comfort. He is more willing to entertain us than we are to come to him.

And for those that have relapsed any kind of way, let them not be discouraged to return again to Christ. The church here was in a drowsy, sleepy estate, and used him unkindly ; yet he is so patient, that he waits her leisure, as it were, and saith, ' Open to me, my sister, my love,' &c. Thomas was so untoward, that he would not believe, ' unless he did see the

* That is, 'stirred up.'—G.   † That is, 'incited.'—G.   ‡ That is ' concentrated.'—G.

print of the nails,' &c., in Christ's body. Yet Christ was so gracious as he condescendeth to poor Thomas, John xx. 27. So to Peter after he was fallen, Mark xvi. 7, and to the church after backsliding.

' Open to me, my sister,' &c. Hence observe further,

That Christ hath never enough of his church till he hath it in heaven, where are indeed the kisses of the spouse, and of Christ. In the mean while ' Open, open,' still. Christ had the heart of the spouse in some measure already ; but yet there were some corners of the heart that were not so filled with Christ as they should be. He was not so much in her understanding, will, joy, delight, and love, as he would be. Therefore, open thy understanding more and more to embrace me, and divine truths that are offered thee. Open thy love to solace me more and more. For God in Christ, having condescended to the terms of friendship, nay, to intimate terms of friendship in marriage with us ; therefore* the church in her right temper, hath never enough of Christ, but desires further union, and communion still. It being the description of the people of God, that ' they love the appearance of Christ,' 2 Tim. iv. 8 ; Rev. xxii. 20, as they loved his first appearance, and waited for 'the consolation of Israel,' Luke ii. 25 ; so they love his second appearing, and are never quiet, till he comes again in the flesh, to consummate the marriage begun here. So Christ also he is as desirous of them, yea, they are his desires that breed their desires. ' Open to me, my sister, my love, my dove,' &c. Again his love and pity moves him to desire further to come into us. Christ knows what is in our hearts. If he be not there, there is that that should not be there. What is in the brain where Christ is not? A deal of worldly projects, nothing worth. What is in our joy if Christ be not there ? Worldly joy, which cleaves to things worse than itself. If a man were anatomised, and seen into, he would be ashamed of himself, if he did see himself. Christ therefore, out of pity to our souls, would not have the devil there. Christ knows it is good for our souls to give way to him, therefore he useth all sweet allurements, ' Open to me, my sister, my love,' &c. Christ hath never his fill, till he close with the soul perfectly ; so that nothing be in the soul above him, nothing equal to him. Therefore ' Open, open,' still.

Again, he sets down, to move the church the more to open to him, the inconveniences that he endured, ' My head is filled with dew,' &c. Wherein he shews what he suffered, which sufferings are of two sorts : in himself ; in his ministers. In himself, and in his own blessed person, what did he endure ! What patience had he in enduring the refractory spirits of men, when he was here ! How many indignities did he digest† in his disciples after their conversion ! Towards his latter end, his head was not only filled with the drops, but his body filled with drops of blood. Drops of blood came from him, because of the anguish of his spirit, and the sense of God's wrath for our sins. Upon the cross, what did he endure there ! That sense of God's anger there, was only for our sins. ' My God, my God, why hast thou forsaken me ?' Mat. xxvii. 46. What should we speak of his going up and down doing good, preaching in his own person, setting whole nights apart for prayer ! And then for what he suffers in his ministers. There he knocks, and saith, ' Open,' in them. And how was he used in the apostles that were after him, and in the ministers of the church ever since ! What have they endured ! for he put a spirit of patience upon them. And what indignities endured they in the primitive church, that were the publishers of the gospel ! Those sweet publishers

* ' As,' deleted here.—G.   † That is, ' bear.'—G.

thereof, drawing men to open to Christ, were killed for preaching. So cruel is the heart, that it offereth violence to them that love them most, that love their souls. And what greater love than the love of the soul ! Yet this is the Satanical temper and disposition of men's hearts. They hate those men most, that deal this way most truly and lovingly with them. It is not that the gospel is such an hard message. It is the word of reconciliation, and the word of life ; but the heart hates it, because it would draw men from their present condition ; and 'therefore condemnation is come into the world, in that men hate the light, because their works are evil,' John iii. 19. Is there anything truly and cordially hated but grace ? and are any persons heartily and cordially hated in the world so much as the promulgers and publishers of grace, and the professors of it ? because it upbraids most of all, and meddles with the corruptions of men, that are dearer to them than their own souls.

Now, what patience is there in Christ to suffer himself in his messengers, and his children to be thus used ! Nor it is not strange to say that Christ stands thus in his ministers ; for it is said, ' That Christ by his Spirit preached in the days of Noah, to the souls now in prison,' 1 Pet. iii. 19. Christ preached in Noah's time, before he was incarnate, much more doth he preach now. And as he was patient then to endure the old world, unto whom Noah preached a hundred and twenty years ; so he is patient now in his ministers to preach still by the same Spirit, even to us still, and yet the entertainment in many places is, as Paul complains, ' Though the more I love you, yet the less I am beloved of you,' 2 Cor. xii. 15.

Use 1. *Let these things move us to be patient towards God and Christ, if we be corrected in any kind,* considering that Christ is so patient towards us, and to wait upon him with patience. How long hath he waited for our conversion ! How long doth he still wait for the thorough giving up of our souls to him ! Shall we think much, then, to wait a little while for him ?

Use 2. *And let this Spirit of Christ strengthen us likewise in our dealing with others,* as to bear with evil men, and as it is, ' to wait, if God will at any time give them repentance,' 2 Tim. ii. 25, 26. Neither may we be so short-spirited, that if we have not an answer, presently to give over. We should imitate Christ here. Never give over as long as God continues life with any advantage and opportunity to do good to any soul. Wait, if God at any time will give them grace. ' Open to me, my sister, my love,' &c.

Use 3. *Let this again work upon us, that our Saviour Christ here would thus set forth his love, and his patience in his love,* in bearing with us thus, under the resemblance of a silly suitor that comes afar off, and stands at the door, and knocks. That Christ should stoop thus in seeking the good of our souls, let this win and quicken our hearts with all readiness and thankfulness to receive him when he comes to work in our souls. Considering that Christ hath such a care of us by himself, his ministers, and the motions of his Spirit, who joins with his ministry, let not us therefore be careless of our own souls, but let it move our hearts to melt to him. The motives may be seen more in the particular compellations. ' Open to me, my sister, my love,' &c.

' My sister.' This was spoken of before in the former verse. The church of God is Christ's sister and spouse. We are knit to him both by consanguinity and by affinity. The nearest affinity is marriage, and the nearest consanguinity is sister. So that there are all bonds to knit us to Christ. Whatsoever is strong in any bond, he knits us to him by it. Is there any love in an husband, a brother, a mother, a friend, in an head to the members ? in anything in the world ? Is there any love scattered in any relation, gather it all into one, and all that love, and a thousand times more than that, is in Christ in a more eminent manner. Therefore he styles himself in all these sweet relations, to shew that he hath the love of all. Will a sister shut out a brother, when the brother comes to visit her, and do her all good ? Is this unkindness even in nature, to look strangely upon a man that is near akin, that comes and saith, ' Open to me, my sister ?' If the sister should shut out the brother, were it not most unnatural ? And is it not monstrous in grace, when our brother comes for our good, and in pity to our souls, to let him stand without doors ? Remember that Christ hath the same affections, to account us brothers and sisters, now in heaven, as he had when he was upon the earth. For after his resurrection, saith he to his disciples, ' I go to my God, and to your God, to my Father, and to your Father,' John xx. 17. He calls himself our brother, having one common Father in heaven, and one Spirit, and one inheritance, &c. This is a sweet relation. Christ being our brother, his heart cannot but melt towards us in any affliction. Joseph dissembled a while, out of politic wisdom, Gen. xlii. 7, *seq.*, but because he had a brother's heart to Benjamin, therefore at last he could not hold, but melted into tears, though he made his countenance as though he had not regarded. So our Joseph, now in heaven, may seem to withdraw all tokens and signs of brotherly love from us, and not to own us ; but it is only in show, he is our brother still. His heart, first or last, will melt towards his brethren, to their wonderful comfort. ' My sister,' &c.

' My love.' That word we had not yet. It is worthy also a little standing on, for all these four words be, as it were, the attractive cords to draw the spouse, not only by shewing what he had suffered, but by sweet titles, ' My love, My dove.'

What, had Christ no love but his spouse ? Did his love go out of his own heart to her, as it were ? It is strange, yet true. Christ's love is so great to his church and children, and so continual* to it, that his church and people and every Christian soul is the seat of his love. That love in his own breast being in them, they are his love, because he himself is there, and one with them, John xvii. 26.

He loves all his creatures. They have all some beams of his goodness, which he must needs love. Therefore he loves them as creatures, and as they be more or less capable of a higher degree of goodness ; but for his church and children, they are his love indeed.

Quest. But what is the ground of such love ?

Ans. 1. He *loves them as he beholds them in his father's choice*, as they are elected of God, and given unto himself in election. ' Thine they are, thou gavest them me,' John xvii. 6. Christ, looking on us in God's election and choice, loves us.

Ans. 2. Again, *he loves us because he sees his own graces in us.* He loves what is his in us. Before we be actually his, he loves us with a love of good will, to wish all good to us. But when we have anything of his Spirit, that our natures are altered and changed, he loves us with a love of the intimatest friendship, with the love of an head, husband, friend, and what we can imagine. He loves his own image. Paul saith ' that the wife is the glory of her husband,' 1 Cor. xi. 7, because whatsoever is in a good husband, the wife expresseth it by reflection. So the church is the glory of Christ ; she reflects his excellencies, though in a weak measure. They

* That is, ' abiding.'—G.

shew forth his virtues or praises, as Peter speaks, 1 Pet. ii. 9. Thus he
sees his own image in her, and the Holy Ghost in his church. He loves
her, and these in her, so as whether we regard the Father or himself or
his Spirit, the church is his love.

Ans. 3. *If we consider also what he hath done and suffered for her,* we may
well say the church is his love. Besides the former favours, not to speak
of election, he choosed us before we were. In time he did choose us by actual
election, by which he called us. We had an existence, but we resisted.
He called us when we resisted. And then also he justified us, and clothed
us with his own righteousness, and after feeds us with his own body. As
the soul is the most excellent thing in the world, so he hath provided for
it the most excellent ornaments. It hath food and ornaments proportionable. What love is this, that he should feed our souls with his own body,
and clothe us with his own righteousness! 'He loved me,' saith Paul,
Gal. ii. 20. What was the effect of his love? 'He gave himself for me.'
He gave himself, both that we might have a righteousness to clothe us with
in the sight of God, and he gave himself that he might be the bread of life,
'My flesh is meat indeed, and my blood is drink indeed,' John vi. 55.
The guilty, the self-accusing soul feeds upon Christ dying for its sins.
Again, Rev. i. 6, you have his love set forth, 'He loved us;' and how doth
he witness it? 'He hath washed us with his own blood, and hath made
us kings, and priests, &c. The like you have, 'He loved us, and gave
himself a sweet sacrifice to God for us,' Eph. v. 2. When this world is at
an end, we shall see what his love is. He is not satisfied till we be all in
one place. What doth he pray for to his Father? 'Father, I will that
those whom thou hast given me be with me where I am,' &c., John xvii. 24.
Run through all the whole course of salvation, election, vocation, justification, glorification, you shall see his love in all of them. But it were an
infinite argument to follow to shew the love of Christ, which is beyond all
knowledge, Eph. iii. 19; and it is too large for us to know all the dimensions of it, to see the height, breadth, depth, and length of it, which we
should ever think, speak, and meditate of, because the soul is then in the
most fit temper to serve, love, and glorify God, when it is most apprehensive of his great love.

1. This phrase imports divers things. 1. *That there is no saving love to
any out of the church,* which is his *love.* It is, as it were, confined in the
church, as if all the beams of his love met in that centre, as we see when
the beams of the sun meet in a glass, they burn, because many are there
united. So in the church all his love doth meet.

2. Then the church is his love also, *because whatsoever she hath or hopes
for is from his love, and is nothing but his love.* The church, as it is a
church, is nothing but the love of Christ. That there is a church so endowed, so graced, so full of the hope of glory, it is out of his love.

And for the properties of it. (1.) It is a *free love, a preventing love.* He
loved us before ever we could love him. He loved us when we resisted
him, and were his enemies.

(2.) It is a most *tender love,* as you have it in Isa. xlix. 15, ' Can a mother
forget her sucking child? If she should, yet will not I forget thee. Thou
art written on the palms of my hands,' &c. He hath us in his heart, in his
eye, in his hand, in a mother's heart, and beyond it. He hath a tender eye
and a powerful hand to maintain his church, Deut. xxxiii. 3.

(3.) It is a *most transcendent and careful love.* All comparisons are under it.

(4.) And it is *a most intimate invincible love,* that nothing could quench it.

As we see here the church droopeth, and had many infirmities, yet she is Christ's love. So that the love of Christ is a kind of love that is unconquerable; no water will ever quench it; no sin of ours; no infirmity. So as it is very comfortable that the church considered under infirmities is yet the love of Christ. 'I sleep, but my heart waketh,' yet Christ comes with 'My love, my dove,' &c.

Quest. But what, cannot Christ see matter of weakness, sinfulness, hatred, and dislike in the church?

Ans. Oh yes, to pity, help, and heal it, but not at all to diminish his love, but to manifest it so much the more. His love is a tender love, sensible of all things wherewith we displease him, yet it is so invincible and unconquerable, that it overcomes all. Again, he sees ill indeed in us, but he sees in us some good of his own also, which moves him more to love, than that that is ill in us, moves him to hate. For what he sees of ours, he sees with a purpose to vanquish, mortify, and eat it out. The Spirit is as fire to consume it. He is as water to wash it. But what he sees of his own, he sees with a purpose to increase it more and more, and to perfect it. Therefore he says, 'my love,' notwithstanding that the church was asleep.

Use. This therefore serves greatly for our comfort, to search what good Christ by his Spirit hath wrought in our hearts; what faith, what love, what sanctified judgment, what fire of holy affections to him, and to the best things. O let us value ourselves by that that is good, that Christ hath in us. We are Christ's love notwithstanding we are sleepy. If we be displeased with this our state; that as Christ dislikes it, so if we by the Spirit dislike it, the matter is not what sin we have in us, but how we are affected to it. Have we that ill in us, which is truly the grief of our hearts and souls, which as Christ dislikes, so we abhor it, and would be purged, and rid of it; and it is the grief of our hearts and souls, that we cannot be better, and more lovely in Christ's eye! then let us not be discouraged. For Christ esteems of his church highly, even as his very love, even at that time when she was sleepy; and may teach us in time of temptation not to hearken to Satan, who then moves us to look altogether upon that which is naught in us, thereby to abate our love to Christ, and our apprehension of his to us. For he knows if we be sensible of the love of Christ to us, we shall love him again. For love is a kind of fire, an active quality, which will set us about glorifying God, and pulling down Satan's kingdom. As we say in nature, fire doth all; (what work almost can a man work without fire, by which all instruments are made and heated? &c.). So grace doth all with love. God first doth manifest to our souls his love to us in Christ, and quicken us by his Spirit, witnessing his love to us, wherewith he warms our hearts, kindles and inflames them so with love, that we love him again; which love hath a constraining, sweet violence to put us upon all duties, to suffer, to do, to resist anything. If a man be in love with Christ, what will be harsh to him in the world? The devil knows this well enough; therefore one of his main engines and temptations is to weaken our hearts in the sense of God's love and of Christ's. Therefore let us be as wise for our souls as he is subtle, and politic against them; as watchful for our own comfort, as he is to discomfort us, and make us despair. Let us be wise to gather all the arguments of Christ's love that we can.

Quest. But how shall we know that Christ loves us in this peculiar manner?

Ans. 1. *First,* search what course he takes and hath taken to *draw thee nearer unto him.* 'He chastiseth every one that he loveth,' Heb. xii. 6. Seasonable corections sanctified, is a sign of Christ's love; when he will

not suffer us to thrive in sin; when we cannot speak nor do amiss; but
either he lasheth us in our conscience for it, and by his Spirit checks us,
or else stirs up others, one thing or other to make us out of love with sin.

2. Again, we may gather Christ's love by this, *if we have any love to
divine things, and can set a great price upon the best things;* upon the word,
because it is Christ's word; upon grace, prizing the image of Christ, and
the new creature. When we can set an high value upon communion with
Christ, the sense of his love in our hearts, and all spiritual prerogatives and
excellencies above all things, this is an excellent argument of Christ's love
to us. Our love is but a reflection of his; and therefore if we have love to
anything that is good, we have it from him first. If a wall that is cold
become hot, we say, the sun of necessity must shine on it first, because it
is nothing but cold stone of itself. So if our hearts, that are naturally
cold, be heated with the love of divine things, certainly we may say, Christ
hath shined here first; for naturally our hearts are of a cold temper. There
is no such thing as spiritual love growing in our natures and hearts.

You have many poor souls helped with this, who cannot tell whether
Christ love them or no; but this helps them a little, they can find undoubted
arguments of their love to Christ, his image, and servants, and of relishing
the word, though they find much corruption : and this their love to divine
things tells them by demonstrations from the effects, *that Christ loves them,*
because there is no love to divine and supernatural things without the love
of Christ first. And the graces in our hearts, they are love tokens given to
the spouse. Common favours he gives, as Abraham gifts to his servants
and others, but special gifts to his spouse. If therefore there be any grace,
a tender and soft heart, a prizing of heavenly things, love to God's people
and truth, then we may comfortably conclude Christ loves us; not only because they are reflections of God's love, but because they are jewels and
ornaments that Christ only bestows upon his spouse; and not upon reprobates, such precious jewels as these, John xv. 15.

3. *By discovering his secrets to us,* Ps. xxv. 14, for that is an argument of love.
Doth Christ by his Spirit discover the secret love he hath borne to us before
all worlds? Doth he discover the breast of his Father, and his own heart to
us? This discovery of secret affections, of entire love, sheweth our happy
state. For that is one prerogative of friendship, and the chiefest discovery
of secrets, when he gives us a particular right to truths, as our own, that
we can go challenge them, these are mine, these belong to me, these promises are mine. This discovery of the secret love of God, and of the
interests we have in the promises, is a sign that Christ loves us, and that
in a peculiar manner we are his love.

Use 1. Let us be like our blessed Saviour, that where we see any saving
goodness in any, let us love them; for should not our love meet with our
Saviour's love? Shall the church of God be the love of Christ, and shall it
be our hatred? Shall a good Christian be Christ's love, and shall he be
the object of my hatred and scorn? Can we imitate a better pattern? O
let us never think our estate to be good, except every child of God be our
love as he is Christ's love. Can I love Christ, and cannot I love * him in
whom I see Christ? It is a sign that I hate himself, when I hate his
image. It is to be wondered at that the devil hath prevailed with any so
much, as to think they should be in a good estate, when they have hearts rising
against the best people, and who, as they grow in grace, so they grow in
their dislike of them. Is here the Spirit of Christ?

* That is, ' can I not love.'—ED.

Use 2. And let them likewise be here reproved that are glad to see any Christian halt, slip, and go awry. The best Christians in the world have that in part, which is wholly in another man ; he hath flesh in him. Shall we utterly distaste a Christian for that ? The church was now in a sleepy condition, and yet, notwithstanding, Christ takes not the advantage of the weakness of the church to cashier,* and to hate her, but he pities her the more, and takes a course to bring her again into a good state and condition. Let us not therefore be glad at the infirmities and failings of any, that discover any true goodness in them. It may be our own case ere long. It casts them not out of Christ's love, but they dwell in his love still ; why should we then cast them out of our love and affections ? Let them be our loves till, as they are the love of Christ, notwithstanding their infirmities.

THE SEVENTH SERMON.

My love, my dove, my undefiled : for my head is filled with dew, and my locks
with the drops of the night. I have put off my coat; how shall I put it on?
I have washed my feet; and how shall I defile them ?—CANT. V. 2, 3.

THAT the life of a Christian is a perpetual conflicting, appears evidently in this book, the passages whereof, joined with our own experiences, sufficiently declare what combats, trials, and temptations the saints are subject unto, after their new birth and change of life; now up, now down, now full of good resolutions, now again sluggish and slow, not to be waked, nor brought forward by the voice of Christ, as it was with the church here. She will not out of her sleep to open unto Christ, though he call, and knock, and stand waiting for entrance. She is now desirous to pity herself, and needs no Peter to stir her up unto it (*g*). The flesh of itself is prone enough to draw back, and make excuses, to hinder the power of grace from its due operation in us. She is laid along, as it were, to rest her ; yet is not she so asleep, but she discerns the voice of Christ. But up and rise she will not.

Thus we may see the truth of that speech of our Saviour verified, ' That which is born of the flesh is flesh, and that which is born of the Spirit is spirit,' John iii. 6. The flesh pulls her back : the Spirit would raise her up to open to Christ. He in the meanwhile makes her inexcusable, and prepares her by his knocking, waiting, and departing; as for a state of further humiliation, so for an estate of further exaltation. But how lovingly doth he speak to her !

1. ' Open unto me, my love.' He calls her my love, especially for two respects ; partly because *his love was settled upon her*. It was in his own breast, but it rested not there, but seated itself upon, and in the heart of his spouse, so that she became Christ's love. We know the heart of a lover is more where it loves than where it lives, as we use to speak ; and indeed, there is a kind of a going out, as it were, to the thing beloved, with a heedlessness of all other things. Where the affection is in any excess, it carries the whole soul with it.

2. But, besides this, when Christ saith my love, he shews, that as his love goes, and plants, and seats itself in the church, *so it is united to that, and is not scattered to other objects.* There are beams of God's general love scattered in the whole world ; but this love, this exceeding love, is only fas-

* That is, ' dismiss.'—G.

tened upon the church. And, indeed, there is no love comparable to this love of Christ, which is above the love of women, of father, or mother, if we consider what course he takes to shew it. For there could be nothing in the world so great to discover his love, as this gift, and gift of himself. And therefore he gave himself, the best thing in heaven or in earth withal, to shew his love. The Father gave him, when he was God equal with his Father. He loved his church, and gave himself for it. How could he discover his love better, than to take our nature to shew how he loved us? How could he come nearer to us, than by being incarnate, so to be bone of our bone, and flesh of our flesh; and took our nature to shew how he loved it, Eph. v. 30. Love draws things nearer wheresoever it is. It drew him out of heaven to the womb of the virgin, there to be incarnate; and, after that, when he was born not only to be a man, but a miserable man, because we could not be his spouse unless he purchased us by his death. We must be his spouse by a satisfaction made to divine justice. God would not give us to him, but with salving* his justice. What sweet love is it to heal us not by searing, or lancing, but by making a plaster of his own blood, which he shed for those that shed his, in malice and hatred. What a wondrous love is it, that he should pour forth tears for those that shed his blood! ' O Jerusalem, Jerusalem,' &c., Mat. xxiii. 37; that he prayed for those that persecuted him, Luke xxiii. 34; and what wondrous love is it now that he sympathiseth with us in heaven, accounting the harm that is done to the least member he hath, as done to himself! ' Saul, Saul, why persecutest thou me?' Acts ix. 4, and that he should take us into one body with himself, to make one Christ, 1 Cor. xii. 27. And he doth not content himself with anything he can do for us here, but his desire is, that we may be one with him more and more, and be for ever with him in the heavens, as you have it in that excellent prayer, John xvii. 24.

Use 1. Now this should stir us up *to be fully persuaded of his love, that loves us so much.* Christ's love in us, is as the loadstone to the iron. Our hearts are heavy and downwards of themselves. We may especially know his love by this, that it draws us upwards, and makes us heavenly minded. It makes us desire further and further communion with him. Still there is a magnetical attractive force in Christ's love. Wheresoever it is, it draws the heart and affections after it.

Use 2. And we may know from hence one argument to prove *the stability of the saints, and the immortality of the soul,* because Christ calls the church his love. The want of love again, where it is entire, and in any great measure, is a misery. Christ therefore should suffer, if those he hath planted his love upon, whom he loves truly, either should fall away for ever, or should not be immortal for ever. Christ will not lose his love. And as it is an argument of persevering in grace, so is it of an everlasting being, that this soul of ours hath; because it is capable of the love of Christ, seeing there is a sweet union and communion between Christ and the soul. It should make Christ miserable, as it were, in heaven, the place of happiness, if there should not be a meeting of him and his spouse. There must therefore be a meeting; which marriage is for ever, that both may be for ever happy one in another, Hos. ii. 20.

Use 3. Let us often *warm our hearts with the consideration hereof, because all our love is from this love of his.* Oh the wonderful love of God, that both such transcendent majesty, and such an infinite love should dwell together. We say majesty and love never dwell together, because love is an abasing of the

---

* That is, ' preserving.'—G.

soul to all services. But herein it is false, for here majesty and love dwell
together in the heart of one Christ, which majesty hath stooped as low as
his almighty power could give leave. Nay, it was an almighty power that
he could stoop so low and yet be God, keeping his majesty still. For God
to beeome man, to hide his majesty for a while, not to be known to be God,
and to hide so far in this nature as to die for us : what an almighty power was
this, that could go so low and yet preserve himself God still ! Yet this we see
in this our blessed Saviour, the greatest majesty met with the greatest
abasement that ever was, and all out of love to our poor souls. There was
no stooping, no abasement that was ever so low as Christ was abased unto
us, to want for a time even the comfort of the presence of his Father.
There was an union of grace ; but the union of solace and comfort that he
had from him was suspended for a time, out of love to us. For he had a
right in his own person to be in heaven presently. Now for him to live
so long out of heaven, and ofttimes, especially towards his suffering, to be
without that solace (that he might be a sacrifice for our sins), to have it
suspended for a time, what a condescending was this ? It is said, Ps. cxiii.
6, that God stoops ' to behold the things done here below.' It is indeed a
wondrous condescending, that God will look upon things below ; but that
he would become man, and out of love to save us, suffer as he did here,
this is wondrous humility to astonishment ! We think humility is not a
proper grace becoming the majesty of God. So it is not indeed, but there
is some resemblance of that grace in God, especially in Christ, that he
should, to reveal himself, veil himself with flesh, and all out of love to us.
The consideration of these things are wondrous effectual, as to strengthen
faith, so to kindle love. Let these be for a taste to˙direct our meditations
herein. It follows,

' My dove.' We know when Christ was baptized, the Holy Ghost
appeared in the shape of a dove, Mat. iii. 16, as a symbol of his presence,
to discover thus much : (1.) *That Christ should have the property and disposition of a dove.* 'And be meek and gentle.' For indeed he became man
for that end, to be ' a merciful Saviour.' ' Learn of me, for I am meek
and lowly,' Mat. xi. 28, 29. ' And I will not quench the smoking flax, nor
break the bruised reed,' &c., Mat. xii. 20, said he ; and therefore the
Spirit appeared upon him in the shape of a dove. As likewise, (2.) *To
shew what his office should be.* For even as the dove in Noah's ark was
sent out, and came home again to the ark with an olive branch, to shew
that the waters were abated ; so Christ was to preach deliverance from
the deluge of God's anger, and to come with an olive leaf of peace in his
mouth, and reconciliation, to shew that God's wrath was appeased. When
he was born, the angels sung, ' Glory to God on high, on earth peace, and
goodwill towards men,' Luke ii. 14. Now, as Christ had the Spirit in the
likeness of a dove ; so all that are Christ's, the spouse of Christ, have the
disposition of Christ. That Spirit that framed him to be like a dove,
frames the church to be a dove ; as the ointment that was poured on Aaron's
head : it ran down upon the lowest skirts of his garments, Ps. cxxxiii. 3.

Now, the church is compared to a dove, partly *for the disposition that is
and should be in the church resembling that creature;* and partly, also, *for
that the church is in a mournful suffering condition.*

I. *For the like disposition as is found in a dove.* There is some good
in all creatures. There is no creature but it hath a beam of God's majesty,
of some attribute ; but some more than others. There is an image of
virtue even in the inferior creatures. Wherefore the Scripture sends us to

them for many virtues, as the sluggard to the ant, Prov. vi. 6. And indeed
we may see the true perfection of the first creation, the state of it, more
in the creatures than in ourselves ; for there is no such degeneration in any
creature as there is in man.

Now, that which in a dove the Scripture aims at, 1, we should resemble
a dove in is, his *meekness* especially. The church is meek both to God and
man, not given to murmurings and revengement. Meek : that is, ' I held
my tongue without murmuring,' as it is in the psalm ; ' I was dumb,' &c.,
Ps. xxxix. 2 : which is a grace that God's Spirit frames in the heart of the
church, and every particular Christian, even to be meek towards God by
an holy silence ; and likewise towards men, to put on the ' bowels of meekness,' as we are exhorted, ' As the elect of God, put on the bowels of meekness and compassion,' &c., Col. iii. 12. Hereby we shall shew ourselves
to be Christ's, and to have the Spirit of Christ. And this grace disposeth
us to a nearer communion with God than other graces. It is a grace that
God most delights in, and would have his spouse to be adorned with, as is
shewed, 1 Pet. iii. 4, where the apostle tells women, it is the best jewel
and ornament that they can wear, and is with God of great price. Moses,
we read, was a mighty man in prayer, and a special means to help and fit him
thereunto, was because he was the meekest man on earth, Num. xii. 3 ; and
therefore, ' seek the Lord, seek meekness,' Zeph. ii. 3 ; and it fits a man for
communion with God, 'for God resisteth the proud, and giveth grace to the
meek and humble,' 1 Pet. v. 5. It is a grace that empties the soul of self-
conceit, to think a man's self unworthy of anything, and so makes it capacious,
low, and fit for God to fill with a larger measure of his Spirit. It takes
away the roughness and swelling of the soul, that keeps out God and grace.
Therefore in that grace we must especially be like this meek creature, which
is no vindictive creature, that hath no way to revenge itself.

Again, 2, *it is a simple creature, without guile.* It hath no way to defend
itself, but only by flight. There is a simplicity that is sinful, when there
is no mixture of wisdom in it. There is a simplicity, that is, a pure simplicity ; and so God is simple, which simplicity of God is the ground of
many other attributes. For thereupon he is eternal, because there is nothing contrary in him ; there is no mixture in him of anything opposite.
So that is a good simplicity in us, when there is no mixture of fraud, no
duplicity in the soul. ' A double-hearted man is inconstant and unstable
in all his ways,' James i. 8. Now simplicity, as it is a virtue, so we must
imitate the dove in it ; for there is a sinful, dove-like silliness. For,
Hos. vii. 11, Ephraim is said there to be ' like a silly dove without heart ;
they call to Egypt, they go to Assyria.' There is a fatal simplicity,
usually going before destruction, when we hate those that defend us, and
account them enemies, and rely more upon them that are enemies indeed
than upon friends. So it was with Ephraim before his destruction : ' He
was a silly dove without heart ; he called to Egypt, and went to Assyria,'
false friends, that were enemies to the church of God ; yet they trusted
them more than God or the prophets. Men have a world of tricks to undermine their friends, to ruin them, and to deserve ill of those that would
with all their hearts deserve well of them, when yet in the mean time they
can gratify the enemy, please them, and hold correspondence with them,
as here Ephraim did. ' Ephraim is a silly dove,' &c. This, therefore, is
not that which we must aim at, but to be simple and children concerning
evil, but not in ignorance and simplicity that way.

3. Again, *this creature is a faithful creature.* That is mainly here aimed

at. It is faithful to the mate. So the Christian soul, by the Spirit of God,
it is made faithful to Christ, it keeps the judgment chaste, is not tainted
with errors and sins. He keeps his affections chaste likewise, sets nothing
in his heart above Christ. ' Whom hath he in heaven but him, and what
is there in earth he desires beside him ?' Ps. lxxiii. 25. You know in the
Revelation, the spouse of Christ is brought in like a virgin contracted, but
the Romish Church like a whore. Therefore the church of God must take
heed of the Roman Church, for that is not a dove. We must be virgins,
who must keep chaste souls to Christ, as you have it—' Those that follow
the Lamb wheresoever he goeth, they have not defiled themselves with
women,' Rev. xiv. 4. The meaning is spiritual, namely, that they have
not defiled themselves with idolatry and spiritual fornication ; they have
chaste hearts to Christ. So in this respect they resemble the dove. These,
therefore, that draw away from the love of religion to mixture, to be mere-
trices* and harlots in religion, they are not Christ's doves. As far as they
yield to this, it is an argument that they have false hearts. Christ's church
is a dove. She keeps close and inviolate to him.

4. Again, *this creature is of a neat† disposition.* It will not lodge where it
shall be troubled with stench, and annoyed that way ; and likewise feeds
neatly on pure grain ; not upon carrion, as you see in the ark, when the
raven was sent out it lights upon carrion, of which there was then plenty,
and therefore never came into the ark again, Gen. viii. 7. But the
dove, when she went out, would not light upon carrion or dead things ;
and so finding no fit food, came back again to the ark. So the Christian
soul in this respect is like a dove, that will not feed upon worldly carrion,
or sinful pleasures, but upon Christ and spiritual things. The soul of a
carnal and a natural man useth to feed upon dust, earth and earthly things.
When the soul of a true Christian, that hath the taste of grace, feeds
neatly, it will not feed on that which is base and earthly, but upon heavenly
and spiritual things.

5. It is *gregaria avis,* a bird that loves communion and fellowship, as the
prophet speaks, ' Who are those that flock to the windows as doves,' Isa.
lx. 8 ; for so they use to flock to their houses by companies. So the children of God love the communion and fellowship one of another, and keep
severed from the world as soon as ever they are separated from it, delighting in all those of the same nature. Doves will consort with doves, Christians with Christians, and none else. They can relish no other company.
These and such like properties may profitably be considered of the dove.
The much standing upon these were to wrong the intendment‡ of the Spirit
of God ; to neglect them altogether were as much. Therefore we have
touched upon some properties only.

II. Now, *for the sufferings of the church* it is like a dove in this. *The
dove is molested by all the birds of prey,* it being the common prey of all
other ravenous birds. So the poor church of God is persecuted and
molested. ' Oh that I had wings like a dove,' &c., saith holy David,
Ps. lv. 6. It is an old speech, and is for ever true, that crows and such,
escape better than doves. The punishment that should light on ravens, ofttimes it lights on doves. Thus God's dove, God's church, is used.

But what defence hath God's poor church ? Why, no defence. But,

First, *flight,* even as the dove hath nothing but flight. It hath no
talons to wound, but it hath flight. So we are to fly to God as to our
mountain ; fly to the ark, that God may take us in. The church of God

* That is, ' courtezans.'—G.   † That is, ' cleanly.'—G.   ‡ That is, ' design.'—G.

hath no other refuge but to be housed in God and Christ, Prov. xviii. 10. He is our ark.

Secondly, and to *mourn;* as Hezekiah saith of himself, 'He mourned as a dove, and chattered like a crane,' Isa. xxxviii. 14. The state of the church of God is like the turtle's, to mourn in all afflictions, desertions, and molestations of wicked men ; to mourn to God, who hears the bemoanings of his own Spirit in them. And woe to all other birds, the birds of prey, when the turtles do mourn because of their cruelty. It is a presage of ruin to them, when they force the turtle to sorrow and mourning.

Thirdly, And then, thirdly, they have another refuge besides flight and mourning, which is *to build high from vermin* that would otherwise molest them. Instinct teacheth them thus to escape their enemies by building high, and so to secure themselves. So there is in God's children a gracious instinct put, an antipathy to the enemies of it; which tends to their safety, in that they mingle not themselves with them. And likewise God breeds in them a familiarity with himself, and stirs them to build in him as on a rock, to be safe in him.

Objec. But you will object, If the church of God be his dove, why is it so with it as it is, that God should suffer his love, and his dove, and his turtle thus as it were to be preyed upon? 'Give not the soul of the turtle to the beasts,' saith the psalmist, Ps. lxxiv. 19. If the church were God's dove, he would esteem more of it than he doth, and not suffer it to be persecuted thus ?

Ans. God never forsakes his dove, but is an ark for it to fly to, a rock for it to build on. The dove hath always a refuge in God and in Christ in the worst times. You have a notable place for this, 'Though you have lien among the pots,' that is, smeared and sullied, 'yet they shall be as the wings of a dove covered with silver, and her feathers with yellow gold. When the Almighty scattered kings in it, it was white as the snow in Salmon,' Ps. lxviii. 13, 14. So though the church of God lies among the pots awhile, all smeared, and soiled, and sullied with the ill-usage of the world, yet as long as it keeps itself a dove, unspotted of the filth of the world and sin (though it be smeared with the ill-usage thereof), we see what God promiseth here, 'yet shall they be as the wings of a dove covered with silver, and her feathers with yellow gold.' So God will bring forth his dove with glory out of all these abasements at length. So much for the title of dove. It follows,

'My undefiled.' Undefiled is a high word to be applied to the church of God here; for the church, groaning under infirmities, to be counted perfect and undefiled. But Christ, who judgeth aright of his church, and knows best what she is, he yet thus judgeth of her. But, how is that? The church is undefiled, especially *in that it is the spouse of Christ, and clothed with the robes of his righteousness.* For there is an exchange so soon as ever we are united to Christ. Our sins are upon him, and his righteousness is made ours; and therefore in Christ the church is undefiled. Christ himself the second person is the first lovely thing next the Father; and in Christ all things as they have relation to him are loved, as they are in him. Christ's human nature is next loved to the second person. It is united, and is first pure, holy, and beloved. Then, because the church is Christ mystical, it is near to him; and, in a manner, as near as that sacred body of his, both making up one Christ mystical. And so is amiable and beloved even of God himself, who hath pure eyes ; yet in this respect looks upon the church as undefiled.

Christ and his church are not to be considered as two when we speak

of this undefiledness, but as one. And the church having Christ, with all
that is Christ's, they have the field, and the pearl * in the field together.
And Christ giving himself to the church, he gives his righteousness, his
perfection, and holiness ; all is the church's.

Quest. But how can it be the church's, when it is not in the church, but
in Christ ?

Ans. It is safe for the church that it is in Christ, who is perfect and undefiled for us ; to make us appear so. And so it is in Christ, the second
Adam, for our good. It is not in him as another person, but it is in him
as the church's Head, that make both one Christ. The hand and
the foot see not; but both hand and foot have benefit by the eye, that
sees for them. There is no member of the body understands, but the
head does all for them. Put the case we have not absolute righteousness
and undefiledness in our own natures and persons inhering in us. Yet we
have it in Christ, that is one with us, who hath it for our good. It is
ours, for all the comfort and good that we may have by it; and thereupon
the church in Christ is undefiled ; yea, even then when it feels its own
defilements. And here ariseth that wondrous contradiction that is found
in a believer's apprehension. The nature of faith is to apprehend righteousness in the sense of sin, happiness in the sense of misery, and favour
in the sense of displeasure.

And the ground of it is, because that at the same time the soul may be
in some measure defiled in itself, and yet notwithstanding be undefiled in
her head and husband Christ. Hence the guilty soul, when it feels corruption and sin, yet notwithstanding doth see itself holy and clean in Christ
the head. And so at once there is a conscience of sin, and no more conscience of sin, as the apostle saith, Heb. x. 2, when we believe in Christ,
and are purged with his blood, that is, there is no more guilt of sin binding over to eternal damnation, yet notwithstanding always there is a conscience of sin, for we are guilty of infirmities, ' And if we say we have no
sin, we lie, and deceive ourselves, 1 John i. 8.

Obj. But, how can this be, that there should be conscience of sin, and
no conscience of sin, a sinner, and yet a perfect saint and undefiled ?

Ans. 1. *The conscience knows its own imperfection, so it is defiled,* and accuseth
of sin. *And as it looks to Christ, so it sees itself pure, and purged from all sin.*
Here is the conquest, fight, and the victory of faith in the deepest sense of
sin, pollution, and defilement in ourselves, at the same time to see an absolute and perfect righteousness in Jesus Christ. Herein is even the triumph
of faith, whereby it answers God. And Christ, who sees our imperfections,
but it is to purge and cleanse them away, not to damn us for them, at the
same time he sees us in his own love clothed with his righteousness, as one
with himself, endowed with whatsoever he hath ; his satisfaction and obedience being ours as verily as anything in the world is. Thus he looks on
us, and thus faith looks upon him too, and together with the sight and sense
of sin, at the same time it apprehends righteousness, perfect righteousness,
and so is undefiled. This is the main point in religion, and the comfort of
Christians, to see their perfection in Christ Jesus, and to be lost in themselves, as it were, and to be only ' found in him, not having their own
righteousness, but the righteousness of God in him,' Phil. iii. 9. This is
a mystery which none knows but a believing soul. None see corruption
more, none see themselves freed more. They have an inward sight to see
corruption, and an inward faith to see God takes not advantage at it. And

* That is, ' treasure.' See Mat. xiii. 44.—G.

surely there can be no greater honour to Christ than this. In the sense of sin, of wants, imperfections, stains, and blemishes, yet to wrap ourselves in the righteousness of Christ, God-man; and by faith , being thus covered with that absolute righteousness of Christ, with boldness to go, clothed in the garments of this our elder brother, to the throne of grace. This is an honour to Christ, to attribute so much to his righteousness, that being clothed therewith, we can boldly break through the fire of God's justice, and all those terrible attributes, when we see them all, as it were, satisfied fully in Christ. For Christ, with his righteousness, could go through the justice of God, having satisfied it to the full for us. And we being clothed with this his righteousness and satisfaction, may go through too.

Ans. 2. But besides that, there is another undefiledness in the church, in respect to which she is called undefiled, that is, *in purity of disposition, tending to perfection.* And God respects her according to her better part, and according to what he will bring her in due time. For we are chosen unto perfection, and to be holy in his sight ; and perfectly holy, undefiled, and pure. We are not chosen to weak beginnings.

In choosing us, what did God aim at ? Did he aim at these imperfect beginnings, to rest there ? No; we were elected and chosen to perfection. For, as it is in this natural life, God purposed that we should not only have all the limbs of men, but grow from infancy to activeness and perfection. As God at first intended so much for our bodies, no question he intends as much also for the soul, that we should not only have the lineaments of Christianity, a sanctified judgment, with affections in part renewed, but he hath chosen us to perfection by degrees. As the seed first lies rotting in the ground, then grows to a stalk, and then to an ear, so God's wisdom shines here, by bringing things by degrees to perfection and undefiledness. His wisdom will have it thus (or else his power might have it otherwise), because he will have us to live by faith, to trust his mercy in Christ, and not to the undefiledness that is begun in us, but to admire that which we have in Christ himself.

And, indeed, it is the character of a judicious believing Christian soul, that he can set a price and value the righteousness of Christ, out of himself, labouring, living, and dying to appear in that; and yet to comfort and sustain himself during this conflict and fight between the flesh and the Spirit, that in time this inherent grace shall be brought to perfection.

And Christ, he looks upon us as he means to perfect the work of grace in us by little and little, as he means to purge and cleanse us, as Eph. v. 26, 27. The end of redemption is, that he might purge his church, and so never leave it till he have made it ' a glorious spouse in heaven.' He looks upon us as we shall be ere long, and therefore we are said ' to be dead to sin,' while we are but dying to it. And, saith he, ' you have crucified the flesh with the affections, and lusts thereof,' Gal. v. 24, when we are but crucifying it. But it is said so because it is as sure to be done as if it were done already. As a man, when he is condemned, and going to his execution, he is a dead man, so there is a sentence passed upon sin and corruption. It shall be abolished and die. Therefore it is dead in sentence, and is dying in execution. It is done ; ' They that are in Christ have crucified the flesh, with the lusts thereof,' Gal. v. 24. It is as sure to faith as if it were done already. So we are said ' to sit in heavenly places with Christ,' Eph. ii. 6. We are with him already. For Christ having taken us so near in affection to himself, he will never leave us till he have made us such as he may have full contentment in, which is in heaven, when the contract between him and us shall be fulfilled in consummation of the marriage. Thus faith looks, and Christ looks thus upon us. Which should comfort us in weakness, that God regards us not in our present imperfections, but as he means to make us ere long. In the mean time, that he may look upon us in love, he looks upon us in the obedience of his son, in whom whatsoever is good shall be perfected at the last.

Use 1. What should we do then, if Christ doth make his church thus, ' his love,' ' his dove,' ' his undefiled,' by making his love to meet in it as the centre thereof, whereunto he doth confine all his love, as it were ? *We should confine our love to him again ; and have no love out of Christ*, since he hath no love out of us. There should be an everlasting mutual shining and reflection between him and the soul. We should lay open our souls to his love, as indeed he desires especially the communion of our affections. We should reflect love to him again. This perpetual everlasting intercourse between Christ and his spouse, is her main happiness here, and her eternal happiness in heaven. In looking on him who hath done so much for us, he shines on us, and we look back again upon him. Doth Christ love us so intimately, and so invincibly, that no indignities nor sin could overcome his love, which made, that he endured that which he hates most, ' to become sin for us,' 2 Cor. v. 21, nay, the want of that, which was more to him than all the world, the want of the sense of the favour of God for a time. ' My God, my God, why hast thou forsaken me ?' Hath Christ thus infinitely loved us, and shall not we back again make him our love ? In their degree the saints of God have all done so. It was a good speech of Ignatius the martyr, ' My love Christ was crucified ! ' (*h*) So a Christian should say, ' My love was crucified,' ' My love died,' ' My love is in heaven.' And for the things on earth, I love them as they have a beam of him in them ; as they lead me to him. But he is my love, there my love is pitched, even upon him. This is the ground of these Scripture phrases, ' But our conversation is in heaven, from whence we look for the Saviour, the Lord Jesus Christ,' &c., Phil. iii. 20 ; and ' set your affections on the things that are above,' Col. iii. 1. Why ? Christ our love is there. The soul is more where it loves, than where its residence is. It dies, as it were, to other things, and lives in the thing it loves. Therefore our thoughts and affections, our joy and delight should be drawn up to Christ ; for indeed his love hath such a magnetical attractive force, that where it is, it will draw up the heavy iron, the gross soul ; and make it heavenly. For there is a binding, a drawing force in this excellent affection of love.

Use 2. ' My love, my dove,' &c. *There are all words of sweetness*. He labours to express all the affection he can. For the conscience is subject to upbraid, and to clamour much. So that there must be a great deal of persuasion to still the accusing conscience of a sinner, to set it down, make it quiet, and persuade it of God's love. Therefore he useth all heavenly rhetoric to persuade and move the affections.

Use 3. In this that the church is undefiled in Christ, let us learn when afflicted in conscience, not so much *to judge of ourselves by what we feel in ourselves, as by what faith suggests*. In Christ therefore let us judge of ourselves by what we are as in him. We are poor in ourselves, but have riches in him. We die in ourselves in regard of this life, but we have a life in him, an eternal life ; and we are sinners in ourselves, but we have a righteousness in him whereby we are righteous in his sight, 1 Cor. v. 21. We are foolish, unskilful, and ignorant in ourselves, but he is our wisdom in all whatsoever is amiss in us. Let us labour to see a full supply of our wants made up in Christ. This is to glorify God as much as if we could fulfil the law perfectly. If we were as undefiled as Adam was, we could not glorify God more, than when we find ourselves and our conscience guilty of sins, yet thus by the Spirit of God to go out of ourselves, and to see ourselves in Christ, and thus to cast ourselves on him, embrace him, and take that gift of God given us, Christ offered to us, because God so commands, John iv. 10. We honour God more than if we had the obedience that Adam had at first before his fall. For now in the covenant of grace, he will be glorified in his mercy, in his forgiving, forbearing, rich, transcendent mercy, and in going beyond all our unworthiness and sins, by shewing that there is a righteousness provided for us, the righteousness of God-man; whose obedience and satisfaction is more than our disobedience, because it is the disobedience of man only, but his obedience and righteousness is the obedience and righteousness of God-man. So it satisfieth divine justice, and therefore ought to satisfy conscience to the full. Our faith must answer Christ's carriage to us. We must therefore account ourselves in him ' undefiled,' because he accounts us so. Not in ourselves, but as we have a being in him, we are undefiled.

Use 4. Again, see here, Christ accounts us, even in regard of habitual grace, *undefiled, though we have for the present many corruptions.* Let us therefore learn a lesson of moderation of so excellent a teacher ; let us not be ashamed to learn of our Saviour. What spirit shall we think they have, that will unchurch churches, because they have some defilement and unbrotherly brethren, accounting them no churches, no brethren, because they have some imperfections ? Why hath not Christ a quarrel to the church then ? is he blind ? doth his love make him blind ? No; he seeth corruption, but he seeth better things ; somewhat of his own, that makes him overlook those imperfections, because they are such as he means to mortify, subdue, wear away, and to fire out by the power of his Spirit, which as fire shall waste all those corruptions in time. So it is with the church. Put the case, she hath some corruptions ; that it be not with her, as it should be, yet she is a church notwithstanding. The church of Corinth, we see, Paul styles them saints and brethren, with all those sweet names, 1 Cor. i. 2, notwithstanding they had many corruptions among them.

Use 5. We have a company of malignant spirits, worse than these a great deal, atheistical persons, that have no religion at all, who, out of malice and envy, *watch for the halting of good Christians ;* who can see nothing but defilement in those that have any good in them, nothing but hypocrisy, moppishness, all that is naught ; who, if they can devise any blemish, put it upon them. Whereas Christ sees a great deal of ill in the church, but he sees it to pardon, subdue, and to pity the church for it, extolling and magnifying its goodness. What spirits are those of that watch to see imperfections in others, that their hearts tell them are better than they, that they may only disgrace them by it ; for goodness they will see none.

Use 6. And likewise, it should teach us *not to wrong ourselves with false judgment.* We should have a double eye : one eye to see that which is amiss in us, our own imperfections, thereby to carry ourselves in a perpetual humility ; but another eye of faith, to see what we have in Christ, our perfection in him, so to account of ourselves, and glory in this our best being, that in him we have a glorious being,—such an one whereby God esteems us perfect, and undefiled in him only. The one of which sights should enforce us to the other, which is one end, why God in this world leaves corruption in his children. Oh, since I am thus undefiled, shall

I rest in myself? Is there any harbour for me to rest in mine own righteousness? Oh, no; it drives a man out of all harbour. Nay, I will rest in that righteousness which God hath wrought by Christ, who is God-man. That will endure the sight of God, being clothed with which, I can endure the presence of God. So, this sight of our own unworthiness and wants should not be a ground of discouragement, but a ground to drive us perfectly out of ourselves, that by faith we might renew our title to that righteousness, wherein is our especial glory. Why should we not judge of ourselves as Christ doth? Can we see more in ourselves than he doth? Yet, notwithstanding all he sees, he accounts us as undefiled.

Use 7. Again, since he accounts us undefiled, because he means to make us so, and now looks on us as we shall be, in all our foils* and infirmities, let us comfort ourselves, *it shall not thus be always with us.* Oh, this flesh of mine shall fall and fall still, and shall decay as Saul's house, and the Spirit at the last shall conquer in all this! I am not chosen to this beginning, to this conflicting course of life. I am chosen to triumph, to perfection of grace: this is my comfort. Thus we should comfort ourselves, and set upon our enemies and conflict in this hope of victory: ' I shall get the better of myself at the last.' Imperfection should not discourage, but comfort us in this world. We are chosen to perfection. Let us still rejoice, in that ' we are chosen to sanctification,' which is a little begun, being an earnest of other blessings. Let us not rest in the pledge or in the earnest, but labour for a further pledge of more strength and grace. For those that have the Spirit of Christ, will strive to be as much unspotted and as heavenly as they can, to fit themselves for that heavenly condition as much as may be. When, because they cannot be in heaven, yet they will converse there as much as they can; and because they cannot be with such company altogether, they will be as much as they may be; labouring as they are able to be that which they shall be hereafter. Imperfection contents them not, and therefore they pray still in the Lord's prayer, ' Thy kingdom come,' Mat. vi. 10. While there is any imperfection, their hearts are enlarged more and more; nothing contents them but perfection. And indeed God accounts us thus unspotted for this end, because he would encourage us. Where he sees the will and endeavour, he gives the title of the thing desired.

I have put off my coat; how shall I put it on? I have washed my feet; how shall I defile them? Verse 3.

Here is an ingenious† confession made by the church of her own unto-wardness. Notwithstanding all Christ's heavenly rhetoric and persuasion that he did use, yet she draws back, and seems to have reason so to do. ' I have put off my coat; how shall I put it on again' to let thee in? ' I have washed my feet, &c. It is a phrase taken from the custom of those hot countries, wherein they used to wash their feet. ' I have washed my feet; how shall I defile them' to rise and open the door to thee? There is a spiritual meaning herein, as if she had said, I have some ease by this sleepy profession, some freedom from evil tongues, and some exemption and immunity from some troubles I was in before. I was then, perhaps, too indiscreet. Now wilt thou call me again to those troubles, that I have wisely avoided? No; ' I have put off my coat; how shall I put it on? I have washed my feet, how shall I defile them?' I affect‡ this estate very well; I am content to be as I am, without troubling of myself. Thus the church puts off Christ. This I take to be the meaning of the words. That which is observable is this: *that it is not an easy*

* That is, 'falls.'—G.   † That is, 'ingenuous.'—G.   ‡ That is, 'like.'—G.

matter to bring the soul and Christ together into near fellowship. We see here how the church draws back ; for the flesh moves either not to yield at all to duty, or to be cold, uncertain, and unsettled therein. The flesh knows that a near communion with Christ cannot stand with favouring any corruption, and therefore the flesh will do something, but not enough. It will yield to something, but not to that that it should do, to that communion and fellowship that we ought to have with Christ. To instance in some particulars, as a rule and measure to somewhat of which we should be.

Obs. 1. *A Christian life should be nothing but a communion and intercourse with Christ,* a walking in the Spirit ; and to be spiritual, and to favour the things of the Spirit altogether, he should study to adorn his profession by a lively and cheerful performance of duty, Mat. v. 16, and be exemplary to others ; and should be in such a frame as he should ' walk continually in the comforts of the Holy Ghost' undismayed and undaunted, ' and abound in the fruits of the Spirit,' Acts ix. 20,' and do all the good he can wheresoever he comes. He should ' keep himself unspotted of the world,' James i. 27, go against the stream, and be continually in such a temper, as it should be the joy of his heart to be dissolved, and to be with Christ, 2 Tim. iv. 6. One might go on thus in a world of particulars, which would be too long. If we could attain to this excellency, it were an happy life, a heaven upon earth. This we should aim at. Will the flesh endure this, think you ? No, it will not ; which you shall see more particularly in this next observation, which is,

Obs. 2. That *one way, whereby the unregenerate part in us hinders this communion with Christ,* and the shining of a believer in a Christian course, *is by false pretences, reasons, and excuses.* ' I have washed my feet ; I have put off my coat,' &c.

The flesh never wants excuses and pretences (there was never any yet came to hell, but they had some seeming pretence for their coming thither) to shift and shuffle off duties. There was never yet any careless, sinful course but it had the flesh to justify it with one reason or other ; and there-fore it is good to understand the sophistical shifts* of the flesh, and pre-tences and shows which it hath. And as it is good to know the truth of God, and of Christ revealed in his word, so is it to know the falseness and deceitfulness of our own hearts. They are both mysteries almost alike, hard to be known. Labour we then more and more to know the falsehood of our own disposition, and to know the truth of God. To give instance in a few particulars. You see in the church the difficulty of her communion with Christ comes from the idle pretences and excuses she hath. Every one hath his several pretexts, as his state and condition is. We think we should be losers if we give ourselves to that degree of goodness which others do ; whereas God doth curse those blessings which men get with neglect of duty to him. If we seek ' first the kingdom of heaven, all other things that are good for us shall be cast upon us,' Mat. vi. 33.

Obj. Thou shalt lose the favour of such a one ?

Ans. Never care for that favour thou canst not keep with God's favour. The favour of man is a snare. Take heed of that favour that snares thee. Thou losest their favour and company, but thou gainest the favour of Christ, and company of angels.

Obj. But they will rail on thee, and reproach thee with thy old sins ?

Ans. Care not, ' God will do thee good for that,' as David said when Shimei cursed him, 2 Sam. xvi. 12.

* That is, ' expedients.'—G.

Obj. But I shall lose my pleasure ?

Ans. O! but such pleasures end in death. They are but pleasures of sin for a season, and thou shalt not lose by the change. ' The ways of wisdom are pleasant ways,' Prov. iii. 17. One day religiously spent in keeping of a good conscience, what a sweet farewell hath it! Joy is in the habitation of the righteous. It becomes the righteous to be joyful. However outwardly it seems, yet there is a paradise within. Many such objections the flesh makes. Some take scandal at the prosperity of the wicked, and affliction of the saints, and from hence take occasion to rot in their dregs of sin. But what saith Christ ? ' Happy is the man who is not offended in me,' Mat. xi. 6. As for the prosperity of the wicked, envy them not. They stand in slippery places, and flourish like a green bay tree, but presently they vanish. Take no offence at them, nor at the cross. Look not at this, but at the ensuing comfort. ' Blessed are they that suffer for righteousness sake,' 1 Pet. iii. 14. Bind such words to your head as your crown. God reserves the best comforts to the worst times ; his people never find it otherwise.

Obj. Ay, but if I be thus precise, the times are so bad, I shall be alone.

Ans. Complain not of the times, when thou makest them worse. Thou shouldst make the times better. The worse the times are, the better be thou ; for this is thy glory, to be good in an evil generation. This was Lot's glory, 2 Pet. ii. 7. Paul tells what ill times they were ; but, saith he, ' our conversation is in heaven, from whence we look for a Saviour,' Phil. iii. 20. What brings destruction on God's people, but their joining with the wicked ? When they joined with the children of men, then came the flood. These and the like pretences keep men altogether from goodness, or else from such a measure as may bring honour to God and comfort to themselves.

Or if men be great, why, this is not honourable to do thus, as you know what Michal said to David, ' How glorious was the king of Israel this day ! like a fool,' &c., 2 Sam. vi. 20. To attend upon the word of God with reverence, to make conscience of religion, Oh ! it stands not with greatness, &c. But the Spirit of God answereth this in him, ' I will yet be more vile for God,' verse 22. It is a man's honour here to stand for God and for good things ; and it is our honour that God will honour us so much.

Those likewise that are worldly have excuses also. ' Alas ! I must tend my calling.' And they have Scripture for it too. ' He that provides not for his family is worse than an infidel,' 1 Tim. v. 8, as if God had set up any callings to hinder the calling of Christianity ; as if that were not the greatest calling, and the best part that will abide with us for ever ; as if it were not the part of a Christian to redeem time from his calling to the duties of Christianity. I have no time, saith the worldling ; what will you have me to do ? Why, what time had David, when he meditated on the law of God day and night ? Ps. i. 2. He was a king. The king is bound to study the Scriptures. And yet whose employment is greater than the employment of the chief magistrate ? Deut. xvii. 18, 19.

And thus every one, as their state and condition is, they have several pretences and excuses. Those that are young, their excuse is, we have time enough for these things hereafter. Others, as those that were negligent to build the second temple, ' the time is not yet, say they,' Hag. i. 2 ; whenas the uncertainty of this life of ours, the weightiness of the business, the danger of the custom of sin, the engaging of our hearts deeper and deeper into the world, makes it a more difficult thing to be a Christian. It more and more darkens our understanding, the more we sin; and the more it estrangeth our affections from good things, the more we have run out in an evil course. Time is a special mercy; but then thou hast not time only, but the means, good company, and good motions. Thou mayest never have such a gale again; thy heart may be hardened through the deceitfulness of sin. Again, who would want the comforts of religion for the present? As Austin saith, ' I have wanted thy sweetness too long.'* What folly is it to want the sweetness and comfort of religion, so long as we may have it.

Some others pretend, the uncomfortableness of religion, I shall want my comforts; whenas indeed there is no sound comfort without having our hearts in a perfect communion with Christ, walking with God, and breaking off from our evil courses. What is the reason of discomforts, unresolvedness, and unsettledness? when we know not where we are, whither we go, or what our condition is. Unsettledness breeds discomfort; and indeed there is no pleasure so much as the pleasure that the serving of God hath with it. As the fire hath light and heat always in it, so there is no holy action that we perform throughly, but as it hath an increase of strength, so there is an increase of comfort and joy annexed to it. There is a present reward annexed to all things that are spiritually good. They carry with them present peace and joy. The conscience hath that present comfort which consumes all discouragements whatsoever, as is always found in the experience of that soul that hath won so much of itself, as to break through discouragements to the practice of holy duties. Believers have a joy and comfort ' that others know not of,' Rev. ii. 7; an hidden kind of manna and contentment.

These and a thousand such like discouragements men frame to themselves: ' My health will not serve,' ' I shall endanger my life.' ' There is a lion in the way,' saith the sluggard, Prov. xxvi. 13, who, with his excuses, ' thinks himself wiser than the wisest in the city,' verse 16. There is none so wise as the sluggard, for belly-policy teacheth him a great many excuses, which he thinks will go for wisdom, because by them he thinks to sleep in a whole skin. He is but a sluggard for all that; and though he plead ' yet a little while,' poverty, not only outward, but spiritual poverty and barrenness of soul, ' will come upon him as an armed man,' Prov. vi. 11, and leave him destitute of grace and comfort, when he shall see at last what an evil course of life he hath led, that he hath yielded so much to his lazy flesh to be drawn away by discouragements from duties that he was convinced were agreeable to the word. Now, what may be the grounds and causes of these false pretences and excuses which hinder us from holy duties? There be many causes.

1. First of all, one cause of this in us is this: Naturally, so far as we are not guided by a better spirit than our own, *we are inclined too much to the earthly present things of this life*, because they are present and pleasant, and we are nuzled up† in them, and whatsoever pulls us from them is unwelcome to us. This is one ground.

2. Again, join with this, that naturally, since the fall, the soul of man having lost wisdom to guide it to that which is truly good, hath wit enough left *to devise untoward shifts,‡ to excuse that which is evil.* In this fallen estate the former abilities to devise things throughly good is turned to a matter of untoward wit, joined with shifting.§ ' God made man right, but

---

* ' Confessions,' Book X. [xxvii.], 38. .'Too late loved I thee, O thou beauty of ancient days, yet ever new! too late I loved thee.'—G.   † That is, ' nestled.'—G
‡ That is, ' expedients.'—G.   § That is, ' expediency.'—G..

he hath sought out many inventions,' Eccles. vii. 29.   Carnal wit serves carnal will very well; and carnal lusts never want an advocate to plead for them, namely, carnal reason.   From the bent, therefore, of the soul to ill things, pleasure, ease, and honour, such a condition as pleaseth the outward man since the fall, the bent and weight of the soul goeth this way, together with wit.   Having lost the image of God in holy wisdom, there is shifting.   This is a ground also why delays are joined with shifts.

3. Again, there is another ground, that *corrupt nature*, in this like the devil and sin, which never appear in their own colours, *sets a man on this way*.   Who would not hate the devil if he should appear in his own likeness? or sin, if it should appear in his own colours?   And therefore wit stretcheth itself to find out shifts.   For, says the heart, unless there be some shifts and pretences to cover my shame, I shall be known to be what I am indeed, which I would be loth were done.   I would have the sweet but not the shame of sin, the credit of religion, but not put myself to the cost which cometh with true religion, to deny myself.   Corrupt courses never appear in their own colours.   They are like the devil for this.

4. And then, again, naturally there is a great deal of *hypocrisy in us*. We may do duties to satisfy conscience, for somewhat must be done, to hear now and then, read and come to prayer betwixt sleeping and waking, yawning prayers, when we can do nothing else.   Somewhat must be done. Conscience else will cry out of us that we are atheists, and shall be damned. Some slubbering service must be done therefore.   Yet notwithstanding, herein is our hypocrisy, that we cannot bring our hearts to do it, as it should be done, to purpose; for though it be true that there is much imperfection in the best actions, the best performances, yet this is hypocrisy when men do not do it as God may accept it, and as it may yield themselves comfort.   The heart draws back.   Duties it will and must do, but yet will not do them as it shall have comfort by them.   This is inbred in the heart naturally.   Conscience forceth to do something, though the flesh and corruption pulls back.   This is the disposition of all men, till they have got the victory of their own atheistical hearts.

5. And then, again, another ground may be this, *a false conceit of God and of Christ*, that they will take anything at our hands.   Because we love ourselves, and think that we do very well, we think that God is such a one as we are, as it is, ' Thou thoughtest that I was like unto thee,' &c., Ps. l. 21, that God will be put off with anything, and any excuse will serve the turn. You have not a swearer, a filthy, careless person, but he thinks God is merciful, and Christ died for sinners; and I was provoked to it, &c.   Still he thinks to have some excuse for it, and that they will stand good with God.   This atheism is in us naturally, and when we are palpably to blame in the judgment of others and ourselves in our sober wits, yet we put more ignorance and carelessness on God than on ourselves.   ' Tush, God regards it not.'   It is the times.   I would be better.   It is company whom I must yield unto, &c.   They think God will accept these things from them.

6. But one main ground thereof is, *the scandals that we meet withal in the world*, which, indeed, is a ground, because our own false hearts are willing to catch at anything.   You see, say they, these men that make profession of religion, what they are; and then the devil will thrust some hypocrisy * into the profession of religion, and they judge all by one or two, and will be sure to do it.   Therein stands their ingenuity; and if they can see any infirmity in them that are incomparably better than themselves, Oh, they are safe.

* Qu. ' hypocrite?'—G.

Here is warrant enough to dislike religion and all good courses, because some do and so,* as if the course of religion were the worse for that. Thus they wrap themselves in those excuses, as men do their hands to defend them from pricks. This is the vile poison of our hearts, that will be naught, and yet, notwithstanding, will have reason to be so. The speech is, wickedness never wanted pretexts, which, as it is true of great wickedness, much more is it of that which goes in the world for drowsy lukewarm profession, under which many sink to hell before they are aware. They never want reason and pretexts to cover their sin. There is a mint and forge of them in the soul. It can coin them suddenly. Thus we see our wits do serve us excellently well to lay blocks in our own way to hinder us from heaven. We are dunces, and dull to do anything that is spiritually good, whereof we are incapable. But if it be to lay blocks in our own way to heaven, to quarrel with God and his ordinances, with the doctrine of salvation, with the instruments, teachers, and those that lead us a better way, that our wit will serve for. But to take a course to do us good another day, to lay up comforts in which we might end and close up our days, there we are backward, and have shift upon shift. This is added for the further explication of it, because of the necessity of the point; for except our hearts be discovered to us, we shall never know what religion means, save to know so much as may, through the winding, turning, shifting, and falsehood of our own nature, bring us to hell. Wherein we are worse enemies to ourselves than the devil is, who could not hurt us unless we did betray ourselves. But he hath factors in us to deal for him. Our own carnal wit and affection, they hold correspondency with him; whence all the mischief that he doth us is by that intercourse that our nature hath with Satan. That is the Delilah which betrayeth all the Sampsons, sound worthy Christians in the world, to their spiritual enemies. Therefore, we can never be sufficiently instructed what a vile nature we have, so opposite to religion, as far as it is saving. Corrupt nature doth not oppose it so far as it is slubbered over, but so far as may bring us to that state we should be in. We have no worse enemies than our own hearts. Therefore, let us watch ourselves continually, and use all blessed means appointed of God whereby we may escape out of this dangerous, sleepy disposition of soul, which cost the church so dear, as we shall hear, God willing, hereafter.

THE EIGHTH SERMON.

I have put off my coat; how shall I put it on?   I have washed my feet; how shall I defile them?—CANT. V. 3.

WE are now, by God's assistance, to speak of *the remedies against the lazy distempers we are prone unto in spiritual things;* where we left off the last day.

Quest. What course should we take, then, to come forth from this distempered laziness? That we may attain a spiritual taste and relish of heavenly things, so as not to loathe religious exercises; or delay and put them off with excuses?

Ans. 1. First of all, *resolve not to consult with flesh and blood in anything.* For it always counsels us for ease, as Peter counselled Christ, 'Master, pity thyself,' Mat. xvi. 22. So we have a nature in us like unto Peter,

* Qu. 'so and so?'—ED.

Spare, favour, pity thyself. Like Eve, and Job's wife, we have a corrupt nature that is always soliciting from* God, and drawing us unto vanity, Gen. iii. 6 and Job ii. 10. Take heed of counselling with flesh and blood; for if men were in a city environed round about with enemies, would they consult with them what they should do for defence of the city? Were it not a mad part? And is it not a greater madness when Christians will consult with flesh and blood what they should do in duties of obedience, which will always put us upon terms of ease, the favour of men, content, and the like, which, if a man yield to, he shall never enter into heaven? Take heed therefore of consulting with our enemy, seeing Satan hath all the correspondency he hath by that enemy which we harbour in our bosom. In which case the hurt he doth us by his sophistry comes by ourselves. We betray ourselves by our carnal reason, whereby Satan mingleth himself with our imaginations and conceits. Let us therefore beware we listen not to the counsel of flesh and blood, especially when the matter comes to suffering once, for there of all other things flesh and blood doth draw back. Every one hath a Peter in himself that saith, 'Spare thyself.' Thou art indiscreet to venture thyself upon this and that hazard. But where the judgment is convinced of the goodness of the cause, whether it be religion or justice (for the first or for the second table, that matters not), if the judgment be convinced of the thing, then consult not with flesh and blood, whatsoever the suffering be. It is not necessary that we should live in riches, honours, pleasures, and estimation with the world. But it is necessary we should live honest men and good Christians. Therefore, when flesh and blood objecteth in this kind, consult not with it. First, because it is an enemy, and therefore is to be suspected and neglected; secondly, because it is said, 'flesh and blood shall not inherit the kingdom of heaven,' 1 Cor. xv. 50.

2. And therefore we should practise that first lesson in religion, *heavenly wisdom*. To aid us wherein, Christ, knowing what an enemy we are to ourselves in the ways of God, saith, 'Let a man deny himself, and take up his cross, and follow me,' Mat. xvi. 24. There is no following of Christ, considering that our flesh is so full of cavils and excuses, unless we practise that heavenly lesson of Christ, 'to deny ourselves,' our whole self, our wit and reason, in the matters of God: our will and affections. Say nay to all the sluggishness of the flesh; silence all presently, as soon as ever they discourage thee from holy ways. Consider whence they come, which is enough; from God's and our enemy, and the worst enemy we have, that lieth in our own bosom. And to enable us the better, mark what Paul saith, 'We are no more debtors to the flesh,' &c., Rom. viii. 12. We owe nothing to it. I owe not such obedience, such subjection, to the flesh and carnal reason; I have renounced it long since. What! am I obnoxious to a man unto whom I owe no service? We owe the flesh no service or obedience. What! shall we yield to that which we have long since renounced?

3. And withal, *in spiritual courses, let us arm ourselves with resolution.* First, conclude is it so or not so. Let our judgments be convinced. For resolution is a disposition arising from the will immediately; but it is of the will, by sound judgment, convinced of the goodness of the thing, after which the will resolves. Get resolution from soundness of conviction that such things are good, and that they are best for us, and best for us at this time, the sooner the better; that there is an absolute necessity to have

* That is, '*away* from.'—G.

them, and that they are everlastingly good. Oh! these considerations will put us on amain to obtain the same. It is our duty, and we shall sin against God, against our conscience, against the Spirit of God, and against others that take like liberty by our examples, if we yield to our base lusts and suggestions in this kind.

And to help resolution the more, let us have before our eyes the examples of God's worthies, who (like unto David's worthies, who brake through the host of the Philistines for water, 2 Sam. xxiii. 16) have in all ages broken through all discouragements, and made a conscience more to please God, to hold communion and fellowship with Christ, than to hold any correspondency with the world. Look to blessed Paul, 'What do ye vexing of me and breaking my heart? I am ready not only to go to Jerusalem, but to die for Christ's sake,' Acts xxi. 13. And look to Christ how he shakes off Peter, 'Get thee behind me, Satan,' &c., Mat. xvi. 23. Look to Moses, how he shook off all the solicitations of a court, 'Because he had an eye to the recompence of the reward,' Heb. xi. 16. Look to Joshua, 'I and mine house will serve the Lord,' Josh. xxiv. 15. Let others of the world do what they will; if others will go to the devil, let them; for myself, I and my house, those that I have charge of, will serve the Lord. This was a noble resolution which was in good Nehemiah, 'Shall such a man as I flee?' Neh. vi. 11. What! shall I flee? shall I do this, yield to this base discouragement? shall I discourage others, like those spies of Canaan, by mine example? Hence it is that Hebrews 11th, in that notable chapter, that little 'book of martyrs,' after the catalogue of those worthies set down there, that which we are exhorted and pointed to in the beginning of the next chapter, is unto the practice of the like virtues, in imitation, having before us 'such a cloud of witnesses,' wherewith being compassed, the exhortation is, 'Let us therefore shake off everything that presseth down, and the sin that hangeth so fast on,' &c., Heb. xii. 1 (i). As the cloud was a guide to them to Canaan out of Egypt, so the cloud of good examples is as it were a light to go before us to the heavenly Canaan.

In this case above all, let us look to Christ, 'who is the author and finisher of our faith,' Heb. xii. 2. This will make us break through discouragements and resolve indeed. What could hinder him? His love is so fiery, that nothing could hinder him to come from heaven to the womb of the virgin; from thence to the cross, and so to the grave, to be abased lower than ever any creature was. His love to us so carried him through all discouragements and disgraces. 'Consider him, who endured such speaking against of sinners,' Heb. xii. 3. The consideration of Christ's love and example will carry us through all discouragements whatsoever.

4. And further, *let us be able by sound reasons to justify the ways of God, and to answer cavils; to give account of what we do to ourselves and others,* with reasons why we sanctify the Sabbath, have such communion with God in prayer, neglect the fashions of the world, &c. To have reasons ready from Scripture is an excellent thing; when we are able to justify whatsoever we do by the word, against all the quarrels of our own hearts and others. When we are led to do things only by the example of others, or by respects, then we are ofttimes put to it on the sudden by temptations, being not able to justify what we do. Let us labour therefore to do things upon good grounds, and be able to justify all the ways of religion, as they are easily justified. For nothing in this world stands with so much reason, as exactness in the ways of God. There is so much reason for nothing in the world, as to be not only Christians, but exact Christians as Paul saith

to Agrippa, ' Would to God you were not almost, but altogether as I am, saving these bonds,' Acts xxvi. 29, to make conscience of all ways and courses. It stands with the most reason of the world, so to justify religion by reasons unanswerable, that may set down corrupt nature, and stop the mouth of the devil himself. And herein let us propound sound and strong questions to ourselves often. Are those things that I am moved to do good, or are they not? If they be good, why do I not do them? If they be bad, why do I do them at all? If they be good, why do I stick at them? How do I prove them to be good? Have alway ready some Scripture, or reason from thence, which is as good. The reasons of the word are most divinely strong, let them be ready against all objections whatsoever, as against slight oaths, think of that of Christ, that we must give an account for all idle words, Mat. xii. 36. How much more for atheistical oaths! So against grosser sins learn reason, a civil man, an heathen, would not do thus.

So also when the flesh moveth us to any backwardness in religious courses, let us have some Scripture ready, or reasons deducted from it. As, 1. *From the dignity of our profession, from the great hopes we have to be glorious another day.* And reason the matter, How doth this that I am moved to, suit with my hopes and expectation to come? How furthers it my journey homewards? And consider this likewise. 2. *That no excuse will serve the turn at the day of judgment, but such an one as ariseth from an invincible infirmity, or an unremovable impediment.* Such an excuse, taken from an invincible infirmity, may then serve the turn. As, when we cannot possibly do a thing, from impediments that all the means in the world cannot remove, as, a poor man cannot be liberal, &c. Excuses also, fetched from impossible impediments, as from invincible weakness, may avail. If a man have an infirm body, that he cannot do that which another man can. These excuses, with a gracious God, will serve the turn : which are not so much excuses, as a just plea. But otherwise, our untoward excuses will not serve the turn. What hindered them in the gospel who were invited to the supper? Luke xiv. Excuses from oxen, wives, &c. Was it not lawful to buy oxen? and was it not lawful for the married to take content in a wife? ' Another had married a wife.' Were not all these things lawful? Very lawful. The farm hurts not, if it hinder not, nor the wife, oxen, nor anything. But in this case, when we regard these things more than the invitation to come to the feast of holy things, here is the malice of the devil, which brings that doleful message, ' They shall never taste of my feast,' Luke xiv. 24. There is such an infinite disproportion between the good of religion, peace of conscience, joy in the Holy Ghost here, and heaven and happiness hereafter, and between anything in this world, that to allege any hindrance whereby we cannot keep a good conscience, and preserve assurance of salvation, is most extreme folly and atheism. I believe not a better life, the disproportion being so great between the state of this life and a better, if I fetch excuses from the things of this life, to keep me from religion, the fear of God, and working out my salvation with fear and trembling. These excuses will not serve the turn. Not only with God at the day of judgment, but also our own consciences will tell us, that we are hypocrites to make such or such a plea. Therefore, when men become false, thereby to provide for wife or children, and take corrupt courses to keep them from religion, with pretext of their callings, lest they should lose one day in seven, this employment cannot prosper, which slights over duties under false pretences. Oh, they can toil for the pelf of the world! But for matters of their souls, they turn off all shamefully, as if there were

not a God to judge them, a heaven to reward them, or a hell to punish
them. Will such excuses serve the turn? Oh, no; they cannot with
conscience, much less with God the Judge, who is greater than our conscience. This is another way to cut off these idle cavils, to consider that
these excuses cannot serve the turn, neither to comfort conscience in this
world, nor to uphold us in our plea at the day of judgment. Remember
that.

5. And then again, *Let us inure ourselves to bear the yoke of religion from
our youth*, which will make it easy afterwards. It were an excellent thing
if those who are young, in the prime of their years, would inure themselves
to the exercise of religion. This would make it easy unto them, to read
the word of God, to open their spirits unto him in prayer. It may please
God hereby (though they be negligent herein), yet they may be called to
religion. But for an old man there is much work to do to read, to get
anything into his brain, when his memory is pestered with other things,
and corrupt nature in him is armed with a world of excuses, that might
have been prevented by a timely and seasonable training up in a course of
religion. Profane young persons know not what they do when they put off
religion. Have they excuses now? They will have many more hereafter,
when Satan and corruption will be much stronger. O! let them bear the
yoke of religion, that is, inure themselves to duties that become Christians,
which may facilitate and make it easy and pliable, that it may not be harsh
to our nature. If a man do not hear, pray, and read, he can never have
faith, grace, knowledge, mortification of corruption, wherein religion stands.
But because these lead to duties that are hard to nature, and harsh, it is
wisdom to inure young ones thereto betimes, that, having used themselves
to these preparing duties, they may be the more fitted for the essential ones;
that, having things in the brain by reading and hearing, grace may be
wrought in the heart, it being a more easy passage from the brain to the
heart. When a man is converted, it is an easy matter to bring it from the
brain unto the heart; whereas a man that hath been negligent in his youth
must then be instructed in the principles of religion. Therefore, it is a
miserable case (though men be never so politic in the world) to have been
negligent herein till age. It breeds a great deal of difficulty to them, ere
they can come to be in such a state as a Christian should be in. Remember this, therefore, to do as Paul adviseth Timothy, a young man, 'to
exercise himself in godliness,' 1 Tim. iv. 7. It is a good thing for all that
are young to exercise themselves to all duties of religion, or else pretences
will grow up with age, whereby they will be indisposed every day more than
other. Experience shews it generally. We may believe it. If we will
not, we shall find it hereafter too true by woful experience.

6. And then again, by little and little, not only to be inured to the yoke
of religion, but likewise *to endure difficulties, opposition, and hardship;* as
the apostle stands upon it to Timothy, 'to endure hardship and afflictions
from the beginning,' 2 Tim. ii. 3. If the thing be good and warrantable,
neglect the speeches of the world. What are the speeches of a company
of men in the state of nature, in their miserable condition, to regard them,
so as not to endure hardship in such things, of the goodness whereof we
are convinced? But in these days men take up a delicate profession of
religion. Men will be religious, but they will suffer nothing, not a taunt
or a scoff. They will part with nothing; be at no loss; suffer no cross;
be at no pains with religion further than may stand with all earthly content
of this world. This delicate profession, if anything among us, threateneth

the removing of the gospel and blessed truths we enjoy, because we will not part with any pleasure now. How will they suffer afflictions for the gospel, if such times come, that will not part with a vain oath, a corrupt fashion of life, a superfluity, that will not part with a rotten unsavoury discourse, which discovereth a rotten spirit, and infecteth others ? Here is a profession of religion, indeed, that cannot have so much mastery of the corrupt heart as to deny and overcome itself in things that are grossly ill ! How will a man part with his blood and life, that will not part with things that he should part withal ? not only with something to the poor and to good uses, but to part with some sinful course of life, and wicked and ungodly lusts that fight against the soul ; who will not endure not so much as a check ; who, rather than they will go under that censure wherewith the world is pleased to disgrace religion, they will live and die like atheists. This extreme tenderness in the matters of God and of salvation is the cause why many eternally perish.

7. Again, to cut off all vain excuses, *let us oft have in thought of our heart what we should be, and what we should all aim at, and how far we come all short of it.* A Christian that hopes of good of his religion should live by faith, and depend upon God in the use of lawful means. If he be as he should be, he ought to walk with God, keep his watch with him, and do nothing unbeseeming the eye of God. When his corruption draws him to be careless, then he is not as he should be ; for in a right temper, he ought to be fitted to every good work, ready for all opportunities of doing anything that is good, because the time of this life is the seedtime, the time of doing good. The time of reaping is in the world to come. When, therefore, the heart is shut, when any opportunity is offered of doing good, he may conclude certainly, I am cold and dull; pretend what I will, I am not as I should be. A Christian ought to ' abound in the work of the Lord,' 1 Cor. xv. 58, especially having such abundance of encouragements as we have. What a world of encouragements hath a Christian ! There are none to * those of religion, from the inward content that it brings here, at the hour of death, and in glory hereafter. When we are drawn to be scanty, niggardly, and base to things that are good, surely this is not as it should be. Pretend what we will to the contrary, this is a fault. A Christian should at all times be fit to yield and to render up his soul unto God, because our life is uncertain. When, therefore, we are moved by corruption to live in a state that we cannot abide to die in, because we are under the guilt of some sin, then certainly, pretend what we will, our state is so far naught, as far as there is unfitness and unwillingness to die. Let us have in the eye of our soul, therefore, what a Christian should be, aim at it, and think that when we stop at a lower measure and pitch, that, pretend what we will, all is but from carnal wit and policy, the greatest enemy that religion hath.

We pray in the Lord's Prayer, ' Thy kingdom come; thy will be done in earth, as it is done in heaven:' great desires, and which should be the desires of all our hearts. But herein we play the hypocrites. Whilst we pray thus, that the kingdom of God may come, that Christ may rule in our hearts over lusts and desires ; yet notwithstanding, we pretend this and that excuse, whereby we may be led with this and that lust. We cross our own prayers. Yet it sheweth what pitch we should aspire to, ' To sanctify the Lord in our hearts,' to delight in him, and trust in him above all. When we do not this, we fall short of our own prayers. And when

* That is, ' there are no encouragements compared with.'—ED.

we cannot bring our hearts to suffer, and to do what God would have us to do, but are led away with our own wills, we are not as we should be. Our wills should be conformable to Christ's in all things. It is our prayer, and therefore we should aim at it. Now, when flesh and blood sets up a pitch of religion, I am well enough; and yet prays, 'Hallowed be thy name; thy kingdom come; thy will be done,' &c.,—such a man is an hypocrite. For his prayer leads him further and further still, till he come to heaven, where is all perfection; until when, our life is a life of endeavour and progress. Though we be never so perfect, yet Christ may more rule and set up his kingdom yet more in the heart, and further bring our will to his in all things. When flesh and blood sets up cavils against this, we play the hypocrites with God, and cross ourselves. Therefore, let us justify a measure of religion beyond our present pitch, whatsoever it is; justify it more and more still. Think, we are never as we should be till we be in heaven; and never bless ourselves, but think that we should always be on the growing hand; and whatsoever excuse comes to hinder us from zealousness and earnestness, though it carry a show of reason in the profession of religion, account it to come from our corrupt hearts.

8. Again, *remember to do all things to God and not to man, in our callings both of religion and in our particular callings;* and then whatsoever discouragement there is from men, we should not be discouraged. We shall hear men continually complain of others, that they are unthankful persons; and why should we do anything for them? Why! do it to God. If it fall within our callings, let us do justice and shew mercy. God will accept, though men do not. It cuts off many discouragements in duties. It is best to have God's reward. In this world it is good to meet with naughty unthankful persons, because else we should meet with all our reward here. It is good to do somewhat for God's sake, and for religion, let people be as unthankful as they will; to say, I did it not to you, but to God. If a man regard the discouragement of the world, he shall never do that which is good, people in the world are so unthankful and regardless to those that wish them best, and that do best to them. But if a man do a thing to God, and do it out of duty and conscience, he may hold on; have he never so many discouragements in the world, he shall lose nothing. All shall be rewarded, and is regarded.

9. Likewise, be sure to carry this in mind, *that sin is the greatest evil, and grace and goodness the best thing in the world.* Therefore, there is no excuse for sin, from anything in the world, for it is the worst thing in the world, which stains the soul, and hinders it from comfort. And for grace and goodness in the inward man, it is the best thing in the world. Therefore, purchase this, though with disadvantage. It is best to avoid sin, though with enduring evil; yea, to avoid the least sin, by enduring the greatest evil. It is wisdom to do good with disadvantage, when the disadvantage is bounded only in this life, the thing that I do being a thing which furthers my reckoning at the day of account. Therefore, have this alway in consideration, whatsoever I suffer in this world, I will not sin. This will cut off a world of excuses.

Therefore, let us labour to cut off all cavils, and to 'arm ourselves.' It is the apostle Peter's exhortation, 1 Pet. iv. 1. As David's worthies brake through the pikes to fetch him water from the well of Bethlehem, 2 Sam. xxiii. 16, so all Christian worthies that look to be crowned, let them be armed inwardly with resolution for good things, take up resolutions that they will do it. As Paul tells his scholar Timothy of his purpose, 'Thou

knowest my purpose, and manner of living,' 2 Tim. iii. 10. This is the
manner of a Christian life : that this, I will not break for all the world.
So, there is a purpose of living honestly a manner of life, not by starts,
now and then to speak a word, and to do a good deed ; but there is a
a purpose and a manner of life for it. He resolves always for the best
things.

And to this end beg of God his Spirit, which is above all impediments.
The more Spirit, the more strength and courage against impediments. The
more we attend upon holy means, the more spiritual and heavenly light and
life is set up in the soul. The more spiritual we are, the more we shall
tread under foot all those things that stand between us and heaven. Let
us therefore labour more and more for the Spirit, and then we shall offer
an holy violence unto good things ; as it was said of John Baptist's time,
'The kingdom of God suffered violence,' Mat. xi. 12. Men were so eager
of it, as that they surprised it as a castle, by violence. There is no way
to take heaven but by offering violence to discouragement, corruption, and
whatsoever stands in the way. The violent only takes heaven by force.*
Now when we are spiritual, we shall not pretend, that 'there is a lion in
the way,' that there are difficulties, as the sluggard doth, that thinks himself wiser than many men who can render a reason. But we shall go boldly
and courageously on ; and know that there are more encouragements for
good, and stronger, than the world hath allurements to be naught, which
are but for the present life ; but we have inward ones, which will hold out
in the hour of death and after. Therefore, go on boldly and resolutely in
good things, always remembering to beg the Spirit of God, that may arm
our spirits with invincible courage.

Now the Spirit of God brings faith with it, which is a conquering, victorious grace over the world, and 'sees him that is invisible,' Heb. xi. 27 ;
which brings love also, 'which is strong as death,' Cant. viii. 6 : wherewith
the soul being warmed, it constraineth us to do duties in spite of all impediments. The Spirit of God will strengthen our hope also of heaven, which
strengthens us against all discouragements which stand in our way. For
this hope is on greater and better grounds than discouragements are ; and
he that giveth us this hope, will enable us to possess it.

Therefore labour first, *to have a clear understanding of the things of God,
and of the excellency of them;* for light will cause heat   Why did the kingdom of heaven in John Baptist's time, 'suffer violence ?' Why were men then
so violent to cleave unto Christ ? Because from that time the gospel was
more clearly manifested. And heavenly truths, the more they are discovered
and laid open (there is such an excellency in them), the more they work
upon the heart and affections. Therefore, 'the kingdom of heaven suffered
violence.' And where are people more earnest after good things, than in
these places where the evangelical truths of God are laid open most? There
they break through all discouragements whatsoever.

And so, *labour for faith to believe those truths:* which is the most victorious
and conquering grace, that will carry us through all discouragements whatsoever; because it will set greater things before us, than the discouragements are. Are we afraid of men ? Faith, it sets hell before us. Are we
allured by the world ? It sets heaven before us. It conquers the world,
with all the discouraging temptations thereof. Are the discouragements

* This recalls the little book of Thomas Watson's, called 'Heaven taken by
Storm,' memorable as having been the occasion of the conversion of the celebrated
Colonel Gardiner, whose life by Doddridge is one of our Christian classics.—G

from impossibilities ?   O, it is hard, I cannot do it.   Aye, but, saith Paul,
' I am able to do all things through Christ that strengthens me,' Phil. iv. 13.
There is a kind of omnipotency in faith, ' O woman, be it unto thee as thou
wilt,' Mark xv. 28.   We have abundance of strength in Christ.   Faith is
but an empty hand, that goes to Christ to draw from him what it hath need
of ; ' In Christ I can do all things.'

So, *to have our hearts warmed with love to him.*   This grace of the Spirit
will make us pass through all discouragements, for it hath a constraining
power.   ' The love of Christ constrains us,' saith the apostle, 2 Cor. v. 14.
If our hearts once be warmed with the love of Christ, this will make us
to think nothing too dear for Christ, and will cut off all excuses and pretences
whatsoever, which come from coldness of affection.   ' Love is strong as
death,' as we have it in this book, ' much water cannot quench it,' Cant.
viii. 6.   All oppositions and discouragements whatsoever, all the water
which the devil and the world hath or useth, cannot quench the heavenly
fire of love, when it is kindled in any measure.   What carried the blessed
saints and martyrs of God in all times through the pikes of all discouragements ?   The Spirit of God, by the spirit of love, from a spirit of faith,
and heavenly conviction of the excellency and truth of the things.   They
saw such a light, which wrought upon their affections, and carried them
amain against the stream (contrary to the stream of the times wherein they
lived), that the worse the times were, the better they were.

10. And let us consider again, *that Christ will not be always thus alluring
us* ; that we shall not always have these encouragements, such truths and
motions of God's Spirit, as perhaps we feel now.   Therefore, when we feel
any good motion stirred up toward Christ, entertain it presently.   Happily
we shall never hear of it again.   The longer we defer and put it off, the
worse.   As a man that is rowing in a boat, let him neglect his stroke, the
neglecting of one may make him tug at it five or six times after to overtake
those that are before him.   So nothing is gotten by sloth and negligence.
We do but cast ourselves back the more.

11. And let us help ourselves *with setting the glory to come before our eyes* ,
with Moses to have a patriarch's eye to him ' that is invisible,' to see ' a
country afar off,' Heb. xi. 27.   Now, ' we are nearer salvation than when
we believed.'   Let us help our backward souls this way : that so, having
still glory in our eyes, it may help us to go through all discouragements,
whatsoever they be.   We know Zaccheus, when he was afraid that he should
not see Christ, went before the multitude ; and getting up upon the top of
a tree, thus helps himself.   So doth grace help itself by glory.   And so far
is grace from objecting and pretending lets,* as it makes supplies in God's
service ; as David, who in this case was pleased to be accounted vile, 2 Sam.
vi. 22.   Let us look unto the recompence of the reward ; not to the present
discouragements, but to the prize at the end of the race.   What makes a
soldier to fight hard for the victory in the end ?   The sweetness of the triumph.   What makes a husbandman go through all discouragements ?   He
hopes to receive a crop in the end.   Consider the issue which followeth
after a conscionable, careful, and Christian life, after a more near and perfect walking with God, maintaining communion with him.   Let there be
what discouragements there will be in the world, ' the end thereof is peace.'
' The end of that man is peace,' Ps. xxxvii. 37.   Upon this ground, the
apostle exhorts us, ' to be fruitful and abundant in the work of the Lord ;
knowing that your labour is not in vain in the Lord,' 1 Cor. xv. 58.

* That is, ' hindrances.'— G.

THE NINTH SERMON.

I rose to open to my beloved ; but my beloved had withdrawn himself.—
CANT. V. 6.

NATURALLY we are prone to delays in heavenly things, and then to cover all
with excuses. A man is a sophister to himself, whom he first deceives,
before the devil or the world deceive him; which is the reason why so oft in
Scripture you have this mentioned: ' Be not deceived, God is not mocked,'
Gal. vi. 7. ' Be not deceived, neither adulterer, nor covetous person, nor
such and such, shall ever enter into the kingdom of heaven,' 1 Cor. vi. 9. 'Be
not deceived,' which is an intimation that naturally we are very prone to be
deceived in points of the greatest consequence in the world, to flatter ourselves, as the church doth here, with false excuses. ' I have put off my
coat,' &c. But we shall now see in this next verse what becomes of all
those excuses and backwardness of the church whereby she puts off
Christ.

' My beloved put in his hand by the hole of the door, and my bowels
were moved for him.

' I rose to open to my beloved ; and my hands dropped with myrrh, and
my fingers with sweet-smelling myrrh, upon the handles of the lock.

' I rose to open to my beloved ; but my beloved had withdrawn himself,' &c., ver. 4–6.

This comes of her sluggishness and drowsiness, that Christ absented and
withdrew himself. There are three things here set down in these verses now
read.

1. *Christ's withdrawing of himself.*

2. *His gracious dealing, having withdrawn himself.*

He doth not altogether leave his church, but ' puts his finger into the
hole of the door,' and then leaves some sweetness behind him before he
goes. After which is set down,

3. *The success of Christ's departure and withdrawing of himself from her.*

(1.) *Her bowels were moved in her*, which were *hard* before.

(2.) *She rose up out of her bed*, wherein formerly she had framed and
composed herself to rest.

(3.) *She seeks and calls after him.*

But the doctrinal points which are to be observed out of these verses are
these,

Obs. 1. *That Christ doth sometimes use to leave his children, as he did the
church here.*

Obs. 2. *That the cause is from the church herself*, as we see how unkindly
she had used Christ, to let him attend her leisure so long. Therefore he,
taking a holy state upon him, leaves the church. The cause of his forsaking us is in ourselves. We may thank ourselves for it.

Obs. 3. *That though Christ deal thus with us, yet notwithstanding he
never leaves us wholly, without some footsteps of his saving grace and everlasting
love ; some remainders and prints he leaves upon the soul*, so as it lingers after
him, and never rests till it find him. He always leaves something. There
is never a total desertion ; as we see here in Christ's dealing, ' he puts his
finger into the hole of the door.' He stands at the door, and leaves myrrh
behind him, something in the heart that causeth a lingering and restless
affection in her towards Christ.

Obs. 4. *That the church, by reason of this gracious dealing of Christ, (leaving somewhat behind him) is sensible of her former unkindness, is restless, and stirs up herself to endeavour more and more, till she have recovered her former communion and sweet fellowship with Christ which she had before.* She never gives over till Christ and she meet again in peace, as we shall see in the prosecution. These be the chief points considerable.

Obs. 1. First, *Christ doth use sometimes to leave his church,* as here he doth, ' My beloved had withdrawn himself,' &c.

But what kind of leaving is it ?

We must distinguish of Christ's leavings and withdrawings of himself. They are either in regard of outward or inward comforts and helps.

1. *Outward,* as Christ leaves his church sometimes *by taking away the means of salvation,* the ministry, or *by taking away outward comforts,* which is a withdrawing of his ; especially if he accompany the taking of them away with some signs of his displeasure or sense of his anger, as usually it falls out. This doth embitter all crosses and losses, namely, when they come from Christ as a testimony of his anger for our former unkindness.

2. Sometimes his forsaking is *more inward,* and that is double, either in regard of *peace and joy,* sweet inward comfort that the soul had wont to feel in the holy ordinances by the Spirit of Christ; or in regard of *strength and assistance.* There is a desertion in regard of comfort and in regard of strength. Sometimes he leaves them to themselves, in regard of strength and supportation, to fall into some sin, to cure some greater sin perhaps.

Now that Christ thus leaves his church, it is true of all, both of the body and of each particular member of the church.

(1.) It is true of the *whole body of the church,* for you have the church complaining, Isa. xlix. 14, ' God hath forgotten me,' ' Can a mother forget her child ?' saith God again. So Ps. xliv. 9; and in other places the church complains of forsakings. The Scripture is full of complaints in this kind.

(2.) It is true of the *several members,* and especially of the most eminent members, as we see holy Job complains, as if God had ' set him,' as it were, ' a butt to shoot at,' Job vi. 4, and had opposed himself against him. So David complains, Ps. lxxxviii. 11, Ps. lxxvii. 9, and Ps. lx. 1, and in other Psalms, of God's anger. ' Correct me not in thine anger,' Ps. vi. 1. The Psalms are full of this, so as it would be time unprofitably spent to be large in a point so clear, that every one knoweth well enough who reads and understands the Psalms. So Jonah likewise felt a kind of forsaking when he was in the midst of the sea, when the waves were without and terrors within, when he was in the midst of hell, as it were, Jonah ii. 2. Thus, you see, the instances clear the point.

The ends that God hath in it are many. (1.) *To endear his presence the more to us,* which we slighted too much before. It is our corruption, the not valuing of things till they be gone. We set not the true price upon them when we enjoy them. When we enjoy good things, we look at the grievances which are mingled with the good, and forget the good ; which, when it is gone, then we remember the good. The Israelites could remember their onions and garlic, and forget their slavery, Num. xi. 5. So, because manna was present, they despised manna, and that upon one inconvenience it had, ' it was ordinary with them,' Num. xxi. 5. Thus the corrupt heart of man is prone in the enjoying of favours. If it have any grievance, it murmurs at that ; and it troubles and makes them forget all the goodness and sweetness of what they enjoy. But, on the contrary,

when God withdraws those good things from us, then we forget those former inconveniences, and begin to think what good we had by them. This
is the poison and corruption of our nature.

(2.) Again, Christ seems to forsake us, *to try the truth of the graces and
affections in us,* whether they be true or not; and to cause us to make after
him, when he seems to forsake us, as undoubtedly we shall, where there is
truth of grace planted in the heart in any measure.

(3.) And in regard of others, he doth it *to teach us heavenly wisdom, how
to deal with those in affliction,* 2 Cor. i. 4.   It makes us wise, tender, and
successful in dealing with others, when we have felt the like particular
grievance ourselves, as Gal. vi. 1, ' Brethren, if a man be overtaken in a
fault, you that are spiritual restore such a one in the spirit of meekness, considering thyself, lest thou also be tempted.'   Experience of spiritual grief in this kind, will make us fit, able, and wise every way to deal
with others.

(4.) This serves likewise *to wean us from the world, in the plenty and
abundance of all earthly things.*   For take a Christian that hath no cross in
the world, let him find some estrangement of Christ from his spirit, that he
finds not the comforts of the Holy Ghost, and that enlargement which in
former times he enjoyed, and all the wealth he hath, the earthly contentments he enjoys, please him not, nor can content that soul, which hath
ever felt sweet communion with Christ.   Again, how should we pray with
earnestness of affection, ' Thy kingdom come,' in the time of prosperity,
except there were somewhat in this kind to raise up the soul to desire to be
gone ?   Now, it is our subjection to these alterations and changes, ebbings
and flowings, sometimes to have the sense of God's love in Christ, and
sometimes to want it; sometimes to feel his love, and sometimes again the
fruits of his anger and displeasure, which serves exceedingly to stir up men's
desires of heaven.

(5.) In this place here, the especial end was *To correct the security, and
ill carriage of the church.*

And, likewise (6.) *to prepare the church, by this desertion and seeming
forsaking, for nearer communion.*   For, indeed, Christ did not forsake her,
but to her feeling, to bring her, in the sequel, to have nearer communion
and union with himself than ever she had before.   God forsakes, that he
may not forsake.   He seems strange, that he may be the more friendly.
This is Christ's usage.   He personates an adversary, when he intends to
shew the greatest effects of his love, as we may see afterwards in the passages following.

And also, (7.) *to make us to know thoroughly the bitterness of sin,* that we
may grow up to a further hatred of that which deprives us of so sweet a
communion.   We think sin a trifle, and never know it enough till the time
of temptation; that conscience be awakened and opened; that it appears
in its right colours.

And then, again, (8.) *that we may know what Christ suffered and underwent for us, in the sense of God's wrath, in the absence of his favour for a
time.*   This the human nature could never have suffered, if his divinity had
withdrawn itself.   Now, all of us must sip of that cup, whereof Christ drank
the dregs, having a taste what it is to have God to forsake us.   For the
most part, those believers who live any time (especially those of great parts),
God deals thus with.   Weaker Christians he is more indulgent unto.   At
such times we know of what use a Mediator is, and how miserable our condition were without such an one, both to have borne and overcome the

wrath of God for us, which burden he could never have undergone, but had sunk under it, but for the hypostatical union.

Use 1. Let us not, therefore, *censure any Christian, when we find that their course hath been good and gracious, yet notwithstanding they seem to want comfort.* Let us not wonder at them, as if God had utterly forsaken them. Indeed, sometimes they think themselves forsaken, and the world thinks them so too, ' that God regards them not,' Ps. lxvi. 18. They are people of no respect either to God or to others, as you have the church in the Psalms complaining, as if God had forsaken them,' Ps. xliv. 9 ; so they think themselves forsaken, and the world thinks them so too, and neglects them. Therefore, in so doing, we shall censure the generation of the righteous. It was thus with the Head of the church, with the whole church, and with every particular member. Neither is it fit we should always enjoy the sense of God's love. Christ by heavenly wisdom dispenseth of his sweetness, comforts, and peace, as may stand with our souls' best good, and we should as much take heed of censuring ourselves in that condition, as if we were rejected and cast away of God. We must judge ourselves at such times by faith, and not by feeling; looking to the promises and word of God, and not to our present sense and apprehension.

Use 2. Again, if this be so, learn *to prepare and look for it beforehand, and to get some grounds of comfort, some promises out of the word, and to keep a good conscience.* O it is a heavy thing, when God shall seem to be angry with us, and our conscience at the same time shall accuse us ; when the devil shall lay sins hard to our charge, and some affliction at the same time lie heavy upon the sore and guilty soul. If we have not somewhat laid up beforehand, what will become of the poor soul, when heaven, and earth, and hell, and all shall seem to be against it. There are few that come to heaven, but they know what these things mean. It is good, therefore, to look for them, and to prepare some comforts beforehand.

But what here should be the inward moving cause? It is in the church herself; for mark the coherence. She had turned off Christ with excuses, pretences, and dilatory answers; and now presently upon it Christ forsakes her in regard of her feeling, and of the sweet comfort she formerly enjoyed. The point is,

Obs. 2. *That the cause rests in ourselves why Christ withdraws comfort from our souls.*

If we search our own hearts we shall find it so, and usually the causes in ourselves are these, as it was in the church here : 1. *When we are unkind to Christ,* and repel the sweet motions of the Spirit. 2. *When we improve not the precious means of salvation that we enjoy.* 3. *When we are careless of our conversation and company.* 4. *When we linger after carnal liberties and ease.* 5. *When we yield to carnal policy* and shifts to keep us off from the power of religion, to go on in a lukewarm course. 6. *When we linger after earthly things and comforts,* and wrap ourselves up in fleshly policy for ease. 7. *When we tremble not at God's judgments and threatenings, and at the signs of them;* with many such things. Where these dispositions are, we need not wonder if we find not the comforts of Christ and of the Holy Ghost in us, with the gracious presence of his Spirit. The cause is in ourselves. But security hath been at large spoken of before, where the church's sleep was handled.* Therefore, the point shall not be here enlarged, but only some use made of it, as may serve for the present purpose.

Use 1. If Christ should take away the comforts that we enjoy, and

* See pp. 35–44, *et seq.*—G.

remove himself and his dwelling from us, for he is now yet among us and knocks at our doors, *do we not give him just cause to depart ?* What a spirit of slumber possesseth us, which will be awaked with nothing to seek after Christ! How few lay hold upon God, press upon him, wrestle with him by prayer, to hide themselves before the evil day come, as they should do! Therefore, if Christ have absented himself a long time from the church in general, and withdrawn the comfort and presence of his ordinances ; and, in particular, withheld the sweet comforts of our spirits and our peace, so that we see him in the contrary signs of his displeasure and anger, as if he did not regard and respect us, we have given him just cause so to do. We see here how the church used Christ ; and so do we, with the like security, and a spirit of slumber, with unkindness. Notwithstanding all the provocations that Christ useth to win us, he leaves us not, until he be left first, for he desires to have nearer acquaintance, communion, and fellowship with the soul, as we have seen in the former verse, ' My love, my dove, my undefiled, open to me,' &c. Therefore, if we do not enjoy more acquaintance with Christ than we do, and walk more in the comforts of the Holy Ghost, it is merely from our own indisposition and security, Acts ix. 31. Therefore, let us censure ourselves in this kind, and not call Christ an enemy, as if he had forgotten, and God had forsaken. Take heed of such a spirit of murmuring. If such a state befall us, let us labour to lay our hand upon our mouth and to justify Christ. It is just with thee thus to leave me, to give me over to this terror, to deal thus with me, that have dealt so unkindly with thee. So to justify God, and accuse ourselves, is the best way to recover spiritual comfort.

Obs. 3. Well, for the third point. *That howsoever Christ be provoked by the church's ingratitude, drowsiness, and careless carriage, to leave her in regard of her feeling, and of inward comfort ; yet notwithstanding he is so gracious, as to leave something behind him, that shews indeed, that he had not left the church altogether, but only in some regard.* For howsoever Christ, in regard of some order of his providence, leave it, yet in regard of another order of his providence, care and mercy, he doth not leave it, so as one way which he takes must sometimes give place to another way of his working in ordering things. Sometimes he is present in a way of comfort, that is one order of his dispensation ; and when he sees that that is neglected, then he withdraws his comforts and hides his gracious countenance. Yet he is then present still in another order and way, though we discern it not, that is, in a way of humbling the soul, letting it see its sin. So here, howsoever Christ had withdrawn himself in regard of this manner of his dealing, in respect of comfort, that the church did not now see his grace, favour ; yet he left behind him a spirit of grace, to affect her heart with grief, sorrow, and shame, and to stir up her endeavours to seek after him, as it is said here: ' I rose to open to my beloved ; and my hands dropped myrrh, and my fingers sweet smelling myrrh, upon the handles of the locks.'

Here observe these three things, which shall be briefly named, because they shall be touched elsewhere.

Obs. 1. *Christ's grace is the cause of our grace.* He first leaves myrrh, and then her fingers drop myrrh. Our oil is from his oil. The head being anointed, ' the oil ran down to the skirts of Aaron's garments,' Ps. cxxxiii. 2, xxxvi. 9 ; ' Out of his fulness we receive grace for grace,' John i. 16, that is, our grace is answerable to the grace of Christ. We have all from him, favour for his favour. Because he is beloved, we are beloved. We have tne grace of sanctification from him. He was sanctified with the Spirit, therefore we are sanctified. We have grace of privilege for his grace. He is the Son of God, therefore we are sons. He is the heir of heaven, therefore we are heirs. So that of his grace it is we receive all. Whether we take grace for favour, or for the grace of sanctification, or the grace of privilege and prerogative, all our graces are from his, ' our myrrh from his myrrh.'

Use. This should teach us, *the necessity of dependence upon Christ,* for whatsoever we have or would have ; which dependence upon Christ is the life of our life, the soul of our souls.

Again, observe from hence, that the church's fingers dropped myrrh when she opened the door, and stirred up herself to endeavour. When first her bowels were moved, then she makes to the door, and then her hands dropped myrrh, so that,

Obs. 2. *We find experience of the grace of Christ, especially when we stir up ourselves to endeavour.* ' Arise and be doing, and the Lord shall be with thee,' 1 Chron. xxviii. 20, saith David to Solomon. So let us rouse up ourselves to endeavour, and we shall find a gracious presence of Christ, and a blessed assistance of the Spirit of Christ, who will shew himself in the midst of endeavours. ' To him that hath shall be given :' what is that ? To him that hath, if he exercise and stir up the grace of God in him, shall be given, Mat. xxv. 29. Therefore, let us stir up the graces of God in us ; let us fall upon actions of obedience, second them with prayer. Whatsoever we pray for and desire, set upon the practice thereof. We mock God else, except we endeavour for that we desire. There was myrrh left on the door, but she feels it not till she arose, opened the door, and laid her hand upon the lock.

I speak to any Christian's experience, if in the midst of obedience they do not find that comfort they looked for, and that it is meat and drink to do God's will. Therefore keep not off and say, I am dead and drowsy, therefore I shall be still so. You are deceived ; fall upon obedience and practising of holy duties, and in the midst thereof thou shalt find the presence and assistance of God's Spirit. That will comfort thee.

Obs. 3. The third thing observable from hence is this, *that God's graces are sweet.* Pleasant and sweet, compared here to myrrh, which was an ingredient in the holy oil. Grace makes us sweet. Prayers are sweet, as it is in Rev. viii. 4. Christ mingleth them with his own sweet odours, and so takes and offers them to God. Holy obedience is sweet and delightful to God and to the conscience. It brings peace and delight to others. Therefore they are called fruits. Fruit doth not only imply and shew the issuing of good things from the root, but there is also a pleasantness in it. So there is a delightfulness in good works, as there is in fruit to the taste. Therefore if we would be sweet and delightful to God, let us labour to have grace. If we would think of ourselves with contentment, and have inward sweetness, let us labour for the graces of God's Spirit. These are like myrrh. ' The wicked are an abomination unto the Lord,' Prov. xv. 8, who abhors them, and whatsoever is in them. But ' the righteous and sincere man is his delight,' Prov. xv. 8. Therefore, if we would approve ourselves to God, and feel that he hath delight in us, labour to be such as he may delight in.

Use. Wherefore let the discouraged soul make this use of it, *not to be afraid to do that which is good, upon fear we should sin.* Indeed, sin will cleave to that we do, but Christ will pardon the sin, and accept that which is sweet of his own Spirit. Let us not esteem basely of that which Christ esteems highly of, nor let that be vile in our eyes that is precious in his. Let us labour to bring our hearts to comfortable obedience, for it is a sweet sacrifice to God.

Now, whence came all this? From this that is mentioned, ' My beloved put in his hand by the hole of the door, and my bowels were moved for him,' ver. 4. First, for that expression, he put his finger in by the hole of the door. It implies here that Christ, before he departed, left by his Spirit an impression on the church's heart, which deeply affected her to seek after him.

The fingers spoken of are nothing but ' the power of his Spirit.' As the usual Scripture phrase is, ' This is God's finger,' ' God's mighty hand,' Exod. viii. 19, without which all ordinances are ineffectual. ' Paul may plant, and Apollos may water,' 1 Cor. iii. 6, 7, but all is nothing without the working of the Spirit, the motions whereof are most strong, being God's finger, whereby he wrought all that affection in the church which is here expressed. Christ, before he leaveth the church, ' puts his finger into the hole of the door,' that is, he works somewhat in the soul by his Spirit, which stirred up a constant endeavour to seek after him. For why else follows it, ' her bowels were moved after him'? which implies a work of the Spirit upon her bowels, expressed in her grief for his absence, and shame for her refusing his entrance, and whereby her heart was moved and turned in her to seek after him. From whence, thus explained, observe,

Obs. 1. *That outward means will do no good, unless the finger of Christ come to do all that is good.*

The finger of Christ is the Spirit of Christ—that is, a kind of divine power goes from him in hearing and speaking the word of God, and in prayer. There is more than a man's power in all this. If these work any effect, Christ ' must put his finger in.' When duties are unfolded to us in the ministry of the word, all is to no purpose, but the sounding of a voice, unless the finger of Christ open the heart, and work in the soul.

Use 1. Let us make this use of it, therefore, *not to rest in any means whatsoever,* but desire the presence of Christ's finger to move and to work upon our hearts and souls. Many careless Christians go about the ordinances of God, and never regard this power of Christ, this mighty power, ' the finger of Christ.' Thereupon they find nothing at all that is divine and spiritual wrought in them. For, as it required a God to redeem us, to take our nature, wherein he might restore us, so likewise it requires the power of God to alter our natures. We could not be brought into the state of grace without divine satisfaction, and we cannot be altered to a frame of grace without a divine finger, the finger of God working upon our hearts and souls. This should move us, in all the ordinances of God that we attend upon, to lift up our hearts in the midst of them, ' Lord, let me feel the finger of thy Spirit writing thy word upon my heart.' ' Turn us, O Lord, and we shall be turned,' Jer. xxxi. 18. Pray for this quickening and enlivening, for this strengthening Spirit. All comes by it.

From this that it is said here, ' that Christ puts his finger into the hole of the door before he removed it,' and withdrew himself, observe,

Obs. 2. How graciously Christ doth deal with us, *that he doth always leave some grace before he doth offer to depart.* Let us therefore, for the time to come, lay and store this up as a ground of comfort, that howsoever Christ may leave us, yet, notwithstanding, he will never leave us wholly; but as he gave us his Holy Spirit at first, so he will continue Him in us by some gracious work or other, either by way of comfort, or of strength to uphold us. Perhaps we may need more sorrow, more humility, than of any other grace. For winter is as good for the growing of things as the spring, because were it not for this, where would be the killing of weeds and worms, and preparing of the ground and land for the spring? So it is as needful for Christians to find the presence of Christ in the way of humiliation and abasement, causing us to afflict our own souls, as to feel his presence in peace, joy, and comfort. In this life we cannot be without this gracious dispensation. We may therefore comfort ourselves, that howsoever Christ leaves us, yet he will always leave somewhat behind him, as here he left some myrrh after him upon the handle of the door. Some myrrh is left always behind him upon the soul, which keeps it in a state and frame of grace, and sweetens it. Myrrh was one of the ingredients in the holy oil, as it is Exod. xxx. 30; and so this leaving of myrrh behind him signifies the oil of grace left upon the soul, that enabled the church to do all these things, which are after spoken of.

Obj. But you will say, How doth this appear, when in some desertion a Christian finds no grace, strength, or comfort at all, that nothing is left?

Ans. It is answered, *they always do.* Take those who at any time have had experience of the love of God, and of Christ formerly, take them at the worst, you shall find from them some sparkles of grace, broken speeches of tried secret comfort, some inward strength and struggling against corruptions; their spirits endeavouring to recover themselves from sinking too low, and with something withstanding both despair and corruption. Take a Christian at the worst, there will be a discovery of the Spirit of Christ left in him, notwithstanding all desertion. This is universally in all in some measure, though perhaps it is not discerned to a Christian himself, but to those that are able to judge. Sometimes others can read our evidences better than ourselves. A Christian that is in temptation cannot judge of his own estate, but others can. And so, at the very worst, he hath always somewhat left in him, whereby he may be comforted. Christ never leaves his church and children that are his wholly. Those that are wholly left, they never had saving grace, as Ahithophel, Cain, Saul, and Judas were left to themselves. But for the children of God, if ever they found the power of sanctifying grace, 'Christ whom he loves, he loves to the end,' John xiii. 1, from whom he departs not, unless he leaves somewhat behind him, that sets an edge upon the desires to seek after him.

Use 2. Make this second use of it, *to magnify the gracious love and mercy of Christ*, that when we deserve the contrary, to be left altogether, yet notwithstanding so graciously he deals with us. Behold, in this his dealing, the mercy of Christ. He will not suffer the church to be in a state of security, but will rather, to cure her, bring her to another opposite state of grief and sorrow, as we shall see in the next point, how that which Christ left in the heart of the church so afflicted her 'that her bowels were turned in her.' Whereupon she riseth, seeks, and inquires after Christ by the watchmen and others. So she saith of herself,

'My bowels were moved in me,' &c. What was that? My heart was affected full of sorrow and grief for my unkind dealing with Christ. Hereby those affections were stirred up, that were afore sleepy and secure, to godly grief, sorrow, and shame. For God hath planted affections in us, and joined them with conscience, as the executioners with the judge. So that, whenas conscience accuseth of any sin, either of omission or commission, affections are ready to be the executioners within us. Thus to prevent eternal damnation, God hath set up a throne in our own hearts, to take revenge and correction by our own affections, godly sorrow and mourning, as here the church saith, ' My bowels were turned in me.' It was a shame and grief, springing out of love to Christ, that had been so kind, patient, and full of forbearance to her. ' My bowels were turned in me;' that is, sorrow and grief were upon me for my unkind dealing.

The observation from hence is,

That security and a cold, dull state produceth a contrary temper. That is, those that are cold, dull, secure, and put off Christ, he suffers them to fall into sharp sorrows and griefs.

We usually say, Cold diseases must have hot and sharp remedies. It is most true spiritually. Security, which is a kind of lethargy, a cold disease, forgetting of God and our duty to him, must have a hot and sharp cure. And the lethargy is best cured by a burning ague. So Christ deals here. He puts his finger in at the hole of the door, and leaves grace behind to work upon the bowels of the church, to make her grieve and be ashamed for her unkind dealing. Thus he cures security by sorrow. This is the best conclusion of sin.

And we may observe withal, *that even sins of omission, they bring grief, shame, and sorrow.* And in the issue, through Christ's sanctifying them, these which they breed consume the parent. That is, sin brings forth sorrow, shame, and grief, which are a means to cure sin. Security breeds this moving of the bowels, which moving helps security. Would we therefore prevent sorrow, shame, and grief? Take heed then of security, the cause that leads to them; yea, of sins of omission, wherein there is more danger than in sins of commission. The sins of carnal, wicked men are usually sins of commission; most which break out outrageously, and thereby taint themselves with open sins. But the sins of God's people, who are nearer to him, are for the most part sins of omission; that is, negligence, coldness, carelessness in duty, want of zeal, and of care they should have in stirring up the graces of God in them; as the church here, which did not give way to Christ, nor shook off security.

Use. Let us esteem as slightly as we will of sins of omission and carelessness, *they are enough to bring men to hell if God be not the more merciful.* It is not required only that we do no harm, and keep ourselves from outward evils; but we must do good in a good manner, and have a care to be fruitful and watchful, which if we do not, this temper will bring grief, shame, and sorrow afterwards. As here, even for sins of omission, deadness, and dulness, we see the church is left by Christ, ' and her bowels are turned in her.' For careless neglect and omission of duty to God is a presage and forerunner of some downfal and dejection. And commonly it is true, when a man is in a secure and careless state, a man may read his destiny (though he have been never so good); nay, the rather if he be good. Such a one is in danger to fall into some sharp punishment, or into some sin; for of all states and tempers, God will not suffer a Christian to be in a secure, lazy, dead state, when he cannot perform things comfortably to God, or himself, or to others. A dead, secure estate is so hateful to him (decay in our first love, this lukewarm temper) that he will not endure it. It either goes before some great sin, cross, affliction, or judgment.

' My bowels were moved in me.' And good reason. It was a suitable correction to the sin wherein she offended. For Christ, his bowels were turned towards her in love and pity, ' My love, my dove, my undefiled,' in which case, she neglecting him, it was fit she should find ' moving of bowels' in another sense, out of love too, but in shame and mourning. Christ here leaves her to seek after him, that had waited and attended her leisure before, as we shall see after.

The next thing we may hence observe in that, 'that her bowels were turned in her,' from something left in the hole of the door by the Spirit of Christ, is,

That Christ hath our affections in his government.

He hath our bowels in his rule and government, more than we ourselves have. We cannot of ourselves rule our grief, shame, sorrow, or such affections as these. The wisest man in the world cannot award* grief and sorrow when God will turn it upon his bowels, and make a man ashamed and confounded in himself. All the wit and policy in the world cannot suppress those affections. For Christ rules our hearts, 'The hearts of kings are in his hand, as the rivers of water,' Prov. xxi. 1, as well as the hearts of ordinary persons.

If he set anything upon the soul to afflict it and cast it down, it shall afflict it, if it be but a conceit. If he will take away the reins from the soul, and leave it to its own passion, removing away its guard; for he by his Spirit guards our souls with peace, by commanding of tranquillity; so as let him but leave it to itself, and it will tear itself in sunder, as Ahithophel, who being left to himself, did tear himself in pieces, 2 Sam. xvii. 23. Cain also being thus left, was disquieted, tormented, and wracked† himself, Gen. iv. 13. So Judas in this case, being divided in himself, you see what became of him, Mat. xxvii. 5. Let Christ but leave us to our own passion of sorrow, what will become of us but misery ? He hath more rule therefore of our passions than we ourselves have, because we cannot rule them graciously, nor can we stay them when we would.

Use. Therefore this should *strike an awe in us of God, with a care to please him.* For there is not the wisest man in the world, but if he remove his guard from his soul, and leave him to himself; if there were no devil in hell, yet he would make him his own tormentor and executioner. Therefore the apostle makes this sweet promise. He bids them pray to God; ' and the peace of God which passeth all understanding should guard their souls,' &c., Philip. iv. 7. So the word is in the original. ‡ It is a great matter for the keeping of God's people, to have their souls guarded.

'Her bowels were turned in her.'

Here again, as the conclusion of all this, we seeing this estate of the church, *may wonder at Christ's carriage towards her in this world.* Christ is wonderful in his saints, and in his goodness towards them, 2 Thess. i. 10; sometimes alluring them, as we see Christ the church here; wondrous in patience, notwithstanding their provocation of him; wondrous in his desertions; wondrous in leaving something behind him in desertions. Those that are his he will not leave them without grace, whereby they shall seek him again. Nay, the falling out of lovers shall be the renewing of fresh and new love, more constant than ever the former was. Thus our blessed Saviour goes beyond us in our deserts, taking advantage even of our security; for our greater good, making all work to good in the issue, Rom. viii. 28; which shall end in a more near and close communion between Christ and his church than ever before. Carnal men feel not these changes, ebbings and flowings. They are not acquainted with God's forsakings. Indeed their whole life is nothing but a forsaking of God, and God's forsaking of them, who gives

---

* That is, ' ward off.'—ED.   ‡ See note *k*, vol I. page 334.—G.
† Qu. ' racked ?'—G.

them outward comforts, peace and friends in the world, wherein they solace themselves. But for inward communion with him, any strength to holy duties, or against sin, for to be instruments for God's honour, and service, to do any good, they are careless. For they live here to serve their own turns, leaving their state and inheritance behind them. The Scripture saith, 'They have no changes, therefore they fear not God,' Ps. lv. 19; and so they go down to hell quietly and securely. Oh! but it is otherwise with God's children. They are tossed up and down. God will not suffer them to prosper, or live long in a secure, drowsy, sinful state, the continuance wherein is a fearful evidence that such an one as yet hath no saving grace, nor that he yet belongs to God, seeing Christ hates such an estate, and will not suffer his to be long therein, but will shift and remove them from vessel to vessel, from condition to condition, till he have wrought in them that disposition of soul that they shall regard and love him more and more, and have nearer and nearer communion with him.

THE TENTH SERMON.

I opened to my beloved; but my beloved had withdrawn himself and was gone: my soul failed when he spake; I sought him, but could not find him; I called him, but he gave no answer.—CANT. V. 6.

THUS we see that the life of a Christian is trouble upon trouble, as wave upon wave. God will not suffer us to rest in security, but one way or other he will fire us out of our starting-holes, and make us to run after him. How much better were it for us, then, to do our works cheerfully and joyfully, 'so to run as we may obtain,' 1 Cor. ix. 24, than to be thus hurried up and down, and through our own default, coming into desertions, and there receiving rebukes and blows and delays ere we have peace again, as it fell out with the church in the sequel; for this text is but the beginning of her seeming misery. The watchmen, after this, 'found her, and wounded her,' &c., verse 7. But heaven is more worth than all, now that her affections are set on fire. From thence she bestirs herself, is resolute to find out her beloved, whom she highly values above all this world. How her affections were stirred by Christ's putting in his finger at the hole of the door, we have heard. Now follows her action thereupon; for here is rising, opening, seeking, calling, and inquiring after Christ.

Action follows affection. After her bowels are moved, she ariseth and openeth; from whence we may further observe—

Obs. 1. *That where truth of affection is, it will discover itself in the outward man, one way or other.* If there be any affection of love and piety to God, there will be eyes lift up, knees bended down, and hands stretched forth to heaven. If there be any grief for sin, there will be the face dejected, the eyes looking down, some expression or other. If there be a desire, there will be a making forth to the thing desired; for the outward man is commanded by the inward, which hath a kind of sovereign commanding power over it, and says, Do this, and it doth it; Speak this, and it speaks it. Therefore, those whose courses of life are not gracious, their affections and their hearts are not good; for where the affections are good, the actions will be suitable. 'Her bowels were moved in her,' and presently she shews the truth of her affection, in that she maketh after him.

1. *Her soul failed when he spake.*
2. *She makes after him.*

' My soul failed when he spake : I sought him, but I could not find him.'
—Of Christ's withdrawing himself, we spake in general before, wherefore
we will leave that and proceed.

' My soul failed when he spake.' That is, her soul failed when she remembered what he had spoke when he stood at the door and said, ' Open
to me, my sister, my love, my dove, my undefiled : for my head is wet with
the dew,' &c. Now, when God's Spirit had wrought upon her, then she
remembered what Christ had said. All those sweet allurements were
effectual now unto her, especially when she saw that after those sweet
allurements Christ had withdrawn himself; for that is the meaning of
these words, ' My soul failed when he spake unto me.' He did not speak
now; but her soul failed after he spake; for so it should be read, that is,
after she remembered his speech to her; for now, when she opened, he was
not there. Therefore, he could not speak to her.

Obs. 2. *The word of Christ, howsoever for the present it be not effectual, yet
afterwards it will be in the remembrance of it.* To those that are gracious,
it will be effectual when the Holy Ghost comes to seal it further upon
their hearts. Christ spake many things to his disciples which they forgot ;
but when afterwards the Holy Ghost the Comforter was come, his office
was, ' to bring all things to their remembrance that they had forgotten
before,' John xiv. 26. The Holy Ghost taught them not new things, but
brought former things to their remembrance ; for God will make the word
effectual at one time or other. Perhaps the word we hear is not effectual
for the present ; it may afterwards, many years after, when God awakes
our consciences.

And as this is true of God's children, the seed now sown in them will
not grow up till many years after, so it is true also of those that are not
God's children. They think they shall never hear again of those things
they hear. Perhaps they will take order by sensuality, hardening of their
hearts, and through God's judgments withal concurring, that conscience
shall not awake in this world. But it shall awake one day; for it is put
into the heart to take God's part, and to witness against us for our sins.
It shall have and perform its office hereafter, use it as you will now ; and it
will preach over those things again that you now hear. You shall hear
again of them, but it shall be a barren hearing. Now we may hear fruitfully to do us good, but afterwards we shall call to mind what we have
heard, and it shall cut us to the heart. Dives, we know, had Moses and
the prophets to instruct him, but he never heeded them in his life, until
afterwards to his torment, Luke xvi. 29. So men never heed what they
hear and read ; they put off all, and lay their consciences asleep ; but God
will bring them afterwards to remembrance. But because it is a point
especially of comfort to the church ;

Labour we all of us to make this use of it, to be diligent and careful to
hear and attend upon the ordinances of God ; for howsoever that we hear
is not effectual for the present, but seems as dead seed cast into the heart,
yet God will give it a body after, as the apostle speaks, at one time or
other, 1 Cor. xv. 38. And that which we hear now, the Holy Ghost will
bring it to our remembrance when we stand in most need of it.

' My soul failed when he spake.' She was in a spiritual swoon and
deliquium * upon his withdrawing, whence the point considerable is,

* That is, ' fainting, sinking.'—G.

That Christ doth leave his church sometimes, and bring it very low in their own apprehensions, that their hearts fail them for want of his presence. So it was with David, Ps. xxxviii. 2, 3 ; so with Jonah, Jonah ii. 2 ; so with the church, Lam. iii. 1, *seq.* We see it at large.

Reason. The necessity of our souls and of our estates require this. As sometimes a body may be so corrupt, that it must be brought as low as possible may be, before there will be a spring of new and good blood and spirits, so we may fall into such a state of security, that nothing will bring us to a right temper but extreme purging. And usually God deals thus with strong wits and parts, if they be holy. David and Solomon were men excellently qualified ; yet when they tasted of the pleasures and contentments of the world too deep, answerably they had ; and so usually others shall have such desertions as will make them smart for their sweetness, as was shewed before.

But upon what occasions doth a Christian think especially that God doth leave, forsake, and fail him ?

First. This failing and fainting of the soul is sometimes upon an apprehension, *as if God and Christ were become enemies,* as Job saith, vii. 20, and as having set us as a butt to shoot at. But this is not all that a gracious and pure heart sinks for.

But also *secondly. For the absence of Christ's love, though it feel no anger.* Even as to a loving wife, her husband not looking lovingly upon her as he used to do, is enough to cast her down, and cause her spirits to fail ; so for God to look upon the soul, put the case, not with an angry, yet with a countenance withdrawn, it is sufficient to cast it down. For any one that hath dependence upon another, to see their countenance withdrawn, and not to shew their face as before, if there be but a sweet disposition in them, it is enough to daunt and dismay them.

Nay, *thirdly.* Moreover, *when they find not that former assistance in holy duties ;* when they find that their hearts are shut up and they cannot pray as formerly when they had the Spirit of God more fully ; and when they find that they cannot bear afflictions with wonted patience—certainly Christ hath withdrawn himself, say they. This is first done when we hear the word of God, not with that delight and profit as we were wont. When they find how they come near to God in holy communion, and yet feel not that sweet taste and relish in the ordinances of God as they were wont to do, they conclude, certainly God hath hid his face. Whereupon they are cast down, their spirits fail. And do not wonder that it should be so, for it is so in nature. When the sun hides itself many days from the world, it is an uncomfortable time ; the spirits of the creatures lower and wither. We see it so in the body, that the animal spirits in the brain, which are the cause of motion and sense, if they be obstructed, there follows an apoplexy and deadness. So it is between Christ and the soul. He is the ' Sun of righteousness,' Mal. iv. 2, by whose beams we are all comforted and cheered, which when they are withheld, then our spirits decay and are discouraged. Summer and winter arise from the presence and absence of the sun. What causeth the spring to be so clothed with all those rich ornaments ? The presence of the sun which comes nearer then. So what makes the summer and winter in the soul, but the absence or presence of Christ ! What makes some so vigorous beyond others, but the presence of the Spirit ! As it is in nature, so it is here. The presence of Christ is the cause of all spiritual life and vigour ; who when he withdraws his presence a little the soul fails.

' My soul failed when he spake to me: I sought him, but I could not find him ; I called, but he gave me no answer.'

Obs. 1. The church redoubleth her complaint to shew her passion. *A large heart hath large expressions.* She took it to heart that Christ did not shew himself in mercy. Therefore she never hath done. I sought him but I could not find him, I called but he gave me no answer. Affection makes eloquent and large expressions.

Obs. 2. But mainly observe from this failing of the church, *the difference between the true children of God and others.* The child of God is cast down when he finds not the presence of God as he was wont; his spirits fail. A carnal man, that never knew what this presence meant, regards it not, can abide the want of it. He finds, indeed, a presence of God in the creature which he thinks not of. There is a sweetness in meat, drink, rest, and a contentment in honour, preferment, and riches ; and thus God is present always with him, but other presence he cares not for. Nay, he shuns all other presence of God, labouring to avoid his spiritual presence. For what is the reason that a carnal man shuns the applying of the word and the thinking of it, but because it brings God near to his heart, and makes him present ? What is the reason he shuns his own conscience ; that he is loath to hear the just and unanswerable accusations that it would charge upon him, but because he cannot abide the presence of God in his conscience ? What is the reason he shuns the sight of holier and better men than himself ? 1 Kings xvii. 18. They present God to him, being his image, and call his sins to memory, and upbraid his wicked life. Hence comes that Satanical hatred more than human in carnal, vile men, to those that are better than themselves ; because they hate all. presence of God, both in the word, ministry, and all God's holy servants. All such presence of God they hate ; whereof one main reason is, because they are malefactors, wicked rebels, and intend to be so. And as a malefactor cannot endure so much as the thought of the judge, so they cannot think of God otherwise, in that course they are in, than of a judge ; whereupon they tremble and quake at the very thought of him, and avoid his presence.

You know that great man, Felix, Paul spake to in the Acts, Acts xxiv. 25, when he spake of the judgment to come, and those virtues, as temperance and righteousness, which he was void of, and guilty of the contrary vices ; he quaked, and could not endure to hear him speak any longer. Wicked men love not to be arraigned, tormented, accused, and condemned before their time, Mark v. 7. Therefore, whatsoever presents to them their future terrible estate, they cannot abide it. It is an evidence of a man in a cursed condition, thus not to endure the presence of God. But what shall God and Christ say to them at the day of judgment ? It was the desire of such men not to have to do with the presence of God here, and it is just with Christ to answer them there as they answer him now ; ' Depart, depart, we will have none of thy ways,' say they, Job xxii. 17. ' Depart, ye cursed,' saith he. He doth but answer in their own language, ' Depart, ye cursed, with the devil and his angels,' Mat. xxv. 41.

But you see the child of God is clean of another temper. He cannot be content to be without the presence of God and of his Spirit, enlightening, quickening, strengthening, and blessing of him in spiritual respects. When he finds not his presence helping him, when he finds Christ his life is absent from him, he is presently discouraged. For ' Christ is our life,' Col. iii. 4. Now, when a man's life fails all fails. When, therefore, a man finds his spiritual taste and comfort not as it was before, then Oh, ' the life

of my life' hath withdrawn himself, and so is never quiet till he have recovered his life again, for ' Christ is his life,' Col. iii. 4.

And because there is a presence of God and of Christ in the word and
sacraments—a sweet presence, the godly soul, he droops and fails if he be
kept from these.   He will not excommunicate himself, as many do, that
perhaps are asleep when they should be at the ordinances of God.   But if
he be excommunicated and banished, O how takes he it to heart !   ' As the
hart panteth after the water brooks, so longeth my soul after thee, O God,'
Ps. xlii. 1.   The whole 84th Psalm is to that purpose, ' O how amiable are
thy tabernacles, O Lord of hosts.'   He finds a presence of God in his word
and sacraments, and when he doth not taste a sweet presence of God therein, he droops and sinks.

A carnal man never heeds these things, because he finds no sweetness in
them ; but the godly, finding Christ in them, they droop in the want of
them, and cannot live without them.   ' Whither shall we go ?' saith Peter to
Christ, ' thou hast the words of eternal life,' John vi. 68.   I find my soul
quickened with thy speaking.   So a soul that feels the quickening power of
the ordinances, he will never be kept from the means of salvation, but he
droops and is never well till he have recovered himself again.

Again, another difference may be observed.   Carnal men, when they find
the sense of God's anger, they seek not God's favour, but think of worse and
worse still, and· so run from God till they be in hell.   But those that are
God's children, when they fail and find the sense of God's displeasure, they
are sensible of it, and give not over seeking to God.   They run not further
and further from him.

The church here, though she found not Christ present with her, yet she
seeks him still and never gives over.   Whence again we may observe,

3. *That although the church be said to fail and not to find Christ, yet he
is present then with her*.   For who enabled her to seek him ?   To explain
this, there is a double presence of Christ.

1. Felt.

2. Not felt.

1. *The presence felt*, is, when Christ is graciously present and is withal
pleased to let us know so much, which is a heaven upon earth.   The soul
is in paradise then, when she feels ' the love of God shed abroad in the
heart,' and the favourable countenance of God shining upon her.   Then she
despiseth the world, the devil, and all, and walks as if she were half in
heaven already.   For she finds a presence and a manifestation of it, a more
glorious state than the world can afford.

2. But, there is a presence of Christ *that is secret;* when he seems to
draw us one way, and to drive us another, that we are both driven and
drawn at once : when he seems to put us away, and yet, notwithstanding,
draws us.   When we find our souls go to Christ, there is a drawing power
and presence ; but when we find him absent, here is a driving away.   As we
see here in the church and in the ' woman of Canaan,' Mat. xv. 21, *seq.*
We see what an answer she had from Christ, at first none, and then an
uncomfortable, and lastly a most unkind answer.   ' We must not give the
children's bread to dogs,' Mat. xv. 27.   Christ seemed to drive her
away, but, at the same time, he by his Spirit draws her to him, and was
thereby secretly present in her heart to increase her faith.   When Christ
wrestled with Jacob, though he contended with him, yet the same time he
gave Jacob power to overcome him, to be Israel, a prevailer over him, Gen.
xxxii. 28.   So, at the same time, the church seems to fail and faint, yet,

notwithstanding, there is a secret, drawing power pulling her to Christ, whereby she never gives over, but seeks and calls still after him.

It is good to observe this kind of Christ's dealing, because it will keep us that we be not discouraged when we find him absent. If still there be any grace left moving us to that which is good, if we find the Spirit of God moving us to love the word and ordinances, to call upon him by prayer, and to be more instant, certainly we may gather there is a hidden, secret presence here that draws us to these things. Nay more, that the end of this seeming forsaking and strangeness is to draw us nearer and nearer, and at length to draw us into heaven to himself. God's people are gainers by all their losses, stronger by all their weaknesses, and the better for all their crosses, whatsoever they are. And you shall find that the Spirit of God is more forcible in them after a strangeness, to stir them up more eagerly after Christ than before, as here the church doth: for her eagerness, constancy, and instantness, it groweth as Christ's withdrawing of himself groweth.

Use 1. Let us therefore learn hence *how to judge of ourselves*, if we be in a dead, lifeless state, both in regard of comfort and of holy performances, whether we be content to be so. If we be not contented, but make towards Christ more and more, it is a good sign that he hath not forsaken us, that he will come again more gloriously than ever before, as here we shall see after, it was with the church. He seems strange, but it is to draw the church to discover her affection, and to make her ashamed of her former unkindness, and to sit surer and hold faster than she did before. All ends in a most sweet communion.

Use 2. We should labour, therefore, *to answer Christ's dealings in suitable apprehensions of soul*, when he is thus present secretly, though he seem, in regard of some comforts and former experience of his love, to withdraw himself. It should teach us to depend upon him, and to believe, though we feel not comfort, yea, against comfort, when we feel signs of displeasure. If he can love and support me, and strengthen my soul, and shew it a presence of that which is fit for me, certainly I should answer thus with my faith, I will depend upon him, though he kill me, as Job did, Job xiii. 15. Our souls should never give over seeking of Christ, praying and endeavouring, for there is true love where he seems to forsake and leave. Therefore I ought in these desertions to cleave to him in life and in death.

THE ELEVENTH SERMON.

I opened to my beloved; but my beloved had withdrawn himself, and was gone: my soul failed when he spake: I sought him, but I could not find him; I called him, but he gave me no answer.—CANT. V. 6, 7.

THE pride and security of the spouse provokes the Lord, her husband, oft to bring her very low, they being incompatible with Christ's residence.

Pride is an affection contrary to his prerogative; for it sets up somewhat in the soul higher than God, the highest.

Security is a dull temper, or rather distemper, that makes the soul neglect her watch, and rely upon some outward privilege. Where this ill couple is entertained, there Christ useth to withdraw himself, even to the failing and fainting of the soul.

The spouse is here in her fainting fit, yet she seeks after Christ. Still she gives not over. So Jonah, ' I am cast out of thy presence,' says he, ' yet notwithstanding I will look toward thy holy temple,' Jonah ii. 4. And David, ' I said in my haste, I am cast out of thy sight ; yet notwithstanding thou heardest the voice of my prayer,' Ps. xxxi. 22. He said it, but he said it in his haste. God's children are surprised on the sudden to think they are cast away ; but it is in haste, and so soon as may be, they recover themselves. ' I said it is my infirmity,' said David, Ps. lxxvii. 10. It is but in a passion. Here then is the difference between the children of God and others in desertions ; they arise, these lie still and despair. There is ' life in the substance of the oak,' Isa. vi. 13, that makes it lift up its head above ground, though it be cut down to the stumps. Nay, we see further here, the church is not taken off for any discouragements, but her faith grows stronger, as the woman's of Canaan did, Mat. xv. 21, *seq.*

The reason whereof is—1, faith looks to the promise, and to the nature of God, not to his present dealing.

And then, 2. God, by a secret work of his Spirit, though he seem to be an enemy, yet notwithstanding draws his children nearer and nearer to him by such his dealing. All this strangeness is but to mortify some former lust, or consume some former dregs of security.

' I sought him, but I could not find him.' Here one of the greatest discouragements of all other is, when prayer, which is left to the church as a salve for all sores, hath no answer. This is the complaint, but indeed an error, of the church ; for Christ did hear the church, though he seemed to turn his back.

But how shall we know that God hears our prayers ?

First. Amongst many other things this is one. When he gives us inward peace, then he hears our prayers, for so is the connection, Phil. iv. 6, 7.

Or secondly. If we find a spirit to pray still, a spirit to wait and to hold out, it is an argument that God either hath or will hear those prayers.

And as it is an argument that God hears our prayers, so is it of the presence of Christ. For how could we pray but from his inward presence ? Christ was now present, and more present with the church when he seemed not to be found of her, than he was when she was secure ; for whence else comes this eagerness of desire, this spirit of prayer, this earnestness of seeking ? ' I called, but he gave no answer,' &c.

Directions how to carry ourselves in such an estate. How shall we carry ourselves when it falls out that our hearts fail of that we seek for, when we pray without success, and find not a present answer, or are in any such-like state of desertion.

1. *We must believe against belief,* as it were, ' hope against hope, and trust in God,' Rom. iv. 18, howsoever he shews himself to us as an opposite.* It is no matter what his present dealing with his church and children here is ; the nature of faith is to break through all opposition, to see the sun behind a cloud, nay, to see one contrary in another, life in death, a calm in a storm, &c., 1 Cor. vi. 8, 9, *seq.*

2. *Labour for an absolute dependence upon Christ, with a poverty of spirit in ourselves.* This is the end of Christ's withdrawing himself, to purge us of self-confidence and pride.

* That is, ' opponent. —G.

3. *Stir up your graces.* For as nature joining with physic helps it to work and carry away the malignant humours, so by the remainder of the Spirit that is in us, let us set all our graces on work until we have carried away that that offends and clogs the soul, and not sink under the burden. For this is a special time for the exercising of faith, hope, love, diligence, care, watchfulness, and such-like graces.

And let us know for our comfort, that even this conflicting condition is a good estate. In a sick body it is a sign of life and health approaching when the humours are stirred, so as that a man complains that the physic works. So when we take to heart our present condition, though we fail and find not what we would, yet this will work to the subduing of corruption at length. It is a sign of future victory when we are discontent with our present ill estate. Grace will get the upper hand, as nature doth when the humours are disturbed.

4. Again, when we are in such a seeming forlorn estate, *let us have recourse to former experience.* What is the reason that God vouchsafes his children for the most part in the beginning of their conversion, in their first love, experience of his love to ravishment ? It is, that afterwards they may have recourse to that love of God then felt, to support themselves, and withal to stir up endeavours, and hope; that finding it not so well with them now as formerly it hath been, by comparing state with state, desires may be stirred up to be as they were, or rather better, Hosea ii. 7.

And as the remembrance of former experiences serve to excite endeavour, so to stir up hope, I hope it shall be as it was, because God is immutable ; I change, but Christ alters not. The inferior elementary world changes. Here is fair weather and foul, but the sun keeps his perpetual course. And as in the gloomiest day that ever was, there was light enough to make it day and to distinguish it from night, though the sun did not shine, so in the most disconsolate state of a Christian soul, there is light enough in the soul to shew that the Sun of righteousness is there, and that Christ hath shined upon the soul, that it is day with the soul, and not night, Ps. cxii. 4.

5. And learn when we are in this condition *to wait God's leisure,* for he hath waited ours. It is for our good, to prepare us for further blessings, to mortify and subdue our corruptions, to enlarge the capacity of the soul, that the Lord absents himself. Therefore Bernard saith well, ' *Tibi accidit,*' &c., ' Christ comes and goes away for our good.' When he withdraws the sense of his love, the soul thereupon is stretched with desire, that it may be as it was in former time, in the days of old. Thus much for that. ' I sought, but could not find him : I called, but he gave me no answer.'

Obj. Here we must answer one objection before we leave the words. This seems to contradict other Scriptures, which promise that those that seek shall find, Matt. vii. 7.

Ans. It is true they that seek shall find, but not presently. God's times are the best and fittest. They that seek shall find, if they seek constantly with their whole heart in all the means. Some do not find, because they seek in one means and not in another. They seek Christ in reading and not in the ordinance of hearing, in private meditation, but not in the communion of saints. We must go through all means to seek Christ, not one must be left. Thus if we will seek him, undoubtedly he will make good his promise. Nay, in some sort, ' he is found before he is sought,' for he is in our souls to stir up desire of seeking him. He prevents us with desires, and answers us in some sort before we pray, Isa. lxv. 24. When he gives us a spirit of prayer, it is a pledge to us, that he means to answer us.

Therefore it is a spiritual deceit when we think Christ is not in us, and we are neglected of him, because we have not all that we would have. Among many other deceits that Christians deceive themselves with in this kind, these be two.

1. That they judge grace *by the quantity and not by the value and price of it;* whereas the least measure of grace and comfort is to be esteemed, because it is an immortal seed cast into the soul by an immortal God, the Father of eternity,* Isa. ix. 6.

2. Another deceit is, that we judge of ourselves *by sense and feeling, and not by faith.*

' The watchman that went about the city found me, and smote me, and took away my veil from me.' Here the poor church, after the setting down of her own exercise in her desertion, now sets out some outward ill dealing she met with, and that from those that should have been her greatest comforters. ' The watchmen that went about the city found me, they wounded me: the keepers of the walls took away my veil from me.'

Thus we see how trouble follows trouble. ' One depth calls upon another.' Inward desertion and outward affliction go many times together. The troubles of the church many times are like Job's messengers. They come fast one upon another, because God means to perfect the work of grace in their hearts. All this is for their good. The sharper the winter the better the spring. Learn hence first of all therefore in general,

That it is no easy thing to be a sound Christian. We see here, when the church had betrothed herself to Christ and entertained him into her garden, thereafter she falls into a state of security and sleep, whence Christ labours to rouse her up. Then she useth him unkindly. After which he withdraws himself, even so far that her heart fails her. Then, as if this were not enough, the watchmen that should have looked to her, ' they smite her, wound her, and take away her veil.' See here the variety of the usage of the church and changes of a Christian ; not long in one state, he is ebbing and flowing.

Therefore let none distaste the way of godliness for this, that it is such a state as is subject to change and variety, whereas carnal men are upon their lees and find no changes.

Obj. But you will say, All Christians are not thus tossed up and down, so deserted of God and persecuted of others.

Ans. I answer, indeed there is difference. Whence comes this difference ? From God's liberty. It is a mystery of the sanctuary, which no man in the world can give a reason of, why of Christians both equally beloved of God, some should have a fairer passage to heaven, others rougher and more rugged. It is a mystery hid in God's breast. It is sufficient for us, if God will bring us any way to heaven, as the blessed apostle saith, ' if by any means I might attain to the resurrection of the dead,' Phil. iii. 11 ; either through thick or thin, if God will bring me to heaven it is no matter. ' If I by any means.'

' The watchmen that went about the city smote me,' &c. By the watchmen here are meant especially governors of state and church.

Why are they called watchmen ?

It is a borrowed speech, taken from the custom of cities that are beleaguered. For policy's sake they have watchmen to descry the danger they are liable unto. So magistrates be watchmen of the state. Ministers are the watchmen for souls, ' watching over our souls for good,' Heb. xiii. 17.

Quest. Why doth God use watchmen ?

* That is, the ' Everlasting Father' of authorised translation.—G.

Ans. 1. Not for any defect of power in him, but for demonstration of his goodness. For he is the great watchman, who watcheth over our commonwealths, churches, and persons. He hath an eye that never sleeps. ' He that watcheth Israel neither slumbers nor sleeps,' Ps. cxxi. 4. Yet notwithstanding he hath subordinate watchmen, not for defect of power, but for demonstration of goodness. He manifests his goodness in that he will use variety of subordinate watchers.

And likewise to shew his power in using many instruments, and his care for us when he keeps us together with his own subordinate means.

And in this that God hath set over us watchers, ministers especially, it implies that *our souls are in danger.* And indeed there is nothing in the world so beset as the soul of a poor Christian. Who hath so many and so bad enemies as a Christian? and amongst them all, the worst and greatest enemy he hath is nearest to him, and converseth daily with him, even himself. Therefore there must needs be watchmen to discover the deceits of Satan and his instruments, and of our own hearts ; to discover the dangers of Jerusalem, and the errors and sins of the times wherein we live. The church is in danger, for God hath set watchmen. Now God and nature doth nothing in vain or needlessly.

Again, in that God takes such care for the soul, it shews the *wondrous worth of it.* Many arguments there be to shew that the soul is a precious thing. It was breathed by God at first. Christ gave his life to redeem it. But this is an especial one, that God hath ordained and established a ministry and watchmen over it. And as God hath set some watchmen over others, so hath he appointed every man to be a watchman to himself. He hath given every man a city to watch over, that is, his own estate and soul. Therefore let us not depend altogether on the watching of others. God hath planted a conscience in every [one] of us, and useth as others to our good, so our own care, wisdom, and foresight, these he elevateth and sanctifieth.

' The watchmen that went about the city found me, they smote me, they wounded me,' &c.

Come we now to the carriage of these watchmen. Those that should have been defensive prove most offensive.

They smote the church and wounded her many ways, though it be not discovered here in particular. As (1.) with their ill and scandalous life ; and (2.) sometimes with corrupt doctrine, and otherwhiles with bitter words ; and (3.) their unjust censures, as we see in the story of the church, especially the Romish Church. They have excommunicated churches and princes. But not to speak of those synagogues of Satan, come we nearer home and we may see amongst ourselves sometimes those that are watchmen, and should be for encouragement, they smite and wound the church, and take away her veil, 3 John 10.

What is it to take away the veil?

You know, in the times of the Old Testament, a veil was that which covered women for modesty, to shew their subjection ; and it was likewise an honourable ornament. ' They took away the veil,' that is, that wherewith the church was covered. They took away that that made the church comely, and laid her open, and as it were naked.

Now both these ways the church's veil is taken away by false and naughty watchmen.

1. As the veil is a token of subjection, when by their false doctrines they labour *to draw people from Christ, and their subjection to him.*

The church is Christ's spouse. The veil was a token of subjection.
Now they that draw the people to themselves, as in popish churches, that
desire to sit high in the consciences of people, and so make the church un-
dutiful, ' they take away the veil of subjection,' and so force Christ to
punish the church, as we see in former ages.

2. As the veil is for honour and comeliness, so ' they take away the veil'
of the church, when they *take away the credit and esteem of the church;* when
they lay open the infirmities and weaknesses of the church.   This is strange
that the watchmen should do this ; yet notwithstanding oftentimes it falls
out so that those that by place are watchmen, are the bitterest enemies of
the church.   Who were bitterer enemies of the poor church in Christ's
time than the scribes, pharisees, and priests ?

And so in the time of the prophets.   Who were the greatest enemies the
church had, but false priests and prophets ?

Quest. What is the ground of this, that those men that by their standing
should be encouragers, are rather dampers of the church's zeal in pursuit
of it ?

Ans. There are many grounds of it.

Sometimes it falls out from a spirit of envy in them at the graces of God's
people, which are wanting in themselves.   They would not have others
better than themselves.

Sometimes from idleness, which makes them hate all such as provoke
them to pains.   They raise up the dignity of outward things too much, as
we see in popery.   They make everything to confer grace, as if they had a
special virtue in them.   But they neglect that wherewith God hath joined
an efficacy, his own ordinances.

Use 1. This should teach us, *to be in love with Christ's government,* and to
see the vanity of all things here below, though they be never so excellent in
their ordinance.   Such is the poison of man's heart, and the malice of
Satan, that they turn the edge of the best things against the good of the
church.

What is more excellent than magistracy ? yet many times the point of
sword is directed the wrong way.   ' I have said ye are gods,' Ps. lxxxii. 6.
They should govern, as God himself would govern, and ask with themselves, Would God now, if he were a watchman of the state, do thus and thus ?
But I wish woeful experience did not witness the contrary.

So ministers are Christ's ambassadors, 2 Cor. v. 20, and should carry themselves even as Christ would do.   They should strengthen the feeble knees
and bind up the broken hearted, nor* discourage ; and not sew pillows under
the armholes of wicked and carnal men, Ezek. xiii. 18.   But, alas! we see
the edge of the ordinance is oftentimes turned another way by the corrupt,
proud, unbroken hearts of men and the malice of Satan.

Use 2. Again, it should teach us *not to think the worse of any for the
disgraces of the times.*   The watchmen here take away the veil of the church,
and her forwardness is disgraced by them.   Take heed, therefore, we entertain not rash conceits of others upon the entertainment they find abroad
in the world, or among those that have a standing in the church, for so we
shall condemn Christ himself.   How was he judged of the priests, scribes,
and pharisees in his times ?   And this hath been the lot of the church in
all ages.   The true members thereof were called heretics and schismatics.
The veil was taken off.   It is the poisonful pride of man's heart that,
when it cannot raise itself by its own worth, it will endeavour to raise itself

* Qu. 'not?'—G.

by the ruin of others' credit through lying slanders. The devil was first a slanderer and liar, and then a murderer, John viii. 44. He cannot murder without he slander first. The credit of the church must first be taken away, and then she is wounded. Otherwise, as it is a usual proverb, Those that kill a dog make the world believe that he was mad first; so they always first traduced the church to the world, and then persecuted her. Truth hath always a scratched face. Falsehood many times goes under better habits than its own, which God suffers, to exercise our skill and wisdom, that we might not depend upon the rash judgment of others, but might consider what grounds they have; not what men do, or whom they oppose, but from what cause, whether from a spirit of envy, idleness, jealousy, and pride, or from good grounds. Else, if Christ himself were on earth again, we should condemn him, as now men do the generation of the just, whom they smite and wound, and take away their veil from them.

THE TWELFTH SERMON.

The watchmen that went about the city found me, they smote me, they wounded me: the keepers of the walls took away my veil from me.—CANT. V. 7.

THE watchmen, those that by their place and standing should be so, they smote the church. As Bernard complains, almost five hundred years ago, ' Alas, alas ! ' saith he, ' those that do seek privileges in the church are the first in persecuting it;' and as his fashion is to speak in a kind of rhetoric, ' they were not pastors, but impostors.' There be two ordinances without which the world cannot stand.

1. Magistracy.
2. Ministry.

Magistrates are nursing fathers and nursing mothers to the church.

Ministers are watchmen by their place and standing.

Now, for shepherds to become wolves, for watchmen to become smiters, what a pitiful thing is it! But thus it is. The church hath been always persecuted with these men under pretence of religion, which is the sharpest persecution of all in the church. It is a grievous thing to suffer of an enemy, but worse of a countryman, worse then that of a friend, and worst of all, of the church. Notwithstanding, by the way, we must know that the persecuted cause is not always the best, as Austin was forced to speak in his time against the Donatists (j). Sarah was a type of the true, and Hagar of the false, church. Now, Sarah, she corrected Hagar. Therefore, it follows not that the suffering cause is alway the better. Therefore, we must judge of things in these kind of passages by the cause, and not by the outward carriage of things.

' They took away my veil.'

Quest. What shall we do in such cases, if we suffer any indignity, if the veil be taken off ? That is, if our shame, infirmities, and weaknesses be laid open by false imputations.

Ans. In this case it is the ' innocency of the dove ' that is to be laboured for, and withal the wisdom of the serpent, Mat. x. 16. If innocency will not serve, labour for wisdom, as indeed it will not alone. The wicked would then labour for subtilty to disgrace righteous persons.

Obj. But what if that will not serve neither? Christ was wisdom itself, yet he suffered most.

Ans. When innocency and wisdom will not do it (because we must be conformable to our head), then we must labour for patience, knowing that one hair of our heads shall not fall to the ground without the providence of the Almighty.

Commend our case, as Christ did, by faith and prayer to God that judgeth.

' I charge you, O daughters of Jerusalem, if you see my beloved, that you tell him that I am sick of love,' &c.

Here the church, after her ill usage of the watchmen, is forced to the society of other Christians not so well acquainted with Christ as herself. ' I charge you, O daughters of Jerusalem, if you find my beloved,' &c., ' tell him,' &c. What shall they tell him?

' Tell him I am sick of love.'

The church is restless in her desire and pursuit after Christ till she find him. No opposition, you see, can take off her endeavour.

1. Christ seems to leave her inwardly.

2. Then she goeth to the watchmen. They ' smite and wound ' her.

3. Then she hath recourse to the daughters of Jerusalem for help.

Generally, before we come to the particulars, from the connection we may observe this,

That love is a fire kindled from heaven.

Nothing in the world will quench this grace, Cant. viii. 7. 8 ; no opposition ; nay, opposition rather whets and kindles endeavour.

The church was nothing discouraged by the ill usage of the watchmen, only she complains ; she is not insensible. A Christian may without sin be sensible of indignities ; only it must be the ' mourning of doves,' Isa. xxxviii. 14, and not the roaring of bears. It must not be murmuring and impatiency, but a humble complaining to God that he may take our case to heart, as the church doth here. But as sensible as she was, she was not a whit discouraged, but seeks after Christ still in other means. If she find him not in one, she will try in another. We see here the nature of love. If it be in any measure perfect, it casteth out all fear of discouragements.

And, indeed, *it is the nature of true grace to grow up with difficulties.* As the ark rose higher with the waters, so likewise the soul grows higher and higher, it mounts up as discouragements and oppositions grow. Nay, the soul takes vigour and strength from discouragements, as the wind increaseth the flame. So the grace of God, the more the winds and waves of affliction oppose it, with so much the more violence it breaks through all oppositions, until it attain the desired hope.

To apply it : those therefore that are soon discouraged, that pull in their horns presently, it is a sign they are very cold, and have but little grace. For where there is any strength of holy affection, they will not be discouraged, nor their zeal be quenched and damped. Therefore they subordinate religion to their own ends, as your temporary believers. Where is any love to Christ, the love of Christ is of a violent nature. It sways in the heart, as the apostle speaks, ' The love of Christ constraineth us,' 2 Cor. v. 14.

If we find this unconquerable resolution in ourselves, notwithstanding all discouragements to go on in a good cause, let us acknowledge that fire to be from heaven ; let us not lose such an argument of the state of grace, as suffering of afflictions with joy. The more we suffer, the more we should rejoice, if the cause be good, as the apostles rejoiced ' that they were accounted worthy to suffer any thing,' Acts v. 41.

'I charge you, O daughters of Jerusalem, if you find my beloved, that ye tell him I am sick of love.'

She goes to the 'daughters of Jerusalem' for help.   Whence we may learn, That, *if we find not comfort in one means, we must have recourse to another*. If we find not Christ present in one, seek him in another; and perhaps we shall find him where we least thought of him.   Sometimes there is more comfort in the society of poor Christians, than of the watchmen themselves.

'I charge you, O daughters of Jerusalem,' &c.

Where we have, 1. A charge given.   'I charge,' &c.

2. The parties charged, 'the daughters of Jerusalem.'

3. The particular thing they are charged with, that is, if they find Christ, 'to tell him she is sick of love.'

The parties charged, are 'the daughters of Jerusalem,' the daughters of the church, which is called Jerusalem, from some resemblances between Jerusalem and the church.   Some few shall be touched, to give light to the point.

1. Jerusalem was a city compact in itself, as the Psalmist saith, Ps. cxxii. 3, so is the church, the body of Christ.

2. Jerusalem was chosen from all places of the world, to be the seat of God; so the church is the seat of Christ.   He dwells there in the hearts of his children.

3. It is said of Jerusalem, they went up to Jerusalem, and down to Egypt, and other places : so the church is from above, Gal. iv. 26.   'The way of wisdom is on high,' Prov. xv. 24.   Religion is upward.   Grace, glory, and comfort come from above; and draw our minds up to have our conversation and our desires above.

4. Jerusalem was 'the joy of the whole earth;' so the church of God, what were the world without it, but a company of incarnate devils?

5. In Jerusalem, records were kept of the names of all the citizens there; so all the true citizens of the church, their names are written in the book of life in heaven, Heb. xii. 23.

The daughters of Jerusalem therefore are the true members of the church that are both bred and fed in the church, 1 Peter i. 20; 1 Peter ii. 2.   Let us take a trial of ourselves, whether we be daughters of Jerusalem or no. That we may make this trial of ourselves.

1. *If we find freedom in our conscience from terrors and fears.*   If we find spiritual liberty and freedom to serve God, it is a sign that we are daughters of Jerusalem, because Jerusalem was free, Gal. iv. 26.

2. Or if we *mind things above, and things of the church.*   If we take to heart the cause of the truth, it is a sign we are true 'daughters of Jerusalem.'   We know what the Psalmist saith, 'Let my right hand forget her cunning if I forget thee, O Jerusalem, if I do not prefer Jerusalem before my chief joy,' Ps. cxxxviii. 5, 6.   If the cause of the church go to our hearts; if we can joy in the church's joy, and mourn in the church's abasement and suffering, it is a sign we are true daughters of Jerusalem, and lively* members of the body of Christ.   Otherwise, when we hear that the church goes down, and that the adverse part prevails, and we joy, it is a sign we are daughters of Babylon and not of Jerusalem.

Therefore let us ask our affections what we are, as Austin writes excellently in his book *De Civitate Dei*.   'Ask thy heart of what city thou art.'

But what saith the church to the daughters of Jerusalem?   In the first place, 'I charge you.'

* That is, 'living.'—G.

It is a kind of admiration supplied thus : ' I charge you, as you love me your sister, as you love Christ, as you tender my case that am thus used, as you will make it good that you are daughters of Jerusalem and not of Babylon, ' tell my beloved, that I am sick of love.' It is a strong charge, a defective speech, which yields us this observation,

That true affections are serious in the things of God and of religion.

She lays a weight upon them, ' I charge you, O daughters of Jerusalem.' True impressions have stong expressions. Therefore are we cold in matters of religion in our discourses ; it is because we want these inward impressions. The church here was full, she could not contain herself, in regard of the largeness of her affections. ' I charge you, O daughters of Jerusalem,' &c.

We may find the truth of grace in the heart, by the discoveries and expressions in the conversation in general.

' I charge you, O daughters of Jerusalem, if you find my beloved, that ye tell him I am sick of love.'

The church here speaks to others meaner than herself. She would have the church tell Christ, by prayer, the surest intelligencer, how she was used, how she languished, and was sick for him, and cannot be without him.

Quest. Why did not the church tell Christ herself ?

Ans. So she did as well as she could, but she desired the help of the church this way also. Sometimes it is so with the children of God that they cannot pray so well as they should, and as they would do ; because the waters of the soul are so troubled, that they can do nothing but utter groans and sighs, especially in a state of desertion, as Hezekiah could but chatter, Isa. xxxviii. 14 ; and Moses could not utter a word at the Red Sea, though he did strive in his spirit, Ex. xiv. 15. In such cases they must be beholden to the help of others.

Sometimes a man is in body sick, as James saith, ' If any man be sick, let him send for the elders, and let them pray,' James v. 14. There may be such distemper of body and soul, that we are unfit to lay open our estate to our own content. It is oft so with the best of God's children ; not that God doth not respect those broken sighs and desires, but they give not content to the soul. The poor palsy man in the gospel, not able to go himself, was carried on the shoulders of others, and let through the house to Christ, Mark ii. 2, 3. Ofttimes we may be in such a palsy estate, that we cannot bring ourselves to Christ, but we must be content to be borne to him by others.

' I charge you, O daughters of Jerusalem, that ye tell my beloved I am sick of love.'

Whence the point that I desire you would observe is,

That at such times as we find not our spirits enlarged from any cause outward and inward, to comfort and joy, then is a time to desire the prayers and help of others.

It is good to have a stock going everywhere ; and those thrive the best that have most prayers made for them ; have a stock going in every country. This is the happiness of the saints. To enforce this instruction, to desire the prayers of others, we must discover, that there is a wondrous force in the prayers of Christians one for another. It is more than a compliment. Would it were so !

The great apostle Paul, see how he desires the Romans, that they would strive and contend with God after a holy violence, by their joint prayers for him, Rom. xv. 30 ; so he desires the Thessalonians that they would

pray for him, ' that he might be delivered from unreasonable men,'
2 Thes. iii. 2. It is usual with him to say, ' Pray, pray,' and for us too;
for such are gracious in the court of heaven. Despise none in this case.
A true, downright, experienced Christian's prayers are of much esteem
with God. Our blessed Saviour himself, when he was to go into the garden, though his poor disciples were sleepy, and very untoward, yet he
would have their society and prayers, Mat. xxvi. 38 (*k*).

' I charge you, O daughters of Jerusalem, if you find my beloved, that
ye tell him I am sick of love.'

To speak a little of the matter of the charge, ' I am sick of love.' I love
him, because I have found former comfort, strength, and sweetness from
him, that I cannot be without him. To be love-sick, then, in the presence
of the church, is to have strong affections to Christ; from which comes
wondrous disquietness of spirit in his absence. Here is somewhat good,
and somewhat ill. This is first her virtue, that she did fervently love. This
was her infirmity, that she was so much distempered with her present
want. These two breed this sickness of love. Whence we observe,

*Where the thing loved is not present, answerable to the desires of the soul
that loves, there follows disquiet and distemper of affections. That is here
termed* * *sickness of love.*

The reason hereof is, *natural contentment is in union with the thing loved.*
The more excellent the thing is that is loved, the more contentment there
is in communion with it; and where it is in any degree or measure hindered, there is disquiet. Answerable to the contentment in enjoying, is the
grief, sorrow, and sickness in parting. The happiness of the church consisting in society with Christ, therefore it is her misery and sickness to be
deprived of him, not to enjoy him whom her soul so dearly loveth. There
are few in the world sick of this disease. I would there were more sick of
the love of Christ. There are many that surfeit rather of fulness, who
think we have too much of this manna, of this preaching, of this gospel.
There is too much of this knowledge of the ordinances. These are not
sick of love.

Use. Make a use, therefore, of trial, whether we be in the state of the
church or no, *by valuing and prizing the presence of Christ in his ordinances,
the word and sacraments.*

There are many fond† sicknesses in the world. There is Amnon's
sickness, that was sick of love for his sister Tamar, 2 Sam. xiii. 2; his
countenance discovered it. And Ahab, he is sick in desiring his neighbour's vineyard, 1 Kings xxi. 1, *seq.* You have many strange sicknesses.
Many sick with fires kindled from the flesh, from hell, but few sick of this
sickness here spoken of.

1. If we find ourselves carried to Christ, to run in that stream as strong
as the affections of those that are distempered with sickness of the love
of other things, *it will discover to us whether we be truly love-sick or not.*

2. Take a man that is sick for any earthly thing, whether of Ahab's or
Amnon's sickness, or of anything, take it as you will, *that which the soul
is sick of in love, it thinks of daily.* It dreams of it in the night. What do
our souls therefore think of? What do our meditations run after? When
we are in our advised and best thoughts, what do we most think of? If
of Christ, of the state of the church here, of grace and glory, all is well.
What makes us, in the midst of all worldly discontentments, to think all
dung and dross in comparison of Christ, but this sickness of love to Christ.

---

     * That is, 'termed.'—G.   † That is, ' foolish.'—G.

If our love be in such a degree as it makes us sick of it, it makes us not to hear what we hear, not to see what we see, not to regard what is present. The soul is in a kind of ecstasy; it is carried so strongly, and taken up with things of heaven. It is deaded to other things, when our eyes are no more led with vanity than if we had none, and the flesh is so mortified as if we were dead men, by reason of the strength of our affections that run another way, to better things which are above.

3. *Thus we see it is in love.* Talk with a man that is in any heat of affections, you talk with one that is not at home, you talk with one absent. The soul is more where it loves than where it dwells. Surely where love is in any strength it draws up the soul, so that a man ofttimes, in his calling and ordinary employments, doth not heed them, but passeth through the world as a man at random. He regards not the things of the world; for Christ is gotten into his heart, and draws all the affections to himself. Where the affection of love is strong, it cares not what it suffers for the party loved, nay, it glories in it. As it is said of the disciples, when they were whipped and scourged for preaching the gospel, it was a matter of glory to them, Acts v. 41. It is not labour, but favour. It is not labour and vexation, but favour that is taken, where love is to the party loved. Where the love of Christ is, which was here in the church, labour is no labour, suffering is no suffering, trouble is no trouble.

4. Again, *it is the property of the party that is sick of this disease, to take little contentment in other things.* Tell a covetous worldling that is in love with the world a discourse of learning, what cares he for learning? Tell him of a good bargain, of a matter of gain, and he will hearken to that. So it is with the soul that hath felt the love of Christ shed abroad in his heart. Tell him of the world, especially if he want* that which he desires, the peace and strength that he found from Christ in former times, he relisheth not your discourse.

Labour we, therefore, every day more and more to have larger and larger affections to Christ. The soul that loves Christ, the nearer to Christ the more joyful it is; when he thinks of those mutual embracings, when Christ and his soul shall meet together there. This happiness is there, where the soul enjoys the thing loved; but that is not here, but in heaven. Therefore, in the mean time, with joy he thankfully frequents the places where Christ is present in the word and sacrament. And, that we may come to have this affection, let us see what our souls are without him; mere dungeons of darkness and confusion, nothing coming from us that is good. This will breed love to the ordinances; and then we shall relish Christ both in the word and sacrament. For he is food for the hungry soul, and requires nothing of us but good appetites; and this will make us desire his love and presence.

THE THIRTEENTH SERMON.

I charge you, O daughters of Jerusalem, if ye find my beloved, that ye tell him I am sick of love. What is thy beloved more than another beloved, O thou fairest among women? &c.—CANT. V. 8, 9.

THE soul, as it is of an immortal substance, so in the right and true temper thereof, [it] aspireth towards immortality, unless when it is clouded and overpressed with that ' which presseth downwards, and the sin which hangeth so fast on,' as the apostle speaks, Heb. xii. 1,* which is the reason of those many and diverse tossings and turmoilings of the enlightened soul, now up, now down, now running amain homewards, and now again sluggish, idle, and lazy ; until roused up by extraordinary means, it puts on again. As the fire mounteth upwards unto its proper place, and as the needle still trembleth till it stand at the north ; so the soul, once inflamed with an heavenly fire, and acquainted with her first original, cannot be at rest until it find itself in that comfortable way which certainly leads homewards.   An instance whereof we have in the church here, who, having lost her sweet communion with Christ, and so paid dearly for her former neglect and slighting his kind invitations, as being troubled, restless in mind, ' beaten and wounded by the watchmen,' bereft of her veil, &c.   Yet this heavenly fire of the blessed Spirit, this ' water of life,' John iv. 10, so restlessly springing in her, makes her sickness of love and ardent desire after Christ to be such, that she cannot contain herself, but breaks forth in this passionate charge and request—

' I charge you, O daughters of Jerusalem, if ye find my beloved, that ye tell him I am sick of love.'

Thus we may see that the way to heaven is full of changes.   The strength of corruption overclouds many times, and damps our joys.   How many several tempers hath the church been in !   Sometimes she is all compounded of joy, vehemently desiring kisses of her best beloved.   She holds her beloved fast, and will not let him go ; and sometimes, again, she is gone, hath lost her beloved, is in a sea of troubles, seeks and cannot find him, becomes sluggish, 'negligent, overtaken with self-love, after which when she hath smarted for her omissions, as here again, she is all a-fire after Christ, as we say, no ground will hold her, away she flies after him, and is restless until she find him.   Where by the way we see, *that permanency and stability is for the life to come; here our portion is to expect changes, storms, and tempests.*   Therefore they must not be strange to particular persons, since it is the portion of the whole church, which thus by sufferings and conformity to the head, 2 Cor. iv. 17, 18, must enter into glory, while God makes his power perfect in our weakness, 2 Cor. xii. 9, overcomes Satan by unlikely means, and so gets himself the glory, even out of our greatest infirmities, temptations, and abasements.

But God, though he make all things work for good unto his children, Rom. viii. 28, even the devil, sin, and death, desertions, afflictions and all; yet we must be warned hereby not to tempt God, by neglecting the means appointed for our comfortable passage, but open to Christ when he knocks, embrace him joyfully in his ordinances, and let our hearts fly open unto him.   For though, through his mercy, our wounds be cured, yet who would be wounded to try such dangerous experiments, as here befell the church in her desertions, for her sluggish negligence, deadness, and self-love ?

So that we see there is nothing gotten by favouring ourselves in carnal liberty, security, or by yielding to the flesh.   The church stood upon terms with Christ when he would ·have come in to her ; but what ensued hereupon ?   She fell into a grievous desertion, and not only so, but finds very hard usage abroad, all which she might have prevented by watchfulness, carefulness, and opening to Christ knocking.   It is a spiritual error, to which we are all prone, to think that much is gained by favouring ourselves,

* See Note *i.*—G.

but we shall find it otherwise. See here, again, that God will bear with nothing, though in his own, but he will sharply punish them even for omissions, and that not only with desertion, but sometimes they shall meet with oppositions in the world.

David cannot scape with a proud thought in numbering of the people, but he must smart for it, and his people also, 2 Sam. xxiv. 1. God is wondrous careful of his children to correct them, when he lets strangers alone, Amos iii. 2. It is a sign of love, when he is at this cost with us. And it should tie us to be careful of our behaviour, not to presume upon God's indulgence; for the nearer we are to him, the more careful he is over us : 'He will be sanctified in all that come near him,' Lev. x. 3. We see the Corinthians, because they come unreverently to the Lord's table, though otherwise they were holy men, ' some of them are sick, some weak, others sleep, that they might not be condemned with the world,' 1 Cor. xi. 30.

Let none, therefore, think the profession of religion to imply an immunity, but rather a straighter* bond ; for 'judgment begins at the house of God,' 1 Pet. iv. 17. Whatsoever he suffers abroad, he will not suffer disorders in his own house, as the prophet says, ' You only have I known of all the families of the earth, therefore you shall not go unpunished,' Amos iii. 2. The church is near him, his spouse whom he loveth, and therefore he will correct her, not enduring any abatement, or decay of the first love in her. And for this very cause he threateneth the church of Ephesus, ' to remove her candlestick,' Rev. ii. 5.

To proceed. The poor church here is not discouraged, but discovers and empties herself to the daughters of Jerusalem. As it is the nature of culinary fire, not only to mount upwards, but also to bewray itself by light and heat, so of this heavenly fire, when it is once kindled from above, not only to aspire in its motion, but to discover itself, in affecting others with its qualities. It could not contain itself here in the church, but that she must go to the daughters of Jerusalem. ' I charge you, O daughters of Jerusalem, if ye find my beloved, that ye tell him that I am sick of love.' Therefore they may doubt that they have not this heavenly fire kindled in them, that express it not seriously ; for of all affections, it will not be concealed. David wonders at his own love : ' Oh, how I love thy law ! Oh, how amiable are thy tabernacles !' Ps. cxix. 97.

Again, we see here, *that where the soul is sick of love, it stands not upon any terms, but it humbleth and abaseth itself.* We say that affection stands not with majesty. Therefore Christ's love to us moved him to abase himself in taking our nature, that he might be one with us. Love stood not upon terms of greatness. We see the church goes to those that were meaner proficients in religion than herself, to pour out her spirit to them, ' to the daughters of Jerusalem.' She abaseth herself to any service, 1 Thess. ii. 8. Love endureth all things, 1 Cor. xiii. 7, anything to attain to the thing loved ; as we see Hamor the son of Shechem,† he would endure painful circumcision for the love he bore to Dinah, Gen. xxxiv. 24. So, Acts v. 41, it is said they went away rejoicing, after they were whipped, because they loved Christ. The spirit of love made them rejoice, when they were most disgracefully used.

Sometimes where this affection of heavenly love is prevalent, so that a man is sick of it, the distempers thereof redounds to the body, and reflects upon that, as we see in David : ' That his moisture became as the drought of summer,' Ps. xxxii. 4 ; because there is a marriage and a sympathy

* Qu. 'straiter ?'—ED.   † ' Shechem the son of Hamor.'—ED.

between the soul and the body, wherein the excessive affections of the one redound and reflect upon the other.

'Tell him that I am sick of love.' Here is a sickness, but not unto death, but unto life ; a sickness that never ends but in comfort and satisfaction. Blessed are those that hunger and thirst after Christ, they shall be satisfied, Mat. v. 6, as we shall see afterwards more at large.

Knowledge gives not the denomination, *for we may know ill and be good, and we may know good and be evil;* but it is the affection of the soul which cleaves to the things known. The truth of our love is that gives the denomination of a state to be good or ill. Love is the weight and wing of the soul, which carries it where it goes ; which, if it carry us to earth, we are base and earthly; if to heaven, heavenly. We should have especial care how we fix this affection ; for thereafter as it is, even so is our condition. 'Ask thy love of what city thou art, whether of Jerusalem or Babylon,' as Austin saith. Now the daughters of Jerusalem reply unto the church, wondering at her earnestness,

'What is thy beloved more than another beloved, O thou fairest among women ? what is thy beloved more than another beloved, that thou dost so charge us ?'

Instead of giving satisfaction to her, they reply with asking new questions, 'What is thy beloved more than another beloved, O thou fairest among women ? what is thy beloved,' &c. Wherein ye have a doubling of the question, to shew the seriousness of it. Of this their answer there are two parts.

1. A loving and sweet compellation, 'O thou fairest among women.'

2. The question doubled, 'What is thy beloved more than another beloved ?' And again, 'What is thy beloved,' &c., 'that thou dost so charge us ?' As if they should say, 'Thou layest a serious charge upon us ; therefore there is some great matter surely in thy beloved that thou makest such inquiry after him.' Thus the weaker Christians being stirred up by the example of the stronger, they make this question, and are thus inquisitive. But to speak of them in their order.

'O thou fairest among women.' Here is the compellation. The church is the fairest among women in the judgment of Christ. So he calls her, 'O thou fairest among women,' Cant. i. 8 ; and here the fellow-members of the church term her so too ; fair, and the fairest, incomparably fair.

Quest. But how cometh she to be thus fair ?

Ans. 1. *It is in regard that she is clothed with Christ's robes.* There is a woman mentioned clothed with the sun, Rev. xii. 1. We were all ennobled with the image of God at the first, but after we had sinned we were bereft of that image. Therefore now all our beauty must be clothing, which is not natural to man, but artificial ; fetched from other things. Our beauty now is borrowed. It is not connatural with us. The beauty of the church now comes from the Head of the church, Christ. She shines in the beams of her husband, not only in justification, but in sanctification also.

2. The church is lovely and fair again, *as from Christ's imputative righteousness, so from his righteousness inherent in her, the graces she hath from him.* For of him we receive grace for grace. There is never a grace but it is beautiful and fair ; for what is grace but the beams of Christ, the Sun of righteousness ? So that all must be fair that comes from the first fair, all beautiful that comes from the first beauty.

This beauty of grace, whereby it makes the church so fair, springs from these grounds.

First. *In that it is from a divine principle and original. It is not basely bred, but from heaven.* And therefore it raiseth the soul above nature, and makes the subjects wherein it is as far surpass all other men, as men do beasts.

Secondly. In regard of the continuance, *it is everlasting, and makes us continue for ever.* 'All flesh is grass, and as the flower of grass,' saith the prophet, Isa. xl. 6 ; and it is repeated in the New Testament in divers places. All worldly excellency is as the flower of grass. 'The grass withereth and the flower fadeth, but the word of the Lord (that is, the grace that is imprinted in the soul by the Spirit with the word), that abideth for ever,' 1 Pet. i. 24, and makes us abide likewise.

Use 1. From this fairness of the church, let us take occasion to contemplate of the excellency of Christ that puts this lustre of beauty upon the church. Moses married a woman that was not beautiful, but could not alter the complexion and condition of his spouse. But Christ doth. He takes us wallowing in our blood, deformed and defiled. He is such a husband as can put into his church his own disposition, and transform her into his own proportion. He is such a head as can quicken his members ; such a root as instils life into all his branches ; such a foundation as makes us living stones. There is a virtue and power in this husband above all.

Obj. But she is black.

Ans. She is so, indeed, and she confesseth herself to be so. 'I am black, but comely,' Cant. i. 5. (1.) Black in regard of the afflictions and persecutions of others she meets with in this world.

(2.) Black, again, in regard of scandals ; for the devil hates the church more than all societies in the world. Therefore, in the society of the church there are often more scandals than in other people ; as the apostle tells the Corinthians there was incest amongst them, the like was not among the heathen, 1 Cor. v. 1.

(3.) She is black through the envy of the world, that looks more at the church's faults than virtues.

(4.) The church is black and unlovely, nothing differing from others, in regard of God's outward dealing. 'All falls alike to all,' Eccles. ix. 2. They are sick and deformed. They have all things outwardly whatsoever in common with others.

(5.) Lastly and principally, she is black, in respect of her infirmities and weaknesses ; subject to weakness and passions, as other men. The beauty of the church is inward, and undiscerned to the carnal eye altogether. The Scribes and Pharisees see no virtue in Christ himself. It is said, 'that he came among his own, and his own could not discern of him : the darkness could not comprehend that light,' John i. 5, 11. Now, as it was with Christ, so it is much more with the church. Let this, then, be the use of it.

Use 2. *Oppose this state of the church to the false judgment of the world.* They see all black, and nothing else that is good. Christ sees that which is black, too ; but then his Spirit in them (together with the sight of their blackness) seeth their beauty, too. 'I am black, but comely,' &c. Be not discouraged, therefore, at the censure of the world. Blind men cannot judge of colours. It is said of Christ, 'he had no form or beauty in him, when we shall see him,' Isa. liii. 2. (1.) Not in outward glory, nor (2.) in the view of the world. If we be, therefore, thought to be black, we are no otherwise thought of than the church and Christ hath been before us.

Use 3. Again, let us make this use of it *against Satan in the time of temptation.* Doth Christ think us fair for the good we have ? Doth he not altogether value us by our ill ? and shall we believe Satan, who joins with the distempers of melancholy or weakness we are in (which he useth as a weapon against the soul), to make us think otherwise ? 'Satan is not only a murderer, but a liar from the beginning,' John viii. 44. We must not believe an enemy and a liar withal. But consider how Christ and the church judgeth, that have better discerning. And let us beware we be not Satans* to ourselves ; for if there were no devil, yet in the time of temptation and desertion we are subject to discouragement, to give false witness against ourselves. We are apt to look on the dark side of the cloud. The cloud that went before the Israelites had a double aspect, one dark, the other light, Exod. xiv. 20. In temptation we look on the dark side of the soul, and are witty in pleading against ourselves. Oh, but consider what Christ judgeth of us, 'O ! thou fairest among women ;' and what those about us that are learned, who can read our evidences better than we ourselves, do judge of us. Let us trust the judgment of others in time of temptation more than our own.

Use 4. Learn again here, *what to judge of the spirits of such kind of men as are all in disgracing and defacing the poor church.* Their table talk is of the infirmities of Christians. They light upon them as flies do upon sore places, and will see nothing that is good in them. Oh ! where is the Spirit of Christ, or of the church of Christ, in them that thus bescratch the face of the church ? when yet ofttimes their hearts tell them these poor despised ones will be better than themselves one day, for grace shall have the upper hand of all excellences.

The church is fair and fairest. Grace is a transcendent good. All the excellency of civility and morality is nothing to this. This denominates the church the fairest. She is not gilt, but pure gold ; not painted, but hath a true natural complexion. All other excellencies are but gilt, painted excellencies. 'The whore of Babylon,' she is wondrous fair ! But wherein doth her beauty consist ? In ornaments and ceremonies to abuse silly people that go no further than fancy. It is an excellency that comes not to the judgment, but the excellency of the church is otherwise. She is 'the fairest among women.' She hath a natural fairness. As gold is pure gold, so the church is of a pure composition, glorious within. It is for the false, whorish church to be glorious without only, but the true church is glorious within. But that which we should especially observe is, *that we should labour to answer this commendation ; not only to be fair, but the fairest ; to be transcendently, singularly good ; to do somewhat more than others can ; to have somewhat more in us than others have.*

For it is answerable to the state of a Christian. Is a Christian in an excellent rank above other men ? Let him shew it by a carriage more gracious, more fruitful and plentiful in good works. There is a kind of excellency affected in other things, much more should we desire to be excellent in that that is good, that we may not be fair only, but the fairest. This the apostle St Paul excellently presseth to Titus, his scholar, Tit. ii. 14,† and to all of us in other places, that we should be 'a peculiar people, zealous of good works,' not only to do them, but to be zealous of them, and to go before others in them, standing as standard-bearers. Therefore those that think they may go too far in religion, that they may be too fruitful, are not worthy the name of the spouse of Christ ; for she is fair, yea, the fairest among women, 'The righteous is more excellent than his neighbour,' Prov. xii. 26. Therefore we should excel in good works, as the apostle

* That is, 'accusers' or 'adversaries.'— G.

† 'Jesus Christ, who gave himself for us that he might redeem us from all iniquity, and purify unto himself a *peculiar* people.'

exhorts us, ' to labour after things that are excellent,' 1 Cor. xii. 31; 2 Pet. i. 8, as if he should say, Is there anything better than other, labour for that. You have some so far from this disposition that they cry down the excellencies of others, lest the fairness of others might discover their blackness. Thus we leave the compellation, and come to the question.

Quest. ' What is thy beloved more than another beloved ?' And they double it, ' What is thy beloved more than another beloved, that thou so chargest us ?'

Questions are of divers natures. We shall not stand upon them. This is not a question merely of ignorance, for they had some knowledge of Christ, though weak. Nor was it a curious nor a catching question, like those of the scribes and pharisees unto Christ, to instance in that of Pilate, ' What is truth ?' John xviii. 38, when Christ had told him the truth. ' What is truth ?' saith he, in a scornful, profane manner (*l*), as indeed profane spirits cannot hear savoury words, but they turn them off with scorn, ' What is truth ?' This here in the text is not such, but a question tending to further resolution and satisfaction, ' What is thy beloved more than another beloved ?'

First of all, observe that these of the church here were stirred up by the examples of other members of the church to be inquisitive after Christ, so to be satisfied. Hence observe *that there is a wondrous force in the examples of Christians to stir up one another.* We see here, when the church was sick of love, the other part of the members began to think, what is the reason the church is so earnest to seek after Christ ? There is some excellency sure in him. For wise men do not use great motions in little matters. Great things are carried with great movings. We use not to stir up tragedies for trifles, to make mountains of mole-hills. The endeavours and carriages of great persons that be wise, judicious, and holy are answerable to the nature of things. And indeed the church judgeth aright in this. Then see the force of good example. Any man that hath his wits about him, when he sees others serious, earnest, and careful about a thing, whereof for the present he can see no reason, especially if they have parts equal or superior to himself, will reason thus presently :—

What is the matter that such a one is so earnest, so careful, watchful, laborious, inquisitive ? It is not for want of wit; surely he hath parts enough, he understands himself well. And then he begins to think, sure I am too cold. Hereupon come competition and co-rivality,* surely I will be as good as he.

Use. Let us labour, therefore, to be exemplary to others, and to express the graces of God ; for thus we shall do more than we are aware. There is a secret influence in good example. Though a man say nothing, saith one, there is a way to profit from a good man though he hold his peace. His course of life speaks loud enough. We owe this to all, even to them that are without, to do them so much good as to give them a good example, and we wrong them when we do not, and hinder their coming on by an evil or a dead example.

Let this be one motive to stir us up to it, *that answerable to the good we shall do in this kind shall be our comfort in life and death, and our reward after death.* For the more spreading our good is either in word, life, or conversation, the more our consciences shall be settled in the consideration of a good life well spent, our reward shall be answerable to our communication and diffusion of good ; and whereas otherwise it will lie heavy on the

* That is, ' mutual emulation.'—G.

conscience, not only in this life, but at the day of judgment and after; when we shall think not only of the personal ill that we stand guilty of, but exemplary ill also.

It should move those therefore of inferior sort to look to all good examples, as the church here to the love of the other part of the church. Wherefore are examples among us but that we should follow them? We shall not only be answerable for abuse of knowledge, but also of good examples we have had and neglected. Doth God kindle lights for us, and shall not we walk by their light? It is a sin not to consider the sun, the moon, the stars, the heavens, and works of nature and providence, much more not to consider the works of grace. But one place of Scripture shall close up all, which is, Rom. xi. 11, that the example of us Gentiles at length shall stir up and provoke the Jews to believe. To those stiff-necked Jews example shall be so forcible that it shall prevail with them to believe and to be converted. If example be of such force as to convert the Jews that are so far off, how much more is it or should it be to convert Christians! Wondrous is the force of good example! So we come to the question itself,

' What is thy beloved more than another beloved?' &c.

We see there is excellent use of holy conference. The church coming to the daughters of Jerusalem, speaking of Christ her beloved, that she is ' sick of love,' &c., the daughters of Jerusalem are inquisitive to know Christ more and more. Here is the benefit of holy conference and good speeches. One thing draws on another, and that draws on another, till at length the soul be warmed and kindled with the consideration and meditation of heavenly things. That that is little in the beginning may bring forth great matters. This question to the church and talking with her, ' I charge you, if you find my beloved, to tell him that I am sick of love,' breeds questions in others, ' What is thy beloved?' &c. Whence, upon the description of her beloved, her heart is kindled, she findeth her beloved; so that talking of holy and heavenly things is good for others and ourselves also.

It is good for others, as it was good for the daughters of Jerusalem here; for thereupon they are stirred up to be inquisitive after Christ. And it was good for the church herself, for hereupon she took occasion to make a large commendation of Christ, wherein she found much comfort.

2. Good conference, then, is *good for ourselves;* for we see a little seed brings forth at length a great tree, a little fire kindleth much fuel, and great things many times rise out of small beginnings. It was a little occasion which Naaman the Assyrian* had to effect his conversion, 2 Kings v. 2. There was a poor banished woman, a stranger, who was a Jewish maid-servant. She told her lord's servants that there was a prophet in Jewry that could heal him, whereupon he came thither, and was converted and healed. And Paul sheweth that the very report of his bonds did a great deal of good in Cæsar's house, Philip. i. 13. Report and fame is a little matter, but little matters make way for the greater.

This may put us in mind *to spend our time fruitfully in good conference, when in discretion it is seasonable.* We know not, when we begin, where we may make an end. Our souls may be carried up to heaven before we are aware, for the Spirit will enlarge itself from one thing to another. ' To him that hath shall be given more and more still,' Mat. xiii. 12. God graciously seconds good beginnings. We see the poor disciples, when they were in a damp for the loss of Christ, after he comes, meets them, and talks of holy things. In that very conference their hearts were warmed and

* ' Syrian.'—ED.

kindled, Luke xxiv. 32. For, next to heaven itself, our meeting together here, it is a kind of paradise. The greatest pleasure in the world is to meet with those here whom we shall ever live with in heaven. Those who are good should not spend such opportunities fruitlessly.

And to this end, labour for the graces of the communion of saints; for there is such a state. We believe it as an article of our creed. How shall we approve ourselves to be such as have interest unto the communion of saints, unless we have spirits able to communicate good to others? pitiful and loving spirits, that we may speak a word in due season.

What a world of precious time is spent in idle conversing, as if the time were a burden, and no improvement to be made of the good parts of others. Sometimes, though we know that which we ask of others as well as they do, yet notwithstanding good speeches will draw us to know it better, by giving occasion to speak more of it, wherewith the Spirit works more effectually and imprints it deeper, so that it shall be a more rooted knowledge than before; for that doth good that is graciously known, and that is graciously known that the Spirit seals upon our souls. Perhaps the knowledge I have is not yet sealed sufficiently; it is not rooted by conference. Though I hear the same things again, yet I may hear them in a fresh manner, and so I may have it sealed deeper than before. Experience finds these things to be true.

Again, *we should labour here to have our hearts inquisitive.* The heathen man accounted it a grace in his scholar, and a sign that he would prove hopeful, because he was full of questions. Christians should be inquisitive of the ways of righteousness; inquisitive of the right path which leads to heaven; how to carry themselves in private, in their families; how in all estates; inquisitive of the excellency of Christ. ' What is thy beloved more than another beloved?' Questions end usually in resolutions; for the soul will not rest but in satisfaction. Rest is the happiness of the soul, as it were. When a question is moved, it will not be quiet till it have satisfaction. Therefore doubting at the first, breeds resolution at the last. It is good therefore to raise questions of the practice of all necessary points; and to improve the good parts and gifts of others that we converse with, to give satisfaction. What an excellent improvement is this of communion and company, when nothing troubles our spirit, but we may have satisfaction from others upon our proposing it. Perhaps God hath laid up in the parts of others, satisfaction to our souls; and hath so determined that we shall be perplexed and vexed with scruples, till we have recourse to some whom he hath appointed to be helpful to us in this kind. Many go mourning a great part of their days in a kind of sullenness this way, because that they do not open their estate to others. You see here the contrary practice of the church. She doubles the question : 'What is thy beloved more than another beloved, O thou fairest among women? what is thy beloved more than another beloved, that thou dost so charge us?

THE FOURTEENTH SERMON.

What is thy beloved more than another beloved, O thou fairest among women?
what is thy beloved more than another beloved, that thou dost so charge us?
My beloved is white and ruddy, the chiefest among ten thousand.—CANT.
V. 9, 10.

THE last time we met we left the church sick of love; which strange affec-

tion in her, together with her passionate charge to the daughters of
Jerusalem, moved them to make this question unto her, ' What is thy beloved more than another beloved,' &c.   To be in love is much ; to conceal
it is grievous ; to vent it with such fervency and passion breeds astonishment in these younger Christians, who wonder what that is which can so
draw away the church's love, and run away with her affections.   They knew
no such excellencies of the person the church so admired, and therefore
they double the question unto her, ' What is thy beloved?' &c. 'what is
thy beloved?' &c.   Whereby we see the excellency of the soul which aspires
still towards perfection ; not resting in any state inferior to the most excellent.   Therefore also is the church's sickness of love here, who desires
a nearer union and communion with Christ than she at this time had.

For there are degrees of spiritual languishing.   *Till we be in heaven we
are always under some degree of this sickness of love;* though the soul have
more communion at one time than at another.   Yea, the angels are under
this wish to see Christ, together with his church, in full perfection.   So
that until we be in heaven, where shall be a perfect reunion of soul and
body, and of all the members of the church together, there is a kind of
sickness attending upon the church and a languishing.

The question asked is,

' What is thy beloved more than another's beloved, O thou fairest among
women ?'

What! now fair when her veil was taken away ? now fair when the
watchmen abased* her? now fair when she was disgraced ?   Yes ; now fair,
and now fair in the sight of the daughters of Jerusalem, and in the sight
of Christ that calls her the fairest among women.   So that under all disgraces, infirmities, and scandals ; under all the shame that riseth in the
soul upon sin ; under all these clouds there is an excellency of the church.
She is, ' the fairest among women,' notwithstanding all these.   ' O thou
fairest among women.'

Quest. Whence comes this fairness, under such seeming foulness and
disgrace ?

Ans. It comes from without.   It is borrowed beauty, as you have it,
Ezek. xvi. 1, 2.   By nature we lie in our blood.   There must be a beauty
put upon us.   We are fair with the beauty that we have out of Christ's
wardrobe.   The church shines in the beams of Christ's righteousness ;
she is not born thus fair, but new-born fairer.   The church of Christ is all
glorious, but it is within, not seen of the world, Ps. xlv. 13.   She hath a
life, but it is a hidden life, ' our glory and our life is hidden in Christ,'
Col. iii. 3.   It is hid sometimes from the church itself, who sees only her
deformity and not her beauty, her death but not her life, because her ' life
is hid.'   Here is a mystery of religion, *The church is never more fair than
when she judgeth herself to be most deformed; never more happy than when
she judgeth herself to be miserable: never more strong than when she feels herself to be weak; never more righteous than when she feels herself to be most
burdened with the guilt of her own sins,* because the sense of one contrary
forceth to another.   The sense of ill forceth us to the fountain of good, to
have supply thence.   ' When I am weak, then am I strong,' saith Paul,
2 Cor. xii. 10.   Grace and strength is perfect in weakness.

Use. This should teach us what to judge of the church and people of
God ; even under their seeming disgraces, yet to judge of them as the excellentest people in the world, 'All my delight is in those that are ex-

* Qu. ' abused?'—G.

cellent,' Ps. xvi. 3; to join ourselves to them. Especially this is here to be understood of the church, as it is the mystical body of Christ; not as a mixed body, as a visible church, 'but as it is the temple of the Holy Ghost,' 1 Cor. iii. 17.

The visible church hath terms of excellency put upon it sometimes, but it is in regard of the better part. As gold unrefined is called gold, because gold is the better part; and a heap of wheat unwinnowed is called wheat, though there be much chaff in it. The body of Christ itself hath always excellent terms given it, ' O thou fairest among women.'

Those that look upon the church with the spectacles of malice can see no such beauty in her, though to espy out faults (as the devil could in Job, Job i. 9, seq.), to quarrel, to slander, they are quick-sighted enough. But we see here the church in the judgment of the ' daughters of Jerusalem,' that she is the 'fairest among women.'

The papists have a painted beauty for their catholic church, but here is no such beauty. It becomes a whore to be painted to be as fair as her hands can make her, with feigned beauty. But the church of Christ hath a beauty from her husband, a real, spiritual beauty, not discerned of the world.

Use. This should be of use to God's children themselves, *to help them in the upbraidings of conscience* (as if they had no goodness in them), *because they have a great deal of ill.* Christians should have a double eye, one to set and fix upon that which is ill in them, to humble them; and another upon that which is supernaturally gracious in them, to encourage themselves. They should look upon themselves as Christ looks upon them, and judge of themselves as he judgeth of them, by the better part. He looks not so much what ill we have, for that shall be wrought out by little and little, and be abolished. It is condemned already, and it shall be executed by little and little, till it be wholly abolished. But he looks upon us in regard of the better part. So should we look upon ourselves, though otherwhiles upon our black feet (our infirmities) when we are tempted to pride and haughtiness. But always let the mean thoughts we conceive of ourselves make us to fly to Christ.

' What is thy beloved more than another beloved?'

Here is a question, and a question answered with a question. Questions they breed knowledge; as the Greek proverb is, doubtings breed resolution. Whereupon the inquisitive soul usually proves the most learned, judicious, and wise soul. Therefore that great philosopher* counted it as a virtue amongst his scholars that they would be inquisitive. So the scholars of righteousness are inquisitive, ' They inquire the way to Canaan, and the way to Zion with their faces thitherwards,' Jer. l. 5.

It is a special part of Christians' wisdom to improve the excellency of others by questions; to have a bucket to draw out of the deep wells of others. As Solomon saith, ' The heart of a wise man is as deep waters, but a man of understanding can tell how to fetch those waters out.' There be many men of deep and excellent parts which are lost in the world, because men know not how to improve them. Therefore it is good, while we have men excellent in any kind, to make use of them. It is an honour to God as well as a commodity to ourselves. Doth God suffer lights to shine in the world that we should take no notice of them? It is a wrong to ourselves and a dishonour to God.

' What is thy beloved more than another beloved?' &c.

A further point from hence is, *that if we would give encouragement to others*

* That is, Socrates in Plato's ' Dialogues.'—G.

to repair to us for any good, we should learn to be so excellent as to adorn religion.

' O thou fairest among women, what is thy beloved ?' &c.   They inquire of her, because they have a good conceit of her.   A world of good might be done if there were bred a good conceit of men in others.   We say in sickness, A good conceit of the physician is half the cure.   So in teaching, a good conceit of the teacher is half the learning.   ' The daughters of Jerusalem' had a good conceit here in their questioning of the church.   ' O thou fairest among women, what is thy beloved more than another beloved ?'

Let us labour, therefore, to be such as may bring honour and credit to religion, and make it lovely ; that what we do may make others think we do what we do to great purpose ; which is ofttimes a special means and occasion of their conversion.   Though properly the cause of conversion be the Spirit of God in the ordinances, yet the inducement, many times, and occasion, is the observation of the course and carriage of those that excel and are known to be eminent in parts and in graces.   Emulation adds spurs to the soul.   Do they take such courses that are wiser than I, and shall not I take the like course too ?   Paul saith, the emulation of the Gentiles shall be a means of the conversion of the Jews, Rom. xi. 11. When they shall see them embrace Christ, they will be encouraged to do so also.   What shall we think, therefore, of them that live so as that they bring an evil report, scandal, and reproach upon religion ?   Great and fearful is their wickedness, that by their ill conversation, like Hophni and Phinehas, discredit the ordinances of the Lord, 1 Sam. ii. 17.

Now the church thus answers the former question touching Christ, ' My beloved is white and ruddy, the chiefest of ten thousand.'   She is not afraid to set out her beloved's beauty ; for there is no envy in spiritual things. It is want of wisdom amongst men to commend a thing that is very lovely to others, and so to set an edge upon their affections when they cannot both share ; and the more one hath, the less another hath of all things here below.   But in spiritual things there is no envy at the sharing of others in that we love ourselves, because all may be loved alike.   Christ hath grace and affection enough for all his.   He hath not, as Esau speaks, but ' one blessing.'   No, he can make all his happy.   Therefore the church stands not upon terms.   When the ' daughters of Jerusalem' inquire about her beloved, I tell you freely, says she, what my beloved is.   First, in general, the answer is, ' My beloved is white and ruddy, the chiefest among ten thousand.' Then afterwards there is a specification of the particulars.   She will not stand upon the gross, but admires* at every parcel in the thing beloved. Every thing is lovely, as we shall see in particulars afterwards.

' My beloved is white and ruddy, the chiefest among ten thousand.'

We will take that which is safe, because we will have sure footing, as near as we can, in this mystical portion of Scripture.

Quest. What is that white and ruddy ?   Why doth the church set forth the spiritual excellencies of Christ by that which is most outwardly excellent and most beautiful ?

Ans. Because of all complexions, the mixed complexion of these two colours, white and ruddy, is the purest and the best.   Therefore she sets out the beauty and the spiritual excellency of Christ by this ' white and ruddy.'   Beauty ariseth of the mixture of these two.   First, she sets out the beauty of Christ positively ; and then, by way of comparison, ' the chiefest among ten thousand.

* That is, ' wonders.'—G.

But what is this white and ruddy ? what is beauty ?

1. To the making of beauty there is required a sound, healthy constitution, so as *the particulars have a due proportion*. There must be a harmony of the parts, one suiting with one another ; for comeliness stands in oneness, when many things, as it were, are one. Uncomeliness is in diversity, when diverse things are jumbled together that belong to many heads ; as we say it is uncomely to have an old man's head on a young man's shoulders. But when all things are so suited that they make one, agreeing exactly, there is beauty and comeliness.

2. Besides soundness of constitution and comeliness of proportion, *there is a grace of colour* that maketh beauty, which ariseth out of the other. So that soundness and goodness of constitution, together with the exact proportion of the variety of parts, having with it this gracefulness of colour and complexion, makes up that which we call beauty. In a word, then, this carnation colour, white and ruddy, may be understood of that excellent and sweet mixture that makes such a gracefulness in Christ. In him there is wonderful purity and holiness, and yet a wonderful weakness. There is God the ' great God' and a piece of earth, of flesh in one person; a bloody, pierced, and a glorious shining body ; humility and glory : justice, wonderful justice, and yet exceeding love and mercy : justice to his enemies, mercy to his children.

Obs. Christ is a most beautiful person, not as God only, but as man, the Mediator, God and man. The person of the Mediator is a beautiful person, as Ps. xlv. 2, there is a notable description of Christ and of his church, ' Thou art fairer than the children of men, grace is poured into thy lips,' &c.

But the loveliness and beauty of Christ *is especially spiritual*, in regard of the graces of his Spirit. A deformed person, man or woman, of a homely complexion and constitution, yet, notwithstanding, when we discern them by their conversation to be very wise and of a lovely and sweet spirit, very able and withal wondrous willing to impart their abilities, being wondrous useful ; what a world of love doth it breed, though we see in their outward man nothing lovely ? The consideration of what sufficiency is in Christ, wisdom, power, goodness, and love, that made him come from heaven to earth, to take our nature upon him, to marry us, and join our nature to his (that he might join us to him in spiritual bonds) : the consideration of his meekness and gentleness, how he never turned any back again that came to him, should make us highly prize him. Indeed some went back of themselves (as the young man in discontent, Mat. xix. 32), Christ turned them not back ; nay, he loved the appearance of goodness in the young man, and embraced him. He is of so sweet a nature that he never upbraided those that followed him with their former sins, as Peter with denial, and the like. He is of so gracious a nature that he took not notice of petty infirmities in his disciples, but tells them of the danger of those sins that might hurt them : being of so sweet a nature that ' he will not quench the smoking flax, nor break the bruised reed,' Isa. xlii. 3 ; his whole life being nothing but a doing of good, ' he did all things well' (as the gospel speaks), excellent well, Mark vii. 37.

Now, the consideration of what a gracious Spirit is in Christ, must needs be a loadstone of love, and make him beautiful. Therefore Bernard saith well, When I think of Christ, I think at once of God, full of majesty and glory ; and, at the same time, of man, full of meekness, gentleness, and sweetness. So, let us consider of Christ as of the ' mighty God,' powerful ; and withal consider of him as a gentle and mild man, that came riding meekly on an ass, as the Scripture sets him out,' Mat. xxi. 5. He was for comers, and gave entertainment to all : ' Come unto me, all ye that are weary and heavy laden,' &c., Mat. xi. 28. For the most weak and miserable person of all had the sweetest entertainment of him, ' He came to seek and to save that which was lost,' Luke xix. 10. Let us, I say, think of him both as of the great God, and withal as of meek man : the one to establish our souls, that he is able to do great matters ; the other to draw us to him because he loves us. We are afraid to go to God, ' a consuming fire,' Heb. xii. 29 ; but now let us think we go to bone of our bone and flesh of our flesh, to our brother, to one that out of his goodness abased himself of purpose that we might be one with him : who loved us more than his own life, and was contented to carry the curse for us, that we might be blessed of God for ever, and to suffer a most painful and shameful death, that so he might make us heirs of everlasting life.

Christ is spiritually lovely, ' the chiefest of ten thousand.' The church sets him out by comparison, ' a standard-bearer,' a carrier of the ' banner of ten thousand.' For, as the goodliest men use to carry the ensign, the banner ; so he, the goodliest of all other, is the standard-bearer.

Obs. Whence we gather, *that Christ, as he is beautiful and good, so he is incomparably, beyond all comparison good ;* ' He is a standard bearer, one among ten thousand ; anointed with the oil of gladness above his fellows,' Ps. xlv. 7.

First, *for that he is so near to God by the personal union.*

And in regard likewise, *that all others have all from him.* Of his fulness we receive grace for grace, John i. 16. Ours is but a derivative fulness. His glory and shining is as the shining of the body of the sun ; ours as the light of the air, which is derived from the glory of the sun. Ours is but the fulness of the stream, and of the vessel, but the fulness of the fountain and of the spring is his. Thereupon he is called ' the head of the church,' Col. i. 18 ; the head is the tower of the body which hath all the five senses in it, and wisdom for the whole body. It seeth, heareth, understandeth, and doth all for the body; having influence into the other parts of it. So Christ is above all, and hath influence into all his church, not only eminence, but influence.

What is excellent in the heavens ? The sun. So Christ is the ' Sun of righteousness,' Mal. iv. 2. The stars. He is the ' bright morning star,' Rev. xxii. 16. The light. He is the ' light of the world,' John ix. 5. Come to all creatures ; you have not any excellent amongst them but Christ is styled from it. He is ' the lion of the tribe of Judah,' Rev. v. 5, the ' lily,' Cant. ii. 1, and the ' rose,' Cant. ii. 1, and ' the Lamb of God that taketh away the sins of the world,' John i. 29, ' the tree of Life,' &c., Rev. xxii. 2. There is not a thing necessary to nature, but you have a style from it given to Christ, to shew that he is as necessary as bread and water, and the food of life, John vi. 35 ; John iv. 14. When we see light, therefore, think of the ' true light,' John ix. 5. When the sun, think of the ' Sun of righteousness,' Mal. iv. 2. So remember ' the bread and water of life,' in our common food. Therefore the sacraments were ordained, that as we go to the sea by the conduct of rivers, so we might go to the sea of all excellency and goodness by the conduct of these rivers of goodness, to be led by every excellency in the creature, to that of our mediator Christ, who is ' the chiefest among ten thousand.'

To come more particularly to speak of his excellencies, omitting his two natures in one person, God and man ; that we may consider his offices, a king, priest and prophet. He being the chief in all these, so all good kings before him were types of him, as also the prophets and priests. He was all in one. Never any before him was king, priest, and prophet, as he was king, priest, and prophet in one. So in every respect he was incomparable above all.

1. *Such a king, as is king of kings;* and subdueth things unconquerable to all other kings, even the greatest enemies of all; such a king as conquered the world, death, hell, and sin, all things that are terrible. Death you know is called ' the king of fears,* because it terrifieth even kings themselves. Christ is such a king as takes away these terrible greatest ills of all; such a king as rules over the soul and conscience, the best part of man, where he settles and stablisheth peace; such a king as sets up his kingdom in our very souls and hearts, guides our thoughts, desires, actions, and affections, setting up a peaceable government there. So he is an incomparable king even in regard of that office. ' He is the chiefest of ten thousand;' such a king as carries the government upon his own shoulders, as it is Isa. ix. 6. He devolves not the care to another, to make it as he list and so be a cypher himself, but he carries all upon his own shoulder. He needs not a pope for his vicar.

2. Again, as a *priest, such a high priest as offered himself a sacrifice by his* eternal Spirit. He as God offered up his manhood. Such a priest as hath satisfied the wrath of God, and reconciled God to man. All other priests were but types of this priest, who is such a priest as never dies, ' but lives for ever to make intercession for us in heaven,' by virtue of that sacrifice which he offered in the days of his flesh. He was both priest and sacrifice. Such a ' priest as is touched with our infirmities ;' so mild and gentle, full of pity and mercy. No priest to this priest. God only smelt a sweet smell from this sacrifice.

3. And for his *prophetical office, he is a prophet beyond all others.* Such a one as can instruct the soul. Other men can propound doctrines, but he can open the understanding, and hath the key of the heart, the ' key of David which can open the soul,' Luke xxiv. 45. By his Holy Spirit he can make the very simple full of knowledge, Prov. i. 4. Such a prophet as hath his chair in the very heart of man ; this great ' Bishop of our souls,' 1 Pet. ii. 25, ' the Angel of the covenant,' that Λογὸς, ' the messenger of the Father.' So he is ' the chief of ten thousand,' consider him as king, as priest, or as prophet.

Use. The use of this is exceeding pregnant, comfortable, and large, that we have such a Saviour, such an eminent person, so near, so peculiar to us. Our beloved, my beloved. If he were *a* ' beloved, the chief of ten thousand,' it were no great matter, but he is mine. He is thus excellent; excellent considered with propriety in it, and a peculiar propriety.† Peculiarity and propriety, together with transcendent excellency, makes happy if there be any enjoying of it. Therefore repent not yourselves of your repentings, but think I have not cast away my love, but have set it upon such an object as deserves it, ' for my beloved is the chiefest of ten thousand.'

---

* Cf. Job. xviii. 14.—G　　　　　　† That is, 'property'= right.—G.

THE FIFTEENTH SERMON.

My beloved is white and ruddy, the chiefest among ten thousand.—CANT. V. 10.

LOVE is such a boundless affection, that where it once breaks forth in praises upon a good foundation, it knows no measure; as we see here in the church, who being provoked and, as it were, exasperated by the ' daughters of Jerusalem' to explain the excellency of him she had with so much affection incessantly sought after, that she might justify her choice (ere she descend into particulars), she breaks forth into this general description of her beloved; whereby she cuts off from all hopes of equalling him, ' My beloved is white and ruddy' (exceeding fair), nay, ' the chief among ten thousand' (none like him). She would not have us think she had bestowed her love but on the most excellent of all, ' the chief of ten thousand.' Well were it for us that we could do so in our love, that we might be able to justify our choice; not to spend it on sinful, vain, and unprofitable things, which cause repentance and mourning in the conclusion, whereof the church here worthily cleareth herself; in that she had chosen ' the chief among ten thousand.'

And most justly did she place her affections upon so excellent an object, who was so full of ' all the treasures of wisdom and knowledge, the life of our life, in whom dwelt all the fulness of the Godhead bodily,' Col. i. 11, 19; in whom was a gracious mixture and compound of all heavenly graces; where greatness and goodness, justice and mercy, God and man, meet in one person. Such an one who breaks no ' bruised reed, nor quenches the smoking flax,' Mat. xii. 20, who refuses not sinners, but invites them unto him, offering to heal all and cure all who come unto him. He is a king indeed, John xviii. 37. But this also approves her choice; he rules all, commands all, judges all. What then can she want who hath such a friend, such a husband? whose government is so winning, mild, and merciful?

He is not such a monarch as loves to get authority by sternness, like Rehoboam, 1 Kings xii. 12, but by those amiable graces of gentleness and love. All the excellencies of holiness, purity, and righteousness, are sweetly tempered with love and meekness in him. You may see, for instance, how he takes his disciples' part against the Pharisees, and the poor woman's that came to wash his feet and kissed them, against the Pharisee that had invited him to dinner, Luke vii. 44. The church is a company of despised people, that are scorned of Pharisaical proud spirits; who perhaps have morality and strength of parts to praise them with. Now Christ takes part with the broken spirits, against all proud spirits. Howsoever he be gone to heaven (where he is full of majesty), yet he hath not forgotten his meekness nor changed his nature, with change of honour. He is now more honoured than he was, for ' he hath a name above all names, in heaven or in earth,' Acts iv. 12; yet he is pitiful still. ' Saul, Saul, why persecutest thou me?' Acts ix. 4. He makes the church's case his own still. Together with beams of glory, there are bowels of pity in him, the same that he had here upon earth; which makes him so lovely to the truly brokenhearted, believing soul, ' My beloved is white and ruddy.'

He is set out likewise by comparing him with all others whatsoever, ' He is the chief of ten thousand;' a certain number for an uncertain, that is, the chief among all. In all things Christ hath the pre-eminence. ' He is the first-born from the dead,' Rom. viii. 29; ' he is the first-born of every creature,' Col.

i. 15; he is the eldest brother; he is the chief among all. For all kings, priests, and prophets before were but types and shadows of him. He, the body, the truth, and the substance. And (as was shewed before) he is all three in one, king, priest, and prophet; the great doctor* and prophet of his church, that spake by all the former prophets, and speaks by his ministers to the end of the world. 'The angel of the covenant,' that Λογὸς, the Word, that expresseth his Father's breast; that as he came from the bosom of his Father, so lays open his counsel to mankind. It was he that spake by Noah, and preached by his Spirit to the souls that are now in prison, as Peter speaks, 1 Pet. iii. 19. So, 'he is the chief among all.' But especially in regard of his righteousness; for which Paul 'accounted all dung and dross, to be found in Christ, not having his own righteousness, but the righteousness that is in Christ,' Phil. iii. 8; which is more than the righteousness of an angel, being the righteousness of God-man, and above all the righteousness of the law.

Quest. But what is this to us or to the church?

Ans. Yes; for his beauty and excellency is the church's, because he is the church's. 'My beloved is white and ruddy, and my beloved is the chief among ten thousand.' It is the peculiar interest that the church hath in Christ that doth relish her spirit; excellency with propriety in him; 'I am my beloved's, and my beloved is mine.' The more excellent the husband is, the more excellent is the wife. She only shines in his beams. Therefore it is the interest that we have in Christ that endears Christ to us. But to come to more particular application of it. Is Christ thus excellent, super-excellent, thus transcendently excellent, 'white and ruddy,' the chief of ten thousand?' This serves,

1. *To draw those that are not yet in Christ unto him.*
2. *To comfort those that are in Christ.*

Use 1. First, those that are not yet in Christ, not contracted to him, to draw them; *what can prevail more than that which is in Christ?* Beauty and excellencies, greatness and goodness. And indeed one main end of our calling, the ministry, is, to lay open and unfold the unsearchable riches of Christ; to dig up the mine, thereby to draw the affections of those that belong to God to Christ.

Use 2. But it is not enough to know that there are excellencies in Christ to draw us to him, but, *there must be a sight of our misery; what beggars we are, and how indebted.* Before we are in Christ we are not our own. The devil lays claim to us that we are his; death lays claim to us. We are under sin; we cannot satisfy one of a thousand; therefore this enforceth to make out to join with him that can discharge all our debts, answer all our suits, and non-suit Satan in the court of heaven. When once we are married to the Lord of heaven and earth, all is ours. We have a large charter, 'All things are yours, and you are Christ's, and Christ is God's,' 1 Cor iii. 22, 23.

Quest. Why are all things ours?

Ans. *Because we are married to Christ, who is Lord of all.* It is the end of our calling to sue for a marriage between Christ and every soul. We are the friends of the bride, to bring the church to him; and the friends of the church, to bring Christ to them. It is the end of our ministry to bring the soul and Christ together; and let no debts, no sins hinder. For especially he invites such as are sensible of their sins. 'Where sin abounds, grace abounds much more,' Rom. v. 20. 'Come unto me, all ye that are

* That is, 'teacher.'—G.

weary and heavy laden,' Mat. xi. 28. And, ' he came to seek and to save
that which was lost,' Luke xix. 10. He requires no more, but that we be
sensible of our debts and miseries, which sense he works likewise by his
Holy Spirit.

Use 3. Again, for those that have entertained Christ, *let them see what an
excellent gracious person they have entertained,* who is ' the chief of ten
thousand.' The world thinks them a company of silly, mean people, that
make choice of Christ, religion, the word, and such things; but there is a
justification of their choice. They choose him that is ' the chief of ten
thousand.' ' Let him kiss me with the kisses of his mouth,' saith the
spouse, ' for thy love is better than wine, nay, than life itself,' Cant. i. 2.
A Christian must justify the choice that he hath made with Mary ' of the
good part,' Luke x. 42 ; against all those that shall disparage his choice.
Let the world account Christians what they will; that they are a company
of deluded, besotted persons, fools and madmen ; the Christian is the only
wise man. Wisdom is seen in choice especially ; and here is the choice of
that which is excellent and most excellent of all, ' the chief of ten thousand.'

Use 4. So also, *we may see here the desperate and base folly of all whatsoever,* save true Christians. What do they make choice of to join to ? that
which is base, the condemned world, vain, transitory things; and refuse
Christ. Are they in their right wits who refuse a husband that is noble for
birth, rich for estate, mighty for power, abundant in kindness and love
itself, every way excellent, and take a base, ignoble, beggarly person ? This
is the choice of the world. God complains, ' Israel would none of me,'
&c., Ps. lxxxi. 11. What shall we judge therefore of those that will none
of Christ when he woos and sues them ; but prefer with Esau a ' mess of
pottage,' before their eternal birthright, Heb. xii. 16 ; with Adam, an apple
before paradise ; and with Judas, thirty pieces of silver before Christ himself. This is the state of many men. To be married to Christ is to take
him for an husband ; to be ruled by him in all things. Now when we prefer base commodities and contentments before peace of conscience and the
enjoying of his love—what is it, but for pelf and commodity, thirty pieces
of silver (perhaps for sixpence, a thing of nothing), to refuse Christ. Yet
this is the condition of base worldlings that live by sense and not by faith.
So then as it serves to comfort those that have made a true choice ; so it
serves to shew the madness and folly of all others, which one day will feel
their hearts full of horror and confusion, and their faces of shame, when
they shall think, What? hath Christ made such suit to my heart to win my
love ? hath he ordained a ministry for to bring me in ? made such large
promises ? is he so excellent ? and was this discovered to me, and yet would
I none of him ? what did I choose, and what did I leave ? I left Christ
with all his riches, and made choice of the ' pleasures and profits of sin,
which are but for a season,' Heb. xi. 25. When the conscience is once
thoroughly awaked, this will torment it,—the punishment of loss, not of loss
simply, as the loss of Christ and the loss of heaven, but the loss of Christ and
of heaven so discovered and opened. Therefore there is no condition in the
world so terrible as of those that live in the church, and hear those things
of Christ crucified unfolded to them before their eyes. As Paul speaks of
the ministry, it makes Christ's cross so open to them as if he had been
crucified before their eyes, Gal. iii. 1. Yet notwithstanding [they] yield to
their base heart's desires and affections before these excellencies ; which if
they had a spirit of faith would draw their hearts to him.

Therefore let us consider how we hear those things. It concerns us

nearly. On the one side we see what we get if we join with Christ; we
have him and his. On the contrary, we lose him; and not only so, but
we gain eternal misery, and perish eternally. O what baseness of mind
possesseth us! Christ left all things in love to us, and we leave Christ for
any paltry thing in the world; almost to please and content the humours
of sinful men, to attain a few empty titles, to get a little wealth, enjoy a
little pleasure. You see then the equity of that terrible commination* that
you have, 'If any man love not the Lord Jesus Christ, let him be Anathema
Maran-atha,' 1 Cor. xvi. 22. Let him be accursed for ever that loves not
the Lord Jesus Christ. If any man sin there is a remedy to discharge his
sin in Jesus Christ, if he will marry him and take him; but when Christ is
offered and we will have none of him, we sin against the gospel; and then
there is no remedy; there is nothing but 'Anathema and Maran-atha.'
Therefore the most dangerous sins of all, are those against the light of the
gospel; when yet we choose rather to live as we list, than to join ourselves
to Christ. To this purpose, Heb. ii., St Paul makes an use of the first
chapter, wherein he sets out the excellency of Christ, whom the angels
adore. He is so beautiful, so lovely that God the Father is in love with
him, and pronounceth, 'This is my beloved Son,' Mat. iii. 17. In the beginning of the second chapter, 'Wherefore,' saith he, 'how shall we escape
if we neglect so great salvation; for if they escaped not that despised Moses'
law, &c., how shall we escape if we neglect so great salvation?' Heb. ii. 3.
He says not, if we oppose Christ, but if we neglect him, if we do not love
so great salvation; as 2 Thess. i. 8, it is said, 'Christ will come in flaming
fire to take vengeance of all those that do not know God, and obey not the
gospel of Christ,' though they do not persecute it.

Use 1. Therefore this *reproves all civil, moral persons that think they have
riches enough.* Not only debauched persons, but self-sufficient persons, that
think they have any righteousness of their own. Let them know that
'Christ shall come in flaming fire, to take vengeance of such.' This is the
scope of the second psalm, which ye know sets out the excellency of Christ,
'I have set my king upon Zion,' Ps. ii. 6. God the Father there anoints
Christ king of the church. To what end? 'That we should kiss the Son,'
kiss him with the kiss of subjection, as subjects do their prince; with the
kiss of love, as the spouse doth her husband; and with the kiss of faith.
But what if we do not kiss him, and subject ourselves to him, love him,
and believe in him? 'If his wrath be once kindled, happy are all those
that trust in him.' He is a lamb, but such a one as can be angry. It is
said, 'The kings and great persons of the world fly from the wrath of the
Lamb,' Rev. vi. 16. He that is so sweet, mild, and gentle, if we join with
him, on the contrary, if we come not unto him, we shall find the wrath of
the Lamb a terrible wrath, which the greatest potentates in the world shall
desire to be hid from. 'If his wrath be once kindled, blessed are all those
that trust in him,' and woe be to them that do not receive him.

Use 2. For us that profess ourselves to be in Christ, and to be joined to
him that is thus excellent, let us make this use, *to make him the rule of our
choice in other things.* In the choice of friends, choose such as are friends
to Christ. Take heed of society with idolaters, or with profane, wretched
persons. If you will be joined to Christ, and profess yourselves to be so,
then let us join to none but those that we can enjoy and Christ too. So
in marriage, let the rule of choice be the love of Christ. And likewise, let
the measure of our respect to all things be the respect to Christ. Let us

* That is, 'denunciation, threatening.'—G.

measure our love to wife and children, to kindred, friends, and to all creatures whatsoever, as it may stand with love to Christ. Obey in the Lord, marry in the Lord, do all things in the Lord, so as may stand with the love and allowance of the Lord, 1 Cor. vii. 39, 40.

Use 3. Make also a use of direction, *how to come to value Christ thus,* as to keep an high esteem of him. For this follows infallibly and undeniably, if Christ be 'the chief of ten thousand,' he must have the chief of our affections 'above ten thousand.' For, as he is in excellency, he must have place in our hearts answerable thereunto; for then our souls are as they should be, when they judge of, and affect things as they are in themselves.

1. First, let us enter into a serious consideration *of the need we have of Christ, of our misery without him, of our happiness if we be joined with him.* The soul being thus convinced, the affections must needs follow the sanctified judgment.

What will come of it if Christ be set in the highest place in our heart? If we crown him there, and make him 'King of kings and Lord of lords,' in a hearty submitting of all the affections of the soul to him? While the soul continues in that frame it cannot be drawn to sin, discomfort, and despair. The honours, pleasures, and profits that are got by base engagements to the humours of men, what are these to Christ? When the soul is rightly possessed of Christ and of his excellency, it disdains that anything should come in competition with him.

2. Again, *it stands firm against all discouragements whatsoever:* for it sets Christ against all, who is the 'chief of ten thousand.' The soul in this case will set Christ against the anger and wrath of God, against Satan, and all our spiritual enemies. Christ is the angel of the covenant. Satan is a lion, a roaring lion; Christ the lion of the tribe of Judah. Satan a serpent, a dragon; but Christ, the true brazen serpent, the very looking upon whom will take away all the stings and fiery darts of Satan whatsoever. Wherefore it is said, 1 John v. 4, that faith is that that 'overcometh the world.' How doth faith overcome the world? Because it overcomes all things in the world, as, on the right hand, pleasures and profits and honours, and on the left hand, threatenings, pains, losses, and disgraces, by setting Christ against all.

3. Again, if we would have a right judgment and esteem of Christ, *let us labour to wean our affections as much as may be from other things.* Fleshly hearts that have run so deeply into the world, and vanities of this present life, it is in a sort an extraordinary task for them to be drawn away and pulled from the world, as a child from a full breast, which they have sucked so long. Now, for sweet affections that are tender, it is an excellent advantage they have to consider betimes that there is that in religion and in the gospel which is worth their best and prime affections, the flower and marrow of them. Let them begin, with young Timothy, 2 Tim. iii. 15, Daniel, and Joseph, to love Christ from their childhood. It is a desperate folly, on the other hand, to put off the regard of good things till after, when we shall be less fit, when the understanding will be darkened, and the affections blunted, when we shall not have that edge, nature being decayed, and the world having taken such possession of the soul that we shall not value this excellency. Therefore let us begin betimes to make up the marriage between Christ and the soul. No time, indeed, is too late, but it were to be wished that those that are young would be thus wise for their souls betimes.

4. Besides, if we would highly value Christ, *beg of God a spirit that we*

*may judge aright of our corruptions, for in what measure we can discern the
height, and breadth, and depth of our corrupt nature, in that measure shall
we judge of the height, and breadth, and depth of the excellency of Christ.*
The sweetest souls are the most humble souls. Those that love Christ
most are those that have been stung most with the sense of their sins.
Where sin most abounds in the sense and feeling of it, grace much more
abounds in the sense and feeling of that, Rom. v. 20. Did ever soul love
Christ more than that woman that had so many devils cast out of her?
Luke viii. 2. And Paul, that had such great sins forgiven? Doth any
man so love his creditor as he that hath much debt forgiven him? It is
our Saviour Christ's own reason. Therefore these two go always with the
true church. 1. The true knowledge of the corruption of nature, and
misery by reason of it; and 2. The true sense and feeling of it, with true
and hearty sorrow for it, &c. In popery they slight original sin, that
mother, breeding sin. Actual sins be venial, and many sins no sins. And
therefore they esteem so slightly of Christ that they join saints, the pope,
works and satisfaction with him. Because they know not the depth of the
malady, how black sin is, what a cursed estate we are in by nature, they
have slight, shallow, and weak conceits of sin. Therefore they have answerable weak and shallow conceits of Christ and of his righteousness and
excellency. Therefore the conviction of our sins goeth before the conviction
of righteousness in Christ, as it is said, ' The Holy Ghost shall convince
the world of sin and then of righteousness,' John xvi. 8. For except the
soul be convinced of sin, and of ill in itself, it will never be truly convinced
of good and of righteousness in Christ.

The Passover was always eaten with sour herbs, because it should add a
relish to the feast. So Christ, the true Passover, we never relish truly
without sour herbs, the consideration of sin, with the desert of it. Christ
savours otherwise to a man humbled for his sins than he doth to another
man not touched therewith; otherwise to a poor man than he doth to a
rich; otherwise to a man that the world goes not well on his side than to
a prosperous man. One savoury discourse of Christ relisheth more to an
afflicted soul than seven discourses with such as are drunk with prosperity,
not having a brain strong enough to conceive, nor an appetite to relish
heavenly things.

Therefore why do we murmur at the cross, when all is to recover our
spiritual taste and relish? Solomon had lost his taste and relish of Christ.
He never made his song of songs when he was in his idolatrous way, nor
was so in love with Christ and his excellencies when he doted so much
upon his wives. No; but when he had recovered his spirit's taste and
relish of heavenly things once, then made he the book of the preacher.
When he had run through variety of things, and saw all to be nothing but
vexation of spirit, and besides that vanity, then he passeth his verdict upon
all things, that they were vanity. So it is with us, we can hardly prize
Christ without some afflictions, some cross or other. Therefore here the
church is fain to endure a spiritual desertion, to set an edge upon her
affections. Now, when she is thus in her desertions, ' Christ is white and
ruddy, the chief of ten thousand.'

We value more, and set a higher price on things in the want of them—
such is our corruption—than in the enjoying of them. And if God remember us not with affliction, then let us afflict, humble, and judge ourselves;
enter into our own souls, to view how we stand affected to Christ, to heaven,
and to heavenly things. How do I relish and esteem them? If I have

lost my esteem and valuing, where have I lost it ? Consider in what sin, in what pleasure, in what company I lost it ; and converse no more with such as dull our affections to heavenly things.

4. And *let us make use likewise of our infirmities and sins to this purpose, to set an high price on the excellencies of Christ.* We carry about us always infirmities and corruptions. What use shall we make of them ? Not to trust to our own righteousness, which is ' as a defiled cloth,' Isa. lxiv. 6, but fly to Christ's righteousness, which is the righteousness of God-man, all being as dung and dross in regard of that. Often think with thyself, What am I? a poor sinful creature; but I have a righteousness in Christ that answers all. I am weak in myself, but Christ is strong, and I am strong in him. I am foolish in myself, but I am wise in him. What I want in myself I have in him. He is mine, and his righteousness is mine, which is the righteousness of God-man. Being clothed with this, I stand safe against conscience, hell, wrath, and whatsoever. Though I have daily experience of my sins, yet there is more righteousness in Christ, who is mine, and who is the chief of ten thousand, than there is sin in me. When thus we shall know Christ, then we shall know him to purpose.

THE SIXTEENTH SERMON.

My beloved is white and ruddy, the chiefest among ten thousand. His head is as fine gold; his locks are bushy and black as a raven; his eyes are as the eyes of doves, by the rivers of waters, washed with milk, and fitly set, &c.—CANT. V. 10, 11, 12, 13.

Obj. Hence likewise we may answer some doubts that may arise; as why the death of one man, Christ, should be of value for satisfaction for the sins of the whole world. How can this be ?

Ans. O but what kind of man was he ? ' The chief among ten thousand,' especially considering that his excellency ariseth from the grace of his personal union of God and man. The first Adam tainted thousands, and would have tainted a world of men more if there had been more ; but he was mere man that did this. And shall not Christ, God and man, the second Adam, advance the world, and ten thousand worlds if there had been more ? He is chief among ten thousand.

' His head is as most fine gold; his locks are bushy and black as a raven,' &c.

1. Positively, ' He is white and ruddy.' 2. Comparatively, ' He is the chiefest of ten thousand.'

The church doth not think it sufficient, in general, to set out Christ thus ; but she descends into a particular description of him by all the parts of a body that are conspicuous. First, in general observe hence, *that it is the nature of love upon all occasions to reflect upon the thing loved.* As the church here, from things that are excellent in the world, borrows phrases and comparisons to set out the excellency of Christ, exalting him above any other thing. Whatsoever the soul of a Christian sees in heaven or earth, it takes occasion thence to think of Christ.

Again, in general, observe from hence, seeing the church fetcheth comparison from doves' eyes, from the body of a man and other things, *that there are some beams of excellency in every creature.* There is somewhat of

God in every creature. This makes the meditation of the creature to be useful. There is none, even the meanest, but it hath a being, and thereby in a sort sets out the being of God. Why doth God style himself a shield, a rock, a buckler, a shadow, and the like ? but to shew that there is something of him in these. And therefore to teach us to rise from them to him, in whom all those excellencies that are scattered in them are united.

In innocency we knew God, and in him we had knowledge of the creature; but now we are fain to help ourselves from the knowledge of the creature to rise to the knowledge of God.

' His head is as fine gold.' A little in general. See the boldness and largeness of the church's affections, who, though she had been ill entreated by the watchmen and others, yet is she not disheartened for all this. No; she goes on and sets out particular commendations of her beloved. Where love hath any strength, no water can quench it. You see the church here found but cold entertainment from the watchmen and others that should have been better.

Nay, she was in desertion, yet she was not discouraged. Nay, not from the desertion that Christ left her in ; but she seeks after him whom her soul loved. Oh ! this is the sign of a true, sanctified soul, touched from heaven, never to give over seeking of Christ; nor setting out his praises. No, though it thinks itself not beloved of Christ. Ask such ones, Do you love God, his children, and his word ? Oh ! you shall have them eloquent. No words are enough to set out their affections.

And this is one reason, which we may note by the way, why God plants in his children, at their first conversion, a sweet love, which we call, ' the first love,' that when desertions come they may call to mind what they felt from Christ, and what they bore to him ; and thereupon the church concludes, ' I will return to my first love, for then was I better than now,' Hos. ii. 7. The church here, from what doth she commend her beloved, but from somewhat that was left in her soul, some inward taste of the love of Christ in her ? She called to mind how it was with her before in the former part of this, and in the latter end of the former chapter ; what an excellent estate she had been in. This helped her to recover herself.

Now you may say, Why is she so exact in reckoning up so many particulars of her beloved, his head, locks, eyes, lips, and such like ?

Why ? 1. It is from largeness of affection. A large heart hath alway large expressions. When we are barren in expressions towards Christ, and of good things, whence comes this but from narrow, poor affections? The church had large affections ; therefore she had suitable expressions.

And then, 2. She is thus particular, because Christ hath not one but many excellencies. Everything in him is excellent, inward and outward, as his head, &c. For indeed beauty consists not in sweetness of colour only, but in affinity and proportion of all parts. Now there is all sweet proportion in Christ. So it should be with Christians. They should not have one excellency, but many. Those that receive grace for grace from Christ, John i. 16, have not only head, eyes, hands, and feet good ; but all lovely, ' grace for grace,' answerable to the variety of graces in Jesus Christ, in whom all things jointly, and everything severally, are lovely.

Then, 3. She sheweth her particular care and study, to be exact in this knowledge of Christ. To rip him up and anatomise him thus, from head to foot, it argueth she had studied Christ well, ere she could attain this excellency. So it should be the study and care of every Christian, to study the excellencies of Christ, not only in the gross, to say as much as you have in the Creed ; he was born for us of the Virgin Mary, was crucified, dead, and buried, &c., which every child can say ; but to be able to particularize the high perfections and excellencies of Christ, as the church here ; to study his nature, offices, the state he was in, and how he carried himself in his humiliation and exaltation ; what good we have by both states, redemption by his abasement ; application of it by his advancement ; what he did for us on earth ; what he doth in heaven ; what in justification, adoption, sanctification, and in the glory to come. Study everything, and warm the heart with the meditation of them.

This particular spreading and laying open the excellencies of Christ is a thing worthy of a Christian. We make slight work of religion. We can be particular and eloquent enough in other things, but in that wherein all eloquence is too little, how barren are we ! how shamefaced to speak of Christ and his excellencies in base company, as if it were a dishonour ! Let us therefore learn this from the church here, to be much in thoughts and meditations of the excellencies of Christ, and so our expressions will be answerable to our meditations. So the holy fathers that were godly (till another kind of divinity came into the world, of querks* and subtilties) there was none of them but was excellent this way. Paul admirable, accounting ' all dung and dross in comparison of Christ.' In speaking of him, when he begins, he goes on from one thing to another, as if he were ravished, and knew not how nor where to end.

The soul hath sights of Christ that God shews to it, and which the soul presents to itself by the help of the Spirit. The sights that God in this kind shews, are to those in affliction especially ; as Daniel and Isaiah saw Christ in his glory in a vision. So Ezekiel had a vision, and John, Rev. i., where Christ was presented to him gloriously. So there is a glorious description of Christ present to the church, Rev. iv. 5.

And as there are sights let down from God into the soul, so there are sights that the soul frames of Christ, such as the church here conceives of him by faith. Thus Moses saw him before he was incarnate, and Abraham saw his day and rejoiced, John viii. 56 : so should we now have spiritual sights, ideas of Christ framed to our souls. This is to bestow our souls as we should do (*m*). So much for general, now we come to some particulars. ' His head is as fine gold ; his locks are bushy and black as a raven.'

' His head is as fine gold.' He begins to set out the excellency of the chief part, the head. The head of Christ is God, as it is 1 Cor. xi. 3. He is above all, and God only is above him. All is yours, and you are Christ's, and Christ is God's, 1 Cor. iii. 22, 23. But that is not so much intended here, as to shew Christ's headship over the church, as God and man. His head is as fine gold, that is, his government and headship is a most sweet and golden government.

Daniel ii. You have an image of the monarchies ; the first whereof had a golden head, which was the Chaldean. The best monarchy is set out by the best metal,—gold ; so Christ, the head of the church, is a precious head, a head of gold.

A head hath an eminency above all others ; an influence and motion above all other parts. It is the seat of the senses. So this golden head is more eminent than all, governs the whole church and hath influence into all. In him we live, and move, and have our being, Acts xvii. 28.

Quest. Why is Christ as king thus resembled to an head of gold ?

Ans. Because gold is the chief, the most precious, durable metal of all

* That is, ' quirks,' = tricks.—G.

others. Christ is a king for ever, and hath an everlasting government.
Gold is also the most pliable metal. You may beat it out to leaves more
than any other metal whatsoever. Christ is all gold indeed. His love hath
beat himself out as low as may be, all for our good. What abasement like
to Christ's ? That which is most precious is most communicating, as the
sun, a glorious creature. What doth so much good as it ? So Christ, as
he is the most excellent of all, ' the chief of ten thousand,' so is he also the
most communicative. What good to the good that Christ did ? He was
beaten, out of love to mankind, to lowest abasement for us. Though this
be not mainly aimed at here, yet, by the way, speaking of gold, we may
present to ourselves such comfortable meditations.

Use 1. Well then, is Christ such an excellent head, a golden head, ' in
whom are hid all the treasures of wisdom, Col. ii. 3, to govern his church ?
What need we then go to that triple crown, having such a golden head ? The
apostasy of the church hath found out another golden head. Is not Christ
precious enough ? Let us take heed of leaving the head Christ, as it is
Col. ii. 19. It is a damnable thing to forsake him. Let the apostatical *
church alone with her antichrist.

2. Again, if Christ be a golden head, let us his members *labour every one
to be suitable.* Though there be difference between the head and the members in many respects, especially in those three formerly named, eminency,
government, and influence, yet for nature they are one. Head and members make but one. So that as the head of the body is gold, so should
every member be. Therefore the seven churches are styled seven golden
candlesticks. Everything in the tabernacle was gold, even to the snuffers,
to shew that in the church everything is excellent. The tabernacle was
gold, most of it, though it was covered with badgers' skins. The church
indeed hath a poor covering as of badgers' skins, not gilded as hypocrites ;
but it is precious within. Again, Christ, as he is gold, so he is fine gold,
whole gold. He hath not only the crown on him, but his head is gold itself.
Other kings, their crowns are of gold, but their heads are not so. But
there is such a precious treasure of wisdom in him that his head is gold.
So let the church and every Christian labour, not to be gilt, but gold ; to
be thoroughly good ; to have the inside as good as the outside, the heart
as good as the conversation. The church is glorious within, Ps. xlv. 13.
Beloved, is Christ an excellent golden head, and shall we have a base body ?
Is he fit to be united to a golden head that is a common drunkard, a swearer,
that is a beast in his life and conversation ? Is this suitable ?

3. Again, is our head so golden, and whatsoever excellency we have, is
it from our head? Therefore as the church in the Revelation, ' *let us cast all
our crowns at his feet,*' Rev. iv. 10. Have we crowns of gold ? anything that
is excellent within, any grace, any comfort ? Let us lay it down at his feet,
for all is from him. Natural men have golden images of their own. Israel
would have golden calves. Nebuchadnezzar sets up a golden image, and all
must worship it. So in the declining times of the church : they framed
golden images, that is, a golden whorish religion, gilded, and painted,
framed by their own brain, whereunto all must stoop. But the true gold
is that we must respect and submit ourselves unto and admire. Others are
but golden dreams and images, as Nebuchadnezzar's was. Christ's head is of
fine gold.

All must be fine gold that comes from this head. His word is gold,
sometimes† purged in the fire. His ordinances gold, in the Scripture

* That is, ' apostate.'—ED.   † Qu. ' seven times ?'—ED.

phrase, Ps. xix. 10. The city, the new Jerusalem, which signifies the state of the church in this world, when it shall be refined to the utmost, all is of gold ; the walls of precious stones ; the gates of pearl ; and the pavement of the streets of pure gold, Rev. xxi. 21, to shew the excellency of reformation ; which golden times are yet to come. In the mean time let us go on and wait for them.

' His locks are bushy, and black as a raven.' I think this is but complemental, to fill up the other. It is nothing but a commendation of his freshness, a foil to beauty. Therefore not particularly to be stood upon.

' His eyes are as doves' eyes by the rivers of waters,' &c. His eyes are as doves' eyes, and such eyes as are by the rivers of waters ; where they are cleansed and washed with milk that they may be the clearer, and fitly set; neither goggle eyes, nor sunk into the head, but fitly set, as a jewel in a ring; neither too much in, nor too much out, to set out the comeliness of this part, the eye, which is the glory of the face.

Quest. Why is Christ said to have the eyes of doves ?

Ans. The dove hath many enemies, especially the white dove is a fair mark for the birds of prey. Therefore God hath given that creature a quick sight, that she might discern her enemies. Thus the Scripture helps us to conceive of the quickness of Christ's eye, Rev. v. 6. There are seven horns and seven eyes, which are the seven Spirits of God. Here Christ the lamb, hath seven eyes and seven horns. What be these ? Christ hath not only horns of power, as the enemies have horns of violence.—He hath horn against horn ; but seven eyes, that is, a quick sight to see all the danger the church is in, and seven eyes. Seven is a word of perfection, that is, he hath many eyes, an accurate sight. He hath not only an eye of providence over the whole world, but an eye of grace and favour, lively, and lovely in regard of his church. All things are naked and open before his eyes, as it is, Heb. iv. 13. He can see through us, he knows our very hearts and reins, which he must do *ex officio*, because he must be our judge. He that is judge of all had need to have eyes that will pierce through all. It had need be a quick eye that must judge of the heart and affections. But what may we learn hence ? That we have a Saviour that hath doves' eyes, that is, clear eyes, able to discern.

Use 1. Take it as a point first, *of all comfort to the church*, that when we have any imputation [that] lies upon us, that we are thus and thus, Christ hath quick eyes, he knows our hearts. Thou knowest, saith Peter, Lord, that I love thee, John xxi. 15. In all false imputations, rest in the eyesight of Christ. He knows it is otherwise with us.

Use 2. Then again, *in all abasement, know that there is an eye that sees all.* He sees with his eye and pities with his heart. As he hath a quick eye, so he hath a tender heart. Though he seems to sleep and to wink, it is but that we may wake him with our prayers ; which when we have done, we shall see that Christ hath seen all this while, and that the violence the enemies of God have offered to his church, the spouse, hath been in his sight, and that they shall know at length to their cost.

Likewise it is a point of terror to all hypocrites and others, that think to blindfold Christ again. Can they blindfold him in heaven that hath this sharp eye ? No ; he sees all their courses and projects, what they are and what they tend to ; and as he sees them, so he will spread them all open ere long.

Use 3. And as it is a point of comfort and terror, so it is a point of *instruction to us all, that we having to deal with a judge that sees all, to wor-*

ship Christ in spirit. If we had knowledge that such an eye of God is fixed upon us in all places, in all our affections and actions, would we give liberty to base and filthy thoughts, to cruel designs, and to treacherous aims and intents? to hatch a hell, as it were, in our hearts, and to carry a fair show outwardly. It could not be. Men are not afraid of their thoughts, affections, desires, and inward delights of their soul, because there is no eye of justice upon them. But if they did consider that the all-seeing God did observe these inward evils, and would call them to account one day for them, then they would be as well afraid to think ill as to do ill.

' His cheeks are as beds of spices, and as sweet flowers.'

Cheeks are the grace of the face. They are used here to denote the presence of Christ, which is sweet as spices and flowers. Not only his presence is glorious in heaven, when we shall see that goodly person of Christ that became man for us, that transforming sight that shall make us like himself, but the spiritual presence of Christ in his ordinances which we are capable of here, this is as spices and flowers.

Obj. But you will say, cheeks, face, and presence present colours to the eye, and not smells, as spices and flowers, which are the peculiar object of another sense.

Ans. Oh, but Christ is the object of all the senses. Beloved, he is not only beauty to the eye, but sweetness to the smell, and to the taste. Therefore faith hath the name of all the senses, to see, hear, taste, and smell, and doth all, because it carries us to Christ, that is instead of all to us. But the point is,

That the manifestation of Christ to his church and children by his Spirit in any of his ordinances, is a sweet manifestation, and delectable as spices and flowers; as it is, Cant. i. 3; 'Because of the savour of thy good ointments, thy name is as an ointment poured out, therefore the virgins love thee.' The very name of Christ, when he is known and laid open by the ministry, is a precious ointment, and the virgins, that is, all chaste souls, follow him by the smell of his ointments. All his ordinances convey a sweetness to the soul. His sacraments are sweet, his word sweet, the communion of saints sweet. The presence of the sun, you know, is known in the spring time by the freshness of all things, which put forth the life and little liveliness they have in them, some in blossoming, and some in flowers. That which lay, as it were, dead in winter, it comes out when the sun draws near; so when Christ comes and shews his presence and face to the soul, he refresheth and delights it.

Hence we see they are enemies to Christ and to the souls of God's people that hinder the manifestation of Christ, whereby his face might be seen, and his lovely cheeks discerned. Those that hate and undermine the ordinances of God, they hinder the comforts of their own souls.

And they are enemies to Christ. For when hath Christ glory but when the virgins follow him in the scent of his sweet ointments? When the soul, in the sense of his sweetness, follows him, and cleaves to him with joy, love, and delight, this makes Christ Christ, and sets him up in the heart above all others. This is the proper work of the ordinances. Those, therefore that are enemies to the ordinances of Christ, are enemies to the souls of God's people, and to the glory and honour of Christ himself. Thus far we may go safely, upon comparison of this with the other Scriptures.

THE SEVENTEENTH SERMON.

*His lips are like lilies, dropping sweet-smelling myrrh ; his hands are as
gold rings set with beryl; his belly is as bright ivory overlaid with sap-
phire : his legs, &c.*—Cant. V. 13.

In speaking of these particulars we are to be very wary, for we have not
that foundation as we have in other generals. For no doubt but the Spirit
of God here did more intend to set out the large affection that the church
had to Christ, than to insinuate any great particularity in every one of these.
Therefore let us only cull out, and take those things that are of more easy
explication.

'His lips are as lilies, dropping down sweet myrrh.'

That is, his doctrine is as sweet as the lilies, and sound as the myrrh,
keeping from putrefaction, it being the nature of myrrh, as it is sound
itself, so to make other things sound. In like manner, the speech of
Christ makes the soul sound that embraceth it. What was ever more
sweet than the truth of Christ? When he spake himself, they all hung
upon his lips, Luke iv. 20, as the phrase is in the gospel (*n*), as a man
hangs upon the lips of another whom he desires and delights to hear speak,
and they marvelled at the gracious words that came out of his lips. Grace
was in his lips, Ps. xlv. 2. All was sweet that came from him, for it came from
the excellency of his Spirit. His words were dyed in these affections of
his heart. In the learned language, the same word signifieth speech and
reason (*o*), to intimate that speech is but the current of reason from the
heart, the seat of reason. Therefore Christ's speeches were sweet, because
his heart was sweet, full of all love, grace, mercy, and goodness, Mat. xii.
34, 35. His heart was a treasure. His lips must needs then be sweet.
Beloved, therefore let us hence take a trial of ourselves, what our condition is, whether the words that come from Christ when he speaks in his
ministry to us be sweet or not.

The word, to some kind of men, is like the northern air, which parcheth
and cutteth. Ahab could not endure the breath of Elias, 1 Kings xxi. 18,
seq., nor Herodias the breath of John Baptist, Mark vi. 16, nor the Pharisees the breath of Stephen and Paul, Luke vii. 54, Acts xxii. 22. So too
many now-a-days cannot endure the breath of divine truth, when it cuts
and pierceth. These words are arrows that stick. If they stick not
savingly, they stick to killing. If we cannot endure Christ's breath, we
are not his spouse, nor have any communion with him.

'His lips are like lilies, dropping sweet myrrh,' &c.

This is one excellency of Christ and of his truth, that it preserves the
soul in a pure estate. It is pure itself, and so it preserves the soul. Myrrh
is a liquor that keeps from putrefaction. There is nothing that keeps the
soul, but the word that endures for ever. Whereas, on the other side, error
is of a putrefying nature, corrupting and defiling the soul.

'His hands are as gold rings set with beryl,' &c.

Hands are the instruments of actions. Christ's actions are precious.
Whatsoever he doth to the church, nay, even when he doth use evil men
to afflict and exercise the church, he hath a hand there, a golden, a precious
hand, in the evil hand of wicked men. God doth all things by Christ. He
is, as it were, God's hand, which all things pass through. Joseph was the
second man of Egypt, through whose hands all things came to the rest,

Heb. i. 2, John v. 22 ; so all things come through Christ's hands to us ;
and whatsoever is his handiwork is good. Even as it is said in the days
of his flesh, ' he did all things well,' Mat. vii. 37, so still, in the church all
his workmanship is exceeding well. Though we cannot see the excellency
of it, it is all well both in the government of the church and his workmanship in our hearts, ' the new creature.'

' His belly is as bright ivory overlaid,' &c.

His belly, that is, his inward parts. In the Hebrew (*p*), it is used for
the inward affections. They are as bright ivory overlaid with sapphires, that
is, they are pure. All the inside of Christ, all his affections that he bears,
are wondrous good. His love, his desires, his joys, his hatred, all pure,
like pure water in a crystal glass. It may be stirred sometimes, but still
it is clear. There are no dregs at the bottom, because there was no taint
of sin in him.

' His legs are as pillars of marble set on sockets of fine gold,' &c.

That is, all his passages and ways are constant and firm, even as pillars
of marble. His children are so likewise, as far as they are endued with his
Spirit. Christ is yesterday, to-day, and the same for ever, Heb. xiii. 8.
In regard of his enemies, he is set out in another manner of similitude, ' as
having legs of brass to trample them all in pieces,' Rev. i. 15. But in
respect of his constant truth and ways of goodness to his church, his legs
are as pillars of marble.

' His countenance is as Lebanon, excellent as the cedars.'

Lebanon was a goodly forest lying on the north side of Judea, wherein
were excellent plants of all kinds, especially cedars. Christ his countenance is as Lebanon, excellent as the cedars, that is, his presnece is goodly,
stately, and majestical. So it is and will be when he shews himself, indeed,
for the vindicating of his church. Then the enemies thereof shall know
that his presence is as Lebanon, and excellent as the cedars.

The children of God are like to cedars, too, for they are Christ mystical.
Other men are as shrubs to them, men of no value ; but they are cedars,
and grow as cedars in Lebanon, from perfection to perfection, bearing most
fruit in their age. Wicked men sometimes are cedars, too, and are said to
grow and flourish as the cedars in Lebanon. But look a while, and you
shall see their place no more. They have no good root, no good foundation, Ps. xxxvii. 10. A Christian is a cedar set in Christ the chief cedar.
He is a plant that grows in him. He hath an eternal root, and, therefore,
he flourisheth eternally.

' His mouth is most sweet, he is altogether lovely.'

His mouth is most sweet. She doubles this commendation. She had
said before, his lips are as lilies dropping sweet myrrh. Here she saith
again of his mouth, it is most sweet, to shew that this is the chief lovely
thing in Christ. The repetition argueth the seriousness of the church's
affection to Christ, and of the excellency of that part. The main lovely
thing is that which comes from his heart by his words and his lips ; as, indeed,
the most excellent thing that we can think of is the expression of the heart
of God in Christ, and of Christ's love to us. ' His mouth is most sweet.'
And, indeed, the best discovery of a true affection to Christ, and of a true
estate in grace, is from our affection to the word of Christ. Wheresoever
there is interest into Christ, there is a high respect to the word. ' My
sheep hear my voice,' John x. 4 ; and you know what Peter saith, John
vi. Many of Christ's hearers and followers forsook him, upon some hard
speeches, as they thought, that came from him. Saith Christ to Peter,

'Will ye also leave me?' Peter answered again, 'Whither, Lord, shall we go? Thou hast the words of eternal life,' John vi. 68. The apostles, that had the Spirit of God, perceived an incredible graciousness to sit on his lips, and therefore they hung upon his lips. 'Whither shall we go? Thou hast the words of eternal life.' If we leave his speech, we leave our comfort, we leave our life.

As a comment hereupon, see Ps. xix., where we have a high commendation of God's excellency; first, from the book of nature, the works of God: 'the heavens declare the glory of God;' then from the word of God; and herein the psalmist is wondrous large. 'The law of the Lord is perfect, converting the soul; the testimonies of the Lord are sure, making wise the simple; the statutes of the Lord are right, and rejoice the heart; the commandments of the Lord are sure, and enlighten the eyes; more to be desired than gold, yea, than fine gold; sweeter also than the honey or the honeycomb.'

But mark the order. When is the word of God precious as gold, sweeter than the honey or the honeycomb, but when the former commendation takes place? Where the word is perfect, converting the soul, and where it is sure, making wise the simple, and where the fear of the Lord is clean, &c., there it is more to be desired than fine gold, and sweeter than the honeycomb. So the church here finding, first of all, the word to be a converting word, and giving understanding to the simple, she cannot but speak of the sweetness of the word of Christ. His lips are as lilies dropping sweet-smelling myrrh. His mouth is most sweet. Thus a man may know his estate in grace by his relish of the word.

There is a divine and a heavenly relish in the word of God; as, for instance, take the doctrine of his providence, 'that all things shall work together for the best to them that love God,' Rom. viii. 28. What a sweet word is this! A whole kingdom is not worth this promise, that whatsoever befalls a Christian in this world, there is an overruling providence to sway all to good, to help forward his eternal good.

That Christ will be present with us in all conditions, what a sweet word and promise is this! Mat. xxviii. 20; 'that he will give his Holy Spirit, if we beg it,' Luke xi. 13; 'that he will not fail us nor forsake us,' Heb. xiii. 5; that 'if we confess our sins, and lay them open, he is merciful to forgive them,' 1 John i. 9; that 'if our sins were as red as scarlet, they shall all be white as wool,' Isa. i. 18. What kind of incredible sweetness is in these to a heart that is prepared for these comforts! The doctrine of reconciliation, of adoption, of glory to come, of the offices of Christ and such like, how sweet are they! They relish wondrously to a sanctified soul.

Let us therefore discern of our estate in grace by this, how do we relish divine truths? Are they connatural and suitable to us? Do we love them more than our appointed food? Are they dearer unto us than thousands of gold and silver? Do we like them above all other truths whatsoever? Ps. cxix. 72, 127. Every truth in its rank is lovely, and is a beam of God. For truth is of God wheresoever we find it. But what are other truths to this heavenly, soul-saving truth? this gospel-truth that is from Christ? 'His mouth is most sweet.'

In our nature there is a contrary disposition and antipathy to divine truth. We love the law better than the gospel, and any truth better than the law. We love a story, any trifling, baubling thing concerning our ordinary callings, better than divine truth. In divine truth, as things are

more spiritual, so the more remote they are naturally from our love and
liking. Evangelical truths will not down with a natural heart; such an
one had rather hear a quaint point of some vice or virtue finely stood upon
than anything in Christ, because he was never truly convinced of his corrupt and miserable estate by nature. But when the grace of God hath
altered him, and his eyes are open to see his misery, then of all truths the
truth of Christ favours* best. Those truths that come out of the mouth of
Christ, and out of the ministry concerning Christ, they are the most sweet
of all. Oh! how sweet are those words in the gospel to the poor man,
' Thy sins are forgiven thee,' Mat. ix. 2. Do you think they went not to
his heart? So to the woman, Luke vii. 47. Her many sins are forgiven her, for she loved much. Oh! they were words that went to her
soul! And to the thief on the cross, ' This day thou shalt be with me in
paradise,' Luke xxiii. 43. How do you think those words affected him?
So it is with us if ever we have been abased in the sense of our sins. Oh!
how sweet is a promise of mercy then! ' He that brings it is as one of
ten thousand, that comes to declare to man his righteousness, Job. xxxiii.
23; to lay open the mercy that belongs to a distressed soul. Oh! the
very feet of those that bring these glad tidings are beautiful! Rom. x. 15.
When our blessed Saviour, after his resurrection, spake to Mary, and
called her by her name, after that she had sought him and could not find
him, ' O Rabboni,' saith she. The words of Christ they melted her presently. Let Christ once call us by our names, for he knows us by name,
as he knew Moses, Exod. xxxiv. 27, Isa. xliii. 1; let him by his Spirit
speak to us by name, and own us, then we call him Rabboni. We own
him again, for what is our love but the reflection of his back again?
Therefore saith the psalmist, ' Let me hear the voice of joy and gladness,
that the bones that thou hast broken may rejoice,' Ps. li. 8. ' Let me
hear;' that is, I long for thy word to hear it; not the bare ministerial
word, but the word of the Spirit. But the church resteth not here, but
saith further,

' He is altogether lovely.' Altogether desirable; as if she should say,
What should I stand upon particulars? he is altogether, from top to toe,
amiable, lovely, and delectable.

' He is altogether lovely.' Lovely to God, to us, to the soul; lovely to
him that can best judge of loveliness. The judgment of God I hope will
go current with us; and what doth God the Father judge of Christ? ' This
is my beloved Son,' Mat. iii. 17. He is the Son of God's love, Col. i. 13,
as God cannot but love his own image. He is lovely also as man, for he
was pure and holy; lovely as mediator by office, for he was anointed by
God to convey the Father's love to us. He must needs be lovely in whom
all others are loved. This is my beloved Son, in whom I am well pleased;
out of him I am well pleased with nobody. And indeed he was filled with
all graces that might make him lovely. All the treasures of wisdom are in
him, and of his fulness we all receive grace for grace. He is made a store-
house of all that is good for us.

He is lovely to God in whatsoever he did. He carried himself lovely,
and pleased his Father in all his doings and sufferings. God loved him
especially, ' because he was obedient, even unto the death of the cross.
Therefore God gave him a name above all names; that at the name of
Jesus every knee should bow, both in heaven and in earth,' Phil. ii. 8–10.
As for the angels, they look upon him with admiration. They attended

* Qu. ' savours?'—ED.

him, and accounted it an honour to wait upon him. He is lovely to all above us, and shall he not be lovely to us?

Obj. But you will say, Was he lovely when he was nailed on the cross, hung between two thieves, when he wore a crown of thorns, was whipped, laid grovelling on the ground, when he sweat water and blood? What loveliness was in him when he was laid in his grave?

Ans. Oh! yes; then he was most lovely of all to us, by how much the more he was abased for us. This makes him more lovely that out of love he would abase himself so low. When greatness and goodness meet together, how goodly is it! That Christ, so great a majesty, should have such bowels of compassion! Majesty alone is not lovely, but awful and fearful; but joined with such condescending grace, is wondrous amiable. How lovely a sight is it to see so great a person to be so meek and gentle! It was so beyond comparison lovely in the eyes of the disciples, that they stood and wondered to see him, who was the eternal Word of the Father, condescend to talk with a poor Samaritan woman, John iv. 6, *seq*. And what loveliness of carriage was in him to Peter, undeserving, after he had denied and forsworn him, yet to restore him to his former place that he had in his heart, loving him as much as ever he did before! In a word, what sweetness, gentleness, bowels of meekness, pity, and compassion did he discover to those that were in misery! We cannot insist upon particulars.

There is a remarkable passage in the story of Alphonsus the king, not very well liked of some. When he saw a poor man pulling of his beast out of a ditch, he put to his hand to help him; after which, as it is recorded, his subjects ever loved him the better. It was a wonderful condescending. And is it not as wonderful that the King of heaven and earth should stoop so low as to help us poor worms out of the ditch of hell and damnation? and that, when he hath set us in a state of deliverance, he should not leave us there, but advance us to such a state and condition as is above our admiration, which neither heart can conceive nor tongue express? Is not this wonderful condescending?

Use 1. That we may further improve this point, Is Christ altogether lovely; so lovely to us, and so beloved of God the Father? *Let us then rest upon his obedience and righteousness;* build upon it, that God cannot refuse that righteousness whose whole subject is altogether lovely. Let us come clothed in the garments of our Elder Brother, and then doubt not of acceptance; for it is in Christ that he loves us. In this well-beloved Son it is that God is well pleased with us. If we put on Christ's righteousness, we put on God's righteousness; and then how can God hate us? No more than he hates his own Son. Nay, he loves us, and that with the same love wherewith he loves him; for he loves whole Christ mystical, Head and members, John xvii. 23. Let this strengthen our faith, that if Christ be so altogether lovely in himself and to the Father, then we may comfortably come before the Father, clothed with the garments of him our Elder Brother, and so rest ourselves on the acceptation of his mediation, that is so beloved a mediator.

Use 2. Again, if Christ be so lovely, 'altogether lovely,' then *let us labour to be in him*, that so we may be lovely to God; because he is the first amiable thing in the world, in whom we are all lovely. All our loveliness is in beloved Christ.

Use 3. Again, if Christ be so lovely, *here only we have whereupon to spend the marrow of our best affections*. Is it not pity we should lose so much of our affections as we do upon other things? Christ is altogether

lovely; why should we doat upon other things so much, and set up idols
in our hearts above Christ? Is he altogether lovely, and shall not he
have altogether our lovely affections, especially when we are commanded,
under pain of a curse, to love the Lord Jesus? *Anathema Maran-atha* to
those that love not Christ, 1 Cor. xvi. 22. Let us therefore labour to
place all our sweet affections that are to be exercised upon good, as love,
joy, and delight, upon this object, this lovely deserving object, Christ, who
is ' altogether lovely.' When we suffer a pure stream, as it were, to run
through a dirty channel, our affections to run after the things of the world,
which are worse than ourselves, we lose our affections and ourselves.

Let, therefore, the whole stream of our affections be carried unto Christ.
Love him, and whatsoever is his; for he being altogether lovely, all that
comes from him is lovely. His promises, his directions, his counsels, his
children, his sacraments, are all lovely. Whatsoever hath the stamp of Christ
upon it, let us love it. We cannot bestow our hearts better, to lose ourselves
in the love of Christ, and to forget ourselves and the love of all. Yea, to hate
all in comparison of him, and to account all ' dung and dross' compared with
Christ, is the only way to find ourselves. And indeed we have a better
condition in him, than in the world or in ourselves. Severed from him,
our condition is vain, and will come to nothing; but that we have in him
is admirable and everlasting. We cannot conceive the happiness which
we poor wretches are advanced to in Christ; and what excellent things
abide for us, which come from the love of God to us in Christ, who is so
altogether lovely. Therefore let us labour to kindle in our hearts an
affection towards Christ, all that we can, considering that he is thus lovely.

Use 4. And let us make an use of trial, *whether he be thus lovely to us, or
no.* We may see hence whether we love Christ or no. We may judge of
our love by our esteem.

1. *How do we value Christ?* what price doth the church set on him?
' He is the chief of ten thousand.' What place, then, should he have in
our hearts? If he be the chief of ten thousand, let us rather offend ten
thousand than offend him. Let us say, with David, ' Whom have I in
heaven but thee?' &c., Ps. lxxiii. 25. And when the soul can say to
Christ, or any that is Christ's (for I speak of him in the latitude of his
truths, promises, sacraments, and communion with his children), ' What
have I in heaven but thee?' &c., then it is in a happy condition. If these
things have the same place in our esteem, as they have in respect of their
own worth, then we may say truly, without hypocrisy, ' He is altogether
lovely to us,' that we truly love him.

2. In the next place, *are we ready to suffer for Christ?* We see the
church here endures anything for Christ. She was misused of the watchmen. They scorned her, and her ' veil is taken away,' yet notwithstanding,
she loves Christ still. Do we stand ready disposed to suffer for Christ?
of the world to be disgraced and censured? and yet are we resolved not to
give over? Nay, do we love Christ the more, and stick to his truth the
faster? Certainly where the love of Christ is, there is a spirit of fortitude,
as we may see in the church here, who is not discouraged from Christ by
any means. He is still the chief of ten thousand. When she was wronged
for seeking after him, yet he was altogether lovely. Whereas, on the
other hand, you have some that, for frowns of greatness, fear of loss, or
for hope of rising, will warp their conscience, and do anything. Where
now is love to Christ and to religion? He that loves Christ, loves him
the more for his cross, as the Holy Ghost hath recorded of some, that they

' rejoiced that they were thought worthy to suffer for Christ,' Acts v. 41.
So the more we suffer for him, the more dear he will be to us. For indeed
he doth present himself in love and comfort most, to those that suffer for his
sake ; therefore their love is increased.

3. Again, where love is, *there it enlargeth the heart*, which being enlarged,
enlargeth the tongue also. The church hath never enough of commending
Christ, and of setting out his praise. The tongue is loosed, because the
heart is loosed. Love will alter a man's disposition. As we see in experience, a man base of nature, love will make him liberal ; he that is tongue-
tied, it will make him eloquent. Let a man love Christ, and though before
he could not speak a word in the commendation of Christ, and for a good
cause, yet, I say, if the love of Christ be in him, you shall have him speak
and labour earnestly in the praises of God. This hot affection, this
heavenly fire, will so mould and alter him, that he shall be clean another
man. As we see in the church here, after that there was kindled a spirit
of love in her, she cannot have done with Christ. When she had spoke
what she could, she adds, ' He is altogether lovely.' Those that cannot
speak of Christ, or for Christ, with large hearts in defence of good causes,
but are tongue-tied and cold in their affections, where is their love ? Put
any worldly man to a worldly theme that he is exercised in, and speaks of
daily, he hath wit and words at will ; but put him to a theme of piety, you
lose him : he is out of his theme, and out of his element. But 'tis not
so with those that have ever felt the love of God in Christ. They have
large affections. How full is Saint Paul ! He cannot speak of Christ, but
he is in the height, breadth, length, and depth of the love of God in Christ,
and the knowledge of God above all knowledge. Thus we may discern
the truth of our love by the expressions of it here as in the church.

4. Again, *the church here is never content till she find Christ* ; whatsoever
she had, nothing contents her. She wanted her beloved. As we see here,
she goes up and down inquisitive after him till she find him. So it is with
a Christian. If he have lost, by his own fault, his former communion with
Christ, he will not rest nor be satisfied ; but searcheth here and there in
the use of this and that means. He runs through all God's ordinances and
means till he find Christ. Nothing in the world will content him, neither
honour, riches, place, or friends, till he find that which he once enjoyed,
but hath now for a season lost, the comfort and assurance of God's love in
Christ.

Now, if we can sit down with other things, and can want Christ and the
assurance of salvation, that sweet report of the Spirit that we are his, and
yet be contented well enough, here is an ill sign that a man is in an ill
condition. The church was not so disposed here. She was never quiet,
nor gives over her inquisition and speaking of Christ (that by speaking of
the object she might warm her affections), until at the last she meets with
Christ. These and the like signs there are of the truth of the love of
Christ. But where there is a flaming love of Christ there is this degree
further, a desire of the appearance of Christ, a desire of his presence. For
if Christ be so lovely in his ordinances, if we find such sweetness in the
word and sacraments, in the communion of saints, in the motions of the
Spirit, what is the sweetness, think you, which the souls in heaven enjoy,
where they see Christ face to face, see him as he is ? Hereupon the spouse
saith, ' Let him kiss me with the kisses of his mouth.' Oh, that I might
live in his presence. This is the desire of a Christian soul when the flame
of love is kindled in any strength, ' Oh, that I might see him.' And there-

fore it longs even for death; for as far as a man is spiritual, he desires to
be dissolved and to be with Christ; as Simeon, when he saw him, though
in his abasement, 'Now I have enough; let thy servant depart in peace,
for mine eyes have seen thy salvation,' Luke ii. 30. The presence of
Christ, though it were but in the womb, when Mary, the mother of Christ,
came to Elizabeth, it caused the babe that was in her womb to spring.
Such comfort there is in the presence of Christ, though he be but in the
womb, as it made John to spring. What, then, shall be his presence in
heaven? How would it make the heart spring there, think you? For that
which is most lovely in Christ is to come. Therefore the saints that have
any degree of grace in the New Testament, they are set out by this description. They were such as loved the appearing of our Lord Jesus Christ.
How can it be otherwise? If they love Christ, they love the appearing of
Christ, wherein we shall be made lovely, as he is lovely.

Here we are not 'altogether lovely;' for we have many dregs of sin,
many infirmities and stains. Shall we not, then, desire that time wherein,
as he is 'altogether lovely,' so shall we be made a fit spouse for so glorious
a husband?

To conclude this point, let us try our affections by the church's affections
in this place, whether Christ be so lovely to us or not. It is said, 'There
is no beauty in him when we shall see him, and he was despised of men,'
Isa. liii. 2. He was so, in regard of his cross and sufferings, to the eye of
the world and of carnal men. Herod scorned him; when Pilate sent him
to him, made nobody of him, as the word in the original is (*q*). They
looked upon the outside of Christ in the flesh when he was abased. 'There
was no form nor beauty in him,' saith the Holy Ghost, that is, to the sight
of carnal men; but those that had the sight of their sins with spiritual eyes,
they could otherwise judge of Christ. The poor centurion saw an excellency in him when he said, 'He was not worthy that he should come under
his roof,' Mat. viii. 8. The poor thief saw the excellency of Christ upon
the cross in those torments. 'Lord, remember me when thou comest into
thy kingdom,' Luke xxiii. 42.

So those souls that were enlightened, that had the sight of their misery
and the sight of God's love in Christ, had a high esteem of Christ in his
greatest abasement. Therefore, if we have a mean esteem of the children
of God as contemptible persons, and of the ordinances of God as mean
things, and of the government of Christ (such as he hath left in his word)
as base, it is an argument of a sinful, unworthy disposition. In such a
soul Christ hath never been effectually by his Spirit; for everything in him
is lovely, even the bitterest thing of all. There is a majesty and excellency
in all things of Christ. The censures of the church are excellent when
they proceed and issue forth with judgment, as they should do, 'to deliver
such a man over to Satan, that he may be saved in the day of the Lord,'
1 Cor. v. 5.

Now, if the ordinances of Christ, the word and sacraments, and the shutting
sinners out of the church, if these things be vilified as powerless things, it
shews a degenerate, wicked heart, not acquainted with the ways of God.
If we have a mean esteem of men that suffer for Christ and stand out for
him, if we account them so and so, shall we think ourselves Christians in
the mean time? When Christ is altogether lovely, shall they be unlovely
that carry the image of Christ? Can we love him that begets, and hate
them that are begotten of him? Can we love Christ, and hate Christians?
It cannot be.

Now, that we may get this affection and esteem of Christ that is so lovely,

Let us labour to make our sins bitter and loathsome, that Christ may be sweet.

Quest. What is the reason we set no higher a price of Christ?

Ans. Because we judge not of ourselves as we are indeed, and want spiritual eye-salve to see into ourselves rightly.

2. *And let us attend upon the means of salvation, to hear the unsearchable riches of Christ.* What makes any man lovely to us, but when we hear of their riches, beauty, and good intent to us? In the word we are made acquainted with the good intent of Christ towards us, the riches of mercy in forgiving our sins, and riches of glory prepared for us. The more we hear of him, of his riches and love to us, the more it will inflame our love to Christ. Those that live where the ordinances of Christ are held forth with life and power, they have more heavenly and enlarged affections than others have, as the experience of Christians will testify.

3. Again, if we would esteem highly of Christ that he may be lovely to us, *let us join with company that highly esteem of Christ, and such as are better than ourselves.* What deads the affections so much as carnal, worldly company, who have nothing in them but civility? By converse with them who have discourse of nothing but the world, if a man have heavenly affections, he shall quickly dull them, and be in danger to lose them. They may be conversed with in civil things, but when we would set to be heavenly and holy minded, let us converse with those that are of an heavenly bent. As we see here, ' the daughters of Jerusalem' are won to love Christ. By what? By conversing with the church. Upon the discourse that the church makes of his excellencies, in particular, they begin to ask, Where is Christ, as in the next chapter; and so are all brought to the love of Christ.

THE EIGHTEENTH SERMON.

His mouth is most sweet; yea, he is altogether lovely. This is my beloved, and this is my friend, O daughters of Jerusalem.—CANT. V. 16.
Whither is thy beloved gone, O thou fairest among women? whither is thy beloved turned aside? that we may seek him with thee? My beloved is gone down, &c.—CANT. VI. 1, 2.

BY this time the church hath well quit herself in that safe subject, commending her beloved; first in general, and then in particular. She affirms in effect, there was none like him in general; which she after makes good, in all the particulars of her description. Now she sums up all with a kind of superabundant expression. What shall I say more of him? if that which is said be not enough, then know farther, he is altogether lovely. There were no end to go through all his perfections; but look on him wholly, ' he is altogether lovely,' and therefore deserves my love. So that there is no cause why you should wonder at the strength of my affections, and care to find out this my beloved and this my friend, O ye daughters of Jerusalem. Thus we see how the pitch of an enlightened soul is bent. It aspires to things suitable to itself; to God-wards; to union and communion with Christ; to supernatural objects. Nothing here below is worthy the name of its beloved. It fastens not on earthly, base things. But this is my beloved, and this is my friend, this so excellent a person, this Jedidiah,* this beloved Son, this judge of all, Lord of all, this chief of ten thousand. Here the church pitches her affections, which she conceals, not as ashamed thereof, but in a kind of triumphing, boasting of her choice. She concludes all with a kind of resolute assurance, that the object of this her choice is far beyond all comparison.

'This is my beloved, and this is my friend, O daughters of Jerusalem.' Which is the closing up of her commendations of Christ. 'This is my beloved, and this my friend,' &c. Which shall only be touched, because we had occasion to speak thereof before. She calls Christ her beloved. Howsoever he had withdrawn himself in regard of the comfort and communion she had with him before, yet he is her beloved still.

That which is specially to be stood upon is, that the church here doth set out not only in parcels, but in general, her beloved Christ. This is my beloved. She doth, as it were, boast in her beloved. Whence observe :

A Christian soul seems to glory as it were in Christ.

'This is my beloved, and this is my friend, O ye daughters of Jerusalem.' But to unfold more fully this point, there be three or four ends why the church thus stands upon the expression of the excellencies of Christ, in particular and in general.

1. The one, *to shew that it is most just that she should love and respect him in whom there is all this to deserve love.* Both in himself, in regard of his own excellencies, so, and in relation to us, in regard of his merits and deserts.

2. Secondly, *to justify her large affections before the world and all opposites.†* For the world thinks, what mean these who are called Christians to haunt the exercises of religion, to spend so much time in good things? They wonder at it for want of better information. Now the church here, to justify her large expressions, says, 'This is my beloved, this is my friend, O ye daughters of Jerusalem.'

3. *And not only to justify, but likewise to glory therein,* as you have it, Ps. xliv. 8. The church there boasts of God, 'I will make my boast of thee all the day long.' So that Christians may not only justify their course of life against enemies, but in some sort boast of Christ, as Paul oft doth. And he shews the reason of it, that God hath made Christ to us all in all, wisdom, righteousness, sanctification, and redemption, 1 Cor. i. 30, that whosoever glorieth might glory in the Lord, ver. 31. For it is not a matter of glorying in the church when she hath such a head and such a husband. 'This is my beloved.' The wife shines in the beams of her husband. Therefore this yields matter not only of justification but of glory.

4. And next, in the fourth place, the church is thus large and shuts up all with a repetition, 'This is my beloved,' *to enlarge her own affections and to feed our‡ own love.* For love feeds upon this fuel, as it were; upon expressions and meditations of the person or thing loved. Love is, as it were, wages of itself. The pains it takes is gain to itself. To the church here, it is an argument pleasing. She dilates upon a copious theme. I may truly say there is no greater comfort to a Christian, nor a readier way to enlarge the affections after Christ, than to speak oft of the excellencies of Christ; to have his tongue as the pen of a ready writer furnished this way, 'This is my beloved,' &c.

* That is, 'beloved of Jehovah.'—G.   † That is, 'opponents.'—ED.
‡ Qu. 'her ?'—ED.

5. In the fifth place, another end of this may be, *to aggravate her own shame*, as indeed God's children are much in this argument; that upon their second thoughts of Christ's worthiness, and therewithal reflecting upon their own unworthiness and unkindness, they may relish Christ the better. Therefore the church here, that it might appear to herself, for her humiliation, how unkind she had been to shut the door against Christ when he knocked (whereupon he deservedly did withdraw himself, and made her seek him so long sorrowing), I tell you, says she, what a kind of beloved he is, thus and thus excellent. How did the consideration of God's kindness and love melt David's heart after that horrible sin in the matter of Uriah, 2 Sam. xii. 13; and the sweet looks of Christ upon Peter, Mat. xxvi. 75, that had been so unkind, melted him. So here the church, when she considered how unkind she had been to Christ her beloved, so incomparably excellent above other beloveds, to let him stand at the door, till his locks were wet with the dew of the night, the consideration hereof made her ashamed of herself. What! so excellent, so deserving a person as my beloved is to me, to be used of me so! what indignity is this! Thus to raise up the aggravation of her unkindness, no question but the church takes this course. For God's children are not as untoward worldlings and hypocrites, afraid to search and to understand themselves. The child of God loves to be well read in his own heart and unworthy ways. Therefore he lays all the blame he can upon himself every way. He knows he loseth nothing by this; for there is more mercy in Christ than there is sin in him. And the more sin abounds in his own feeling, the more grace shall abound. He knows the mystery of God's carriage in this kind. Therefore for this end, amongst the rest, she says, 'This is my beloved, and this is my friend,' whom I have so unkindly used.

6. And the last reason why the church is thus large was, *to draw and wind up the affections of those well-meaning Christians that were comers on, who were inquisitive of the way to Zion.* O ye daughters of Jerusalem, that you may know that there is some cause to seek after Christ more than you have done before, I tell you what an excellent person my beloved is; to whet their affections more and more. And we see the success of this excellent discourse in the beginning of the next chapter. 'Whither is thy beloved gone?' &c.

These and the like reasons there are of the large expressions of the church, of the excellencies of Christ. 'This is my beloved, and this is my friend, O ye daughters of Jerusalem.' But we will single out of these reasons for use, that which I think fittest for us to make use of.

Let us then oft think of the excellencies of Christ for this end, *to justify our endeavours and pains we take in the exercises of religion, and to justify God's people from the false imputations of the world, that they lay upon them*; as if they were negligent in other matters, and were too much busied in spiritual things. You see how large the church is in setting out the excellencies of her beloved, and then she shuts up all (being able to say no more) justifying our cause, 'This is my beloved, and this is my friend.' Do you wonder that I seek so much after him then? or wonder you at Christians, when they take such pains to keep their communion with Christ in a holy walking with, and depending upon God? These are no wonders, if you consider how excellent Christ is, what he hath done for us, and what he keeps for us in another world? that he will preserve us to his heavenly kingdom, till he put us into possession of that glorious condition that he hath purchased? Let the hearts of men dwell upon the consideration of these things, and then you shall see that God's children are rather to be blamed that they are no more careful, watchful, and industrious, than to be taxed that they are so much. Our Saviour Christ said, ' Wisdom is justified of all her children,' Mat. xi. 19. If you will make good that you are children of wisdom, you must be able to justify the wisdom of God every way, to justify your reading, hearing, your communion of saints ; to justify all the exercises of religion from an experimental taste and sweetness of them, as the church doth here, ' This is my beloved.' What says Joshua ? ' This choice I have made; do you what you will, it matters me not, but I and my house will serve the Lord,' Josh. xxiv. 15. So Paul makes a voluntary profession of his affection, Rom. i. 2, ' I am not ashamed of the gospel of Jesus Christ.' Let the gospel be entertained in the world as it will, and let others think of me as they will, that I am forward in the preaching of it ; I am not ashamed of it. And good reason he had not to be ashamed ; for it is the power of God to salvation, to all that believe ; yea the saving power to us. And have not I cause to stand in the defence of it ? And so he saith, ' I know whom I have believed,' &c., 2 Tim. i. 12. I am not ashamed to suffer bonds for his sake. Though the world thought him a mean person, ' I will not be scorned out of my faith and religion by shallow, empty persons, that know not what Christ and religion meaneth.' No ; ' I know whom I have believed ; he is able to keep that that I have committed to him against that day.' Let us therefore be able to justify from a judicious apprehension, sweet divine truths. You see what justifications there are of the church of God, ' Wherefore should the heathen say, Where is now their God ?' Micah vii. 10, and Ps. xlii. 10. Oh, it went to David's heart, when they said, ' Where is now their God,' ' What was become of his God,' when he was left in trouble, as the church here. And what doth he answer ? Doth he let it go with a question ? No, says he; our God is in heaven, Ps. cxiii. 4, and hath done whatsoever he pleased.

And this justification of religion, you may know by this sign. It is with the desertion of all discourses opposite to religion whatsoever. He that justifies the truth, he esteems meanly of other courses and discourses. Therefore in the next verse the church vilifies the idols. Our God is in heaven, and doth whatsoever he pleaseth ; the idols are silver and gold, the work of men's hands : they have eyes and see not, ears and hear not, Ps. cxv. 6. And the more we justify Christ, the more we will be against antichrist and his religion. We may know the owning of the one truth by the vilifying the other. Let us labour therefore to grow to such a convincing knowledge of Christ ; the good things in him ; and the ways of God, as we may be able to stand out against all opposition of the gates of hell whatsoever.

And to this end proceed in the study of Christ, and to a deeper search of him, and of the excellencies and good things in him, that we may say as Micah vii. 18, ' Who is a God like to thee, that pardons sins and iniquities ?' and as David, Ps. cxiii., ' Who is a God like our God, that humbleth himself to behold the things done here below ?'

And desire also to this purpose, the spirit of revelation, that which Paul prays for, Eph. iii. 18, ' that we may know that knowledge that is above all knowledge, the height, depth, and breadth of God's love in Christ.' So sweet is God in the greatest abasements of his children, that he leaves such a taste in the soul of a Christian, that from thence he may be able to say, ' This is my beloved,' when his beloved seems not to care for him. When the church seemed to be disrespected and neglected of Christ, yet she says, ' This is my beloved, and this is my friend, O ye daughters of Jerusalem.'

Shall rich men boast of their riches ? Shall men that are in favour, boast
of the favour of great persons ? Shall a man that hath large possessions
boast and think himself as good and as great as his estate is ? Shall a base-
minded worldling be able to boast ?   ' Why boastest thou thyself, O mighty
man ?' Ps. lii. 1.   Nay, you shall have malignant-spirited men boast of
their malignant destructive power.   I can do this and that mischief.   Shall
a man boast of. mischief, that he is able to do mischief ? and hath not a
Christian more cause to boast in God and in salvation ?   Lord, shine on me,
says David, Ps. iv. 6, let me enjoy the light of thy countenance ; and that
shall bring me more joy than they have, when their corn and wine increaseth.   Know this, as he goes on in the same psalm, that God accepts
the righteous man.

Therefore let us think we have much more cause to boast of God and of
Christ in a spiritual manner, than the worldling hath of the world.   Is not
God and Christ our portion ? and having Christ, have we not all things
with Christ ?   Put case all things be took from us.   If a man have Christ,
he is rich though he have nothing else.   If he have all without him, his
plenty is (as a father saith, and as it is in truth) beggary.   But whosoever
hath Christ may thus rejoice with David, ' The lot is fallen to me in pleasant places ; yea, I have a goodly heritage,' Ps. xvi. 6.   Would we have
more than God in Christ, a ring with a diamond very precious in it ?   Now
the daughters of Jerusalem, hearing this large expression of affection, ask,

' Whither is thy beloved gone, O thou fairest among women ? whither is
thy beloved turned aside ? that we may seek him with thee,' chap. vi. 1.

Here is another question.   The first which the daughters of Jerusalem
ask is, ' What is thy beloved ?' whereupon the church took occasion to express what her beloved was : upon her expression closing up all with this
general, ' This is my beloved, and this is my friend.'

Then the second question is, ' Whither is thy beloved gone ?'   One question begets another ; and indeed if this question be well satisfied, what is
Christ above others ? this will follow again.   Where is he ?   How shall I
get him ?   How shall I seek him ?   What is the reason this second question is seldom made ?   Whither is he gone ? how shall I get Christ ?   Because the former question, namely, ' What is Christ ? is so seldom made.
For if we did once know what Christ is, we would be sure with the daughters
of Jerusalem to ask whither is he gone, that we may seek him with thee.

We see here is a growth in the desires of the daughters of Jerusalem,
whence we learn,

*That grace, though it be in never so little proportion at the first, it is grow-
ing still.*

From the first question, ' What is thy beloved ?' here is a second, upon
better information, ' Whither is thy beloved gone, that we may seek him
with thee ?'   Nothing is less than grace at the first, nothing in the world
so little in proportion.   The kingdom of heaven is compared to a grain of
mustard seed, Mat. xiii. 31, *seq.*   That is, the work of grace in the heart, as
well as in the preaching of the gospel, in the beginning is little.   It is true
of the work of grace, as well as of the word of grace, that it is like a grain
of mustard seed at first.   ' What is thy beloved ?' inquires the church at
first ; but when she hears of the excellency of Christ, then, ' Whither is thy
beloved gone ?'   Grace begets grace.   There is a connection and knitting
together in religion.   Good things beget good things.   It is a strange thing
in religion how great a matter ariseth of a little beginning.   The woman of
Samaria had but a small beginning of grace, and yet she presently drew

many of her neighbours to believe in Christ. So Andrew, John i. 41. As soon as he was converted, he finds his brother Simon, and tells him that he had found the Messiah, and so brings him to Christ. And Philip, as soon as he had got a spark of faith himself, he draws also Nathanael to come to Christ. Paul speaks of his bonds, how the noise of them was in Cæsar's court, Philip. i. 13, and many believed the very report, which, howsoever it is not a working cause, yet it may be a preparing, inducing, leading cause to such things, from one thing to another, till there follow this change and full conversion. You see here the daughters of Jerusalem growing. Therefore, let us labour to be under good means. Some of the Romists and others, which are ill affected and grounded in that point, they think that the efficacy of grace is, as we call it, from the congruity, fitness, and proportion of the means to the heart and will of man. And thereupon God converts one and not another, because there is a congruous and fit offering of means to him when he is fitly disposed, and another is not fitly disposed. Therefore, there follows not upon it effectual calling. So that the virtue of the means offered depends upon suitableness and fitness in the party to whom the means are offered, and not upon the power and blessing of God. Verily, this is plausible, and goes down very roundly with many weak persons; but this is a false and a gross error, for unless God by his Holy Spirit do work by the means, no planting and watering will bring any increase, and change the heart and mind. Though there were greater means in Christ's time when he wrought these miracles, than any time before, yet all those could not convert that froward generation; and it was Moses's complaint in the wilderness, where they had abundance of means, ' God hath not given you a heart to perceive, and eyes to see, and ears to hear until this day,' Deut. xxix. 4. When a man is planted under good means and frequents them, then ordinarily it pleaseth God, by the inward workings of his own powerful Spirit, to work greater matters; and those that keep out of God's reach, that will not come into places where they may hear good things, there is no hope of them. Though there be many ill fish in the net, yet there is no hope to catch them that are without the net. So those that are kept out of all opportunities and occasions whereby God's Spirit may work upon them, there is no hope of them.

Let us learn this heavenly wisdom, to advantage ourselves this way, by improving all good opportunities whatsoever whereby we may learn; for God works by outward means. Good company and good discourse, these breed excellent thoughts. As, therefore, we love our souls, take all advantages wherein the Spirit of God works. We shall find incredible fruit thereof, more than we would believe. But to come to the question.

1. See here, first of all, in this question *the blessed success of the church's inquiry after Christ* in the daughters of Jerusalem after they heard the large explications of the excellencies of Christ, especially by the church, whom they had a good conceit of, for they call her ' the fairest among women.'

And seeing, likewise, the confidence of the church, she stands to it, ' This is my beloved;' yea, also, eagerness in the church to seek after him, they would seek him with her. So that where these meet, a large unfolding of the truth of God, and that by persons that are known to be good, well accepted, and conceited of, and where there is a large demonstration of real affection, and the things are spoken of with confidence, as knowing what they say; the word, I say, so managed, it is never without wondrous success.

(1.) For in the course of reason, what can I have to say, considering the party who speaks is an excellent person? He is wiser and holier than I; he takes to heart these things; and shall not I affect that which those that have better parts and graces do?

(2.) Then, withal, I see not only excellent persons do it, but I see how earnest they are. Surely there is some matter in it; for persons so holy, so wise, and gracious to be so earnest, surely either they are to blame, or I am too dull and too dead; but I have most cause to suspect myself.

(3.) And to see them carried with a spirit of confidence, as if they were well enough advised when they deliver this, 'This is my beloved,' in particular, and then to shut up all in general, 'This is my beloved, and this is my friend;' I say, when there is grace and life in the heart, and earnestness with confidence, this, together with the explication of the heavenly excellencies of Christ and of religion, it hath admirable success. As here in the church, 'the fairest among women,' the 'daughters of Jerusalem,' seeing the church was so earnest, confident, and so large in the explication of the excellencies of Christ, see how it works. It draws out this question with resolution. They join with the church in seeking Christ, 'Whither is thy beloved gone, O thou fairest among women? whither is thy beloved turned aside? that we may seek him with thee.' Where by the way observe, as the church before doubles it, 'This is my beloved, and this is my friend,' so they answer with a double question, 'Whither is thy beloved gone? whither is he turned aside? O thou fairest among women,' &c. From this appellation note,

2. If we would be happy instruments to convert others, being converted ourselves, *labour to be such as the world may think to be good and gracious.* 'O thou fairest among women,' fair in the robes of Christ took * out of his wardrobe. All the beauty and ornaments that the church hath she hath from Christ. Let us labour to be such as the world may conceit are good persons. We say of physicians, when the patient hath a good conceit of them, the cure is half wrought. So the doctrine is half persuaded when there is a good conceit of the speaker.

3. Again, *labour to be earnest.* If we would kindle others, we must be warmed ourselves; if we would make others weep, we must weep ourselves. Naturalists could observe this. The church spake this with large expressions, indeed, more than can be expressed. Let us labour to be deeply affected with what we speak, and speak with confidence as if we knew what we spoke, as the apostle John doth, in the beginning of his epistle, to bring others to be better persuaded of his doctrine. He affirmeth 'that which was from the beginning, which we have heard, which we have seen with these our eyes, which we have looked upon, and these hands of ours have handled of the word of life' he delivered to them, 1 John i. 1.

For when we are confident from spiritual experience, it is wonderful how we shall be instruments of God to gain upon others. So Peter. 'We followed not,' says he, 'deceivable fables, when we opened unto you the power and coming of our Lord Jesus Christ, but with our eyes we saw his majesty,' 2 Pet. i. 16.

Do not think it belongs only to the ministry. There is an art of conversion that belongs to every one that is a grown Christian, to win others.

'Whither is thy beloved gone, O thou fairest among women?'

The next observation out of the words, because it is the especial, which works upon the daughters of Jerusalem, is from the large explication of Christ.

* That is, 'taken.'—G

That which most of all stirs up holy affections to search after Christ is the large explications of his excellencies.

Then be in love with the ministry of the gospel and the communion of saints, who have their tongues and their hearts taught of God to speak excellently. Their tongues are as refined silver; their hearts are enriched to increase the communion of saints, Prov. x. 20. Mark this one excellency of that excellent ordinance of God in Christ, whereof Paul saith, Eph. iii. 7, 8, ' To me is committed this excellent office, to lay open the unsearchable riches of Christ;' such riches as may draw you to wonder, such ' as eye hath never seen, nor ear heard, nor hath entered into the heart of man to conceive,' 1 Cor. ii. 9; and so to draw the affections of people after them.

And because it is the special office of the ministry to lay Him open, to hold up the tapestry, to unfold the hidden mysteries of Christ, labour we, therefore, to be alway speaking somewhat about Christ, or tending that way. When we speak of the law, let it drive us to Christ; when of moral duties, to teach us to walk worthy of Christ. Christ, or somewhat tending to Christ, should be our theme and mark to aim at.

Therefore what shall we judge of those that are hinderers of this glorious ordinance of Christ in the gospel? They are enemies of conversion and of the calling of God's people; enemies of their comfort. And what shall we think of those wretched and miserable creatures that, like Cain, are vagabonds? who wander, and will not submit themselves to any ordinance meekly, but keep themselves out of this blessed opportunity of hearing the excellencies of Christ, which might draw their hearts to him? We are made for ever, if Christ and we be one. If we have all the world without him, it is nothing; if we have nothing in the world but Christ, we are happy. Oh! happy then when this match is made between Christ and the soul! The friends of the bride and of Christ, they, laying open the unsearchable riches of Christ to the spouse, draw the affections, work faith, and so bring the bride and the bridegroom together.

Thus far of the question. Now we have the church's answer to the daughters of Jerusalem.

' My beloved is gone into his garden, to the beds of spices, to feed in the gardens, and to gather lilies.'

The question was not for a bare satisfaction, but from a desire the church had to seek Christ. ' Whither is thy beloved gone, that we may seek him?' It was not a curious question, but a question of inquisition tending to practice. Many are inquisitive; but when they know another man's meaning, it is all they desire. Now I know your meaning, will they say, but I mean not to follow your counsel. The daughters of Jerusalem had a more sincere intention, ' O thou fairest among women, whither is thy beloved turned aside? *that we may seek him with thee.*' Whereunto the church answered,

' My beloved is gone into his garden, to the beds of spices, to feed in the gardens.' Where we see,

The church is not squeamish, but directly answers to the question. For there is no envy in spiritual things, because they may be divided *in solidum.* One may have as much as another, and all alike. Envy is not in those things that are not divisible; in other things, the more one hath, another hath the less. But there is no envy in grace and glory, because all may share alike. Therefore here is no envy in the answer, as if she denied the daughters of Jerusalem the enjoying of her beloved. No. If you will know, says she, I will tell you directly whither my beloved is gone.

' My beloved is gone into his garden, to the bed of spices,' &c.

God hath two gardens. The church catholic is his garden, and every particular church are gardens and beds of spices, in regard that many Christians are sown there that Christ's soul delights in, as in sweet spices. This was spoken of before at large in chapter v. 1, why the church is called a garden, being a severed place from the waste.* The church is severed from the wilderness of the world in God's care and love ; likewise he tends and weeds his church and garden. As for the waste of the world, he is content the wilderness should have barren plants, but he will not endure such in his garden. Therefore those that give themselves liberty to be naught in the church of God, he will have a time to root them out. Trees that are not for fruit shall be for the fire ; and above all other trees their doom shall be the heaviest that grow in God's garden without fruit. That fig-tree shall be cursed, Luke xiii. 6–9.

Men are pleased with answering the bill of accusation against them thus : Are we not baptized ? and do we not come to church ? &c. What do you make of us ? Yet they are abominable swearers, and filthy in their lives. To such I say, the more God hath lift you up and honoured you in the use of the means, the more just shall your damnation be, that you bring forth nothing but briers and brambles, Heb. vi. 4, *seq.*, the grapes of Sodom and the vine of Gomorrah, Deut. xxxii. 32. Heavy will the doom be of many that live in the church's bosom, to whom it had been better to have been born in America (*r*), in Turkey, or in the most barbarous parts in the world. They have a heavy account to make that have been such ill proficients under abundance of means. Therefore it ought to be taken to heart.

' My beloved is gone into his garden, to the beds of spices, to feed in the gardens, and to gather lilies.'

That is, having first planted them lilies here, to gather them, and to transport them out of the garden here to the garden in heaven, where there shall be nothing but lilies. For the church of God hath two gardens or paradises since the first paradise (whereof that was a resemblance), the paradise of the church and the paradise of heaven. As Christ saith to the good thief, ' This day thou shalt be with me in paradise,' Luke xxiii. 43 ; so those that are good plants in the paradise of the church, they shall be glorious plants also in the paradise of heaven. We must not alway be here ; we shall change our soil, and be taken into heaven. ' He is gone into his garden to gather lilies.'

1. Christians are compared to lilies for their *purity and whiteness*, unspotted in justification ; and for their endeavours in sanctity and holiness, wherein also at length they shall be wholly unspotted. It is the end they are chosen to, ' to be holy without blame before him in love,' Eph. i. 4. God and Christ looks upon them without blame, not as they are here defiled and spotted, but as they intend, by little and little, to purge and purify themselves by the Spirit that is in them, that they may be altogether without blame. They are lilies, being clothed with the white garment of Christ's righteousness, not having a natural whiteness and purity (*s*). The whiteness and purity of God's children is borrowed. All their beauty and garments are taken out of another's wardrobe. The church is all glorious within ; but she borrows her glory, as the moon borrows all her light from the sun. The church's excellency is borrowed. It is her own, but by gift ; but being once her own, it is her own for ever.

The church before was likened to a garden culled out, an Eden, a para-

* See pp. 8–10.—G.

dise. Now there, you know, were four streams, sweet and goodly rivers, which watered paradise; the heads of which rivers were without it. So the church of God, her graces are her own; that is, the Spirit of God comes through her nature, purgeth and purifieth it; but the spring of those graces, as in paradise, is out of herself.

2. And then the lily is *a tall, goodly plant.* Therefore the church is compared to them. Other men are compared to thorns, not only for a noxious, hurtful quality in them, but for their baseness likewise. What are thorns good for, but to cumber the ground, to eat out the heart of it, to hide snakes, and for the fire? Wicked men are not lilies, but thorns. They are base, mean persons. Antiochus, Dan. xi. 21, is said to be a vile person, though he were a king, because he was a naughty* man. Wicked men, though they be never so great, being void of the grace of God, are vile persons. Though we must respect them in regard of their places, yet as they are in their qualification, they are vile and base thorns. But the church is not so, but as a lily among thorns, that is, among vile and abominable persons.

Use 1. The use is *to comfort God's children.* They have an excellency and glory in them, which, howsoever it is not from them, yet it is theirs by gift, and eternally theirs. Therefore let them comfort themselves against all the censures of sinful persons that labour to trample them under foot, and think basely and meanly of them, as of the offscouring of the world. Let the unworthy world think of them as they will, they are lilies in God's esteem, and are so indeed; glorious persons that have the Spirit of glory resting upon them, 1 Pet. iv. 14, and whom the world is not worthy of, Heb. xi. 38, though their glory be within. Therefore let us glory in it, that God vouchsafeth saving grace to us above any other privilege.

Use 2. Again, it comforts us in all our wants whatsoever, that *God will take care for us.* Christ useth this argument. God saith, he clotheth the lilies of the field with an excellent beauty; he cares even for the meanest plants, and will he not take care for you, O ye of little faith? Mat. vi. 29. Doth he care for lilies, that are to-day, and to-morrow are cast into the oven? and shall he not care for the lilies of paradise, the living lilies, those holy reasonable lilies? Undoubtedly he will. Our Saviour Christ's reason is undeniable. He that puts such a beauty upon the poor plants, that flourish to-day in the morning, and wither before night; he that puts such a beauty upon the grass of the field; will he not put more excellency upon his children? will he not provide for them, feed them? Undoubtedly he will. Thus we have shewed why God's children in the church of God are compared to lilies.

'To gather lilies.' Christ is said to gather these lilies, that is, he will gather them together. Christ will not have his lilies alone, scattered. Though he leaves them oft alone for a while, yet he will gather them to congregations and churches. The name of a church in the original is *Ecclesia* (t). It is nothing but a company gathered out of the world. Do we think that we are lilies by nature? No; we are thorns and briers. God makes us lilies, and then gathers us to other lilies, that one may strengthen another. The Spirit of God in his children is not a spirit of separation of Christians from Christians, but a spirit of separation from the waste, wild wilderness of the world, as we say of fire, *Congregat homogenea et disgregat heterogenea.* It congregates all homogeneal things, as gold, which it gathers, but disgregates heterogeneal things, consumeth dross. So the

* That is, 'wicked.'—G.

Spirit of God severs thorns, and gathers lilies ; gathers Christians together in the church, and will gather them for ever in heaven.

Thus we see the answer of the church to the daughters of Jerusalem, what it was, with the occasion thereof ; the question of the daughters of Jerusalem, ' Whither is thy beloved gone ? ' So that the church was be-holden to the daughters of Jerusalem for ministering such a question, to give her occasion to know better what her beloved was. Indeed, we many times gain by weaker Christians. Good questions, though from weak ones, minister suitable answers. It is a Greek proverb, that ' doubting begets plenty and abundance,' for doubting at the first begets resolution at last. O ! that we could take occasion hence to think of this. What excellent virtue is in the communion of saints, when they meet about heavenly exercises ! What a blessing follows when, though at the entry their affections may be flat and dull, yet they part not so ! Christ heats and inflames their hearts to do much good to one another. O ! those that shall for ever live together in heaven, should they not delight to live more together on earth ?

THE NINETEENTH SERMON.

I am my beloved's, and my beloved is mine ; he feedeth among the lilies.—
CANT. VI. 3.

THESE words are a kind of triumphant acclamation upon all the former passages ; as it were, the foot of the song. For when the church had spoken formerly of her ill-dealing with Christ, and how he thereupon ab-sented himself from her, with many other passages, she shuts up all at last with this, ' I am my beloved's, and my beloved is mine.'

Now she begins to feel some comfort from Christ, who had estranged himself from her. O ! saith she, notwithstanding all my sufferings, deser-tions, crosses, and the like, ' I am my beloved's, and my beloved is mine,' words expressing the wondrous comfort, joy, and contentment the church now had in Christ ; having her heart inflamed with love unto him, upon his manifesting of himself to her soul. ' I am my beloved's, and my beloved is mine : he feedeth among the lilies.'

There is a mutual intercourse and vicissitude of claiming interest betwixt Christ and his church. I am Christ's, and Christ is mine. ' I am my beloved's, and my beloved is mine.'

From the dependence and order of the words coming in after a desertion for a while, observe,

That Christ will not be long from his church.

The spiritual desertions (forsakings, as we use to call them), howsoever they be very irksome to the church (that loves communion with Christ), and to a loving soul to be deprived of the sense of her beloved, yet notwith-standing they are but short. Christ will not be long from his church. His love and her desire will not let him. They offer violence. Why art thou absent ? say they. Why art thou so far off, and hidest thyself ? Joseph may conceal himself for a space, but he will have much ado so to hold long, to be straitened to his brethren. Passion will break out. So Christ may seem hard to be entreated, and to cross his own sweet disposition, as to the woman of Canaan, but he will not long keep at this distance. He is soon overcome. ' O ! woman, great is thy faith ; have what thou wilt,' Mat. xv. 28. When she strove with him a little (as faith is a striving grace), see how she did win upon him ! So the angel and Jacob may strive for a while, but Jacob at the length proves Israel; he prevails with God, Gen. xxxii. 24, *seq*. So it is with the Christian soul and Christ. Howsoever there be desertion, for causes before mentioned, because the church was negligent, as we hear, and partly for the time to come, that Christ, by his estrangement, might sweeten his coming again howsoever there may be strangeness for a time, yet Christ will return again to his spouse.

Use 1. The use should be not only *for comfort to stay us in such times, but to teach us likewise to wait, and never give over*. If the church had given over here, she had not had such gracious manifestations of Christ to her. Learn hence, therefore, this use, to wait God's leisure. God will wait to do good to them that wait on him, Isa. xxx. 18. If we wait his leisure, he will wait an opportunity of doing good to us. When God seems not to answer our prayers, let us yet wait. We shall not lose by our tarrying. He will wait to do us good.

Use 2. In the next place, observe, after this temporary desertion, *Christ visits his church with more abundant comfort than ever before*.

Now, the church cannot hold, ' My beloved is mine, and I am his ;' and Christ cannot hold, but falls into a large commendation of his spouse back again. As she was large in his commendations, so he is large in hers, and more large. He will have the last word. Therefore, learn by this experience, ' that all things work together for the best to them that love God,' Rom. viii. 28. All things. What? evil ? Ay, evil. Why, even sin turns to their humiliation ; yea, and desertion (those spiritual ills), turns to their good ; for Christ seems to forsake for a while, that he may come after with more abundance of comfort. When once he hath enlarged the soul before with a spacious desire of his coming, to say, O ! that he would come ; when the soul is thus stretched with desire in the sense of want, then he fills it again till it burst forth, ' My beloved is mine, and I am his.' It was a good experiment of Bernard, an holy man in ill times, *tibi accidit*, &c., speaking of Christ's dealing with his church. He comes and he goeth away for thy good. He comes for thy good to comfort thee ; after which, if thou be not careful to maintain communion with him, then he goeth away for thy good, to correct thy error, and to enlarge thy desire of him again, to teach thee to lay sure and faster hold upon him when thou hast him, not to let him go again.

If you would see a parallel place to this, look in Cant. iii., where there is the like case of the spouse and Christ, ' By night on my bed I sought him.' The church sought Christ not only by day, but by night, ' I sought him whom my soul loved.' Though she wanted him, yet her soul loved him constantly. Though a Christian's soul have not present communion with Christ, yet he may truly say, My soul loves him, because he seeks him diligently and constantly in the use of all the means. So we see the church, before my text, calls him my beloved still, though she wanted communion with him. Well, she goes on, ' I sought him, but I found him not.' Would the church give over there ? No ; then she riseth and goeth about the city, and about the streets, and ' seeks him whom her soul loved,' seeks him, and will not give over. So I sought him, but I wanted the issue of my seeking, I found him not. What comes upon that ? ' The watchmen go about the city, and find her.' Of whom, when by her own seeking she could not find Christ, she inquires, ' Saw you him whom my soul loveth ?' She inquires of the watchmen, the guides of God's people, who could not satisfy her fully. She could not find her beloved, yet what doth she, she shews, verse 4. It was but a little that she stayed, after she had used all means, private and public—in her bed, out of her bed—by the watchmen and others, yet, saith she, it was but a little that I was past from them. She had not an answer presently, though the watchmen gave her some good counsel. It was not presently, yet not long after. Christ will exercise us a while with waiting : ' It was but a little that I passed from them, but I found him whom my soul loved.' After all our seeking, there must be waiting, and then we shall find him whom our soul loveth. Perhaps we have used all means, private and public, and yet find not that comfort we look for. Oh, but wait a while ! God hath a long time waited for thee. Be thou content to wait a while for him. We shall not lose by it, for it follows in the next verse ; after she had found him whom her soul loved, ' I held him, I would not let him go.' So this is the issue of desertions. They stir up diligence and searching, in the use of means, private and public ; and exercise patience to wait God's leisure, who will not suffer a gracious soul to fail of its expectation. At length he will fulfil the desires of them that fear him, Ps. cxlv. 19 ; and this comes of their patience. Grace grows greater and stronger. ' I held him, and would not let him go, until I had brought him unto my mother's house.' Thus you see how the Spirit expresseth the same truth in another state of the church. Compare place with place. To go on.

' I am my beloved's, and my beloved is mine.' The words themselves are a passionate expression of long-looked-for consolation. Affections have eloquence of their own beyond words. Fear hath a proper expression. Love vents itself in broken words and sighs, delighting in a peculiar eloquence suitable to the height and pitch of the affection, that no words can reach unto. So that here is more in the words breathed from such an inflamed heart, than in ordinary construction can be picked out, ' I am my beloved's,' &c., coming from a full and large heart, expressing the union and communion between Christ and the church, especially after a desertion. ' I am my beloved's, and my beloved is mine.'

First, I say, the union, viz., the union of persons, which is before all comfort and communion of graces, ' I am my beloved's, and my beloved is mine.' Christ's person is ours, and our persons are his. For, as it is in marriage, if the person of the husband be not the wife's, his goods are not hers, nor his titles of honour ; for these come all to her, because his person is hers : he having passed over the right of his own body and of his person to his wife, as she hath passed over all the right of herself to her husband. So it is in this mystical marriage. That that entitles us to communion of graces is union of persons between Christ and his church. ' I am my beloved's, and my beloved himself is mine.' And indeed nothing else will content a Christian's heart. He would not care so much for heaven itself, if he had not Christ there. The sacrament, word, and comforts, why doth he esteem them ? As they come from Christ, and as they lead to Christ. It is but an adulterous and base affection to love anything severed from Christ.

Now, from this union of persons comes a communion of all other things whatsoever. ' I am my beloved's, and my beloved is mine.' If Christ himself be mine, then all is mine (u). What he hath done, what he hath suffered, is mine; the benefit of all is mine. What he hath is mine. His prerogatives and privileges to be the Son of God, and heir of heaven,

and the like, all is mine. Why? Himself is mine. Union is the foundation of communion. So it is here with the church, 'I am my beloved's.'
My person is his, my life is his, to glorify him, and to lay it down when
he will. My goods are his, my reputation his. I am content to sacrifice
all for him. I am his, all mine is his. So you see there is union and
communion mutually, between Christ and his church. The original and
spring hereof is Christ's uniting and communicating himself to his church
first. The spring begins to* the stream. What hath the stream or cistern
in it, but what is had from the spring? First we love him, because he
loved us first, 1 John iv. 19. It was a true speech of Augustine, *Quicquid
bonum*, &c.: whatsoever is good in the world or lovely, it is either God or
from God; it is either Christ or from Christ. He begins it. It is said in
nature, love descends. The father and the mother love the child before
the child can love them. Love, indeed, is of a fiery nature. Only here is
the dissimilitude, fire ascends, love descends. It is stronger, descending
from the greater to the less, than ascending up from the meaner to the
greater, and that for this amongst other reasons,

Because the greater person looks upon the lesser as a piece of himself—sees
himself in it. The father and mother see themselves in their child. So
God loves us more than we can love him, because he sees his image in us.
Neither is there only a priority of order. He loves us first, and then we
love him. But also.of causality. He is the cause of our love, not by way
of motive only. He loves us, and therefore from an ingenuous spirit we
must love him again. But he gives us his Spirit, circumciseth our hearts
to love him, Deut. xxx. 6; for all the motives or moral persuasions in the
world, without the Spirit, cannot make us love, 1 Thess. iv. 9. We are
taught of God to love one another, our brethren whom we see daily, saith
Paul, much more need we to be taught to love him whom we never saw,
so that his love kindles ours by way of reflection.

In the new covenant God works both parts, his own and our parts too.
Our love to him, our fear of him, our faith in him, he works all, even as he
shews his own love to us.

If God love us thus, what must we do? Meditate upon his love. Let
our hearts be warmed with the consideration of it. Let us bring them to
that fire of his love, and then they will wax hot within us, and beg the
Spirit, 'Lord, thou hast promised to give thy Spirit to them that ask it,'
Luke xi. 10, and to circumcise our hearts to love thee, and to love one
another, 'give thy Holy Spirit, as thou hast promised.'

In a word, these words, "I am my beloved's, and my beloved is mine,'
to join them both together.

1. They imply a *mutual propriety*,† Christ hath a propriety in me, and I
in Christ. Peculiar propriety. Christ is mine, so as I have none in the
world. So mine, 'whom have I in heaven but Christ?' and what is there
in earth in comparison of him? He is mine, and mine in a peculiar manner, and I am his in a peculiar manner. There is propriety with peculiarity.

2. Then, again, these words, 'I am his,' implies *mutual love*. All is
mutual in them, mutual propriety, mutual peculiarity, and mutual love. I
love Christ so as I love nothing else. There is nothing above him in my
heart, as Christ loves me more than anything else, saith the church, and
every Christian. He loves all, and gives outward benefits to all, but to me

---

* That is, 'originates, or gives its beginning to.'—ED.
† That is, 'property.'—G.

he hath given himself, so love I him.   As the husband loves all in the
family, his cattle and his servants, but he gives himself to his spouse.   So
Christ is mine, himself is mine, and myself am Christ's.   He hath my soul,
my affections, my body, and all.   He hath a propriety in me, and a peculiarity in me.   He hath my affection and love to the uttermost, as I have
his, for there is an intercourse in these words.

3. Then, again, they imply *mutual familiarity*.   Christ is familiar to my
soul, and I to Christ.   He discovers himself to me in the secret of his love,
and I discover myself to him in prayer and meditation, opening my soul to
him upon all occasions.   God's children have a spirit of prayer, which is
a spirit of fellowship, and talks, as it were, to God in Christ.   It is the
language of a new-born Christian.   He cries to his Father.   There is a
kind of familiarity between him and his God in Christ, who gives the entrance and access to God.   So that where there is not a kind of familiarity
in prayer and opening of the soul to Christ upon all occasions, there is not
this holy communion.   Those that are not given to prayer, they cannot in
truth speak these words, as the church doth here, ' I am my beloved's, and
my beloved is mine,' for they imply sweet familiarity.

4. Then, again, they imply *mutual likeness* one to another.   He is
mine, and I am his.   The one is a glass to the other.   Christ sees himself
in me, I see myself in him.   For this is the issue of spiritual love, especially, that it breeds likeness and resemblance of the party loved in the
soul that loveth ; for love frameth the soul to the likeness of the party
loved.   I am his, I resemble him.   I am his, I have given myself to him.
I carry his picture and resemblance in my soul, for they are words of mutual conformity.   Christ, out of love, became like me in all things, wherein
I am not like the devil, that is, sin excepted.   If he became like me, taking
my nature that I might be near him in the fellowship of grace, ' My beloved is mine,' I will be as like him as possibly I can, I am his.   Every
Christian carries a character of Christ's disposition as far as weakness will
suffer.   You may know Christ in every Christian ; for as the king's coin
carries the stamp of the king (Cæsar's coin bears Cæsar's superscription),
so every Christian soul is God's coin, and he sets his own stamp upon it.
If we be Christ's, there is a mutual conformity betwixt him and us.

Now, where you see a malicious, unclean, worldly spirit, know that is
a stamp of the devil, none of Christ's.   He that hath not the Spirit of God
is none of his.   Now, where the Spirit of Christ is, it stamps Christ's likeness upon the soul.   Therefore we are exhorted, Phil. ii. 5, to be like-
minded to Christ.

5. Again, these words, ' I am my beloved's, and my beloved is mine,'
imply a *mutual care* that Christ and the soul have of the good of one another,
of each other's honour and reputation.   As Christ hath a care of our good,
so a Christian soul, if it can say with truth and sincerity I am Christ's, it
must needs have care of Christ's good, of his children, religion, and truth.
What ! will such a soul say, Shall Christ care for my body, soul, and salvation, and stoop to come from heaven to save me, and shall I have no care for
him and his glory ?   He hath left his truth and his church behind him, and
shall not I defend his truth, and stand for the poor church to the utmost
of my power against all contrary power ?   Shall not I stand for religion ?
Shall it be all one to me what opinions are held ?   Shall I pretend he cares
for me, and shall I not care for that I should care for ?   Is it not an honour to me that he hath trusted me to care for anything ? that he will be
honoured by my care ?   Beloved, it is an honour for us that we may speak

a good word for religion, for Christ's cause, for his church, against ma-
ligners and opposers; and we shall know one day that Christ will be a
rewarder of every good word.   Where this is said in sincerity, that Christ
is mine, and I am Christ's, there will be this mutual care.

6. Likewise there is implied a *mutual complacency* in these words.   By
a complacency I mean a resting, contenting love.   Christ hath a complacency and resting in the church; and the church hath a sweet resting
.contentment in Christ.   Christ in us and we in him.   A true Christian
soul that hath yielded up its consent to Christ, when it is beaten in the
world, vexed and turmoiled, it can rely on this, 'I have yet a loving
husband;' yet I have Christ.

Let this put us upon a search into ourselves, what we retire to, when we
meet with afflictions.   Those that have brutish and beastly souls retire to
carnal contentments, to good fellowship; forget, besot, and fly away from
themselves; their own consciences and thought of their own trouble.
Whereas a soul that hath any acquaintance with God in Christ, or any interest into Christ, so that it may say, that Christ is mine, and I am Christ's,
there will be contentment and rest in such a soul, whatsoever it meets with
in the world.

7. The last thing implied is *courage*, a branch of the former.   Say all
against it what they can, saith the resolved soul, I will be Christ's.   Here
is courage with resolution.   Agreeable hereto is that, 'One shall say I
am the Lord's, and another shall call himself by the name of Jacob; another shall subscribe and surname himself by the name of Israel,' Isa. xliv. 5.
Where there is not this resolution in good causes, there is not the Spirit of
Christ; there is no interest into Christ.   It is but a delusion and self-
flattery to say I am Christ's, when there is not resolution to stand to Christ.
These words are the expression of a resolved heart, I am, and I will be
Christ's; I am not ashamed of my bargain; of the consent I have given
him; I am and I will be his.   You have the like in Micah iv. 5, ' All people will
walk every one in the name of his god, they will resolve on that, and we
will walk in the name of the Lord our God for ever and for ever.'   So
that where these words are spoken in truth, that ' I am Christ's,' there is
necessarily implied, I will own him and his cause for ever and ever.

He hath married me for ever and ever; therefore, if I hope to have
interest in him for comfort for ever and ever, I must be sure to yield myself to him for ever and ever; and stand for his cause, in all oppositions,
against all enemies whatsoever.   These and such like places in Scripture
run parallel with this in the text, ' I am my beloved's, and my beloved is
mine,' not only holding in the person, but in the cause of Christ.   Every
man hopes his god will stand for him against the devil, who accuseth us
daily.   If we will have Christ to stand for us, and to be an advocate to
plead our cause as he doth in heaven, we must resolve to stand for him
against all enemies, heretics, schismatics, persecutors whatsoever; that we
will walk in the name of our God for ever and ever.

Quest. But when the case is not thus with us, and that neither we can
feel comfort from Christ, nor have this assurance of his love to us, what
should we judge of such?

Solution. We should not wonder to see poor souls distempered when
they are in spiritual desertions, considering how the spouse cannot endure
the absence of Christ.   It is out of love therefore in the deepest plunge
she hath this in her mouth, '*my* beloved.'   Therefore let us not judge
amiss of ourselves or others, when we are impatient in this kind.

But for a more full answer, in want of feeling of the love of Christ in regard of that measure we would (for there is never altogether a want of feeling, there is so much as keeps from despair alway, yet), if we carry a constant love towards him, mourn to him and seek after him as the church here ; if the desire of our souls be after him, that we make after him in the use of means, and are willing to speak of him as the church here, feel or feel not, we are his, and he will at length discover himself to us.

Let such drooping spirits consider, that as he will not be long from us, nor wholly, so it shall not be for our disadvantage that he retires at all. His absence at length will end in a sweet discovery of himself more abundantly than before. He absents himself for our good, to make us more humble and watchful for the time to come ; more pitiful to others ; more to prize our former condition ; to justify the ways of God more strictly ; to walk with him ; to regain that sweet communion which by our negligence and security we lost. When we are thus prepared by his absence, there ensues a more satisfying discovery of himself than ever before.

But when is the time that he comes ? Compare this with the former chapter. He comes after long waiting for him. The church waited for him, and waited in the use of all means. She runs to the watchmen, and then inquires after him of the daughters of Jerusalem. After this she finds him. After we have waited and expected Christ in the use of means, Christ at length will discover himself to us ; and yet more immediately, it was after the church had so deservedly exalted him in such lofty praises, ' This is my beloved, the chief of ten thousand ; he is altogether lovely.' When we set our hearts to the high exaltation of Christ above all things in the world, proclaiming him ' the chief of ten thousand,' this at the last breeds a gracious discovery, ' I am my beloved's, and my beloved is mine,' for Christ when he sees us faithful, and so loving that we will not endure his absence, and so constantly loving, that we love him notwithstanding some discouragements, it melts him at the last, as Joseph was melted by his brethren.

' I am my beloved's, and my beloved is mine.'

In the words, you see a mutual interest and owning between Christ and the church. Howsoever in the order of words, the church saith, ' I am my beloved's ' first, yet in order of nature Christ is ours first, though not in order of discovery. There is one order of knowing, and another order of causing. Many things are known by the effect, but they issue from a cause. I know he is mine, because I am his. I have given myself to him. I know it is day, because the sun is up. There is a proof from the effect. So I know a man is alive, because he walks. There is a proof of the cause by the effect. ' I am his ; ' I have grace to give myself up to him. Therefore I know he loves me. He is mine. Thus I say in order of discovery ; but in order of nature, he is first mine, and then I am his. ' My beloved is mine, and I am my beloved's.'

The union and communion betwixt us and Christ hath been already spoken of.

Now to speak of the branches, ' I am my beloved's, and my beloved is mine.' That Christ is first ours ; and then we are his, because he is ours ; and the wondrous comfort that issues hence—that Christ himself is ours.

How comes Christ to be ours ? (1.) Christ is ours by his Father's gift. God hath given him for us. (2.) Christ is ours by his own gift. He hath given himself for us. (3.) And Christ is ours by his Spirit that witnesseth so much to our spirits. For the Spirit is given for this purpose, to shew us all things that are given us of God, whereof Christ is the chief. Therefore the Spirit of Christ tells us that Christ is ours ; and Christ being ours, all that he hath is ours.

If he be ours, if we have the field, we have all the treasures in the field. If we have him, we have all his. He was born for us ; his birth was for us ; he became man for us ; he was given to death for us. And so likewise, he is ours in his other estate of exaltation. His rising is for our good. He will cause us to rise also, and ascend with him, and sit in heavenly places, judging the world and the angels. We recover in this second, what we lost in the first, Adam.

Use 1. This is a point of wondrous comfort *to shew the riches of a Christian*, his high estate, that Christ is his.

And Christ being ours, God the Father and the Holy Spirit and all things else in the world, the rich promises, are ours ; for in Christ they are all made, and for him they shall be performed. For, indeed, he is the chief promise of all himself, and all are ' yea and amen in him,' 2 Cor. i. 20. Can we want righteousness, while we have Christ's righteousness ? Is not his garment large enough for himself and us, too ? Is not his obedience enough for us ? Shall we need to patch it up with our own righteousness ? He is ours, therefore his obedience is ours.

Use 2. And this should be a ground likewise of *contentation* in our condition and state whatsoever*,—Christ himself is ours. In the dividing of all things, some men have wealth, honours, friends, and greatness, but not Christ, nor the love of God in Christ, and therefore they have nothing in mercy. But a Christian, he hath Christ himself. Christ is his by faith and by the Spirit's witness. Therefore, what if he want those appendencies,† the lesser things ? He hath the main ; what if he want a riveret, a stream ? He hath the spring, the ocean ; him, in whom all things are, and shall he not be content ? Put case a man be very covetous, yet God might satisfy him. What ! should anxious thoughts disquiet us, when we have such bills, such obligations from him who is faithfulness itself ? When a Christian cannot say, honour, favour, or great persons are his, yet he can say, he hath that that is worth all, more than all ; Christ is his.

Obj. Oh ! may some say, this is but a speculation,—Christ is yours. A man may want and be in misery for all that.

Ans. No ; it is a reality. Christ is ours, and all things else are ours. He that can command all things is mine. Why then, do I want other things ? Because he sees they are not for my good. If they were, he would not withhold them from me. If there were none to be had without a miracle, no comfort, no friends, he could and would make new out of nothing, nay, out of contraries, were it not better for me to be without them.

Use 3. That you may the more fully feed on this comfort, *study the excellencies of Christ* in the Scripture, the riches and honour that he hath, the favour he is in with his Father, with the intercession that he makes in heaven, John xvii. Study his mercy, goodness, offices, power, &c., and then come home to yourselves, ' All this is mine, for he is mine ; the love of God is mine.' God loves him, and therefore he loves me, because we are both one. He loves me with the same love that he loves his Son. Thus we should make use of this, that Christ is ours. I come to the second.

' I am my beloved's.'

This is a speech of reflection, second in nature, though first in place and

* That is, ' contentment.'—G.　　　　　　　† That is, ' additions.'—G.

in discovery to us. Sometimes we can know our own love, when we feel
not so much the love of Christ, but Christ's love must be there first. ' I
am my beloved's,' 1 John iv. 19.

How are we Christ's beloved ?

1. We are his, first of all, *by his Father's gift;* for God in his eternal
purpose gave him for us, and gives us to him, as it is in the excellent
prayer, 'Father, thine they were, and thou gavest them me,' John xvii. 6. I
had not them of myself first, but thine they were before all worlds were.
Thou gavest them me to redeem them, and my commission doth not extend
beyond thy gift. I die for all those that thou gavest me. I sanctify
myself for them, that they may be sanctified. So we are Christ's in his
Father's gift. But that is not all, though it be the chief, fundamental,
principal ground of all.

For, 2. We are his likewise by *redemption.* Christ took our nature, that
he might die for us, to purchase us. We cost him dear. We are a bloody
spouse to Christ. As that froward woman wrongfully said to Moses, ' Thou
art a bloody husband unto me,' Exod. iv. 25, so Christ may without wrong
say to the church, ' Thou art a spouse of blood to me.' We were, indeed,
to be his spouse, but first he must win us by conquest in regard of Satan,
and then satisfy justice. We were in such debt by sin, lying under God's
wrath, so as, till all debts were paid, we could not in the way of justice be
given as a spouse to Christ.

3. Nor is this all ; but we are Christ's *by marriage* also. For when he
purchased us, and paid so dear for us, when he died and satisfied divine
justice, he did it with a purpose to marry us to himself. We have nothing
to bring him but debt and misery ; yet he took upon him our nature to
discharge all, that he might marry us, and take us to himself. So we are
his by marriage.

4. Then again, we are his *by consent.* We have passed ourselves over
unto him. He hath given himself to us, and we have given ourselves to
him back again. To come to some use of it, if we be Christ's, as Christ
is ours.

Use 1. First, it is a point of *wondrous comfort.* God will not suffer his
own to want. He is worse than an infidel that will suffer his family to
perish. When we are once of Christ's family, and not only of his family,
but of his body, his spouse, can we think he will suffer us to want that
which is needful ?

2. Then again, as it comforts us against want, so it likewise *fenceth us
against all the accusations of Satan.* I am Christ's ; I am Christ's. If he
have anything to say, lo ! we may bid him go to Christ. If the creditor
comes to the wife, she is not liable to pay her own debts, but saith, Go to
my husband. So in all temptations, learn hence to send Satan whither he
should be sent. When we cannot answer him, send him to Christ.

3. And for the time to come, what a ground of comfort is this, that we
are Christ's, as well as he is ours. What a plea doth this put into our
mouths for all things that are beneficial to us. 'Lord, I am thine ; save
me,' saith the psalmist. Why? ' Save me, because I am thine, I am
thine ; Lord, teach me and direct me,' Ps. xxvii. 11. The husband is to
direct the spouse. The head should direct all the senses. All the treasures of wisdom are in Christ, as all the senses are in the head for the good
of the body. All fulness dwells in him. Therefore, plead with him, I
want wisdom ; teach me and instruct me how to behave myself in troubles,
in dangers, in fears. If it be an argument strong enough amongst men,

weak men, I am thine, I am thy child, I am thy spouse, &c, shall we attribute more pity and mercy to ourselves than to the God of mercy and comfort, who planted these affections in the creature ? Shall he make men tender and careful over others, and shall not he himself be careful of his own flock ? Do we think that he will neglect his jewels, his spouse, his diadem, and crown ? Isa. lxii. 3. He will not.

But you will urge experience. We see how the church is used, even as a forlorn widow, as if she had no husband in the world, as an orphan that had no father. Therefore, how doth this stand good ?

Ans. 1. The answer is, all that the church or any particular Christian suffers in this world, it is but that there may be *a conformity between the spouse and the husband.* The Head wore a crown of thorns, and went to heaven and happiness through a great deal of misery and abasement in the world, the lowest that ever was. And it is not meet that the church should go to heaven another way.

Ans. 2. Then again, all this is but *to fashion the spouse to be like to Christ,* but to bring the church and Christ nearer together. That is all the hurt they do, to drive the church nearer to Christ than before. Christ is as near to his church as ever in the greatest afflictions, by his Spirit. Christ cries out on the cross, ' My God, my God, why hast thou forsaken me ? ' It is a strange voice, that God should be his God, and yet, notwithstanding, seem to forsake him. But God was never more his God than at that present. Indeed, he was not his God in regard of some feelings that he had enjoyed in former times. He seemed to be forsaken in regard of some sense, as Christ seems to forsake the church in regard of some sense and feeling, but yet his God still. So the church may say, I am thine still. Though she seem to be forsaken in regard of some feelings, yet she is not deserted in regard of God's care for support of the inward man and fashioning to Christ. The church hath never sweeter communion with Christ than under the greatest crosses ; and, therefore, they many times have proved the ground of the greatest comforts. For Christ leads the church into the wilderness, and then speaks to her heart, Hos. ii. 14. Christ speaks to the heart of his spouse in the wilderness, that is, in a place of no comfort. There are no orchards or pleasures, but all discomforts there. A man must have it from heaven, if he have any good in the wilderness. In that wilderness, that is, in a desolate, disconsolate estate, Christ speaks to the heart of his children. There is in the wilderness oftentimes a sweet intercourse of love, incomparably beyond the time of prosperity.

Ans. 3 Again, to stay your hearts, *know this will not be long ;* as we see here, the church seemed to be forsaken and neglected, fell into the hands of cruel watchmen, and was fain to go through this and that means, but it was not long ere she met with him whom she sought after. It may be midnight at this time, but the night continues not long ; it will be morning ere long. Therefore the church may well say, ' Rejoice not against me, O mine enemy ; for though I be fallen, I shall rise again ; though I sit in darkness, the Lord will be a light unto me,' as it is Mic. vii. 8. It shall not be always ill with the church. Those that survive us shall see other manner of days than we see yet, whatsoever we shall ourselves.

4. Hence we have also an use of trial. Whosoever are Christ's, they have hearts to give themselves to him. As he gives himself, not his goods or his honours, but himself for his church, so the church gives herself to Christ. My delight is in him ; he hath myself, my heart, my love and affection, my joy and delight, and all with myself. If I have any honour,

he shall have it. I will use it for his glory. My riches I will give them
to him and his church and ministry and children, as occasion shall serve.
I am his, therefore all that I have is his, if he ask it at my hands. It is
said of the Macedonians, they gave themselves to Christ, and then their
riches and goods, 2 Cor. viii. 5. It is an easy matter to give our riches to
Christ when we have given ourselves first. A Christian, as soon as ever
he becomes a Christian, and ever after, to death, and in death too, he gives
up himself to Christ. They that stand with Christ, and will give this or
that particular, will part only with idle things that they may spare, are they
Christ's? No. A Christian gives himself and all his to Christ. So we
see here what we should do if Christ be ours. Let us give up ourselves to
him, as it is Rom. xii. 1. The issue of all that learned profound discourse in
the former part of the epistle, that Christ justifieth us by his righteousness
and merit, and sanctifies us by his Spirit, and hath predestinated and elected
us, and refused others, is this, ' I beseech you, give up your bodies and
souls, and all as a living sacrifice, holy and acceptable unto God.

In brief, these words imply renunciation and resignation. ' I am his,'
that is, I have given up myself to him, therefore I renounce all others that
stand not with his love and liking. I am not only his by way of service,
which I owe him above all that call for it, but I am his by way of resignation. If he will have me die, I will die. If he will have me live here, I
will. I have not myself to dispose of any longer. I have altogether alien-
ated myself from myself. I am his to serve him, his to be disposed of by
him. I have renounced all other.

Therefore here we have another answer to Satan, if he come to us and
solicit us to sin. Let the Christian's heart make this answer, *I am not mine
own*. What hath Satan and his instruments to do with me? Is my body
his to defile? Is my tongue his to swear at his pleasure? Shall I make
the temple of God the member of an harlot? As the apostle reasons,
' Shall I defile my vessel with sin?' 1 Cor. vi. 15. What saith converted
Ephraim? ' What have I any more to do with idols? for I have seen and observed him?' Hos. xiv. 8. We ought to have such resolutions ready in our
hearts. Indeed, when a Christian is resolute, the world counts such to be
lost. He is gone. We have lost him, say your dissolute, profane persons.
It is true they have lost him indeed, for he is not his own, much less theirs,
any longer. But he is found to God and himself and the church. Thus
we see what springs from this, that Christ is ours, and that we are Christ's
back again. Let us carry this with us even to death; and if times should
come that God should honour us by serving himself of us in our lives, if
Christ will have us spend our blood, consider this, I am not mine own in
life nor death, and it is my happiness that I am not my own. For if I
were mine own, what should I do with myself? I should lose myself, as
Adam did. It is therefore my happiness that I am not mine own, that I
am not the world's, that I am not the devil's, that none else hath to do with
me, to claim any interest in me, but I am Christ's. If I do anything for
others, it is for Christ's sake. Remember this for the time to come. If
there be anything that we will not part with for Christ's sake, it will be our
bane. We shall lose Christ and it too. If we will not say with a perfect
spirit, I am his, my life, my credit, my person is his, anything his; look
what we will not give for him, at length we shall lose and part with it and
him too.

THE TWENTIETH SERMON.

I am my beloved's, and my beloved is mine; he feedeth among the lilies.—
Cant. VI. 3.

The church, you see here, though she stood out a while against all Christ's
invitation and knocking, yet at length she is brought to yield herself up
wholly unto Christ, and to renounce herself, which course God takes with
most, yea, in a manner with all his people, ere they go out of this world,
to lay all high things low, beat down every high thought and imagination
which exalteth itself against him, 2 Cor. x. 5, that they may give themselves and all they have to Christ, Luke xiv. 26, if he call for it. For he
that doth not so is not worthy of Christ. If we do not this, at least in
preparation of mind, let us not own the name of Christians, lest we own
that which shall further increase and aggravate our condemnation, professing religion one way, and yet alienating our minds to our lusts and pleasures of the world another way. To have peculiar love-fits of our own,
distinct from Christ, how stands this with ' I am my beloved's, and my
beloved is mine' ? How stands it with the self-resignation that was spoken
of before ?

Now this follows upon apprehension of Christ being ours. ' I am my
beloved's, because my beloved is mine first.' There are four reasons why
Christ must be given to us before we can give ourselves to him by this self-
resignation.

1. *Because he is the chief spring of all good affections*, which he must
place in us ; loving us, ere we can love him, 1 John iv. 10, 19.

2. *Because love descends.* Though it be of a fiery nature, yet in this it
is contrary, for love descends, whereas fire ascends. The superior, first
loves the inferior. Christ must descend in his love to us, ere we can
ascend to him in our affections.

3. *Because our nature is such that we cannot love but where we know ourselves to be loved first.* Therefore God is indulgent to us herein ; and that we
may love him, he manifests his love first to us.

4. *Because naturally ourselves, being conscious of guilt, are full of fears from
thence.* So that if the soul be not persuaded first of Christ's love, it runs
away from him, as Adam did from God, and as Peter from Christ, ' Depart
from me, for I am but a sinful man,' Luke v. 8. So the soul of every man
would say, if first it were not persuaded of God's love in Christ, ' Who amongst
us shall dwell with the everlasting burnings ?' Isa. xxxiii. 14. Therefore
to prevent that disposition of soul which would rise out of the sense of guilt
and unworthiness, God first speaks to us in Christ ; at length saying unto
our souls, ' I am thy salvation,' whereupon the soul first finding his love,
loves him back again, of whom it finds itself so much beloved ; so that our
love is but a reflection of his, ' I am my beloved's, because my beloved is
mine.'

It is with the Spirit of God as with the spirits in the soul and body of a
man, there is a marriage betwixt the body and soul. The spirits join both
together, being of a middle nature ; for they have somewhat spiritual near
the soul, and somewhat bodily near the body. Therefore they come between the body and the soul, and are the instruments thereof, whereby it
works. So it is with the Spirit of God. The same Spirit that tells the

soul that Christ is ours, the same Spirit makes up the match on our part, and gives us up to Christ again.

Let this then be the trial that we are Christ's, by the spiritual echo that our souls make to that report which Christ makes to our souls, whether in promises or in instructions.

Use 1. See hence likewise the nature of faith, for these are the words of faith as well as of love. Faith hath two branches, it doth give as well as take. Faith receives Christ, and says, Christ is mine; and the same faith saith, I am Christ's again. Indeed, our souls are empty; so that the main work of faith is to be an empty hand, *mendica manus* (as Luther calls it); a beggar's hand to receive. But when it hath received it gives back again, both ourselves and all that we can do. The churches of Macedonia 'gave themselves,' and then 'they gave their goods,' 2 Cor. viii. 5. Where faith is, there will be a giving of ourselves and our goods; and, by a proportion, our strength, wits, and all back again. This discovers a great deal of empty false faith in the world; for undoubtedly if it were true faith there would be a yielding back again.

Use 2. And again, these words discover the mutual coherence of justification and sanctification, and the dependence one upon another. 'I am my beloved's,' and my beloved is mine.' Christ is mine; his righteousness is mine for my justification; I am clothed with Christ as it is, 'The spouse there is clothed with the sun,' Rev. xii. 1, with the beams of Christ. But is that all? No. 'I am my beloved's;' I am Christ's. There is a return of faith in sanctification. The same Spirit that witnesseth Christ is ours, it sanctifies and alters our disposition, that we can say, I am Christ's. It serves to instruct us therefore in the necessary connection of these two, justification and sanctification, against the idle slander of papists, that sinfully traduce that doctrine, as if we were Solifideans (*v*), as if we severed justification from sanctification. No. We hold here that whensoever Christ is ours, there is a spirit of sanctification in us, to yield all to Christ, though this resignation be not presently perfect.

Use 3. This likewise helps us, by way of direction, to understand the covenant of grace, and the seals of the covenant, what they enforce and comprise; not only what God will do to us, but the duty we are to do to him again, though we do it in his strength. A covenant holds not on one side, but on both. Christ is mine, and I am Christ's again. 'I will be their God,' but they must have grace 'to be my people,' Lev. xxvi. 12; and then the covenant is made up. The covenant of grace is so called, because God is so gracious as to enable us to perform our own part.

And so in the seals of the covenant in baptism. God doth not only bind himself to do thus and thus to us, but binds us also to do back again to him. So in the communion, we promise to lead a new life, renewing our covenant; and therefore we must not think that all is well (when we have received our Maker), though we continue in a scandalous, fruitless course of life. No. There is a promise in the sacrament (the seal of the covenant of grace), to yield up ourselves to God, to return to Christ again with our duty. Then we come as we should do when we come thus disposed. This for direction, 'My beloved is mine, and I am my beloved's.'

Use 4. To proceed to make an use of comfort *to poor, doubting Christians.* 'I am my beloved's,' is the voice of the whole church, that all ranks of Christians, if they be true, may without presumption take up. I have not so much faith, so much love, so much grace, so much patience

as another, saith a poor Christian; therefore I am none of Christ's. But
we must know that Christ hath in his church of all ranks, and they are all
his spouse, one as well as another, there is no exception.   There is a little
spirit of emulation, and a spice of envy, in Christians that are weaker.   If
they have not all that great measure of grace which they see in others, they
fear they have none at all; as if there were no babes in Christ's school as
well as men and grown persons.

Then again, we see here the nature of faith in the whole church.   It is
the same that is in every particular, and the same in every particular as it
is in the whole church.   The whole church saith, 'I am my beloved's,
and my beloved is mine.'   I appropriate him.   There is a spirit of appro-
priation in the whole, and there is so in each particular.   Every Christian
may say with Paul, 'I live by faith in the Son of God, that hath loved me,
and gave himself for me,' Gal. ii. 20; and with Thomas, 'My God, and my
Lord,' John xx. 28.

The ground hereof is, because they are all one in Christ, and there is
one and the same Spirit in the whole church and every particular Christian, as in pipes, though of different sounds, yet there is the same breath
in them.   So Christians may have different sounds, from the greater or
lesser strength of grace that is in the one and in the other, but all comes
from the same breath, the same Spirit.   The Spirit in the bride saith Come,
Rev. xxii. 17, the whole church saith it, and every particular Christian
must say it; because, as the body is acted by one spirit, and makes but
one natural body, though consisting of many parts weaker and stronger,
so should there be a harmony in this mystical body acted by that one
Spirit of Christ, who so regards all, as if there were but one, and regards
every one so, as he doth not forget the whole.   *Sic omnibus attentus ut non
detentus, &c.*   Christ so attends to all, that he is not detained from any
particular, and he so attends every particular, that he is not restrained
from all.   There is the same love to all as to one, and to every one, as if
there were no other.   He so loves each one, that every Christian may say
as well as the whole church, Christ is mine, and I am Christ's.

In those things that we call homogeneal, there is the same nature in
each quantity as in the whole, as there is the same nature in one drop of
water as in the whole ocean, all is water; and the same respect of a spark,
and of all the element of fire.   So Christ bears the same respect to the
church as to every particular, and to every particular as to the church.

Use 5. To come to make an use of direction, *how to come to be able to
say this,* 'I am my beloved's, and my beloved is mine.'   For answer hereto, take notice in the first place, from the dependence.   Christ must be
first ours, before we can give ourselves to him.

(1.) Therefore, we must dwell on the consideration of Christ's love.
This must direct and lead our method in this thing.   Would we have our
hearts to love Christ, to trust in him, and to embrace him, why then think
what he is to us.   Begin there; nay, and what we are : weak, and in our
apprehension, lost.   Then go to consider his love, his constant love to his
church and children.   'Whom he loves, he loves to the end,' John xiii. 1.
We must warm our souls with the consideration of the love of God in him
to us, and this will stir up our faith to him back again.   For we are more
safe in that he is ours, Gal. iv. 9, Philip. iii. 12, than that we give ourselves
to him.   We are more safe in his comprehending of us, than in our clasp-
ing and holding of him.   As we say of the mother and the child, both
hold, but the safety of the child is that the mother holds him.   If Christ

once give himself to us, he will make good his own part alway. Our safety is more on his side than on ours. If ever we have felt the love of Christ, we may comfort ourselves with the constancy and perpetuity thereof. Though, perhaps, we find not our affections warmed to him at all times, nor alike, yet the strength of a Christian's comfort lies in this, that first, ' Christ is mine,' and then, in the second place, that ' I am his.' Now, I say, that we may be able to maintain this blessed tradition of giving ourselves to Christ,

(2.) Let us dwell on the consideration of his love to us, and of the necessity that we have of him ; how miserable we are without him, poor, beggarly, in bondage to the devil. Therefore we must have him to recover us out of debt, and to enrich us. For Christ's love carries him forth, not only to pay all our debts for us, but to enrich us ; and it is a protecting, preserving love, till he brings us to heaven, his own place, where we shall ever be with him. The consideration of these things will warm our hearts, and for this purpose serves the ministry.

(3.) We should therefore, in the next place, attend upon the word, for this very end. Wherefore serves the ministry ? Among many others, this is one main end—' to lay open the unsearchable riches of Christ.' Therein you have something of Christ unfolded, of his natures, offices, and benefits we have by him,—redemption, and freedom, and a right to all things in him, the excellencies of another world. Therefore attend upon the means of salvation, that we may know what riches we have in him. This will keep our affections close to Christ, so as to say, ' I am his.'

(4.) And labour we also every day more and more to bring all our love to him. We see in burning-glasses, where the beams of the sun meet in one, how forcible they are, because there is an union of the beams in a little point. Let it be our labour that all the beams of our love may meet in Christ, that he may be as the church saith, our beloved. ' My beloved is mine, and I am my beloved's,' saith she, as if the church had no love out of Christ. And is it love lost ? No ; but as Christ is the church's beloved, so the church is Christ's love again, as we see in this book oft, ' My love, my dove.' As all streams meet in the great ocean, so let all our loves meet in Christ. We may love other things, and we should do so, but no otherwise than as they convey love to us from Christ, and may be means of drawing up our affections unto Christ. We may love our friends, and we ought to do so, and other blessings of God ; but how ? No otherwise than as tokens of his love to us. We love a thing that our friends send to us. O, but it is as it doth convey his affection to us. So must we love all things, as they come from God's love to us in Christ.

And, indeed, whatsoever we have is a love-token, even our very afflictions themselves. ' Whom I love, I rebuke and chastise,' Heb. xii. 6.

(5.) Again, that we may inflame our hearts with the love of Christ, as we are exhorted by Jude, 21, let us consider the vanity of all things that entice us from Christ, and labour every day more and more to draw our affections from them, as we are exhorted—' Hearken, O daughter, and consider, and incline thine ear ; forget also thine own people, and thy father's house : so shall the king greatly desire thy beauty,' Ps. xlv. 10. So, if we will have Christ to delight in us, that we may say we are his, let us labour to sequester our affections more and more from all earthly things, that we may not have such hearts, as St James speaketh of, adulterous hearts. ' O ye adulterers and adulteresses ! know ye not that the love of the world is enmity with God ?' James iv. 4.

Indeed there is reason for this exhortation ; for all earthly things, they are all vain and empty things. There is an emptiness in whatsoever is in the world, save Christ. Therefore we should not set our affections too much upon them. A man cannot be wise in loving anything but Christ, and what he loves for Christ. Therefore let us follow that counsel, to draw ourselves from our former company, acquaintance, pleasures, delights, and vanities. We cannot bestow our love and our affections better than upon Christ. It is a happiness that we have such affections, as joy, delight, and love, planted in us by God ; and what a happiness is it, that we should have such an excellent object to fill those affections, yea, to transcend and more than satisfy them ! Therefore the apostle wisheth that they might know all the dimensions of God's love in Christ. There is a ' height, breadth, length, and depth of the love of God,' Eph. iii. 18.

And let us think of the dimensions, the height, breadth, and depth of our misery out of Christ. The more excellent our natures are, the more miserable they are if not changed ; for look what degree of excellency we have, if it be not advanced in Christ, we have so much misery being out of him. Therefore let us labour to see this, as to value our being in him, so to be able, upon good grounds, to say, ' I am my beloved's, and my beloved is mine.'

(6.) Again, let us labour to walk in the light of a sanctified knowledge to be attained by the gospel, for as it is, ' the end of all our preaching is to assure Christ to the soul,' 1 John v. 13, that we may be able to say without deceiving our own souls, ' I am my beloved's, and my beloved is mine.' All preaching, I say, is for this end. The terror of the law and the discovery of corruption is to drive us out of ourselves to him; and then to provoke us to grow up into him more and more. Therefore saith John, ' All our preaching is that we may have fellowship with the Father and the Son, and they with us,' 1 John i. 7. And what doth he make an evidence of that fellowship? ' walking in the light, as he is light,' or else we are liars. He is bold in plain terms to give us the lie, to say we are Christ's, and have communion with the Father and the Son, when yet we walk in darkness. In sins against conscience, in wilful ignorance, the darkness of an evil life, we have no communion with Christ. Therefore if we will have communion with him, let us walk in the light, and labour to be lightsome in our understandings, to have a great deal of knowledge, and then to walk answerable to that light and revelation that we have. Those that live in sins against conscience, and are friends to the darkness of ignorance, of an evil life, Oh they never think of the fellowship with Christ and with God! These things are mere riddles to them ; they have no hope of them, or if any, their hope is in vain. They bar themselves of ever having comfortable communion with Christ here ; much less shall they enjoy him hereafter in heaven.

Therefore labour every day more and more to grow rich in knowledge, to get light, and to walk in that light; to which end pray with the holy apostle, ' That you may have the Spirit of revelation,' Eph. i. 17, that excellent Spirit of God, to reveal the things of God, that we may have the light discovered to us.

What a world of comfort hath a Christian that hath light in him and walks in that light, above another man. Whether he live or die, the light brings him into fellowship with the Father of lights. He that hath this light knows his condition and his way, and whither he goeth. When he dieth he knows in what condition he dieth, and upon what grounds. The very light of nature is comfortable, much more that of grace. Therefore labour to grow daily more and more in the knowledge and obedience of the light.

All professors of the gospel are either such as are not Christ's, or such as are his. For such as are not yet, that you may be provoked to draw to fellowship with Christ, do but consider you are as branches cut off, that will wither and die, and be cast into the fire, unless you be grafted into the living stock, Christ. You are as naked persons in a storm, not clothed with anything to stand against the storm of God's wrath. Let this force you to get into Christ.

Use 6. And next for encouragement consider, *Christ offereth himself to all in the gospel;* and that is the end of the ministry, to bring Christ and our souls together, to make a spiritual marriage, to lay open his riches and to draw you to him, 1 John i. 9. If you confess your sins, he will forgive them, and you shall have mercy, ' He relieves those that are wearied and heavy laden,' Mat. xi. 28, and bids those come to him that are thirsty, Isa. lv. 1. Christ came to seek and to save that which was lost. Christ offers himself in mercy to the worst soul.

Therefore if there be any that have lived in evil courses, in former times, consider that upon repentance all shall be forgotten, and as a mist scattered away and cast into the bottom of the sea. Christ offers himself to you. These are the times, this is the hour of grace. Now the water is stirring for you to enter; do but entertain Christ, and desire that he may be yours to rule you and guide you, and all will be well for the time to come.

Obj. Do not object, *I am a loathsome creature, full of rebellions.*

Ans. Christ doth not match with you, *because you are good, but to make you good.* Christ takes you not with any dowry. All that he requires is to confess your beggary and to come with emptiness. He takes us not because we are clean, but because he will purge us. He takes us in our blood when he first takes us, Ezek. xvi. 9. Let none despair either for want of worth or of strength, Eph. v. 27. Christ seeth that for strength we are dead, and for worth we are enemies; but he gives us both spiritual strength and worth, takes us near to himself and enricheth us. Let none therefore be discouraged. It is our office, thus to lay open and offer the riches of Christ. If you will not come in, but love your sinful courses more than Christ, then you perish in your blood, and we free our hands, and may free our souls from the guilt thereof. Therefore as you love your own souls, come in at length and stand out no longer.

And for those that have in some measure given themselves up to Christ, and can say, ' He is mine and I am his,' let them go on with comfort, and never be discouraged for the infirmities that hang about them. For one part of Christ's office is to purge his church by his Spirit more and more ; not to cast her away for her infirmities, ' but to wash and cleanse it more and more till it be a glorious spouse like himself,' Eph. v. 27. For if the husband will, by the bond of nature, bear with the infirmities of the wife, as the weaker vessel, doth not Christ bind himself by that which he accounts us bound ? Is there more love and mercy, and pity in us to those that we take near us, than there is in Christ to us ? What a most blasphemous thought were this to conceive so ! Only let us take heed of being in league with sin ; for we cannot give our souls to Christ, and to sinful courses too. Christ will allow of no bigamy or double marriage. Where he hath anything to do, we must have single hearts, resolving, though I fall, yet I purpose to please Christ, and to go on in a good conversation ; and if our hearts tell us so, daily infirmities ought not to discourage us.

We have helps enough for these. First, Christ bids us ask forgiveness; and then we have the mercy of Christ to bear with weaker vessels. Then his advocation.* He is now in heaven to plead for us. If we were perfect, we needed not that office, 1 John ii. 2. Let none be discouraged therefore; but let us labour more and more that we may be able to comprehend in some measure the love of Christ, so will all duties come off sweetly and easily; and then we shall be enabled to suffer all things, not only willingly, but cheerfully, and rejoice in them. Love is of the nature of fire, which as it severeth and consumeth all that is opposite, all dross and dregs, and dissolves coldness, so it quickens and makes active and lively. It hath a kind of constraining force, a sweet violence. As the apostle saith, ' the love of Christ constraineth,' 2 Cor. v. 24.

Let a man that loves the Lord Jesus Christ in sincerity, be called to part with his life, he will yield it as a sacrifice with comfort. Come what will, all is welcome, when we are inflamed with the love of Christ; and the more we suffer, the more we find his love. For he reserves the manifestation of his love most for times of suffering; and the more we find the manifestation of his love, the more we love him back again, and rejoice in suffering for him that we love so. Whether they be duties of obedience, active or passive, doing or suffering, all comes off with abundance of cheerfulness and ease, where the love of Christ is, that the soul can say, ' I am my beloved's, and my beloved is mine.' Nothing in the world is able to make such a soul miserable. It follows.

' He feedeth among the lilies. The church here shews where Christ feeds.

Quest. But the question is, Whether it be the feeding of the church and people that is meant, or whether he feeds himself?

Ans. For answer, he both feeds his church among the lilies, and delights himself to be there. The one follows the other. Especially it is meant of the church. Those that are his, he feeds them among the lilies. How?

Lilies are such kind of flowers as require a great deal of nourishment, and grow best in valleys and fat ground. Therefore when she saith, ' He feeds among the lilies,' the meaning is, he feeds his church and people in fat pastures, as sheep in such grounds as are sweet and fruitful. Such are his holy word and the communion of saints. These are especially the pastures wherein he feeds his church. The holy truths of God are the food of the soul, whereby it is cherished and nourished up to life everlasting. This whole book is a kind of pastoral (to understand the word a little better), a ' song of a beloved' concerning a beloved. Therefore Christ in many places of this book, he takes upon him the term and carriage, as it were, of a loving shepherd, who labours to find out for his sheep the fattest, fruitfulest, best, and sweetest pastures, that they may grow up as calves of the stall, as it is Malachi iv. 2, that they may grow and be well liking.

You have, to give light to this place, a phrase somewhat like this, where he follows the point more at large, Cant. i. 7. The church there prays to Christ, ' Tell me, O thou whom my soul loveth, where thou feedest, where thou makest thy flocks to rest at noon.' Those that are coming up in the church desire to know with whom they may join, and what truths they may embrace. ' Tell me where thou feedest, and where thou makest thy flock to rest at noon :' that is, in the greatest heat and storm of persecution, as at noon-day the sun is hottest. ' For why should I be as one that turns aside by the flocks of thy companions?' that is, by those that are not true

* That is, ' advocacy.'—ED.

friends, that are false shepherds ; why should I be drawn away by them ?
I desire to feed where thou feedest among thy sheep.   Why should I be as
one that turns aside by the flocks of those that are emulators to thee ? as
antichrist is to Christ.   Thus the church puts forth to Christ, whereunto
Christ replies, verse 8.   ' If thou know not, O thou fairest among women,
go thy way forth by the footsteps of the flocks, and feed thy kids beside the
shepherds' tents :' that is, if thou know not, go thy way forth, get thee out
of thyself, out of the world, out of thy former course, put thyself forward,
stay not complaining, go on, put thyself to endeavour, go thy way forth.
Whither ? ' In the footsteps of the flocks.'   See the steps of Christians in
the best times of the church in former times.   Tread in the steps of those
that lived in the best ages of the church.   ' Feed thy kids,' thy Christians,
' beside the shepherds' tents,' the best shepherds.   Mark where the apostles
and prophets fed their sheep ; there feed thou.   And mark the footsteps of
the flock that have lived in the best times ; for of all times since the apostles
and prophets, we must follow those virgin best times.   All churches are so
far true churches, as they have consanguinity with the primitive apostolical
and prophetical churches.

Therefore, ' we are now to go out by the footsteps of the flock.'   Mark the
footsteps of former Christians, Abraham, Moses, and David ; and in Christ's
time, of John, Peter, and the rest.   Blessed saints ! walk as they walked,
go their way, and ' feed yourselves by the shepherds' tents.'   Mark the
shepherds where they have their tents !   So these words have reference to
the prophetical, especially to the evangelical times, whereunto we must conform ourselves ; for the latter times are apostate times.   After a certain
season the church kept not her purity ; which the Scriptures foretold directly,
that we should not take scandal at it.   The church did fall to a kind of
admiration of antichrist, and embraced doctrines of devils, 1 Tim. iv. 1.
Therefore now we must not follow these companies that lead into by-paths,
contrary to the apostolical ways, but see wherein our church agrees with
the apostolical churches and truth, and embrace no truth for the food of
our souls, but that we find in the gospel.   For antichrist feeds his flocks with
wind, and with poison, and with empty things.   For what hath been the
food in popery ?   Sweet and goodly titles ; as if they, poor souls, had the
best pastors in the world, whenas they administer to them nothing but that
which will be the bane of their souls, full of poison and fraud.   This is
spoken to unfold that place which gives light to this, spoken of the pastoral
care of Christ, ' he feeds his flock among the lilies,' plentifully and sweetly.
From hence may be briefly observed, first,

That Christ feeds as well as breeds.   And we have need of feeding as well
as breeding.   Where dost thou feed ? that is, build up thy children, and
go on with the work begun in them.   We have need to be fed after we are
bred ; and Christ (answerable to our exigence and necessity) he feeds as
well as breeds ; and that word which is the seed to beget us, is that which
feeds too, 1 Peter i. 23.   What is the seed of the new birth ?   The word
of God, the holy promises, they are the seed, the Spirit mingling with them,
whereby a Christian is born, and being born, is cherished and bred.   Therefore, ' as new-born babes,' saith the apostle, ' desire the sincere milk of
the word, that you may grow thereby,' 1 Peter ii. 1.   So that the same
thing is both the seed of a Christian, and that which breeds him ; the blessed
truth and promises of God.

Quest. If you ask, why we must grow up and be fed still ?

Ans. 1. Do but ask your own souls, whether there be not a perpetual re-

newing of corruption, which still breaks out into new guilt every day. Therefore we have need to feed every day anew upon the promises, upon old promises with new affections. Somewhat breaks out ever and anon which
abaseth the soul of a Christian, that makes him go with a sharp appetite to
the blessed truths that feed his soul.

Ans. 2. And then again, we need a great deal of strength, which is
maintained by feeding. Besides the guilt of the soul, there needs strength
for duty, which must be fetched from the blessed word of God; and the comforts thence, whereby we are able to withstand and resist, to stand and do
all that we do.

Ans. 3. And then we are set upon by variety of temptations within and
without, which require variety of wisdom and strength, all which must be
gotten by feeding ; and therefore you see a Christian for his subsistence and
being, hath need of a feeding, cherishing, and maintaining still, by the sweet
and blessed directions and promises out of the word of God.

Therefore you may see what kind of atheistical creatures those are, and
how much they are to be regarded, that turn off all with a *compendium* in
religion, Tush, if we know that we must love God above all, and our neighbours as ourselves, and that Christ died for all, we know enough, more
than we can practise. They think these *compendiums* will serve the turn,
as if there were not a necessity of growing still further and further in distinct
knowledge. Alas ! the soul needs to be fed continually. It will stagger
else, and be insufficient to stand against temptation, or to perform duties.

A second general point out of the text is this, *that as Christ feedeth still
his flock and people, so he feeds them fully, plentifully, and sweetly among the
lilies.* There are saving truths enough. There is an all-sufficiency in the
book of God. What need we go out to man's inventions, seeing there is a
fulness and all-sufficiency of truth there ? Whatsoever is not in that is
wind, or poison. In the word is a full kind of feeding. In former times
when they had not the Scriptures, and the comforts of them to feed
on, what did the poor souls then ? and what do those remaining in popery
feed on ? Upon stones as it were. There was a dream of an holy man in
those times, divers hundred years agone, that he saw one having a deal of
manchet* to feed on, and yet all the while the poor wretch he fed on stones.
What folly and misery is this, when there are delicate things to feed on,
to gnaw upon stones ! And what is all the school learning almost, (except
one or two that had better spirits than the rest) but a gnawing upon stones,
barren distinctions, empty things, that had no substance in them ? They had
the Scriptures, though they were locked up in Latin, an unknown tongue.
They had the sweet pastures of Christ to feed in ; and yet all this while
they fed, as it were, on stones.

*This should shew us, likewise, our own blessedness that live in these times,
wherein the streams of the gospel run abundantly, sweetly, and pleasantly.*
There is a fulness among us, even in the spirits of the worst sort. There
is a fulness almost to loathing of that heavenly manna : but those souls,
who ever were acquainted with the necessity of it, rather find a want than
a fulness ; and still desire to grow up to a further desire, that as they have
plentiful means, so they may have plentiful affections after, and strength by
those means. Let us know our own happiness in these times. Is it not
a comfort to know where to feed and to have pastures to go to, without
suspicion of poison ? that we may feed ourselves with comforts fully without
fear of bane, or noisome mingling of *coloquintida* in the pot, which would

* That is, ' white-bread.' See Holinshed, Description of England, B. ii. c. 6.—G.

disrelish all the rest? to know that there are truths that we may feed on safely? This the church in the former place, Cant. i. 6, 7, accounted a great privilege, ' Oh, shew me where thou feedest at noon.' In the greatest heat of persecution, that I may feed among them. So then it is a great privilege to know where to feed, and so to be esteemed, that thereby we may be stirred up to be thankful for our own good, and to improve these privileges to our souls' comfort.

But the second branch that must be touched a little is, *that there is fulness nowhere but in God's house; and that there, and there only, is that which satisfieth the soul with fatness and sweetness.*

Nay, not only the promises, but the very rebukes, of Scripture, are sweet. The rebukes of a friend, they feed the soul. For we have many corruptions which hinder our communion with God, so that a Christian delights to have his corruptions rebuked; for he knows, if he leave them, he shall grow into further communion with Christ, wherein stands his happiness in this world, and the fulness of his happiness in the world to come.

If this be so, let us know then that when we come to religion we lose not the sweetness of our lives, but only translate them to a far more excellent and better condition. Perhaps we fed before upon vain authors, upon (as it were) gravel, vain company; but now we have our delight (and perhaps find more pleasure) in better things. Instead of that which fed our idle fancy (vain treatises and the like), now we have holy truths to delight our souls. Believe it, a Christian never knows what comfort is to purpose till he be downright and sincere in religion. Therefore Austin saith of himself, ' Lord, I have wanted thy sweetness over long. I see all my former life (that I thought had such sweetness in it) was nothing at all but husks, empty things. Now I know where sweetness is, it is in the word and truth.'* Therefore let us not misconceive of religion as of a mopish and dull thing, wherein we must lose all comfort. If we give ourselves over to the study thereof, must we so? Must we lose our comfort? Nay, we have no comfort till we be religious indeed. Christ feeds not his among thorns and briers and stinking weeds, but among lilies. Dost thou think he feeds thee among unsavoury, harsh, fretting, galling things? No; ' he feeds among lilies.' Therefore when thou comest to religion, think that thou comest to comfort, to refresh thy soul. Let us make use of this for our soul's comfort, to make us in love more with the ways of Christ.

Now, to seal this further, see what the Scripture saith in some parallel places. ' The Lord is my shepherd;' and what is the use that David presently makes hereof? Why, ' I shall want nothing,' Ps. xxiii. 1. He will feed me plentifully and abundantly. The whole psalm is nothing but a commenting upon that word, ' the Lord is my shepherd.' How doth he perform the duty of a shepherd? ' He makes me to lie down in green pastures, and leads me by the still waters.' It is not only meant of the body, but of the soul chiefly, ' he restoreth my soul;' that is, when my soul languisheth and is ready to faint, he restores it, and gives me as it were a new soul; he refresheth it. We see say,* re-creation is the creating of a thing anew. So he restores my soul; he gives me my soul anew, with fresh comforts. Thus the blessed Shepherd doth, and how? Because ' he feeds among the lilies,' the promises of the gospel. Then he doth not only do good to the body and soul, but he guides all our ways, all our goings out, ' he leads us in the paths of righteousness.' And why?

---

* Confessions, b. x. p. [xxviii.] 38.—G.

† That is, ' we see that people, etymologists, say.'—ED.

Because I deserve so much at his hands ? No ; 'for his own name's sake,' because he hath a love to me; because he hath purchased me with his blood, and given his life for his sheep; hath bought me so dear, though there be no worth in me. He goes on, 'Though I walk through all temptations and troubles,' which are as 'the valley of the shadow of death,' that is, where there is nothing but disconsolation and misery; 'yet I will fear none ill; thou, with thy rod and staff, dost comfort me.' If I, as a wandering sheep, venture to go out of the way, thou, out of thy care, being a sweet and loving shepherd, wilt pull me in with thy hook and staff again. He hath not care only to feed us, but to govern us also. What a sweet Shepherd and Saviour have we in covenant, that deals thus with us! And so he proceeds, 'Thou wilt prepare my table in the presence of mine enemies.' And for the time to come he promiseth himself as much, that God, as he hath been a Shepherd for the present, to provide all things necessary for body and soul and guidance, so surely the goodness of the Lord shall follow me all the days of my life; for he is a perpetual Shepherd. He will not leave us till he hath brought us to heaven. Thus we see in this place the sweet care of Christ.

The like place you have—'He shall feed his flock like a shepherd; he shall gather the lambs with his arms, and carry them in his bosom, and shall gently lead those that are with young,' Isa. xl. 11. So he leads them into the pastures, and feeds them plentifully and sweetly, not only with sweet things, but with a tender care, which is sweeter. As a shepherd, he takes into his bosom the poor lambs that cannot walk themselves, and the sheep that are heavy with young. He cares for them; 'he gently leads them' that are poor, weak Christians, that struggle and conflict with many temptations and corruptions. Christ hath a tender care of them. He carries them, as it were, in his bosom and in his 'arms, and leads them gently ; for indeed all Christ's sheep are weak. Every one hath somewhat to complain of. Therefore he hath a tender care ; he feeds them tenderly and sweetly, or else they might perish.

Another place notable for this purpose, see Ezek. xxxiv. 14, *seq.*, wherein you have the same metaphor from a loving shepherd ; and it is but a comment upon the text. Therefore, being parallel places, they may help our memories : 'I will feed them in good pastures upon the high mountains of Israel; there shall their fold be; there shall they lie in a good fold, and in a fat pasture. I will feed my flock, and cause them to lie down, saith the Lord God. I will seek that which is lost, and bring back that which was driven away ; I will bind up that which was broken, and strengthen that which is sick, and destroy the fat and the strong, and feed them with judgment.' Those that are Christ's true sheep have somewhat to complain of. Either they are sick, or broken, or driven away. Somewhat is amiss or other. But Christ's care preventeth all the necessities of his sheep. He hath a fit salve for all their sores.* And, to apply this to the business in hand,† doth not Christ feed us ' among the lilies ? ' Doth he not now feed us with his own body and blood in the sacrament ? Would you have better food ? ' My body is meat indeed, and my blood is drink indeed,'—that is, it is the only meat, with an emphasis ; the only meat and drink that our souls could feed upon. God gave his Son to death, to shed his blood for my sins. What would become of the hunger-bitten, thirsty soul, that is

* This is the title of one of Thomas Powell's excellent practical treatises, viz. :— ' Salve for Soul-Sores.'—G.

† That is, celebration of the sacrament.—G.

stung with Satan and his temptations, were it not for the blood of Christ to quench our thirst, and the body of Christ given by the Father to death for sin ? Were it not that the soul could think upon this, where were the comfort of the soul ? All this is represented to us here in the sacrament. We feed on the body and blood of Christ spiritually, and are refreshed thereby, as verily as our bodies are refreshed with the bread and wine. For God doth not feed us with empty symbols and representations, but with things themselves, that the soul which comes prepared by faith is partaker of Christ crucified, and is knit to him, though now in heaven. There is as sure an union and communion between Christ and the Christian soul, as there is between the food and the body, when it is once digested.

Therefore let us come to this blessed, to this sweet food of our souls with hungry appetites and thankful hearts, that God hath given us the best comforts of his word, and fed us with the sweet comforts of the sacraments, as a seal of the word. We should even spend our lives much in thankfulness for this, that he will feed us so sweetly, that thinks nothing is good enough for our food, but his own self, with his own gracious word and truth. Thus we should be very thankful unto God, and now at this time labour to get hungry appetites fit for this blessed food to receive it.

How shall we do that ?

1. Think seriously of the former part of thy life, and this week past. For Christ, the food of the soul, relisheth well with the sour herbs of repentance. Let us stir up in our hearts repentance for our sins, and sorrow in the consideration of our own corrupt nature and life ; and when we have felt our corruptions and have the sense of our want, then Christ will be sweet to us. The paschal lamb was to be eaten with sour herbs ; so Christ our passover must be eaten with repentance.

2. Then withal there must be purging. There are many things which clog the stomach. Come not with worldly, wicked, malicious affections, which puff up the soul, James i. 21 ; ' but lay aside,' as the apostle wisheth, ' all guile, malice, and superfluity,' 1 Pet. ii. 1. Empty the soul of all sin and prepossessing* thoughts or affections.

3. And then consider the necessity of spiritual strength, that we have need to grow up more and more in Christianity, to be feeding still. We have need of strong faith and strong assurance that Christ is ours, and that we are his. Let us often frequent this ordinance, and come prepared as we should, and we shall find Christ making good his own ordinance, in his own best time ; so as we shall be able to say, in truth of heart, experimentally and feelingly with the church, ' My beloved is mine, and I am his. He feedeth among the lilies.'

FINIS.

———

NOTES.

(a) P. 4.—' Some would have Solomon, by a spirit of prophecy, to take a view here of all the time,' &c. For a very full and valuable, though, in respect of the early English expositors (of whom there are many in whole or part), defective and meagre, ' *Historical Sketch of the Exegesis of the Book*,' consult Ginsburg's ' Song of Songs, ... with a Commentary, Historical and Critical,' (London, Longman, 1857, 8vo) pp. 20–101. The opinions referred to by Sibbes will be found duly recorded.

* That is, ' pre-occupying.'—G.

(*b*) P. 35.—' One soul in two bodies.' This definition of friendship, which is
again and again introduced by Sibbes and his contemporaries, is ascribed to Aristotle
by Diogenes Laertius (v. § 20), as follows: ἐρωτηθεὶς τί 'εστι φίλος, 'έφη, μία
ψυχὴ δύο σώμασιν 'ενοικοῦσα. Cf. Aristotle, Eth. Nic., ix. 8, § 2, Ovid. Trist.,
iv. 4, 72. Probably Sibbes derived it from Augustine (a favourite with him), who
applies it to his friend Nebridius. Materials for an interesting paper on this saying,
in its multiform variations, have accumulated in my hands.

(*c*) P. 37.—' This goeth in the world for unnecessary *nicety*.' This reminds us of
an anecdote of the saintly Richard Rogers, who was remarkable for seriousness and
gravity in all kinds of company. Being once engaged in conversation with one of
the ' wits,' who said to him, ' Mr Rogers, I like you and your company very well,
only you are *too precise*;' he replied, ' Oh, sir, I serve a *precise God*.'—Firmin's
Real Christian, p. 67, ed. 1670.

(*d*) P. 38.—' Postill-like.' The allusion, no doubt, is to the over-subtle distinctions
and uselessly curious speculations of the *scholastic* expositions of Scripture, which
are called ' Postilla.' Various had been translated in the time of Sibbes, under the
title of ' Postils.'

(*e*) P. 48.—' *Da mihi cor.*' Jesuitism, even in its present working, proceeds on
this maxim, of which there have been many startling evidences.

(*f*) P. 60.—' God spake in me oft, and I knew it not.' This is the touching burden of the early chapters of Augustine's *Confessions.*

(*f**) P. 61.—' Ballarmine makes this objection,' &c. An ignorat eos aperire non
posse? An stultus non esset, qui ostium vicini pulsaret, si certo sciret neminem
intus esse qui aperire posset. Bell. de gratia et lib.: arbit. lib. i., cap. xi.

(*g*) P. 74.—' She is now desirous to pity herself, and needs no Peter to stir her up
to it.' The allusion is to Mat. xvi. 22. In our translation it is rendered, ' Be it far
from thee, Lord,' which obscures the pathos of the devoted apostle's mistaken, but
most loving appeal. It should be ' *Pity thyself.*' Hence Sibbes's reference.

(*h*) P. 84.—' It was a good speech of Ignatius the martyr,' &c. There are
various sayings resembling this in the epistles of Ignatius, *e.g.*, to the Ephesians,
c. xviii., to the Trallians, c. ix–xi., to the Romans, c. ii.–iv., and vi. Probably Sibbes
refers to the ancient narrative of the ' martyrdom of Ignatius.' Cf. § 2. Patrum
Apostolicorum Opera, ed. Hefele. 8vo. 1847.

(*i*) P. 93.—Hebrews xii. 1. Cf. Sibbes's translation, with Alford, Webster and
Wilkinson, and Dr Sampson, *in loc.* He repeats this and other renderings in his
various books.

(*j*) P. 121.—' Austin was forced to speak in his time against the *Donatists.*' For
a very masterly account of this and other of the great fathers' controversies, consult
Wigger's ' Historical Presentation of Augustinism and Pelagianism from the Original Sources,' (ed. by Emerson. Andover, 1840. 8vo).

(*k*) P. 125.—' He [the Lord] . . . would have their [disciples'] society and *prayers.*'
This is the popular view, but, like the popular understanding of Thomas, thrusting
his fingers into the side and nail-prints of the risen Saviour, (See note *a*, vol. i.,
p. 101), is probably a popular mistake. Our Lord sought the society of his disciples
certainly; but nowhere do we read of his asking any one to pray *for* him. It is an
awful peculiarity of the divine man ' Emanuel,' that he never did that,—one of a
multitude of subsidiary assertions of his divinity.

(*l*) P. 132.—' " What is truth?" saith he, in a scornful, profane manner.' This,
almost verbatim the opening words of Bacon's Essay on ' Truth,' reminds one, with
others, of Sibbes's intercourse with him, noticed in our memoir.

(*m*) P. 149.—' So should we now . . . . have ideas of Christ framed to our souls,'
&c. For a very valuable, and, in many respects, remarkably acute and suggestive
discussion of the question of framing ' ideas of Christ,' a subject keenly debated in
the last century in Scotland, consult the following little-known book, by Ralph
Erskine—' Faith no Fancy; or a Treatise of Mental Images . . . . . shewing that
our imaginary idea of Christ as Man (when supposed to belong to saving faith,
whether in its act or object), imports nothing but ignorance, atheism, idolatry, great
falsehood, and gross delusion.' . . . . . Edinburgh, 1745, 12mo. This little work
may be pronounced the pioneer of the philosophy known as Scottish. Apart from
its bearing on the passage of Sibbes, it will be found to contain much uncommon
thought on ' ideas.' equal, to say the least, to the subsequent writings of Reid.

(*n*) P. 153.—' All hung upon his lips, as the phrase is in the gospel.' The reference is to Luke iv. 20, which is here given in the original, to confirm Sibbes's

remark,—Καὶ πτύξας τὸ βιβλίον ἀποδοὺς τῷ ὑπηρέτῃ, ἐκάθισε καὶ πάντων ἐν τῇ συναγωγῇ οἱ ὀφθαλμοὶ ἦσαν ἀτενίζοντες αὐτῷ. ἀτενής = 'intent,' 'earnestly fixed,' from τείνω, cf. xxii. 56.   Acts iii. 12, x. 4, xiv. 9.

(*o*) P. 153.—'In the learned language, the same word signifieth speech and reason.'   Query—Is the allusion to λογος ?

(*p*) P. 154.—'His belly . . . . In the Hebrew it is used for the inward affections.'   See prefatory note to the present treatise of ' Bowels Opened.'

(*q*) P. 160.—' When Pilate sent him to him, [Herod] made *nobody* of him, as the word in the original is.' Sibbes's reference is to Luke xxiii. 11, rendered in authorised version, 'set him at nought,' but literally runs, 'having set him at nought,' *i.e.*, etymologically, treated him as if he were nobody, or of no consideration. The verb is ἐξουθενέω.

(*r*) P. 169.—'Heavy will the doom be of many that live in the church's bosom, to whom it had been better to have been born in America, in Turkey' . . . . . The juxtaposition of America *and* Turkey is in curious contrast with the present position of America among the *Christian* nations of the world. Yet with all this idea of the ' barbarousness' of America (which was common to Sibbes with his contemporaries), the Puritans shrank not from exiling themselves thither when the question of their religious liberties came up. Hooker, Davenport, Cotton, Stone, and numerous others of Sibbes's friends thus expatriated themselves.

(*s*) P. 169.—' They are lilies, being clothed with the white garment,' &c. It is pity to destroy the ' fine fancies ' of Sibbes on the supposed ' whiteness ' of the lily ; but he was thinking of the home, not of the eastern ' lily,' which is purple coloured, not 'white.' The ' purple ' gives greater vividness to the Lord's allusion to the imperial robes of Solomon, Mat. vi. 28, 29.

(*t*) P. 170.—'The name of a church in the original is Ecclesia,' *i.e.*, ἐκκλησία. Cf. 1 Cor. xi. 18, and Robinson and Liddell and Scott, *sub voce.*

(*u*) P. 173.—'If Christ himself be mine, then all is mine.' The well-known hymn, ' If God be mine ' *(anonymous)*, is little more than a paraphrase of these sweet words of Sibbes.

(*v*) P. 183.—'As if we were Solifideans.' This sect derived its name from *solus*, alone, and *fides*, faith. The following quotations will illustrate Sibbes :—

' Such is first the persuasion of the *solifidians*, that all religion consists in *believing* aright, that the being of orthodox (as that is opposed to erroneous) opinions is all that is on our part required to render our condition safe, and our persons acceptable in the sight of God.'—Hammond. Works, i., p. 480.

' That we may be able to answer the Papists, who charge us with *solifidianism*, as if we were of this opinion, that if a man do but trust in Christ, that is, be but confidently persuaded that he will save him, and pardon him, this is sufficient, and, consequently, he that is thus persuaded need not take any farther care of his salvation, but may live as he list.'—Tillotson, iii., ser. 174.   G.

THE SPOUSE,

HER EARNEST DESIRE AFTER CHRIST.

NOTE.

'The Spouse' is one of two sermons published together, but independent, in 1638. The general title-page of both is given below [*]; also the separate title of 'The Spouse' [†]. Prefixed is an 'Epistle Dedicatory,' which will be found on the opposite page. 'The Spouse,' though from an earlier chapter of Canticles, as being subordinate, follows 'Bowels Opened.'   **G.**

* and † Title-pages—·

TWO
SERMONS :
PREACHED
By that Faithfull
and Reverend Divine,
RICHARD SIBBES,
D.D. and sometimes Prea-
cher to the Honourable So-
ciety of *Grayes-Inne;*
And Master of *Katherine*
Hall in CAMBRIDGE.
Printed at *London* by *T. Cotes,** and
are to sold by *Andr. Kembe,* at his Shop
at S *Margarets* Hill in *Southwarke,* 1638.

On the back of this title we read, 'Imprimator [sic] Tho. Wykes. **Aprill 12. 1638.'**

THE
S P O V S E,
HER
Earnest desire after
Christ her Husband.
OR,
A Sermon preached on
CANT. I. Vers. 5.

By that Faithfull and Reverend Divine, *Richard Sibbes,*
D. D. and sometimes preacher
to the Honorable Societie
of *Grayes-Inne ;*
And Master of *Katherine* Hall in
Cambridge.

PSAL. 73. 25.
Whom have I in Heaven but thee ?
and there is none upon earth that I
desire besides thee.

* It may be noted here that Coates was the publisher of the famous second folio of the works of Shakespeare, 1632.—G.

SIR JOHN HOWLAND, KNIGHT.

SIR,—These two sermons were brought unto me for that learned and religious divine, whose name they bear; and so far as I am able to judge, the style and spiritualness of the matter argue no less. Being earnestly requested to peruse them, I thought fit to commend them to the world under your name, because I know that you so well affected the author. My request unto you is, that you would be pleased to accept the dedication of them as a testimony of his sincere affection, who labours, and prays for your good in the best things.

Your Worship's to be commanded in all Christian service,

R. T.*

---

* These initials R. T., probably represent Robert Town or Towne. In the 'Nonconformist's Memorial,' (iii. 438) he is stated to have been one of the 'Ejected' of 1662, being at the time in Howorth, Yorkshire, the same it is presumable with Haworth, since rendered so renowned by the Brontës, and a little earlier by Grimshawe. He had at a former period been Vicar of Ealand, Halifax. He died in 1663, aged about 70. Palmer adds, 'It was said that he had imbibed some unsound principles, but he was a man of good character.' Neither Calamy, nor Palmer, nor any of the Puritan historians, enumerate writings by him. But at the end of Burrough's 'Saint's Happiness,' (4to 1660), Nathanael Brook announces the following: 'Reassertion of grace? *Vindiciæ Evangelii*, or the Vindication of the Gospel; a reply to Mr Anthony Bridges [*sic* but Burgess is meant] *Vindiciæ Legis*, and to Mr Rutherford, by Robert Town.'—G.

THE SPOUSE, HER EARNEST DESIRE AFTER CHRIST.

Let him kiss me with the kisses of his mouth : for thy love is better than wine.
—CANT. I. 2.

THE Holy Ghost is pleased here to condescend to our infirmities ; and, that we might help ourselves in our spiritual estate by our bodies, he speaketh here of heavenly things after an earthly manner, and with a comfortable mystery. As in other places the Holy Ghost sets out the joys of heaven by a sweet banquet, so here he sets out the union that we have with Christ by the union of the husband with the wife ; and that we might the better understand what this union is, he condescends to our weakness, that we might see that in a glass which we through our corruptions cannot otherwise discern. This book is nothing else but a plain demonstration and setting forth of the love of Christ to his church, and of the love of the church to Christ ; so familiarly and plainly, that the Jews take great scandal at it, and would not have any to read this book till they are come to the age of thirty years, lest they thereby should be tempted to incontinency ; wherein they would seem wiser than God himself. But the Holy Ghost is pleased thus by corporeal to set out these spiritual things, which are of a higher nature, that by thinking and tasting of the one they might be stirred up to translate their affections (which in youthful age are most strong) from the heat of natural love to spiritual things, to the things of God ; and all those who are spiritually minded (for whom chiefly the Scriptures were written) will take special comfort and instruction thereby, though others take offence and scandal at it. So here, the union between Christ and his spouse is so familiarly and livelily set forth by that union which is between the husband and the wife, that, though ungodly men might take offence at it, yet the godly may be bettered by it.

' Let him kiss,' &c. These words are the words of the spouse to Christ, containing in them two particulars.

First, *an earnest desire*, in these words, ' Let him kiss me with the kisses of his mouth.'

In which note three parts.

First, the person desiring, the church.

Secondly, the person desired, Christ.

Thirdly, the things desired, a familiar kiss of his mouth.

Secondly, *the ground of the desire,* fetched from the excellency of the thing desired, in these words, ' For thy love is sweeter than wine.'

From the whole in general observe *a spiritual contract between Christ and his church.* There is a civil contract between man and wife, answerable to which the spiritual contract between Christ and his church holds firm resemblance.

1. That this civil contract may hold, *both parties must consent.* So it is between Christ and his spouse. He was so in love with mankind, that he hath taken our nature upon him ; and this his incarnation is the ground of all our union with Christ. First, his incarnation is the cause or ground of our union with him in grace here ; and, secondly, our union in grace is the ground of our union in glory. Now, that we may be a spouse to him, he gives us his Spirit to testify his love to us, that we might give our consent to him again, as also that we might be made a fit spouse for him.

2. Likewise in marriage there is *a communicating of all good things.* So it is here. Christ here in this spiritual contract gives himself, and with himself all good things. The Spirit is the church's. His happiness is the church's. His graces are the church's. His righteousness is the church's. In a word, all his privileges and prerogatives are the church's ; as saith the apostle, ' All things are Christ's, and Christ is yours,' 1 Cor. iii. 21 ; for all are Christ's, and all that are Christ's are yours by this spiritual contract. This excellency is set down by the prophet Hosea in his second chapter and latter end, where he, speaking of this spiritual contract between Christ and his church, saith, Hos. ii. 19, &c. ' In that day when he shall marry her unto himself in faithfulness, he will make a covenant for her with all creatures, with the beasts of the field, the fowls of heaven, and all that creepeth upon the earth.' So that upon this contract cometh in a league between the church and all the creatures. All that he hath done, all that he hath suffered by this contract is made ours. We have the benefit of all.

Obj. But what have we to bestow upon him again ?

Solution. Nothing at all ; neither portion nor proportion, beauty nor riches, but our miserable and base condition that he took upon him.

Use. This is *a well-spring of much comfort,* and *a ground of much duty.*

1. Christ condescended so far unto us, to such a near league, as to take us to be his spouse, who hath all things. What then can we want when we are at the fountain of all things ? We can want no protection, for that is the covering of this well. We can want no good thing but he will supply it. We have free access unto him, as the wife hath to her husband. Who hath free access to the husband if the wife hath not ? So who hath free access to Christ but the spouse ?

Obj. Yea, but we have infirmities.

Solution. True, indeed ; but shall man bear with his wife because she is the ' weaker vessel,' 1 Pet. iii. 7, and shall not Christ much more with his spouse ? Herein then is our chiefest comfort, that this union, this contract, is not for a time, but for ever : ' I have married thee unto myself for ever,' Hos. ii. 19. And therefore we shall never want protection nor direction, nor anything that is good for us.

2. Now, the duty on our part is to love him again with a mutual love, and obedient love ; to honour him as Sarah did Abraham, by calling him Lord, 1 Pet. iii. 6 ; and manifest it by doing what he would have thee to do, and by suffering what he would have thee to suffer.

To come to particulars.

First, *of the person desiring,* 'Let him kiss me.'

'Me' is here the speech of the whole church, and so of every particular member which is the spouse of Christ.

Doct. All Christian favours belong to all Christians alike. We have one faith, one baptism, one Spirit. As every Christian may say 'me,' so may the whole church, and every Christian as well as the church. All Christian privileges belong to all alike.

Use 1. Herein have comfort then, that whatsoever belongs to the church in general, belongs to every member in particular.

Use 2. This teacheth us to reason from one spiritual thing to another, as thus Abraham believed, 'and it was counted to him for righteousness,' Rom. iv. 22; and therefore if I believe I shall be counted righteous. David sinned, and David repented and found mercy; and therefore if I, &c. So all privileges belong alike to all Christians. Every Christian soul is the spouse of Christ as the whole church is. Therefore St Paul propounds himself an example to all that would believe in Christ. 'God had mercy on him,' 1 Tim. i. 16, and therefore he encourageth all to come unto Christ, by this, that he will have mercy on thee, as he had on him. Whatsoever is promised to the whole church, that apply to thy own soul in particular; and whatsoever is required of the whole church, that is required of thee in particular by Christ, if thou be a member. But though in spiritual favours all have a like portion, yet it is not so in outward things; but some are rich, some are poor, some honourable, some base. But in the best privileges and best gifts there is an equal extending to all alike, to the poor Christian as well as to the rich, to him that is base in the eye of the world, as well as to him that is honourable.

Secondly, *of the person desired,* 'Let him.'

Many make love to the spouse; as the devil, the world, and the flesh. The devil and carnal persons make love to the soul, to draw her away from Christ, but she looks to Christ still. 'Let *him* kiss me.' She goes not as the papists do, to Peter and Paul, but to Christ and to Christ alone. He 'is my well-beloved, and I am his,' Cant. ii. 16; he is my peculiar, and I am his peculiar; none have 'I in heaven but him, and there is none that I desire in comparison of him,' Ps. lxxiii. 25. He hath singled out me, and I have singled out him, 'Let him kiss me.'

Thirdly, *of the thing desired,* 'Let him kiss me,' &c.

The thing desired, it is a kiss. There are divers sorts of kisses spoken of in Scripture. There is a kiss of superiors to inferiors, and of inferiors to superiors. There is an holy kiss, Rom. xvi. 16, 1 Cor. xvi. 20, and an hypocritical kiss, as Joab to Amasa, 2 Sam. xx. 9, and as Judas to Christ, Mat. xxvi. 49. There are kisses of love; so Jonathan kissed David, 1 Sam. xx. 41. There are kisses also of subjection, as, Kiss ye the Son, &c., Ps. ii. 12. But here is the kiss of a superior to an inferior. 'Let him kiss me with the kisses of his mouth,' that is, let him shew me further testimony of his love by his presence; let me enjoy further communion with him still; let him further assure me of his love. Consider what the church meant; howsoever she had interest in this spiritual contract and covenant at the first, yet the church, according to the different degrees of time, had different degrees of desires to be further and further assured of his love. As in Solomon's time, so before from the beginning, there was a desire in the church of the kisses of Christ, that is, that he would come in our nature, and that he would manifest by little and little, clearer and clearer, his coming in the flesh; and accordingly he did by degrees reveal himself, as first in paradise, ' The seed of the woman shall break the serpent's head, Gen. iii. 15; then to Abraham, ' In thy seed shall all the families of the earth be blessed,' Gen. xii. 3. After that to one tribe, Gen. xlix. 10, the tribe of Judah, Heb. vii. 14; then to one family of that tribe, the house of David, Luke i. 27; then a virgin shall conceive, Isa. vii. 14; and after that pointed out by the finger of John the Baptist, ' Behold the Lamb of God that takes away the sins of the world,' John i. 29. So you see how Christ did reveal himself more and more by degrees unto his church. Answerable to these degrees were the desires of the church for the coming of Christ, as the prophet Isaiah saith, ' Come down and break the heavens,' Isa. lxiv. 1.; and then prophesied of by those that waited for the consummation of Israel. So that before Christ came in the flesh the church had a longing desire after his incarnation, as here, ' Let him kiss me with the kisses of his mouth.' But that is not all. For she knew this should not be till the last days, and therefore desireth some further means of acquaintance and knowledge of him, desiring that he would manifest himself more and more by his word, by his grace, and by his Spirit; and therefore as then the desire of the church was for the coming of Christ, so now that which Christians desire and long after is, to go to him that they may remain with him in glory. They love his appearance, but because this shall not be yet, though the church be still in expectation of it, therefore she desireth to hear his words, and to have him kiss her with his mouth in his word. But this is not all; but let me find his Spirit now walking with me here, and further, ' kiss me with his mouth,' by increasing his graces in me, manifesting his love unto me more and more. This is the desire of the church, and of every Christian soul, that Christ would thus kiss her; that he would reveal himself every day more and more unto her, in his word, in his sacraments, by his Spirit, by his graces, by increasing of them. This is the desire of the church and of every Christian soul, that Christ would thus ' kiss her with the kisses of his mouth.'

Now we are come to the ground of this desire, taken from the excellency of the love of Christ, which is here said by experience of the whole church, and of every Christian soul, to be ' sweeter than wine.'

From hence we note two things.

Doct. 1. *First, that every Christian soul and the spouse in general hath a sweet taste of the love of Christ even in this life.*

Doct. 2. *That after this contract and taste of this love, she hath ever springing up in her a further desire of the increase and manifestation of it.*

Doct. 1. For the first, as after the contract there is a more manifestation of love than was before, yet not a full manifestation of love till after the marriage, so Christ, though he do give his spouse a taste of his love here, and sends love-tokens unto her, some graces whereby his love is made more manifest than before (as Isaac sent to Rebekah some jewels and bracelets to manifest his love to her, Gen. xxiv. 53); yet his love is not fully manifested in this life, but is kept until the great solemnity. Christ cannot delight in the spouse unless she be decked with his graces, and therefore he gives her of them; and these are not only a taste of his favours, but the fruit of his favours.

The reasons are diverse.

Reason 1. The first reason is *to solace their long absence,* that they may not faint, but having a sweet taste of his love here, may stay their hearts thereupon until the day wherein he will fully manifest his love unto them. The Lord seeth his children are subject to be oppressed with heaviness here; therefore he gives them a taste of his love here, that thereby they might be comforted, when nothing else can.

Reason 2. The Lord gives his children a sweet taste of his love here, *that when they by weakness and frailty fall away and lose their first love, when by their former taste they might return and recover themselves again,* considering how sweet, and how strong that love was, that once they had enjoyed from Christ, and hereby they might say with the church, ' I will return,' &c., Hos. ii. 7.

Reason 3. The third reason is, *because the manifestation of this his love doth wonderfully strengthen a Christian to go lightly through the heaviest affliction;* for when Christ assures a Christian of his love, then affliction will seem grievous, but he will through all, he will suffer whatsoever shall befall him for Christ's sake with joy.

Reason 4. Lastly, Christ gives his church, and so every Christian, a taste of his love in this life, *because he knows we have many temptations in this world which are ready to steal away our affections,* as carnal pleasures, riches, honours, and the like. Now that these might not draw away our affections, he gives us a taste of his love, which is better than all other things, ' which is sweeter than wine,' that by this our affections might be preserved chaste to him. So then Christ gives us, his spouse, a sweet taste of his love in this life, that afflictions on our left hand might not too much press us down and discomfort us ; nor the pleasures and delights on our right hand steal away our hearts from him.

Use. The use is to teach us to *admire** *at the goodness of God* in this, that he is pleased so to provide for us, as to keep us from being too much overcome with heaviness through the multitude of temptations and afflictions which in this life we are subject unto ; expelling the bitterness thereof with the sweetness of his love, thereby preserving our affections chaste unto himself.

Now we come to the second doctrine.

Doct. 2. *That the church (and so every Christian) after this contract and taste of Christ's love, hath evermore springing up in them an insatiable desire for a further taste and assurance of his love.*

The reasons of this doctrine are two.

Reason 1. The first reason is taken from the nature of true love, *which is never satisfied.* And hence it is, that though Christ give his spouse a taste of his love in his word, by sending his ambassadors, his ministers with his love-letters, the gospel of peace, giving therein a taste of his love, as also by his Spirit, by his sacraments, by his graces ; yet all this will not satisfy her soul, but Christ having once manifested his love unto her, there is a continual desire to have a further taste and assurance of it.

Reason 2. The second reason is drawn *from Christ's infinite riches,* infinite in his glory, in his power, in his beauty, in his pleasures, and joys, and the like. He hath all things, ' All power is given him in heaven and in earth,' Mat. xxviii. 18 ; every way infinite in himself; and hence it is, that the spouse hath an infinite desire to have a further taste of his love, and a nearer communion with him. So you see whether we regard the nature of love, which is never satisfied, or whether we consider his infinite riches, both manifest this truth, that there is an insatiable desire in a Christian, to be further filled with, and more fully assured of, the love of Christ.

* That is, ' wonder.'—G.

Where grace is, there is a further desire of growth in grace. It is an higher degree of love to desire the enjoying of the presence of Christ, than to enjoy heaven itself; but this will not be yet.

Use 1. Therefore let us try our love *by our labouring for that sight of Christ which we may have;* as in his ordinances where he manifests himself in a special manner. Is it the great grief of thy soul that thou art shut from the presence of Christ in his ordinances, from the congregation of the saints, where he by familiar kisses useth to manifest his love to thee more and more? I can but wonder that some persons dare to take upon them the name of Christianity, and yet think that men be too holy. These want this character of a Christian, viz., a further desire of the manifestation of Christ's love. Many of them neglect the ordinances of God, or if they do come there, they desire not further inward kisses of his love, but content themselves with the outward.

When the Spirit should witness and seal up the love, the love of Christ to their souls, by an inward kiss, they only content themselves with the outward, the bare hearing of the word. But where this further desire of familiarity with Christ is not, there is but a barren soul, there is no taste of Christ's love. If there were a taste, there would be a further desire of growth in that love. There are some that make a profession of religion, as many that marry to cloak their adultery; so these profess Christ, to cover their strong covetousness and strong faults, that they may have the more strength to commit sin. We must not content ourselves without these outward kisses, but give, as the outward man, so sacrifice the inward man, Rom. vii. 22, the soul unto God. Let those that find, after this trial, these desires springing up in them, comfort themselves in this, that they are Christ's, and Christ shall manifest his love more and more unto them. For God hath promised to grant the desires of the righteous, Ps. xxxvii. 4. Hast thou then a longing desire to have a further taste of the love of Christ? Use the means, and then be sure that Christ will manifest his love more and more unto thy soul.

Use 2. The second use is for exhortation and spiritual direction *how we shall come to a further assurance, sign, and fruit of Christ's love.* If we desire this, we must labour to have, first, *chaste judgments*, and secondly, *chaste affections. A chaste judgment* from error, heresy, and schism; and our affections chaste from the world, from pleasures and the like. For Christ is wonderful jealous of our judgments, and of our love. Therefore Paul desires to present the Corinths* a ' pure virgin unto Christ,' 2 Cor. xi. 2. So then, as we must affect† goodness, so we must profess truth. We must have chaste judgments as well as chaste affections. The spouse of Christ, as she is pure in affections, so she is pure in judgment; she hears his voice and follows him. Whatsoever comes not from the word, receive it not, but reject it. Thus much for the judgment.

So likewise labour for *chaste affections.* Christ will not have us to divide our affections; partly for him, and partly for the world, or partly to pleasures, and partly to him. He will not have it so. He will have the whole heart and whole affections, or he will have neither heart nor affections. If we give our hearts to the world or to the pleasures of the world, the love of which is enmity with God, James iv. 4, then have we an adulterous heart; which to do is a double sin. As for a wife to commit whoredom is a double sin, there is adultery and breach of marriage covenant; so to embrace the world after we are contracted unto Christ, is spiritual whoredom and a

* That is, ' Corinthians.'—G.   † That is, ' love.'—G.

breach of our covenant in spiritual contract. Take heed of worldly-minded ness, which will glue thy affections to the earth, and will not suffer them to be lifted up to Christ. Take heed of the pleasures of the world, lest they drown thy soul, as they do the souls of many that profess themselves to be Christians.

Use 3. Thirdly, if we will grow in the assurance of the love of Christ, and have more familiar kisses of his mouth, then labour *to get an humble heart*, by searching out our own unworthiness in respect of what we are, or were by nature. Indeed, we may disparage our credits by abasing our selves in respect of men, but never can we be too much humbled to our Saviour in acknowledging ourselves unworthy of all that we have. There is no danger in thus debasing ourselves to our Saviour, nay, it is for our honour with God. For those that thus honour him he will honour with his graces ; for he giveth grace to the humble, and with such a spirit he delights to dwell, Isa. lxvi. 2. Let us with humility, then, acknowledge all to be from his free grace, and with Jacob, acknowledge ourselves to be less than the least of his mercies, Gen. xxxii. 10.

Use 4. Fourthly, if we will grow in the assurance of the love of Christ, *we must give Christ no peace.* Take no nay of him, till he hath given thee the kisses of his love. Many times he delays the manifesting of his love— what though ? Yet wait his pleasure, for he hath waited long upon thee. We see Mary Magdalen, what ado she made when she could not find Christ. He having manifested himself unto her at the beginning, at length he calleth her by her name, demanding for what she wept, and whom she sought, Luke vii. 47. Give him no rest, take no denial, till he answer thee, for he will do it. What did the woman of Canaan ? She gave him no rest till he did apply himself unto her, Mat. xv. 22, *seq.* Jacob wrestled with God, and would not let him go, till he had assured him of his love and favour, Gen. xxxii. 24, *seq.* He hath promised to grant the desires of the righteous, Ps. xxxvii. 4. Hath he given us such strong desires after him ? Then continue constant importuning him by prayer, and he cannot stand out with us long ; he cannot deny us some further assurance of his love.

Use 5. Again, *take everything to thine advantage,* as his former love and favour, his power, fidelity, and stability. Take advantage from these, and plead for thy desires, as the woman of Canaan. Christ accounts her a dog, Mat. xv. 26. I am indeed so, saith she. She taketh advantage of his words, and thereby pleads for her desire. As the servants of Benhadad catch at words of comfort from Ahab, 1 Kings xx. 33 ; so continually take advantage from your own experience. He hath been thus and thus good unto thee, these and these means thou hast enjoyed, and thus and thus hath it wrought for my good; I will therefore follow him now until he assure me of his love in a further degree.

Use 6. Again, consider thou must be *modest in thy desires of this kind.* Desire no great matter at the first. I mean, not full assurance of the love of Christ at the first ; but observe the degrees of his kisses, and manifestation of his love. The thief on the cross desired but to be remembered of Christ when he came into his kingdom, Luke xxiii. 42,—no great matter ; so do thou desire any taste of his love, though never so little. Indeed, so the children of God do. First they desire the pardon of their sins, and having obtained this, they grow more and more in desiring the graces of the Spirit, as seals to assure them of the pardon of them, and of his love unto them, and nearer communion with him.

Obj. But this communion is not alway felt.

Sol. 1. I answer, if Christ be strange to us, *it is from ourselves, not from Christ;* for he is all love. It is either because our loose hearts run after some carnal contents ; and then no marvel though Christ shew himself strange unto us, and we go mourning all the day long, without a sense of his love.

Or else, 2, It is when *we will not seek for his kisses,* a further taste of his love, as we should, in his ordinances, nor exercise those graces that we have as we should, in attending upon the ordinance, resting by faith upon God's promise for a blessing.

Or else, 3, *We are so negligent, that we do not stir up those graces of God in us by private duties.*

Or else, 4, *We join ourselves to evil company,* or to persons led with an evil spirit. These are the causes why Christ is strange to us.

Or else, 5, It is to exercise and try our faith, and to let us see ourselves and our own weakness. Thus he left Peter. Otherwise, it is Christ, his nature, to manifest himself and his love by familiar kisses of his mouth. Search into your hearts, and you shall find that these and such like are the causes why Christ is strange unto you, and why you are senseless* of your communion with him.

Use 7. Consider, again, when it is, *at what time is it that we have the sweetest kisses, and are most refreshed with Christ's love.* Is it not when we put our strength to good means, as when we strive with God in prayer, and labour in humility rightly, and profitably to use all his ordinances ? Mark these two well as a means to preserve and increase the assurance of Christ's love in you.

First, *how you fall into deadness,* and the causes of it.

Secondly, *how you come to have most communion with Christ,* and at what time, and after what performances. Canst thou say, I was thus and thus dead and senseless of Christ's love, but now I am thus and thus comforted and refreshed ? either when thou deniedst anything to thyself, which thy heart stood strongly for, or when thou hadst been most careful in holy duties. If we deny ourselves in anything, that our hearts stand strongly for, because it hinders us in holy courses, God will be sure to recompense us in spiritual things abundantly, yea, and in temporal things many times.

Use 8. Consider, again, *when I was afflicted and had none else to comfort me, then the Lord was most sweet unto me, then he refreshed my soul with a sense of his love.*

These may help us much in getting a further assurance of Christ's love. Be stirred up, then, to desire to be where Christ is, and to have the kisses of his love in his ordinances, as further testimonies of his favour, and never rest from having a desire to increase in grace and communion with Christ. So shall you never want assurance of a good estate, nor comfort in any good estate. Cast such a man into a dungeon, he hath paradise there. Why ? Because Christ comes to him. And if we have this communion with Christ, then though we are compassed about with death, yet it cannot affright us, because the great God is with us, Ps. xxiii. 4. Do with such a one what you will ; cast him into hell, if it were possible ; he having a sweet communion with Christ, will be joyful still ; and the more sense we have of the love of Christ, the less we shall regard the pleasures or riches of the world. For what joy can be compared with this, that

* That is, 'unconscious of,' 'without assurance of.'—G.

the soul hath communion with Christ ?   All the world is nothing in comparison.

Now, then, seeing you cannot requite this love of Christ again, yet shew your love to Christ in manifesting love to his members, to the poor, to such poor especially as have the church of God in their families.   As the woman poured oil on the head of Christ, so shall we do well to pour some oil upon the feet of Christ.   That which we would do to him, if he were here, let us do to his members, that thereby we may further our communion with Christ.

FINIS.

A BREATHING AFTER GOD.

A BREATHING AFTER GOD.

NOTE.

The 'Breathing after God' is placed immediately after the sermons from Canticles, as being not only on the same subject, though from a different portion of Holy Scripture, but also as partaking very much of their spirit. The original title-page is given below.* Prefixed is the miniature portrait, by Marshall, found in several of Sibbes's smaller volumes. **G.**

* Title-page :—

A
BREATHING
AFTER GOD,
OR
A CHRISTIANS
DESIRE OF GODS
PRESENCE,
BY
The late Reverent [*sic*] and worthy
Divine RICHARD SIBS,
Doctor in Divinity, Master of
Katherine Hall in *Cambridge*, and
sometime Preacher of
Graies-Inne.
Psal. 42. 1.
As the Hart panteth after the water brooks;
so panteth my soul after thee, O God.
Lam. 3. 56.
Hide not thine eare at my breathing.
LONDON
Printed by *John Dawson* for *R. M.*
and are to be sold by *Thomas Slater,*
at the Swan in *Duck-lane.* 1639.

TO THE CHRISTIAN READER.

MAN in this world, especially since his defection from God, standing at a distance from his happiness in respect of full possession, it is not the least part of his bliss to be happy in expectation. Happiness being by all men desirable, the desire of it is naturally engrafted in every man ; and is the centre of all the searchings of his heart and turnings of his life. But the most of men, like the men of Sodom, grope and find not the right door, Gen. xix. 11. Only to a true Christian, by a supernatural light, is discovered both the right object, and the right way to felicity. Upon this discovery, finding himself, while he is here, a stranger to his happiness, he desires to take leave of this sublunary condition, that he may enjoy him who is ' the desire of all nations,' Hag. ii. 7.

Now although God cast common blessings promiscuously upon good and bad ; yet he holds his best favours at a distance, as parents do cherries or apples from their children, to whet their appetites the more after them. And indeed the best perfection of a Christian in his military* condition, is, in desire and expectation ; and it is enough to him that ; for that he hath God's acceptation, who knowing whereof we are made, and how unable to hold weight in the ' balance of the sanctuary,' Dan. v. 27, takes his best gold with grains of allowance.

The soul of man is like a cipher, which is valued by that which is set before it. If it weary itself in the desire of earthly things, like the silk-worm, it finisheth its work with its own destruction. But if on things above, when this earthly tabernacle is turned to ashes, there shall result a glorious phœnix for immortality.

There are no characters better distinguishing a Christian, than those that are inward (hypocrisy like sale-work, may make a fair show outward ; an hypocrite may perform external works, but cannot dissemble inward affections), and amongst them, none better discovers his temper, than the beating of the pulse of his desires, which this worthy author (who departed not without being much desired† and no less lamented) hath most livelily set forth in the ensuing treatise ; which a Christian, holding as a glass before him, may discern whether he have life or no by these breathings.

---

* That is 'militant.'—G.   † That is, ' longed after.'—G

For the object here propounded, what more desirable than the chief good? For the place, where can it be more desired, than in his house, where his presence is manifested? What better end to be in that house, than to behold God in the 'beauty of holiness?' Ps. xxix. 2. What term of happiness better than 'for ever'? This was the desire of the holy prophet David, and that it may be thy desire, is the desire of

Thy Christian friend,

H. I.*

---

* These initials are in all probability those of John Hill, reversed, intentionally or by a misprint. See note on p. 251.—G.

A BREATHING AFTER GOD.

*One thing have I desired of the Lord, that I will seek after ; that I may dwell
in the house of the Lord all the days of my life ; to behold th   uty of the
Lord, and to inquire in his temple.*—Ps. XXVII. 4.

This psalm is partly a prophecy. It was made after some great deliverance
out of some great trouble. The blessed prophet David, having experience
of God's goodness suitable to the trouble he was in, in the first part of this
excellent psalm he shews—

I. His *comfort;* and, II. His *courage;* and, III. His *care.*

I. His *comfort.* It was altogether *in the Lord,* whom he sets out in all
the beauties and excellency of speech he can. He propounds the Lord to
him in borrowed terms. ' The Lord is my light and my salvation, the
strength of my life,' Ps. xxvii. 1. So he fetcheth comfort from God, the
spring of comfort, ' the Father of all comfort,' 2 Cor. i. 4. He labours to
present God to him in the sweetest manner that may be. He opposeth
him to every difficulty and distress. In darkness, he is ' my light ;' in
danger, he is ' my salvation ;' in weakness, he is ' my strength ;' in all my
afflictions and straits, he is the ' strength of my life.' Here is the art of
faith in all perplexities whatsoever, to be able to set somewhat in God
against every malady in ourselves. And this is not simply set out, but
likewise with a holy insultation.* ' The Lord is my light and salvation ;
whom shall I fear ?' Ps. xxvii. 1. It is a question proceeding from a holy
insultation, and daring of all other things. ' The Lord is the strength of
my life ; of whom shall I be afraid ?' That is one branch of his comfort.

The second branch and ground of his comfort is, 2. *The goodness of God
in the ruin and destruction of his enemies.* ' When the wicked, even mine
enemies and foes, came upon me to eat up my flesh, they stumbled and
fell,' Ps. xxvii. 2. He describes his enemies by their malice, and by their
ruin.

[1.] His enemies were *cruel enemies,* blood-suckers, eaters of flesh. We
call them cannibals. As indeed men that have not grace, if they have
greatness, and be opposed, their greatness is inaccessible ; one man is a
devil to another. The Scripture calls them ' wolves, that leave nothing

* That is, ' defiance.'—G.

till morning,' Zeph. iii. 3. As the great fishes eat up the little ones, so great men they make no more conscience of eating up other men, than of eating bread ; they make no more bones of overthrowing men and undoing them, than of eating bread. 'They eat up my people as they eat bread,' Ps. xxvii. 2.

[2.] But notwithstanding their cruelty, *they were overthrown*. Saith David, 'when my foes came upon me to eat up my flesh, they stumbled and fell.' For, indeed, God's children, when they are delivered, it is usually with the confusion of their enemies. God doth two things at once, because the special grievance of God's children it is from inward and outward enemies. He seldom or never delivers them but with the confusion of their enemies. So he sets down his own comfort in the Lord, by the confusion of his enemies. This will be most apparent at the day of judgment, when Satan, and all that are led by his spirit, all the malignant church, shall be sent to their own place, and the church shall be for ever free from all kind of enemies. When the church is most free, then the enemies of the church are nearest to destruction ; like a pair of balances, when they are up at the one end, they are down at the other. So when it is up with the church, down go the enemies. So here are the two branches of his comfort.

II. Now his *courage* for the time to come, that is, in the third verse. 'Though an host encamp against me, my heart shall not fear.' He puts the case of the greatest danger that can be. Though an host of men should encompass me, 'my heart shall not fear ; though war rise against me, in this I will be confident.' Here is great courage for the time to come. *Experience breeds hope and confidence.* David was not so courageous a man of himself ; but upon experience of God's former comfort and assistance, his faith brake as fire out of the smoke, or as the sun out of a cloud. Though I was in such and such perplexities, yet for the time to come I have such confidence and experience of God's goodness, that I will not fear. He that seeth God by a spirit of faith in his greatness and power, he sees all other things below as nothing. Therefore he saith here, he cares not for the time to come for any opposition ; no, not of an army. 'If God be with us, who can be against us ?' Rom. viii. 31. He saw God in his power ; and then, looking from God to the creature, alas ! who was he ? As Micah, when he had seen God sitting upon his throne ; what was Ahab to him, when he had seen God once ? So when the prophet David had seen God once, then 'though an host encamp against me, I will not fear,' &c. Thus you have his comfort in the double branch of it ; his courage, also, and his confidence for the time to come.

III. What is his *care ?* That is the next. I will not analyse the psalm farther than the text. After his comfort in the Lord, and in the confusion of his enemies, and his courage for the time to come, he sets down his care, 'One thing have I desired of the Lord, and that will I seek after, that I may dwell in the house of the Lord all the days of my life,' &c. This was his care. He had so sweet experience of the goodness and power of God, being light, and salvation and strength to him in confounding his enemies, that he studied with himself how to be thankful to God ; and this he thought fittest in the open great congregation, in the church of God, among many others. Therefore he saith, 'One thing have I desired of the Lord, and that will I seek after still, that I may dwell in the house of the Lord all the days of my life.'

Now, in the words of the text that I have read, there is contained the holy prophet's care and desire, set down first in general, 'One thing have I desired of the Lord, and that I will seek after.'

And then a specification of that desire he specifies. What is that one thing he desired? That 'I may dwell in the house of the Lord,' with the circumstance of time, 'all the days of my life.'

Now, after the desire in general, set out here by the object in general, the transcendent object, 'One thing have I desired of the Lord,' and likewise by the frequency and fervency of the desire, 'I will seek after it still.' I have desired it, and I will not cease. So my desire, it shall not be a flash soon kindled, and soon put out. No; but 'one thing have I desired of the Lord, and that I will seek still.' I will not be quiet till my desire be accomplished. There is the general desire, and the degrees of it.

The particular is, 'that I may dwell in the house of the Lord.'

Then the grounds and ends of the particular desire of dwelling in the 'house of the Lord,' because it is 'the house of God.' There is a strong argument to move him to dwell in the house of God. It is good dwelling where God dwells, where his angels dwell, and where his Spirit dwells, 'in the house of the Lord.' There is one argument that moved him, 'I desire to dwell there,' because it is the house of God, which is set out by the extent of time, that 'I may dwell in the house of God all the days of my life,' till I be housed in heaven, where I shall need none of these ordinances that I stand in need of in this world. 'I desire to dwell in the house of the Lord all the days of my life.'

Then the second end is, 'To behold the beauty of God.' That was one end of his desire, to dwell in the house of God; not to feed his eyes with speculations and goodly sights (as indeed there were in the tabernacle goodly things to be seen). No; he had a more spiritual sight than that. He saw the inward spiritual beauty of those spiritual things. The other were but outward things, as the apostle calls them. I desire to dwell in the house of the Lord, 'to behold the beauty of the Lord,' the inward beauty of the Lord especially.

And then the third end of his desire is, 'that I may inquire in his temple.' He desired to dwell in the house of God, because it was the house of God, and to see the beauty of God, the sweet, alluring beauty of God, that appeared in his ordinances; and then his desire was to dwell in the house of God, that he might inquire more and more of the meaning of God still, because there is an unfathomed bottom, and an endless depth of excellency in divine things, that the more we know, the more we may, and the more we seek, the more we may seek. They are beyond our capacity; they do not only satisfy, but transcend it. Therefore, he desires still further and further to wade deeper into these things, 'to inquire in God's temple.' Thus ye see the state of the verse. There is a general desire propounded. 'One thing have I desired of the Lord, and that will I seek after.'

And then the desire specified, 'to dwell in the house of the Lord, and to see the beauty of the Lord, and to inquire in his temple.' These be the three ends.

'One thing have I desired of the Lord,' &c.

To speak first of this desire generally propounded, 'One thing have I desired,' &c.

And then of the increase of it, in that he saith, 'I will seek after it still.' He desired it, and he would seek more and more after it.

In the desire, consider—

First, the *object*, ' one thing.'

And then the *desire* or *seeking itself*.

First, the *object*, ' one thing.'

Quest. Was there but one thing for holy David to make the object of his desire? Was there but one thing needful? Alas! this poor life of ours, it is a life of necessities. How many things are needful for our bodies? How many things are needful for the decency of our condition? How many things need we for our souls? It is a life of necessities. How, then, doth he say, ' One thing have I desired?'

Ans. Yes. His meaning is, comparatively, I seek for other things in their order and rank, and as they may stand with the main; but, indeed, one thing principally. All the rest will follow. ' Seek ye first the kingdom of God, and all the rest will be cast on you,' Mat. vi. 33. The best way to have all other things, is to seek one thing in the first place. Therefore, in heavenly wisdom he saith, I desire *unum unicè*; one thing after an entire manner. That I desire more than all things else.

Hence we may see that,

There is a difference of degrees of things. God hath established in the world degrees of things. There are some good and some ill by his permission; and of good, there are some that are greater goods, and some less. There are spiritual goods, and outward goods; and of spiritual good, there are some that are means leading to that which is spiritually good, and some that are spiritual good things in their own essence and nature. The leading preparing things are the means of salvation, the word, and sacraments, and being in the visible church. The true spiritual good, the good that we get by these things, faith and love, and spiritual inward strength. Now that there is degrees of things, the prophet here insinuates when he saith, ' One thing have I desired;' that is, of all these variety of things, he desired the best, that includes all in it. God, to exercise the wisdom that he hath given to man, hath planted a difference in the creatures, and hath given a faculty to man to make a right choice in those differences; and then man makes a right choice when he chooseth as God chooseth. Now, God makes choice of spiritual things to be the best things, and them he gives to his best friends. He knows they will make us good, and supply all outward wants whatsoever, and sanctify all estates and conditions to us, and they are eternal, suitable to the spiritual nature of our souls. God knows this very well. Therefore, God hath set spiritual things, as the one only thing; and so the soul, when it is made spiritual, and hath the image of God upon it, it chooseth as God chooseth.

' One thing have I desired.'

Quest. But here it may be asked, why doth he say, ' one thing?' He desired not only to live near the tabernacle, but to hear and see, to have the word read, and he desired thereupon grace, and then nearer communion with God by grace, to have more communion here, and fuller communion in heaven. Here is more than one thing.

Ans. I answer, it is all one. As a chain that hath many links, yet it is but one chain; so all these are but one. ' I desire one thing.' What is that? To live in the church of God, to enjoy the ordinances of God, and they will draw on faith and fear, &c. The Spirit accompanying the ordinances, it will be a spirit of faith, and repentance, and grace; and by those graces of faith, and the rest that accompany the ordinances, I shall have nearer communion with God here, and eternal and everlasting communion with God in heaven ; and all these are but one, because they are all links of one chain. Therefore, when he saith, 'One thing have I desired,' he means that one thing that will draw on all other.

That is the scope of a gracious heart, when it attends upon the means of salvation, and lives in the church ; not to hear that it may hear, and there an end, and to read that it may read, to perform it as a task, and all is done ; but to have the work of the Spirit together with it, to have the ministry of the Spirit in the gospel, and the Spirit to increase faith, and faith to increase all other graces, and so by grace to grow into nearer communion with God in Christ. That is the scope of every good hearer. Therefore, he speaks to purpose when he saith, ' One thing have I desired.'

But to speak a little more of the object, why doth he say, ' One thing ?'

First, *it is from the nature of God*. We must have the whole bent and sway of our souls to him. He will have no halting. The devil is content with half, if we will sin, because then he is sure of all ; but God will have the whole heart. ' My son, give me thy whole heart,' Prov. xxiii. 26 ; and ' Thou shalt love the Lord with all thy heart, and with all thy soul,' Luke x. 27. The bent and sway of the soul must be that way ; for it is the nature of excellent things, except we desire them in the chief place, they take state upon them.* God takes state upon him in this case. He will not have us serve him and Mammon, Mat. vi. 24. He will not have the heart divided.

Second. Then again, *it is from the nature of the soul*. Therefore, he saith, ' One thing.' It is the nature of the soul, when it is upon many things, it can do nothing well. Therefore, that I may be religious to purpose, ' One thing have I desired.' A stream cut into many channels runs weakly, and is unfit to carry anything. Babylon was so taken. They cut the river into many channels, and then he that took it easily passed over them. (a) When the soul is divided into many channels, to many things, that it looks after this thing and that thing, and that with expense and intention of care and endeavour, alas ! where is the desire of one thing necessary all the while ? For the soul cannot go with that strength as it should, except it mind one thing. The soul of man is a finite thing. Therefore, except it gather its strength, as a stream, that riseth of many particular lesser rivers, which makes it run stronger ; so the soul it cannot desire one thing as it should, except it bring all other petty streams to it, and make that the main desire, to be saved in another world, and to have communion and fellowship with God in Christ Jesus, by the Spirit of grace in this world, in the use of the means. Unless this be the main care, the soul takes no good when it is so much set on other things.

Then, *thirdly*, he sets down this ' one thing,' to ' dwell in the house of God,' to grow in grace there ' as a cedar,' to be a ' tree planted there,' *from the very nature of grace*, which is to unite things to the main. The Spirit of grace sets before the eye of the soul heavenly spiritual things in their greatness and excellency ; and the Spirit of grace, seeing there are many useful things in this world, it hath an uniting, knitting, subordinating power, to rank all things so as they may agree to and help the main. Grace confines the soul to one thing. Man, after his fall, ' sought out many inventions,' Eccles. vii. 29, saith the wise man. He was not content with his condition when he stood, but ' he sought out many inventions. When man falls to the creature, he knows not where to stay. No creature can afford a stay and rest for the soul long. The soul is never quiet till it come

* That is, ' are offended.'—G.

to God again,* and that is the one thing the soul desireth. The soul being sanctified by the Spirit of God, it subordinates all things to this one thing. David desired many things besides this one thing, but not in that degree, but as they might stand with the desire of this one thing necessary. Grace subordinates and ranks all things so as that the best things have the pre-eminence. Therefore, he might well say, ' one thing,' from the disposition that grace hath to rank all things to one. It is a promise in the covenant of grace. Saith God, ' I will give you one heart,' Jer. xxxii. 39. As soon as a man becomes a Christian, he hath one heart.' His heart before was divided. There was variety of objects it was set upon; God had the least piece. The flesh had a piece, and this delight and that delight had a piece; but saith God, ' I will give you one heart,' that is, a heart uniting itself in desire to the best things, and regulating all things, so as all shall be but one, that a man shall ' use the world as though he used it not,' so as it shall help to the main. As I said, little streams they help the main stream running into it, so grace hath a subordinating power over all things in the world, as they may help the main. ' One thing have I desired,' and I desire other things, as they may help the main. Grace will teach us that art. It hath a special art that way. So we see both in regard of God, and in regard of the soul being finite, and in respect of the wise disposing of grace that aims at the main, and ranks all things as they may help the main, he doth well say, ' One thing have I desired.'

Use. This shews *the vanity and baseness of every worldly man, that makes the main work and labour his by-work, and the by-work his main work.* That that is the ' one thing necessary,' Luke x. 42, is set after all. Indeed, without grace, this is so. The first work of grace is to set the soul in order, to subdue base affections, to sanctify the judgment; and when it hath set the soul in tune and order, then it is fitted to set a right price on things, to rank and order them as it should. So much shall be sufficient to unfold the object itself in general, ' One thing have I desired.'

Now I come to the affection itself, set forth here by the degrees.

' One thing have I desired, *and that I will seek after.*

I have desired it, and I will desire it still. Desires are the issues of the heart. Thoughts and desires are the two primitive issues of the heart, the births of the heart. Thoughts breed desires. Thoughts in the mind or brain, the brain strikes the heart presently. It goes from the understanding to the will and affections. What we think of, that we desire, if it be good. So thoughts and desires, they immediately spring from the soul ; and where they are in any efficacy and strength, they stir up motion in the outward man. The desires of the soul, being the inward motion, they stir up outward motion, till there be an attaining of the thing desired, and then there is rest. Desire to the thing desired is like *motus ad quietem*, as motion is to rest. When motion comes once to rest, it is quiet. So desire, which is the inward motion, it stirs up outward motion, till the thing desired be accomplished, and then the soul rests in a loving content, and enjoying of the thing desired.

Now this desire, it was a spiritual desire. ' One thing have I desired of the Lord.' Holy desires, they issue from choice. A holy, wise desire, when it is not a mere notion, it ariseth from a choice of a thing that is good ; for desire is nothing but the embracing and closing with a thing that is good. The understanding must choose the good first, before the soul embrace it. The will is but the carriage of the soul, the furthering and

* Augustine.—See note *h*, vol. I., page 214.—G.

promotion of the soul to the good things discovered; so it supposeth a choice of good things.

And choice supposeth an esteem of the things before we choose them; and that supposeth a deliberate judging that works an esteem. So that it was no hasty, sudden thing this desire; but it rose from the sanctified judgment of David, that bred a holy esteem of these excellent things ; the means of salvation, having the Spirit of God accompanying of them, containing such excellent comforts as they do. I say this desire supposes a right judgment, and thence an esteem ; thence a choice upon all, choosing these things above all other contentments and things in the world besides. For at this time he wanted in his family the comfort of his wife and house, &c. Tush, what do I regard these things ? If I could enjoy the sweet, and strong, and comfortable presence of God in his ordinances, other things I could bear well enough, the want of house, and wife and children, the pleasures and contentments of my country. Therefore, ' One thing have I desired.' It was a desire out of a high esteem and choice of that one thing he speaks of.

The point of doctrine that I will observe in brief, because I hasten to the main thing, is this,

That the Spirit of God in the hearts of his children is effectual in stirring up holy desires.

There is nothing that characteriseth and sets a stamp upon a Christian so much as desires. All other things may be counterfeit. Words and actions may be counterfeit, but the desires and affections cannot, because they are the immediate issues and productions of the soul ; they are that that comes immediately from the soul, as fire cannot be counterfeit. A man may ask his desires what he is ? According to the pulse of the desires, so is the temper of the man. Desires are better than actions a great deal ; for a man may do a good action, that he doth not love, and he may abstain from an ill action, that he hates not. But God is a Spirit, and looks to the spirit especially. It is a good character of a Christian, that his desire, for the most part, is to good ; the tenor and sway and bent of his desire is to good. ' One thing have I desired.' The Spirit of God is effectual in stirring up these desires.

Quest. But how shall we know that these desires are the chief things to distinguish an hypocrite from a true Christian, and whether they be true or no ?

Ans. To go no farther than the text : desires are holy and spiritual,

If they be about holy and spiritual things. ' One thing have I desired,' saith David. What was that ? To be rich and great in the world, and to be revenged on my enemies ? No, no ; that is not the matter. I have many enemies ; God will take a course that they shall fall. That that I desire, is to have nearer communion with God ; I desire to enjoy the ordinances of God. So his desire it was set on spiritual objects, and that argued it was a holy desire.

2. And then again, his desire. It was a *fervent desire*, as he saith, ' One thing have I desired, and that will I seek after.' It was not a blaze or flash, that was soon in and soon out. It was not a mere velleity, a kind of inefficacious desire. Fervency shewed that his desire was sound. He would not be quieted without the thing accomplished.

3. And then *constancy*, when a man will not be taken off. There is not the wickedest man in the world, but he hath good flashes, good offers, and desires sometimes. ' Lord, have mercy upon me,' &c. He hath good

ejaculations sometimes. Ay, but what is the bent and sway of his desires? This was David's constant desire. As it was about spiritual, and was a fervent and eager desire, that he would not be quieted, so it was constant. That that is natural is constant, and that that is supernaturally natural. That that is natural in spiritual things, it is constant; nature is constant. For how doth nature differ from art? Artificial things are for a time. Teach a creature beyond his nature, he will shew his naturals. So let an hypocrite act a part, if it be not his nature, he will soon turn to his naturals, and shew that he is an hypocrite again. Constancy and perpetuity in good things, a tenor of good desires, shew that the heart is good, because it is constant.

4. And then again, this desire here, of David, it was kindled *from the love of God, and not out of base ends.* Holy desires are kindled in the soul from the love of God; for what saith he here? 'One thing have I desired.' What was that? 'To dwell in the house of the Lord.' What to do? 'To behold the beauty of God;' to see God in his excellency and beauty and worthiness. All his desire was from this, that his soul was enamoured with the beauty of God's house. The love of God stirred up this blessed desire in the prophet. Therefore, it was a holy and spiritual desire.

5. Again, as they spring from the love of God, *so they tend to the honour of God;* for what comes from heaven, goes to heaven back again. As waters that come from a spring, they go as high as the place they come from; so holy desires, being kindled from heaven from a spirit of love, they go to heaven again. The love of God stirs them up, and he seeks God's glory, and honour, and inward communion with God in this. For a man out of a natural desire may desire holy things sometimes, to be free from such or such a sin, and to have such and such a grace, not out of a desire to honour God; but if he had grace, he sees he might escape troubles, he might be free from temporal judgments, and he might ingratiate himself, and commend himself to this or that person, whom he desires to benefit by. Therefore, he desires as much grace as may help forward his intentions in the world. He joins the world and God together. Oh! no, these are not the desires that distinguish a Christian from another man; but those that spring from the love of God, that proceed inwardly from the truth of the heart, and that the things themselves please God, and that there is a loveliness in them, and that they tend to the honour of God especially, and our own good in a secondary place. This is a character of good desires. Thus we see, though I should go no further than the text, how we may distinguish holy and heavenly desires from other desires. 'One thing have I desired, and that will I seek,' &c.

Therefore, let us examine what our desires are, what our bent is. Desires issue from the will and affections, and they shew the frame of the soul more than anything in the world. As the springs in low places are discovered by the steams and vapours that come out of the place, men gather that there is a spring below, because of the ascent of vapours; so the vapouring out of these desires shew that there is a spring of grace in the heart; they discover that there is a spring within.

And let those that mourn in Sion, that have some evidence (though they are not so good as they would be), let them look to their hearts. What is thy desire? What is the bent of thy soul? When a man is once converted and turned, wherein is his turning? Especially, his mind and judgment and esteem of things are altered. There is a change of mind, and withal the desire and bent of the soul is altered; that if a man ask

him, and examine what the bent is of all the course of his life, oh! that
God might be glorified, that his church and cause might prosper, that
others might be converted; this is the bent of his soul; not that he might
be great in the world, and ruin those that stand in his way (this shews that
a man is a rotten hypocrite). The bent and sway of the soul shews what
a man is.

Because I would not have any deceived in the point, take one evidence
and sign more with you, and that shall be instead of all, and it is out of
the text too, ' One thing have I desired, and that will I seek after,' not by
prayer only, but in the use of all means; as, indeed, he was never quiet
till he was settled again in Sion, nor then neither till he had gotten materials
for the temple, and a place for God's honour ' to dwell in,' Deut. xii. 11.
If desires be not the desires of the sluggard, there will be endeavour; as
we see in the desire of David here, ' One thing have I desired, and that will
I seek.' He used all means to enjoy communion with God sweetly.

The sluggard lusts and hath nothing. So there are many spiritual sluggards that lust and have nothing, because they shew not their desire in
their endeavours. There will be endeavour where the desire is true. For
desire springs from the will, the will being the appetite of the whole man,
Voluntas appetitus, &c. The understanding carries not, but the will. When
the will will have a thing, it carries all the parts. Hereupon, when the
desire is true, it stirs up all the powers and faculties to do their duty, to
seek to attain the accomplishment and possession of that that is desired.

Those, therefore, that pretend they have good desires to God, and yet
live scandalously and negligently, and will take no pains with their souls,
alas! it is the sluggard's desire, if they take not pains to remove all lets and
hindrances. For a man may know the desire of a thing is good when he
labours to set the hindrances out of the way, if he can. If the lets and
hindrances be not impossible, he will remove it, if he can. Therefore, those
that pretend this and that, ' There is a lion in the way,' Prov. xxvi. 13,
when they might remove it, if they would, there is no true desire; for
desire is with the removing of all possible hindrances of the thing desired.

Quest. But to resolve one question. How shall I know whether my
desire be strong enough and ripe enough or no to give me comfort?

Ans. I answer, if the desire of grace *be above the desire of any earthly
thing*, that a man may say with David, ' One thing have I desired,' I desire
to be free from sin, as a greater blessing to my soul, than to be free from
any calamity, Oh! it is a good sign. And surely a man can never have
comfort of his desire till his desires be raised to that pitch. For none ever
shall come to heaven that do not desire the things that tend to heaven,
above all earthly things; nor none shall ever escape hell that do not think
it worse and more terrible than all earthly miseries. God brings no fools
to heaven that cannot discern the difference of things. Therefore, let us
know, that our desires are to little purpose if we have some desire to be
good, &c.; but we have a greater desire to be rich and great in the world,
to have such and such place. If the desire of that be greater than to be
gracious with God, if we hate poverty, and disgrace, and want, and this and
that more than sin and hell, to which sin leads, it is a sign that our judgments are rotten and corrupt, and that our desire is no pure spiritual desire.
For it is not answerable to the thing desired; there is no proportion. David
saith here, ' One thing have I desired.' His desire carried him amain to
' one thing necessary,' above all other things whatsoever. Thus you see
out of the text, what are the distinguishing notes of true desires from those

that are false. I need name no more, if we consider what hath been spoken.

Now for our comfort, if we find these holy desires: Oh! let us take comfort in ourselves : for ' God will fulfil the desires of them that fear him,' Ps. xxxvii. 4. Holy desires, they are the birth of God's Spirit, and there is not one of them that shall be lost; for God regards those desires, 'My groanings are not hid from thee,' Ps. xxxviii. 9 ; my groanings in trouble, and desires of grace. There is not the least thing stirred up in the soul by the Spirit of God, but it prevails with God in some degree, answerable to the degree of worth in it. Therefore, if we have holy desires stirred up by God, God promotes those desires. God will regard his own work, and to ' him that hath shall be given,' Mat. xiii. 12. ' Lord, be merciful to thy servants, that desire to fear thy name,' saith Nehemiah, i. 11.* It is a plea that we may bring to God, ' Lord, I desire to please thee,' as it is, ' The desire of our souls is to thy name, O Lord,' Isa. xxvi. 8. We fail sometimes, that we cannot perform actions with that zeal and earnestness as we should ; but the desire and bent of our soul is to thy name. A Christian may make it his plea to God,—truly our desires are towards thy name, and we have some suitable endeavours ; and our desires are more that way than to anything in the world. It is a good plea, though we be much hindered and pulled back by our corruptions. So much for that, the act upon this object, ' One thing have I desired.'

Of whom doth he desire it ? Of the Lord.

' One thing have I desired of the Lord.'

It was not a blind desire of the thing, *but a desire directed to the right object, to God,* to fulfil it. Holy desires are such as we are not ashamed of, but dare open them to God himself in prayer, and desires to God. A Christian, what he desires as a Christian, he prays for, and what he prays for he desires ; he is a hypocrite else. If a man pray, as St Austin, in his confessions,† that God would free him from temptations, and yet is unwilling to have those loving baits from him, he prays, but he doth not desire. There are many that pray ; they say in their prayers, ' Lead us not into temptation,' Mat. vi. 13, and yet they run into temptation ; they feed their eyes, and ears, and senses with vain things. You know what they are well enough, their lives are nothing but a satisfying of their lusts, and yet they pray, ' Lead us not in temptation.' And there are many persons that desire that, that they dare not pray for, they desire to be so bad. But a Christian what he desires, he prays for. I desire in earnest to be in the house of the Lord, I desire it of the Lord, I put up my request to him; and what I pray to him for, I earnestly desire indeed. Learn this in a word, hence, that,

When we have holy desires stirred up by God, turn them to prayers.

A prayer is more than a desire. It is a desire put up to God. Let us turn our desires into prayers. That is the way to have them speed.

' One thing have I desired of the Lord.'

The reason why we should, in all our desires, make our desires known to God, is to keep our acquaintance continually with God. We have continual use of desires of grace, and desires of mortification of corruptions, and of freedom from this and that evil that is upon us. As many desires as we have, let them be so many prayers; turn our desires into prayers to God, and so maintain our acquaintance with God. And we shall never come from God

* Misprinted ' Ezechias' = Hezekiah.—G.

† Conf. A reminiscence rather than translation, of a recurring sentiment in the ' Confessions.'—G.

without a blessing and comfort. He never sends any out of his presence empty, that come with a gracious heart, that know what they desire. And it brings peace with it, when we make our desires known to God by our prayer. It brings ' peace that passeth understanding,' Philip. iv. Put case God doth not hear our request, that he doth not grant what we ask. ' The peace of God which passeth understanding, shall keep your hearts and minds.' So that when we put up our requests to God with thankfulness for what we have received, the soul will find peace. Therefore I say, let us turn all our desires into prayers, to maintain perpetual communion and acquaintance with God. Oh! it is a gainful and comfortable acquaintance.

It is an argument, and sign of a good conscience, for a man to go oft to God with his desires. It is a sign that he is not in a wicked course ; for then he dares not appeal to the presence of God. Sore eyes cannot endure the light ; and a galled conscience cannot endure God's presence. There-fore it is good to come oft into the presence of God. It shews that the heart doth not regard iniquity. ' If I regard iniquity in my heart, God will not hear my prayers.' Ps. lxvi. 18. It is an argument of a good con-science to come oft into the presence of God. But I will not enter into the common place of prayer.

We see next his earnestness, ' I have desired it of the Lord, *and I will seek after it.*'

I will follow God still. Here is his importunity in prayer, his fervency, his uncessancy and perseverance, as the apostle exhorts, he persevered in prayer, Eph. vi. 18. ' I will seek after it.' In prayer, and in the use of all good means, I will do what I can. So you see one qualification of prayer, *it must be with perseverance and importunity.* God loves importunate suitors. Though we cannot endure to be troubled with such persons, yet God loves importunate suitors, as we see in Luke xviii. 1–8, in the parable of the widow. God there vouchsafes to compare himself to an unrighteous judge, that ' cared neither for God nor man,' yet the importunity of the widow moved him to regard her. So the poor church of God, she is like a widow, with her hair hanging about her. ' This is Zion, whom none regardeth ;' yet this widow, the poor church of God, and every particular member of it, they are importunate with the Judge of heaven and earth, with God ; and will not he more regard the importunity of his children whom he loves, and delights in, that ' call upon him day and night' ? Ps. cii. 2, will not he re-gard their petitions, when an unrighteous judge shall care for the impor-tunity of a poor widow ? Thus you see the excellent fruit of importunity in our blessed Saviour himself, and here in David, ' I will seek after it,' I will have no nay. Therefore we are exhorted in the Scriptures, not to keep silence, to give God no rest. ' You that are the Lord's remembrancers, keep not silence, give him no rest.' As Jacob with the angel, wrestle with him, leave him not till we have a blessing. As the woman of Canaan, let us follow him still, and take no nay. Oh this is a blessed violence, be-loved, when we can set upon God, and will have no nay, but renew suit upon suit, and desire on desire, and never leave till our petitions be answered. Can the hypocrite pray alway ? Would you know a comfort-able note to distinguish an hypocrite from a true Christian ? take it hence, will the hypocrite pray alway ? Sometimes he will pray ; but if God answer him not presently he gives over ; but God's children pray always, if the ground be good, if they see the excellency of the thing, and the neces-sity, and withal join at the amiableness of it, that it may be gotten. When they see the excellency, and the necessity and usefulness of the thing, and the attainableness of it, and that it is attainable in the use of means, they need no more, they will never give over. That is the reason of that in the petitions, ' Thy kingdom come, thy will be done in earth as it is in heaven,' Mat. vi. 10. But can we do the will of God on earth as it is done in heaven ? and doth God's glorious kingdom of heaven come while we are here on earth ? No ; it doth not, but the soul that is guided with the spirit of prayer, it rests not in this or that degree, but prays till it be in heaven, ' Thy kingdom come.' I have grace now, but I desire glory. ' Thy will be done.' I desire to do it as thy saints in heaven, though I cannot do it ; but I desire, and I will not give God rest, but pray, till all my prayers be answered in heaven ; and then I shall do the will of God as it is done in heaven indeed. Thus we ought eagerly, and constantly to persevere in our desires, till they be fully satisfied, or else we are but hypo-crites.

Let us make conscience, I beseech you, of this duty more than we have done, and never give God over for grace ; for strength against our corrup-tions ; for his church ; for the prosperity of the means of salvation ; for those things that we have ground for ; let us never give him over till we see he hath answered our desires. And when he hath answered our desires, let us go on still to desire more ; for this life is a life of desires. The life of accomplishment is heaven. Then all our desires shall be ac-complished, and all promises performed, and not before then. This is a life of desires, and we must be in a state of desires and prayers still till we be in heaven.

Quest. What is the reason that God doth not presently accomplish our desires ?

Ans. There be diverse reasons. *First* of all *he loves to hear the desires of his servants*, he loves to be sued unto ; because he knows it is for our good. It is music that best pleaseth God's ears to hear a soul come to him to re-quest, especially spiritual things of him, which he delights most to give, which he knows is most useful and best for us. This pleaseth him so marvellously, that he will not presently grant it, but leads us along and along, that still he may hear more and more from us.

2. And then *to keep us in a perpetual humble subjection and dependence on him*, he grants not all at once, but leads us along, by yielding a little and a little, that so he may keep us in a humble dependence.

3. And then *to exercise all our graces ;* for a spirit of prayer is a spirit of exercise of all grace. We cannot pray, but we must exercise faith, and love to God and his church ; and a sanctified judgment to esteem what are the best things to be prayed for ; and to exercise mortification. ' If I regard sin, God will not regard my prayers,' Ps. lxvi. 18. A spirit of prayer is a spirit that puts all into exercise ; therefore God, to keep us in the exercise of all grace, answers not at the first.

4. And then he would have us *to set a high price upon what we desire and seek after.* If we had it at the first, we should not set so high an esteem and price of it.

5. And then, that *we might better use it when we have it.* Then we use things as we should do when we have gotten them with much ado ; when we have won them from God with great importunity, then we keep and pre-serve them as we should. These and the like reasons may be given, and you may easily conceive them yourselves. Therefore let us not be offended with God's gracious dispensation if he answer not our desires presently, but pray still ; and if we have the spirit of prayer continued to us, that

spirit of prayer is better than the thing we beg a great deal. Ofttimes God answers us in a better kind, when he gives us a spirit of prayer; for increasing a spirit of prayer in us, he increaseth all graces in us. What is it we would have? this or that particular grace. But when God gives us a spirit of prayer, he answers us better than in the thing we ask, for there is all grace. He will answer in one kind or other. But I will not be large in these points. You see then what was the affection of the holy prophet, to that one thing. 'One thing have I desired.' And he did not only desire it, but turned his desire into a prayer. He prayed to God; and he not only prayed once or twice, but he seeks it still, till God vouchsafed to grant it.

Obj. Well, but that that he prayed for, he was assured of, and therefore what need he pray for it? He had a promise, 'He shall prepare a table before mine enemies, my cup doth overflow,' Ps. xxiii. 5, 6. But what is that to this? These be things of this life. Oh! but, saith he, God will be good to me in the things of another life, and all the days of my life too. 'Doubtless the lovingkindness of the Lord shall follow me all the days of my life, and I shall dwell in the house of the Lord.' He takes in trust his dwelling in the house of God; and that the lovingkindness of God should follow him all the days of his life, he was assured of it, and yet here he seeks it and prays for it.

Ans. I note it, to shew that the assurance of the thing takes not away the earnestness of prayer. Daniel was assured (Dan. ix. 4, *seq.*) that God would deliver the Jews out of Babylon. He had read Jeremiah's prophecies, he knew the time was accomplished; yet we see what an earnest prayer he makes there. Christ knew that God heard him in all his desires, that he should have all good from God, being his only Son, yet he prayed whole nights sometimes, and a whole chapter, John xvii., is an excellent prayer of his. So that the assurance of the thing takes not away prayer to God; nay, it stablisheth it, for God so makes good his promises for the time to come, as that he makes them good this way, he will be sought to by prayer. And I may know hence that he will make good his promises for the time to come to me, if I have a spirit of prayer for them; if I pray for perseverance to the end, that God would vouchsafe me grace to live in the church, and to grow up as a cedar. God surely means to grant this, because he hath given me holy and gracious desires, which he would not have given me, but that he means to give the thing. For this is an encouragement to pray, when I know I shall not lose my labour. I pray, because I have a promise to have it, and I know the promise runs upon this. 'But I will be sought unto of the house of Judah for this,' Ezek. xxxvi. 37. For if we have it, and have not sought it by prayer, for the most part we cannot have a comfortable use of it, unless we have things as the fruit of our prayers. Though there be not a particular prayer for every particular thing we have of God, yet unless it be the fruit of the general prayer, that we put up daily, we cannot have comfort in it; if God give it by a general providence, as he fills 'the bellies of the wicked with good things,' Ps. xvii. 14. But if we will have things for our good in particular, we must receive them as the fruit of our prayers from God. You see here he seeks, and desires that that he had a promise to have, 'One thing have I desired of the Lord, and that will I seek.'

'That I may dwell in the house of the Lord.'

It was generally propounded before. 'One thing have I desired, and that will I seek after,' with all my might. And what is that? The specification of it is this:

'That I may dwell in the house of the Lord for ever.'

His desire is, not only to be in God's house, but to dwell in it, to abide; and not for a little while, but to dwell, and to dwell ' all the days of my life.'

The house of God then was the tabernacle, the sanctuary. The temple was not yet built. He desired to be near the tabernacle, to dwell in the sanctuary, the place of God's worship. In the tabernacle, which in those times was the house of God, there was the ark and the mercy-seat, types of many glorious things in the New Testament; the holy of holies, &c. And he desired to dwell in the tabernacle, to be near the ark, the house of God. Why? Because God manifested his presence there, more than in other places. The ark hath God's name in diverse places of Scripture; because God gave his answers in the ark, in the propitiatory, or mercy-seat. They came there to know his meaning, what he would have; he gave his answer there. He is said to dwell between the cherubins. There were two cherubins upon the mercy-seat, and God is said to dwell between the cherubins, Exod. xxxv. 22; that is, there he was present to give answers to the high priest, when he came to ask. David knew this well enough, that God had vouchsafed a more special presence in the tabernacle, than in all the places of the world, and therefore, saith he, ' I desire to dwell in the house of the Lord all the days of my life.'

' House,' we take for the persons that are in it, and persons that are ordered, or else it is a confusion, and not a house. It is a company of those that are voluntary. They come not by chance into our house, those that are members of our society; but there is an order. There is a governor in a house, and some that are under government, and there is a voluntary conjunction and combination. So the church is a voluntary company of people that is orderly, some to teach, and some to be instructed; and thereupon it is called a house.

And it is called the house of God, because he is present there, as a man delights to be present in his house. It is the place where God will be met withal. As a man will be found in his house, and there he will have suitors come to him, where he reveals his secrets. A man rests, he lies, and lodgeth in his house. Where is a man so familiar as in his house? And what other place hath he such care to protect and provide for as his house? And he lays up his treasures, and his jewels in his house. So God lays up all the treasures of grace and comfort in the visible church. In the church he is to be spoken with as a man is in his house. There he gives us sweet meetings; there are mutual spiritual kisses. ' Let him kiss me with the kisses of his mouth,' Cant. i. 2. A man's house is his castle, as we say, that he will protect and provide for. God will be sure to protect and provide for his church. Therefore he calls the church of God, that is, the tabernacle (that was the church at that time), the house of God. If we apply it to our times, that that answers the tabernacle now, is particular visible churches under particular pastors, where the means of salvation are set up. Particular visible churches now are God's tabernacle (b). The church of the Jews was a national church. There was but one church, but one place, and one tabernacle; but now God hath erected particular tabernacles. Every particular church and congregation under one pastor, their meeting is the church of God, a several church independent. Our national church, that is, the Church of England, because it is under a government civil, which is not dependent upon any other foreign prince, it is a particular church from other nations.

In that God calls the church his house, it shews the special respect that he hath to his church. God, though he be present everywhere, yet he is present in another manner in his church. As for instance, the soul is present in all the parts of the body; but the soul, as far as it understands, is only in the brain; as far as it is the fountain of life, it is in the heart. It hath offices and functions in all the parts; but in the special function, the rational function of it, as it discourseth and reasoneth, it is in the brain. So for our apprehension's sake, God is everywhere; but as he sanctifies and pours out his blessings, and opens, and manifests his secrets, so he is in his church especially. God is everywhere, but he is in another way in heaven than in other places. He is there gloriously. So in earth he is everywhere, but he is in another manner in the church (the heaven upon earth), than in other places. He is there as in his house to protect them, and provide for them as his family; and there he abides by his ordinances, and takes solace, and delight. God delights himself in his church and children that attend upon his ordinances. ' Where two or three are met together, I will be in the midst of them,' Mat. xviii. 20. When God's people meet together in the church, God is present among them. So you see in what respect the tabernacle then, and particular churches now, which answer it, are called the house of God.

Let us learn this for our duty, as well as consider our comfort, in that the church is the house of God, *let us carry ourselves as we should, decently, in the house of God.* Those that are to look to the house of God, they should purge out all unclean corners, that God may delight to dwell in his house still, that we give him no cause to depart out of his house. ' That I may *dwell in the house of the Lord,*' &c.

The act here is, that I ' may dwell in house of the Lord.' He did not desire to be in it for a day or a little time, to salute it, and so leave to it; but to ' dwell in the house of the Lord,' and to dwell there for ever. You see here that Christians have a constant love to the best things, a constant desire to dwell in the house of God. You may think it a strange desire of this holy man to dwell in the house of God; but think then of the continuedness of his desire, it was even to heaven itself; he desired ' to dwell in the house of God for ever.'

For what end ?

1. I desire to dwell in the house of God, that I may dwell *in the love of God, and in the care of God to me in Christ for ever.* I do not desire to dwell in the house of God, as it is a meeting, and there an end; but I desire to dwell in the house of God, that I may dwell in the love and care of God, and not only dwell in his care and love to me, and his care and esteem of me; but,

2. That I may dwell *in my love to him,* that I may ' abide in his love,' and faith in him; that I may abide in Christ. It is not only for a man to abide in the house of God, and go no further than so, but to abide in the love of God; and in our love, and care, and faith, and dependence upon him, to make God our house, to live, and walk, and abide in, ' to dwell in God,' as St John saith, 1 John iv. 13; not only in the house of God, but God himself. And the upshot of all his desire, was to abide in heaven for ever. The desires of God's people never rest till they come to their proper centre, and there they are quiet. There is a rest of all desires in heaven; as fire, it never rests till it come to its element above, and heavy bodies rest not till they come to the centre below. So holy desires, that are the motion of the soul, they rest not till they come to the centre, the place of rest. So we must conceive of David's desire to dwell in the

house of the Lord, to dwell in the care, and love, and protection of God
for ever, to dwell in love, and faith, and dependence, and in the whole
stream of my soul for ever while I live ; and then abide in heaven,
where there are 'pleasures for evermore,' as he saith in another place,
Ps. xvi. 11.

Therefore when we have any thoughts and desires, while we are here
below, of grace and comfort, &c., let us extend, and stretch our desires to
the last, to heaven itself, where all desires shall be accomplished, where all
promises shall have their full performance.   It is a poor thing only to
desire to live in the church militant, and there is an end.   No ; here is the
comfort of God's people, that in their prayers and desires, and their endeavours suitable to their prayers and desires, they all lead them to heaven ;
and there they have their full accomplishment.   They have a constant desire
to dwell in the house of God.

1. The reason is, because the soul in this world *is never fully satisfied
with the good things of God's house till it be in heaven.*   This life is a life of
desires and longing ; the church is but contracted to Christ in this world ;
the marriage shall be consummate in another world.   Therefore the church
desires still further and further communion with Christ in his ordinances
here, and for ever in heaven.

2. And then *there are remainders of corruptions still, that dead and dull
our performances, and put us on to actions that grieve our spirits and the Spirit
of God ;* to this end, that we may have a perpetual supply of the Spirit.
We desire to dwell in the house of the Lord, because there is corruption in
us still, till grace hath wrought it out fully.

3. *There is more and more to be had still in the house of God.*   We
never come to be full.   The soul it is wondrous capable, being a spiritual
essence.   It is capable of more grace and comfort than we can have
in this world.   Therefore we pray, 'Thy will be done on earth as
it is in heaven.'   A Christian desires to dwell in the house of the
Lord here, till he come to dwell in heaven, till he be translated from the
temple here, to the temple in heaven.   In Ephes. iv. 11, *seq.*, God hath ordained
a ministry to the edification of the church, not only to constitute the church,
as some think and say, that preaching must constitute a church, and after
praying must edify it.   Oh! let both go together.   'God gave gifts to men,'
to preach, to edify the church more and more.   So long as there is use of
building more and more, so long there is need of the ministry.   Therefore
he desired to 'dwell in the house of the Lord.'

4. But the especial reason why he desired it, was *because he knew God
was also present in his own house, and there is no good thing can be wanting
where God is present.*   It is the presence of God that makes all things sweet
and comfortable.   What makes heaven to be heaven, but because God is
there ?   If the soul of a Christian were among angels, angelical comforts
would not be desired, if God were not there.   If there were all the delights
in the world, it would not care for them, except God were present.   Heaven
were not heaven without the presence of God.   The presence of God in a
dungeon, in a lion's den, makes it a paradise, a place of pleasure ; the
presence of God makes all conditions comfortable.   If there be not the
presence of God, the greatest comfort in the world is nothing.   What
makes the church esteemed of by holy men ?   God is present there ; and
wheresoever God is present, in the communion of saints, especially in his
ordinances, we should esteem them by this, that God is present.   What
makes hell to be hell ?   There is no presence of God there ; no testi-

mony of his presence in hell; nothing but 'utter darkness.' What makes the life of man comfortable? There is some presence of God in everything. There is a presence of God in meat, in drink, in friends, that a man may say, Oh, here is a good God, here is some presence of God. There is not the vilest reprobate in the world, but he hath some testimony of God's presence. He tastes of God in somewhat or other; though he see not God in it (but like a beast is drowned in the use of the creature), yet God shews himself to him in some comfort. But when God shall remove all his presence from a man, that is hell itself. What is hell but where there is no presence of God? When there is no communion with the chief good, that the fountain of good is removed, a man is in darkness, and horror, that is hell, as we see in Dives, Luke xvi. 4, *seq.* It is the presence of God that makes things comfortable. That is heaven, to enjoy nearer and nearer communion with God.

Therefore let us labour to enjoy the presence of God in his ordinances, that we may have a heaven upon earth, that we may desire still more and more to delight in them, till we come to heaven, where all desires shall be accomplished, and there shall be no more desire. David knowing that God was present in his church, he saith, ' Oh that I might dwell in the house of God all the days of my life.'

See the constant disposition of God's children hence. It is a torment to carnal men to watch one hour with Christ. ' Could you not watch with me one hour?' Mat. xxvi. 40, saith he to his disciples. It is a torment to give God the hearing; to sanctify the Lord's day. Alas! it cannot stand with their carnal dispositions. But God's people long, and have a longing desire. ' One thing have I desired, that I may dwell in the house of the Lord.' Men that have not depth of grace, they are like comets. They blaze for a time; but when they are not fed with vapours from below, there is a dispartition not long after. But fixed stars are always in the firmament; they never vary. So a true Christian is as a fixed star, he is fixed in the firmament, in his desire. ' One thing have I desired, that I may dwell in the house of the Lord all the days of my life;' and God seconds his desire, and saith amen to it; as I shall have occasion to press after, in the use in the latter part of the verse. ' That I may dwell in the house of the Lord.'

' To behold the beauty of the Lord.'

This was another ground of the eager, constant, unsatisfied desire, ' To dwell in the house of the Lord,' that he might 'see the beauty of the Lord,' or the delight, the sweetness of God. Beauty is too particular a word to express the fulness of the Holy Ghost, the pleasantness or the delight of God. Take the word in a general sense, in your apprehensions. It may be the object of all senses, inward and outward. Delight is most transcendent for pleasantness; for indeed God in his ordinances, is not only beauty to the eye of the soul, but is ointment to the smell, and sweetness to the taste, and all in all to all the powers of the soul. God in Christ, therefore, he is delightful and sweet. ' That I may see the beauty of the Lord.'

In this clause here are discovered these two things, the object and the act.

There are these two points. *That God is beautiful.* And this is seen in his ordinances, and in his church, especially, ' to see the beauty' of God's house. And *it is the happiness of a Christian*, and he esteems it so by the Spirit of God, to see, and to be partaker of this beauty of God. Sight is put for the more full enjoying, one sense put for another, as indeed sight

is taken for all the senses, inward and outward. It is no benefit to us,
though there be beauty, if we have not eyes to see it, all is lost ; therefore
he desired to dwell in the house of the Lord, that he might ' see the beauty
of the Lord.'

Now, concerning the beauty of God, I will not speak of it at large, or
singly of the excellencies of God. The text aims especially at the beauty
of God, *as discovered in his ordinances, in his church.* A man may speak
gloriously, and largely of the beauty of God, of his excellency. That his
wisdom is wondrous excellent, and beautiful, that is seen in the ordering of
things, and his power is wonderful beautiful, and his mercy, &c. All this
is true ; but what is all to us, though God be never so beautiful in himself,
if he be not beautiful to us in Christ, and in his church ? Therefore we
will come to that that the holy prophet here aims at, ' The beauty of the
Lord ;' that is, God is especially beautiful in his church, in his ordinances,
and that was the ground of his desire. *Omne pulchrum est amabile,* every
beautiful thing is an attractive of love. It is no wonder he desired to dwell
in the house of the Lord, because there was the beauty of the Lord, and the
most excellent beauty of all.

The beauty of the Lord is especially the amiable things of God, which
is his mercy and love, that makes all other things beautiful that is in the
church.

What makes his power sweet to his children ? and his justice, in confounding their enemies, and giving rewards ? and his wisdom sweet, in reconciling justice and mercy together wisely in Christ ? All that makes this
so lovely, is his grace and love, that set his wisdom on work, to devise a
way to reconcile justice and mercy by Christ Emmanuel, God and man.
So that that is most beautiful in God is grace ; as you have it, Exod.
xxxiv. 6. When Moses desired to see the glory of God, how doth God describe himself to Moses ? ' Jehovah, Jehovah strong, gracious, merciful,
longsuffering, full of kindness.' So that if we would see the glory of God,
it appears most in grace, and mercy, and lovingkindness, and such sweet
attributes. This makes all things in God amiable ; for now we can think
of his justice, and not fear. It is fully satisfied in Christ. We can
think of his power with comfort. It serves for our good to subdue
all our enemies. There is no atttibute, though it be terrible in itself,
but it is sweet and amiable, because God looks graciously on us in his
beloved.

Now this grace and love and mercy of God shines to us in the face of
Christ as beloved, as I have shewed out of that text, 2 Cor. iii. 18, ' We
all behold the glory of God as in a glass (*c*), that is, we behold the love of
God in Jesus Christ, in the mirror of the gospel. We must take God, not
as considered abstractively* and simply, but God in Christ ; for other notions of God are terrible. God will not otherwise be seen by the eye of the
soul, nor otherwise known, than in Christ. Now God in the Messiah is
very delightful in his house. This beauteous grace of God shines in the
face of Jesus Christ, 2 Cor. iv. 6. For God is so gracious and merciful, as
that his justice must be fully satisfied, that is, only in Christ ; that being
satisfied, God in Christ looks on us with a gracious look. So that God is
beautiful now in regard of his mercy and grace, as it is revealed in Jesus
Christ, as he looks upon us in the face of his beloved Son. There are
two objects of religious worship. God the Father, Son, and Holy Ghost,
and Christ Mediator. The beauty of both is wondrous in the church,

* That is, ' abstractly.'—G.

wondrous towards the church of God, and it is most apparent in the ordinances of God in the church. Christ is 'altogether lovely,' Cant. v. 16. Christ in whom God is a Father, and reconciled to us; and now we can sweetly think of, ' He is altogether lovely, the chief of ten thousand.' The church sets him out there particularly, his head, his arms, his breasts, his eyes. ' His lips drop myrrh,' Cant. v. 13. She singles out every excellency of Christ, and dwells upon it in her meditation, and sums up all together, ' Christ is lovely.' What makes beauty but a mixture of diverse colours ? as we say, white and red mix together sweetly. Now to see justice and mercy in Christ so sweetly mixed, what an excellent beauty it makes ! To see the justice of God fully satisfied, that his mercy might run amain to us now. Here is a sea indeed if we should enter into it, to see the love of God, which is the most beautiful and amiable grace of all ; the love of God in Christ, and the love of Christ towards us.

Christ was never more lovely to his church than when he was most deformed for his church ; ' there was no form nor beauty in him,' Isa. liii. 2, when he hung upon the cross. Oh ! there was a beauty to a guilty soul, to see his surety enduring the wrath of God, overcoming all his enemies, and nailing the law to his cross. And that should endear Christ to us above all things. He should be the dearer to us, the more vile and base he was made for us, and he should be most lovely in our eyes, when he was least lovely in his own, and when he was deformed, when our sins were upon him. We should consider those times especially. The world is most offended at that, that a Christian most joys in. ' God forbid that I should joy in anything but in the cross of Christ,' Gal. vi. 14, saith St Paul; so we should joy in and love that especially in Christ.

Now this love of God in Christ, and this love of Christ, is expressed to us in the Scriptures at large; it is published by the ministry, sealed by the sacrament. It is too large an argument for me to wade into. I need but only give you a touch and taste of it.

Now, that that makes the house of God so beautiful, then, *is the love of God, and the love of Christ shewed and manifested, and the presence of God, of Christ, and of the Holy Ghost in the church.* Take it for the persons ; God the Father, as he hath revealed himself a Father in Christ, he is among the people of God in the church, and there is God the Son, and the Holy Ghost, dispensing graces and comfort there. It is the presence of the king that makes the court, and it is the presence of God in the church that makes it so glorious and so excellent as it is. ' Glorious things are spoken of thee, thou city of God,' Ps. lxxxvii. 3.

The church likewise is beautiful *in regard of the angels, that are alway attending in our assemblies*, and see how we carry ourselves. Here is not only the Father, Son, and Holy Ghost distributing grace and mercy, but likewise the blessed angels, as pure instruments are in our assemblies. Therefore in the curtains, in the hangings of the ark, there were pictures of cherubins, to shew that the angels attend about the church, especially the church gathered together ; for God more respects the church gathered together than any several member. We are all temples severally, but especially the church is the temple when it is met together. Now by the cherubins in the curtains of the tabernacle, was set forth the angels' attendance upon the church. They are servants to do good to the church ; and they are fellow-students with us. They study the mysteries of salvation, the beauty of God, the wonderful transcendent love, and grace, and mercy of God to his church, as it is in 1 Pet. i. 10, 11, ' The angels pry into the mysteries of salvation;' they are students with us of those blessed mysteries. Something is revealed to them, some grace and mercy to the church, that they knew not before experimentally.

And it is beautiful likewise in regard *of the church itself.* The people of God themselves are beautiful ; for order is beautiful. Now it is an orderly thing to see many together to submit themselves to the ordinance of God. ' The glory of a king is in the multitude of subjects,' Prov. xiv. 28 ; and it is a glorious thing for God to have many subjects meekly meeting together to attend his pleasure. An army is a beautiful thing, because of the order, and of the well disposed ranks that are within it. In this regard the church is beautiful.

That which makes the house of God beautiful more especially, *is the means of salvation :* not only God's presence, but the means, solemn and public prayer, the word and sacraments, and likewise the government, that should be in purging the church,—all make the church of God beautiful and lovely. All the ordinances of God in the church of God have a delight in them to spiritual senses.

1. *As for the ordinance of the word,* it is wondrous delightful, ' sweeter than the honeycomb,' Ps. xix. 10, especially the ordinance unfolding the word, the word as it is preached, which is the ' opening of the box.' A box of sweet ointment, if it be not opened, it casts not a sweet savour all the house over ; but when the box is opened, the savour comes over all the house. So the publishing of the word in the ordinance, is the opening of the box, the lifting up of the brazen serpent. If the serpent were [not] lift up for the wounded person, he could not behold it. Now [that] Christ is lift up in the ordinance, every wounded soul may look to Christ. The preaching of the word, is the lifting up of the banner of Christ's love. As it is in the Canticles, Christ's love as a banner draws all after him. When the beauty of Christ is unfolded, it draws the wounded, hungry soul unto him. The preaching of the word doth that that shews the sweet love of God in Jesus Christ. This makes the ordinance of the ministry so sweet. The ordinance of the ministry is that that distributes the portion to every child of God. The ministers of God are stewards, as it were, to distribute comfort and reproof to whom it belongs. Now where there is a convenient distributing of the portion to every one, that makes the ordinance of God so beautiful, when the waters of life are derived from the spring of the Scripture to every particular man's use. The word, in the application of it, is a sweet thing. For good things, the nearer they are brought home, the more delightful they are. This ordinance of preaching, it lays open the ' riches of Christ.' There may be a great deal of riches wrapped up in a treasury, but this opens the treasury, as St Paul saith, ' to lay open the unsearchable riches of Christ,' Eph. iii. 8. The ministry of the word is ordained to lay open the treasure to God's people, that they may know what riches they have by Christ ; and the end of the ministry is to win the people's love to Christ. Therefore they come between the bride and bridegroom to procure the marriage ; therefore they lay open that that procures the contract here, and the consummation in heaven ; so to woo for Christ, and ' beseech them to be reconciled to God,' 2 Cor. v. 20. This is the end of the ministry. This makes the church of God so beautiful, that it hath this ordinance in it, to bring God, and Christ, and his people together : to contract them together. There be rich mines in the Scripture, but they must be digged up. The ministry serves to dig up those mines. God hath therefore set apart this calling of the ministry, to shew what belongs

to God's people. Thus you see in this respect, of the ordinance of the ministry, God is beautiful in his house.

2. Then likewise for the other ordinance, *the sacrament, it is a sweet and delightful thing.* There is a wondrous beauty in the sacrament; for therein we taste the love of God, and the love of Christ. That they would condescend so low, as to seal our faith with the sacrament, to help our souls by our bodies, by outward things; to help our souls by that that feeds our bodies, to teach us what feeds our souls, namely, the death of Christ, as satisfying divine justice,—the thinking and digesting of this is wondrous comfortable, as any food is to the body, and incomparably more sweet, considering our continual necessity to relish that spiritual food, and our daily sins and breaches, that enforce a daily necessity to relish Christ. That God should appoint such means, that he should in the sacrament feed us with his own body and blood. He thought he could not manifest his love enough, unless he had told us that he would give himself to us, and make over himself wholly to us: You shall have me, my body and blood; as in the sacrament we are as verily partakers of the body and blood of Christ, as we are of the bread and wine. Our souls have as much spiritual growth by Christ, and his benefits, as our bodies have by the outward elements. He feeds us with himself; he esteems and prizeth our souls that are bought with his blood, so that he thinks no food good enough but his own body and blood. What a gracious sweet love is this! He is both the inviter and the banquet, and all. He invites us to himself.

3. There is a loveliness likewise *in all other ordinances that belong to the church; as in the good order and government of the church, in purging the church of offenders;* the discipline that is in the church, which is as the snuffers in the sanctuary to purge the lights; so that there should be a casting out of persons that are openly scandalous. The lights should be purged, the temple should be cleansed, scandals should be removed, that God's house might be the more beautiful. They are blemishes of God's house, open swearers and blasphemers. Those that live in scandalous sins, they are spots in the assembly, they are leaven, and this leaven should be purged out; and where there is the vigour of this, there is a great beauty of the church. Where these things are looked to as they should be, they are the bonds, and nerves, and sinews that knit and tie a church together. It makes a church wondrous lovely, the neglect of which makes the church as a garden overgrown. So you see how, in respect of the ordinances of the word, and of the sacrament, and this government that should be, that the house of God is a beautiful place.

4. Then again, it is a comfortable, a sweet and delightful thing, *the praises of God.* It is a marvellous sweet thing, when all as one man hear together, pray together, sing together hymns, and spiritual songs, and praise God together, and receive the sacrament together, all as one man,—what a comely thing is this to a spiritual eye! Every Christian hath a beauty severed in himself; but when all meet together, this is more excellent. As we say of the *via lactea,* or milky way in the heavens (we call it so), it is nothing but a deal of light from a company of little stars, that makes a glorious lustre. So if there be a beauty in every poor Christian, what a beauty is there when all meet together! A beauty, nay, strength too; for the prayer and the praise of such, they offer a holy violence to God, they can obtain anything at his hands. We see burning glasses, when there is a confluence, and meeting of divers beams in one point, it strengthens the heat, and inflames a thing; so when there are many sweet desires meet

together, many strong desires of spiritual things, they bind God. There is
not only beauty but strength in the prayers of the church. They are in
Christ's own esteem comeliness. He loves to see his church, especially when
they are together. ' Let me see thy face, and hear thy voice, thou that hidest
thyself in the clefts of the rock,' Cant. ii. 14. He marvellously desires to
see his children, and to hear them speak, especially when they present
themselves before him. Harmony is a sweet and pleasant thing. The
comparing of the state of the church in former times with the present, is a
harmonious thing. David, he lived under the Old Testament, and yet he
saw under that the New, so we should see the Old in the New, compare
them together, to see shadows in substances, types in truths. So that
there is nothing in the church, but it gives special delight.

5. God's beauty likewise appears, his gracious, amiable, sweet beauty,
in his house, his church in regard *of the evidences of his love that he bears to
his church, in protecting it, and providing for it.* ' They shall not need a
wall,' saith he in Zechariah, ' I will be a wall of fire,' Zech. ii. 5. God
hath a special care of his congregation. ' God dwells in the congregation
of the righteous,' Ps. lxxxii. 1. He hath his dwelling, his special residence
there, where his name is called on. This will appear more if we see all the
sweet privileges and comforts that are in the house of God. God is not
only beautiful in himself, but in regard of the privileges that the church
hath from him. For all our beauty and excellency is borrowed. The
church shines in the beams and beauty of Christ. Now these privileges
that the church hath by Christ, to name a few. (1.) *We see in the golden
chain of salvation,* what sweet, amiable love is in all those links; as what
a wondrous sweet love of God is it. (2.) *To call men out of the wilderness of
the world,* out of the kingdom of Satan, to be his children ! A marvellous
love to single us out of the rest of mankind to be Christians, and being
Christians, to be professors of the truth, and being so, to be true professors
of the truth. What a wondrous love of God was it to call us, and thereby
to have the eternal purpose of God opened to us. As when we are drawn
to God by his Spirit and by the ministry, then the good pleasure of God,
that was hid from eternity, is discovered to the soul. Here is the amiable
love of God.

(3.) And then in *the pardon, and forgiveness of sins, and justification after*
—what a wondrous grace is that forgiveness of sins, and adoption to be the
sons and heirs of God, ' fellow-heirs with Jesus Christ,' Rom. viii. 17, and
thereupon to have angels our attendants. What beauty have we in justification, to be clothed with the righteousness of Christ; that perfect righteousness, that can answer the justice of God much more Satan's cavils and the
troubles of our own consciences. That that satisfieth the justice of God,
being the righteousness of God-man, it will satisfy conscience, and Satan's
temptations. It is a garment without spot. Satan can pick no hole in
that glorious garment, the righteousness of Christ. If we have the wardrobe of Christ, we shall be beautiful in that we have from Christ, we shall
shine in his beams.

(4.) So go to *sanctification.* How amiable is God in the privilege of sanctification, to set his image upon us, to make us new creatures, to be like his
Son, that before were like the devils, full of malice and base affections.
Now for God by his Spirit to frame a new temple for his Spirit to dwell
in, to set his stamp upon us, what a wondrous beauty is this ! The
church of God is the house where God frameth new creatures. There he
sets a stamp upon his creatures.

The graces that belong to the church of God are wondrous delight. 'Wisdom makes a man's face to shine,' Eccles. viii. 1 ; and there is no wisdom out of the church. All is but darkness and folly. So of all other graces whatsoever. Graces are the anointing of the Spirit, the oil of the Spirit. They make sweet and delightful, delightful to God, and to the church, and to one another. They are anointed with the oil of gladness and of grace. It ran first upon Christ's head, upon Aaron's head, but then upon the skirts, the meanest Christian.

And so the beginning of glory here; for all is not kept for the life to come. For God distils some drops of glory beforehand. We see the beauty of God here, marvellously even in this world, in regard of the beginning of glory. For upon justification, and the beginning of holiness wrought in our nature by the Spirit, we have inward peace of conscience, and joy and comfort in all discomforts whatsoever. We have not only the oil of grace, but the oil of comfort. Oh! the comfort of the children of God, that are members of the church, that are so in the church, that they are of the church too, that are of the church visible, so as they are of the church invisible. Oh! the comfort that belongs to them, all the comfort in God's book. So you see the wondrous sweet prerogatives and privileges we have in all the passages of salvation in the house of God, and in God reconciled in Jesus Christ.

Nay, God is so lovely to those that are his, his church and people, he is so good to Israel, that he makes everything good to them in the issue. 'All things work for the best to them that love God,' Rom. viii. 28, in the issue. He makes a covenant between everything. So that all the endeavours of Satan and his instruments, all their plottings, shall turn for the good of the church. When they think to do most hurt, they do most good ; so sweet, and good, and gracious is God.

Indeed, 'glorious things are spoken,' Ps. lxxxvii. 3, of the people of God. Take the church for a visible congregation, a mixed congregation; glorious things are spoken of that. It is the house of God. Take it as visible, 'the vessels of honour and dishonour,' 2 Tim. ii. 20, and the field, the 'tares and the wheat,' Mat. xiii. 1, seq., it is God's field. Though we take the church as visible, it hath a glorious name for the good that is in it, specially for the wheat. But take the church of God for the company of his children that are gathered by the means dwelling in the visible church, enjoying the visible means: so they are the house and temple of Christ, the 'temple of the Holy Ghost, the body of Christ, the spouse of Christ.' They are God's delight, they are spiritual kings and priests, &c. The most glorious things that can be, all other excellencies in the world, are but titular things, mere shadows of things. There is some little reality, but it is nothing in comparison, it is scarce worth the name of reality, but Solomon calls them 'vanity of vanities.' In comparison of the excellencies of the church all is nothing. I might be large in these particulars. It is enough to give you the generals of the delights and excellencies of God's house, 'the beauty of the Lord.' We see amiableness of God in Christ, in his ordinances, the privileges that we have in the ordinances, graces, and comforts. Indeed the church of God, beloved, is a paradise. Since we were cast out of the first paradise, this second paradise is the church of God, and the third is heaven itself. This paradise, this church, it is the seminary* of young plants, that must be transplanted hence to heaven in due time. In paradise there was the tree of life, Gen. iii. 22 ; in the church, there is the tree of life,

* That is, 'seed-plot.'—G.

Christ. In paradise there was waters, streams, the rivers of paradise, Gen. ii. 10; so there ' is a river that makes glad the city of God,' Ps. xlvi. 4, streams of grace and comfort that run through the church of God.

In the church we are as plants by the rivers of waters, that bring forth fruit in due season, as it is in Ps. i. 3, *seq.* Speaking of blessed men that live in the church, ' Blessed is the man that meditates in the word day and night,' that attends upon the ordinances. He is ' planted as a tree by the waters' side,' his leaf is alway green. What food to that food that is ministered to us in the word, and sacraments—Christ himself to feed us to life eternal ! And what raiment to the raiment of justification ; for Christ to clothe these poor souls of ours, poor, naked, beggarly souls ! What riches to the riches of God's graces and comforts ! What strength to that that is in the church, to overcome our own corruptions and lusts! What beauty to the image of God shining and stamped on his children ! What company so sweet, as those that we meet with in the earth, in good exercises, and that we shall live ever with in heaven ! What company to God the Father, Son, and Holy Ghost, and the angels, that we enjoy in the church ! What discourse so sweet, as that of God, hearing him speak in his word, and us speaking to him by prayer, so that it is a resemblance of heaven upon earth, the church of God !

Therefore we should be in love with the beauty of God's temple and sanctuary. And the rather because all things now in this age of the church wherein we live are in a more glorious manner than in David's time. David when he saw the beauty of God's sanctuary, it was but in a shadow ; and when he looked upon the mercy-seat, then he did think of Christ, the true propitiatory, the true mercy-seat. When he looked on the high priest, he thought on Christ the true high priest. When he thought of Canaan, it put him in mind of heaven, whereof Canaan was a type. When he saw the sacrifices, he thought of the true sacrifice for our sins, Christ. When he thought of the oblations and incense, he thought of the sacrifice of thankfulness. When he thought of the passover, he thought of Christ the true passover, whose blood is sprinkled on our souls, that the destroying angel hath nothing to do with us. He saw all in shadows; we see them naked. So our condition is more glorious in this latter age of the church, than it was in David's time. Therefore our desires should be more stirred up; for instead of the shadow we have the substance. Then the Spirit was but dropped, but the Father hath poured out the Spirit since Christ's time. Then the pale of the church was straitened, now it is enlarged. Then there was but one church, the national church of the Jews. Then the service of God was wondrous burdensome, and chargeable, but it is not so now. So that there be many differences. All things are more lightsome and clear now than they were then. Therefore having many things to commend the frequenting of the congregation more than David had in his time, we should much more make this one thing our desire ' to dwell in the house of the Lord, all the days of our life, to *behold the beauty of the Lord.*'

Quest. If this be so, that there is such a beauty in the house of God, then what shall we think of those that see no such beauty at all, that see no such delight and contentment in the house of God?

Ans. I answer, it is a discovery to them, if they would think of it, *that they have no spiritual senses at all;* as St Austin saith of men that complain, that they do not taste and relish these things. Surely, saith he, thou wantest a spiritual palate to taste these things. What do swine care for sweet marjoram or roses? They care more for a dunghill or a puddle. What do your base filthy swine in men's shape care for these things? They care more for pleasures and such things, that they may spend their lives as beasts. Now when we speak of the delights, and dainties, and excellencies of God's house, we speak to those that we wish, and we hope have spiritual senses answerable to these things. Every creature delights in its proper element. These things are the element of a Christian. Beetles delight in dirt, and swine in mire, the fish in the sea, man hath his element here, and spiritual things are the element of a Christian, so far as he is a Christian, and that is his *ubi*, the place that he delights in. I speak to such. They can make it good in some measure, that ' one day in the house of God is better than a thousand elsewhere,' Ps. lxxxiv. 10, that one hour in the unfolding the sweet mysteries of salvation, it is worth twenty-four hours in other employment; and they are so taken with the sweetness, that they are content that God should take them out of the world, in the unfolding of these sweet things. When they hear the promises of salvation opened, though by a poor weak man, yet when it is in the ministry, it so ravisheth their hearts, that they are content to go to heaven at the same time; it so convinceth them of the excellency of religion. I speak to such of the beauty of God.

Now David here, he desires to behold God's beauty, to see or consider this excellency of God in his church, for to true delight these things must concur. There must be something sweet in the thing itself. There must be a power in the soul to apprehend it. There must be an affection in the soul to that good thing. If the affection be flat, though there be never so beautiful and sweet things, and a power to apprehend them, if there be not affection, they are nothing; and then, upon the affection, there must be complacency and contentment in the thing when we have it. All these things are in delight from that that is beautiful and pleasant, David desired to see. He knew there was a beauty in the presence of God in his ordinances and gifts and graces; but he desired to see and to contemplate these things, that the faculties and powers of his soul might be answerable to the things, that as they were excellent, so he might have a power in his soul answerable. And then he had affections to carry that power of his soul to the things, ' One thing have I desired.' And then there was a complacency and delight in the things, upon enjoining,* answerable, as we see how he expressed his delight when he danced before the ark. We see what a psalm he made when he did but purpose ' to build the temple,' Ps. cxxxii. He had a wondrous joy. So answerable to our delights is our joy and complacency in the thing when we have it.

Now that he might have the sweeter complacency, he desired to see the beauty and the things in God's house. Of all senses, sight hath this property above the rest (as it is more spiritual, more refined, and more capable; a man may see many things at once, it is a quick sense; so), it hath this privilege, it stirs affections more than any sense, more than hearing, that is a more dull sense. Things stir affections more that are seen, than by that we hear. He desired therefore to see the beauty of God's house, that he might be enamoured. Of sight comes love.

David had spiritual eyes, and he desired to feed his spiritual eye-sight with the best object that could be, for therein is the happiness of man. Wherein stands a man's happiness? When there is a concurrence of the most excellent object, with the most excellent power and faculty of the

* Qu. 'enjoying?'—ED.

soul, with delight and content in it.　Now he desired to see the beauty of God in his house, that his soul might be ravished in the excellency of the object, and that the highest powers of his soul, his understanding, will, and affections might be fully satisfied, that he might have full contentment. Since the fall, all our happiness is out of ourselves, it is derived from God in Christ ; and it is taken out of the promises of God in the word. For God will be seen in Christ, and God and Christ will be seen in the glass of the ordinances till we come to heaven, and there we shall see ' face to face,' 1 Cor. xiii. 12.　So that now all our happiness is fetched by looking on the love of God, out of ourselves, fetched out of the ordinances. David desired to see the beauty of God.　God's love is diffusive.　It spreads and communicates itself to his church in the ordinances.　Thus he, knowing, desired more and more to communicate of this diffusive, abundant, transcendent love of God.

Quest. But how shall we come to have these desires that David had, to see the beauty of God ?

Ans. In a word—we must have *spiritual senses.* The spiritual life of a Christian is furnished with spiritual senses.　He hath a spiritual eye and a spiritual taste to relish spiritual things, and a spiritual ear to judge of holy things, and a spiritual feeling.　As every life, so this excellent life hath senses and motion suitable to it.　Now we should labour to have this spiritual life quickened in us, that we may have a quick sight of heavenly things ; and a taste of heavenly things, that we may smell the ointment of Christ.　'For the sweetness of thy ointments the virgins run after thee,' Cant. i. 3.　The soul hath senses answerable to the body, let us desire God *to cleanse all our senses, and to reveal himself in Christ more and more in the ordinances.*

This St Paul calleth the ' Spirit of revelation,' Eph. i. 17.　Let us pray to God that in his ordinances he would discover that amiable love of his in Christ, to shine on us in the face of his Son, in his ordinances ; for the Spirit must help us to see the beauty of God.　When we have spiritual senses, except the Spirit give us a spiritual light to see, we cannot see. Therefore let us desire that God would give us spiritual senses, to the spiritual light.

When God made the world, light was the first creature.　Why ?　That all the excellency of the creature might be discerned by light.　If God had made never so many excellent creatures, if the light had not discovered them, where had been his glory ?　So there are many excellent, beautiful things in Christ, wonderful grace and comfort ; if these be discovered in the word and we have no senses, and no light, if there be not light in the understanding, God shall want his glory, and we the comfort.

It is light that makes things that are beautiful to be beautiful to us.　A blind man cannot judge of colours, nor a deaf man of sounds and harmony. A man that hath lost his taste cannot judge of sweetness, so that there must be senses, and the Spirit of God must reveal these things unto us.

And likewise let us labour more and more to *see our own deformity, and then we shall see Christ's beauty, the more we desire to know our own vileness.* Indeed the Spirit of God carries these parallel one with another.　He discovers by the same light our own deformity and necessity, and the beauty and excellency of God in Jesus Christ.　The one will set an edge on the other, and he that will come to see the height and breadth, and depth of God's love in Christ, must see the height, and breadth, and depth of his own corruption, and our misery by it out of Christ.　And they are good thoughts for us, every day to think of these two objects, the misery of the condition of man out of Christ, and the excellency now that we have in Jesus Christ; the amiableness of Christ towards us, and our amiable condition in him. He delights in us, as we delight in him. The consideration of this, and of the loathsome, terrible, fearful condition out of him, will keep us closer to Christ, and make us value the ordinances more, that we may grow up in faith and knowledge of Christ more and more, till we come to a fulness in Christ.

And present to the eye of our souls, God in Christ *in the relations he hath taken upon him,* to be a Father in Christ. Let us make that benefit of this beauty that is presented to us in the gospel, especially when it is unfolded in the ministry, because Satan hath a special policy to present God and Christ otherwise to us. Especially in the time of temptation, he presents God as a judge, sitting upon his throne, and God as a 'consuming fire,' Heb. xii. 29. It is true he is so out of Christ, but in him he hath taken the relation of a father, and looketh on us sweetly in the relation of sons. Christ must be considered in the sweet relation of a Saviour, and the Holy Ghost in the sweet relation of a comforter ; and the word is all written for our comfort, if we believe, and the sacraments feed us to eternal life. Let us represent these things beautifully to the soul, and this will strengthen faith, and cherish affection, that Satan shall not rob us of our comfort, nor say to us, what do you, ye unclean persons, loathsome creatures, what do you come to the sacrament, and come to the holy things of God? It is true, if we mean to be so still, but as soon as ever the desire of our souls is to come to God, and that there is a divorce between us and our sins, and we desire to leave them, let us have all the sweet conceits of God that may be. We see in Revelations, Laodicea was lukewarm, and that is a hateful temper. 'Behold,' saith he, 'I stand and knock, if any man open to me, I will come, and sup with them,' Rev. iii. 20. A strange love, to come to them that were in such a lukewarm estate. He was ready to cast them out. His stomach was loaden with them. 'I stand at the door and knock,' yet if any of you lukewarm professors will open, I will come and sup with him, and refresh him with the refreshings of God. So in Cant. v., when the church slighted Christ and offended him, yet he woos his church. 'My locks are wet with the dew of the night,' Cant. v. 2. Oh! marvellous patience, that notwithstanding her lukewarmness and neglect, yet Christ gives not over! Let us not entertain hard conceits of God in Christ, but labour to present them sweetly to our meditations.

This is the wisdom of a Christian, to have sights of faith, that is, to present several things that faith may work on to strengthen itself, as for faith to have a sight of God in Christ, a gracious Father; and to have a spiritual sight of Christ sending ambassadors wooing and beseeching us to be reconciled ; and a sight of the joys of heaven, that we shall have full possession of after. Let us think of them, and present them to our souls ; and present to our souls by meditation, the excellency, and royalty, and prerogative of God's children, that they are the most excellent people in the world. These sights that faith helps itself by, are an excellent means to make us in love with the beauty of God's house. But to answer two or three objections briefly before I proceed to more particulars.

Obj. Some will object, what need we now in these glorious times of the church stand upon the ordinances so much? Indeed in darker times there was more need, &c.

Ans. I will not be large, but to answer in a word. *The more God dis-*

covers himself, and his excellent things here, the more we should express our thankfulness in labouring to grow in knowledge ; for there is such a breadth in them, that we can never have enough of them, and there is such a daily exigence of spiritual things, of comforts and graces, that are all conveyed in the use of means, that a Christian cannot be without them ; he can no more be without the use of the ordinances than he can without his daily food.

Obj. Oh ! but what need we be so eager and earnest after these things as some are ?   Is not now and then enough ?

Ans. Are we better than David ?   See how earnest he was, Ps. lxxxiv. and Ps. xlii. ' As the hart panteth after the rivers of water, so my soul thirsteth after thee, O God,' Ps. xlii. 1, lxxiv. 2.   For there is a presence of God in his ordinances that other men are not sensible of. There is a presence to their spirits that they feel that they marvellously love, and are affected with.   And if they want the presence of God, as David here, they are wondrously discouraged.   As good Nehemiah, when he heard it went not well with the church, he grew sad ; and David, we see how he takes it here when he was banished, as it were, from the house and ordinances of God.   But I will not stand long upon these objections.

Obj. Some think they may as well read at home good books and sermons, and not come to the ordinances.

Ans. But David *loved the ordinances ; he loved the place.* Might not he think of what he heard before ? might not he have help of the prophets ? Oh ! but there is a blessing in the very meeting, ' Where two or three are met together, I will be in the midst of them,' Mat. xviii. 20.   And Christ walks in the midst ' of the golden candlesticks,' Rev. i. 12.   There is a more powerful, gracious presence in the very assemblies of God's people. Put case thou mayest do much good in private, with contempt of the public ordinance ; it is a cursed study.   Like manna that did stink when it was gathered out of season.   When it was gathered when it should not, it putrefied.   There is a curse upon that study, and upon that knowledge that we get when we should attend upon the public means.   For it is not knowledge that will bring to heaven, for the devil hath that, but it is knowledge sanctified, seizing upon the affections.   Now, what is it that maketh us good ?   The Spirit working with the ordinance ; and will the Spirit work when we neglect the ordinance ?   It is but a pretence.   They spend their time otherwise, it is to be feared not so well.   But put the case they should, there never comes good of it.   It may enrich them in knowledge to grow more devilish ; but more holy they cannot be, for holiness comes from the Spirit, and the Spirit will work by his own ordinances.   So much for that, and of all other objections in regard of the beauty of God.

I will not raise any objections, but only answer those that commonly popish spirits trouble some withal.   I will answer, I say, some of them briefly.

Obj. They trouble us about our churches.   Indeed, if your particular churches were churches of God, if you could make that good, then you might delight in them, but you are heretics and schismatics ; your churches are not good churches.   Thus they trouble good Christians that are of the simpler sort ; especially with this, where was your church a hundred years ago ? before Luther's time ? (*d*)   Your church is an upstart, and your congregations are nothing but a meeting of a company of heretics together.*

---

* The commonplaces of the popish controversy.   Consult Faber's ' Difficulties of Romanism.'—G.

Ans. Beloved, that *that makes a church to be a catholic church, to be a branch of the catholic church*, which we believe in the creed, *it is the catholic faith*. The faith and truth that is the seed of the church, it is begotten of the word of God. Wheresoever the word, the catholic truth of God, is, there is the church, a branch of the catholic church. Now our faith that we believe hath consanguinity with the first churches; for what do we believe, but it is fetched out of the Testament, and from the primitive church? And indeed in their own confession, if they would be modest, that might be extorted from them, that we are more catholic, and our doctrine is more catholic than theirs. Why? For that that agrees with the ancient truth, ' and faith once given,' as St Jude saith, ver. 3, it runs through all ages; and that wherein we agree with them is more agreeable and catholic than that they hold severed from us. It is more catholic in regard of all times, before Christ, and in Christ's time, and in the apostles' times; and that that the papists themselves hold with us, is more catholic than that they hold severed. Now wherein they differ from us, and we account them heretics, they differ from the Scriptures, and from the church six hundred years after Christ; and many of them are of late standing. Therefore in those tenets of ours we agree with the papists, and with the primitive church. What do we hold but they hold? But they add traditions that are pernicious. We hold the Scriptures. They hold that, and traditions too. We hold two sacraments. They add five more. We hold Christ to be the Mediator. They make saints mediators too. Whatsoever we hold they hold, but they add their own patcheries* to them. Therefore our doctrine is more catholic, because we have the evidence of Scripture for all ours, and we have them to justify ours; and wherein they differ from us, they have neither Scripture nor antiquity; but they are only a company, a mass of things of their own. But I will not be much in this point. And then, say they, where was your church before Luther's time, and two hundred years ago? Where was it? Where their church was. Our church was amongst them, in the midst of them. Witness their fire and inquisition, and persecution! They found out our church well enough.

But to make it a little clearer. The church of God, take it in general for good and bad in it, and for the means of salvation that they had in some measure, it may be called a kind of visible church, though very corruptly; and so considered, our church, those that possessed our religion, was the best of that church in the declining times of it. As in a lump of gold that is not yet refined to bullion there is gold, and a great deal of earth: take it in the whole, we say it is gold; but when it is refined to bullion, we say it is gold severed. Now our church in the midst of popery was as gold in the midst of earth unrefined; that is, there were† many Romish Churches, and ours was in the midst of them, the temple in the midst of the court; that is, the true church in the visible church. There were a great company that held the tenets of the gospel, especially at the hours of death, that denied popery. But then there were some that were refined as bullion after, as the Waldenses,‡ that were a severed company of people, besides other holy men and women that grew up by hearing somewhat of Christ in their sermons, and somewhat in the sacrament. They left out that that was bad, and took that that was good. Besides the lump of gold, there was some refined gold, when popery was in its perfection; and those they termed Waldenses, and the like. There was alway a company that held the

---

* That is, 'patchwork,' = additions.—G. † Misprinted 'was.'—G.
‡ Consult Stanley Faber's 'Waldenses and Albigenses'—able and trustworthy.—G.

truth against them. I am sorry to mention these things, in a point tending more to edification. Our churches therefore are refined churches, that is, gold singled out of the dross of popery. They are a corrupt, and our church a refined, a visible congregation.

Now to cut off these objections, to come nearer to ourselves, to make good our particular congregations, and to shew that of necessity we ought to frequent them, and to take heed of all objections that the devil and the flesh may make to bring us out of love with our particular congregations, know therefore these three or four rules in a word.

First, that there hath been *a church from the beginning af the world, where God hath been worshipped.* Christ is a King, and he must have a kingdom. To believe a catholic church is an article of our faith, and there cannot be an act without an object. I have faith, I believe a visible church, therefore there must be a church. So that there hath been a church from the beginning of the world. It is an article of our faith.*

Secondly, the mark whereby this church is known *is especially the truth of God.* That is the seed of the church, the truth of God discovered by his word and ordinance. To which is annexed the sacraments and ecclesiastical government; but the former most necessary. And these three were typified in the ark; for there was the law signifying the word, and the pot of manna signifying the sacrament, and the rod to shew the discipline. Those three were, as it were, types of the three marks of the church. But especially the word. For that is the seed of the new birth. Wheresoever the word hath been published, and there hath been an order of teachers, and people submitting themselves, there is a church, though perhaps there might be some weakness in other regards. A man is a man though he want the ornaments of a man; and a city without walls is a city. Put case there might be some weakness in some things, yet as long as the vitals of the church remain it is a church.

The third thing that I observe, to clear this point, to hasten to things of more edification, is this, *abuse takes not away the use.* A neglectful use or abuse takes not away the true use of things. Put case the Scripture be abused many ways, that the sacraments have many additions, that these things are not so pure; yet it takes not away the just use; for then we take away the cause of things. Then the conclusion of all is this, that of necessity, notwithstanding somewhat may be found fault with in all visible churches, some errors there may be; yet we ought to cleave to a visible church, because it hath been alway, and we ought to know it by these marks. If the word of God be taught there, then of necessity we must cleave to it. 'God added to the church such as should be saved,' Acts ii. 47, to the visible church. Those that are saved must be saved in submission to the visible church. But these things I list not† to be large in. This may give satisfaction.

Use 1. If this be so, that we ought to submit to the ordinance of God in the visible church, to come into the ark as it were (the visible church is called the ark), or else we must be drowned and perish, *what shall we think then of those that are cast out of the church by excommunication* (but that is for their good)? But their case is very ill, because they are cut off from the house and beauty of God. Their case is miserable. But it is worse with those that depart out of themselves, as apostates, &c. Some are cast out, some are apostates and go out. They fall away from the church of God to the Romish strumpet,

* Consult Pearson, and also John Smith, *in loc.*—G.
† That is, 'choose not.'—G.

to Babylon ; being dazzled with the pomp of that church, not seeing the spiritual beauty of the ordinances of God with us. What think we of those that ought to join with visible congregations, that excommunicate themselves willingly, such as schismatics, and such profane separatists, that when they may, will not; partly because they will not have their consciences awaked, and partly because they will give liberty to the flesh to other things at that time. Some are cast out, and some go out, some excommunicate themselves. They are of the disposition of the devils, that will not be ' tormented before their time,' Mat. viii. 29. They think they shall hear somewhat that will awake their conscience, and they are very unwilling to have conscience awaked, but they will have all their torment at once. All these are in a woeful condition. If the gracious presence of God be in the church above all other places in the world (as we see David desired ' to dwell in the house of God, that he might see the beauty of God') if there be a beauty in the divine ordinances, how miserable are those that are cast out, or that go out ! that rent themselves from the church, or willingly excommunicate themselves like wild creatures ? They are worse than Cain. He grieved when he was to depart the presence of God. He fell into a desperate temper. They are worse than he, that when they have the liberty of the ordinances of God, they go on in a wild licentious course, and neglect all means that God hath sanctified to bring them to heaven.

Use 2. But to come nearer, to make an use of trial, *how shall we know whether we have benefit by, and whether we be truly in love with, the beauty of God's house or no, because many come hither ?* As in Noah's ark there were beasts that were clean and unclean, so there are many that come to the visible congregations; they are in the church (as excrements are in the body), but they are not of it.

To know therefore whether we come to purpose, and heartily love the beauty of God in his ordinances, and comforts and graces, as David did here or no, we may know it easily, *for sight*, as I said before, *it works affection.* We may know by our affection whether we see the excellency of God or no in his ordinances. There is no sense that stirs up affection answerable to sight ; the affection of love especially.

How shall we know that we love the ordinances of God ?

That is an affection that of all others is least to be concealed. What we love we will boldly profess; we will joy and delight in it if we have it. You see how David joyed in the ordinance of God, how he danced before the ark. There was no joy that he had comparable. He preferred it before all other joy that he had whatsoever. It was a transcendent joy. And what we love and delight in we meditate much on. ' Oh how I love thy law ! my meditation is on it continually,' Ps. cxix. 97. Our minds will run on it. Therefore we are exhorted to think of the word of God, to have it before our eyes, to have it written before us in our courses, that we may meditate upon it at home and abroad. Moses he gave those helps. Where there is love there is meditation. Those that love the good things of God, their minds will be often on them.

Again, there will be *zeal for the holy things of God.* A man will not endure them to be disgraced, but he will have a good word to speak in the defence of God's ordinances, of holy things and religion. Those that suffer religion to be betrayed in the company of base carnal people, they have never seen the beauty of God's house ; [they] that have not a word to say. Those that have seen God's beauty, and felt the comfort of the delights of

God's house, they are able to justify it against all opposers whatsoever, that there is good to be taken and done there, by their own experience, by the comfort they have felt. They will be able to tell others what ' the Lord hath done for their souls,' Ps. lxvi. 16, and in their souls, what graces they have been strengthened in, what comfort they have felt. They can discover this, and can justify all the ordinances of God from their own experience. Do not we see daily under the ordinance of God by weak men, the blind see, the spiritually deaf hear, the spiritually dumb be able to speak, to pray to God; the dead, those that are dead in sin, they receive life. Do not all these justify the excellency of God's ordinance, which gives spiritual life, and spiritual senses? Those therefore that have been dead in former time in sinful courses, and have found the power of God's Spirit with his ordinances, they are able to justify it. Those that are not able to justify these things by some experience, they never felt any good by them. By these and the like evidences, we may try the truth of our affection, whether we have seen this beauty or no to purpose.

Quest. If we find that we have little comfort and strength by the word of God, that we have not seen the beauty of it, what shall we do, what course shall we take?

Ans. 1. *Wait still.* Wait still at the pool for the angel's stirring, John v. 4; for God at length will discover his power by his Spirit; he will discover his goodness, if not at the first, yet at length. Therefore let us use all sanctified means. And know this for a rule, that God's Spirit is an excellent worker. He will only work by his own instruments.

2. And *come to the ordinances with a spirit of faith,* because they are God's ordinances. God will discover himself in some excellency or other; he will discover some comfort and grace, somewhat that is useful to our souls to build us up to eternal life. Let us come with a particular faith that he will do so. Faith must answer God's promise. God hath promised, ' where two or three are met together in his name, he will be in the midst of them.' He hath made a promise to bless all his ordinances. Therefore let our particular faith answer God's ordinances. Lord, I go to thy house to hear thy word, to receive thy sacrament in thy fear, in reverence of thy majesty, and in a spirit of faith, I expect thee to make good thy own ordinance. This brings a marvellous efficacy with it. If we go with a particular faith, know that God will be as good as his word. This course we must take to see the beauty of the Lord.

3. And then, as I said before, *often let our thoughts be upon these spiritual excellencies.* Let us balance and weigh things in our thoughts. Love comes from judgment, love comes from an esteem of things, of the goodness of things, and that comes from a right judgment. Let us therefore labour to have a right judgment of things to be as they are. Solomon was the wisest man, next to him that was God-man, that ever was, and he knew what spiritual things were, and what all other things in the world were, and what verdict doth he give? This is the whole man, ' to fear God and keep his commandments, Eccl. xii. 13. And how doth he commend wisdom in Prov. viii. 1, *seq.* All precious things are nothing in comparison of the wisdom of God's word. But what saith he of other things? He that had run through all things by experience, and thought to extract the quintessence of all that the creature could give, he saith they were but ' vanity and vexation of spirit,' Eccles. i. 2; trust my experience. Therefore let us be able to lay in the balance the good that we get or may get by the blessed ordinances of God, with other things whatsoever. Oh the beauty and excel-

lency of spiritual things, it is above all other beauty whatsoever! Alas! what is outward beauty? it is but a lump of well-coloured earth.* What is gold, and all the lustre of it? It is but earth refined. And what are all honours and goodly delights that way? It is but a puff of smoke, it is nothing; in one word, it is vanity, and experience proves this every day. Oh! but the 'word of the Lord endureth for ever,' 1 Pet. i. 25, that is, the comforts, and the privileges that we have by the word of God, they endure for ever; and then more especially the comfort of them when outward comforts fail most, even upon our deathbed. When conscience is awakened then, and hath presented to it the former life, and the guilt of many sins, what will comfort a man then? his goodly apparel, or his goodly feature, or his great place and honour? (Perhaps these will increase his grief as they have been instruments of sin.) Oh no; this will do him good. Such a comfort I heard in such a sermon; such good things I heard read, and such good things come to my mind; such experience I have of God's Spirit working at such and such a time; these will testify that God's Spirit went with his ordinance to fasten somewhat on my soul, and they will comfort when nothing else will.

Let us oft compare all other things with the beauty of God, and his ordinances, as if all were nothing to them. Thus holy Moses, he saw a beauty and a glory in the despised people of God that made brick; he saw they were the people that God set his delight on, and that the church of God was there. When he saw that, he despised all the glory of Pharaoh's court, and accounted the worst thing in religion, 'the reproach and shame,' better than all the pleasures of sin, Heb. xi. 23. Beloved, the bitterest things in the ordinance of God are better than any worldly thing. What is the bitterest thing in the ordinance of God? Reproofs! They are as precious balm. If the ordinance of God meet with our particular sins, and tell us, and discover to us what an enemy it is, that it will be the bane of our souls if we live in it, and it send us away to look to ourselves, this will be as a precious balm; our souls will come to be saved by it. And if for religion we suffer reproach and shame, it will be as a crown, as holy Moses accounted the reproach of Christ better than the treasures of Egypt, Heb. xi. 26. If the worst and bitterest things in God's ordinance be so sweet, what are the best things of all? The comforts of religion. What is the peace of conscience and joy in the Holy Ghost, and eternal glory in heaven? What are the excellencies of religion, when the shame and disgrace are to be preferred before all other things whatsoever?

So blessed St Paul, he weighed things after this fashion. He was an excellent man, and had excellent privileges to glory in. Oh but, saith he, I account all 'dung and dross' in comparison of the excellent knowledge of Christ that he had, Phil. iii. 8. Our blessed Saviour, that was the most able of all to judge, he would have all 'sold for the pearl,' that is, for the field where the pearl is (e), to buy that, to get the ordinances of God. He accounts him a wise man that will sell all for that. And when Martha and Mary entertained him, Mary sat at his feet to hear him expound the truth of God; 'she chose the better part,' Luke x. 42, saith Christ. If we will believe him 'in whom all the treasures of wisdom are,' in his judgment, 'Mary chose the better part;' 'One thing is necessary,' saith he. He justified David's choice, 'One thing have I desired;' and saith Christ, 'One thing is necessary.' All things in comparison of that are not necessary; they may well enough be spared. Thus we see how we may come to love God

* See note a, vol. I., p. 31.—G.

in his ordinances, and to see the ' beauty of holiness,' the beauty of God in his sanctuary.

4. And because there are two things needful to see a beauty, *an object revealed, and a sight*, let us desire God *to reveal himself in his ordinances to us more and more, and desire him to give us spiritual eyes more and more to see him.* Sometimes he hides himself in his ordinances, that we cannot see the beauty of things. Let us therefore desire him to reveal himself, to take away that veil that is between us and holy things, and between us and grace, and comfort, that he would take away that spiritual veil, and reveal himself to us, and shine on us in Christ, that he would manifest his love to us, and give us spiritual eyes to see him.

Prayer is an excellent means before we come ; and when we are there, and oft in attending on the ordinances, let us lift up our hearts to God to reveal his truths to us.

There are many veils between us and holy things. Let us desire God to take them all away—of error, and ignorance, and unbelief—and to shine so clearly to us by his Spirit, that we may see him more clearly. And objects have a special influence when they are clearly discerned. Now a man may more clearly see and feel God at peace with him by the Spirit, and clearly see and feel the comfort of forgiveness of sins, and of any promise that is unfolded ; and it hath a marvellous influence upon the affections, to comfort and to breed peace and joy. And that is one sign that we profit by the ordinance of God, when it is so with us ; when we find an influence from the things, upon our daily prayers, to work peace and comfort, and spiritual strength against temptations and corruptions. All in the ordinance is by the power of the Spirit. Therefore we are to pray to God that he would join his Holy Spirit, that he would reveal his secrets to us, and with revelation work an influence into our souls, that there may be a distilling of grace and comfort through the ordinances to our souls. Prayer must accompany the ordinances ; because the ordinance of itself is an empty thing unless the Spirit accompany it.

To stir us up a little to this, more and more to see the beauty of God in his ordinances, to see the glory of God, as the Scripture speaks—indeed God is not only delightful and beautiful, but glorious in his ordinances ; and the ark is called the ' glory of God,' Exod. xl. 34 ; and the knowledge of God in Christ it is a glorious knowledge, and the gospel is called a ' glorious gospel,' 1 Tim. i. 11—*this will only* * *make us truly glorious.* These things, they put a glory upon our souls. St Paul calls it ' the glorious grace,' Eph. i. 6. What a glorious thing is it when, by the ordinance of God, a weak man shall have power against the strong devil, against all the ' gates of hell,' Mat. xvi. 18 ; when a poor creature, ' flesh and blood,' by some virtue distilled through the ordinance by the Spirit of God, shall have such a strong faith in the promise of forgiveness of sins ; such a faith in the promise that all such † turn to his good ; that God is reconciled to him in Christ ; that all the gates of hell shall not prevail over a weak soul. And what a glorious grace is it when, by the use and attendance upon the ordinance of God, a poor soul shall have strength over these corruptions and sins that others are slaves to, and cannot get the victory over, that when they see the spiritual beauty in God's ordinances, they grow out of taste with all other things that others are besotted with, that are of more excellent natural parts than they, what a glory of grace is this! Therefore let us with all fear and reverence attend upon the ordinances of

* That is, ' this only.'—G.   † Qu. ' shall ?'—ED.

God, that God may be glorious in us by his Spirit, and strengthen us against Satan and our beloved corruptions.

2. *And let us know what our souls were made for.* What are our souls more for than to dwell in the meditation of the beauty of God? What are our souls made for, but for excellent things? and what is excellent but in God's ordinances? Is the soul made to study debates and jars between man and man in our particular callings? Is the soul made to get a little wealth, that we shall leave perhaps to an unthrifty generation after? Are our souls, that are the most excellent things under heaven (the world is not worth a soul; they are the price of the blood of the Son of God; in his judgment the world is not worth a soul), are they for these things? No. They are for union and communion with God in his ordinances, to grow in nearer communion with God by his Spirit, to have more knowledge and affection, more love and joy and delight in the best things daily. Our souls are for these things that will make us gracious here, and glorious for ever after in heaven.

It is a great deordination,* when we study and care only for earthly things, and have slight conceits of those things that are incomparably the best things, in the judgment of God and of Christ himself, and of Solomon, and of all good men.

3. And the rather let us be stirred up to affect these things, *lest God depart from us.* The glory of God departed out [of] the temple before the destruction of Jerusalem, Ezek. xi. 23; so the glory of God, that is, a visible sign of his glory, it departs from a church; the beauty and excellency of God departs when we esteem them not. And if anything in the world make God to leave a church, as he left the Jews, and as he may leave any particular church (he will alway have a catholic church in the world; but he is not tied to England or France, or any country), if anything move him to this, it is because there is not a prizing of the heavenly things we have; of the blessed liberty we have to meet God in his ordinances; that we have not a care to improve these ordinances, to get grace and comfort against the evil day. For however we esteem these things, God sets a high price on them; and if we do not, God will deprive us of them, or of the power and beauty of them. Therefore as we desire God to continue his ordinances, and his blessing, and power in his ordinances, let us improve them the best way to get grace and comfort. He hath made a great progress in religion, that hath gotten a high esteem and a sanctified judgment of the best things. Though perhaps he find himself dull and dead, and complain of it, yet when God shines so far that he is able to approve, and to justify the best things, that they touch his affections so much, that the bent of his soul is that way, and he cannot be long without them, and he finds much comfort by them, though it be joined with much corruption, these things argue a good temper and frame of soul.

And of all other dispositions of soul, let us preserve that spiritual disposition of soul, whereby our soul is fitted to the things themselves. The things of God's Spirit are holy and excellent, when there is such a taste and relish wrought in the soul suitable to the things. There is a happy combination then. We may know there is a powerful work of the things upon the soul, for all grace wrought by the things of God, we may know it when the soul hath a suitable relish of them, and longs after them, and delights in them, and improves them to the best; and such a soul never wants evidence of a good Christian. Ask a Christian what is the best evidence of

* That is, 'disordering,' = placing out of order.—G.

salvation, and that you belong to God ? ' My sheep hear my voice,' John x. 4, saith Christ, ' and as children new born, desire the sincere milk of the word, that ye may grow thereby,' 1 Pet. ii. 2. A man may know he is a true child of the church if he desire the sincere milk of the word, to grow better and more holy and comfortable. If he delight in the voice of God in the ministry, and so be affected to the truth and ordinances of God, it is a comfortable character of a good Christian. There are more hidden evidences sometimes, but this for an ordinary evidence is a good one and comfortable. David marvellously comforted himself with this. ' Oh! how do I love thy law,' Ps. cxix. 97. Oh! that we could say as he did, ' Oh how do I love thy law, and love thy truth,' that we could wonder at our own affections, that we could delight in this beauty of God, as David saith here, ' One thing have I desired of the Lord, and that will I seek after, that I may dwell in the house of the Lord all the days of my life, to behold the beauty of the Lord,' &c.

FINIS.

NOTES.

(*a*) P. 217.—'Babylon was so taken,' &c. Consult Herodotus, I. 177, *seq.*, with the annotations and illustrations of Rawlinson, *in loc.;* also Xenophon, *Cyrop.* vii. 5. For very interesting explorations confirmatory of the fact cf. Rich, ' Babylon and Persepolis;' Ainsworth, ' Researches in Assyria;' and Chesney, ' Exped. for Survey of Euphrates.' It need hardly be stated that it was Cyrus who took Babylon in the manner referred to by Sibbes.

(*b*) P. 226.—' Particular visible churches are now God's tabernacle.' In a tract by Philip Nye, entitled ' The Lawfulness of the Oath of Supremacy, and Power of the King in Ecclesiastical Affairs ' (4to, 1683, p. 41), the above and other context is quoted. On the margin is placed ' Gospel Anointings,' which misled us into inquiring after such a book (of which none had ever heard) by Sibbes. Another tractate, by Bartlet, his ' Model of the Primitive Congregational Way ' (4to, 1647), explains the mistake of Nye. The following was evidently his authority :—' I shall produce only one more that was famous for his *Gospell-anointings* [in italics, the usual mode of expressing quotations], and little thought by most men to have been of this judgment [in the margin here, " see Dr Sibbs "]. And yet you shall find in a little treatise of his (printed before these troubles brake forth in England), called *A Breathing after God*, that he speaks fully to this purpose, his subject leading him to discover himself herein, being, as I suppose, a little before his death.' Bartlet then quotes the passages to which the present note refers. The manner in which Nye was led into his mistake is quite apparent on an examination of Bartlet's tractate. Sibbes's name in the margin is exactly opposite the words ' his *Gospell Anointings,*' while the title of the book actually quoted does not apppear till several lines lower on the page.

(*c*) P. 230.—' As I have shewed out of that text, 2 Cor. iii. 18,' &c. The sermons here referred to comprise the second half of Sibbes's ' Excellency of the Gospel above the Law.' 18mo, 1639.

(*d*) P. 240.—' Where was your church before Luther ? ' &c. There have been many polemical answers to this taunting question. For *thoroughness* none perhaps excels the old Scottish tractate by Andrew Logie, ' Answer to the question, Where was your religion before Luther ? ' Aberdeen, 1634, 4to.

(*e*) P. 245.—' The field where the pearl is.' Either Sibbes uses pearl as = treasure, or here, and elsewhere, he makes a slip. It is ' treasure,' not a ' pearl,' that is hidden in the ' field.'—Mat. xiii. 44.   G.

THE RETURNING BACKSLIDER.

THE RETURNING BACKSLIDER.

NOTE.

'The Returning Backslider' passed through three editions, viz. :—

(a) 1st, 1639, 4to, ⎱ Portrait *ætat* 58 prefixed, without the verses. (See prefatory
(b) 2d, 1641, 4to, ⎰ note to 'Bowels Opened.')
(c) 3d, 1650, 4to.

It will be remembered that it is on a copy of this work that Isaak Walton's memorable couplet is found (Memoir of Sibbes, vol. i., page xx). Our text follows *c*. Its title-page is given below.* The 'Saint's Privilege' therein mentioned is an admirable little treatise on John xvi. 8–10, which will be included, with other of Sibbes's minor writings, in a subsequent volume. It will be remembered that Bishop Reynolds also has a series of expository sermons on 14th chapter of Hosea, entitled 'Israel's Prayer in Time of Trouble, with God's gracious Answer,' 4to, 1638.

G.

* Title-page :—

THE
RETVRNING
BACKSLIDER:
OR,
A COMMENTARIE
upon the whole XIV. Chapter
of the Prophecy of the Prophet HOSEA.
Wherein is shewed the large extent of GODS free Mercy,
even unto the most miserable forlorne and wretched sinners
that may be, upon their Humiliation and Repentance.
Also the Saints Priviledge, *&c.*
Preached by that Learned and Iudicious Divine, Dr. SIBS, late Preacher to the Honourable Society of *Grayes Inne*, and Master of
Katherine-Hall in CAMBRIDGE.
Published by his own Permission before his Death.
The third Edition.
JEREM. 3. 12, 13.

Goe and Proclaime these words towards the North, and say, Return thou Backsliding Israel, saith the LORD ; *and I will not cause mine Anger to fall upon you : for I am merciful, saith the* LORD, *and I will not keep anger for ever. Onely acknowledge thine iniqnity,* &c.

LONDON.
Printed by *T. Mab* and *A. Coles* for JOHN SAYWELL dwelling in *Little Brittain* without *Aldersgate* at the signe
of the *Grey-hound.* M D C L.

TO THE READER.

GOOD READER ! this treatise begs the favour of those concerning whom especially it is said Christ came for, poor trembling sinners, 'the blind,' 'the prisoners of hope,'* and such who by the assiduity, iteration, and multitude of Satan's discouragements and temptations, sit, as it were, in darkness, and in the valley of death, to whom every sour thing is sweet. Because these, most of all, relish and stand in need of mercy ; for when the least flame of that unsupportable wrath breaks forth in show, which is poured out like fire, and 'kindled by the breath of the Lord of Hosts, like a river of brimstone,'† which can make 'the mountains quake, the hills melt,'‡ 'burn up the earth, and all that is therein,'§ the poor soul for the time thinking on nothing but 'blackness and darkness of tempest,'|| whilst bypast sins, without sight of the Mediator, stares them in the face, with millions of unconceivable horrors and astonishments : then to see light in darkness, mercy in wrath, the sunshine of righteousness, a gracious God appeased by a Mediator, with some sight and sense of its interest therein, this must needs overjoy the troubled soul, which is the main subject of this book. How gracious God is to encourage miserable sinners to return ! What encouragements and helps he gives them, what effects his gracious working hath in them, and how sweetly they close with him again ! Wherefore, though this mess comes not unto thee set forth in a 'lordly dish,'¶ not having passed, since the preaching thereof, under the exquisite hand of the most worthy author, yet despise it not. For many times, though things of greater judgment affect the understanding most, yet things of lesser conciseness work more upon the affections in a plain flowing way, which happiness, with all other felicities, he wisheth thee, who is ever

Thine in the best bonds,

J. H.**

* Isa. lxi. 1.   † Isa. xxx. 33.   ‡ Amos ix. 5, 13.   § 2 Peter iii. 12.
|| Heb. xii. 18.   ¶ Judges v. 25.
** This J. H. was probably the John Hill who writes an 'Epistle Dedicatory' to Elton's work on the 'Ten Commandments,' entitled, 'God's Holy Mind Tovching Matters Morall,' &c. (4to, 1625). He therein addresses the parishioners of 'St Marie Magdalen's in Barmondsey,' (i.e., Bermondsey), who were formerly under the charge of Elton, as his ; but there appears to be little known of him beyond this. He is not the 'John Hill' noticed in the Nonconformist's Memorial, ii. 54.—G.

THE RETURNING BACKSLIDER.

SERMON I.

O Israel, return unto the Lord thy God; for thou hast fallen by thine iniquity.
Take with you words, and turn to the Lord; say unto him, Take away all ini-
quity, &c.—Hos. XIV. 1, 2.

THE whole frame of godliness is a mystery, Col. i. 26. The apostle called
it 'a great mystery,' comprehending all under these particulars: 'God was
manifested in the flesh, justified in the Spirit, seen of angels, preached unto
the Gentiles, believed on in the world, received up into glory,' 1 Tim. iii.
16. Amongst which mysteries, this may well be the 'mystery of mysteries.'
'God was manifest in the flesh,' which includeth also another mystery,
the graciousness and abundant tender mercy of God towards miserable,
wretched, and sinful creatures; even in the height of their rebellion,
appointing such a remedy to heal them. Which is the subject of this
chapter, and last part of this prophecy: which, as it thunders out terrible
judgments against hard-hearted impenitent sinners (such as were the most
part of Israel), so is it mingled full of many and sweet consolations to the
faithful, in those times, scattered amongst the wicked troop of idolaters
then living.

The time when Hosea prophesied was under the reign of Uzziah, Jotham,
Ahaz, and Hezekiah, kings of Judah; and in the days of Jeroboam, the son
of Joash, king of Israel, in whose days idolatry was first universally set up,
and countenanced by regal power. This Jeroboam, 'who caused Israel to sin,'
1 Kings xv. 34, that he might strengthen himself, made use of religion,
and profanely mixed it with his civil affairs in carnal policy, and so leavened
the whole lump of Israel with idolatry, that shortly after, the whole ten
tribes, for their sin, and their injustice, cruelty, lust, security, and such
other sins as accompanied and sprang from this brutish idolatry, were led
away captive by the king of Assyria, and the Lord's righteous judgment
made manifest upon them.

There being, notwithstanding, amongst these some faithful ones, though
thinly scattered, who mourned for, and by their good examples, reproved
these abominable courses: there being also a seed of the elect unconverted;
and of the converted, some that were carried down too far in the strength
of this stream of wickedness: in this chapter, therefore, being the con-

clusion of this prophecy, there are many excellent and heavenly encouragements ; also many earnest incitements to repentance and returning to the
Lord, with free and gracious promises, not only of pardon and acceptance,
but of great rewards in things spiritual and temporal to such as should thus
return.

' O Israel, return unto the Lord thy God, for thou hast fallen by thine
iniquity.'

' Take with you words, and turn to the Lord; say unto him, Take away
all iniquity,' &c.

In this chapter we have,

1. *An exhortation to repentance, with the motives enforcing the same :* ' O
Israel, return unto the Lord thy God,' ver. 1.

2. *The form :* ' Take with you words, and say unto the Lord,' &c., ver. 2.

3. *A restipulation, what they should do : and return back again, having their
prayers granted.* 1. *Thanksgiving :* ' So will we render the calves of our
lips.' 2. *Sound reformation of their beloved sin :* ' Ashur shall not save us,'
&c.; *with the reason thereof :* ' For in thee the fatherless findeth mercy,'
ver. 3.

4. *God's answer to their petitions.* 1. *In what he will do for them :* ' Heal
their backsliding, love them freely, and be as the dew unto Israel;' *with the
reason thereof :* ' For mine anger is turned away from him,' ver. 4.   2. *What
he will work in them, a proportionable speedy growth in height, breadth, and
depth :* ' He shall grow as the lily, and cast forth his roots as Lebanon,'
&c.; which mercy is further amplified *by a blessing poured out also upon their
families :* ' They that dwell under his shadow shall return,' ver. 5–7.

5. There is set down a further effect of this repentance and gracious
work in them, *a sound and strong well-rooted indignation against their former
darling sins ;* ' Ephraim shall say, What have I any more to do with idols?'
backed with a *strong consolation :* ' I have heard him and observed him,'
&c., ver. 8.

6. *The diverse event and issue* of this God's so gracious dealing, is shewed
both in the godly and wicked.   1. The wise and prudent understand and
know that the ways of the Lord are right, and shall walk in them; but, 2.
' The transgressors shall fall therein,' ver. 9.

' O Israel, return unto the Lord thy God, for thou hast fallen by thine
iniquity.'

Every word hath his weight, and, in a manner, is an argument to enforce this returning.

' O Israel !' Israel, we know, 1, is a word *of covenant.* Jacob was
Israel, a prince and wrestler with God, as they also ought to be. Therefore he enforceth, You also ought to return, because you are Israel. And,
2, It was also an *encouragement* for them to return, because God so acknowledgeth them to be Israel, and will be gracious unto them, though they were
such hideous sinners.

' Return,' saith he, ' unto the Lord Jehovah,' who is the chief good. For
when a man returneth to the creature, which is a particular, changeable
good, unsatisfying [to] the soul, he is restless still until he come unto
Jehovah, who is the all-sufficient, universal good, who fills and fills the soul
abundantly.   Therefore, ' return ' to him who is the fountain of all good,
and giveth a being unto all things, and not to ' broken cisterns,' Jer. ii. 13.
He is Jehovah, like himself, and ' changeth not.'   And then he is *thy* God.
Therefore, return to him who is thy God in covenant, who will make good
his gracious covenant unto thee, and did choose thee to be ' his people be-

fore all the nations of the world.' This, therefore, is also an encouragement to return. And then,

' Thou hast fallen by thine iniquity.' Therefore, because thou art fallen by thy iniquities, and thine own inventions have brought these miseries upon thee, and none but God can help thee out of these miseries, seeing he only can, and is willing to forgive thy sins and revive thee, therefore,

' O Israel, return unto the Lord thy God, for thou hast fallen by thine iniquity.'

Now, in that he forewarneth them of the fearful judgments to come, which were to fall upon them unless they were prevented by true repentance, hence in general it is to be observed,

That *God comes not as a sudden storm upon his people, but gives them warning before he smites them.*

This is verified in Scripture. When the cry of Sodom and Gomorrah was great, the Lord said, ' Because the cry of Sodom and Gomorrah is great, and because their sin is very grievous, I will go down now and see whether they have done altogether according to the cry of it which is come unto me; and if not, I will know,' Gen. xviii. 20, 21. And wherefore was the ark of Noah so long in building, but to give warning to that sinful age, which were nothing bettered by it. The like we have of Pharaoh and all the Egyptians, who had so many warnings and miracles shewed before their destruction came, Exod. xi. 1, *seq.* Thus God dealt in Amos : ' Therefore, thus will I do unto thee; and because I will do this unto thee, prepare to meet thy God, O Israel,' Amos iv. 12. ' O Jerusalem, Jerusalem,' saith Christ, ' thou that killest the prophets, and stonest them which are sent unto thee, how often would I have gathered thy children together, even as a hen gathereth the chickens under her wings, and ye would not,' Mat. xxiii. 37. What need we stand upon proofs? Are not all the threatenings of Scripture as so many warning-pieces of approaching judgments?

1. The reason hereof is, *his own nature.* ' He is a God of long-suffering,' Exod. xxxiv. 6. He made the world in six days, yet hath continued it six thousand years, notwithstanding the many sins and provocations thereof, ' his mercies being over all his works,' Ps. cxlv. 9.

2. And partly *from a special regard to his own dear children*, these terrible threatenings not being killing and wounding, but, like Jonathan's warning arrows, who, though he shot, yet meant no other harm to David save to forewarn him of harm, 1 Sam. xx. 20.

Use. Let us, therefore, observe God's gracious and mild dealing in so much mercy, who giveth us so many warnings by his servants, and lesser judgments which we have had amongst us; let us take notice and believe, so as belief may stir up fear, and fear may provoke care, and care stir up endeavours to provide us an ark, even a hiding-place betimes, before winter and worse times come upon us.

Hence issueth another general point, that

The best provision for preventing of destruction is spiritual means.

God himself is a spirit, and spiritual means reach unto him who is the first mover of the great wheel of all the affairs of this world. It is preposterous to begin at the second cause. We trouble ourselves in vain there, when we neglect the first. We should therefore begin the work in heaven, and first of all take up that quarrel which is between God and our souls. If this be done first, we need not fear the carriage of second things, all which God, out of his good providence and gracious care, will frame to work for good to his, Rom. viii. 28, for whose sakes, rather than help should fail, he will create new helps, Isa. iv. 5. Wherefore, in all things it is best to begin with God.

The third general point is this, that

Of all spiritual means, the best is to return to the Lord.

In this returning, 1. *There must be a stop.* Those who have run on in evil ways must first stop their lewd courses. For naturally from our birth and childhood we are posting on to hell; and yet such is our madness (unless the Spirit of God shew us ourselves) to be angry with those who stand in our way.

To make this stop, then (which is always before returning).

(1.) There must be *examination and consideration whither our ways tend.* There be stopping considerations, which both waken a man and likewise put rubs in his way; if a man, upon examination, find his ways displeasing unto God, disagreeing from the rule, and consider what will be the end and issue of them (nothing but death and damnation), and withal consider of the day of judgment, the hour of death, the all-seeing eye of God, and the like. So the consideration of a man's own ways, and of God's ways towards him, partly when God meets him with goodness;—I have hitherto been a vile wretch, and God hath been good to me, and spared me;—and partly when God stops a wicked man's ways with thorns, meets him with crosses and afflictions. These will work upon an ingenious* spirit, to make him have better thoughts and deeper considerations of true happiness, and the way unto it. God puts into the heart of a man, whom he intends to save, serious and sad considerations, what estate he is in, whither his course leads; and withal he lets them feel some displeasure of his, towards them, in those ways, by his ways towards them; whereupon they make a stop.

(2.) There must be *humiliation, with displeasure against ourselves,* judging and taking revenge of ourselves, working and reflecting on our hearts, taking shame to ourselves for our ways and courses; and withal, there must concur some hope of mercy. For so long as there is hue and cry, as we say, after a traitor, he returns not, but flies still and hastes away; but offer a pardon, and he returneth. So, unless there be hope of pardon, to draw a man again to God, as the prodigal was moved to return by hope of mercy and favour from his father, Luke xv. 18, we will not, we dare not else return.

(3.) There must be a *resolution to overcome impediments.* For when a man thinks or resolves to turn to God, Satan will stir up all his instruments, and labour to kill Christ in his infancy, and to quench good while it is in the purpose only. The dragon stood watching for the birth of the child, Rev. xii. 4; so doth Satan observe the birth of every good resolution and purpose, so far as he can know them, to destroy them.

Use. Let it be thought of by us in all our distresses, and in whatsoever other evidences of God's anger, whether this means have been taken up by us. It will be thus known.

[1.] Turning is a change of the posture of the body; so is this *of the frame of the mind.* By this we know a man is in a state of turning. The look of his intentions, purposes, the whole bent of his soul is set another way, even upon God; and his word is the star of direction towards which he bends all his thoughts.

[2.] *His present actions, also, be contrary to his former.* There is not only a change of the disposition of his soul, 'Behold all things are become new;' not some things, but all; not only 'new,' but with a 'behold' new, 2 Cor.

* That is, 'ingenuous.'—G.

v. 17. This change undoubtedly sheweth that there is a true conversion and unfeigned.

[3.] *By our association.* He that turns to God, turns presently to the company of God's people. Together with the change of his nature and course of life, there is a change of company; that is, of such as we make choice of for amity and friendship, Isa. xi. 10, *seq.* Other company, by reason of our callings, and occasionally, may be frequented.

[4.] It is a sign that one is not only turned, but hath gone backwards from sin a great way, *when the things of heaven only are great things in his eyes.* For, as the further a man goeth from a place, the lesser the things behind him seem, so the greater the things before, he being nearer to them. The more sublime and high thoughts a man hath of the ways of God, and the meaner thoughts of the world and worldly matters he esteemed so highly of in the days of his vanity, the more he is turned unto God.

This returning is further enforced, saying, 'Return unto the Lord thy God.'

It is very emphatical and significant in the original (*a*). Return, *usque ad Jehovam*, even to Jehovah, as though he should say, Do not only begin to return towards Jehovah, but so return as you never cease coming till you come to Jehovah.

'Even unto the Lord thy God.'

It is not enough to make a stop, and forbear the practising of our former sins; but we must come home, even unto the Lord our God, to be pardoned and healed of him.

The prodigal son had been never a whit the better to see his sin and misery, and to be grieved for his wicked life past, unless he had come unto his father for pardon and comfort, Luke xv. 20. And when those were pricked in their hearts at Peter's sermon, asking Peter ' what they should do ?' he exhorted them, ' To repent, every one to be baptized in the name of Jesus Christ, for the remission of sins, and so they should receive the Holy Ghost,' Acts ii. 38. And when Christ invites all those who ' are weary and heavy laden to come unto him,' Mat. xi. 28, he bids them not now be further humbled and grieved for their sins, but by faith to come unto him to be healed, and so they should find rest and peace to their souls. It is not sufficient for a wounded man to be sorry for his brawling and fighting, and to say, he will fight no more ; but he must come to the surgeon to have his wounds stopped, dressed, and healed, or else it may cost him his life. So it is not enough to be humbled and grieved for sin, and to resolve against it. We shall relapse again, do what we can, unless we come under the wing of Christ, to be healed by his blood.

Use. Many think they have repented, and are deceived upon this false ground. They are and have been grieved for their sins and offences ; are determined to leave and forsake them, and that is all they do. They never lay hold on Christ, and come home to God.

'For thou hast fallen by thine iniquity.'

Here divers points might be insisted on.

1. *That where there is a falling into sin, there will be a falling into misery and judgment.*

This is made good in the experience of all times, ages, persons, and states. Still the more sinful any were, the more fearful judgments fell upon them ; and as soon as any man came into a sinful state, he entered into a declining state ; as Jacob said of his son Reuben, who had defiled his bed, ' Unstable as water, thou shalt not excel ; because thou wentest up to thy father's bed,' Gen. xlix. 4. So sin still debaseth a man. So much sin, so much loss of excellency.

The use hereof is, *first*, against those that complain of their troubles and miseries, as though God and men had dealt hardly with them ; whereas their own ways, indeed, have brought all these evils upon them, Lam. iii. 39. God is a sufficient, wise, and holy disposer and orderer of all the ways of men, and rewarder of good and evil doings. God being wise and just in his disposing of all things, it must needs follow, that it shall go well with those that are good ; as the prophet speaks, ' Say unto the just, that it shall be well with them, for the reward of their works shall be given them,' Isa. iii. 10. And if it fall out otherwise than well with men, the blame must be laid on their own sin. As the church confesseth, and therefore resolveth, ' I will bear the indignation of the Lord, because I have sinned against him, until he plead my cause, and execute judgment for me ; he will bring me forth in the light, and I shall see his righteousness,' Micah vii. 9. If Adam sin, he shall find a hell in a paradise. If Paul return, and return to God, he shall find a heaven in a dungeon.

Secondly, It should move us therefore to seek unto God by unfeigned repentance, to have our sins taken away and pardoned; or else, however we may change our plagues, yet they shall not be taken away ; nay, we shall still, like Pharoah, change for the worst ; who, though he had his judgments changed, yet sin, the cause, remaining, he was never a whit the better, but the worse, for changing, until his final ruin came.

' The wages of sin is death,' Rom. vi. 23. Sin will cry till it hath its wages. Where iniquity is, there cannot but be falling into judgment. Therefore they are cruel to their own souls that walk in evil ways ; for undoubtedly God will turn their own ways upon their own heads. We should not therefore envy any man, be he what he will, who goeth on in ill courses, seeing some judgment is owing him first or last, unless he stop the current of God's wrath by repentance. God, in much mercy, hath set up a court in our hearts to this end, that, if we judge ourselves in this inferior court, we may escape, and not be brought up into the higher. If first they be judged rightly in the inferior court, then there needs no review. But otherwise, if we by repentance take not up the matter, sin must be judged somewhere, either in the tribunal of the heart and conscience, or else afterwards there must be a reckoning for it.

Thirdly, Hence we learn, since the cause of every man's misery is his own sin, *that therefore all the power of the world, and of hell, cannot keep a man in misery, nor hinder him from comfort and happiness, if he will part with his sins by true and unfeigned repentance.* As we know, Manasseh, as soon as he put away sin, the Lord had mercy upon him, and turned his captivity, 2 Chron. xxxiii. 12, 13. So the people of Israel, in the Judges. Look how often they were humbled and returned to God, still he forgave them all their sins. As soon as they put away sin, God and they met again. So that, if we come to Christ by true repentance, neither sin nor punishment can cleave to us, Ps. cvi. 43, 44; cvii. 1, 9.

' Thou hast fallen,' &c. Fallen blindly, as it were. Thou couldst not see which way thou wentest, or to what end thy courses did tend. Therefore thou art come into misery before thou knowest where thou art. A sinner is blind, ' The god of this world hath put out his eyes,' 2 Cor. iv. 4. They see not their way, nor foresee their success. The devil is ever for our falling. That we fall into sin, and then fall into misery, and so fall into despair, and into hell, this pleaseth him. ' Cast thyself down,' saith he to Christ, Mat. iv. 6. 'Down with it, down with it,' saith Edom, Ps. cxxxvii. 7. Hell is beneath. The devil drives all that way.

Use. Take heed of sin! take heed of blindness! Ponder the path of your feet! keep your thoughts heavenward! stop the beginnings, the first stumblings! pray to God to make our way plain before us, and not to lead us into temptation!

'Take with you words, and turn to the Lord: say unto him,' &c., ver. 2. These Israelites were but a rude people, and had not so good means to thrive in grace as Judah had. Therefore he prompts them here with such words as they might use to God in their returning. 'Take with you words,' whereby we see how gracious God is unto us in using such helps for our recovery, and pitying us more than we pity ourselves. Is not this a sufficient warrant and invitation to return, when the party offended, who is the superior, desires, entreats, and sues unto the offending, guilty inferior, to be reconciled?' 2 Cor. v. 5.

But this is not all. He further sheweth his willingness in teaching us, who are ignorant of the way, in what manner and with what expressions we should return to the Lord. He giveth us not only words, and tells us what we shall say, but also giveth his Spirit so effectually therewith, as that they shall not be lifeless and dead words, but 'with unexpressible sighs and groans unto God,' Rom. viii. 26, who heareth the requests of his own Spirit. Christ likewise teacheth us how to pray. We have words dictated, and a spirit of prayer poured upon us; as if a great person should dictate and frame a petition for one who were afraid to speak unto him. Such is God's graciousness; and so ready is he in Jesus Christ to receive sinners unto mercy.

'Take unto you words.' None were to appear empty before the Lord at Jerusalem, but were to bring something. So it is with us. We must not appear empty before our God. If we can bring nothing else, let us bring words; yea, though broken words, yet if out of a broken and contrite heart, it will be a sacrifice acceptable.

This same taking of words or petitions, in all our troubles and afflictions, must needs be a special remedy, it being of God's own prescription, who is so infinite in knowledge and skill. Whence we observe, that

They who would have help and comfort against all sins and sorrows, must come to God with words of prayer.

As we see in Jonah's case, in a matchless distress, words were inforcive,[*] and did him more good than all the world besides could. For after that he had been humbled, and prayed out of the whale's belly, the whale was forced to cast him out again, Jonah ii. 10. So the prodigal son being undone, having neither credit nor coin, but all in a manner against him, yet he had words left him : 'Father, I have sinned against heaven and before thee, and am no more worthy to be called thy son: make me as one of thy hired servants,' Luke xv. 18, *seq.* After which, his father had compassion on him. And good Hezekiah, being desperately sick of a desperate disease, yet when he set his faith a-work, and took with him words, which comfort only now was left unto him, we know how after he had turned his face towards the wall, and prayed with words, God not only healed him of that dangerous disease, but also wrought a great miracle for his sake, causing the sun to come back ten degrees, Isa. xxxviii. 2, 8. Thus, when life seemed impossible, yet words, prayers, and tears prevailed with God. Jehoshaphat, also, going to war with Ahab, against God's commandment,

[*] That is, 'prevailing, or invested with a power of enforcing.'—ED.

and in the battle, being encompassed with enemies, yet had words with him ready, and after prayer found deliverance, 1 Kings xxii. 32. Elijah, likewise, after a great drowth and famine, when rain had been three years wanting, and all in a manner out of frame for a long time, ' took with him words,' James v. 18 ; and God sent rain abundantly upon the earth again.

The reason is, because prayer sets God on work ; and God, who is able and willing to go through with his works, sets all the creatures on work, Hos. ii. 21, 22. As we heard of Elijah, when he prayed for rain, the creatures were set a-work to effect it, 1 Kings xviii. 45, *seq.*

Obj. Where it may be objected, Oh, but rain might come too late in that hot country, where all the roots and herbs might be withered and dried up in three years' space.

Ans. Yet all was well again. The land brought forth her increase as formerly. For faithful prayer never comes too late, because God can never come too late. If our prayers come to him, we shall find him come to us. Jehoshaphat, we read, was in great distress when three kings came against him ; yet when he went to God by unfeigned and hearty fasting and prayer, God heard him, fought for him, and destroyed all his enemies, 2 Chron. xx. 3. *seq.* The Scripture sheweth, also, how after Hezekiah's prayer against Sennacherib's blasphemies and threatenings, the Lord sent forth his angel, and destroyed in one night a hundred fourscore and five thousand of the Assyrians, 2 Chron. xxxii. 21, *seq.*

Use 1. This is, first, *for reproof* of those who, in their distresses, set their wit, wealth, friends, and all a-work, but never set God a-work, as Hezekiah did in Sennacherib's case. The first time he turned him off to his cost, with enduring a heavy taxation, and yet was never a whit the better for it, 2 Kings xviii. 15, *seq.;* for Sennacherib came shortly after and besieged Jerusalem, until Hezekiah had humbled himself and prayed ; and then God chased all away and destroyed them. He had better have done so at first, and so saved his money and pains, too. The like weakness we have a proof of in Asa, who, when a greater army came against him of ten hundred thousand men, laid about him, prayed and trusted in God, and so was delivered, with the destruction of his enemies, 2 Chron. xiv. 11, yet in a lesser danger, 2 Chron. xvi. 2, against Baasha, king of Israel, distrusted God, and sent out the treasures of the house of God and of his own house unto Benhadad, king of Syria, to have help of him, by a diverting[*] war against Baasha, king of Israel, which his plot, though it prospered, yet was he reproved by the prophet Hanani, and wars thenceforth denounced against him, 2 Chron. xvi. 7. This Asa, notwithstanding this experiment, afterwards sought unto the physician, before he sought unto God, 2 Chron. xvi. 12.

Use 2. Secondly. *This blameth that barrenness and want of words to go unto God,* which, for want of hearts, we often find in ourselves. It were a strange thing to see a wife have words enough for her maids and servants, and yet not to be able to speak to her husband. We all profess to be the spouse of Christ. What a strange thing, then, is it to be full when we speak to men, yet be so empty and want words to speak to him ! A beggar, we know, wants no words, nay, he aboundeth with variety of expressions ; and what makes him thus fruitful in words ? His necessity, and, in part, his hope of obtaining.

These two make beggars so earnest. So would it be with us. If we found sufficiently our great need of Christ, and therewith had hope, it

---

[*] That is, ' diverging or dividing.—G.

would embolden us so to go to God in Christ, that we should not want words. But we want this hope, and the feeling of our necessities, which makes us so barren in prayer.

Prepare thyself, therefore, to prayer, by getting unto thee a true sense of thy need, acquaintance with God, and hope to obtain, and it will make thee fervent in prayer, and copious in thy requests.

Use 3. Thirdly, this is for *consolation*. Though one should want all other means, yet whatsoever their misery be, if they can take words, and can pray well, they shall speed well, Isa. xxxviii. 3. If the misery be for sin, confess it, and ask pardon for it, and they shall have it, 'and be cleansed from all unrighteousness,' 1 John i. 9. Words fetch the comfort to us, though it be the 'blood of Christ only that hath paid the debt,' Isa. liii. 5.

THE SECOND SERMON.

Take with you words, and turn to the Lord ; say unto him, Take away all iniquity, and receive us graciously : so will we render the calves of our lips.
—Hos. XIV. 2.

As we lost ourselves in the first Adam, so the mercy of God, in the covenant of grace, found out a way to restore us again by the 'second Adam,' 1 Cor. xv. 47, Jesus Christ, in whom all the promises are 'yea and amen ; yesterday and to-day, and the same for ever,' Heb. xiii. 8. And as the wisdom of God did freely find out this way at first, comforting our first parents with it in paradise ; so this bowels of incomprehensible love of his hath so gone on from time,* in all ages of the church, comforting and raising up the dejected spirits of his church, from time to time, and awakening them out of their drowsiness and sleepy condition. And many times, the greater sinners he dealt with, the greater mercies and tender bowels of compassion were opened unto them, in many sweet and gracious promises tendering forgiveness, and inviting to repentance ; as here in this chapter, and whole prophecy, is shewed. What tribe so wicked, so full of idolatry and rebellion, as Ephraim ? and yet here Ephraim and Israel are taught a lesson of repentance. As the tender nurse feeds her child, and puts meat in its mouth, so here the Lord puts words in the mouth of this rebellious people.

'Take with you words, and turn unto the Lord.'

Obj. What need God words, he knows our hearts before we speak unto him ?

Ans. It is true : God needs no words, but we do, to stir up our hearts and affections ; and because he will have us take shame unto ourselves, having given us our tongues as an instrument of glorifying him, he will have our 'glory,' Ps. xvi. 9 ; lvii. 8, used in our petitions and thanksgivings. And therefore, in regard of ourselves, he will, as was said, have us take words unto ourselves, for exciting of the graces of God in us by words, blowing up of the affections, and for manifestation of the hidden man of the heart. God will be glorified by the outward, as well as by the inward man.

'And turn to the Lord.' He repeats the exhortation of returning, to

* That is, 'from time to time,' or 'through all time.'—ED.

shew that *words must not be empty, but such as are joined with a purpose of turning to God.* For otherwise, to turn to him with a purpose to live in any sin, is the extremity of profane impudence. To come to ask a pardon of the king, with a resolution to live still in rebellion against him, what is this but mockery, as if one should come with a dagg* to shoot him? Such is our case, when we come to ask forgiveness, with a purpose to offend. It is the extremity of profaneness, to come to ask a pardon, to the intent that we may sin still. Therefore he repeats it again, ' Take unto you words, and turn to the Lord.' The form is—

' Take away all iniquity, and receive us graciously,' or ' do good to us : ' ' so will we render the calves of our lips ;' wherein we have,

1. A *petition:* (1.) *To take away all iniquity;* (2.) *To receive them graciously.*

2. A *re-stipulation,* or promise of thankfulness back again to the Lord, ' So will we render the calves of our lips.' So that we may observe, hence—

What God will grant us. He will have us ask of him. ' Yet for all these things I will be sought unto of the house of Israel,' Ezek. xx. 31, saith God ; because he will have us acknowledge our homage and dependence upon him. Therefore we must ask what he hath purposed to give. ' Take away all iniquity,' &c., where there is an implication of a confession of their sins and great iniquities. ' Take away iniquity,' and ' Take away all iniquity,' that is, our manifold guilt. So, before petition, there must be a free and full confession, as was shewed before.

Now, this confession here is made to God, and to God only, saith Austin in this case. Because it is a point in controversy, it is good to hear what the ancients say. There are a curious sort of men, who are busy to search into other men's lives, and are careless in amending their own. Saith he, ' What have I to do with men to hear me confess, when I have offended God ? We must confess to God, and to God only.' † But in some cases there may be public and private confession to men. Public, in public offences, for the satisfaction of the church, and the glory of God ; for preventing of scandal. Private, to ministers, for the quieting of conscience. But this is only in some cases. Men go not to the chirurgeon, as the papists would have it, for every little prick of their finger. No ; but yet in some cases it is good to open the matter to a minister, ' who hath the tongue of the learned,' Isa. l. 4. But the sin is toward God, against him, he only being able to forgive sins, as the Pharisees confessed : ' None can forgive sins but God,' Mark ii. 7. The papists, therefore, herein are worse than the Pharisees.

The petition is, ' Take away iniquity,' and ' all iniquity.' Why all ?

First. Because where there is any true goodness in the heart, that hatred which carries the bent of the soul against one sin, is alike against all, as I shewed ; and the devil carries thousands to hell by this partial obedience, because he knows at any time where to have such. God and a purpose to sin will not stand together, nor dwell in a heart that allows itself in any sin, be it never so small. He saith, Take away all, because the Spirit of God works in a man renewed, such a disposition of sincerity to hate all alike.

Secondly, he saith, ' Take away all iniquity,' because the heart, which desires to be at peace with God, desires also to be like God, who hates all sin. Therefore, saith the sanctified soul, forgive all sin. Take all away, that I may have nothing in me displeasing unto thee. I desire to join

---

* That is, ' small pistol.'—G.　　　　　† Augustine, Conf. Introd., *et alibi.*—G.

with the Lord; to hate what he hateth, and as he hateth; to carry a perfect hatred to the whole kind. ' Take away all iniquity.' Hatred is not satisfied, but with the utter abolishing of the thing hated. Therefore it hath this extent here. ' Take away all sin,' both the guilt and the reign of every sin, that none may rule in me; nay, by little and little, purge out all. ' Take away iniquity,' and the train of all which it draws after it—judgments. ' Take away iniquity,' that is, forgive the sin, and overcome the power of it by sanctifying grace, and remit the judgments attending it.

' Take it away.' That is, take away the guilt of it utterly by pardon, and the remainders thereof by sanctifying grace, so as the Spirit may rule, and be all in all in us. They see sin is an offensive thing, and therefore they say, ' Take it away,' as an offensive, odious thing, and as a burden. For howsoever it be sweet as honey in the committing it, afterwards, when the conscience is thoroughly awaked, it is most offensive and bitter. So as in this case, a sinner would gladly run from his own conscience, and from himself; run anywhere from the tormenting and racking thoughts of conscience awaked, and withal hates the place where it was committed, and the company with whom, yea, the thoughts of them. As Absalom hated Tamar after he had lien with her, so a sinner awaked from sin hates what he formerly loved. As good men love the circumstances of anything which puts them in mind of any good they have done, loving both place and person. So it is with a sinner. When his conscience is awaked, he hates all things which puts him in mind of his sins. Therefore, ' Take it away,' forgive it, cast it into the bottom of the sea, blot it out of thy remembrance, cover it, impute it not; all which phrases shew a taking away.

Therefore, I beseech you, let us examine ourselves hereby, whether our desire of forgiveness be sound or not. If we desire sin should be taken away, we cannot think of it with comfort. For in that many think with delight of their old sins, what do they else, but repeat them over again and again? But where the heart is soundly touched with a saving sense of sin, O then he cries, ' Take it away;' take it out of my conscience, that it cause not despair there; and out of thy remembrance, that no advantage be taken against me for it. ' Take it away.' But it is no otherwise taken away than by satisfying of divine justice. How much are we beholden to Christ, therefore, who hath borne and taken away our sins, and as the scape-goat, gone away with the burden of all into the wilderness of oblivion. Blessed be God, and the Lamb of God, that taketh away the sins of the world! We can never bless God too much, nor sufficiently, for Christ. ' Blessed be God, the Father of our Lord Jesus Christ,' Eph. i. 3. Now we may think of sin without shame and despair. O blessed state, when a man can think of his former odious, and filthy, loathsome sins, and yet not despair! Because, when he believes in Christ, the blood of Christ purgeth all away, takes away all sin. He hath taken them away.

You see here, in the first place, they pray for the taking away of their iniquity. For, take away this, and all other mercies follow after, because this only is it which stops the current of God's favours, which removed, the current of his mercies run amain. As when the clouds are gone, the sun shines out; so let our sins be removed, and God's favour immediately shines upon us. Therefore, first ' Take away all iniquity,' and then we shall see nothing but thy fatherly face in Christ. You see what the care of God's children is, to seek mercy and favour in the first place; as David, ' Have mercy on me, O Lord!' Ps. li. 1. This he begs first of all. Whereas God had threatened other terrible judgments, as that the sword should never depart from his house, &c., yet he neglects all, as it were, and begs only for mercy, ' to take away iniquity.' For a sinner is never in such a blessed condition as he should be in, until he prize and desire mercy above all ; because, though we be in misery, until then, with sinful Ephraim, Hos. vii. 14, we howl upon our beds for corn and wine, preferring earthly, sensual things before all. But that soul and conscience which is acquainted with God, and the odiousness of sin, that soul God intends to speak peace unto in the end, desires pardon of sin and mercy above all. For it knows that God is goodness itself, and that, when the interposing clouds are vanished, God cannot shew himself otherwise than in goodness, grace, and mercy. ' Take away all iniquity.'

Quest. Before I go further, let me answer one question. Ought we not to think of our former sins ? Shall God take them away altogether out of the soul ?

Ans. Oh no ! Take them away out of the conscience, O Lord, that it do not accuse for them ; but not out of the memory. It is good that sin be remembered, to humble us, to make us more thankful, pitiful, and tender-hearted unto others, to abase us and keep us low all the days of our life, and to make us deal gently and mercifully with others, being sensible of our own frailties. As they are naught in the conscience, so they are good to the memory. Therefore, let us think often of this, what the chief desire of our souls to God should be for—mercy, to have sin taken away. In all the articles of our creed, that of chiefest comfort is, that of ' remission of sins.'* Wherefore are all the other articles of Christ, his birth, death, and crucifying, but that he might get the church ? and that the privileges thereof might be, ' forgiveness of sins, resurrection of the body, and life everlasting;' but forgiveness of sins is in the first place.

Quest. But may some say, How shall I know whether or no my sins be forgiven ?

1. By something that goes before.
2. By something which follows after.

Ans. There is somewhat which goes before, viz.:—

First, an humble and hearty confession, as, ' If we confess our sins, he is faithful and just to forgive us our sins, and to cleanse us from all unrighteousness,' 1 John i. 9. Therefore, whether I feel it or not, if I have heartily, fully, and freely confessed, my sins are forgiven. God in wisdom and mercy may suspend the feeling thereof, for our humiliation, and for being over-bold with Satan's baits ; yet I ought to believe it. For I make God a liar else, if I confess heartily, and acknowledge my debt, to think that he hath not cancelled the bond.

Secondly, sin is certainly pardoned, *when a man finds strength against it ;* for where God forgives, he gives strength withal : as to the man whom he healed of the palsy, ' Thy sins are forgiven thee; take up thy bed and walk,' Mat. ix. 2, 6. When a man hath strength to return to God, to run the way of his commandments, and to go on in a Christian course, his sins are forgiven, because he hath a spirit of faith to go on and lead him forward still. Those who find no strength of grace, may question forgiveness of sins. For God, where he takes away sin, and pardons it, as we see here in this text, after prayer made to take away iniquity, he ' doth good to us.'

The *third* evidence is, *some peace of conscience ;* though not much, perhaps, yet so much as supports us from despair, as, ' Therefore, being justified by faith, we have peace with God through our Lord Jesus Christ,' Rom. v. 1 ;

* Creed, Article X.—G.

that is, being acquitted from our sins by faith, we have peace with God ;
so much peace, as makes us go boldly to him. So that one may know his
bonds are cancelled, and his sins forgiven, when with some boldness he dare
look God in the face in Jesus Christ. A Judas, an Ahithophel, a Saul,
because they are in the guilt of their sins, cannot confess comfortably, and
go to God, which, when with some boldness we can do, it is a sign that
peace is made for us.

Fourth. Again, where sin is pardoned, *our hearts will be much enlarged
with love to God;* as Christ said to the woman, ' Her sins, which are many,
are forgiven her, because she loved much,' Luke vii. 47.   Therefore, when
we find our hearts inflamed with love to God, we may know that God hath
shined upon our souls in the pardon of sin ; and proportionably to our
measure of love is our assurance of pardon.   Therefore we should labour
for a greater measure thereof, that our hearts may be the more inflamed in
the love of God. It is impossible that the soul should at all love God
angry, offended, and unappeased ; nay, such a soul wisheth that there were
no God at all, for the very thoughts thereof terrify him.

Fifthly. Again, where sin is forgiven, *it frames the soul suitably,* to be
gentle, merciful, and to pardon others. For, usually, those who have
peaceable consciences themselves are peaceable unto others ; and those
who have forgiveness of sins, can also forgive others.   Those who have
found mercy have merciful hearts, shewing that they have found mercy with
God. And, on the contrary, he that is a cruel, merciless man, it is a sign
that his heart was never warmed nor melted with the sense of God's mercy
in Christ. Therefore, ' as the elect of God,' saith the apostle, ' put on
bowels of compassion,' 1 Peter iii. 8, as you will make it good that you are
the elect of God, members of Christ, and God's children.

Therefore, let us labour for the forgiveness of our sins, that God would
remove and subdue the power of them, take them away, and the judgments
due to them, or else we are but miserable men, though we enjoyed all the
pleasures of the world, which to a worldly man are but like the liberty of the
tower* to a condemned traitor, who though he have all wants supplied with
all possible attendance, yet when he thinks of his estate, it makes his heart
cold, damps his courage, and makes him think the poorest car-man or
tankard-bearer, at liberty, happier than he, who would not change estates
with him. So it is with a man that hath not sued out his pardon, nor is
at peace with God. He hath no comfort, so long as he knows his sins are
on the file,† that God in heaven is not at peace with him, who can arm all
the creatures against him to be revenged of him. In which case, who shall
be umpire betwixt God and us, if we take not up the controversy betwixt
him and our souls ?   Therefore, it being so miserable a case to want
assurance of the forgiveness of sins, it should make us be never an hour
quiet till we have gotten it, seeing the uncertainty of this life, wherein there
is but a step betwixt hell, damnation, and us. Therefore sue unto God,
ply him with broken and humble hearts, that he would pardon all the sins
of our youth and after-age, known and unknown, that he would pardon all
whatsoever. ' Take away all iniquity.'

' And do good to us.' For so it is in the original,‡ but it is all one,
' Receive us graciously, and do good to us.' All the goodness we have from
God, it is out of his grace, from his free grace and goodness.   All grace,
every little thing from God is grace. As we say of favours received of

* That is, the state-prison.—G.   † See note *b*, vol. I. p. 289.—G.
‡ See note *a*.—G.

great persons, this is his grace, his favour ; so this is a respect which is put upon all things which we receive from God, when we are in covenant, all is gracious. Take we the words as they are, the more plain, in the original. ' Take good, and do good to us :' take good out of thy treasure of goodness, and do good to us, bestow upon us thy own good. First, ' take away our iniquities,' and then take good out of thy bounty, ' and do good to us.' Whence we see—

Doct. That God's mercy to his children is complete and full.

For he takes away ill, and doth good. Men may pardon, but withal they think that they have done wondrous bountifully when they have pardoned. But God goes further. He takes away ill, and doth good ; takes good out of his fountain, and doth good to us.

Use. Therefore, let us make this use of it, to be encouraged, when we have the first blessing of all, forgiveness of sins, to go to him for more and more, and gather upon God further and further still. For because he is a fountain of goodness that can never be drawn dry, he is wondrously pleased with this. We cannot honour him more than by making use of his mercy in the forgiveness of sins ; and of his goodness, in going to him for it ; and having interested ourselves in his goodness, go to him for more. Lord, thou hast begun : make an end ; thou hast forgiven my sins ; I want this and that good ; together with the pardon of my sins, do me good. ' Receive us graciously,' or, ' do us good.' Now, good is the loadstone of the soul, the attractive that draws it. Therefore, after forgiveness of sins, he saith, ' do good.' The petition is easy, God will soon grant it. For nothing else interposeth betwixt God and us, and makes two, but sin, which being removed, he is all goodness and mercy. ' All his ways are mercy and truth,' Ps. xxv. 10. Yea, even his sharpest ways are mercy, all mercy. When sin is forgiven, there is goodness in all, in the greatest cross and affliction. ' Do good to us.'

The soul, we see, desires good, and needs good. It is a transcendent word here, and must be understood according to the taste of God's people, of a sanctified soul. ' Do good.' Especially do spiritual good to us. Together with the forgiveness of sins, give us the righteousness of Jesus Christ, sanctifying grace, such good as may make us good first. For the desire must be such as the person is, who makes it. Wicked men, as it is said of Balaam, have good gifts, without the good God ; but we must not be so pleased with gifts, unless we be good ourselves, and see God making us good. ' Can an evil tree bring forth good fruit ?' Mat. vii. 18. Therefore, the apostle calls the regenerate person ' God's workmanship,' &c., Eph. ii. 10. We are God's good work, and then we do good works ; being made good, good comes from us. ' Do good to us.'

It is an acknowledgment of their own emptiness, ' Do good to us.' We are blind in our own understandings, enlighten us. We are perplexed, set us right. We are dull, quicken us. We are empty, fill us. We are dark, shine upon us. We are ready to go out of the way, establish us. Every way do good to us suitable to our wants. The best that we can bring to thee is emptiness. Therefore do thou good to us ; fill us with thy fulness. Do good to us every way, whereby thou usest to convey spiritual things to thy servants' souls. Give us first thy grace, thy Spirit, which is the spring of all good things ; for the Spirit of God is a Spirit of direction, of strength, of comfort, and all. Therefore he who hath the Spirit of God hath the spring of all. That is begged in the first place. And then give us good magistrates, to rule us well, and good ministers, who are the dispensers of grace, instruments of our salvation, the conduit pipes whereby thou derivest and conveyest good to us. When thou hast made us good, continue the means of salvation for our good every way. The church, when she saith, ' Do good to us,' hath a large desire. Here be seeds of wondrous large things in these two short petitions, ' Take away all iniquity,' and ' do good to us.' *A bono Deo*, &c. From the good God nothing can come but what is good. Therefore do good to us in all spiritual things. The prophet David aims at this excellent good, saying that other men are for corn, wine, and oil, and say, ' Who will shew us any good? But, Lord, lift thou up the light of thy countenance upon us,' Ps. iv. 6, 7. Thy lovingkindness is better than life, therefore do good to us. When thou hast forgiven our sins, shine graciously upon us in Jesus Christ.

And it extends its limits likewise to outward prosperity, this desire of doing good. Let us have happy days! Sweeten our pilgrimage here! Let our profession of religion be comfortable! Do not lay more crosses upon us than thou wilt give us strength to bear! Do good to us every way! But mark the wisdom of the Holy Ghost in dictating of this prayer to them. He speaks in general, ' Do good to us;' not to do this or that good, but he leaves it to the wisdom of God, as they here frame their hearts unto the will of God. ' Do good to us,' spiritual. That needs no limitation, because we cannot more honour God than to depend upon him for all spiritual good things. Thou art wiser, and knowest what is good for us better than we ourselves. Beggars ought to be no choosers. Therefore ' do good to us,' for the particulars we leave them to thy wisdom. Oh, beloved, it is a happy and blessed privilege to be under the conduct of so wise and all-sufficient a God, who is good, and as he is good, knows best what is good for us. We would have riches, liberty, and health; aye, but it may be it is not good for us. ' Do good to us.' Thou, Lord, knowest what is best. Do in thine own wisdom what is best.

Use. Which should teach us not to limit the Holy One of Israel in our desires of any outward thing whatsoever. Especially desire forgiveness and spiritual good things, leaving the rest to his wise disposing. Yet notwithstanding, out of the sense of pain and grief, we may pray either for the mitigation or removing of a cross, if God be so pleased. Because he hath put in us self-love, not sinful, but love of preserving our nature, therefore he permits us, if it may stand with his good pleasure, to desire the good of our outward man, as, Lord, give us bodily health, for we cannot else be instruments of serving thee. With reservation of God's good pleasure, we may desire such and such things, conditionally, that when we see God will have it otherwise, we rest contented, sit down quietly, knowing that whatsoever health, sickness, or crosses he sends, it comes from his goodness and love, and shall turn to our good at length. If we love God, all shall work for good.

' Take away our iniquity, and do us good.' We should make this petition for the church and ourselves. Pardon our sins, and do good to us, to our persons, to the state, to the times wherein we live, to the church at home and abroad, do good to all.

And we may observe this from the order, and know what good we have. It comes from God in love, when it comes after forgiveness of sins. How then, may we take comfort of all the good things we have enjoyed, having seen many good days, enjoyed many good blessings, in health, wealth, good magistracy, ministry, peace, plenty, and the like! If all this goodness of God lead us to God, and draw us nearer to him, ' after forgiveness of sins,' grounded on the former evidences I spake of, then they come in love.   But never let us think to have true comfort with a blessing, or any good thing we enjoy, till we have assurance of God's love and mercy in the forgiveness of sins, lest God strip us naked of all the good things we have, and make us as naked as Dives in hell, who had not anything that was good to refresh his body or soul.   So that all good things we enjoy here without this, will only aggravate our condemnation.   Let us observe, therefore, how all our good things are joined with spiritual good (whether we ourselves are made better by them or not), having our sins pardoned.   I beseech you, let us renew our requests for forgiveness of sins every day, making our accounts even with God, desiring grace to set our souls in a holy and sanctified frame with God, that ourselves may be good, our conversation good, and that then he would ' do good to us' all other ways, and sanctify all other things. This is the method of God's Spirit in setting us right onwards in our heavenly journey, first to have forgiveness of sins, then sanctification, to be better ourselves, and then to look for peaceable and comfortable days in this world, if God see it good.   What can be more ?   ' Take away all iniquity, and do us good,' all manner of good.

Therefore, since all good comes from God, the first and chief good, let us labour to have communion with him by all sanctified means, that so he may take away our ill, and do us every way good to our souls, bodies, conditions.   Oh, what a blessed thing is it for a Christian to keep a strict and near communion with the fountain of goodness, who can do more for us than all the world besides !   When we are sick on our deathbeds, or when conscience is thoroughly awaked, then to speak peace comfortably to us in this great extremity, is more worth than all this world.   Therefore let us labour to keep communion with God, that he may speak peace to our souls when nothing else can.

I beseech you, therefore, let us take heed how we break or walk loosely with God, seeing we can have no further comfort of any good thing we enjoy, than we are careful to keep and maintain our peace and communion with him at all times.   And when we run into arrearages with God, then be sure we lie not in sin, but say, ' Take away all iniquity, and do good to us,' labouring to be in such an estate as God may give us his Holy Spirit, both to make us good and to sanctify unto us all other good.   There be good things which are good of themselves, and which make all other things good.   Thus, by communion with God, we ourselves are made good, and all other things likewise are made good to us, all his ways being mercy and truth unto those who fear him.   Therefore resign we ourselves and all that we have unto his wisdom and disposing, because ofttimes there is good where we imagine the worst of evils to be, as it is sometimes good to have a vein opened to be purged.   The physician thinks so, when yet the patient, impatient of reason's issue, thinks not so.   But as the physician is wiser than the patient, to know what is best for him, so God is wiser than man, to know what is good for him, who intends us no hurt when he purgeth us by affliction.

All our care, therefore, should be to annihilate ourselves, to come with empty, poor souls to God, ' Do good to us.'   In which case it is no matter what our ill be, if he do us good, who hath both pardon and rich grace to remove the evil of sin, and convey all grace unto us out of his rich treasury.

' So will we render the calves of our lips.'

Here is the re-stipulation or promise.   They return back again to God, for there is no friendship maintained without rendering.   When God hath entered into covenant with us, then there is a kind of friendship knit up betwixt him and us, he becoming our friend. We must not, therefore, be like graves, to swallow up all, and return nothing, for then the intercourse betwixt God and us is cut off. Therefore the same Spirit which teacheth them to pray, and to ' take to them words,' teacheth them likewise to take unto them words of praise, that there may be a rendering according to receiving, without which we are worse than the poorest creature that is, which rendereth according to its receipt. The earth, when it is ploughed and sowed, it yields us fruit. Trees being set, yield increase. Beasts being fed, render in their kind. Yea, the fiercest, untamed beasts, as we read of the lion, have been thankful in their kind. The heavens, saith the psalmist, declare the glory of God, and the firmament shews forth his praise, Ps. xix. 1. So there must be a return, if we be not worse than beasts. Therefore the church here promiseth a return by the same Spirit which stirred her up to pray. ' So will we render the calves of our lips.'

Now, this promise which the church makes here of praise, is a kind of vow, ' So will we render,' &c. To bind one's-self is a kind of vow. The church therefore binds herself, that she may bind God; for binding herself by vow to thankfulness, she thereby binds God; who is moved with nothing we can do so much as with setting forth of his praise, which was his end in all the creation, the setting forth of his glory. The end of the new creature is the end of all things both in nature and grace; the end whereof is God's glory, from whence all things come and wherein all things end: as we say of a circle, all things begin and end in it. All other things are for man, and man for God's glory. When the soul can say, ' Lord, this shall be for thy honour, to set forth thy praise,' it binds God. Hence, that they might move God to yield to their prayers, they bind themselves by a kind of vow. Do thus, O Lord, and thou shalt not lose by it, thou shalt have praise; ' so will we render thee the calves of our lips.'

So promises and vows of praise are alleged as an argument to prevail with God, for the obtaining of that the church begs for: ' So will we render,' &c. Not to enter into the commonplace of vows, only thus much I say, that there is a good use of them, to vow and promise thankfulness when we would obtain blessings from God. That which a promise is to men, that a vow is to God; and usually they go together in Scripture, as it is said of David, that ' he vowed unto God, and sware unto the mighty God of Jacob,' Ps. cxxxii. 2. So we have all in baptism vowed a vow. So that it is good to renew our vows often, especially that of new obedience; and in this particular to vow unto him that we will praise him, and strive that his glory be no loser by us.

1. It is good thus to vow, if it were but *to excite and quicken our dulness and forgetfulness of our general vow;* to put us in mind of our duty, the more to oblige us to God and refresh our memories. This bond, that having promised, now I must do it, provokes the soul to it. As it helps the memory, so it quickens the affections.

2. Besides, as by nature we are forgetful, *so we are inconstant;* in which respect it is a tie to our inconstant and unsteady natures. For there are none who have the Spirit of God at all, with any tenderness of heart, but will thus think: I have vowed to God. If it be a heinous thing to break with men, what is it wittingly and willingly to break with the great God? A vow is a kind of oath. This is the sacrifice of fools, to come to God, and yet neither to make good our vows, nor endeavour to do it.

Let us consider therefore what we have done in this case. By permission of authority, there was a fast lately, when we all renewed our vows (we mocked God else), [and] received the communion. Will God be mocked, think you? No; but howsoever man may forget, God will not, but will come upon us for non-payment of our vows and covenants. Lay we it to heart therefore what covenants we have made with God of late. And then, for the time to come, be not discouraged if you have been faulty in it. There is a general vow, wherein, though we have failed (if we be his children, and break not with God in the main, cleaving to him in purpose of heart, occasionally renewing our purposes and covenants), yet let not Satan discourage us for our unfaithfulness therein. But be ashamed of it, watch more, look better to it for the time to come, and make use of the gracious covenant; and, upon recovery, say with the church, ' So will we render the calves of our lips.'

It was the custom under the Jewish policy, you know, to offer sacrifices of all sorts. But the Spirit of God speaks here of the church of the Jews under the New Testament; especially what they should be after their conversion, having reference to the Jews in Christ's time, and to the believing Jews in all times, implying thus much; howsoever, not legal sacrifices of calves, bullocks, sheep, and lambs, yet the ' calves of the lips,' which God likes better, are acceptable to him. And it likewise implies some humiliation of the church. Lord, whatsoever else we could offer unto thee, it is thine own, though it were the beasts upon a thousand mountains; but this, by thy grace, we can do, to ' praise thee,' Ps. l. 23. For God must open and circumcise our lips and hearts before we can offer him the ' calves of our lips.' Thus much the poorest creature in the world may say to God, Lord, ' I will render thee the calves of my lips.' Other things I have not. This I have by thy gracious Spirit, a heart somewhat touched by the sense of thy favour. Therefore ' I will render thee the calves of my lips;' that is, praise, as the apostle hath it, ' By him therefore let us offer the sacrifice of praise to God continually; that is, the fruit of our lips, giving thanks to his name,' Heb. xiii. 15. ' So will we render thee the calves of our lips.' Whence the point is,

Doct. That God's children at all times have their sacrifices.

There is indeed one kind of sacrificing determined* and finished by the coming of Christ, who was the last sacrifice of propitiation for our sins. The more to blame those who yet maintain a daily sacrifice, not of laud and praise, but of cozening and deluding the world, in saying mass for the sins of the quick and the dead; all such sacrifices being finished and closed up in him, our blessed Saviour; who, ' by one sacrifice,' as the apostle speaks, ' hath perfected them that are sanctified,' Heb. x. 14, vii. 27; and that, ' by one sacrifice, when he offered up himself,' Heb. x. 12; when all the Jewish sacrifices ended. Since which, all ours are but a commemoration of Christ's last sacrifice, as the fathers say: the Lord's supper, with the rest, which remain still; and the sacrifice of praise, with a few others, I desire to name.

1. First, The sacrifice of a broken heart, whereof David speaks, Ps. li. 17; which sacrifice of a wounded, broken heart, by the knife of repentance, pleaseth God wondrously well.

2. And then, a broken heart that offers Christ to God every day; who, though he were offered once for all, yet our believing in him, and daily presenting his atonement made for us, is a new offering of him. Christ is

* That is, ' abolished ' = fulfilled.—G.

crucified and sacrificed for thee as oft as thou believest in Christ crucified. Now, upon all occasions we manifest our belief in Christ, to wash and bathe ourselves in his blood, who justifieth the ungodly. So that, upon a fresh sight of sin, with contrition for it, he continually justifieth us. Thus, when we believe, we offer him to God daily ; a broken heart first, and then Christ with a broken heart.

3. And then when we believe in Christ, we offer and sacrifice ourselves to God ; in which respect we must, as it were, be killed ere we be offered. For we may not offer ourselves as we are in our lusts, but as mortified and killed by repentance. Then we offer ourselves to God as a reasonable and living sacrifice, when we offer ourselves wholly unto him, wit, understanding, judgment, affections, and endeavour ; as Paul saith of the Macedonians, ' they gave themselves to God first, and then their goods,' 2 Cor. viii. 5. In sum, it is that sacrifice Paul speaks of, ' to present our bodies a living sacrifice, holy, acceptable unto God,' &c., Rom. xii. 1. For a Christian who believeth in the Lord Jesus is not his own, but sacrificeth himself to him that was sacrificed for him. As Christ is given to us, so he that believes in Christ gives himself back again to Christ. Hereby a man may know if he be a true Christian, and that Christ is his, if he yields up himself to God. For ' Christ died and rose again,' saith the apostle, ' that he might be Lord both of quick and dead,' Rom. xiv. 9. ' Therefore,' saith he, ' whether we live or die, we are not our own,' Rom. xiv. 8. What we do or suffer in the world, in all we are sacrificed. So saith a sanctified soul, My wit, my will, my life, my good, my affections are thine ; of thee I received them, and I resign all to thee as a sacrifice. Thus the martyrs, to seal the truth, as a sacrifice, yielded up their blood. He that hath not obtained of himself so much as to yield himself to God, he knows not what the gospel means. For Christian religion is not only to believe in Christ for forgiveness of sin ; but the same faith which takes this great benefit, renders back ourselves in lieu of thankfulness.

So that, whatsoever we have, after we believe, we give all back again. Lord, I have my life, my will, my wit, and all from thee ; and to thee I return all back again. For when I gave myself to believe in thy dear Son, I yielded myself and all I have to thee ; and now, having nothing but by thy gift, if thou wilt have all I will return all unto thee again ; if thou wilt have my life, my goods, my liberty, thou shalt have them. This is the state of a Christian who hath denied himself. For we cannot believe as we should unless we deny ourselves. Christianity is not altogether in believing this and that ; but the faith which moves me to believe forgiveness of sins, carries us also unto God to yield all back again to him.

4. More especially, among the sacrifices of the New Testament are alms, as, ' To do good and to communicate forget not, for with such sacrifices God is well pleased,' Heb. xiii. 16.

5. And among the rest, the sacrifice of praise, which is in the same chapter, verse 15. First, he saith, By him, that is, by Christ, let us offer the sacrifice of praise to God continually, that is, the fruit of our lips : which is but an exposition of this place, which, because it is especially here intended, I will a little enlarge myself in.

The ' calves of our lips ' implies two things :

Not only thankfulness to God, but glorifying of God, in setting out his praise. Otherwise to thank God for his goodness to us, or for what we hope to receive, without glorifying of him, is nothing at all worth. For in glorifying there are two things.

1. *A supposition of excellency.* For that cannot be glorified, which hath no excellency in it. Glory in sublimity hath alway excellency attending it. And

2. *The manifestation of this glory.*

Now, when all the excellencies of God, as they are, are discovered and set out, his wisdom, mercy, power, goodness, all-sufficiency, &c., then we glorify him. To praise God for his favours to us, and accordingly to glorify him, is ' the calves of our lips ; ' but especially to praise him. Whence the point is—

That the yielding of praise to God is a wondrous acceptable sacrifice.

Which is instead of all the sacrifices of the Old Testament, than which the greatest can do no more, nor the least less ; for it is the sacrifice and fruit of the lips. But to open it. It is not merely the sacrifice of our lips ; for the praise we yield to God, it must be begotten in the heart. Hereupon the word, λογός, speech, signifieth both reason and speech, there being one word in the learned language for both.* Because speech is nothing but that stream which issues from the spring of reason and understanding : therefore, in thanksgiving there must not be a lip-labour only, but a thanksgiving from the lips, first begotten in the heart, coming from the inward man, as the prophet saith, ' Bless the Lord, O my soul ; and all that is within me, bless his holy name,' Ps. ciii. 1. Praise must come from a sound judgment of the worth of the thing we praise for. It must come from an affection which desires that God may have the glory, by the powers of the whole inward man, which is a hard matter, to rouse up ourselves to praise God with all the powers of our soul, ' all that is within me, praise his holy name,' Ps. ciii. 1. There goeth judgment, resolution of the will, strength of affections, and all with it.

And then again, besides this, ' the calves of our lips ' carries us to work. The oral thanksgiving must be justified by our works and deeds ; or else our actions will give our tongue the lie, that we praise him with the one, but deny him in the other. This is a solecism, as if one should look to the earth, and cry, O ye heavens ! So when we say, God be praised, when yet our life speaks the contrary, it is a dishonouring of God. So the praise of our lips must be made good and justified by our life, actions, and conversation. This we must suppose for the full understanding of the words, ' We will render,' from our hearts, ' the calves of our lips ; ' which we must make good in our lives and conversations, ever to set forth thy praise in our whole life.

Quest. But why doth the prophet especially mention lips, ' the calves of our lips,' which are our words ?

Ans. 1. Partly, because Christ, who is the Word, delights in our words.

2. Because our tongue is our glory, and that whereby we glorify God.

3. And especially because our tongue is that which excites others, being a trumpet of praise, ordained of God for this purpose. Therefore, ' the calves of our lips ; ' partly, because it stirs up ourselves and others, and partly, because God delights in words, especially of his own dictating. To come then to speak more fully of praise and thanksgiving, let us consider what a sweet, excellent, and prevailing duty this is, which the church, to bind God, promiseth unto him, ' the calves of our lips.' I will not be long in the point, but only come to some helps how we may come to do it.

First, this praising of God must be *from an humble, broken heart.* The

* Cf. p. 153 and note *o*, p. 195.—G.

humble soul that sees itself not worthy of any favour, and confesseth sin before God, is alway a thankful soul. ' Take away our iniquity, and then do good to us.' We are empty ourselves. Then will ' we render thee the calves of our lips.' What made David so thankful a man ? He was an humble man ; and so Jacob, what abased him so in his own eyes ? His humility : ' Lord, I am less than the least of thy mercies,' Gen. xxxii. 10. He that thinks himself unworthy of anything, will be thankful for everything ; and he who thinks himself unworthy of any blessing, will be contented with the least. Therefore, let us work our hearts to humility, in consideration of our sinfulness, vileness, and unworthiness, which will make us thankful : especially of the best blessings, when we consider their greatness, and our unworthiness of them. A proud man can never be thankful. Therefore, that religion which teacheth pride, cannot be a thankful religion. Popery is compounded of spiritual pride : merit of congruity, before conversion ; merit of condignity, and desert of heaven, after ; free will, and the like, to puff up nature. What a religion is this ! Must we light a candle before the devil ? Is not nature proud enough, but we must light a candle to it ? To be spiritually proud is worst of all.

2. And with our own unworthiness, add this : *a consideration of the greatness of the thing we bless God for ;* setting as high a price upon it as we can, by considering what and how miserable we were without it. He will bless God joyfully for pardon of sin, who sees how miserable he were without it, in misery next to devils, ready to drop into hell every moment. And the more excellent we are, so much the more accursed, without the forgiveness of sins. For the soul, by reason of the largeness thereof, is so much the more capable and comprehensible of misery ; as the devils are more capable than we, therefore are most accursed. Oh, this will make us bless God for the pardon of sin ! And likewise, let us set a price upon all God's blessings, considering what we were without our senses, speech, meat, drink, rest, &c. O beloved ! we forget to praise God sufficiently for our senses. This little spark of reason in us is an excellent thing ; grace is founded upon it. If we were without reason, what were we ? If we wanted sight, hearing, speech, rest, and other daily blessings, how uncomfortable were our lives ! This consideration will add and set a price to their worth, and make us thankful, to consider our misery without them. But, such is our corruption, that favours are more known by the want, than by the enjoying of them. When too late, we many times find how dark and uncomfortable we are without them ; then smarting the more soundly, because in time we did not sufficiently prize, and were thankful for them.

3. And then, *labour to get further and further assurance that we are God's children, beloved of him.* This will make us thankful both for what we have and hope for. It lets out the life-blood of thankfulness, to teach doubting or falling from grace. What is the end, I beseech you, why the glory to come is revealed before the time ? That we shall be sons and daughters, kings and queens, heirs and co-heirs with Christ, and [that] ' all that he hath is ours ?' Rom. viii. 17. Is not this knowledge revealed beforehand, that our praise and thanksgiving should beforehand be suitable to this revelation, being set with Christ in heavenly places already. Whence comes those strong phrases ? ' We are raised with Christ ; sit with him in heavenly places,' Eph. ii. 6 ; ' are translated from death to life,' Col. i. 13 ; ' transformed into his image ;' ' partakers of the divine nature,' &c., 2 Pet. i. 4. If anything that can come betwixt our believing,

and our sitting there, could disappoint us thereof, or unsettle us, it may as well put Christ out of heaven, for we sit with him. If we yield to the uncomfortable popish doctrine of doubting, we cannot be heartily thankful for blessings ; for still there will rise in the soul surmises, I know not whether God favour me or not : it may be, I am only fatted for the day of slaughter ; God gives me outward things to damn me, and make me the more inexcusable. What a cooler of praise is this, to be ever doubting, and to have no assurance of God's favour ! But when upon good evidence, which cannot deceive, we have somewhat wrought in us, distinct from the greater number of worldlings, God's stamp set upon us ; having evidences of the state of grace, by conformity to Christ, and walking humbly by the rule of the word in all God's ways : then we may heartily be thankful, yea, and we shall break forth in thanksgiving ; this being an estate of peace, and ' joy unspeakable and glorious,' 1 Pet. i. 8, wherein we take everything as an evidence of God's love.

Thus the assurance of our being in the state of grace makes us thankful for everything. So by the contrary, being not in some measure assured of God's love in Christ, we cannot be thankful for everything. For it will always come in our mind, I know not how I have these things, and what account I shall give for them. Therefore, even for the honour of God, and that we may praise him the more cheerfully, let us labour to have further and further evidences of the state of grace, to make us thankful both for things present and to come, seeing faith takes to trust things to come, as if it had them in possession. Whereby we are assured of this, that we shall come to heaven, as sure as if we were there already. This makes us praise God beforehand for all favours ; as blessed Peter begins his epistle, ' Blessed be the God and Father of our Lord Jesus Christ, which, according to his abundant mercy, hath begotten us again unto a lively hope, by the resurrection of Jesus Christ from the dead, to an inheritance incorruptible and undefiled, and that fadeth not away, reserved in heaven for you,' &c., 1 Pet. i. 3, 4. As soon as we are newborn, we are begotten to a kingdom and an inheritance. Therefore, assurance that we are God's children will make us thankful for grace present, and that to come, as if we were in heaven already. We begin then the employment of heaven in thanksgiving here, to praise God beforehand with cherubims and angels. Let us, then, be stirred up to give God his due beforehand, to begin heaven upon earth ; for we are so much in heaven already, as we abound and are conversant in thanksgiving upon earth.

THE THIRD SERMON.

So will we render the calves of our lips. Asshur shall not save us ; we will not ride upon horses : neither will we say any more to the works of our hands, Ye are our gods : for in thee the fatherless findeth mercy.—Hos. XIV. 2, 3.

THE words, as we heard heretofore, contain a most sweet and excellent form of returning unto God, for miserable, lost, and forlorn sinners ; wherein so far God discovers his willingness to have his people return unto him, that he dictates unto them a form of prayer, ' Take with you words, and turn to the Lord ; say unto him, Take away iniquity.' Wherein we see how

detestation of sin must be as general as the desire of pardon, and that none
heartily pray to God to ' take away all iniquity ' who have not grace truly
to hate all iniquity. ' And do good to us,' or do graciously to us ; for there
is no good to us till sin be removed. Though God be goodness itself, there
is no provoking or meriting cause of mercy in us. But he finds cause from
his own gracious nature and bowels of mercy to pity his poor people and
servants. It is his nature to shew mercy, as the fire to burn, a spring to
run, the sun to shine. Therefore, it is easily done. As the prophet
speaks, ' Who is a God like unto thee ? ' Micah vii. 18.

Where we come to speak of the re-stipulation, ' So will we render the
calves of our lips.' Where God's favour shines, there will be a reflection.
Love is not idle, but a working thing. It must render or die. And what
doth it render ? Divers sacrifices of the New Testament, which I spake
of ; that of a broken heart ; of Christ offered to the Father, to stand betwixt God's wrath and us ; ourselves as a living sacrifice ; alms-deeds and
praise, which must be with the whole inward powers of the soul.

' Praise is not comely in the mouth of a fool,' saith the wise man, nor of
a wicked man. Saith God to such, ' What hast thou to do to take my
words in thy mouth, since thou hatest to be reformed, and hast cast my
words behind thee ? ' Ps. l. 16, 17. There are a company who are ordinary swearers and filthy speakers. For them to praise God, James tells
them that these contrary streams cannot flow out of a good heart, James
iii. 10, 11. Oh, no ; God requires not the praise of such fools.

I gave you also some directions how to praise God, and to stir up yourselves to this most excellent duty, which I will not insist on now, but add a
little unto that I then delivered, which is, *that we must watch all advantages
of praising God from our dispositions.* ' Is any merry ? let him sing,' saith
James, v. 13. Oh ! it is a great point of wisdom to take advantages with
the stream of our temper to praise God. When he doth encourage us by
his favours and blessings, and enlarge our spirits, then we are in a right
temper to bless him. Let us not lose the occasion. This is one branch of
redeeming of time, to observe what state and temper of soul we are in, and
to take advantage from thence. Is any man in heaviness ? he is fit to
mourn for sin. Let him take the opportunity of that temper. Is any disposed to cheerfulness ? Let him sacrifice that marrow, oil, and sweetness
of spirit to God. We see the poor birds in the spring-time, when those
little spirits they have are cherished with the sunbeams, how they express
it in singing. So when God warms us with his favours, let him have the
praise of all.

And here I cannot but take up a lamentation of the horrible ingratitude
of men, who are so far from taking advantage by God's blessings to praise
him, that they fight like rebels against him with his own favours. Those
tongues which he hath given them for his glory, they abuse to pierce him
with blasphemy ; and those other benefits of his, lent them to honour him
with, they turn to his dishonour ; like children who importunately ask for
divers things, which, when they have, they throw them to the dog. So
favours they will have, which, when they have obtained, they give them to
the devil ; unto whom they sacrifice their strength and cheerfulness, and
cannot be merry, unless they be mad and sinful. Are these things to be
tolerated in these days of light ? How few shall we find, who, in a temper
of mirth, turn it the right way ?

1. But to add some encouragements to incite us to praise God unto the
former, I beseech you let this be one, that *we honour God by it.* It is a

well-pleasing sacrifice to him. If we would study to please him, we cannot do it better than by praising him.

2. And *it is a gainful trading with God*. For in bestowing his seed, where he finds there is improvement in a good soil, with such a sanctified disposition as to bless him upon all occasions, that there comes not a good thought, a good motion in the mind, but we bless God who hath injected such a good thought in our heart; there, I say, God delights to shower down more and more blessings, making us fruitful in every good work to the praise of his name. Sometimes we shall have holy and gracious persons make a law that no good or holy motion shall come into their hearts, which they will not be thankful for. Oh! when God seeth a heart so excellently disposed, how doth it enrich the soul! It is a gainful trade. As we delight to bestow our seed in soils of great increase, which yield sixty and an hundredfold, if possible, so God delights in a disposition inclined to bless him upon all occasions, on whom he multiplies his favours.

3. And then, in itself, *it is a most noble act of religion*, it being a more base thing to be always begging of God; but it argueth a more noble, raised, and elevated spirit, to be disposed to praise God. And it is an argument of less self-love and respect, being therefore more gainful to us. Yea, it is a more noble and royal disposition, fit for spiritual kings and priests thus to sacrifice.

4. Again, indeed, *we have more cause to praise God than to pray;* having many things to praise him for, which we never prayed for. Who ever prayed for his election, care of parents in our infancy, their affection to us, care to breed and train us to years of discretion, besides those many favours daily heaped upon us, above all that we are able to think or speak? Therefore, praise being a more large sacrifice than prayer, we ought to be abundant in it. For those that begin not heaven upon earth, of which this praise is a main function, they shall never come to heaven, after they are taken from the earth; for there is no heavenly action, but it is begun upon earth, especially this main one, of joining with angels, seraphim, and cherubim, in lauding God. Shall they praise him on our behalf, and shall not we for our own? We see the choir of angels, when Christ was born, sang, ' Glory be to God on high, on earth peace, and goodwill towards men,' Luke ii. 14. What was this for? Because Christ the Saviour of the world was born; whereby they shew that we have more benefit by it than they. Therefore, if we would ever join with them in heaven, let us join with them upon earth. For this is one of the great privileges mentioned by the author to the Hebrews, unto which we be come to, ' communion with the spirits of just men made perfect, and to the company of innumerable angels,' Heb. xii. 22, 23. We cannot better shew that we are come to that blessed estate and society spoken of, than by praising God.

5. And lastly, if we be much in praising God, *we shall be much in joy*, which easeth misery. For a man can never be miserable that can be joyful; and a man is always joyful when he is thankful. When one is joyful and cheerful, what misery can lie upon him? Therefore, it is a wondrous help in misery to stir up the heart to this spiritual sacrifice of thanksgiving by all arguments, means, and occasions. Our hearts are temples, and we are priests. We should alway, therefore, have this light and incense burning in our hearts, as the fire did alway burn on the altar in Moses's time, that we may have these spiritual sacrifices to offer continually. Where this is not, the heart of that man or woman is like ' the abomination of desolation,'

Dan. xii. 11, which, when the daily sacrifice was taken away, was set up in the temple. And certainly where there is not praising of God, the heart is ' an abomination of desolation,' having nothing in it save monsters of base lusts and earthly affections.

Ques. But how shall we know that God accepts these sacrifices of praise ?

Ans. How did he witness the acceptation of those sacrifices under the old law ? ' By fire from heaven,' Judges vi. 21 ; 1 Kings xviii. 24, *et seq.* This was ordinary with them. So, if we find our hearts warm, cheered and encouraged with joy, peace, and comfort in praising God ; this is as it were a witness by fire from heaven that our sacrifices are accepted. Let this now said be effectual to stir you up to this excellent and useful duty of thanksgiving, without multiplying of more arguments, save to put you in mind of this, that as we are exhorted to ' delight ourselves in the Lord,' Ps. xxxvii. 4, one way, among the rest, to do it, is to ' serve him with cheerfulness.' It is an excellent thing to make us delight in God, who loves a cheerful giver and thanksgiver. ' So will we render the calves of our lips.' But to proceed.

After this their solemn covenant and promise of yielding praise to God, that if he would forgive all their sins, and do good to them, then he should have the best they could do to him again : praise here is a promise of new obedience, which hath two branches,

1. *A renunciation of the ill courses they took before.*

' Asshur shall not save us ; we will not ride upon horses; neither will we say any more to the works of our hands, Ye are our gods.'

2. Then there is *a positive duty implied* in these words, ' For in thee the fatherless findeth mercy.'

Whereof, the one springs from the other ; ' Asshur shall not save us, we will not ride upon horses; neither will we say any more to the works of our hands, Ye are our gods.' Whence comes all these ? ' For in thee the fatherless findeth mercy.' Thou shalt be our rock, our trust, our confidence for ever. What will follow upon this ? ' Asshur shall not save us any longer ; we will not ride upon horses,' &c. For we have pitched and placed our confidence better ; on him in whom ' the fatherless findeth mercy.'

' Asshur shall not save us.' The confidence which this people had placed partly in Asshur, their friends and associates, and partly in their own strength at home, now promising repentance, they renounce all such confidence in Asshur, horses and idols. ' Asshur shall not save us,' &c.

First, for this, ' Asshur shall not save us,' that is, the Assyrians, whom they had on the one side, and the Egyptians on the other : it being, as we see in the prophecies of Isaiah and Jeremiah, ordinary with God's people, in any distress, to have recourse to the Assyrians, or Egyptians, as if God had not been sufficient to be their rock and their shield. We see how often the Lord complains of this manner of dealing. ' Woe unto them that go down into Egypt for help, and stay on horses, and trust in chariots, because they are many,' &c., Isa. xxx. 2, and xxxi. 1. The prophets, and so this prophet, are very full of such complaints : it being one of the chief arguments he presseth, their falseness in this, that in any fear or peril, they ran to the shelter of other nations, especially these two, Egypt and Assyria, as you have it, ' Ephraim feedeth on wind, and followeth after the east wind ; he daily increaseth lies and desolation, and they do make a covenant with the Assyrians, and oil is carried into Egypt,' Hosea xii. 1, that is, balm, who had this privilege above all other nations, to abound in precious balms ; which balm and oil they carried into Egypt, to win their favour against the Assyrians.   Sometimes they relied on the one, and sometimes on the other, the story and causes whereof were too tedious to relate. Wherefore I come to the useful points arising hence.   ' Asshur shall not save us.'

1. That man, naturally, is prone to put confidence in the creature.

2. That the creature is insufficient and unable to yield us this prop to uphold our confidence.

3. That God's people, when they are endowed with light supernatural to discern and be convinced hereof, are of that mind to say, ' Asshur shall not save us.'

But, to make way to these things, we must first observe two things for a preparative.

Doct. First, *That reformation of life must be joined with prayer and praise.* There was prayer before, and a promise of praise ; but, as here, there must be joined reformation of their sin.   That it must be so, it appears, first, for *prayer.*   It is said, ' If I regard iniquity in my heart, the Lord will not hear my prayer,' Ps. lxvi. 18.   And for *praise,* ' The very sacrifice of the wicked (who reforms not his ways) is abominable,' Prov. xv. 8.   So that, without reformation, prayer and praise is to no purpose.   Therefore it is brought here after a promise of praise.   Lord, as we mean to praise thee, so we intend a thorough reformation of former sins, whereof we were guilty. We will renounce Asshur, and confidence in horses, idols, and the like. Therefore let us, when we come to God with prayer and praise, think also of reforming what is amiss.   Out with Achan, Josh. vii. 19.   If there be any dead fly, Eccles. x. 1, or Achan uncast out, prayer and praise is in vain. ' Will you steal, lie, commit adultery, swear falsely, and come and stand before me,' saith the Lord, by the prophet Jeremiah, Jer. vii. 9.   Will you offer to pray to me, and praise me, living in these and these sins ? No ; God will abhor both that prayer and praise, where there is no reformation. ' What hast thou to do to take my name in thy mouth, since thou hatest to be reformed, and hast cast my words behind thee, saith God,' Ps. l. 16, where he pleads with the hypocrite for this audacious boldness in severing things conjoined by God.   Therefore, as we would not have our prayers turned back from heaven, which should bring a blessing upon all other things else : as we would not have our sacrifices abominable to God, labour to reform what is amiss, amend all, or else never think our lip-labour will prove anything but a lost labour without this reformation.

A *second* thing, which I observe in general, before I come to the particulars, is,

Doct. *That true repentance is, of the particular sin which we are most addicted to, and most guilty of.*

The particular sin of this people, whom God so instructs here, was their confidence in Assyria, horses, and idols.   Now therefore repenting, they repent of the particular, main sins they were most guilty of ; which being stricken down, all the lesser will be easy to conquer.   As when Goliath himself was stricken down, all the host of the Philistines ran away, 1 Sam. xvii. 51.   So when Goliath shall be slain in us, the reigning, ruling, domineering sin, the rest will easily be conquered.

Use. Therefore let us make an use of *examination* and trial of our repentance.   If it be sound, it draws with it a reformation ; as in general, so especially of our particular sins.   As those confess and say, ' Above all

other things we have sinned in this, in asking a king,' 1 Sam. xii. 8. We
were naught, and had offended God many ways before ; but herein we have
been exceeding sinful, in seeking another governor, being weary of God's
gracious government over us.   So a gracious heart will say, I have been a
wretch in all other things, but in this and that sin above all other.   Thus
it was with the woman of Samaria, when she was put in mind by Christ of
her particular grand sin, that she had been a light woman, and had had
many husbands, he whom she lived with now not being her husband, John
iv. 18.   This discovery, when Christ touched the galled part, did so work
upon her conscience that it occasioned a general repentance of all her
other sins whatsoever.   And, indeed, sound repentance of one main sin
will draw with it all the rest.   And, for the most part, when God brings
any man home to him, he so carries our repentance, that, discovering
unto us our sinfulness, he especially shews us our Delilah, Isaac, Herodias,
our particular sin ; which being cast out, we prevail easily against the rest.
As the charge was given by the king of Aram against Ahab, ' Fight neither
against great nor small, but only against the king of Israel,' 2 Chron. xviii.
30 ; kill him, and then there will be an end of the battle.   So let us not
stand striking at this and that sin (which we are not so much tempted to),
if we will indeed prove our repentance to be sound ; but at that main sin
which by nature, calling, or custom we are most prone unto.   Repentance
for this causes repentance for all the rest ; as here the church saith, ' Asshur
shall not save us ; we will not ride upon horses,' &c.

It is a grand imposture, which carries many to hell; they will cherish
themselves in some gross main sin, which pleases corrupt nature, and is
advantageous to them ; and by way of compensation with God, they will
do many other things well, but leave a dead fly to mar all ; whereas they
should begin here especially.   Thus much in general, which things premised, I come to the forenamed particulars.   First,

*Doct. That naturally we are apt and prone to confidence in outward helps
and present things.*

This came to our nature from the first fall.   What was our fall at first ?
A turning from the all-sufficient, unchangeable God, to the creature.   If I
should describe sin, it is nothing but a turning from God to one creature
or other.   When we find not contentment and sufficiency in one creature,
we run to another.   As the bird flies from one tree and bough to another,
so we seek variety of contentments from one thing to another.   Such is
the pravity of our nature since the fall.   This is a fundamental conclusion.
Man naturally will, and must, have somewhat to rely on.   The soul must
have a bottom, a foundation to rest on, either such as the world affords, or
a better.   Weak things must have their supports.   As we see, the vine
being a weak thing, is commonly supported by the elm, or the like supply.
So is it with the soul since the fall.   Because it is weak, and cannot uphold nor satisfy itself with itself, therefore it looks out of itself.   Look to
God it cannot, till it be in the state of grace ; for being his enemy, it loves
not to look to him or his ways, or have dealing with him.   Therefore it
looks unto the creature, that next hand unto itself.   This being naturally
since the fall, that what we had in God before when we stood, we now
labour to have in the creature.

Reason 1. Because, as was said, having lost communion with God, somewhat we must have to stay the soul.

2. *Secondly,* Because Satan joins with our sense and fancy, by which we
are naturally prone to live, esteeming of things not by faith and by deeper

grounds, but by fancy. Now, fancy having communion with sense, what it discovers and presents for good and great, fancy makes it greater. And the devil, above all, having communion with that faculty of fancy, and so a spirit of error being mixed therewith, to make our fancy think the riches of the world to be the only riches; the greatness and goodness of the creature to be the only greatness and goodness; and the strength thereof the only strength. This spirit of error joining with our own spirits, and with the deceit of our natures, makes us set a higher value on the creature, enlargeth and enrageth the fancy, making it spiritually drunk, so as to conceive amiss of things.

Use. Briefly for use hereof, it being but a directing point to others. Let us take notice of our corruption herein, and be humbled for it; taking in good part those afflictions and crosses which God sends us, to convince and let us see that there is no such thing in the creature as we imagined; because naturally, we are desperately given to think that there is somewhat more therein than there is. Now affliction helps this sickness of fancy, embittering unto us all confidence in the creature. Therefore it is a happy and a blessed thing to be crossed in that which we over-value, as these Israelites here did the Assyrians and the Egyptians: for being enemies, they trusted in a ' broken reed,' 2 Kings xviii. 21, as we shall see further in the second point.

Doct. How these outward things cannot help us.

How prone soever we are to rely upon them, they are in effect nothing. They cannot help us, and so are not to be relied upon. ' Asshur shall not save us.' Indeed it will not, it cannot. These things cannot aid us at our most need. So that that which we most pitch upon, fails us when we should especially have help. Some present vanishing supply they yield, but little to purpose. They have not that in them which should support the soul at a strait, or great pinch, as we say.

Reason. The reason is largely given by Solomon in the whole book of Ecclesiastes, ' All is vanity and vexation of spirit,' Eccles. i. 14. There is a vanity in all the creatures, being empty and not able to support the soul. They are vain in their continuance, and empty in regard of their strength. They are gone when we have need of them. Riches, as the wise man saith, are gone, and have wings to fly away, in our most need, Prov. xxiii. 5. So friends are fugitive good things, being like to the brooks mentioned in Job, vi. 15: which when in summer there is need of, then they are dried up, and yet run amain in winter, when there is no need of them. So, earthly supports, when there is no need of them, then they are at hand; but when we have most need of them, are gone. ' They are broken cisterns,' as the prophet calls them, Jer. ii. 13. Cisterns, that is, they have a limited capacity. A cistern is not a spring. So all their support, at the best, is but a bounded and a mixed sufficiency; and that also which will quickly fail: like water in a cistern, which if it be not fed with a continual spring, fails or putrefies presently. Likewise these outward things are not sufficient for the grievance; for being limited and bounded, the grievance will be above the strength of the creature; which though sometime it be present and do not fail, yet the trouble is such, that it is above the strength of the creature to help. So that for these and the like respects, there is no sufficiency, nor help to be expected from the creature. ' Asshur shall not save us.' He is not a sufficient ground of trust. Why?

1. He is but a creature.

2. He is an enemy.

3. He is an idolater.

So that, take him in all these three relations, he is not to be trusted.

1. *He is a creature.* What is a creature ? Nothing, as it were. Saith the prophet, ' All creatures before him are as nothing, and as a very little thing.' And what it is, when he pleaseth, he can dissolve it into nothing, turn it into dust. Man's breath is in his nostrils, Isa. ii. 22. ' All flesh is grass, and all his glory as the flower of grass,' Ps. ciii. 15. If a man trust the creature, he may outlive his trust. His prop may be taken from him, and down he falls. Asshur must not be trusted, therefore, as a creature, nor as a man, for that brings us within the curse. Thus saith the Lord, ' Cursed be the man that trusteth in man, and maketh flesh his arm,' &c., Jer. xvii. 5. So trusting in the creature not only deceives us, but brings us within the curse. In that respect, Asshur must not be trusted.

2. But Asshur likewise was an *enemy,* and a secret enemy. For howsoever the ten tribes unto whom Hosea prophesied were great idolaters, yet they were somewhat better than Asshur, who was without the pale of the church, and a wholly corrupted church. Therefore, they were enemies to the ten tribes, and, amongst other reasons, because they were not so bad as they, nor deeply enough dyed with idolatry.

Many think they may comply with popery in some few things, to gain their love, and that there may be joining with them in this and that ; but do we think that they will ever trust us for all this ? No ; they will alway hate us, till we be as bad as they, and then they will despise us, and secure themselves of us. Therefore, there is no trusting of papists, as papists ; not only creatures, but as false, and as enemies. For this is the nature of wicked men. They will never trust better than themselves, till they become as bad as they are, after which they despise them. Say they, Now we may trust such and such a one ; he is as bad as we, becom'd * one of us. Which is the reason why some of a naughty dispositson take away the chastity and virginity of men's consciences, making them take this and that evil course, and then they think they have such safe, being as bad as themselves. Wherein they deal as Ahithophel's politic, devilish counsel was, that Absalom should do that which was naught, and then he should be sure that David and he should never agree after that, 2 Sam. xvi. 21 ; and that then by this discovery the wicked Jews, set on mischief, might secure themselves of Absalom. So they, now that they join with us, God will forsake them ; we shall have them our instruments for anything. First, they would have the ten tribes as bad as they, and then give them the slip whensoever they trusted them.

3. Again, neither were they to be trusted *as idolaters,* to have league and society with them. There may be some commerce and traffic with them, but amity and trust, none. Asshur and Egypt were horrible idolaters, and therefore not to be trusted in that respect. As we see the prophet in this case reproved good Jehoshaphat, when he had joined with wicked Ahab, king of the ten tribes, ' Shouldst thou help the ungodly, and love them that hate the Lord ? therefore wrath is upon thee from before the Lord,' 2 Chron. xix. 2. So we see it is a dangerous thing to be in league with idolaters, even such as the ten tribes were, who had some religion amongst them. This good king was chidden for it.

' We will not ride upon horses.'

What kind of creature a horse is, it is worth the seeing. What a description God gives of him, that we may see what reason the Spirit of God hath

* That is, ' become.'—G.

to instance in the horse. Saith God to Job, 'Hast thou given the horse
strength? hast thou clothed his neck with thunder? canst thou make
him afraid as a grasshopper? the glory of his nostrils is terrible. He
paweth in the valley, and rejoiceth in his strength: he goeth on to meet
the armed men. He mocketh at fear, and is not affrighted; neither turneth
he back from the sword. The quiver rattleth against him, the glittering
spear and the shield. He swalloweth the ground with fierceness and rage:
neither believeth he that it is the sound of the trumpet. He saith among
the trumpets, Ha, ha; and he smelleth the battle afar off, the thunder of
the captains, and the shouting,' Job xxxix. 19–21. A notable and excellent
description of this warlike creature. And yet for all this excellency, so
described by the Spirit of God, in another place the psalmist saith, 'A horse
is a vain thing for safety, neither shall he deliver any by his great strength,'
Ps. xxxiii. 17. 'Some trust in chariots, and some in horses; but we will
remember the name of the Lord our God,' Ps. xx. 7. So in another place,
'The horse is prepared against the day of battle, but victory is of the Lord,'
Prov. xxi. 31.

How oft have you in the Psalms that proud warlike creature disparaged,
because naturally men are more bewitched with that than with any other
creature. If they have store of horses, then they think they are strong.
Therefore God forbids the king 'to multiply horses to himself, nor cause
the people to return to Egypt, to the end he should multiply horses,' &c.,
Deut. xvii. 16, because God is the strength of his church, when there is no
multitude of horses. You see it is a bewitching creature, and yet a vain
help. A place like this we have, Isa. ii. 7, complaining there of the naughty
people which were among the Jews, at that time as bad as the Israelites.
Saith he, 'Their land also is full of silver and gold; neither is there
any end of their treasures; their land is also full of horses, neither is
there any end of their chariots.' What, is there a fault in that? No.
Luther saith, 'Good works are good, but the confidence in them is damnable.' So gold and silver, horses and chariots, are good creatures of God.
But this was their sin, confidence in these things. 'There is no end of
their treasures.' If they had treasure enough, they should do well enough.
'Their land also was full of horses.' Was this a fault? No; but their
confidence in them. They thought they were a wise people to have such
furniture and provision of munition for war. But God was their king, and
the chief governor of his people; and for them to heap up these things, to
trust over-much in them, it was a matter of complaint. 'Their land also
is full of idols.'

Thus you see there is no confidence to be put neither in the one nor the
other, neither in the association of foreign friends, who will prove deceitful, 'reeds of Egypt,' that not only deceive, but the splinters thereof fly
about, and may run up into the hand. Such are idolaters and false friends,
deceitful and hurtful. Nor in home. There is no trust in horses, munition, or such like. What doth this imply? That to war and have provision in that kind is unlawful and unnecessary, because he finds fault here
with horses and the like? No; take heed of that; for John Baptist, if
the soldier's profession had been unlawful, he would have bid them cast
away their weapons; but he bids them 'do violence to no man, neither
accuse any falsely,' &c., Luke iii. 14. And God would never style himself
'the Lord of hosts, and a man of war,' Isa. xlii. 13, and 'he that teacheth
our hands to war, and our fingers to fight,' Ps. xviii. 34, unless it were

good in the season. Therefore war is lawful, seeing in the way to heaven we live in the midst of enemies.

Therefore it is but an anabaptistical fancy to judge war to be unlawful. No, no; it is clean another thing which the Holy Ghost aims at: to beat back carnal confidence. For it is an equal fault to multiply help and to neglect them. Either of both are fatal many times: to multiply horses, trusting in them, or to spoil horses and other helps vainly, so to weaken a kingdom. Therefore there is a middle way for all outward things, a fit care to serve God's providence, and when we have done, trust in God without tempting of him; for to neglect these helps is to tempt him, and to trust in them, when we have them, is to commit idolatry with them. Beware of both these extremes, for God will have his providence served in the use of lawful means. When there is this great care in a Christian commonwealth, there is a promise of good success, because God is with us. Otherwise, what is all, if he be our enemy? So we see the second point made good, *that these outward things of themselves cannot help.* Therefore comes this in the third place:—

Obs. That when God alters and changes and mouldeth anew the heart of a man to repentance, he altereth his confidence in the creature.

A Christian State will not trust in Asshur, nor in horses. It is true both of State and persons. The reason will follow after in the end of the verse, ' For in thee the fatherless findeth mercy.' Because, when a man hath once repented, there is a closing between God and him, and he seeth an all-sufficiency in God to satisfy all his desires. Therefore he will use all other things as helps, and as far as it may stand with his favour. For he hath Moses's eye put in him, a new eye to see him that is invisible, Heb. xi. 27, to see God in his greatness, and other things in their right estimate as vain things. What is repentance but a change of the mind, when a man comes to be wise and judicious, as indeed repentant men are the only wise men? Then a man hath an esteem of God to be *El-shadai*, all-sufficient, and all other things to be as they are, uncertain; that is, they are so to-day, as that they may be otherwise to-morrow, for that is the nature of the creatures. They are *in potentia*, in a possibility to be other things than they are. God is alway ' I AM,' alway the same. There is not so much as a shadow of changing in him. Wherefore, when the soul hath attained unto this spiritual eyesight and wisdom, if it be a sinful association with Egypt or Asshur, with this idolater or that, he will not meddle; and as for other helps, he will not use them further than as subordinate means. When a man is converted, he hath not a double, not a divided heart, to trust partly to God and partly to the creature. If God fail him,* he hath Asshur and horses enough, and association with all round about. But a Christian he will use all helps, as they may stand with the favour of God, and are subordinate under him. Now for trial.

Quest. How shall we know whether we exceed in this confidence in the creature or not?

Sol. 1. We may know it by *adventuring on ill courses and causes,* thinking to bear them out with Asshur and with horses. But all the mercenary soldiers in the world, and all the horses at home and abroad, what can they do when God is angry? Now, when there is such confidence in these things as for to out-dare God, then there is too much trust in them. That trust will end in confusion, if it be not repented of, for that lifts up the heart in the creature. And as the heathen man observes, ' God delights

* That is, the ' double-minded' man.—G.

to make great little, and little great.' It is his daily work to ' cast down mountains, and exalt the valleys,' Isa. xl. 4. Those that are great, and boast in their greatness, as if they would command heaven and earth, God delights to make their greatness little, and at length nothing, and to raise up the day of small things. Therefore the apostle saith, ' If I rejoice, it shall be in my infirmities,' 2 Cor. xii. 9, in nothing else; for God delights to shew strength in weakness.

2. *By security and resting of the soul in meaner things*, never seeking to divine and religious helps when we are supplied with those that are outward. For these people, when they trusted to Assyria and Egypt, those false supports and sandy foundations, they were careless of God, and therefore must trust in somewhat else. Wherefore, if we see a man secure and careless, certainly he trusts too much to uncertain riches, to Asshur, to Egypt, to friends, or to outward helps. His security bewrays that. If a man trust God in the use of the means, his care will be to keep God his friend by repentance and daily exercises of religion, by making conscience of his duty. But if he trust the means and not God, he will be careless and weak in good duties, dull and slow, and, out of the atheism of his heart, cry, Tush! if God do not help me, I shall have help from friends abroad, and be supported with this and that at home, horses and the like, and shall be well.

Use 1. Let us therefore enter into our own souls, and examine ourselves, how far forth we are guilty of this sin, and think we come so far short of repentance. For the ten tribes here, the people of God, when they repented, say, 'Asshur shall not save us ; we will not ride upon horses.' He speaks comparatively, as trusted in. Therefore, let us take heed of that boasting, vain-glorious disposition, arising from the supply of the creature. Saith God, ' Let not the wise man glory in his wisdom ; neither let the mighty man glory in his might: let not the rich man glory in his riches ; but let him that glorieth glory in this, that he understandeth and knoweth this, that I am the Lord, which exercise lovingkindness, judgment, and righteousness in the earth,' &c., Jer. ix. 23, 24. Let a man glory that he knows God in Christ to be his God in the covenant of grace ; that he hath the God of all strength, the King of kings and Lord of lords to be his : who hath all other things at his command, who is independent and all-sufficient. If a man will boast, let him go out of himself to God, and plant himself there ; and for other things, take heed the heart be not lift up with them.

1. Consider what kind of thing boasting is. It is idolatry, for it sets the creature in the place and room of God.

2. And it is also spiritual adultery, whereby we fix our affections upon the creature, which should be placed on God ; as it is in James, ' Ye adulterers and adulteresses, know ye not that the friendship of the world is enmity with God ?' &c., James iv. 4.

3. Habakkuk calls it drunkennness, Hab. ii. 4, 5, for it makes the soul drunk with sottishness and conceitedness, so as a man in this case is never sober, until God strip him of all.

4. And then again, it puts forth the eye of the soul. It is a kind of white, that mars the sight. When a man looks to Asshur, horses, and to outward strength, where is God all this while ? These are so many clouds, that they cannot see God, but altogether pore upon the creature. He sees so much greatness there, that God seems nothing. But when a man sees God in his greatness and almightiness, then the creature is

nothing, Job xlii. 6. But until this be, there is a mist and blindness in the eye of the soul.

And when we have seen our guiltiness this way (as who of us in this case may not be confounded and ashamed of relying too much on outward helps ?), then let us labour to take off our souls from these outward things, whether it be strength abroad or at home. Which that we may do, we must labour for that obedience which our Saviour Christ exhorts us unto in self-denial, Mat. xvi. 24, not to trust to our own devices, policy, or strength, wit, will, or conceits, that this or that may help us, nor anything. Make it general ; for when conversion is wrought, and the heart is turned to God, it turns from the creature, only using it as subordinate to God. We see, usually, men that exalt themselves in confidence, either of strength, of wit, or whatsoever, they are successless in their issue. For God delights to confound them, and go beyond their wit, as we have it, Isa. xxx. 3. They thought to go beyond God with their policy, they would have help out of Egypt, this and that way. Oh, saith the prophet, but for all this, God is wise to see through all your devices ; secretly hereby touching them to the quick, as sottish persons, who thought by their shallow brains to go beyond God. You think religious courses, and the obedience God pre-scribeth to you, to be idle, needless courses ; but, notwithstanding, God is wise. He will go beyond you, and catch you in your own craft. ' There-fore, the strength of Pharaoh shall be your shame, and the trust in the shadow of Egypt your confusion,' Isa. xxx. 3. Thus God loves to scatter Babels fabrics, Gen. xi. 8, and holds that are erected in confidence of human strength against him. He delights to catch the wise in their own craft, to beat all down, lay all high imaginations and things flat before him, that no flesh may glory in his sight. There is to this purpose a notable place in Isaiah : ' Behold, all ye that kindle a fire, that compass yourselves about with sparks,' Isa. l. 11. For they kindled a fire, and had a light of their own, and would not borrow light from God : ' Walk in the light of your fire, and in the sparks that ye have kindled.' But what is the con-clusion of all ? ' This shall ye have of mine hand.' I dare assure you of this, saith the prophet. ' You shall lie down in sorrow.' Those that walk by the light and spark of their own fire, this they shall have at God's hands : ' they shall lie down in sorrow.'

Let us therefore take heed of carnal confidence. You have a number who love to sleep in a whole skin, and will be sure to take the safest courses, as they think, not consulting with God, but with ' flesh and blood.' It might be instanced in stories of former times, how God hath crossed emperors, and great men in this kind, were it not too tedious. But for present instance, you have many who will be of no settled religion. Oh, they cannot tell, there may be a change. Therefore they will be sure to offend neither part. This is their policy, and if they be in place, they will reform nothing. Oh, I shall lay myself open to advantages, and stir up enemies against me. And so they will not trust God, but have carnal devices to turn off all duty whatsoever. It is an ordinary speech, but very true, policy overthrows policy. It is true of carnal policy. When a man goes by carnal rules to be governed by God's enemy and his own, with his own wit and understanding, which leads him to outward things, this kind of policy overthrows all policy, and outward government at length. Those that walk religiously and by rule, they walk most confidently and securely, as the issue will shew. Therefore, consider that, set God aside, all is but vanity. And that,

First, In regard they do not yield that which we expect they should yield. There is a falsehood in the things. They promise this and that in shows, but when we possess them, they yield it not. As they have no strength indeed, so they deceive.

2. Then, also, there is a mutability in them; for there is nothing in the world but changes. There is a vanity of corruption in them. All things at last come to an end, save God, who is unchangeable.

3. Then again, besides the intrinsical vanity in all outward things, and whatsoever carnal reason leads unto, they are snares and baits unto us, to draw us away from God, by reason of the vanity of our nature, vainer than the things themselves. Therefore take heed of confidence in anything, or else this will be the issue: we shall be worse than the things we trust. 'Vanity of vanities, all things are vanity,' Eccles. i. 1; and man himself is lighter than vanity, saith the psalmist, Ps. lxii. 9. He that trusts to vanity, is worse than vanity. A man cannot stand on a thing that cannot stand itself,—*stare non stante*. A man cannot stand on a thing that is mutable and changeable. If he doth, he is vain with the thing. Even as a picture drawn upon ice, as the ice dissolves, so the picture vanisheth away. So it is with all confidence in the creature whatsoever. It is like a picture upon ice, which vanisheth with the things themselves. He that stands upon a slippery thing, slips with the thing he stands on. If there were no word of God against it, yet thus much may be sufficient out of the principles of reason, to shew the folly of trusting to Asshur, and horses, and the like.

Let this be the end of all, then, touching this carnal confidence: to beware that we do not fasten our affections too much upon any earthly thing, at home or abroad, within or without ourselves. For 'God will destroy the wisdom of the wise,' 1 Cor. i. 19. Let us take heed, therefore, of all false confidence whatsoever. Let us use all outward helps, yet so as to rely upon God for his blessing in the use of all. And when they all fail, be of Jehoshaphat's mind: 'Lord, we know not what to do,' 2 Chron. xx. 12. The creature fails us, our helps fail us; 'but our eyes are upon thee.' So when all outward Asshurs, and horses, and helps fail, despair not; for the less help there is in the creature, the more there is in God. As Gideon with his army, when he thought to carry it away with multitudes, God told him there were too many of them to get the victory by, lest Israel should vaunt themselves of their number, and so lessened the army to three hundred, Jud. vii. 2; so it is not the means, but the blessing on the means which helps us. If we be never so low, despair not. Let us make God ours, who is all-sufficient and almighty, and then if we were brought a hundred times lower than we are, God will help and raise us. Those who labour not to have God, the Lord of hosts, to go out with their armies, if they had all the Asshurs and horses in the world, all were in vain. It was therefore a good resolution of Moses. Saith he to God, 'If thy presence go not with us, carry us not hence,' Exod. xxxiii. 15. He would not go one step forward without God. So, if we cannot make God our friend to go out before us, in vain it is to go one step forward. Let us therefore double our care in holy duties, renewing our covenant with God, before the decree come out against us. The more religious, the more secure we shall be. If we had all the creatures in the world to help us, what are they but vanity and nothing, if God be our enemy! These things we know well enough for notion; but let us labour to bring them home for use, in these dangerous times abroad. Let us begin where we should, that our work may be especially in heaven. Let us reform our

lives, being moderately careful, as Christians should, without tempting
God's providence, using rightly all civil supports and helps seasonably, and
to the best advantage ; for, as was said, the carelessness herein for defence
may prove as dangerous and fatal to a State, as the too much confidence
and trust in them.

THE FOURTH SERMON.

*Asshur shall not save us ; we will not ride upon horses ; neither will we say any
more to the works of our hands, Ye are our gods: for in thee the fatherless
findeth mercy.*—Hos. xiv. 3.

WE shewed you heretofore at large, how the Spirit of God, by the prophet,
doth here dictate a form of turning unto these Israelites, ' Take unto you
words ;' and then teacheth them what they should return back again,
thanks. ' So will we render the calves of our lips.' Wherein they shew
two things. 1. They that have no great matters to render, oxen or sheep,
&c. 2. They shew what is most pleasing unto God, the calves of our lips ;
that is, thanksgiving from a broken heart, which, as the Psalmist speaks,
pleaseth God better than ' a bullock that hath horns and hoofs,' Ps. lxix. 31.
But this is not enough. The Holy Ghost therefore doth prescribe them,
together with prayer and thanksgiving, reformation. ' Asshur shall not save
us ; we will not ride upon horses ; neither will we say any more to the works
of our hands, Ye are our gods : for in thee the fatherless findeth mercy.'
So that here you have reformation joined with prayer and praise. Whence
we observed divers things : that without reformation our prayers are abominable ; that in repentance there must be reformation of our special sin ;
which here they do. Take this one thing more in the third place, which
shall be added to the former.

*Obs. In reformation, we must go not only to the outward delinquencies, but
to the spring of them, which is some breach of the first table.*

The root of all sin, is the deficiency of obedience to some command of the
first table. When confidence is not pitched aright in God, or when it is mis-
applied, and misfastened to the creature : when the soul sets up somewhat for
a stay and prop unto it, which it should not do, this is a spiritual and subtle
sin, and must be repented of, as here, ' Asshur shall not save us,' &c. It
were good therefore for all those who seriously intend the work of repentance, to take this course. If the gross fault be of the second table, take
occasion of sorrow and mourning thence. But when you have begun there,
resolve and bring all to the breeding sin of all, which is the fastening of the
soul falsely, when it is not well fastened and bottomed in the root. And
therefore it was well done by Luther, who, in a Catechism of his, brings in
the first commandment into all the commandments of the first and second
table, ' Thou shalt have no other gods but me.' Therefore thou shalt
sanctify the Sabbath, honour thy father and mother, shalt not take my name
in vain, shalt not commit adultery, shalt not steal, &c., (*b*). Because he
that hath no God but that God in his heart, will be sure to sanctify the
Sabbath, honour his father and mother, not commit adultery, nor steal.
And whence come all the breaches of the second table ? Hence, that there
is not the true fear and love of God in our hearts ; and it is just with God,
for their spiritual sins, to give them up to carnal and gross sins. Therefore,

though the Israelites here had many gross sins to repent of, yet they go to the spring-head, the breeding sin of all, false confidence. This is to deal thoroughly, to go to the core. ' Asshur shall not save us ; we will not ride upon horses.' From whence, in the third place, may descend to the next branch of their sin, idolatry.

'Neither will we say any more to the works of our hands, Ye are our gods.' All false confidence hath two objects : for it is always either,

1. Out of religion ; or,
2. In religion.

For the first, all ill confidence and trust, if it be out of religion, it is in the creature ; either,

1. Out of us ; or,
2. In ourselves.

Secondly, if it be in religion, it is in a false god, as here, ' Neither will we say any more to the works of our hands, Ye are our gods.' Observe hence in the first place.

Obs. Man naturally is prone to idolatry.

The story of the Bible, and of all ages, sheweth how prone men are to idolatry and will-worship, and what miseries ensued thereupon. Amongst other instances, we see how presently after that breach in the kingdom of David and Solomon, by Jeroboam's setting up of two calves, how suddenly they fell to idolatry, 1 Kings xiii. 33, *seq.*; 2 Chron. xiii. 8. So that after that, there was not one good king amongst them all, until the nation was destroyed. And so in the story of their antiquities, see how prone they were to idolatry in the wilderness. Moses doth but go up to the mount, and they fall to idolatry, cause Aaron to make a calf, and dance round about it, Exod. xxxii. 4, *seq.*; Ps. cvi. 19. The thing is so palpable, that it need not be stood upon, that man's nature is prone to idolatry which will not raise itself up to God, but fetch God to itself, and conceive of him according to its false imaginations.

Now idolatry is two ways committed, in the false, hollow, and deceitful heart of man : either,

1. By attributing to the creature that which is proper to God only, investing it with God's properties ; or,
2. By worshipping the true God in a false manner.

1. So that, in the *first* place, idolatry *is to invest the creature with God's properties.* Go to the highest creature, Christ's human nature. We have some bitter spirits (Lutherans they call them) Protestants, who attribute to the human nature of Christ, that which only is proper to God, to be every where, and therefore to be in the sacrament, (*c*). You have some come near them, both in their opinion and in their bitterness. They will have a *nescio quomodo.* Christ is there though they know not how. But this is to make Christ's human nature a god, to make an idol of it. So prayers to saints and angels, this makes idols of them, because it invests them with properties to know our hearts, which he must know unto whom we pray. And then, it gives unto them that which is proper to God, worship and prayer. But, we must call upon none but whom we must believe in, and we must believe in none but God. Therefore, worshipping of saints or angels is idolatry.

Secondly, idolatry *is to worship the true God in a false manner ;* to fix his presence to that we should not fix it to; to annex it to statues, images, crucifixes, the picture of the Virgin Mary and the like. Not to run into the common place of idolatry, but to come home unto ourselves.

Quest. Whether are the papists idolaters or not, like unto these Israelites, who say (being converted), ' Neither will we say unto the works of our hands, Ye are our gods ?'

Ans. I answer, Yes ; as gross as ever the heathens were, and worse. The very Egyptians, they worshipped none for gods but those who were alive ; as a papist himself saith (though he were an honest papist), the Egyptians worshipped living creatures, but we are worse than they ; for we worship stocks and stones, and a piece of bread in the sacrament. And to this purpose, one of their Jesuits confesseth this, and yielded the question for granted, that if there be not a transubstantiation of the bread turned into the body and blood of Christ, we are worse idolaters than these and these nations ; because we worship a piece of bread, which is a dead thing. But we assume (according to the Scriptures, the judgment of the church, and of the truth itself), the bread is not transubstantiated, at least it is a doubtful matter, for if it be not the intention of the priest, it is not. See here upon what hazard they put the souls of people !

Obj. But they have many shifts for themselves ; as, among the rest, this is one, that *they do not worship the image, but God or Christ before the image.*

Ans. To which the answer is, that the fathers who wrote against the heathens meet with this pretence. The Pagans had this excuse. We worship not this statue of Jupiter, but Jupiter himself. Thus they have no allegation for themselves, but the heathen had the same, which the ancient Fathers confuted. They are guilty of idolatry in both the forenamed kinds. For, first, they worship things that they should not, as appears by their invocation of saints, vows to them ; their temples, altars, and the like, full of their images, giving them honour due unto God. And then, they worship the true God in a false manner before their images. There is no kind of idolatry but they are grossly guilty of it. Whereof let this be the use.

Use 1. First of all, of *thankfulness*, that God hath brought us into Goshen, into a kingdom of light ; that we are born in a time and place of knowledge of the true God, wherein is the true worship of the true God. It is a matter that we cannot be too thankful to God for.

Quest. How shall we shew ourselves thankful ?

Ans. In keeping fast the true worship of God we have, and keeping out idolatry ; in reviving laws in that kind, if not making new. What if there were liberty given for men to go about the country to poison people ! Would we endure such persons, and not lay hold of them ? So in that we are freed from Jesuits who go about to poison the souls of God's people, let us shew our thankfulness for this, and shun idolatry of all sorts whatsoever.

Use 2. *Secondly*, See from hence that there can be *no toleration of that religion*, no more, as was said, than to suffer and tolerate poisoners. As they said of coloquintida in their pottage, 2 Kings iv. 40, so ' there is death in the pot' of Romish religion. Therefore it were good to compel them to come in and serve the Lord their God. As it is said, good Josiah compelled those in his time to serve the Lord, 2 Chron, xxxiv. 33, so it were good such courses were taken to reform and reclaim them. As Saint Augustine said of himself in his time, being a Donatist, he altered his judgment by force. In which case it would be with them as with children, who, when they are young, must be forced to school, but afterwards they thank them who forced them. So it is in religion, though it cannot be forced, yet such might afterwards bless God for them who brought them to the means; who, instead of their blindness, trained them up in more knowledge, by forcing them to use the means for which, when God should open their eyes, they might bless God another day. But this point of gross idolatry, so largely handled in books, is only touched by the way, that we may hate idolatry the more; which could not be left out, the words leading to say somewhat of it, seeing how these converts here hate it, and out of that hatred make this profession, ' Neither will we say any more to the works of our hands, Ye are our gods,' &c.

But this is not all; we must know that there be other idols than the idols which we make with our hands. Besides these religious idols, there be secular idols in the world, such as men set up to themselves in their own hearts. Whatsoever takes up the heart most, which they attribute more to than to God, that is their idol, their god. A man's love, a man's fear, is his god. If a man fear greatness rather than God, that he had rather displease God than any great person, they are his idols for the time. ' The fear of a man brings a snare,' Prov. xxix. 25, saith the wise man. And those who get the favour of any in place, sacrifice therefore their credit, profession, religion, and souls, it is gross idolatry; dangerous to the party, and dangerous to themselves. It was the ruin of Herod to have that applause given to him, and taken by him, ' The voice of God, and not of man,' Acts xii. 22. So for any to be blown up with flatterers, that lift them up above their due measure, it is an exceeding wrong to them, prejudiceth their comfort, and will prove ill in the conclusion; indeed, treason against their souls.

So there is a baser sort of idolaters, who sacrifice their credit and state, whatsoever is good within them, their whole powers, to their base and filthy pleasures. Thus man is degenerate since his fall, that he makes that his god which is meaner than himself. Man, that was ordained for everlasting happiness and communion with God, is now brought to place his happiness and contentment in base pleasures. Whereas it is with the soul of man for good or ill, as it applies itself to that which is greater or meaner than itself. If it apply itself to confidence and affiance in God, then it is better. For it is the happiness of the soul to have communion with the Spring of goodness, as David speaks, ' It is good for me to draw near to God,' &c., Ps. lxxiii. 28. When we suffer the soul to cleave in affiance to earthly things, it grows in some measure to the nature of the things adhered to. When we love the world and earthly things, we are earthly. Till the Spirit of God touch the soul, as the loadstone doth the heavy iron, drawing it up, as it were, it will cleave to the creature, to baser things than itself, and so makes the creature an idol, which is the common idolatry of these times. Some make favour, as the ambitious person; some their pleasures, as baser persons of meaner condition; and some riches. Every man as their temper and as their temptations are.

Now, it is not enough to be sound in religion one way in the main; but we must be sound every way, without any touch of idolatry. In a special manner the apostle calls the ' covetous man an idolater,' Eph. v. 5, because he makes riches his castle, thinking to carry anything with his wealth. But his riches oftentimes prove his ruin; for whatsoever a man loves more than God, God will make it his bane and ruin; at least, be sure to take it away, if God mean to save the party. Therefore, here they say, ' Asshur shall not save us; we will not ride upon horses; neither will we say any more to the works of our hands, Ye are our gods.'

' For in thee the fatherless findeth mercy.'

Here he shews the reason of their rejecting of all false confidence in

Asshur, in horses, in idols; because they had planted their confidence in the true God. They said so when they had smarted by Asshur, and by idolatry. Then 'Asshur shall not save us,' &c. They knew it by rule before; but till God plagued them, as he did oft by Asshur and by Egypt, when he broke the reed that it did not only not uphold them, but run into their hands, they made no such acknowledgment. Hence observe,

Obs. Usually it is thus with man, he never repents till sin be embittered to him. He never alters his confidence till his trusts be taken away. When God overthrows the mould of his devices, or brings them upon his own head, setting him to reap the fruit of his own ways, embittering sinful courses to him, then he returns. Instruction without correction doth for the most part little good. When Asshur had dealt falsely with them, and idolatry would do them no good, then they begin to alter their judgment. What makes men, after too much confidence in their wit, when they have, by their plots and devices, gone beyond what they should do, and wrapped and entangled themselves in a net of their own weaving, as we say, alter their judgment? They are then become sick of their own devices. This makes the change. For till then the brain hath a kind of net to wrap our devices in. So, many have nets in their brains, wherewith they entangle themselves and others with their idle devices; which, when they have done, and so woven the web of their own misery, then they begin to say, as the heathen saith when he was deceived, ' O fool am I, I was never a wise man!' Then they begin to say, I was a fool to trust such and such. I have tried such and such policies, and they have deceived me. I will now alter my course. And surely men of great parts are seldom converted till God confound their plots, and lays flat all their false confidence. When Asshur disappoints them, then 'Asshur shall not save us,' &c.

Use. Therefore make this use of it, *not to be discouraged when God doth confound any carnal plot or policy of ours,* as to think that God hates either a nation or a person when they have ill success in plots and projects which are not good. Nay, it is a sign rather that God intends good, if they make a right use it. God intends conversion, to translate false confidence from the creature to himself, and to learn us to make God wise for us. It is a happy thing when in this world God will disappoint a man's courses and counsels, and bring him to shame, rather than he should go on and thrive in an evil and carnal course, and so end his days. There is no evidence at all which can be given of a reprobate, because there may be final repentance, repentance at the last. But this is one and as fearful a sign as may be, to thrive and go on in an evil course to the end. When God shall disappoint and bring a man to shame in that he prided in and built upon, it is a good sign. If thereupon we take advantage to turn to God, and lay a better bottom and foundation, as we see here, 'Asshur shall not save us; we will not ride upon horses,' &c.

' For in thee the fatherless findeth mercy.'

As if he should say, We have that supply of strength and comfort from thee that Asshur, horses, and idols cannot give. Therefore we will alter our confidence, to fix and pitch it upon thee, and trust thee; because ' in thee the fatherless findeth mercy.' We shall not need to say, In thee will we trust; for, if God be apprehended thus, as one in whom ' the fatherless findeth mercy,' affiance will follow. For the object is the attractive and loadstone of the soul; so that if a fit object be presented unto it, affiance, confidence, and trust will of itself follow. Therefore the Spirit of God forbears multiplication of words, and sets down this, ' For in thee the fatherless findeth mercy;' and doth not say, In thee will I trust, for that is implied.   Whatsoever conceives that God is so gracious and merciful to despicable, miserable persons, such as are set down in this one particular, 'fatherless,' they cannot but trust in God.   Therefore the one is put for the other, 'for in thee the fatherless findeth mercy.'   Whence, from the dependence of the words, observe,

Obs. That it is not sufficient to disclaim affiance in the creature, but we must pitch that affiance aright upon God.

We must not only take it off where it should not be placed, but set it where it should be. 'Cease from evil, and learn to do well,' Isa. i. 16, 17.   Trust not in the creature. 'Cease from man,' as the prophet saith, 'whose breath is in his nostrils,' Isa. ii. 22; 'Commit thy ways to God, trust in him,' Ps. xxxvii. 5.   The heathen, by the light of nature, knew this, that for the *negative* there is no trusting in the creature, which is a vain thing.   They could speak wonderful wittily* and to purpose of these things, especially the Stoics.   They could see the vanity of the creature. But for the *positive* part, where to place their confidence, that they were ignorant in.   And so for the other part here, 'Neither will we say any more to the works of our hands, Ye are our gods.'   Idolaters can see the vanity of false gods well enough.   In Italy you have thousands of the wittier and learneder sort, who see the folly and madness of their religion. And among ourselves, how many witty men can disclaim† against popery, who yet in their lives and conversations are not the better for it ; because they think it enough to see the error that misleads them, though they never pitch their confidence as they should do.   It is not enough therefore to rest in the negative part.   A negative Christian is no Christian ; not to be an idolater, not to be a papist ; no, there must be somewhat else.   We must bring forth good fruit, Mat. iii. 10, or else we are for the fire, and are near to cursing and burning, Heb. vi. 8.   This is spoken, the rather because many think themselves well when they can disclaim against the errors of popery ; and that they are good Christians, because they can argue well. Oh ! such make religion nothing but a matter of opinion, of canvassing an argument, &c.   But it is another manner of matter, a divine power exercised upon the soul, whereby it is transformed into the obedience of divine truth, and moulded into it.   So that there must be a positive as well as a negative religion ; a cleaving to God as well as a forsaking of idols.

Again, in the severing of these idols from God, we must know and observe hence,

Obs. That there is no communion between God and idols.

'Neither will we say any more to the works of our hands, Ye are our gods : for in thee the fatherless findeth mercy.'   There must be a renouncing of false worship, religion, and confidence, before we can trust in God. 'Ye cannot serve God and Mammon,' saith Christ, Mat. vi. 24. We cannot serve Christ and Antichrist together.   We may as well bring north and south, east and west together, and mingle light and darkness, as mix two opposite religions.   You see here, one of them is disclaimed ere affiance be placed in the other.   Therefore the halters betwixt two religions are here condemned.   It was excellent well said by Joshua. They had there some mixture of false worship, and thought therewith to serve also Jevovah. 'No,' saith he, 'you cannot serve Jehovah,' Josh. xxiv. 19.   What is Joshua's meaning when he saith they could not ?   Not only that they had no power of themselves ; but, you are a naughty, false

---

* That is, 'with wit' = wisdom.—G.   † That is, 'declaim.'—G.

people, you think to jumble God's worship and that of heathens together; 'you cannot serve God' thus. So a man may say to those who look Romewards, for worldly ends, and yet will be Protestants, You cannot serve God; you cannot be sound Christians, halting thus betwixt both. These are not compatible, they cannot stand together; you must disclaim the one if you will cleave to the other. We see the ground here, 'Neither will we say any more to the works of our hands, Ye are our gods: for in thee the fatherless findeth mercy.'

Again, whereas upon disclaiming of false confidence in the creatures and idols, they name this as a ground, 'For in thee the fatherless findeth mercy,' observe,

In what measure and degree we apprehend God aright to be the all-sufficient true God, in that measure we cast away all false confidence whatsoever.

The more or less we conceive of God as we should do, so the more or less we disclaim confidence in the creature. Those who in their affections of joy, love, affiance, and delight, are taken up too much with the creature, say what they will, profess to all the world by their practice that they know not God. By the contrary, those who know and apprehend him in his greatness and goodness as he should be apprehended, in that proportion they withdraw their affections from the creature and all things else. It is with the soul in this case as with a balance. If the one scale be drawn down by a weight put in it, the other is lifted up. So where God weighs down in the soul, all other things are light; and where other things prevail, there God is set light. 'Asshur shall not save us,' for he can do us no good; nor 'horses,' because they are vain helps. How attained they to this light esteem of Asshur and horses? 'For in thee the fatherless findeth mercy.' That which is taken from the creature, they find in God. And this is the reason why the world so malign good and sound Christians. They think, when God gets, that they lose a feather, as we say, some of their strength. Surely so it is; for when a Christian turns to God and becomes sound, he comes to have a mean esteem of that which formerly was great in his sight. His judgment is otherwise, as we see here, Asshur, horses, idols, and all, they esteem nothing of them. Horses and the like are good, useful, and necessary to serve God's providence in the use of means; not to trust in, or make co-ordinate with God. In the world especially, great persons would be gods in the hearts of people; therefore, when they see any make conscience of their ways, they think they lose them; because now they will do nothing but what may stand with the favour of God. Thus far from the connection. Now to the words themselves.

'For in thee the fatherless findeth mercy.'

Wherein we have set forth unto us for our consideration of God's rich goodness towards poor miserable sinners—

ι. The attribute of God, *mercy.*

2. The fit object thereof, *the fatherless.*

Mercy is God's sweetest attribute, which sweeteneth all his other attributes; for, but for mercy, whatsoever else is in God were matter of terror to us. His justice would affright us. His holiness likewise (considering our impurity) would drive us from him. 'Depart from me,' saith Peter to our Saviour, 'for I am a sinful man,' Luke v. 8. And when the prophet Isaiah saw God in his excellency a little, then he said, 'Woe is me, for I am undone, because I am a man of unclean lips,' &c., Isa. vi. 5. His ower is terrible; it would confound us; his majesty astonish us. Oh!

but mercy mitigates all. He that is great in majesty, is abounding in mercy ; he that hath beams of majesty, hath bowels of mercy. Oh ! this draweth especially miserable persons. ' In thee the fatherless findeth mercy.' And now, in the covenant of grace, this mercy sets all awork. For it is the mercy of God by which we triumph now in the covenant of grace ; in that mercy which stirred up his wisdom to find out a way for mercy by satisfying his justice. So that the first moving attribute of God that set him awork about that great work of our salvation by Jesus Christ, in the covenant of grace, was mercy, his tender mercy, his bowels of mercy. Therefore, of all others, that attribute is here named. ' For in thee the fatherless findeth mercy.'

Mercy in God, supposeth misery in the creature, either present or possible ; for there is, 1. A preventing ; 2. A rescuing mercy.

A *preventing mercy*, whereby the creature is freed from possible misery that it might fall into ; as it is his mercy that we are not such sinners in that degree as others are. And every man that hath understanding is beholden to God for their preventing, as well as for their rescuing mercy. We think God is merciful only to those unto whom he forgives great sins. Oh ! he is merciful to thee that standeth. Thou mightst have fallen foully else. Mercy supposeth misery, either that we are in, or may fall into. So that mercy in God may admit of a threefold consideration.

1. It supposeth *sin*. So there is a *pardoning mercy* for that. Or,
2. *Misery ;* that is, a *delivering mercy.* Or,
3. *Defect or want in the creature*, which is, *supplying mercy.*

Wheresoever mercy is conversant, it is usually about one of these three, either sin, or misery, or defects and wants ; that is, to persons in misery. For, indeed, the word is more general than fatherless. Deserted persons, that are forsaken of others, and have no strength of their own, they are here meant by the fatherless, who have no means, wisdom, power, or ability of their own, but are deserted and forsaken of others. Whence the chief truth that offers itself to be considered of us is this,

That God is especially merciful to those persons who stand most in need of mercy.

First, Because *these do relish mercy most*, and give him the glory of it, applying themselves most to his mercy, being beaten out of the creature ; and the more we have communion with God, being driven out of the creature and other comforts, the more he discovers himself to us. As the nearer we are to the fire, the hotter it is ; so the nearer we are to God, the more good and gracious he every way shews himself unto us. Now, what makes us near him, but extremity of misery, whereby we are beaten from all other holds whatsoever ? It is acknowledged to be his work, when he doth it for those that are deserted of all others, Hosea v. 15. Then he hath the chief glory of it. This is one end why God suffers his children to fall into extremity of great sorrows and perplexities, to fall very low in depths of miseries (as the Scripture speaks), Ps. cxxx. 1, that he might discover a depth of his mercy beyond the depth of their misery, to shew that there is a depth deeper than that depth, for their misery is finite. Oh ! but the bowels of his compassions are infinite, both in measure and time. ' His mercy endureth for ever,' Ps. cxxxvi. 1, *seq.*

Again, *God is jealous of their affiance and confidence*, knowing that naturally, unless we fall into some straits and weaning extremities, we shall place our affiance upon the creature. Therefore, he deals thus with us. He knows our sickness well enough, that we are desperately addicted to present things. Therefore, to cure this sickness in us, he draws us by extremities from the creature to himself, which, when it fails, we go to him. 'Help, Lord!' Why? 'For vain is the help of man,' Ps. lx. 11. It is time then to help. 'Help, Lord, for the godly are perished from the earth,' Ps. xii. 1. It is time to help, Lord, for if thou do not, none will; whereby they come to have their confidence upon the rock, which is worth all. Other men, they run from creature to creature, from help to help, as sick bodies do to this and to that drug, and to this and that potion. They seek to many things to beg comfort from; but a Christian hath a sure foundation that he may stay upon. 'In thee the fatherless findeth mercy.'

To come now to speak of the words as they lie in the whole. They carry another instruction,

That God is very gracious and merciful to fatherless and distressed persons. As we have it, Ps. x. 18, 'that God will judge the fatherless and oppressed; that the man of the earth may no more oppress;' so Ps. cxlvi. 9, it is said, 'The Lord preserveth the strangers, he relieveth the fatherless and widow,' &c. And for the general we have it, 'The Lord relieveth all that fall, and raiseth up all that be bowed down,' Ps. cxlv. 14. God he opens his ear to hear their cry, to judge the fatherless and the oppressed. The like we have in Exodus, 'Also thou shalt not oppress a stranger,' for ye know the heart of a stranger, seeing ye were strangers in the land of Egypt,' Exod. xxiii. 9. And saith he, 'Thou shalt not afflict any widow or fatherless child. If thou afflict them in any wise, and they cry at all unto me, I will surely hear their cry,' Exod. xxii. 21. These, among many, are direct places to shew the truth of this, that God is merciful, not only in general, but to those persons set down by a *synecdoche*, a figure where one is set down for all of the same kind. God is merciful to all persons, in any kind of misery or distress whatsoever. As the apostle speaks, God is he 'who comforteth the abject person,' 2 Cor. vii. 6, the forlorn, the castaway persons of the world; and he is 'a very present help in trouble,' Ps. xlvi. 1. So as when there are none to help, then he awaketh and rouseth up himself to lay hold for us. 'His own arm brings salvation for his own sake.'* So when there is misery, and none to help, God will find cause and ground from his own bowels to shew mercy, to take pity and compassion upon his poor church and children. Which should teach us,

Use 1. First of all, *to take notice of this most excellent attribute of God,* and to make use of it upon all occasions at our most need, then to present to our souls God thus described and set out by his own Spirit, to be 'he that comforteth the abject,' and sheweth mercy to the fatherless and oppressed. This we should make use of for the church in general, and for every one of ourselves in particular. The church hath been a long time like a forlorn widow, as it were. God hath promised that he will have a care of the 'widow and the fatherless,' and so he will of his poor church.

We see in the parable, the widow, with her importunity, prevailed with an unrighteous judge, Luke xviii. 5. The church now being like a widow, what is wanting but a spirit of supplication and prayer? Which spirit, if the church had to wrestle with God, and lay hold upon him as Jacob did, Hos. xii. 4, and not suffer God to rest till he had mercy on his poor church, certainly it would be better with it than it is, for God comforteth the widow, Isa. lxii. 7. If one, what will he do for the whole spouse, which hath so long been a despicable and forlorn widow? And for the time to come it ought to minister matter of comfort for the church. Certainly, God that

* Isa. xli. 17, lix. 16, lxiii. 5, xlviii. 9.

is merciful to the fatherless, he will be merciful to the poor church. We see in the Revelation, though the woman was persecuted by the dragon, yet there were given two wings of a great eagle to her, that she might fly unto the wilderness, where she had a place provided of God, Rev. xii. 14. It alludes to the story of the Israelites when they came out of Egypt. God provided for them in the wilderness. They had manna from heaven, and water out of the rock; and till they came to Canaan, God provided every way for them in a marvellous manner. So God will be sure to provide for his in the wilderness of this world. He will have a harbour still for the church, and a hiding-place from the stormy tempests of her adversaries, Isa. iv. 5, 6. Therefore let us not despair, but stir up a spirit of prayer for the church, that he who shews mercy to the fatherless, and commands mercy to be shewed to the widow, that he would shew that himself which he requires of us. And why may not we hope and trust for it. The church in this world is, as it were, a fatherless person, a pupil, an orphan, a sheep in the midst of wolves, as Daniel in the lions' den, as a ship tossed in the waves, as a lily among thorns. It is environed with enemies, and of itself, like the poor sheep, is shiftless.* What is the church but a company of weak persons? Not so witty† for the world as worldly-wise men are, not so strong in the arm of flesh, nor so defenced, but a company of persons who have a hidden dependence upon God we know not how, and hang, as it were, by a thread, as the church in this land, and abroad in other places. The true church is maintained, we know not how. God keeps up religion, the church, and all, because he is merciful to the fatherless, who have no shifting wits, as the worldly Ahithophels have. God is wise for them that are not wise for themselves, and powerful for them that have little strength of their own. Therefore let us not be discouraged though we be weak creatures, a little flock, like a company of sheep, yet notwithstanding we have a strong shepherd, Ps. xxiii 1. The church is like a vine, a poor, despicable, withered, crooked, weak plant, which winds about, and must be supported, or else it sinks to the ground; yet it is a fruitful plant, Isa. v. 1, 7. So the church of God, a number of weak Christians professing religion, they want many helps, yet God supports them, and hath ordained this and that haven for them, as this magistrate and that person. God hath one support or other for them. While they are fruitful and true vines, God will have a care of them, though they be never so weak and despised in the eye of the world, Isa. liv. 11.

Use 2. Again, this should teach us *to make God our all-sufficiency in all estates whatsoever*, and not to go one hair's breadth from a good conscience, for fear of after-claps.‡ I may be cast into prison, I may lose my goods. What of all this? Is not God all-sufficient? And is not he especially seen in comforting of those who stand in most need of comfort, who want other helps? And will he be indebted to any man who stands out in a good quarrel for his cause? Isa. xli. 17. Will he not give needful supply, if not in this world, yet in a better, of all comforts whatsoever? It is a good supply when the loss is in outward things, and the supply in inward peace, grace, and strength. It is a happy loss that is lost to the advantage, Isa. lx. 17; lxiv. 5. There was never any man yet, from the beginning of the world, who lost by cleaving to religion and good causes. God ever made it up one way or other. Therefore this is a ground of courage to cast ourselves upon doing good when God offers the occasion, relying upon

---

* That is, 'without expedients.'—G.   † That is, 'wise.'—G.
‡ That is, 'judgments, trials.'—G.

God, as Esther did, ' If I perish, I perish,' Esther iv. 16. She meant, ' If I perish, I shall not perish.' Such have a better condition in the love and favour of God than they had before, or should have had, if they had not perished. It is the way not to perish, so to perish. It is as clear and true as the sunshine, but we want faith to believe it.

Use 3. And then, again, let us make use of it in another kind, to resist another temptation. What will become of my poor children, if I do thus and thus, stand thus and thus, and go on in my innocency ? What will become of thy children ? It was well spoken by Lactantius, ' Because God would have men stand out and die in a good cause willingly, therefore he hath promised in a special manner to be a father to the fatherless, and a husband to the widow' (*d*). Are we the chief fathers of our children ? No ; we are but under God, to bring those who are his children into the world. We are but instruments. God is the chief father, best and last father, ' The everlasting father,' Isa. ix. 6, who takes upon him to be a father to the fatherless, whom he chargeth all not to hurt. Experience shews how he blesseth the posterity of the righteous, who have stood in defence of the truth. Therefore let us make no pretences either for baseness, dejection of spirit, or covetousness, to keep us from well doing, for God will reward all.

Quest. Oh, say some, I could be content not to be so worldly, but it is for my children.

Ans. What saith the apostle ? ' Let those who are married be as if they were not married,' 1 Cor. vii. 29, meaning in regard of this scraping of wealth together by unlawful means of covetousness, or in regard of readiness to do works of mercy. What, doth God appoint one ordinance of marriage, to take a man off of all duties ? No ; notwithstanding this we must do fitting works of mercy. God will be the father of the fatherless. Many use oppression, and go to hell themselves to make their children rich. Who commands us to make our children, in show, a while happy here, to make our souls and bodies miserable for ever ? There is a moderate care, as the apostle speaks, so that ' he who cares not for his own, is worse than an infidel,' 1 Tim. v. 8 ; but we must not make this pretence to excuse injurious and extortive courses. But let God alone. He will do all things well ; trust him. Or, if anything should befall us otherwise than well, what if it do ? God is the God of the fatherless. Whatsoever he takes away, he supplies it better another way. For whence have the creatures that infusion to help ? Is it not from God ? And when the creature is taken away, is not God where he was ?

Use 4. And let us also learn hence that we answer God's dealing, in shewing mercy to the fatherless and such as stand in need, as the apostle exhorts, ' Put on, therefore, as the elect of God, holy and beloved, bowels of mercy,' &c., Col. iii. 12, as if he should say, as you would prove yourselves to be elect members of Christ and children of God, so shew your likeness in this particular, ' The bowels of mercy and compassion.' This hath ever been, and yet is at all times, a character of God's children, and shall be to the end of the world. It is a sign such a one hath found bowels of mercy, that is ready upon all occasions to pour forth those bowels of compassion upon others, as hard-heartedness this way shews a disposition which yet hath not rightly tasted of mercy. As we say in another case, those that are appeased in their consciences, in the sense of the forgiveness of sins, they are peaceable to others, because they feel peace. So here, those that feel mercy will be merciful, those that have felt love will be loving to others.

' A good man is merciful to his beast, but the mercies of the wicked are
cruel,' Prov. xii. 10.   Those, therefore, that are hard-hearted and unmerciful, hardening themselves against the complaints of the miserable, there
is, for the present, no comfort for them, that the Spirit of God hath wrought
any change in their hearts ; for then it would stamp the image of God upon
them, they would be merciful to the fatherless, widow, and distressed persons.   What shall we think, then, of a generation of men who, by gripping
usury and the like courses, have made many widows miserable ?   Let such
profess what they will, whilst they are thus hard-hearted they have not the
bowels of Christ.   God is so merciful that you see, as the Jews call them
(e), he hath hedges of the commandments, that is, he hath some remote
commands which are not of the main, and all to hedge from cruelty, as,
' Thou shalt not kill the dam upon the nest,' Deut. xxii. 6 ; ' Thou shalt
not seethe a kid in his mother's milk,' Exod. xxiii. 19.   What tends this
to ?   Nothing but to shew the mercy and bowels of God, and that he would
have us to abstain from cruelty.   He that would not have us murder, would
have us keep aloof off, and not be merciless to the very dumb creatures,
birds and beasts.   Therefore let us labour to express the image of our heavenly father in this.

Use 5.   Again, we should use this *as a plea against dejectedness at the hour
of death*, in regard of those we leave behind us, not to be troubled what
shall become of them, when we are to yield up our souls to God ; but
know that he hath undertaken to be ' the Father of the fatherless, and of
the widow.'   Therefore, for shame, for shame ! learn, as to live, so to die
by faith ; and as to die by faith in other things, so to die in this faith ;
that God, as he will receive thy soul, so he will receive the care of thy
posterity.   Canst thou with affiance yield up thy soul unto God, and wilt
thou not with the same confidence yield thy posterity ?   Thou art an
hypocrite, if this distract and vex thee, when yet thou pretendest to die in
the faith of Christ.   Canst thou yield thy soul, and yet art grieved for thy
posterity ?   No ; leave it to God.   He is all-sufficient.   ' The earth is the
Lord's, and the fulness thereof,' Ps. xxiv. 1.   We need not fear to put our
portion in his hands.   He is rich enough.   ' The earth and all is his.'
Therefore, when we are in any extremity whatsoever, rely on this mercy of
so rich and powerful a God ; improve it, for it is our portion, especially in
a distressed condition.   Were it not for faith, wrought by the blessed
Spirit of God, he would lose the glory of this attribute of mercy.   Now,
faith is a wise power of the soul, that sees in God what is fit for it, singling out in God what is fit for the present occasion of distress.   Is a man
in any extremity of misery ? let him look to mercy.   Is a man oppressed ?
let him look to mercy, to be revenged of his enemies.   Is a man in any
perplexity ? let him look to mercy, joined with wisdom, which is able to
deliver him.   Religion is nothing else but an application of the soul to
God, and a fetching out of him somewhat (as he hath discovered himself in the covenant) fit for all our exigents ; as there is somewhat
in God, and in the promises, for all estates of the soul.   Faith, therefore, is witty to look to that in God which is fit for its turn.   Let us
therefore take heed of Satan's policy herein, who in our extremity, useth
this as a weapon to shake our faith.   ' Tush,' as it is in the psalm, ' God
hath forsaken and forgotten him,' Ps. x. 11.   Hath he so ?   Nay ; because
I am in extremity, and deserted above others, rather God now regards me
more than before ; because, ' he scourgeth every son whom he receiveth,'
Heb. xii. 6.   So retort Satan's fiery darts back again.   For indeed, that

is the time wherein God exalts and shews himself most glorious and triumphant in mercy, where misery is greatest. 'Where sin abounds, there grace abounds much more,' Rom. v. 20. So where misery abounds, mercy superabounds much more. Therefore let us be as wise for our souls, as Satan can be malicious against them. What he useth for a weapon to wound the soul, use the same as a weapon against him.

To end all, *let faith in God's mercy answer this his description;* and let it be a description ingrafted into us at such a time. Doth God care for the fatherless, and mean persons, who are cast down and afflicted? Why, then, I will trust that God who doth so, being in this case myself. If he will help in extremity, trust him in extremity; if he will help in distress, trust him in distress; if he will help when all forsake, trust him when we are forsaken of all, Hab. iii. 17. What if a stream be taken away? yet none can take away God from thee. What if a beam be taken away? thou hast the sun itself. What if a particular comfort be taken away? So long as God, 'who comforteth the abject,' and is merciful to the distressed, fatherless, and widows, continues with thee, thou needst not fear. A man cannot want comfort and mercy, so long as the Father of mercies is in covenant with him. If he sin, he hath pardoning mercy for him; if weak, he hath strengthening mercy; if in darkness, he hath quickening mercy; if we be dull, dead, and in danger, there is rescuing mercy; and if subject to dangers we may fall in, there is for that preventing mercy, Ps. xxxii. 10. Therefore there is mercy ready to compass God's children about in all conditions. When they are environed with dangers, yet God is nearer to guard their souls, than the danger is to hurt them.

Therefore let us take the counsel of the blessed apostle. 'Be careful for nothing; but in everything, by prayer and supplication, with thanksgiving, let your requests be known to God.' And what then? Will God grant that I pray for? Perhaps he will not; but yet, 'the peace of God, which passeth all understanding, shall guard your hearts and minds through Christ Jesus,' Philip. iv. 6, 7. As if he should say, in nothing be overcareful. Let your care be, when ye have used the means, to depend upon God for support in the event and issue of all. If God deny you what you pray for, he will grant you that which is better. He will set up an excellent inward peace there, whereby he will stablish the soul in assurance of his love, pardon of sins, and reconciliation: whereby their souls shall be guarded, and their hearts and minds preserved in Christ. So they become impregnable in all miseries whatsoever, when they have 'the peace of God, which passeth all understanding,' to guard them within. Therefore let us not betray and lose our comforts for want of making use of them, or for fear some should call us hypocrites. And, on the other side, let us not flatter ourselves in an evil course; but make the conscience good, which will bear us out in all miseries, dangers, and difficulties whatsoever. Nothing makes losses, crosses, banishment, imprisonment, and death so terrible and out of measure dreadful unto us, but the inward guilt and sting in the inside, the tumults of conscience, Gen. xlii. 21. Clear this well once, make all whole within, let conscience be right and straight, let it have its just use and measure of truth and uprightness, and go thy way in peace; I warrant thee, thou shalt hold up thy head, and wind thyself out of all dangers well enough: nothing shall daunt or appal thy courage. For, saith Solomon, 'The righteous is bold as a lion,' Prov. xxviii. 1. What can, what should he fear, who is heir of all things,' Rev. xxi. 7, whose all things are, and who is reconciled to God in Christ, having all the angels and creatures for his servants, Heb. i. 14, for whose sake ' all things must needs work together for good ?' Rom. viii. 28.

THE FIFTH SERMON.

I will heal their backsliding, I will love them freely: for mine anger is turned away from them.—Hos. XIV. 4.

THE superabounding mercies and marvellous lovingkindnesses of a gracious and loving God to wretched and miserable sinners, as we have heard, is the substance and sum of this short, sweet chapter, wherein their ignorance is taught, their bashfulness is encouraged, their deadness is quickened, their untowardness is pardoned, their wounds are cured, all their objections and petitions answered; so as a large and open passage is made unto them, and all other miserable penitent sinners, for access unto the throne of grace. If they want words, they are taught what to say; if discouraged for sins past, they are encouraged that sin may be taken away ; yea, all iniquity may be taken away. ' Take away all iniquity.' If their unworthiness hinder them, they are taught for this, that God is gracious. ' Receive us graciously.' If their by-past unthankfulness be any bar of hindrance unto them, they are taught to promise thankfulness. ' So will we render the calves of our lips.' And that their repentance may appear to be sound and unfeigned, they are brought in, making profession of their detestation of their bosom sins, of false confidence and idolatry. ' Asshur shall not save us; we will not ride upon horses ; neither will we say any more to the works of our hands, Ye are our gods.' And not only do they reject their false confidence, to cease from evil, but they do good, and pitch their affiance where it should be. For ' in thee the fatherless findeth mercy.'

None must therefore be discouraged, or run away from God, for what they have been, for there may be a returning. God may have a time for them, who, in his wise dispensation, doth bring his children to distress, that their delivery may be so much the more admired by themselves and others, to his glory and their good. He knows us better than we ourselves. How prone we are to lean upon the creature. Therefore he is fain to take from us all our props and supports, whereupon we are forced to rely upon him. If we could do this of ourselves, it were an excellent work, and an undoubted evidence of the child of God, that hath a weaned soul in the midst of outward supports, to enjoy them, as if he possessed them not ; not to be puffed up with present greatness, not to swell with riches, nor be high-minded ; to consider of things to be as they are, weak things, subordinate to God, which can help no further than as he blesseth them. But to come to the words now read.

' I will heal their backsliding, and love them freely,' &c.

After that the church had shewed her repentance and truth of returning to God : now in these words, and the other verses, unto the end of the chapter (saving the last verse, which is a kind of acclamation issuing from all the rest of the foregoing verses, ' Who is wise, and he shall understand these things ?' &c.), is set down an answer unto that prayer, repentance, and reformation which the church made ; all the branches of which their former suit the Lord doth punctually * answer. For they had formerly

* That is, ' point by point.'—ED.

prayed, 'Take away all iniquity, and receive us graciously; do good untc us.' Unto which he answers here, 'I will heal their backsliding,' &c.

Which is thus much: I will pardon their iniquities, I will accept graciously of them, I will love them freely, and so of the rest, as will appear afterwards; and, in sum, God answers all those desires which formerly he had stirred up in his people. Whence, ere we come to the particulars, observe in general, *Obs. Where God doth give a spirit of prayer, he will answer.*

It needs no proof, the point is so clear and experimental. All the saints can say thus much from their experience of God's gracious dealing with them; and the Scriptures are full of such instances and promises, which we all know. To name a place or two for all the rest, 'Call upon me in the day of trouble, I will deliver thee, and thou shalt glorify me,' Ps. l. 15. So in another place, 'And it shall come to pass that before they call, I will answer; and whilst they speak, I will hear,' Isa. lxv. 24. It hath been made good to persons, as Daniel, Elijah, Solomon, Jacob, and others; and it hath been, and is, made good unto all ages of the church, from time to time, and shall be unto the end of the world. And therefore the prophet sets down this as a conclusion undeniable from the premises, ' O thou that hearest prayer, unto thee shall all flesh come,' Ps. lxv. 2. Whence he draws this excellent consolation, 'Iniquities prevail against me; as for our transgressions, thou shalt purge them away.'

Reason. The reason is strong, because they are the motions of his own Spirit, which he stirs up in us. For he dictates this prayer unto them, 'Take with you words,' &c., 'and say unto the Lord, Take away all iniquity, and receive us graciously.' So that, where God stirs up holy desires by his Spirit, he will answer exactly; there shall not a sigh be lost. ' Likewise,' saith the apostle, ' the Spirit also helps our infirmities : for we know not what we should pray for as we ought: but the Spirit itself makes intercession for us, with groanings which cannot be uttered,' Rom. viii. 26. Therefore there cannot a groan be lost, nor a darting of a sigh. Whatsoever is spiritual must be effectual, though it cannot be vented in words. For God hath an ear, not only near a man's tongue, to know what he saith; but also in a man's heart, to know what he desires, or would have. As the observing, careful, tender mother many times knows what the child would have though it cannot speak; so God, he knows the desires, sighs, and groans of the heart when we cannot speak. For sometimes there may be such a confusion upon the soul, by reason of divers disturbances, that it cannot express nor vent itself in words. Therefore the Spirit vents itself then in sighs and groans, which are heard and accepted, because they are the desires of his own Spirit. Thus much the prophet David excellently sheweth, ' Lord, thou hast heard the desire of the humble : thou wilt prepare their heart, thou wilt cause thine ear to hear,' Ps. x. 17. God, he first prepares the heart to pray, then his ear to hear their prayers and desires. If this will not encourage us to be much in suit to God, and put up our petitions to him, to labour for a spirit of prayer, I know not what will prevail; when we know that no petition shall be turned back again unanswered. When we are to deal with princes upon earth, they oftentimes regard neither the persons nor their petitions, but turn their backs upon both. Oh! but a Christian hath the ear of God and heaven open upon him; such credit in heaven, that his desires and groans are respected and heard. And undoubtedly a man may know that he shall be heard when he hath a spirit of prayer; in one kind or other, though not in the particulars or kinds we ask, hear he will for our good.

God will not lose the incense of his own Spirit, of a spirit of prayer which he stirs up, it is so precious. Therefore let us labour to have a spirit of prayer, which God regards so much; seeing for a certain, wheresoever he gives a spirit of prayer, he means to give that we pray for; but according to his heavenly wisdom, as here his answer is,

'I will heal their backsliding, I will love them freely,' &c.

God answers them exactly unto all they prayed for, beginning first with the ground of all our comfort, 'forgiveness of sins.' According to their petition, 'Take away all iniquity,' he answers, 'I will heal their backsliding,' or their rebellion. Backsliding is an aggravation of sin. Every sin is not a rebellion, apostasy, or backsliding · for there be also sins of infirmities. We usually rank sins thus, in

1. Sins of ignorance.
2. Sins of infirmity.
3. Sins against knowledge, with a higher hand; and
4. The sins against the Holy Ghost.

Now, this is more than to cure sins of ignorance and of infirmity when he saith, 'I will heal their backsliding.'

Quest. But why doth he answer the higher pitch of an aggravation, when their petition was in a lower strain only, 'Take away all mine iniquity'?

Ans. To shew that he would answer them fully; that is, that he would heal all sins whatsoever, not only of ignorance and of infirmity, but also sins willingly committed, their rebellions and backslidings. For, indeed, they were backsliding. From the time of Jeroboam, that made the rent, the ten tribes grew worse and worse continually, so that they had been utterly extinguished, but that God was wondrous gracious to send them prophets to preserve many that they should not bow the knee to Baal, being merciful to them to bear with their backsliding so long. For besides their calves, they had false gods. They did not only worship the true God in a false manner by the calves, but they had Baals also. So that we see, God, when he will comfort, will comfort to purpose, and take away all objections that the soul can make, a guilty soul being full of objections. Oh! my sins are many, great, rebellions and apostasies. But, be they what they will, God's mercy in Christ is greater and more. 'I will heal their backsliding,' or their rebellion. God is above conscience. Let Satan terrify the conscience as he will, and let conscience speak the worst it can against itself, yet God is greater. Therefore, let the sin be what it will, God will pardon all manner of sins. As they pray to pardon all, so he will 'take away all iniquity, heal their backsliding.' But to come nearer the words.

'I will heal,' &c. The healing meant here is especially in the pardon of their sins, answerable to their desires in justification. And there is a healing also in sanctification by the Spirit. When God takes away the venom from the wound, then God cures in sanctification. Both are meant, but especially the first. In a wound we know there is,

1. The malignity and venom of it; and then,
2. The wound itself, so festered and rankled.

Now, pardoning grace in justification takes away the anguish and malice of the wound, so that it ceaseth to be so malignant and deadly as to kill or infect. And then sanctification purgeth and cleanseth the wound and heals it up. Now, God through Christ doth both. The blood of Christ doth heal the guilt of sin, which is the anger and malignity of it; and by the Spirit of Christ he heals the wound itself, and purgeth out the sick and peccant humour by little and little through sanctification. God is a perfect healer. ' I will heal their backsliding.' See here the state of the church and children of God. They are prone to backsliding and turning away. We are naturally prone to decline further and further from God. So the church of God, planted in a family in the beginning of the world, how soon was it prone to backsliding. This is one weakness since the fall. It is incident to our nature to be unsettled and unsteady in our holy resolutions. And whilst we live in the midst of temptations, the world, together with the fickleness of our own nature, evil examples, and Satan's perpetual malice against God and the poor church, are ill pilots to lead us out of the way. This is spoken to make us careful how to shun backsliding. For we see how many opinions are foisted in amongst us, and have got some head, that durst not before once be named amongst us. Popery spreads itself amain. Even churches are prone to backsliding. Therefore, St Paul's advice is, ' Be not high-minded, but fear; for if God spared not the natural branches, take heed lest he also spare not thee,' Rom. xi. 20, 21. What is become of Rome ? So the same will become of us if we stop not our backslidings.

Now, in that God's promise is, ' I will heal their backslidings,' observe, in the first place,

That sin is a wound and a disease.

Now, as in sickness there is, 1, grief troubling and vexing the party who feels it; and, 2, deformity of the place affected, which comes by wounds and weaknesses; so in all sin, when we are sensible of it, there is first grief, vexation, and torment of conscience, and then, again, deformity. For it takes away the beauty and vigour of the soul, and dejects the countenance. It debaseth a man, and takes away his excellency. As Jacob saith of Reuben, ' Unstable as water, thou shalt not excel, because thou wentest up to thy father's bed,' Gen. xlix. 4. Saith God to Cain, ' Why art thou wroth, and why is thy countenance fallen ?' Gen. iv. 6. And the prophet David, he confesseth, ' When I kept silence, my bones waxed old through my roaring all the day long,' Ps. xxxii. 3, 4. So again, ' There is no soundness in my flesh, because of thine anger ; neither is there any rest in my bones, because of my sin,' Ps. xxxviii. 3. So that sin is a wound and a disease, whether we consider the miseries it brings on soul and body, or both. Therefore, howsoever a sinful person think himself a goodly person, and wear his sins as ornaments about him, pride, lust, and the like, yet he is a deformed, loathsome person in the eyes and presence of God ; and when conscience is awakened, sin will be loathsome, irksome, and odious unto himself, fill him full of grief and shame, so that he cannot endure the sight of his own soul.

Now, all sins whatsoever are diseases. The first sin of all sins, which we call hereditary, original sin, what was * it but an hereditary disease ? A leprosy, which we drew from our first parents, spread over all the soul, having the seeds and spawn of all sin in it. The church of Rome makes it less than other sins, as indeed popery is ignorant both of the height of grace and of the depth of corruption, for if they knew the one, they would be more capable of the other. Why do they not conceive aright of grace and of the height of it ? Because they know not the depth of original sin. And, indeed, the true knowledge of this disease is proper only to the child of God in the true church. None but he knows what original sin is. Others can dispute and talk of it, but none feels it but the child of God. Now, all other particular, actual sins be diseases flowing from hence. So that all diseases in this kind arise either, 1, from ourselves, as we have a

* Qu. ' is it ?'—G.

seminary of them in our own hearts; or else, 2, from the infection and contagion of others; or, 3, from Satan, who hath society with our spirits, as men have with the outward man, coming in by his suggestions, and our entertaining of them. So that in that respect sin is like unto a wound and a disease, in regard of the cause of them.

And, in regard of the effects, sin is like a disease. Diseases, if they be neglected, breed death itself, and become incurable. So it is with the diseases and sins of the soul. Neglect them, and the best end of them will be despair in this world. Whereupon we may have advantage to fly unto the mercy of God in Christ. This is the end of sin, either to end in a good despair or in a fruitless barren despair, at the hour of death leading to hell, when they have no grace to repent. 'The wages of sin is death,' &c., Rom. vi. 23. Sin itself is a wound, and that which riseth from sin is a wound too, doubting and despair; for this disease and wound of sin breeds that other disease, a despair of mercy, which is the beginning of hell, the second death. These things might be further enlarged. But for the present only in general know that sin is *a disease and a wound of the soul;* so much worse than the diseases of the body, by how much the soul is more precious than it, and the death of the soul more terrible than the death of the body. Sin is a disease and a wound; for what is pride but a swelling? What is anger but an intemperate heat of the soul, like an ague, as it were? What is revenge but a wildfire in the soul? What is lust but a spreading canker in the soul, tending to a consumption? What is covetousness but a sword, a perpetual wounder of the soul, piercing it through with many sorrows? What is security but, as it were, the lethargy and apoplexy of the soul? And so we might go on in other resemblances (*f*).

Quest. But, it may be demanded, how shall we know that we are sick of this sickness and disease you speak of?

Ans. How do we know that we are sick in body? If the body be extreme cold we know there is a distemper, or if it be extreme hot. So if the soul be so extreme cold that no heavenly motives or sweet promises can work upon it, stir it up, then certainly there is a disease upon the soul. If the soul be inflamed with revenge and anger, that soul is certainly diseased. The temper of the soul is according to the passions thereof. A man may know by his passions when he hath a sick soul.

If a man cannot relish good diet, then we count him a sick man; so when a man cannot relish holy discourse nor the ordinances of God. You have some men that can relish nothing but profits and pleasures, and such vanities, but no divine thing. Such have sick souls undoubtedly.

So, again, a man may know there is a deadly sickness and soreness upon the soul, 1, when it is senseless of its wounds; and, 2, is senseless of that which passeth from it. As men, we say, are ready to die when excremental things pass from them without any sense, so a man may know that he is desperately soul-sick when oaths, lies, and deceitful speeches pass from him, and yet he is senseless of them. They think not of them. They mean no harm. Doth that argue a sound state of body, when a man is so desperately ill that he feels not his bodily hurts? And is this a good state of soul, when these filthy things come out from it insensibly? It is an argument of extreme deadness of spirit and irreverence, and of a desperate sin-sick soul, when there is no dread or awe of the majesty of God. Let such look about them. It is an aggravation of the danger of the soul this kind of temper. We usually say, when the stomach is so weak that it can hold no nourishment without casting it up again as fast as it receives it, certainly such an one is sick, and in a dangerous state of body. So when a man hears and hears, and reads and reads, and digests nothing into nourishment, but all is left where he heard it, it is a sign they have sick souls when their retentive power is so weak. And there is certainly some sickness, some dangerous obstruction in that soul that cannot digest the wholesome word of God, to make use of it; some noisome lust then certainly obstructs the soul, which must be purged out.

It is a pitiful thing to see the desperate condition of many now, who, though they live under the tyranny of sin, yet flatter their own disease, and account them their greatest enemies who any way oppose their sick humour. What do they most cordially hate? The sound preaching of the word. The very sight of such an one whose calling hath been to put us in mind of our sins, evil courses, and vanities of the world, is loathsome and offensive to carnal men, in whom corruption is grown up to such a tyranny that it sways the whole soul to devise how to satisfy it. Man is so diseased that those lusts in him, which he should labour to subdue and mortify by the power of the Spirit, do so oversway him that all his life is nothing else but a disease and backsliding into sin. And as if we were not corrupt enough ourselves, how many are there who feed their corruptions when they frequent ill places and company, whom they cannot do without, and are as fish in the water, feeding the old man in them. So that such are not only sick, but defend, maintain, and feed their sickness, their whole life being spent this way, which they laugh at, and make ' pride their chain and ornament,' Ps. lxxiii. 6, as the prophet speaks. This is spoken that we may take up a lamentation for the vileness of man's nature, and to teach us how to judge aright of men when they devise how to have their liberty strengthened to go to hell, as it were, with an high hand, having their will so fortified that no man is able to deal with them, thwart them, or teach them anything. If it were offered to most men to have what estate they would in this world, what are their wishes and desires? O that I might live as I list, that I might have what would content my pleasures without control, that I might have no crosses, but go smoothly on! Yet this, which is the desire of most men, is the most cursed estate of all, and most to be lamented. Thus it appeareth sin is a wound and a disease. What use may we make of it?

Use 1. If this be so, then, in the first place, let us know and consider, *that no man who lives in sins unrepented of and uncured, is to be envied, be they never so great.* Who will envy a man that hath a rotten body, covered over with glorious attire? when every man knows that he carries a rotten disease about him; either some disease in the vital parts, or from the rottenness of sin, which puts a kind of shame and scorn. Can we pity a man thus in glorious attire, having a filthy body under it? thus covering their nakedness, in whose case we would not for anything be. And are they not much more to be pitied, who have ulcerous souls, galled and pierced through with many sins? When we see men that are blasphemers, swearers, men guilty of much blood and filthiness, and of many sins hanging upon them, to envy such a man's greatness is extreme folly. Oh, he carries his death's wound about him, as we say. He is stricken already in his side with a deadly dart. Without the healing mercy of God, there is but a step betwixt him and eternal death; wherefore no man is to be envied for his sinful greatness.

Use 2. Again, if this be so, that sin is a disease and wound of the soul, *let us therefore labour to cure it presently.* It is desperate folly in men to neglect their bodies, when they know that they are prone to such and such diseases, which are growing upon them every day. How careful are men, perceiving thus much, to prevent diseases by timely physic ! All sins are diseases, and growing like diseases, run from ill to worse, worse and worse. ' Wicked men,' saith the apostle, ' grow worse and worse,' 2 Tim. iii. 13. Therefore, if sin be a disease, prevent it presently. For as we see, heretics and other the like are hardly sound but at the first, and then are hardly cured. So, if we neglect the diseases of our souls, they will breed a consumption of grace, or such an ill temper of soul, as that it cannot well desire to repent. Nay, when a man lives in wicked, rebellious courses long, God will give him up to such terrors of conscience, that it will not be pacified, but upbraid itself. I have been a sinful, wretched creature; mercy hath been offered me again and again, but now it is too late, having outstood all the means of grace, and rejected them. When they have considered that their lives have for a long time been a mere rebellion, and that they have put off the checks of conscience, the admonitions of the word and Spirit, with the motions thereof. It is long in this case before a man can have peace. For answerable to the continuance in sin, is the hardness of the cure, if it be cured at all.

Therefore there is no dallying with sin. I shall repent at length, but not now. Yet a while I will continue these and these courses, I shall do well enough, &c.; as if a man who were sick, or desperately wounded, should say, I shall do well, and yet neglect to send for the physician. None are so desperately foolish in case of the body, why should we for our souls? Is not that in much more hazard than the body, if we had spiritual eyes to consider of it ? The truth is, people are not convinced of this, that sin is such a sickness, which is the reason they are so careless of it. But when the conscience is awaked, as it will be one day, here or in hell, then they will be of another mind. Nay, in this world, when friends, nor riches, nor anything can comfort, then they cry out, O that they had not been so foolish ! They would give a world, if they had it, for peace of conscience ! This will be the best of it, for men that go on in sin. Therefore, before hardness of heart grow upon us, that disease following the disease of sin, let us take heed, and labour to have our souls healed in time. Thus we have found that sin is a sickness ; for so much is implied, when he saith, ' I will heal their backsliding.' Whence the direct observation is,

That God is the great physician of the soul.

For he saith here, ' I will heal their backsliding ;' so that healing implies the taking away of—

1. The guilt of sin, which is the venom of it, by justification.
2. The rage of sin, which is the spreading of it, by sanctification.
3. The removing the judgment upon our estate.

For, unless God be the more merciful, these things follow. Where there is sin, and breaking of his law, there is a state binding over to damnation and guilt. When there is a sinful disposition raging, and bringing us from one degree of sin to another, then there is God's judgment and wrath revealed from heaven against this. Now, when God heals, he heals perfectly, but in some regards slowly, as we shall see hereafter. In regard of forgiveness of sins, he healeth perfectly. But by little and little in regard of the other, of sanctification. He stops up the issues of our corruption by little and little. For other things, and judgments in this world, he removes the malice, and takes away the sting of them, which is the venom ; as he saith afterward, ' For mine anger is turned away,' which being removed and turned from things, then they are no more judgments. What cared Paul for imprisonment, when he knew God's wrath accompanied not the stocks? Acts xvi. 19, *seq.*   Let wrath be taken from the suffering, that the soul be sound, then it is no matter what condition a man be in, he carries heaven and paradise with him.   Therefore, so far God removes those diseases and sicknesses of condition, as they carry venom in them ; so changing the condition, that whatsoever we suffer, it hath the nature of an exercise, medicine, or correction only.   But that which envenoms all, and makes the least cross a curse, and sinks deep, is the anger of God joined with things, Ps. lxxxix. 46.   The least cross, when it carrieth with it the anger and vengeance of God, and reports that to the soul, I have offended God, and it is just with him thus to inflict wrath upon me : this is terrible, and it puts a sting to the cross.   Now, God here promiseth to remove that, ' I will heal their backsliding.'   This principally, in the first place, is meant of healing in regard of justification ; taking away that guilt from the soul which enthrals it, and binds it over to condemnation and judgment.   God will set the soul at a spiritual liberty, and so heal it. Thus you see the point clear, that God is the great physician of the soul.

Reason 1. For God who made the soul, *knows all the diseases, windings, and turnings of it.*   He is an excellent anatomist : 'all things are naked and open before his eyes,' Heb. iv. 13.   He knows the inward part of the soul, the seat of all sin.   We know not ourselves as he knows us.   There is a mystery of self-deceit in the heart, which he knows who can search all the hidden corners of the heart, which is the reason why he is so good a physician, and so excellent.   Because he is a discerner and searcher of the heart, who can see all, and so can cure all, being above the sting of conscience, he hath a remedy above the malady.   He is greater than our conscience.   Therefore he can cure our conscience.

Reason 2. And in the next place, *as he can heal our souls, so he is willing to do it,* which his willingness we may know by the medicine he doth it by, his own dear Son.   He hath provided a plaster of his Son's blood to heal us.   And besides his own inward willingness, being now a gracious father to us in Christ Jesus, he sends his ambassadors to heal and cure us in his name, 2 Cor. v. 20, to apply his medicines, and to beseech and entreat us to be reconciled.   God, by them, entreats us to entreat him for pardon and mercy, and is so willing to be entreated, that ere we shall set out he teacheth us words, as we heard, ' Take unto you words,' &c.   As he is an able, so he is a willing physician.   Christ, the great physician, together with his Father, expects not that we should first come to him, but he comes first, and sends to us.   The physician came to the sick, though for the most part the sick, if able, go to the physician, 1 John iv. 9, 10.   But here is the contrary.   He came from heaven, took our nature upon him, and therein died, by which his blood-shedding, he satisfied the wrath of God, justly offended with us, Isa. liii. 10.   So he heals our souls that way, having undergone the anger and wrath of God, that his blood might quench and appease that anger by a plaster thereof made, and applied to our souls, Isa. liii. 11, 12.

Do we doubt of his willingness, when he comes to us and calls us, ' Come unto me, all ye that labour and are heavy laden, and I will give you rest'? Mat. xi. 28.   It is his office which he hath assumed to heal our soul.   The many cures he hath done sheweth the ability and willingness of the physician ; cures whereof we are incapable, by reason of our mean condition. A king, as his place is greater, so sometimes his sins are greater than others are ; yet he cured Manasseh, that sinful king, 2 Chron. xxxiii. 23, together with Mary Magdalen, Paul, Peter, and the rest, who were a company healed by this physician. Therefore all this is for the glory of our physician. We may see what he can do by what he hath done; as amongst us physicians are sought after according to their skill and cures done. Consider in the sacrament how ready God is to cure and to heal us, how gracious he is in the sacrament of baptism, wherein he engageth us to believe, admitting us into the covenant, and preventing us with mercy, before we knew what a covenant or seal was, Ezek. xvi. 6, *seq.* And so to persuade us of his willingness to forgive our sins and heal our rebellions, he hath ordained the sacrament, not for his sake, but to strengthen our weak faith, and help us. The point is easy for matter of our understanding, but hard in regard of use and application, especially when it should be made use of, in time of temptation. Then let us lay it up as a comfortable point, this gracious promise of God, ' I will heal their backsliding, I will love them freely,' &c. Lay this up against the hour of temptation, make use of it then, alleging unto God his own promise and nature, as David did, ' Lord, remember the promise wherein thou hast caused me to trust,' Ps. cxix. 49. Thou hast promised pardoning and healing [of] all our trangressions, &c. Remember thy free promises made in Jesus Christ. God cannot deny himself nor his word, but loves to have his bonds sued. Remember this. And when conscience is surprised with any sin, though it be never so great, look not on the disease so much as who is the physician, and what his plaster and medicine is. God is the physician, and the blood of Christ is the plaster. What if our sins be mountains! There is an ocean and a sea of mercy to swell above and cover these mountains of our sins, Mic. vii. 18, 19. Our sins in this case are like fire, which, falling into the sea, is by and by quenched. What if our sins be of never so long standing (as these their backslidings here had continued hundreds of years, wherein they were a backsliding generation), yet it is no matter of what standing or continuance the disease is, so long as God hath promised to be the physician, and the blood of Christ is the plaster that healeth us, Isa. i. 18, 19. The question is not, What ? How many ? How great ? and of what continuance our sins ? but how we stand affected towards them, hate them, and resolve against them ? That sin cannot hurt us which we fight against, mourn for, complain of, resolve to leave, and truly hate. Let us never stand, then, in comparisons with our sins, which bear no proportion to the infinite skill and power of our great physician, and to the infinite work of Christ's all-sufficient satisfaction. What canst thou object, O man ? ' It is Christ that justifieth the ungodly, who art thou that condemneth ? It is he that died, yea, rather, who is risen again, who is also at the right hand of God, and also maketh intercession for us,' Rom. viii. 33, 34. Thou canst not satisfy for the least sin. God hath laid upon him the iniquities of us all, Lev. xvi. 21. ' The chastisements of our peace was upon him, and with his stripes we are healed,' Isa. liii. 5.

Let us, therefore, be wise for afterwards, hear, read, lay up, and meditate for the time to come. For times will come, if we belong to God, that nothing will content or pacify the soul but the infinite worth and merit of an infinite and free mercy apprehended in the face of Jesus Christ. When our sins are set in order before us, the sins of our youth, middle, and old age, our sins against conscience, against the law and gospel, against examples, vows, promises, resolutions, and admonitions of the Spirit and

servants of God; when there shall be such a terrible accuser, and God
shall perhaps let the wounds of conscience fly open and join against us;
when wrath shall appear, be in some sort felt, and God presented to the
soul as ' a consuming fire,' Heb. xii. 29, no comfort in heaven or earth
appearing, hell beneath seeming ready to revenge against us the quarrel
of God's covenant, Oh then for faith to look through all these clouds! to
see mercy in wrath! love in correction! Heb. xii. 6, life in death! the
sweetness of the promises! the virtue and merit of Christ's sufferings,
death, resurrection, and intercession at the right hand! the sting of death
removed, 1 Cor. xv. 55, sin pardoned and done away, and glory at hand!
In sum, this promise made good, which leads unto all this happiness, as
we shall by and by hear, ' I will heal their backsliding, I will love them
freely, for mine anger is turned away.' Oh, this is a marvellous matter,
then, to be persuaded of! Therefore let us make a right use of these
words in due season, for they are ' like apples of gold, with pictures of
silver,' Prov. xxv. 11, like balm to a green wound, like delivery in a ship-
wreck. But, indeed, all comparisons come far short of this illustration, as
the terror of incensed wrath in the fearful apprehension of eternal, unspeakable misery, is beyond any other fear, apprehension, or joy.

But lest this grace be abused by others (for we must not withhold the
children's bread, for fear others partake with them unto whom it belongs
not), let them know thus much: that those who turn this grace into wan-
tonness, and will be evil, because God is thus gracious—that there is no
word of comfort in the whole Scripture for them, who stand resolved to go
on in their sins, presuming of mercy. See what God saith in this case,
' Lest there should be among you a root that beareth gall and wormwood;
and it come to pass when he heareth the words of this curse, that he bless
himself in his heart, saying, I shall have peace, though I walk in the imagination of mine heart, to add drunkenness to thirst: the Lord will not
spare him, but then the anger of the Lord and his jealousy shall smoke
against that man, and all the curses that are written in this book shall lie
upon him, and the Lord shall blot out his name from under heaven,' Deut.
xxix. 18–20. 'God will wound the hairy scalp of such an one,' Ps. lxviii.
21, who goes on in his wickedness, and means to be so. And in the New
Testament those who thus make a progress in sin, what do they? They
are said ' to treasure up unto themselves wrath against the day of wrath,
and revelation of the righteous judgment of God,' Rom. ii. 5. Therefore
God's word speaks no comfort to those who purpose to live in any sin.
All the comfort that can be spoken to such is, that yet they are not in
hell; that yet they have time to return to this great Physician of the soul.
But take such an one in his present condition, he can have no comfort in
this estate, wherein there is but a step between him and hell. So as
when the rotten thread of this uncertain life shall fail, or is cut asunder,
down they fall. We have no comfort here for them, till they return.
This precious balm belongs to the wounded conscience. Briefly for
use then.

Use. Seeing that our God is a healing God, as we can admire the wisdom,
skill, and excellency of our physician, so let us much more make use of
him upon all occasions. Trust and cleave to him, not like good Asa (but
not good in this), who forgot himself, and sent first to the physicians,
2 Chron. xvi. 12. But let us especially rely upon God, and look to him,
who can ' create help,' Isa. iv. 5, and must bless all means whatsoever.
He is a healing God, who will heal all rebellions, and the most grievous

sicknesses. He is a physician that is good for all turns. There are some diseases which are called the scorn of physicians, as the gout, the ague, and the like; wherein, in some cases, they are put to a stand, and know not what to do. But God is never at a loss. His skill cannot be set down. He is good at all diseases, to pardon all manner of sins. Therefore let us go to him for cure, seeing there is neither sin, nor grief, nor terror of conscience arising thereupon, which can be so great but God can cure both the sin and the terror, if we take a right course, and speak peace to the soul. God is a healing God, arising when he comes 'with healing in his wings,' Mal. iv. 2. As he saith, 'I will heal their rebellion,' &c. And as he is a healing physician, so he puts his patients to no charge. For as he saith, 'I will heal their backslidings;' so he saith, 'I will love them freely.'

Therefore let us the more build upon this truth, which is indeed the sum of all godliness. For what is the gospel but the triumph of mercy? Do but consider the scope of God in the new covenant, whereof the sacrament is a seal, which is only to shew forth the exaltation of the grace and mercy of God in Jesus Christ, above all unworthiness whatsoever. For all there is for the glory of his mercy. For in the covenant of grace, mercy doth triumph against judgment and justice; which mercy of God in Christ is said by the apostle 'to reign unto life everlasting, by Jesus Christ our Lord,' Rom. v. 21. It reigns, and hath a regiment* above, and over all. For mercy in God stirred up his wisdom to devise a way, by shedding of the blood of Christ Jesus, God-man, to satisfy divine justice, and rejoice against it. But whence comes this, that justice should be so satisfied? Because a way is found out, how none of God's attributes are losers by mercy. Wherefore in any temptation, when we are prone to doubt of God's love, say, What! shall we wrong God more, by calling in question his mercy, and the excellency of his lovingkindness, which is more than any other sin we have committed? This is a sin superadded against his mercy, power, goodness, graciousness, and love in healing of sin; which takes away the glory of God in that attribute, wherein he labours to triumph, reign, and glorify himself most, and 'which is over all his works,' Ps. cxlv. 9. Therefore he that offends herein, in denying God the glory of his great, tender, unspeakable mercy, whereby he would glorify himself most in the covenant of grace, he offends God most.

Therefore let us, at such times as God awakens conscience, be so far from thinking that God is unwilling to cure and help us, as to think that hereby we shall honour God more by believing than we dishonoured him by our sin. For the faith of an humble, contrite sinner, it glorifies God more than our better obedience in other things doth; because it gives him the glory of that wherein he delights, and will be most glorified, the glory of his mercy and truth, of his rich, abundant mercy that hath no bounds. There is no comparison between the mercy of God in the covenant of grace, and that to Adam in the state of nature. For in the first he did good to a good man; first he made him good, and then did him good. But when man did degenerate, and was fallen into such a cursed estate as we are, for God then to be good to a sinner, and freely to do good, here is goodness indeed, triumphant goodness. Cain was a cursed person, who said, 'My punishment is greater than can be borne,' Gen. iv. 13. We know who spake it. No; God is a physician for all diseases. If they be 'crimson sins,' he can make them 'white as wool,' Isa. i. 18.

That is, 'government.'—G.

Who would not be careful therefore to search his wounds, his sins to the bottom ? Let the search be as deep as we can, considering that there is more mercy in God, than there can be sin in us. Who would favour his soul ? especially considering, if he neglect searching of it, sins will grow deadly and incurable upon that neglect. Let this therefore encourage us not to spare ourselves, in opening the wounds of our souls to God, that he may spare all. Thus we saw formerly, the church here is brought in dealing plainly with God, and confessing all (for she had an excellent teacher), and God answers all ; beginning with this, ' I will heal their backsliding.' They were idolaters, and guilty of the sins of the second table in a high measure (no petty sins), yet God saith, ' I will heal their backsliding,' &c. Which being healed, then an open highway is made for all other mercies whatsoever, which is the next point we observe hence :

Obs. That the chief mercy of all, which leads unto all the rest, is the pardon and forgiveness of sins.

Healing of the guilt of sin, we see, is set in the front of these petitions formerly shewed ; which as it is the first thing in the church's desire, ' Take away all iniquity,' &c, so it is the first thing yielded to in God's promise, ' I will heal their backsliding,' &c. Pardon of sin, and cure of sin, whereby the conscience ceaseth to be bound over to condemnation, is the first and chiefest blessing of God, and is that for which the church falls out in a triumph. ' Who is a God like unto thee, that pardoneth iniquity, and passeth by the transgression of the remnant of his heritage, because he delighteth in mercy,' &c., Micah vii. 18, 19, 20. And this is that excellent and sweet conclusion of the new covenant also, whereupon all the rest of those former foregoing mercies there are grounded. For, ' I will forgive their iniquity, and I will remember their sin no more,' Jer. xxxi. 34. Yea, this is the effect of that grand promise made to his church after the return of their captivity. ' In those days, and at that time, saith the Lord, the iniquity of Israel shall be sought for, and there shall be none ; and the sins of Judah, and they shall not be found ; for I will pardon them whom I reserve,' Jer. l. 20. The point is plain and clear enough ; it needs no following. The reason is,

Because it takes away the interposing cloud. God is gracious in himself. Pardon of sin removes the cloud betwixt God's gracious face and the soul. Naturally, God is a spring of mercy ; but our sins stop the spring. But when sin is pardoned, the stop is taken away, and the spring runs amain. God is not merciful as a flint yields fire, by force ; but as a spring, whence water naturally issues.

Quest. Seeing forgiveness of sins unstops this spring, why do we not feel this mercy ?

Ans. Surely, because some sin or other is upon the file uncancelled,* perhaps unconfessed ; or because we are stuffed with pride, that we believe not ; or are so troubled, or trouble ourselves, that we apprehend not, or believe not the pardon of sins confessed and hated. But sure it is, forgiveness of sins unstops the spring of mercy, and unveils God's gracious face in Jesus Christ unto us. Sin being not pardoned, this stops, as the prophet speaks. Our iniquity is that which keeps good things from us. Therefore the chief mercy is that which removes, that which unstops the current of all mercy. ' I will heal their backsliding,' &c. Look at a condemned prisoner in the tower ! Let him have all contentment ; as long as he is in the displeasure of the prince, stands condemned, and the sentence

* See note *b*, vol. I., p. 289.—G.

unreversed, what true contentment can he have? None at all. So it is
with a sinner, that hath not his pardon and *quietus est* from heaven. Yield
him all contentment which the world can afford; all the satisfaction that
can issue from the creature; yet what is this to him, as long as he hath
not mercy, and that his conscience is not pacified, because it is not cleansed
and washed with the blood of Christ?

Sin is like Jonah: whilst he was in the ship, there was nothing but tem-
pest, Jonah i. 4; like Achan in the army, Joshua vii. 11, 12: whilst he
was not found out, God's judgment followed the camp. Sin is that which
troubleth all. Therefore it must be taken away first; and therewith all
evil is taken away. Therefore, the first mercy is a forgiving, pardoning,
and quieting mercy. When the blood of Jesus Christ, by the hand of faith,
is sprinkled upon the soul, God creating a hand of faith to sprinkle and shed
it upon the soul, ' Christ loved me, and gave himself for me,' then the
soul saith, Though my sins be great, yet the satisfaction of Christ is
greater. God hath loved me, and gave his own Son for me; and I apply
this to myself, as it is offered to me, and take the offer. This pacifieth the
soul, as it is written, ' The blood of Christ, who through the eternal Spirit
offered himself without spot to God, is that which purgeth our conscience
from dead works to serve the living God,' Heb. ix. 14. To a repentant
sinner, this ' blood of sprinkling speaks better things than the blood of
Abel,' Heb. xii. 24: not as his blood cried for vengeance, but mercy,
mercy. When the soul is thus pacified, there is the foundation of all other
mercy whatsoever. The order is this: when God is reconciled, all is reconciled; when God is at peace with us in the forgiveness of sins, then all is
peaceable at home and abroad. Conscience is in peace within, and all the
creatures at peace without; all which, with all that befalls us, have a command to do us no hurt; as David gave charge to the people, of Absalom.
When God is reconciled and at peace, all things are at peace with us. For
is not he Lord of hosts, who hath the command of all the creatures? Therefore this grace of forgiveness is the chief grace.

To shew it in one instance more. David was a king and a prophet, a
comely and a valorous person. But what esteemed he most? Did he
say, Blessed is the man who is a king, or a prophet, or a valiant warrior,
or hath dominion, obedience, or great possessions, as I have? Oh, no.
' Blessed is the man whose sins are forgiven, and whose iniquities are
covered,' Ps. xxxii. 1. You see wherein this holy man David sets and
pitcheth happiness, in the forgiveness of sins. Blessed is such a man.
Though he were a king, he knew well enough that if his sins were not pardoned and covered he had been a wretched man.

Use 1. Therefore, this should teach us to desire of God continually *the
pardon of our sins;* and we should make it the chief desire of our souls
that God would shine upon them in Jesus Christ, pardon and accept us in
his beloved. They go together.

Use 2. And *bless him for this above all other blessings,* as it is Ps. ciii.
1, 3, ' Bless the Lord, O my soul; and all that is within me, bless his holy
name,' &c. Why? ' Who forgiveth all thy iniquities, and healeth all thy
diseases.' We should bless God most of all for this, that he hath devised
a way by Christ to receive satisfaction for sin, to pardon it, and say unto
our souls, ' I am thy salvation,' Ps. xxxv. 3. This is the greatest favour
of all.

Quest. But you ask, How shall I know that God hath healed my soul in
regard of the forgiveness of sins?

Ans. The answer is, *If, together with pardon of sin, he heal sin.* For God, when he takes away the venom of a wound that endangers death, the deadly disease, he takes away also the swelling of the wound and glowing of it. When he ceaseth to make it deadly, he heals the soul withal, and *subdues our iniquities*, as his promise is, Micah vii. 19. So there is, together with pardoning mercy, curing mercy in regard of sanctification. Where God is a Father to make us sons, he is a Father to beget us anew. So where Christ comes by blood to wash away our sins, he comes by water also and the Holy Ghost; where he is a Comforter in the forgiveness of sins, he is a sanctifier. And the soul of a distressed sinner looks to the one as well as the other. Ask the soul of any man who is truly humbled, What do you chiefly desire? Oh, that God would pardon my sins! But is that all? No; that he would also heal my sins and subdue my rebellions, that I may not any longer be under the government and tyranny of my lusts, but under God's gracious government, who will guide me better than before, Hos. ii. 7. This we see to be the order in the Lord's prayer. After we are taught to say, 'Forgive us our trespasses,' it follows, 'And lead us not into temptation, but deliver us from evil,' which is for the time to come, Mat. vi. 12, 13. So David, 'Cleanse me from my secret sins, and keep me, that presumptuous sins have not dominion over me,' &c., Ps. xix. 12, 13. So that this is the desire of an afflicted conscience truly humbled, curing as well as covering of sin. This is a sure evidence that our sins are pardoned.

2. Then again, *when there is peace:* when the soul feels this, it is a sign that God hath healed the soul. 'For,' saith the apostle, 'being justified by faith, we have peace with God through our Lord Jesus Christ,' Rom. v. 1. The blood of Christ hath a pacifying power in forgiveness of sins. When Jonah was cast out, there was a calm, Jonah i. 12; so when sin is cast out and pardoned, there is a calm in the soul, which comes from the forgiveness of sins.

3. Again, healing is known by this, *if we have hearts willing to be searched,* for then our will is cured, which in the state of grace is more than our obedience. When we would be better than we are, then certainly our will is not in league with corruptions. Now, where the will is so much sanctified, I resolve to be better, I would be better, and I use all means, being glad when any joins with me against my corruptions, I am glad of all such advantages, here is a good sign. As now, when a man goes to church, and desires, 'O that my corruptions might be met withal! O that I might be laid open to myself, and know myself better than I have formerly done!' this is the desire of an ingenuous soul. Where there is no guile of soul, a man is glad to have himself and his corruptions discovered, whereas another frets and kicks, and rageth against the word of God, which is a sign that there is some league betwixt him and his sin. You have some that, above all things in the world, they would not have such and such downright ministers. O take heed; this is a sign of a hollow heart, and that a man is in love with his disease. Can there be a cure where there is a love of the disease?

4. Not to name many, the last, which is a high pitch, shall be, *by our estimation of things here and above.* What hath this healing wrought in thee? What estimation of things? How is thy heart weaned from the world? How are thy affections set on things which are above? Col. iii. 1. When a sick man is soundly recovered, though his distempered palate could not relish the best meats in his sickness, yet now he relishes and

loves the best most of all. Look, then, to ourselves. How forget we,
with blessed St Paul, ' the things which are behind, pressing hard to the
mark which is before, for the high prize of that calling' ? Philip. iii. 13.
How stand we affected, to long for our country? this world being only the
place of our pilgrimage. Surely a soul that is soundly healed is an undervaluing soul, to use this world and all things therein as though we used
them not; and it is also a valuing soul, to covet spiritual things above all,
1 Cor. vii. 29, 31. ' O,' saith David, ' how I love thy law, it is my meditation all the day; I love thy commandments above gold, yea, above fine
gold,' Ps. cxix. 97, 127. The joy of this estate ' is a joy unspeakable and
glorious,' 1 Pet. i. 8, of which 'it is said ' the stranger shall not meddle
with,' Pro. xiv. 10. Thus much concerning the disease. Before we come
to the cure a question ariseth.

Quest. Whence, then, comes a calm in a carnal person ?

Ans. From ignorance and deadness of conscience, or from diversion.
As a sick man, when he talks with another man that is his friend, his mind
is diverted that he feeleth not his sickness all the while, so wicked men,
either their consciences are seared, and they go on in sin, or else they have
diversions. Great persons are loath to hear, and are usually full of diversions from the time they rise till they sleep again. All diversions busy
conscience about other things; so they keep themselves, that it may not
trouble them. But the peace of a true Christian comes from another
ground, from sound knowledge of his disease, and from sound satisfaction,
by faith knowing Christ, the Spirit of God sealing this knowledge to the
soul. If peace be thus settled, it is a sign of a sound cure.

Quest. But you will say, How shall I know that my sins are pardoned
when I am subject to those sins still ?

Ans. Not to speak of transient actual sins, that are past and pardoned,
when we have repented of them ; but of the root of all sin, which is weakness and corruption in us, fortified, and, as it were, intrenched by nature,
occasions and custom. Of this the question is, How to discern of pardon,
the root of sin remaining, and now and then foiling us? The answer is
affirmative. We may have that sin pardoned, which yet occasionally may
foil us still. For a man is in the state of health, though he have the dregs
of a disease hanging upon him, whereby a man ofttimes hath some little fit
of the disease. When nature and physic hath prevailed over the disease,
yet after that, there may be grudgings. So when God hath cured the soul
by pardon, and hath begun to cure in sanctification, the cure is wrought,
though some dregs remain, because those dregs are carried away with daily
physic, and daily flying to God, ' Lord, forgive our debts ; Lord, heal us.'
Every prayer and renewing of repentance carries some debt away, till
death comes, that excellent physician, which once for all perfectly
cures both soul and body, bringing both there where both shall have
perfection.

Quest. But you will say, Is God's grace weak, that it cannot carry away
all dregs of corruption as well as pardon ? Why is pardon in the forgiveness of sins absolute, when yet God suffers the dregs to remain, so as we
still are subject to the disease of sin ?

Ans. God is wise. Let us not quarrel with our physician, for he is
wiser than we ourselves. For he makes these relics medicinal to us, as
thus : naturally we are prone to security and spiritual pride, therefore he
makes a medicine of our infirmities, to cure spiritual pride and security,
and to set us a-work. Therefore the Jebusites, and the residue of that

kind, were left uncast out from among Israel, that thereby he might prove Israel, and lest they should be a prey unto wild beasts to devour them, Judges iii. 1. So some remainders of the flesh are left still in the best, that these wild beasts might not prey upon their souls. Spiritual pride, which is a detestable sin, robbing and denying God of his prerogative, and security, the grave of the soul, to cure these two especially, God makes the relics and remainders of sin a medicine unto us.

Quest. Why doth God suffer these infirmities and diseases to remain in us ?

Ans. Diseases are suffered, to put us in mind of infirmities in the root, which we knew not before. For if these should not sometimes break forth into a disease, we would think our nature were pure. Therefore God suffers them to break forth into diseases. Who would have thought that Moses had been passionate ? Certainly, himself did not know himself, at the waters of strife, that the seeds of anger should be in the meekest man in the world ! Num. xx. 2. Who would have thought that David, whose heart smote him for cutting off the lap of Saul's garment, 1 Sam. xxiv. 4, that so mild a man should have cruelty in him, and yet after that he committed murder ? Who would have thought that Peter, who made such protestations of love to Christ, that though all men forsook him, yet he would not ; yet after that should deny his Master, and forswear him ? Matt. xxiii. 33, 69, &c. All which was to shew us, that it is useful for us sometimes to have our corruptions break out, to put us in mind what inward weaknesses we have unknown and unsearched in us, and that we may know the depth of our corruption. God's children are gainers by all their infirmities and weaknesses, whereby they learn to stand stronger. Here is a main difference betwixt the slips of God's children, and the ordinary evil courses of others. They grow worse and worse. The oftener they fall into sin, the more they are settled upon their dregs. But God's child hath the remainders of corruption in him, from whence he hath infirmities, and whence he breaks into diseases. But notwithstanding, corruption is a loser hereby. For the oftener he falls into sin, it is the weaker and weaker. For the more he sees the root of it, the more he hates it, resolves and strives against it, till it be consummated by repentance and sanctifying grace. Let no man therefore be too much cast down for infirmities, though ofttimes they break out, if thereupon we find a renewed hatred, repentance, and strength against them. For God looks not so much, how much corruption there is in us, as how we stand affected to it, and what good there is, whether we be in league with it, and resist it. It is not sin that damns men, but sin with the ill qualities, sin unconfessed, not grieved for, and unresisted, else God hath holy ends in leaving corruption in us, to exercise, try us, and keep us from other sins. Therefore sin is left uncured.

Now the way to have it cured, both in the pardon and likewise in sanctification, we have it in the context. What doth God say ? ' I will heal their backsliding,' &c. After they had searched their hearts, and thereupon found iniquity, and then prayed, ' Take away all iniquity ;' after they had desired a divorce from their sins, ' Asshur shall not save us ;' and when they had some faith that God would cure them, and accordingly put confidence in God, ' the Father of the fatherless ;' then saith God, ' I will heal their backsliding.' So that sense of pardon in the forgiveness of sins, and sense of grace, comes after sight, sense, weariness, and confession of sin. God doth not pardon sin, when it is not seen, sorrowed for, nor confessed, and where there is not some degree of faith, to come to God, ' the

Father of the fatherless,' and the great Physician of souls. When we do this, as it is said in the context, then we find the forgiveness of sins, with the gracious power of God's Spirit healing of our diseases, 'I will heal their backsliding.'

Let us therefore remember this, lest we deceive our souls, for it is not so easy a thing to attain unto forgiveness of sins as we think.

And then again, though forgiveness of sins be free, yet notwithstanding there is a way whereby we come to forgiveness of sins that costs us somewhat. God humbles the soul first, brings a man to himself, to think of his course, to lay open his sins and spread them before God in confession, and working upon the soul hearty repentance; so to come to God, and wait for forgiveness of sins, perhaps a good while before there be a report of it. There are none who have sins forgiven, but they know how they come by it. For there is a predisposition wrought in man's soul by the Spirit, which teacheth him what estate he is in, and what his danger is, whereupon follows confession; and upon that, peace. God keeps his children many times a long while upon the rack before he speaks peace unto them in the forgiveness of sins, because he would not have them think slightly of the riches of his mercy. It is no easy matter to attain unto the sense of the forgiveness of sins, though indeed we should strive to attain it, that so we may walk in the comforts of the Holy Ghost. The difficulty of obtaining or recovering the sense of forgiveness, may be seen in David after his fall. Did he easily obtain sense of pardon? Oh no! God held him on the rack a long time, 'He roared all the day long, his moisture was turned into the drought of summer,' Ps. xxxii. 3, 4. But when he had resolved a thorough, and no slight, confession; when he had resolved to shame himself and glorify God; then saith he, 'And thou forgavest my sin.' But till he dealt thoroughly with his soul without all guile, he felt no comfort. So it is with the children of God. When in the state of grace they fall into sin, it is no slight 'Lord, have mercy upon me' that will serve the turn; but a thorough shaming of themselves before God, and a thorough confession, resolving and determining to be under another government; to have Christ to govern them as well as to pardon them. God will no otherwise do it. Because he would glorify his rich mercy herein; for who would give mercy its due glory, if forgiveness were easily attained, without shaming of ourselves? If it came easily, without protestation and waiting upon God, as the church here, we should never be thoroughly humbled for our sins, and God would never have the glory of his mercy, nor known to be so just in hating of sin in his dear children, who long ago upon such terms have attained sense of forgiveness of sins. It is worth our trouble to search our souls and to wait at Christ's feet, never to give over until we have attained the sense of forgiveness of sin. It is heaven upon earth to have our consciences enlarged with God's favour in the pardon of sin.

What is the reason that many profess that God is merciful, and Christ hath pardoned their sins, &c.? If the ground be right, it is a high conceit of mercy; and such have been soundly humbled for their sins. But dost thou profess so, who livest carelessly in thy sins, and licentiously still? Surely * thy ground is naught, for hadst thou been upon the rack, in God's scalding-house, and smarted soundly for sin, wouldst thou take pleasure still to live in sin? Oh no! Those that go on carelessly in their actions and speeches, not caring what they are, did they ever smart for sin,

* That is, ' assuredly.'—G.

who carry themselves thus ? Surely these were never soundly humbled for sin, nor confessed them with loathing and detestation. Therefore let us mark the context here inferred. After they had confessed, prayed, and waited, resolving reformation in their false confidence, then God promiseth, 'I will heal their backsliding.' It is a fundamental error in a Christian course, the slighting of true humiliation, which goes along in all the fabric and frame of a Christian course. Let a man not be soundly humbled with the sight of his sins, his faith is weaker, and his sanctification and comfort the slighter. Whereas, if a man would deal truly with his own heart, set up a court there, and arraign, judge, and condemn himself (which is God's end in all his dealings, afflictions, and judgments inflicted upon us), the deeper we went in this course, the more would our comfort be, and the report of God's mercy, in the sense of that which follows, 'I will love them freely : for mine anger is turned away.'

THE SIXTH SERMON.

I will love them freely : for mine anger is turned away. I will be as the dew unto Israel ; he shall grow as the lily, and cast forth his root as Lebanon. —Hos. XIV. 4, 5.

IT was a good speech of St Austin, ' Those that are to petition great persons, they will obtain some who are skilful, to frame their petitions ; lest by their unskilfulness they provoke anger, instead of carrying away the benefit desired.' So it is here with God's people, being to deal with the great God, and not being able to frame their own petitions, God, as we heard before, doth it for them, and answers them graciously with the same mercies which he had suggested them to ask ; his answer being exact to their petitions, 'I will heal their backsliding, I will love them freely,' &c., wherein God exceeds all physicians in the world whatsoever. For they have nature to help them. Physic is the midwife of nature, helping it to do that which it cannot do itself. Physic can do nothing to a dead man. But God is so great a physician, that he first gives life, and after that spiritual life is in some degrees begun ; by little and little he heals more and more. ' I will heal their backslidings.'

We have an error crept in amongst some of the meaner, ignorant sort of people, who think that God sees no sin when he hath once pardoned men in justification ; who falsely smooth themselves in this wicked, sensual conceit, think they can commit no sin offensive to God ; as though God should frame such a justification for men, to blindfold him, and cast dust, as it were, in his eyes ; or justify men, to make them loose and idle. No ; it is false, as appeareth by this place ; for how can God heal that he sees not ? He sees it not to be revenged on them for it ; but he sees sin, to correct it and to heal it. He sees it not after a revengeful, wrathful justice, to cast us into hell and damn us for it ; but he sees it after a sort, to make us smart and lament for it, and to have many times a bitter sense of his wrath and forsaking, as men undone without a new supply of comfort and peace from heaven. Let a man neglect sanctification, daily sorrow and confession of sin, and now and then even craving new pardon for sins past, casting all upon a fantastic conceit of faith in their justification : what follows but pride, hardness of heart, contempt of others, and neglect of better than themselves, and proneness out of God's judgment, to fall from ill to worse, from one error to another? In this case the heart is false and deceitful. For whilst it pretends a glorious faith to look back to Christ, to live by faith, and lay all on him by justification, it winds itself out of all tasks of religion, sets the heart at liberty, neglects sanctification and mortification of lusts, and beautifying the image of God in them, giving too much way to the flesh. Therefore, away with this false and self-conceited opinion, which draws poison out of that which God speaks to confirm and stablish us, ' That he sees no iniquity in Jacob,' &c., Num. xxiii. 21. Whence from these hyperbolical speeches, they think that God seeth not that which we ourselves see. But, ' He heals our backslidings,' therefore he sees them. For how can he heal a wound, if he see it not? He sees it, but not to their destruction who are freely justified by his grace. But we will leave this point, it being too much honour to them to spend time in confutation of it, and will rather say unto it, as Isaiah speaks of a menstruous cloth, ' Get thee hence,' Isa. xxx. 22.

Now as God is a most gracious God, never weary of well-doing and comforting his people, because it is his nature to be merciful, so he hath suitable expressions of it; he goes on with mercy upon mercy, lovingkindness upon lovingkindness. He had promised before, ' I will heal their backslidings,' take in sum all their apostasy, all shall be healed. But this is not all. He answers all the accusations and doubts of Satan, who is still objecting against us our unworthiness, misery, wretchedness to have such favours conferred on such filthy creatures. Therefore, he takes off all with this which followeth. As they had prayed, ' Receive us graciously ;' so the answer is full, and suitable to their request, ' I will love them freely.'

Put case, they out of conscience of their own guilt should see no worth in themselves, or cause why they should be respected, yet I see reason in mine own love. ' I will love them freely.'

Quest. But may some say, How can God love freely?

Ans. Ask thyself. Doth not a father and mother love their child freely? What doth the child deserve of the father and mother a great while? Nothing. But the mother hath many a weary night and foul hand with it. Hath God planted an affection in us to love our children freely; and shall not God much more, who gives this love and plants it in us, be admitted to love freely? But indeed there is absurdity and infidelity in distrust. For it is against reason, to deny the mighty God that which we have in ourselves. If he did not love freely, how could he love us at all? What could he foresee in us to love for beforehand? The very manhood of Christ deserved not the grace of union, it was freely given.

' I will love them freely.' That which, first of all, we observe hence is thus much, *that God loves his people freely.* So saith the apostle, ' God commendeth his love towards us, in that while we were yet sinners, Christ died for us ; much more being justified by his blood, we shall be saved from wrath through him,' Rom. v. 8, 9. The like we have in Ezekiel. Saith God, ' Therefore, say unto the house of Israel, Thus saith the Lord God, I do not this for your sakes, O house of Israel, but for mine holy name's sake, which ye have profaned among the heathen whither ye went,' Ezek. xxxvi. 22. Adam when he had sinned that main, great sin, what did he? Fly from God, run away; and when God called to him, and debated the matter with him, he accused God, and excused himself, Gen.

iii. 12, 13. Yet for all this God pitied him, and clothed him, and made him that promise of the blessed seed. What desert was there here in Adam! nay, rather the quite contrary; yet God loved him freely. The same may be said of St Paul, for the time past a persecutor, what deserving was there in him? None at all; yet he found God's free love in his conversion; for, saith God to Ananias, 'He is a chosen vessel unto me, to bear my name before the Gentiles,' Acts ix. 15. Here was no deserving in St Paul, but God's free election, which in time took place, Acts ix. 5. And so we may say of the prodigal, having spent all, his father pardoned all, and loved him freely, Luke xv. 20.

Reason 1. The reason hereof is, *because it is his name and nature to be gracious*, and to love freely; and whatsoever is God's nature, that hath a freedom in the working.

Reason 2. *Because no creature can deserve anything at God's hands.* (1.) Because by nature we are all God's enemies; and therefore what can enemies deserve? Nothing but wrath and vengeance. (2.) If we have any graces, they are the gift of God; and therefore we deserve nothing by them, they being of his own gift. So St James speaks, 'Every good gift, and every perfect gift, is from above, and cometh down from the Father of lights, with whom is no variableness, nor shadow of turning,' James i. 17. And St Paul saith, 'That of him, and through him, and to him, are all things,' Rom. xi. 36. What should follow hereupon? 'To him be glory for ever.'

Use 1. This, in the *first place*, serves for *reproof of our adversaries of the Romish Church*, who say that God loves us for something foreseen in us, which is good, or for somewhat which in time we would do to deserve favour at his hands. But both are false. The cause of love is free from himself; for, 'when we have done our best,' yet, saith the Holy Ghost, 'we are unprofitable servants.' Luke xvii. 10.

Use 2. *Secondly*, It is for reproof of *God's own dear children*, who, because they find no deserving in themselves, are therefore discouraged at the sight of their own unworthiness; whereas, quite contrary, the sight of our own unworthiness should make us the more fit subjects for Christ's free love, which hath nothing to do with them that stand upon deserving. Many of God's dear children are troubled with temptations, doubts, and fears of God's love and favour towards them, because they expect to find it in the fruits of grace, and not in free grace itself. If we would have any sound peace, let us look for it in free grace. Therefore the blessed apostle, in the entrance of his salutations in his epistles, still joineth grace, and then peace, to shew us that if we look for sound peace, we can nowhere find it but in grace. We would find peace in the grace that is in us, but it is labour in vain, for we shall never find it but in free grace.

Use 3. Hence we may also be *comforted in the certainty of our salvation;* for that grace, and love, and favour, whereby we are saved, is in God, not in us. Now, whatsoever is in him is immutable and sure. So saith the apostle, 'Nevertheless, the foundation of God standeth sure, having this seal, the Lord knoweth them that are his; and let every one that nameth the name of Christ depart from iniquity,' 2 Tim. ii. 19. Where speaking of election, which comes from the free love of God, he makes that a sure foundation to build on. If there be a reformation 'to depart from iniquity,' we may be comfortably assured of our salvation. And as it is with election, so is it with all the other fruits of God's love: vocation, adoption, justification, and perseverance. The foundation of God, fastly

sealed in the way of holiness, stands good and sure in all, Rom. iii. 24 ;
John xiii. 1.

Use 4. This further teacheth us *thankfulness unto God*, who hath so
freely loved us ; for if there were deserving on our part, what place were
left for thankfulness ?   We know, one who deserves nothing, and hath
small matters bestowed upon him, at least will be thankful for such favours.
But when one is so far from deserving anything, that by the contrary he
deserveth all plagues and punishments, hath yet many and abundant mercies bestowed freely upon him, this doth exceedingly provoke (especially a
generous spirit) to a suitable thankfulness, as much as may be.

Use 5. And let it likewise breed *confidence in us to God, in all our
miseries*, both for pardon of sin, help in distress, and comfort in sorrows,
because he ' loves us freely,' and did love us whilst we were enemies.
Make, therefore, upon all occasions, the apostle's use of it.   ' For if, when
we were enemies, we were reconciled to God by the death of his Son, much
more, being reconciled, we shall be saved by his life,' Rom. v. 10.

' I will love them freely.'

In the next place, from hence we observe another point, which necessarily followeth upon the former,—*that God did not then begin to love them,
when he said, ' I will love them freely;' but to discover that love unto them,
which he carried unto them from all eternity.*   For instance hereof, St Paul
was beloved of God, ere God manifested his love unto him ; as he testifieth
to himself, that the discovery of this free love was, ' when it pleased God,
who separated me from my mother's womb, and called me by his grace, to
reveal his son in me,' &c., Gal. i. 15, 16.   So the apostle blesseth God,
in his salutation unto them, ' who had blessed them with all spiritual
blessings in heavenly places in Christ,' Eph. i. 3.   But whence fetcheth
he the ground hereof ?   ' According as he hath chosen us in him, before
the foundatiom of the world, that we should be holy and unblameable
before him in love,' verse 4.   We need not multiply places more to prove
it.   Our adversaries would fain seem to clear God only in all,* and so
shroud their arguments under such needless pretences, shift off all places,
name we never so many, with their strong heads, distinctions, and sophisms.
But God will one day give them no thanks for their labour : the will of God
(how unequal soever in our eyes, who cannot with our shallow conceits sound
the depth of such mysteries) being ground enough to justify all his actions
whatsoever.   We will therefore come to some reasons of the point.

Reason 1. Because *whatsoever is in God*, manifested in time, *is eternal and
everlasting in him, without beginning and ending ;* for whatsoever is in God
is God.   God is not loving, but love, 1 John iv. 8 ; and he is not only
true, but truth itself, John xiv. 6.   He is not wise only, but wisdom itself,
1 Cor. i. 24.   And therefore his love, discovered in time, must needs be
from all eternity.

Secondly, If God did then first begin to love us, when he manifested his
love unto us, *then there should be a change in God*, because he should love
them now that he did not formerly love.   As we see, those who loved Paul
after his conversion loved him not before.   There was then a change in
the church.   In which case, if God should so love, he should be changeable, and so be like unto man.

Thirdly, And then, again, *Christ's prayer*, John xvii., *makes it clear* that
the love of God beginneth not with the manifestation thereof ; for Christ
there, knowing all the Father's secrets, as coming out of the bosom of the

* That is, ' would fain seem only to clear God in all.'—G.

Father, intimates the contrary, where he makes one end of his prayer for them to be, ' That the world may know that thou hast loved them, as thou hast loved me,' John xvii. 23. Now, how he loved Christ is also shewed a little after, ' For thou lovedst me before the foundation of the world,' verse 24. Therefore the saints and children of God are loved with an everlasting former love, not beginning at that instant discovery thereof.

Use 1. The use hereof is, first of all, against those *who measure God's love and favour by their own feeling*, because, as God loved them before, so he loves them as well and as dearly still ; when he hideth his face from them, as when he suffered his lovingkindness to shine most comfortably upon them. He loved Christ as dearly when he hanged on the tree, in torment of soul and body, as he did when he said,' This is my beloved son, in whom I am well pleased,' Mat. iii. 17 ; yea, and when he received him up into glory. The sun shineth as clearly in the darkest day as it doth in the brightest. The difference is not in the sun, but in some clouds which hinder the manifestation of the light thereof. So God loveth us as well when he shineth not in the brightness of his countenance upon us as when he doth. Job was as much beloved of God in the midst of his miseries as he was afterwards when he came to enjoy the abundance of his mercies, Job xlii. 7.

' I will love them freely,' &c.

The last point which we gather from hence, as a special ground of comfort, is this,

That this free love and favour of God is the cause of all other mercies and free favours, whereby he discovereth his love unto us.

(1.) It is the cause *of election*, ' Even so, then, at this present time also there is a remnant, according to the election of grace,' Rom. xi. 5. So (2.), For *vocation*. When the apostle had shewed that the Ephesians were saved by grace, he adds, ' That in the ages to come he might shew the exceeding riches of his grace, in his kindness towards us through Christ Jesus,' Eph. ii. 7. He afterwards sheweth, when this grace began first to have being, ' For we are his workmanship, created unto good works, which God hath before ordained that we should walk therein,' Eph. ii. 10. (3.) *Forgiveness of sins*. ' In whom we have a redemption through his blood, even the forgiveness of sins, according to the riches of his grace.' Eph. i. 7. So (4.), For the *grace of love*. ' We love him because he loved us first,' 1 John iv. 19. (5.) For *justification and sanctification*. It is said ' that Christ hath loved us.' Why ? ' For he hath washed us from our sins in his own blood,' Rev. i. 5 ; and St John saith, ' He hath made us kings and priests unto God and his Father.' [1.] Kings to fight against the world, the flesh, and the devil. [2.] Priests to teach, instruct, reprove, and comfort ourselves and others by the word of God, and then to offer up the sacrifice of a broken heart, in prayers and praises. All comes from freedom of love. (6.) So *every good inclination* comes hence, ' for it is God which worketh in us, both to will and to do of his good pleasure,' Phil. ii. 13. So (7.) *Every good work*. ' For we are his workmanship, created in Christ Jesus unto good works, which he had before ordained that we should walk therein,' ' for by grace ye are saved,' saith he, ' through faith,' Eph. ii. 8, 10. So (8.) For *eternal life*. The apostle sheweth, ' It is the gift of God, through Jesus Christ our Lord,' Rom. vi. 23.

Use 1. This should teach us, in the first place, *to be humbled*, in that we are so miserable, naughty servants, doing so little work, nay, nothing as we

should, yet should have so good wages. But ' God loves us freely,' &c.
It should rather humble us the more than puff us up in pride, in regard
that there was nothing in us which might deserve anything at God's hand,
1 Cor. iv. 7; Eph. ii. 9.

Use 2. And hence also it followeth that if he loved us from everlasting
with a free love, John xvii. 23, 24, in a sort as he loved Christ, that therefore the *effects of his love towards us shall never fail,* as the apostle sheweth,
' The gifts and calling of God are without repentance,' Rom. xi. 29.   Faith
and repentance, being fruits of his love wrought in us, shall hold out. Therefore the weakness of these graces, as they shall not hinder our salvation,
no more should they discourage us, or hinder the comfort of our profession; because that faith and repentance which we have is not any work
of ours, but the work of God's free love in us.   Therefore they shall be
continued and accepted.   For our perseverance doth not stand in this, that
we have strength in ourselves to continue faithful to God, but because he,
out of his free love, continueth faithful to us, and will never fail nor forsake
them whom he hath once taken into his everlasting favour, on whom he
hath set his everlasting free love, as the apostle speaks of Christ, ' Who
also shall confirm you unto the end, that ye may be blameless in the day
of our Lord Jesus Christ.'   But upon what ground ?   ' God is faithful, by
whom we were called unto the fellowship of his Son, Jesus Christ our Lord,'
1 Cor. i. 8, 9. So that if any of the elect should fall away, God should be un-
faithful.   The case in perseverance is not how faithful we are, but how faithful God is, who ' guides us here with his counsel in all things, and afterwards receiveth us into glory,' Ps. lxxiii. 24. So in another place, after
the apostle had prayed, ' Now the very God of peace sanctify you wholly ;
and I pray God your whole spirit and soul and body be preserved blameless unto the coming of the Lord Jesus Christ.'   What maketh the ground
of this his prayer ?   ' Faithful is he that calleth you, who also will do it,'
1 Thess. v. 23, 24.

Use 3. If, then, we would have God to manifest his free love to us, let us
strive to be *obedient to his commandments,* and stir up our hearts by all means
to love him who hath so freely loved us.

Quest. Now, how should we manifest our love toward God ?

Ans. First, in *loving his word,* as Ps. xix. and Ps. cxix.   Secondly, in
loving his people, 1 John v. 1, 2. Thirdly, in *longing for* and loving his
second coming, Rev. xxii. 20.

Now followeth the reason of the discovery of this free love shewed now
in time to them.

' For mine anger is turned away from him.'

Here is the third branch of God's answer to their petition, ' Mine anger is
turned away from him,' which is included and implied in the former, ' I
will heal their backsliding.' How could he do this if he were angry ? No;
he saith, ' I will love them freely,' which argues that his anger was appeased. God knoweth that variety of words and expressions are all little
enough to raise up and comfort a doubting, wounded, galled soul, which,
when it is touched with a sense of sin and of his displeasure, cannot hear
words enough of comfort. This God knows well enough, and therefore he
adds expression upon expression, ' I will heal their backsliding, I will love
them freely, for mine anger is turned away from him.' The soul which is
touched with the sense of wrath, and defiled with the stains of sin's dreadful impressions, receives all this cheerfully, and more too. Therefore, in
such cases we must take in good part the largeness of God's expressions,

' For mine anger is turned away from him.' To unfold the words, therefore,

Anger is the inward displeasure which God hath against sin, and his purpose to punish it, accompanied with threatenings upon his purpose, and execution upon his threatenings. The point to be observed in the first place is,

That there is anger in God against sin.

We need not stand to prove the point, it is so manifest to every man. The Scripture is copious in it. If we consider either judgments executed upon sinners, threatenings against sin, or the saint's complaining of it, as Ps. lxxiv. 1, Job xlii. 7, Ps. vi. 1, Ps. xc. 11, Ps. xxxviii. 1, 3, Isa. lxiii. 6, with many the like places, prove that there is anger in God against sin. We will rather see the reason of it.

Because there is an antipathy betwixt him and sin, which is contrary to his pure nature. Sin, as it opposeth God, so it is contrary unto him; and, indeed, sin would turn him out of his sovereignty. For what doth a man, when he sins wittingly and willingly, but turn God out of his government, and causes the devil to take up God's room in the heart? When a man gives way to sin, then the devil rules, and he thinks his own lusts better than God's will, and his own carnal reason in contriving of sin above God's wisdom in his word; therefore, he is a proud rebel. Sin is such a kind of thing, that it labours to take away God; for it not only puts him out of that part of his throne, man's heart, but for the time a man sins, he could wish there were no God to take vengeance of him. Can you wonder, therefore, that God is so opposite to that which is so opposite to his prerogative royal as sin is?

The truth is, God is angry with nothing else but with sin, which is the only object of his anger. That which foolish persons make a trifle and sport of, swearing, filthy speaking, and lying, is the object of God's anger, Ps. xiv. 1. For this offence of sin he did not spare the angels of heaven, 2 Pet. ii. 4, but tumbled them thence, never to return again. Sin also thrust Adam out of paradise, Gen. iii. 23, and made God angry with him and the whole world, so as to destroy it with a flood of water, Gen. vi. 13, and will at last make him burn and consume all with a deluge of fire, 2 Pet. iii. 12. Yea, it made him in a sort angry with his own dear Son, when he underwent the punishment of sin as our surety, so that he cried out, ' My God, my God, why hast thou forsaken me?' Mat. xxvii. 46. If God thus shewed his anger against sin, in punishing it in Christ our surety, who was made sin for us, and yet had no sin in himself, how will he punish it much more in those who are not in Christ? Those who stand in their own sin and guilt, what will become of them? So that God is angry with sin, and with nothing else.

The second thing we gather from this, where he saith, ' My anger is turned away from him,' God's anger being taken especially for judgments, is,

That God's anger is the special thing in afflictions.

They come from his anger, as hath been shewed. Therefore he saith, ' I will take mine anger from you,' whereby he means judgments, the effect of his anger. For in the Scriptures anger is ordinarily taken for the fruits and effects of God's anger, which are terrible judgments, as we may see, Deut. xxix. 20, and so in many other places.

Quest. [Why are] judgments, then, called God's anger?

Ans, 1. Because they issue from his anger and displeasure; for it is not the judgments, but the anger in them, which lies heavy upon the soul,

When they come from God's anger, they are intolerable to the conscience : else, when we suffer ill, knowing that it is not from God's anger, but for trial of our graces, or for exercise, we bear it patiently. Therefore God saith, ' Mine anger is turned away from him :' for this, unremoved, embittereth every cross, though it be never so small. Let God's anger be upon a man, and he will make a conceit, a very light thing, to be as a heavy cross upon him, and vex him both in body and state more than mightier crosses at some other time shall. Will you see this in one instance, where God threatened his own dear people thus : ' And the Lord will smite thee with the botch of Egypt, and with the emrods, and with the scab, and with the itch, whereof thou canst not be healed,' Deut. xxviii. 27. What! is a scab, and an itch, and the like, such a terrible judgment, which in these days is set so light by ? O yes ! When it comes with God's displeasure ; when the least scratch is set on fire by God's anger, it shall consume us, it proves uncurable, as there it is threatened : ' whereof thou canst not be healed.' When the vermin came in God's anger upon that hardhearted king, all Pharaoh's skill, and his magicians' skill, could not beat them out, because, as they confessed, ' this was the finger of God,' Exod. viii. 19. Let any thing come as a messenger of God's anger, it comes with vengeance, and sticks to the soul, like a ' fretting leprosy,' Lev. xiv. 45, 46, which, when it entered into a house, many times could not be gotten out again with pulling out stones, or scraping them, till the house were demolished. So, when God's anger is raised and kindled against a person, you may remove this and that, change place and company, and use of helps ; yet it will never leave fretting till it have consumed him, unless it be removed by repentance. If it be never so small a scratch or itch, all the physic in the world shall not cure it. For as the love of God makes all other things in God comfortable unto us, so it is his anger which makes all his attributes terrible. As, for his power, the more he loves me, the more he is able to do me good. But otherwise, the more he is angry and displeased, the more his other attributes are terrible. If he be wise, the more he will find out my sins : if he be powerful and angry, the more he can revenge himself on me. Is he angry and just ? the more woe to me. So there is nothing in God when he is angry, but it is so much the more terrible. For this puts a sting in everything : which, when it is removed out of malignant creatures armed with a sting, then they are no more hurtful. The sting of every evil and cross, is God's anger and wrath. This being removed, nothing hurts. All crosses then are gentle, mild, tractable, and medicinal, when God hath once said, ' For mine anger is turned away from him.' After that's gone, whatsoever remaineth is good for us, when we feel no anger in it. What is that which blows the coals of hell, and makes hell hell, but the anger of God, seizing upon the conscience ? This kindles Tophet, and sets it a-fire like a river of brimstone, Isa. xxx. 33. Therefore this is a wondrous sweet comfort and encouragement when he saith, ' For mine anger is turned away from him.' Whence, in the next place, we may observe,

That God will turn away his anger upon repentance.

When there is this course taken, formerly mentioned, to turn unto the Lord and to sue for pardon, to vow reformation, ' Asshur shall not save us,' and a thorough reformation of the particular sin ; and when there is wrought in the heart faith to rely on God's mercy, as the ' Father of the fatherless,' in whom they ' find mercy,' then God's anger is turned away. God, upon repentance, will turn away his anger. The point is clear. We see, when the Lord hath threatened many grievous judgments and plagues for sin, one upon the neck of another, denounced with all variety of expressions in the most terrible manner; yet, after all that thundering, Deut. xxviii. and xxix., it follows, ' And it shall come to pass, when all these things are come upon thee, the blessings and the curses, which I have set before thee, and thou shalt call them to mind among all the nations whither the Lord thy God hath driven thee, and shalt return unto the Lord thy God, &c.; that then the Lord thy God will turn thy captivity, and have compassion upon thee,' &c., Deut. xxx. 1, 2, 3. After repentance, you see the promise comes presently after; not that the one is the meritorious cause of the other; but there is an order of things. God will have the one come with the other. Where there is not sense of sin and humiliation, and thence prayer to God for pardon, with reformation and trusting in his mercy, there the anger of God abides still. But where these are, ' his anger is turned away.' God hath established his order, that the one of these must still follow the other.

Another excellent place to the forenamed, we have in the Chronicles, ' If my people that are called by my name shall humble themselves and pray,' (as they did here in this chapter, ' take words unto yourselves') ' and seek my face and turn from their wicked ways,' 2 Chron. vii. 14; as they did here, ' Asshur shall not save us, we will not ride upon horses,' &c. We will no more rely on the barren false helps of foreign strength. What then ? ' I will hear from heaven, and will forgive their sin, and will heal their land,' 2 Chron. vii. 14. Here is the promise, whereof this text is a proof. So in all the prophets there is a multiplication of the like instances and promises; which we will not stand upon now, as not being controversial. It is God's name so to do, as we may see in that well known place of Exodus. ' Jehovah, Jehovah, God, merciful and gracious, longsuffering, and abundant in goodness and truth; keeping mercy for thousands, forgiving iniquity, and transgression, and sin,' &c., Exod. xxxiv. 6, 7. And so it is said, ' At what time soever a sinner repents himself of his sins from the bottom of his heart, I will put all his sins out of my remembrance, saith the Lord God,' Hebrews viii. 12. The Scripture is plentiful in nothing more; especially it is the burden of Ezek. xviii. and xxxiii., forgiveness of sins, and removal of wrath upon repentance.

And for example. See one for all the rest. Let the greater include the lesser. Manasseh was a greater sinner than any of us all can be; because he was enabled* with a greater authority to do mischief, (all which no private man, nor ordinary great man, is capable of, not having the like power); which he exercised to the full in all manner of cruelty, joined with other gross and deadly sins; and yet the Scripture shews that, upon his humiliation and praying, he found mercy. God turned away his anger, 2 Chron. xxxiii. 12, 13.

That of the prodigal is a parable also fitted for this purpose, who had no sooner a resolution to return to his father, Luke xv. 23. *Filius timet convitium, &c.* The son fears chiding; the father provides a banquet. So God doth transcend our thoughts in that kind. We can no sooner humble ourselves to pray to him heartily, resolving to amend our ways and come to him, but he lays his anger aside to entertain terms of love and friendship with us. As we see in David, who was a good man, though he slubbered over the matter of repentance, all which while God's hand was so heavy upon him, that his moisture was turned into the drought of summer, he

* That is, ' endued.'—G.

roaring all the day long, Ps. xxxii. 3, 4. But when once he dealt throughly in the business, and resolved, 'I will confess my transgression unto the Lord; and thou forgavest the iniquity of my sin.' Let our humiliation be real and thorough, with prayer for pardon, and purpose to reform, and presently God will shew mercy.

The reason is clear, because it is his nature so to do. His nature is more inclined to mercy than anger. For him to be angry, it is still upon supposition of our sins. But to be merciful and gracious, it always proceeds from his own bowels, whether we be sinners or not. Without all supposition, God is still merciful unto whom he will shew mercy. ' Who is a God like unto thee,' saith the prophet, 'that pardoneth iniquity? he passeth by the transgression of the remnant of his heritage, and retaineth not his anger for ever; because he delighteth in mercy.' Things naturally come easily, without pain; as beams from the sun, water from the spring, and as heat from fire; all which come easily, because they are natural. So mercy and love from God come easily and willingly. It is his nature to be gracious and merciful. Though we be sinners, if we take this course here, as the church doth, to pray and be humbled, then it will follow, ' Mine anger is turned away from him.' The use is,

First, to observe *God's truth in the performance of his gracious promises*, who, as he makes gracious promises to us, so he makes them good. His promise is, ' If we confess our sins, he will forgive them and be merciful,' Prov. xxviii. 13. So here he says, ' Mine anger is turned away.' As they confess, so he is merciful to forgive them. It is good to observe the experiments* of God's truth. Every word of God is a shield, that is, we may take it as a shield. It is an experimental truth, whereby we may arm our souls. This is an experimental truth, that when we are humbled for our sins, God, he will be merciful unto our sins, and allay his anger, as it is in this text. Therefore it is said, ' Those that know thy name will trust in thee, for thou never failest those who put their trust in thee,' Ps. ix. 10. Let us then open our hearts unto God, and confess our sins unto him; and if we resolve amendment, we shall find the truth of his gracious promises. He will turn aside his anger, and will never fail us, if we put trust in him. ' The name of the Lord is a strong tower, and the righteous fly to it and are safe,' Prov. xviii. 10. This name of mercy, grace, and favour, is a strong tower to distressed consciences. Let us therefore remember to fly unto it, when our consciences are awaked and distressed with sin, and sense of God's displeasure. Seeing these kinds of promises are as a city of refuge, let us run unto them, and we shall not be pulled from the horns of this altar, as Joab once was from his, 1 Kings ii. 28; but shall at all times find grace and mercy to help us at the time of need. It is a comfortable point, ' Mine anger is turned away from him.'

Quest. But it may be said, How is God's anger turned away from his children, when they feel it ofttimes after in the course of their lives?

Ans. The answer is, that there is a double anger of God, whereby we must judge of things, for either it is,

1. Vindicative; or, 2. Fatherly anger.

God, ofter our first conversion, he removeth his vindicative anger, after which, though sometimes he threaten and frown upon us, yet it is with a fatherly anger, which God also removes, with the shame and correction attending it, when we reform and amend our wicked ways.

There is, 1. A child of anger; 2. A child under anger.

God's children are never ' children of wrath,' Eph. ii. 3, and anger, after

---

* That is, 'experiences' = trials of.— G.

their first conversion. But sometimes children under wrath, if they make bold with sin, so as they cannot use their right of sonship, to go boldly to the throne of grace. Because then, though they have the right of fear,* they conceive of God as angry with them, and cannot use it, so long as they live in any sin against conscience, and so continue, until they reform and humble themselves, as the church doth here ; after which they can and do rejoice again, claim their right, and are not either children of wrath, or under wrath. David, after he had sinned that foul sin, Ps. li. was a child under wrath, not a child of wrath. So, if we make bold to sin, we are children under wrath, for ofttimes God begins correction at his own house, if there be any disorder there, 1 Pet. iv. 17. You know God was so angry with Moses, that he was not suffered to enter into the land of Canaan, Num. xx. 12. And David, when he had numbered the people, God was angry with him, 2 Sam. xxiv. 1 ; and with the Corinthians also, for unreverent receiving of the Lord's Supper, 1 Cor. xi. 30. But here is a course prescribed to remove his fatherly anger, and to enjoy the beams of his countenance, and sunshine of his favour in Christ. If we humble ourselves, confess our sins, and fly unto him, as the church here doth, then we shall find this made good, ' For mine anger is turned away from him.' But it may be asked,

Quest. In times of affliction, how may we know God's anger to be removed, when yet we endure the affliction ?

Ans. The answer is, that God is infinitely wise, and in one affliction hath many ends ; as,

1. When he afflicts them, it is to correct them for their sins ; after which, when they have pulled out the sting of sin by confession and humiliation, if afflictions continue, his anger doth not continue.

2. Affliction sometimes is for an exercise of patience and faith, and trial of their graces, and for the exemplary manifestation to others of God's goodness to them.

But even then they may know that things come not in anger unto them by this ; that after repentance God speaks peace unto their conscience ; so that, though the grievance continue, it is with much joy in the Holy Ghost, and peace of conscience, in which case, the soul knows that it is for other ends that God continues it. Therefore the first thing in any affliction is, to remove away the core and sting thereof by humbling ourselves, as the church here doth, after which our consciences will be at peace for other things. God hath many ends in correcting us. He will humble us, improve our afflictions to the good of others, and will gain himself honour by our afflictions, sufferings, and crosses. When God hath shed abroad his love in our hearts by his Spirit, then we can rejoice in tribulation, and rejoice under hope, Rom. v. 5. Though the afflictions continue, because the sting is gone, anger is removed.

' For mine anger is turned away from him.'

The last point we observe from hence, and gather from all these general truths, is this,

Where there is not humiliation for sin, and hearty prayer to God, with reformation of our ways, flying unto God for mercy, who is merciful to the fatherless, there God's wrath continues.

For as where they are performed his anger is turned away, so must it needs follow, that where they are not performed, his anger continueth. Therefore, let us examine ourselves. The Spirit of God here speaks of

* Qu. ' the right, of fear they conceive ? ' &c.—ED.

' healing backslidings,' and of ' turning away iniquity.' Let us look well to ourselves, and to the present state of things, that our diseases be soundly cured, our personal diseases ; and then let us be sensible of the diseases of the land, and pray for them. For there are universal diseases and sins of a kingdom, as well as personal. And we are guilty of the sins of the times, as far as we are not humbled for them. Paul tells those who did not punish the incestuous person, 'Why are you not humbled rather for this deed ?' 1 Cor. v. 2. Where there is a public disease, there is a public anger hanging over upon that disease ; the cure whereof is here prescribed, to be humbled, as for ourselves, so for others. Therefore let us beware of sin (if we would shun wrath), especially of idolatry, or else we shall be sure to smart for it, as Ephraim did, of whom the Spirit of God saith, ' When Ephraim spake trembling, he exalted himself in Israel ; but when he offended in Baal, he died,' Hosea xiii. 1. Ephraim had got such authority, what with his former victories, and by the signs of God's favour among them, that when he spake ' there was trembling,' and he ' exalted himself in Israel ;' but when he ' offended once in Baal,' that is, when he became an idolater, ' he died.' It is meant of the civil death especially, that he lost his former credit and reputation. We see then the dangerous effects of sin, especially of idolatry. Wherefore let us fortify ourselves against it, and bless God that we live under such a gracious, just, and mild king, and good government, where there are such laws against this great sin especially, and beseech God long to continue his life and prosperity for our good amongst us. For use then.

Remember, when we are to deal with God, *that he is the great Mover of all things;* who, if he be angry, can overturn all things, and cross us in all things ; and can also heal us of all our diseases. But what must we do if we would be healed ? We must take the course prescribed here, ' Take unto us words ;' humble ourselves, and have no confidence in Asshur, munition, people, or in ' the works of our hands ;' but trust in God, so shall we be happy and blessed. Whatsoever our enemies be, yet if we can make God our rock, fortress, and shield, then it is no matter who be our enemies. ' If he be on our side, who can be against us ?' Rom. viii. 31. Let us all, ministers and all, reform ourselves, and stand in the gap, after the course here prescribed, and go to God in a right manner ; so we may dissipate all the clouds of anger which may seem to hang over our heads, and find God experimentally making this promise good to us, which he made then to his people, ' I will heal their backsliding, I will love them freely : for mine anger is turned away from him.'

Therefore let us do as Jacob did with Esau, when he came incensed with mighty displeasure against his brother. Jacob comes before him humbly, prostrates himself before him, and so turns away his anger, Gen. xxxiii. 3. So when God is angry with us, and comes against us, let us humble ourselves before him to appease him. As Abigail quieted David, by humbling herself before him, when he had a purpose to destroy her family, 1 Sam. xxv. 23, *seq.*, so let us come before God in humility of soul, and God will turn away his anger. As when there was a great plague begun in the army, Aaron stood with his censer betwixt the living and the dead, offering incense and making atonement for them, whereby the plague was stayed, Num. xvi. 48 ; so in any wrath felt or feared, for ourselves or the State we live in, let every one hold his censer and offer the incense of prayer, ' Take with you words,' Rev. viii. 4. God is wondrously moved to pity by the incense of these sweet odours offered up by

Christ unto the Father. Believe it, it is the only safe course to begin in heaven. Such a beginning will have a blessed ending. Other courses, politic and subordinate helps must also be taken, but all is to no purpose, unless we begin in heaven; because all things under God are ruled and moved by him; who, when he is favourable, makes all the creatures pliable unto us, but especially makes this good, ' I will heal their backsliding, I will love them freely; for mine anger is turned away from him.'

THE SEVENTH SERMON.

I will be as the dew unto Israel: he shall grow as the lily, and cast forth his root as Lebanon. His branches shall spread, and his beauty shall be as the olive tree, and his smell as Lebanon.—HOSEA XIV. 5, 6.

THE church, as we heard, had been humbled, and therefore is comforted. It is usual in the Scriptures, especially in the prophetical parts thereof, after terrible threatenings to come with sweet promises; because God in all ages hath a church.* Therefore God in this chapter takes this course. He makes gracious promises to this people, grounded upon the former part of the chapter, wherein God had dictated unto them a form of prayer, repentance, and reformation. 'Take with you words, and turn to the Lord: say unto him, Take away all iniquity, and receive us graciously,' &c. Whereupon a reformation is promised, 'Asshur shall not save us, we will not ride upon horses,' &c. Which was a reformation of that national sin which they were guilty of, false confidence. Now, as we have heard, God answers them to every particular. He makes a gracious promise, 'that he will heal their backsliding,' according to their prayer, 'Take away all iniquity.' And to that, 'receive us graciously,' he answers, 'I will love them freely, for mine anger is turned away from him.'

Now, it cannot be but that God should regard the desires of his own Spirit, when both the words and Spirit proceed from him. Therefore he goes on more fully to answer their desire of 'doing good to them,' saying, 'I will be as the dew to Israel,' &c.

In which words the holy prophet doth first, by a metaphor and borrowed speech, set down the ground of all happiness. So that there is here given a more full satisfaction to the desires of the church.

1. The cause of all—' I will be as the dew,' &c.

2. The particular persons to whom—' to Israel.'

3. The fruit of this follows—' he shall grow as the lily, and cast forth his root as Lebanon.'

Now the words read are a fuller satisfaction to the desires of God's people, which were stirred up by his own Spirit. 'I will be as dew unto Israel.' Where,

1. You have set down the cause of all, which follows. God by his gracious Spirit will be ' as the dew unto Israel.'

2. And then upon that, the prosperous success this dew of God's Spirit hath in them, ' They shall grow as the lily.'

Obj. 1. Aye, but the lily grows, but hath no stability. Everything that grows is not well rooted. Therefore he adds, in the second place, ' They

* Joel ii. 27, 28; Hos. ii. 14, 15; Isa. i. 18, 19; Deut. iii. 1, *seq;* Jer. iii. 12; Jer. xxx. 1, *seq.*

shall cast out their roots as Lebanon;' that is, with growth they shall have stability; not only grow in height speedily, but also grow fast in the root with firmness.

Obj. 2. And likewise, as everything that grows in root and firmness, doth not spread itself, he says, he shall not only grow upward, and take root downwards, ' but his branches shall spread;' whereby he shall be more fruitful and comfortable to others.

Obj. 3. Oh! but everything that grows, is rooted and spread, is not for all that fruitful; therefore, he saith, they shall be as the olive tree, ' His beauty shall be as the olive tree for fruitfulness.'

Obj. 4. Yet, though the olive be fruitful, it hath no pleasant smell nor good taste. Therefore he adds another blessing to that. They shall, in regard of their pleasantness to God and man, that shall delight in them, be ' as the smell of Lebanon;' which was a wondrous pleasant, delightful place, which yielded a pleasant savour round about. So we see what a complete kind of growth this is, wherein blessing upon blessing is promised. The Holy Ghost cannot enough satisfy himself in variety of comfortable expressions. Nothing is left unsatisfied that the heart can propound. He will make them grow, be stedfast, fruitful, delightful, and pleasant. So that we have here to consider:

1. The favour and blessing that he promiseth, to be ' as the dew to Israel.'

2. The excellency of it in divers particulars.

3. The order wherein it is promised.

Before we come to the words themselves, if we remember and read over the former part of the prophecy, we shall find it full of terrible curses, all opposite unto that here promised : to shew,

We can never be in so disconsolate a state, but God can alter all.

He hath a right hand as well as a left; blessings as well as curses; mercy as well as justice; which is more proper to his nature than that. Therefore let Christian souls never be discouraged with their condition and state whatsoever it is.

Reason. For, as there are many maladies, so there are many remedies opposite to them. As Solomon saith, ' This is set over against that,' &c., Eccles. vii. 14. If there be a thousand kinds of ills, there are many thousand kinds of remedies. For God is larger in his helps than we can be in our diseases and distresses, whatsoever they are, Zech. i. 19, 20, 21. Therefore it is good to make this use of it, to be so conceited of God, as may draw us nearer unto him upon all occasions.

Again, we see here how large the Spirit of God is in expressions of the particulars. ' I will be as the dew unto Israel: and he shall grow as the lily, and cast forth his roots as Lebanon. His branches shall spread, and his beauty be large,' &c. Whereunto tends all this largeness of expression ? God doth it in mercy unto us, who especially need it, being in a distressed, disconsolate estate. Therefore they are not words wastefully spent. We may marvel sometimes, in Isaiah, and so in some other prophets, to see the same things in substance so often repeated, though with variety of lively expressions, as it is, for the most part, the manner of every prophet. Surely, because it is useful and profitable, the people of God need it. There is, nor never was any man in a drooping, sinking condition, but he desires line upon line, word upon word, promise upon promise, expression upon expression.

Obj. One would think, is not a word of God sufficient ?

Ans. Yes, for him, but not for us. We have doubting and drooping hearts, and therefore God adds sacraments and seals ; not only one sacrament, but two; and in the sacrament not only bread, but wine also ; to shew that Christ is all in all. What large expressions are here, thinks a profane heart, what needs this ? As if God knew us not better than we know ourselves. Whensoever thou art touched in conscience with the sense of thy sins, and knowest how great, how powerful, how holy a God thou hast to deal with, who can endure no impure thing, thou wilt never find fault with his large expressions in his word and sacraments ; and with the variety of his promises, when he translates out of the book of nature into his own book, all expressions of excellent things to spread forth his mercy and love. Is this needless ? No ; we need all. He that made us, redeemed us, preserves us, knows us better than we know ourselves. He who is infinite in wisdom and love takes this course.

And mark again, in the next place, how the Holy Ghost fetcheth here this comfort from things that are most excellent in their kind. ' They shall grow as the lily,' that grows fairly and speedily ; ' and they shall take root as Lebanon.' To shew that a Christian should be the excellent in his kind, he compares him in his right temper and state, to the most excellent things in nature ; to the sun, to lions, trees of Lebanon, cedars, and olive trees for fruitfulness ; and all to shew that a Christian should not be an ordinary man. All the excellencies of nature are little enough to set out the excellency of a Christian. He must be an extraordinary singular man. Saith Christ, ' What singular thing do ye ?' Mat. v. 47. He must not be a common man. Therefore, when God would raise his people, he tells them, they should not be common men, but grow as lilies, be rooted as trees, fruitful as olives, and pleasant, beautiful, as the goodly, sweet-smelling trees of Libanus. How graciously doth God condescend unto us, to teach us by outward things, how to help our souls by our senses, that when we see the growth, fruitfulness, and sweetness of other things, we should call to mind what we should be, and what God hath promised we shall be, if we take this course and order formerly prescribed. Indeed, a wise Christian, endowed with the Spirit of God, extracts a quintessence out of everything, especially from those that God singles out to teach him his duty by. When he looks upon any plant, fruit, or tree that is pleasant, delightful, and fruitful, it should put him in mind of his duty.

' I will be as the dew to Israel,' &c.

These sweet promises in their order follow immediately upon this, that God would freely love them, and cease to be angry with them. Then he adds the fruits of his love to their souls, and the effects of those fruits in many particulars; whence first of all we observe,

God's love is a fruitful love.

Wheresoever he loves, he makes the things lovely. We see things lovely, and then we love them ; but God so loves us that in loving us he makes us lovely. So saith God by the prophet, ' I have seen his ways, and will heal him ; I will lead him also, and restore comforts unto him and to his mourners,' Isa. lvii. 18. And from this experience of the fruitfulness of God's love, the church is brought in rejoicing, ' I will greatly rejoice in the Lord ; my soul shall be joyful in my God : for he hath clothed me with the garments of salvation, he hath covered me with the robe of righteousness, as a bridegroom decketh himself with ornaments, and as a bride adorneth herself with her jewels,' Isa. lxi. 10. Thus he makes us such as may be amiable objects of his love that he may delight in.

Reason. For his love is the love, as of a gracious, so of a powerful, God, that can alter all things to us, and us to all things. He can bring us good out of everything, and do us good at all times, according to the church's prayer, ' Do good unto us.'

Use. Wherefore, seeing God can do us good, and since his love is not only a pardoning love, to take away his anger, but also so complete and fruitful a love, so full of spiritual favours, ' I will be as the dew unto Israel, and he shall grow up as the lily,' &c., let us stand more upon God's love than we have formerly done, and strive to have our hearts inflamed with love towards God again, as the prophet David doth, ' I love the Lord, because he hath heard my voice and my supplications,' Ps. cxvi. 1.   It may be for outward condition that even where God loves they may go backwards so and so ; but for their best part, their souls, God will be as the ' dew to them,' and ' they shall grow as Lebanon.'   God will be good to them in the best things ; and a Christian, when he begins to know what the best things are, concerning a better life, he then learneth to value spiritual blessings and favours above all other whatsoever.   Therefore God suits his promises to the desires of his children, that he would water their dry souls, that he would be as the dew unto them.   God's love is a fruitful love, and fruitful in the best things.   As we know what David saith, ' There be many who say, Who will shew us any good ?   Lord, lift thou up the light of thy countenance upon us.   Thou hast put gladness in my heart, more than in the time that their corn and their wine increased,' Ps. iv. 6, 7.   So God fits his gracious promise, answerable to the desires of a gracious heart, ' I will be as the dew to Israel.'

2. To come to the words, in particular, for this is the ground of all that follows, ' I will be as the dew unto Israel.'

Quest. How will God be as the dew to Israel ?

Ans. This is especially meant of, and performed to, the church under the New Testament, especially next unto Christ's time, when the dew of grace fell in greatest abundance upon the church.   The comfortable, sanctifying, fruitful grace of God is compared to dew in many respects.

First, *the dew doth come from above.*   God sends it, it drops from above, and cannot be commanded by the creature.   So all other gifts, and especially this perfect gift, the grace of God, comes from above, from the Father of lights.   There is no principle of grace naturally within a man.   It is as childish to think that grace comes from any principle within us, as to think that the dew which falls upon a stone is the sweat of the stone, as children think that the stone sweats, when it is the dew that has fallen upon it. Certainly our hearts, in regard of themselves, are barren and dry.   Wherefore, God's grace, in regard of the original, is compared to dew, which should teach us to go to God, as the church doth here, and pray him to deal graciously with us, to do good to us, for this cause laying open our souls unto him, to shed his grace into them.

Secondly, *the dew doth fall insensibly and invisibly.*   So the grace of God. We feel the comfort, sweetness, and operation of it, but it falls insensibly without observation.   Inferior things here feel the sweet and comfortable influence of the heavens, but who sees the active influence upon them ? which, how it is derived from superior bodies to the inferior, is not observable.   As our Saviour speaks of the beginnings of grace and workings of it, ' The wind bloweth where it listeth, and thou hearest the sound thereof, but canst not tell whence it cometh or whither it goeth : so is every one that is born of the Spirit,' John iii. 8.   It works we know not how. We feel the work, but the manner of working is unknown to us. Grace, therefore, is wrought undiscernibly. No man can see the conversion of another; nay, no man almost can discern his own conversion at first. Therefore, this question should not much trouble you, Shew us the first hour, the first time of your conversion and entrance into the state of grace. Grace, to many, falls like the dew, by little and little, drop and drop, line upon line. It falls sweetly and undiscernibly upon them at the first. Therefore, it is hard to set down the first time, seeing, as our blessed Saviour speaks, grace at the first is wondrous little, likened to a grain of mustardseed; but though it be small at first, yet nothing is more glorious and beautiful afterwards, for from a small seed it grows to overspread and be great, shooting out branches, Mark iv. 31, 32. And as the root of Jesse was a despised stock, and in show a dead root, yet thence Christ rose, a branch as high as heaven; so the beginning of a Christian is despised and little, like a dead stock, as it were; but they grow upward and upward still, till they come to heaven itself, Prov. iv. 18. Thus we see there is nothing in the world more undiscernible in the beginning than the work of grace, which must make us not over-curious to examine exactly the first beginnings thereof, because it' is as the falling of the dew, or ' the blowing of the wind.'

Thirdly, Again, as it falls undiscernibly and invisibly, so *very sweetly and mildly*, not violating the nature or course of anything, but rather helping and cherishing the same; or if it make any change in anything, it doth it mildly and gently. So usually, unless it be in some extraordinary case, God works sweetly upon the soul by his grace mildly and sweetly. Grace works sweetly upon the soul, preserving its freedom; so as man, when he begins to be good, shall be freely good, from inward principles wrought in him. His judgment shall like the course he takes, and be clean opposite to others that are contrary, from an inward principle; as free now in altering his course, as formerly he was in following the other. There is no violence, but in regard of corruption. God works strongly and mildly: strongly, for he changeth a stone into a fleshly heart; and yet sweetly: he breaks not any power of nature, but advanceth it. For grace doth not take away or imprison nature, but lifts it up, and sets it at liberty. For it makes the will stronger and freer, the judgment sounder, the understanding clearer, the affections more orderly. It makes all things better, so that no violence is offered to nature.

Fourthly, Again, grace is compared to dew, *in regard of the operations of dew*. For, what effects hath dew upon the earth?

(1.) *It cools the air when it falls*, and then with coolness it hath a fructifying virtue; for falling especially on tender herbs and plants, it soaks into the root of them, and makes them fruitful. So it is with the grace of God's Spirit. It cools the soul, scorched with the sense of God's anger; as indeed all our souls will be, when we have to deal with God, who is 'a consuming fire,' Heb. xii. 29, till we take that course to look upon him in Christ for the pardon of sin; after which his grace and the sense of it cooleth, assuageth, and speaks peace to an uncomfortable, disconsolate heart. This voice, ' Son, be of good comfort, thy sins are forgiven thee.' Oh, this hath a cooling in it! and this also, ' This day shalt thou be with me in paradise.' Oh, how it cooled and cheered the good thief, and comforted him! And so when God says unto the soul, ' I am thy salvation;' Oh, when the soul feels this, how is it cooled and refreshed!

(2.) And the soul is not only cooled and refreshed, but *it is also sweetened and made fruitful with comfort to the soul.* If we were to see a man in the pangs of conscience, stung with fiery temptations, as with so many fiery serpents and poisoned darts, which drink up the spirits, and presents God a consuming fire ; and hell beneath, full of insupportable torments, set on by the insupportable wrath of God : then we should know what it were to have grace in this efficacious manner, cooling and refreshing the soul, that hath these fiery darts stuck into it of violent strong temptations, which to the present sense are the flashes and beginnings of hell. Oh, it is an excellent thing to have the grace of God in such a case to assuage and cool the maladies of a distressed soul, which for the present seems to burn in a flame of wrath ! As it cools, so also it makes the heart fruitful, our hearts of themselves being as the barren wilderness and wild desert. Now God by his grace turns ' the wilderness into water-springs,' as it appeareth in many places of the prophets. Saith God, ' For I will pour water upon him that is thirsty, and floods upon the dry ground ; I will pour my Spirit upon thy seed,' &c., Isa. xliv. 3 ; xlv. 8. So grace, it turns the barren wilderness, the heart, dry of itself, and makes it fruitful. We know what Paul said of Onesimus, a fruitless servant, nay, a fugitive thief. He is unfruitful no longer, saith he, now that he is become a convert, another, a new man, now he will do good service, Phil. xvi. A man is no sooner altered by the dew of grace, but howsoever formerly he were a naughty, hurtful person, of whom every man was afraid because of his wickedness, yet now he is a fruitful person, and strives to bring forth fruits worthy of amendment of life, Mat. iii. 8.

Fifthly, And we may add one more, in the next place, *in regard of the unresistibleness thereof;* for as nothing can hinder the dew from falling from the sweet influence of heaven unto us, or hinder the working of those superior bodies upon the inferior, or hinder the wind from blowing ; so who can hinder God's grace ? Job xxxviii. 37. They may, out of malice, hinder the means of it, and hinder the gracious working of the Spirit, by discouragements in others ; which is a sign of a devilish spirit, when yet God hath a hand in that too after a sort. For it raineth in one city, and not in another, by God's appointment ; but nothing can hinder, where God will have the dew and water, and shine of the influence of grace, work. Nothing in the world can stop it. So it is said in that excellent prophecy of Christ and his kingdom, ' He shall come down like rain upon the mown grass, as showers that water the earth,' which as they cool and fructify, so come they unresistibly, Ps. lxxii. 6.

Use. Let none, therefore, be discouraged with the deadness, dryness, and barrenness of their own hearts; but let them know that God doth graciously promise, if they will take the course formerly set down, to be ' as the dew unto them.' Therefore let them come unto the ordinances of God, with wondrous hope, confidence, and faith, that he will be as dew unto them ; that, seeing he hath appointed variety of ordinances, the word and sacraments, he will bless those means of his own ordaining and appointing, for his own ends. He that hath graciously appointed such means of grace, will he not bless them ? especially having promised, ' I will be as the dew unto Israel.' Therefore let us attend upon the ordinances, and not keep away, though our hearts be barren, dry, and unfruitful. God is above the heart, and able to turn the wilderness into a fruitful place. He can make the heart a fit habitation for himself to dwell in. Let us by faith attend upon the ordinances. If we find not comfort in one ordinance, let us go unto another, and another. Comfort and help shall come, especially if, with

the church, we ' go a little further,' Cant. iii. 4 ; for the promise is, ' I
will be as the dew unto Israel.'

But mark the order wherein he makes this promise.

First, He gives grace to pray to him. ' Take away all iniquity, and receive
us graciously ; ' ' Do good to us.'

Then, *second, he gives a spirit of reformation,* promising amendment ;
whereupon this followeth, 'that he will forgive their sins, love them freely,'
&c., and be ' as the dew unto Israel.'   He will be as the dew unto Israel ;
but he will give them grace first to be humbled, confess sin, and pray to
God for grace and forgiveness.   There is an order of working in the soul.
God giveth justification before sanctification ; and before he freeth from the
guilt of sin, he gives grace to confess sin.   ' If we confess our sins, he is
faithful and just to forgive us our sins, and to cleanse us from them,' saith
St John, 1 John i. 9.   Where these go before, grace will follow ; and
where they do not, there will be no sanctification.   Therefore let us consider the order ; for wheresoever God ' takes away iniquity,' and heals their
souls, in regard of the guilt of their sins, unto those he will be as dew.
Therefore, if we have still barren souls, without desires or strength to
goodness, certainly our sins are still upon the file ;* for justification is
never without holiness of life.   ' Whosoever is in Christ, he is a new
creature,' 2 Cor. v. 17.   When this is done, God will be ' as the dew ; '
because he doth pardon our sins for this cause, that he may thereby fit us
to be entertained in the covenant ; and are we fit to be in covenant with
him, until our natures be altered ?   Therefore, whensoever he enters into
covenant with any, he changeth their natures, that they may be friends,
and have communion with him.   Then the same soul which crieth, ' Take
away all iniquity,' desireth also the dew of grace to make it better.   This
order is not only necessary on God's part, but in regard of the soul also.
For was there ever any soul, from the beginning of the world, that truly
desired forgiveness of sins, which did not also therewith desire grace ?   Such
a soul were but a hypocritical soul.   For if it be rightly touched with sorrow,
it desires as well ability to subdue sin, as forgiveness of sin ; holiness and
righteousness, with forgiveness, Luke i. 75.

Use 1.   Therefore, lest we deceive ourselves, let this be an use of trial
from the order, *that if we find not grace wrought in our natures to restrain sin,
and alter our former lewd courses, our sins are not yet forgiven.*   For, wheresoever God takes away sin, and ' loves freely,' there also he gives the best
fruits of his love, bestows the dew of his grace, to work upon and alter our
natures.   Christ came not by blood alone, to die for us ; but by water also,
to sanctify us, 1 John v. 6.   He will not only ' love freely,' but he will be
' as the dew,' where he loves freely.   Therefore, if we have not sanctifying
grace, we have not as yet pardoning grace.   For we know the prophet joins
them both together.   ' Blessed is the man unto whom the Lord imputeth
not iniquity, and in whose spirit there is no guile,' Ps. xxxii. 1, 2.   If we
retain a guileful, false spirit, our sins are not forgiven.   We see both these
are put together.

Use 2.   And seeing all these good things come from God, it is necessary
to take notice of what hath been said of God's goodness, *that we do not rob
God of his due glory, nor ourselves of the due comfort that we may draw
thence.*   The Egyptians had the river Nylus, that overflowed the land every
year, caused by anniversary winds, which so blew into the mouth of the
river, that it could not discharge itself into the sea ; whereupon it over-

* See Note *b*, vol. I. p. 289.—G.

flowed the banks, and left a fruitful slime upon the ground, so that they needed not rain as other countries, because it was watered with Nylus. Hereupon they did not depend upon God's blessing, nor were so holy as they should; but were proud of their river, as is intimated by Moses unto the people. ' But the land whither thou goest in to possess it, is not as the land of Egypt, from whence ye came out, where thou sowest thy seed, and wateredst it with thy foot, as a garden of herbs : but the land whither ye go to possess it is a land of hills and valleys, and drinketh water of the rain of heaven : a land which the Lord thy God careth for,' &c., Deut. xi. 10, 11. They having more immediately rain from heaven, saw God's hand in watering it, whereas the Egyptians did not. And what makes a papist to be so unthankful ? He thinks he can with his own industry water his own ground with somewhat in himself. What makes another man thankful, on the other side ? Because he knoweth he hath all things by dependence from the first Cause : for as in nature, ' In God we live, move, and have our being,' Acts xvii. 28, much more in grace. We have all our nourishment, spiritual being, moving, and life from the dew of heaven. All our heat is from the Sun of righteousness,' Mal. iv. 2, which makes a Christian life to be nothing else but a gracious dependence. ' I can do all things,' saith St Paul,' Philip. iv. 13. Big and great words ! Oh, but it is ' through Christ that strengthens me.' These things must not be forgotten. For a child of the church is a child of grace. By grace he is what he is ; he hath all from heaven. Suitable to the former place is that in Ezekiel. ' And the land of Egypt shall be desolate and waste ; and they shall know that I am the Lord ; because he hath said, The river is mine, and I have made it,' Ezek. xxix. 9. He shall be desolate, because he boasts and brags of his river, and depends not upon God for the sweet showers of the former and the latter rain. They boasted because it was a fat, fruitful country, which the Romans called their granary. But we must look for all from heaven. God by his Spirit will be as the dew.

You know in paradise there were four rivers that watered the garden of God, that sweet place, and made it fruitful; but the heads of all these rivers were out of paradise, Gen. ii. 10. So it is with the church of God, ' There is a river, the streams whereof makes glad the city of God,' as the Psalmist speaks, Ps. xlvi. 4 : many precious comfortable graces, the particulars whereof follow. But where is the head-spring of the river ? It is in heaven. We have all from God, through Christ the Mediator. So, though we have of the water and dew, yet notwithstanding the head and spring of all is from without the church; in heaven, in Christ, in the Mediator. And, therefore, in all the excellent things we enjoy in the church, let us look to the original first cause, Christ by his Spirit. He is ' as the dew' to his church.

Use 3. This affords likewise an *use of direction*, how to come to have grace to sanctify and alter our natures.

Ans. Do as the church doth here ; desire it of God. Lord, teach me to see and know my sins : Lord, ' Take away all iniquity, and receive me graciously ;' Heal my soul, for I have sinned against thee. O love me freely. Turn away thy angry face from my sins, and be as the dew unto my barren soul; my dead soul, O quicken it; make good thy promise, come swiftly, come speedily, come unresistibly, ' like rain upon the mown grass,' Ps. lxxii. 6 ; as showers, to water with the dew of grace, and fructify my dry, parched soul. Thus we should be earnest with God for grace for ourselves, and for the churches abroad, for our church and state at home. Therefore, let such an use be made of it generally, as God, and not other foreign helps, may especially be trusted in: for it is the only way to destruction, to let God alone, and to trust to this body and that body. For in this case, many times, God makes those we trust in our destruction, as the Assyrians and Babylonians were the ruin of the ten tribes. But begin always first in heaven: set that great wheel a-working, and he will make all things comfortable, especially for our souls. Then we shall not only find him to make good this promise, ' I will be as the dew unto Israel;' but the residue which follow after.

' He shall grow as the lily,' &c.

Those unto whom God is dew, [he gives] a double blessing. He will make them grow, and so grow as they shall grow up as the lily. Thistles, and nettles, and ill weeds grow apace also, but not as lilies. But God's children are lilies, and then they grow as lilies.

Quest. How do Christians grow like lilies?

Ans. First, *for beauty and glory.* There is such a kind of glory and beauty in that plant, that it is said by our Saviour, that Solomon ' in all his royalty was not arrayed like one of these,' Mat. vi. 29. Because his was a borrowed glory from the creature, but the lily hath a native beauty of its own.

2. Again, the lily hath *a sweet and fragrant smell.* So have Christians a sweetness and shining expressed in their conversation; as we have it a little after, ' His smell shall be as Lebanon,' &c.

3. And then again, in regard *of purity and whiteness.* So, Christians are pure and unspotted in their conversation, and their aim is purity and unspottedness. Whiteness betokens an unstained conversation. So the people and children of God, they are lilies, beautiful and glorious in the eyes of God, and of all those who have spiritual eyes, to discern what spiritual excellency is; howsoever in regard of the world, their life be hidden. Their excellency is veiled with infirmities, afflictions, and disgraces by the malignant church; yet in God's esteem, and in the esteem of his children, they are lilies. All the dirt in the world cast upon a pearl cannot alter the nature of it. So, though the world go about to besmear these lilies with false imputations, yet they are lilies still, and have a glory upon them. For they have a better spirit and nature than the world hath. And they are sweeter in their conversation than the world; for when they have begun to be Christians, they sweeten their speeches and discourses. There is no Christian who is not of a sweet conversation. So far as grace hath altered him, he is beautiful, lovely, and sweet, and hath the whiteness of sincerity.

4. Now as God's children are lilies, and then grow as lilies for sweetness, glory, and beauty; so they are like lilies, especially in regard of *sudden growth.* When God gives a blessing, there is a strange growth on a sudden, as it is observed of this plant, that it grows very much in a night. So God's children, when his blessing is upon them, they thrive marvellously in a short space. To make this clear. When the dew of grace fell in our Saviour's time upon the Christian world, what a world of lilies grew suddenly! Three thousand in one day, at one sermon, converted by Peter, Acts ii. 41. The kingdom of heaven suffered violence in John Baptist's time, that is, the people thronged after the means of grace, and offered a holy violence to the things of God, Mat. xi. 12. So when this dew of grace fell, it was prophesied of it, ' The youth of thy womb,' saith he, ' shall be as the morning dew,' Ps. cx. 3. The dew comes out of the womb

of the morning, for the morning begets it : ' Thy youth shall be as the dew of the morning,' that is, they shall come in great abundance, as we see it fell out in the first spring of the gospel.   In the space of forty years, by the preaching of the apostles, what a deal of good was done through a great part of the world !   How did the gospel then break out like lightning, by means of that blessed apostle Paul, who himself carried it through a great part of the world !

And now, in the second spring of the gospel, when Luther began to preach, in the period of a few years, how many countries were converted and turned to the gospel !   England, Scotland, Swethland,* Denmark, the Palatinate, a great part of France, Bohemia, and of the Netherlands.   How many lilies grew up here on a sudden !   Sudden growths are suspected, and well they may be.   But when God will bless, in a short space a great deal of work shall be done.   For God is not tied to length of time.   He makes water to be wine every year in tract of time ; for he turns the water of heaven into the juice of the grape.   So there is water turned into wine ; that done in tract of time, which he can do in a shorter time, as he did in the gospel, John ii. 1, &c.   Where is the difference ?   That he did that miraculously in a short time, which he usually effects in continuance of time.   So now many times he doth great matters in a short time, that his power may be known and seen the more, as we see now in these wars of Germany (g) how quickly God hath turned his hand to help his church, and hiss for a despised, forgotten nation to trample down the insulting, afflicting, menacing power of the proud enemy.   And he can do so still, if our sins hinder him not.   Surely if we stand still and behold the salvation of the Lord, we shall see great matters effected in a little time.   ' They shall grow as the lily.'   The accomplishment of this promise is not wholly yet come, for there be blessed times approaching, wherein, when the Jews are converted, ' they shall grow as the lily ' in those glorious times there spoken of, at the conversion of the Jews and ' fulness of the Gentiles ' coming in, Rom. xi. 12, the accomplishment whereof we expect, to the rejoicing of our hearts, that they should at length prove indeed with us the true children of Abraham.

Use 1.   Therefore, we should make this use of all.   Labour that the dew of God may prove the dew of grace, that God would make us lilies.   If we would be beautiful and glorious, have a lustre upon us, and be as much beyond others as pearls are beyond common stones, and as lilies are better than thorns and briers, let us labour to have the grace of God, so to be accounted lilies, whatsoever the world accounts of us.

Use 2.   Again, if the work be wrought upon us, though the imputations of the world be otherwise, let us comfort ourselves, God accounts me a lily.   Set this against the base esteem of the world, considering how God judgeth, and those who are led by his Spirit, who judge better of us.   And in all association, combination, and linking in acquaintance, labour to join with those that are lilies, who cast a good and a sweet savour.   For we shall gain by their acquaintance whom Solomon affirmeth to be better and more excellent than their brethren, Prov. xii. 26.   What are other people then ?   They are but thorns.   Therefore, let not those which are lilies have too much or near acquaintance with thorns, lest they prick us, and, as our blessed Savour saith, turning again all to be-rent † us, Mat. vii. 6. It is said of our blessed Saviour in the Canticles, ' He feedeth among the lilies,' ii. 16.   And, indeed, where is there any true delight to be had under

* That is, ' Sweden.'—G.   † That is, ' rend.'—G.

heaven but in their company who are gracious ?   What can a man receive
from profane spirits in regard of comfort of soul ?   Nothing.   They are as
the barren wilderness that can yield nothing.   Their hearts are empty.
Therefore, their tongues are worth nothing.   But let our delight be with
David, toward the most excellent of the land, Ps. ci. 6, and then we shall
not only ' grow as the lily,' but, as it followeth, ' we shall cast forth our
roots as Lebanon.'

' And cast forth his roots as Lebanon.'

Because we have spoken of growth, and shall have occasion to touch it
hereafter, we will not be large in the point.   God here promiseth a growth
not only to the church, but to every particular Christian ; and it is very
necessary it should be so.   For without growth neither can we give God
his due honour, nor he receive the smell of a sweet sacrifice from us, as is
fit.   Nor can we without it withstand our enemies, or bear our crosses that
God may call us to.   Again, without growth and strength we cannot perform those great duties that God requires at our hands, of thankfulness ;
nor do things so cheerfully and sweetly as may be comfortable to us.   In
some* without growth we can do nothing acceptably either to God or his
people.   The more grace, the more acceptance, which is spoken that we
may value the promises, this especially, that we shall grow up in grace and
knowledge ' as the lily, and cast forth our roots as Lebanon.'

Quest. But how shall we come to grow ?

Ans. 1. Go to God, *that we may continually have from him the sanctifying dew of his grace.*   Go first for pardon of sin, then for a heart to reform
our ways, to enter in a new covenant for the time to come, that we will not
' trust in Asshur,' but will renounce our particular personal sins ; after
which we shall find sanctifying grace, so as the dew of God's Spirit will
make us grow.   Therefore take this order to improve the promises.   Go
to God for his love in Christ, for the pardoning of sin, and accepting of us
in him, that we may find a sense of his love in accepting of our persons,
in the pardoning of our sin, which is the ground of love ; for then this
sense of his love will kindle our love towards him again, feeling that we are
in the state of grace.   Then go to God for his promise in this order : Lord,
thou hast promised that thou wilt be as the dew, and that we shall grow as
lilies.   Make good thy promise then, that I may find the effectual power of
it transforming my soul into the blessed image of thy dear Son !

2. And know *that we must use all the means of growth, together with the
promise ;* for, in the things of this life, if a man were assured that the next
year would be a very plentiful year, would men therefore, because they
were thus forewarned, hang up their ploughs, and not prepare their ground?
No ; but they would the rather be encouraged to take pains, because they
know that howsoever God be pleased to vouchsafe plenty, yet he will do it
in the use of means, observing and depending on his providence.   So when
he hath made gracious promises of the dew of his grace, and of growth as
lilies, &c., this implieth a subordinate serving of his gracious providence.
Therefore it is a way to stir us up unto the use of all means rather, and
not to take us off from them.   Even as God, when he told the Israelites,
' I will give you the land of Canaan,' Gen. xvii. 8, did only promise it,
leaving the remainder to their conquest in the use of means.   Should this
have made them cast away their swords ?   No ; but it was that they
might fight, and fight the more courageously.   So when God hath promised
growth in grace, should this make us careless ?   Oh no ; it should make us

* Qu. 'in sum ?'—ED.

more diligent and careful, and comfort us in the use of means, knowing
that our labour shall not be in vain in the Lord, 1 Cor. xv. 58. Now,
Lord, I know I shall not lose my labour in hearing, in receiving of the sacrament, in the communion of saints, and use of sanctified means, for thou
hast made a gracious promise that ' I shall grow as the lily,' and that thou
wilt be ' as the dew unto me.' Therefore make thy good work begun, effectual unto my poor soul, that it may flourish and be refreshed as a watered
garden. But there are several sorts of growth formerly touched, either

1. A growing upward; or
2. A growing in the root ; or
3. A spreading and growing in the fruit, and sweetness.

Therefore Christians must not always look to have their growth in one
and the same place, but must wisely consider of God's prudent dealing with
his children in this kind, as will be further seen hereafter in the particulars.

' He shall cast forth his roots as Lebanon.'

That is, he shall cast and spread, and so put forth his roots as Lebanon.
He shall grow upward and downward. In regard of firmness, he shall be
more rooted. In what proportion? Trees grow upwards, in that proportion they take root downwards, because otherwise they may be top-heavy
and overturn, a blast of wind taking advantage of their tallness and weakness, to root them out the sooner. Therefore, proportionable to their
spreading above, there must be a rooting in the ground. As the prophet
speaks to Hezekiah of God's people, ' And the remnant that is escaped of
the house of Judah shall yet again take root downward, and bear fruit upward,' 2 Kings xix. 30. There must be firmness in the root, as well as
growth in the branches, for which cause God here promiseth to the church
and every Christian stability and fixedness, that as he groweth upward like
the lily, so he should grow downward, firm and strong.

Quest. Now, whence comes this rootedness and firm stability of God's
children ?

Ans. Especially from this, that they are now in the covenant of grace,
rooted in Christ, who is God-man, in whom they are firmly rooted. In
Adam we had a root of our own, but now our root is in Christ. All grace
is first poured into Christ's blessed nature, John i. 16, and then at a second
hand, ' out of his fulness we all receive grace for grace.' Being rooted in
Christ we become firm, for there is in him an everlasting marriage and
union. ' The root beareth us, we bear not the root,' Rom. xi. 18. Christ
beareth us, we bear not him. So now, in the covenant of grace, all the
firmness is out of us. Even as salvation itself was wrought out of us by a
mediator, so it is kept by a mediator out of us. All goodness, grace, and
favour of God to us is not in us, but in Christ; but it is so out of us, as
Christ and we are one. But now we only speak of the cause of our firmness and stability, that because we are in the state of grace we have an
everlasting firmness, as we are in Christ Jesus. God now making a second
covenant, he will not have it disannulled as the first was, for his second
works are better than his first. His first covenant was, ' Do this and live,'
Lev. xviii. 5 ; but his second is, ' Believe this and live,' Rom. x. 9. So
as howsoever our state in grace be but little, yet it is of a blessed, growing,
spreading, firm nature, so sure as what is begun in grace will end in glory.
Where God gives the first fruits he will give tenths, yea, the full harvest
and all, because by the covenant of grace we are one with Christ, who is
an everlasting head that never dies. Subservient to this now we have promised in the covenant of grace that we shall never depart from him, and

that he will never depart from us to do us good. He puts an awe-band into our hearts, that we shall never depart from him. But this point being often touched, leaving it, we will come to answer some objections.

Obj. 1. It may seem that these things are not so. God's children do not always grow and spread themselves, but they are often overturned and fall.

Ans 1. This is nothing. They are moved, but not removed. They are as Mount Zion, which cannot be removed, but abideth for ever, Ps. cxxv. 1, which, though it may be shaken with earthquakes, yet is not removed thereby. The gates of hell and sorrows of death may set sore upon them, but not prevail against them, Mat. xvi. 18. They may fall, but not fall away. They may be as a weather-beaten tree, but not as a tree pulled up by the roots. Therefore they are compared here to a tree whose root stands fast still. Thus much the church, after a sore trial and endurance of much affliction, confesseth, 'All this is come upon us, yet have we not forgotten thee, neither have we dealt falsely in thy covenant; our heart is not turned back, neither have our steps declined from thy way, though thou hast broken us in the place of dragons, and covered us with the shadow of death,' &c., Ps. xliv. 17, 18, 19.

And again, though they fall, yet they learn to stand fast by their falls, are gainers by their losses, and become stronger by their weaknesses. As tall cedars, the more they are shaken by the winds, the more deeply they take rooting; so Christians, the more storms and blasts they have, the more they are fastly rooted. That which we think to be the overthrow of God's children, doth but root them deeper. As Peter after his fall took deeper rooting, and David, &c., so after all outward storms and declinings, here is the fruit of all. They take deeper rooting, whilst their sins are purged away by their fiery afflictions, Isa. xxx. 15.

Qbject. 2. But why then are they not more comfortable in their lives, in feeling and seeing of God's wise ordering of things ?

Ans. 1. First, Because though God work strongly and surely in them, *yet he doth it for the most part slowly*, as the wise man speaks, ' all his works being beautiful in time,' Eccl. iii. 11. Therefore they apprehend not their comforts as they ought, and so go mourning the longer : the time of knitting divine experiences together not being yet come.

Secondly, Because the anguish of the cross, if it be quick and sharp, many times *takes away the apprehensions of God's excellent ends in the same ;* as the children of Israel could not hearken unto Moses, for anguish and vexation of spirit, Exod. vi. 9. ' No affliction,' saith the apostle, ' for the present is joyous,' though afterwards it brings forth the quiet fruit of righteousness, Heb. xii. 11.

Thirdly, Then again, *Satan's malice*, who casts in floods of temptations, *is great.* So that the soul cannot enjoy that sweet tranquillity and peace it otherwise might, casting in doubts and numbers of what-ifs into the soul. So that for a time, he causes a strong diversion in them, whence after that, there followeth peace again, when those temptations are seen and overcome.

Fourthly, It is long also of ourselves, who are not armed for crosses and afflictions, until we are suddenly surprised by them. And then leaving our watchfulness, and forgetting our consolation, we are struck down for the present by them, and cannot support ourselves against them.

Fifthly, and lastly, It comes also *from God's wise ordering and disposing providence*, who will not do all at once. Our comforts must come by degrees, now a little and then a little. Our experience, and so our comforts,

come together, after we have honoured God in dependence upon his will
and pleasure. And yet this hinders not, but a Christian grows still, though
he be for the present insensible of it, as a man is alive and grows whilst he
sleeps, though he be not sensible of it. Other objections have been
formerly touched.

' He shall cast forth his roots as Lebanon.'

We see then that the state of God's children is a firm and a stable condition, whence we may observe the difference betwixt God's people and
others. God's people are rooted, and spread their root; but the other
have rottenness in their root, being cursed, without any foundation. For
take a man who is not a good Christian, where is his foundation? Only
in the things of this world. Now all here is vanity, and we ourselves by
trusting vanity become vain, ' Every man in his best estate is altogether
vanity,' Ps. lxii. 9, vanity in himself, and trusts in vanity. What stable-
ness can there be in vanity? Can a man, *stare non stante*, stand in a thing
that stands not in itself? Will a picture continue that is drawn upon the
ice? Will it not fail and melt away, when the ice upon which it is drawn
thaws? So all these who have not the dew of God's grace, they are as a
picture upon the water, have no foundation, and stand upon that which cannot stand itself. Therefore the Scripture compareth them to the worst of
grass, which hath no good root; grass upon the housetop, which hath no
blessing of those that come by, but there stands perking up above others,
Ps. cxxix. 6. So it is with men that have no grace, they can perk up above
others; but as they have no stable root, nor the blessing of God's people,
stability with the Spirit of God inwardly, and the prayers of God's people
to water and bless them, so they perish and wither quickly. Nay, whole
nations, if wicked, have no foundation. What is become of the great
monarchies of the world, the Assyrian, Persian, Grecian and Roman
monarchies? And for cities themselves, they have died like men, and had
their periods. Only a Christian hath a kingdom, a stable condition which
cannot be shaken, Heb. xii. 28. He takes his root strongly, and grows
stronger and stronger till he grows to heaven, nay, indeed, while he lives,
he is rooted in heaven before his time; for though we be in earth, we are rooted
in heaven. Christ our root is in heaven, and his faith which is wrought
from heaven, carrieth us to Christ in heaven; and love, that grace of union,
following the union of faith, carrieth us to Christ also. Even before our
time, we are there in faith, love, and joy. Therefore a poor Christian is
firm and stable even in this life, having union with Christ. Though he
creep upon the earth, and seem a despised person, yet his root is heaven,
where he hath union with Christ. ' His life is hid with God in Christ,'
who ' when he shall appear,' he shall appear with him likewise in glory,
Col. iii. 3, 4. Therefore, if Christ be firm, the estate of a Christian
must needs be firm, for he is a cedar. Another man is as grass or corn
upon the house-top. ' All flesh is grass,' saith the prophet, Isa. xl. 6.

Obj. Aye, but they have wit, and memory, and parts, &c. Yet they
are but as the flower of the grass, perhaps better than ordinary grass, ' but
the grass withereth, and the flower fadeth.' What continueth then? Oh,
the word of the Lord, and comfort and grace by that word, ' endures for
ever,' 1 Pet. i. 25, and makes us endure for ever. This is excellently set
down by the prophet David. We see there, the righteous man is compared
to a tree planted by the water side, his leaf fails not, Ps. i. 3. So a Christian is planted in Christ, he is still on the growing hand, and his leaf shall
not wither : ' Those who are planted in the house of the Lord, shall flourish

in the courts of our God, they shall still bring fruit in their old age, they shall be fat and flourishing, they shall grow like a cedar in Lebanon,' Ps. xcii. 13.

Use 1. This clear difference should stir us up to *be comforted in our condition, which is firm and stable.* Why do we value crystal above glass ? Because it is brighter, and of more continuance. Why do we value continuing things ? inheritance above annuities ? Because they continue. If by the strength of our discourse, we value things answerable to their lasting, why should we not value the best things ? Our estate in grace, this is a lasting condition : for a Christian is like a cedar that is rooted, and takes deeper and deeper root, and never leaves growing till he grow to heaven. ' He shall cast forth his roots as Lebanon.'

Use 2. Again, let all them make use of it, *that find not the work of grace upon their hearts.* Oh ! let them consider what a fading condition they are in. They think they can do great matters. Perhaps they have a destructive power. They labour to do mischief, to crush whom they will in this world. But what is all this ? We see what the psalmist saith of a Doeg, a cursed man, who had a destroying power. ' Why boastest thou thyself in mischief, O mighty man ? the goodness of God endureth continually,' Ps. lii. 1. Why boastest thou thyself, that thou canst do mischief and overturn God's people ? &c. Know this, that the good will of God continues. Boast not thyself ; thy tongue deviseth mischief, as a sharp razor ; God shall destroy thee for ever. He shall cast thee away and pull thee out of thy dwelling, and root thee out of the land of the living. Those men that rejoice in a destructive power, in their ability to do mischief, and exercising of that ability all they can, they shall be plucked out of their place, and rooted out of the land of the living. And as it is in Job, they shall be hurled away as a man hurls a stone out of a sling, Job. xxvii. 21. Then what shall the righteous say ? They shall see and fear, and say, ' Lo, this is the man that made not God his strength, but trusted in the abundance of his riches, and strengthened himself in wickedness,' Ps. lii. 7. He thought to root himself so fast, that he should never be removed ; but at the last it shall come to pass, that all that see him shall say, ' Lo, see what is become of him ! this is the man that trusted in his riches, and made not God his strength.' What is become of him? Saith David of himself, ' I am like a green olive tree in the house of God ; I trust in the mercy of God for ever and ever,' Ps. lii. 8. Let them trust, if they will, in riches, power, strength, and favour with Saul and great men ; yet notwithstanding, be Doeg what he will, ' I shall be a green olive planted in the house of God,' &c.

So here is a double use the Scripture makes of these things. 1. The godly man rejoiceth in his condition ; and 2, Other men fear and grow wise, not to trust to their fading condition. They are, as the prophet speaks, ' as a bay tree,' Ps. xxxvii. 35, that flourishes for a time, and then after come to nothing, ' their place is nowhere found.' They keep a great deal of do in the world for a time, but afterwards, where is such an one ? Their place is nowhere found, nowhere comfortably. They have a place in hell, but comfortably a place nowhere. This is the estate of all those who have not a good root. For, saith Christ, ' Every plant that my heavenly Father hath not planted, shall be rooted up,' Mat. xv. 13. It is true of every condition, and of every man, if God have not planted him in that excellent state, or do not in time, he shall be rooted up. For the time will come that the earth will hold him no longer. He roots himself now in the earth, which then shall cast him out. He cannot stay here long. Heaven will not receive him, then hell must.   What a miserable thing is this, when we place and bottom ourselves upon things that will not last! when ourselves shall outlast our foundation! when a man shall live for ever, and that which he builds on is fading!   What extremity of folly is this, to build on riches, favour, greatness, power, inheritance, which either must be taken from him, or he from them, he knoweth not how soon!

What makes a man miserable, but the disappointing of his hopes and crossing of his affections?   Now when a man pitcheth his soul too much upon his worldly things, from which there must be a parting, this is, as it were, the rending of the skin from the flesh, and the flesh from the bones. When a man's soul is rent from that he pitcheth his happiness on, this maketh a man miserable; for misery is in disappointing the hopes, and crossing the affections.   Now only a Christian plants his heart and affections on that which is everlasting, of equal continuance with his soul.   As he shall live for ever, so he is rooted for ever in that which must make him everlastingly happy.   These things we hear, and they are undeniably true. But how few make use of them, to desist from going on in a plodding, swelling desire of an earthly condition, to overtop other men.   Such labour to grow in tallness and height, but strive not to be rooted.   Now that which grows perking up in height, overtopping other things, yet without root, what will become of it?   It will be turned up by the roots.

Now, how shall we grow to be rooted?   For to attain hereunto, it is not only necessary to apply the promises, and challenge God with them, but to consider also what ways he will make them good.

First, Labour to know God and his free grace in Jesus Christ.   ' Grow in grace, and in the knowledge of our Lord Jesus Christ,' 2 Pet. iii. 18.   They go both together.   The more we grow in the knowledge of our Lord Jesus Christ, and of the grace of God in him, the more grace and rootedness we shall have.   For that which the soul doth clearly apprehend, it fastens upon in that measure it apprehendeth it.   Clearness in the understanding breeds earnestness in the affections, and fastness too.   So the more we grow in knowledge, the more we root ourselves in that we know.   And therefore the apostle prays for the Ephesians, that they might have the Spirit of revelation, &c., that they might know the height, breadth, depth, and length of God's love that passeth knowledge.   ' For this cause I bow my knees unto the Father of our Lord Jesus Christ, of whom the whole family of heaven and earth is named, that he would grant you, according to the riches of his glory, to be strengthened by his Spirit in the inner man; that Christ may dwell in your hearts by faith; that ye, being rooted and grounded in love,' in the sense of God's love to us, and so of our love to him again (for we are not rooted in love to God, till we be rooted in the sense of God's love to us), ' that you may be able to comprehend with all saints the height and breadth,' &c., Ephes. iii. 14.

Second, And withal, *labour to know the gracious promises of Christ.*   For we are knit to him by virtue of his word and promises, which like himself are ' yea and amen.'   ' Jehovah, yesterday, to-day, and the same for ever,' 2 Cor. i. 20.   So all his promises made in him, they are ' yea and amen,' in themselves firm, and firm to us in him.   They are ' yea and amen;' that is, they are made and performed in Christ, in whom they are sure to be performed; and thereupon they are firm too.   God made them, who is Jehovah, and they are made in Christ that is Jehovah.   So God the Father Jehovah, he promiseth, and he makes them good in Christ Jehovah, who is unchangeable.

Thirdly, But this is not enough. We must *labour to have our hearts stablished*, that they may rely firmly on that which is firm. For if a thing be never so firm, except we rely firmly on it, there is no stability or strength from it. Now, when there is strength in the thing, and strength in the soul, that strength is impregnable and unconquerable strength. In Christ they are ' yea and amen ;' in whom he stablisheth us, anoints us, seals us, and gives us the earnest of the Spirit in our hearts.

How doth God stablish us upon the promises ? The rest which followeth is an explication of this. When he gives us the ' earnest of the Spirit,' 2 Cor. i. 22, and seals us to be his, in token he means to make good the bargain, then we are established. But we are never firmly established till we get the assurance of salvation. Then, as the promises are yea and amen in themselves, so we are stablished upon them when we are sealed and have earnest of the Spirit. Let us labour therefore to grow in the knowledge of God's love in Christ, to know the height, breadth, depth, and length of it, and to grow in all the gracious promises which are made in Christ, who is Amen himself, as his promises are ; and then, when we are sealed and anointed by the Spirit, we shall be so stablished that nothing shall move us. Therefore let us use all means for the establishing of growth in us, the word and sacraments especially. For as baptism admits us into the house of God, so by the sacrament of the Lord's supper, the blessed food of the soul, we are strengthened. In the use of these means, let us make suit unto God to make good his gracious promise unto us, that we shall ' grow as lilies, and take root as the cedars in Lebanon.'

Let us know, that we ought every day to labour to be more and more rooted. Do we know what times may befall us ? We have need to grow every day, to grow upward, and in breadth and in depth. If we considered what times we may live to, it should force us to grow every way, especially in humility, that root and mother of graces, to grow downward in that ; to grow in knowledge and faith, until we be filled with the fulness of God.

Obj. A poor Christian ofttimes makes this objection, Oh ! I do not grow ! Therefore I fear my state ; I am oft shaken ! Therefore this promise is not fulfilled to me !

Ans. To this I answer, Christians may be deceived ; for they do grow ofttimes in firmness, strength, and stability, though they do not spread out. They may grow in refinedness, that that which comes from them may be more pure, and less mixed with natural corruption, pride, self-love, and the like. This is a temptation that old men are subject to especially, in whom the heat of nature decays, who think withal that grace decays. But it is not so ; for ofttimes when grace is carried with the heat of nature, it makes a greater show, being helped by nature. The demonstration, but not the truth, of grace is thus helped. Therefore this clause of the promise is made good in old Christians. They are every day more and more rooted, firm, stable, and judicious, and more able in those graces which belong to their place and condition. Therefore they should not be discouraged though they be not carried with the stream and tide of nature, helped with that vigour that sometime was in them. They grow in judiciousness, mortifiedness, in heavenly-mindedness, and in ability to give good counsel to others. This is well, for we grow not in grace one way, but divers ways ; not only when we grow in outward demonstration, and in many fruits and actions, but when we grow in refinedness and judiciousness, as was said, then we are said to grow likewise.

Yet notwithstanding it should be the endeavour of all to grow what they can in grace. When, if they grow not so fast as others, let them know that there are several ages in Christ. A young Christian cannot be so planted and so deeply rooted as another that is of a greater standing. This should not discourage any, seeing there are 'babes in Christ,' 1 Cor. iii. 1, as well as 'strong men,' Rom. xv. 1. Therefore where there is truth of heart, with endeavour to grow better and better, and to use all means, let no man be discouraged. Remember alway this for a truth, that we may grow, and we ought to grow, and the children of God ordinarily have grown more and more, both in fruitfulness and stedfastness every way, but not with a like growth in measure or time. Therefore labour to make use of these promises, and not to favour ourselves in an ungrowing estate, for grace is of a growing nature. If it grow not in fruitfulness, yet it grows in the root; as a plant sometimes grows in fruitfulness, sometimes in the root. There is more virtue in winter time in the root than in the fruit which is gone. So a Christian groweth one way if not another; though not in outward demonstration, yet in humiliation. God sometimes sees it necessary that our branches should not spread for a while, but that we should grow in humility; by some faults and sins we fall and slip into, that we may see our own weakness and look up.

Let us labour therefore, who have so long enjoyed such store of blessed means, under the dew of God's grace and the influence of his Spirit, in the paradise of God, his house and church. Having so long lived in this Eden, let us labour now to spread and grow in fruitfulness, that so we may be filled with the fulness of God. It is the chief thing of all, to be rooted and grow in grace. You see, God when he would single out a blessing, he tells them not that they shall grow rich, that they shall spread out and grow rich in the world. No! But, you whom I love freely, take this as a fruit of it, 'you shall grow as the lily,' you shall grow fruitful 'as the olive,' &c. This is the comfort of a Christian. Though he grows downward oft in the world, and things of this natural life, yet he grows upward in another condition: as lilies and cedars, they grow downwards one way, but they grow upwards another. Perhaps they may decay in their state and favour, and in their practice and cunning in this life; but a Christian, if he be in the use of right means, and put in suit the gracious promises, he is sure still to grow in grace, in faith, in love, and in the inner man.

Is not this a comfort, that a Christian hath a comfortable meditation of the time to come in all his crosses? that it is for better and better still; that as in time he is nearer heaven, so he shall be fitter and fitter, and nearer and nearer still, with a disposition suitable to the place; that the time to come is the best time; and that he shall grow every way, in height, in breadth, in depth and length, and apprehension of God's love, and that the more he grows in knowledge of these things, the more he shall grow in all dimensions, being as sure of things to come as of things past, and that neither things present nor to come shall ever separate him from the love of God in Christ? Rom. viii. 35. What a comfortable state is a Christian in, who is always on the mending hand, that is such a child of hope, when the hope of the wicked shall perish! Let us labour, therefore, that we may be in such a case and state of soul as that thoughts of the time to come may be comfortable, that when we think we must be transplanted hence out of the paradise and Eden of God's church into a heavenly paradise, that all our changes shall be for the better. What a fearful thing is it to be in the state of nature! What foundation hath a man in that estate, who hath no root here, and that root he hath will fail him ere long? How fearful is it for such a man to think of a change, when it is not a change for the better?

Here is wisdom. If we will be wise to purpose, let us be wise this way. Labour, in the first place, to prize God's favours, and to know how to come by them in the use of all means. Look to God for the performance of these gracious promises. For they are not of what we shall do in ourselves, but what God will do in the covenant of grace. And if a Christian should not be rooted and grow stronger and stronger, we should not fail, but God and Christ should fail, who is our root and bears us up. Therefore, God hath taken upon him the performance of all these things. What remaineth for us but a careful using of all means? and in the use of all, a going out of ourselves to God, that he would be ' as the dew to us,' and cause us, by the dew of his Spirit, to grow more and more rooted in grace as long as we live in this world? And then our rooting and stability lies upon God, not upon us. He fails if we fail, who hath undertaken that ' we shall grow as the lily, and cast forth our roots as Lebanon.'

THE EIGHTH SERMON.

His branches shall spread, his beauty shall be as the olive-tree, and his smell as Lebanon. They that dwell under his shadow shall return; they shall revive as the corn, and grow as the vine: the scent thereof shall be as the vine of Lebanon.—Hos. XIV. 6, 7.

WE have heard at large heretofore what petitions God put into the heart and mouth of his church, as also what gracious answer God gives his own petitions. He cannot deny the prayers made by his own Spirit; and as he is goodness in itself, so he shews it in this, that he goes beyond all that we can desire, think, or speak. His answer is more transcendent, as the apostle speaks. He does ' exceeding abundantly above all that we ask or think,' &c., Ephes. iii. 19, 20. For whereas they in particular and in brief say, ' Do good to us, and receive us graciously,' he tells them, ' He will be as the dew unto them.' And from thence, being dew to them, is their spreading and growing as a lily, and casting of their roots as Lebanon. ' And their branches shall spread,' &c. And all this to encourage us to come to so powerful and large-hearted a God, who, as he is able to do more than we desire of him, so he will also do it. ' He will be as the dew unto us.' This is the general of all, for all other fruitfulness comes from this: 1. God will be as the dew; and then, 2. They shall grow as the lily, and cast their roots as the cedars in Lebanon. They shall not only grow upward, but downward, for the lily quickly spreads itself forth; but they shall be like the trees of Lebanon for stedfastness, and then spread in breadth, grow in all dimensions, which is fulfilled of the church in general, and of every particular Christian, when once he is in Christ, using sanctified means. They grow, then, in the root, and upright, and in every dimension. ' His branches shall spread.' And then,

' His beauty shall be as the olive-tree.'

Which, though fruitful and excellent, yet because it hath no sweet smell, it is added,

' His smell shall be as Lebanon.'

These excellencies promised to the church of God are not all in one tree, but yet they are in some sort in every Christian. What agrees not all to one plant agrees to the ' plants of righteousness.' They grow upwards and downwards, spread, and are savoury and fruitful. All agrees to a tree of righteousness. We say of man, He is a little world, a compendium of this great world, as indeed there is a comprising of all the excellencies of the world in man, for he hath a being with those creatures who have only that, and therewith he hath growing sense and reason, whereby he hath communion with God, and those understanding spirits, the angels. So that he is, as it were, a sum of all the excellencies of the creatures, a little world indeed (h). The great world hath nothing, but the little world hath the same in some proportion. So it is in grace. A Christian hath all excellencies in him, that are in the world. There is not an excellency in any thing, but it is an higher kind in a Christian. He hath the beauty of the lily, and he grows up in spreading, smell, and fruitfulness. His wisdom exceeds that of all the creatures. There is not an excellency in nature, but we have some proportionable excellency in grace which is above it. God useth these outward things to help us, that we should do both body and soul good by the creatures. Whatsoever doth our bodies good, either by necessity or delight, they help our souls; as plants and trees not only refresh the outward man, and the senses, but also they teach our souls, as here the Holy Ghost teacheth them by outward things. First it is said,

' His branches shall spread.'

When God enriches the soul with saving grace, one shall grow every way and flourish abundantly, extending forth their goodness on every side largely to the knowledge and open view of others ; and then further,

' His beauty shall be as the olive-tree.'

What is the beauty of the olive-tree ? To be useful, fruitful, and to bring forth good fruit. Indeed, the glory of a tree is to be loaden with fruit, and useful fruit ; which is the best property of fruit, to be useful and delightful. So the glory of a Christian, who is a plant of righteousness, of God's own planting, is to abound in fruits of righteousness. Indeed, the olive is a very fruitful tree, and the oil which comes and distils from it hath many excellent properties agreeing to graces.

1. Amongst the rest, it is a royal kind of liquor, that will be above the rest. So grace it commands all other things ; it gives a sanctified use of the creature, and subdues all corruption.

2. And then it is unmixed. It will mingle with nothing. Light and darkness will not mingle, no more will grace and corruption ; for the one is hostile to the other, as Solomon speaks, ' The just is abomination to the wicked,' Prov. xxix. 27.

3. Further, it is sweet, strengthening, and feeding the life, as in Zechariah there is mention made of two olives before the Lord, which feed the two candlesticks, Zech. iv. 3. And olives of grace have always fatness distilling from Christ to feed his lamp with oil. God's church hath always oil ; and those that are olives, they keep the church by their particular calling.

1. He shall be fruitful as the olive ; and,

2. Abundant in fruit, as the olive.

3. Constant in fruit, like the olive.

For it bears fruit much, and never fails, no not in winter, and hath a perpetual greenness. Indeed, the child of God hath a perpetual verdure ; as it is, Ps. i. 3, ' His leaf never fails,' because that which is the cause of flourishing never fails him. Which causes are two,

1. Moisture.

2. Heat.

For we know, moisture and heat, these two are the causes of all kindly growth. If a tree have more moisture than heat, then it is waterish; if it have more heat than moisture, then there is no bigness in the fruit. So true it is, that moisture and heat are the causes of fruitfulness in a good proportion. So God's children, having the Sun of righteousness always shining upon them, and being always under the dew of grace (the promise being, ' to be as the dew to Israel'), having all dew to fall upon them for moisture, and having the Sun of righteousness to shine upon them to make them fruitful, their leaf never fails, they never give over bringing forth fruit ; because they have in them causes perpetuating fruitfulness, though not alike ; because Christ by his Spirit is a voluntary, and not a natural, cause of their fruitfulness, that is, he is such a cause, as works sometimes more and sometimes less, to shew that grace springs not from ourselves, and to acquaint us with our own weakness and insufficiency. Heaven is the perfection of all, both graces and comforts. Wherefore Peter calls the state of heaven, ' an inheritance, immortal and undefiled, that fades not away,' 1 Peter i. 4. Why is that an estate of grace and comfort, more than this of this world ? Because it is a never-fading estate. There they are alway in one tenure ; and because Christ shews himself alway there. There is abundance of water to moisten them, and heat to cherish them. There is no intermingling or stopping in growth, as is here. Therefore it is an inheritance that fadeth not away, having the supply of a perpetual cause of flourishing.

This in some degree is true of the church on earth. It is the inheritance of God that fades not, and Christians therein are olives that bring forth fruit constantly, having a perpetual freshness and greenness. So the righteous man is compared to the cedars of Lebanon, Ps. xcii. 12, which bring forth much fruit in their age. He shall be fruitful as the olive. From all which this point, formerly touched, followeth :

That it is the excellency and glory of a Christian, to be fruitful in his place.

Both to be fruitful in his place as a Christian, and in his particular calling ; to be fruitful as a magistrate, as a minister, as a governor of a family, as a neighbour, as a friend ; to be fruitful in all. Because in religion, every near relation is as it were a joining together of the body in Christ, one to another, by which some good is derived from one to another. God uses these relations as conduits to convey graces. A good Christian, the meanest of them is a good neighbour, and doth a great deal of good, being fruitful as a neighbour, fruitful as a friend ; much more as a husband, as a magistrate, as a minister. These relations are a knitting to Christ, by which fatness and sap are derived from the head for the good of the whole body. Therefore a Christian in all relations is fruitful. When he comes to be a Christian, he considers, like good Mordecai, what good he may do ; as he told Esther, ' What if thou be called to the kingdom for this purpose,' Esther iv. 14 ? So a Christian will reason with himself, What if I be called to be a magistrate, or a minister, for this purpose ? What if I be called to be a friend, for such or such a purpose, to do this or this good ? Indeed such are gracious *quære's** made to a man's soul, to inquire for what purpose hath God raised me ? To do this or that ? To be idle, or barren, or noisome ? O no ; to be a plant of God's planting. My glory shall be my fruitfulness in my place.

* That is, ' queries.'—G.

Therefore let us every one consider with ourselves, wherefore God hath set us in the church in our particular standings. Wherein let us remember this, that howsoever God may endure barrenness out of the church, in want of means, yet he will never endure it under means. It is better for a bramble to be in the wilderness, than in an orchard ; for a weed to be abroad, than in a garden, where it is sure to be weeded out, as the other to be cut down. If a man will be unprofitable, let him be unprofitable out of the church. But to be so where he hath the dew of grace falling on him, in the means of salvation, where are all God's sweet favours, to be a bramble in the orchard, to be a weed in the garden, to be noisome in a place where we should be fruitful, will God the great husbandman endure this ? He will not long put it up. But that he exerciseth his children with such noisome trees to try them, as he hath some service for these thorns to do, to scratch them. So, were it not for such-like services for a time, he would weed them out and burn them. For whatsoever is not for fruit, is for the fire. ' Yea, every tree that bringeth forth not good fruit, shall be hewn down and cast into the fire,' Mat. iii. 10.

And the more to stir us up hereunto, let us know that wheresoever the dew of grace falls, and where there is the means of salvation, that at that very time there is an axe, an instrument of vengeance, laid to the root of the tree, which is not struck down presently, but ' it is laid to the root,' Mat. iii. 10; that is, vengeance is threatened to the tree, to that plant which hath the means, and brings not forth good fruit in time and season. What is the end thereof ? To be hewn down and cast into the fire. As we see the church of the Jews, when Christ came, the Messiah, the great prophet of the church, never was there more means of salvation ; yet even then, what saith John Baptist ? ' Now,' even now, ' is the axe laid unto the root of the tree,' Mat. iii. 10 ; and indeed, in a few years after, the whole tree, the church of the Jews, was cut down. And, Rev. vi. 2, 4, we see, after the rider on the ' white horse,' which is the preaching of the gospel, there comes a ' red, bloody horse,' and ' a pale horse,' war and famine. After the ' white horse,' his triumphant chariot, the preaching of the gospel. If this take not place, that it win and gain not, what follows after ? ' The red and the pale horse,' war, famine, and destruction. It will not be always with us as it is ; for the gospel having been so long preached, we having been so long planted in God's paradise, the church, if we bear not fruit, ' the axe is laid to the root of the tree.' God will strike at the root, and root up all. Therefore let every one in their place be fruitful.

Every one that is fruitful, God hath a special care of. If any tree were fruitful, the Israelites in their conquest were to spare that, because it was useful, and they might have use of it, Deut. xx. 19, 20. So God will always spare fruitful trees, and have a special care of such in common calamities. Let us therefore be exhorted not only to bring forth fruit, but to bring forth fruit in abundance, to study to excel in good works. The word in the original is, ' a standard-bearer ' (i), to stand before others in good works. As it is in Titus, ' labour to be as standard-bearers,' Titus iii. 8, to go before others in good works. Strive to out-go others in fruitfulness ; for therein is the excellency. For those both in the sight of God and men are in most esteem who are most fruitful in their callings and places. The more we excel in fruitfulness, the more we excel in comfort ; and the more we excel this way, the more we may excel. For God will tend and prune good trees, that they may bring forth more and better fruit, John xv. 2. And the more majesty we walk with, the more we damp the enemies, seeing them all under our feet. A growing Christian never wants abundance of encouragements, for he sees such grounds of comfort, as that he walks impregnable and invincible in all the discouragements of this world, breaking through all. As Solomon saith, it is a comely thing to see a lion walk, Prov. xxx. 29, 30. So much more it is to see a valiant, strong, well-grown Christian, who is bold as a lion, abound in good works.

It is said, ' His beauty shall be as the olive, and his smell as Lebanon.' The olive of itself hath no sweet smell. Therefore it is made up by another resemblance,

' His smell shall be as Lebanon.'

Lebanon stood on the north side of Judea, and was a place abounding with goodly trees, and all sweet plants whatsoever, which cast a wondrous sweet scent and smell afar off ; as some countries abound so in sweet fruits and simples, as oranges, lemons and the like, that the fragrancy of the smell is smelt of passengers as they sail along the coast (j). So was this Lebanon a place full of rare fruits and fragrant flowers, which cast a scent afar off. Now, hence the Holy Ghost fetcheth the comparison. ' They shall smell as Lebanon,' that is, as those plants in Lebanon which cast a sweet and delightful smell afar off. Whence we will only observe this ;

That a Christian by his fruitfulness doth delight others.

He is sweet to God and man, as the olive and the vine speak of their fruitfulness. ' They delight God and man,' Judges ix. 9, 13. So a Christian, both alive and dead, he is pleasing and delightful to the spirits of others, to God, and all that have the Spirit of God. As for God himself, we know that works of mercy are, as it were, a sweet odour. He is delighted with good works, as with sacrifice, Philip. iv. 18, smelling a sweet savour from them ; and their prayers ascend as sweet incense before him, Ps. cxli. 2. Every good work is pleasing and delightful to God, who dwells in an humble heart, and broken spirit. ' The upright are his delight,' Prov. xi. 20. We see likewise how Christ commends the graces of his church, which whole book is full of praises in this kind one of another. The church sets out the praises of Christ, and Christ the praises of the church. The church is sweet : ' Oh, let me hear thy voice, for it is sweet and lovely,' Cant. ii. 14. The church's voice is sweet, praying to God, or praising him. So whatsoever comes from the Spirit of God in the hearts of his children, is sweet. God lays to heart the voice of his children.

And as it is true of God, so is it of God's people. They are delighted with the favour of those things that come from other of God's people. For they have graces in them, and therewith the Spirit of God, which is as fire to set a-work all those graces in them. For it is the nature of fire, where it encounters with sweet things, to kindle them, and make them smell more fragrant and sweet. So a spirit of love makes all sweet and pleasing whatsoever, in the children of God. It puts a gracefulness upon their words, making their reproofs, admonitions, comforts, and whatsoever comes from them, to have a delightfulness in them ; because all is done in love, and comes from the Spirit of God, which carrieth a sweetness in it, to all those endowed with the same Spirit.

Use 1. Let this be an encouragement to be in love with the state of God's children, that so our works, and whatsoever comes from us, as far as it is spiritual, may be acceptable unto God and to the church, while we are living, nay, when we are dead. The very works of holy men, when they are dead, are as a box of ointment, as the ointment of the apothecary ; as the wise man says of Josiah, whose very name was like the ointment of the apothecary.* So the name of those who have stood out for good, and have been good in their times, it carries a sweetness with it when they are gone. The church of God riseth out of the ashes of the martyrs, which hitherto smells sweet, and puts life in those who come after, so precious are they both dead and alive (*k*).

Use 2. And then, let it be an encouragement to be led by God's Spirit, and planted in God's house, and to be fruitful in our places, that so we may delight God and man, and when we are gone, leave a good scent behind us. Good men, as it were, with their good scent they leave behind them, perfume the times, which are the better for them dead and alive. What a sweet savour hath Paul left behind him, by his writings to the church, even to the end of the world! What fragrancy of delightful smells have the holy ancient fathers and martyrs left behind them! A good man should be like the box of ointment spoken of in the gospel, which when it was opened, the whole house was filled with the sweetness thereof, Mat. xxvi. 7, *seq.* So a good man should labour to be full of sweetness, willingness and abilities to do good, all kindled by a spirit of love in him; that when he is opened, all should be pleasing and delightful that cometh from him. Christ never opened his mouth, but good came from him; and the heavens never opened in vain. Therefore, in opening of our mouths, we should labour to fill the places where we are with a good savour. Oh, how contrary is this to the condition of many! What comes from them? Filthy speeches and oaths; nay, that which should be their shame they glory in. We see it is the glory of a tree to be fruitful, and to cast forth a good savour, like the trees of Lebanon. What vile spirits, then, are such men led withal, who delight to offend God and man with their impious speeches! who yet are so bold as to shew their faces, to outdare others that are better than themselves. Such are contrary to all God's senses. The Scripture condescends so far to our capacity, as to attribute senses unto God, of feeling, smelling, and touching, &c. So God is said to look upon his children with delight, and to hear their prayers. 'Let me hear thy voice,' &c., Cant. ii. 14. And he tastes the fruit that comes from them. So, on the contrary, all his senses are annoyed with wicked men and vile persons, who are abominable to God, as the Scripture speaks. As a man that goes by a stinking dunghill, stops his nose, and cannot endure the scent, so the blasphemous breath of graceless persons, it is abominable to God, as it were; God cannot endure such an odious smell; and for his eyes, he cannot endure iniquity, to look upon the wicked; and for his ears, their prayers are abominable. How abominable, then, are their persons whence those prayers proceed! They have proud hearts, hating God and man. Wherefore, praying out of necessity, not love to him, they are abominable. And so for feeling. Your sacrifices are a burden unto me, I cannot bear them, Isa. i. 11; and the prophet complaineth that God was burdened and loaded under their sins, 'as a cart pressed till it be ready to break under the sheaves,' Amos ii. 13. All his senses are offended with wicked men. This, hardened wretches think not of, that, whilst God fills their bellies with good things, go on in sin-security. But the time will come when they shall know the truth of these things, what it is to lead an odious, abominable life, contrary to God and all good men. Hence we see what we should be, that we may give a sweet scent: 'His smell shall be as Lebanon.'

* The passage is in Ecclesiasticus xlix. 1. This is the first reference that we have found in Sibbes to the Apocrypha.—ED..

Wicked men know this very well, that the lives, speeches, and courses of good men, for the most part, are fruitful beyond theirs. Therefore, what they can, they labour to cast aspersions upon them, that they may not smell so sweet. So, crying down those who are better than themselves, that they may be the less ill thought of, and setting a price upon all things in themselves, and their companions. Take me a knot of cursed companions, and they are the only stout, the only wise and learned men : all learning it must live and die with them ; and all other men, though incomparable beyond them in abilities, in grace, in fruitfulness to do good, they are nobody. And this policy the devil teacheth them. But this will not serve the turn; for God, both in life and after death, will raise up the esteem of such who have been fruitful, when ' the memory of the wicked shall rot,' Prov. x. 7, and not be mentioned without a kind of loathing. Therefore let no man trust to this foolish policy, to cry down all others that are better than themselves, thinking thereby themselves shall be better esteemed. This will not do ; for as all other things, so our good name is at God's disposing. It is not in the world to take away the good name or acceptance of good people ; for they shall have, in spite of the world, a place in the hearts of God's people, who are best able to judge. The next thing promised is,

' They that dwell under his shadow shall return.'

The Holy Ghost, it seems, cannot express in words and comparisons enough, the excellent condition of the church, and of the children of God, when they are once brought into the state of grace. The former words concern the excellency of the children of God in themselves, and these the fruitfulness and goodness of them that are under them, who shall be brought into the families and places where they live. ' They that dwell under his shadow,' under the shadow of Israel, ' shall return and revive as the corn, and grow as the vine,' &c. For so it is most fitly meant of Israel. For formerly it is said, ' I will be as the dew unto Israel.' Originally it is meant of Christ's shadow ; but because whosoever dwells under the church's shadow dwells under Christ's, therefore it is most fitly applied to Israel. They that dwell under Israel's shadow shall return.' What returning ? Return to God by repentance. This is supposed ; for those that dwell in the church of God, if they belong to God, by the help of good means they shall attain to reformation and repentance. But it is especially meant of that which follows upon it, ' They shall return;' that is, they shall revive, as a man's spirits after a swoon are said to return, and things after a seeming decay and deadness are said to be quickened and return again. So all that dwell under the shadow of Israel, they shall return to God by repentance. ' They shall return,' having a greater vigour and liveliness, recovering that which they seemed to have lost before.

' They that dwell under his shadow shall return.'

When God will bless any people, he will bless all that belong to them and are under them, because they are blessed in blessing them, even as we are touched when our children are stricken. God strikes the father in the child, the husband in the wife, the master in the servant, because there is some relation and dependence betwixt them. As it is in ill so it is in good: God blesseth the father in the child, the king in the subject, and the subject in the king. God blesseth one in another. And in blessing, because God loves the church, all the friends of the church are the better for it. They prosper that love the church, Ps. cxxii. 6, though they be not members of it. All that bless Abraham shall be blessed. Though they be not actually good, yet if they wish him well, a blessing is promised. So when

God blesseth a man to purpose, he blesseth all that belong to him. All that be under his shadow fare the better. The point to be handled is this, *That the church itself yields a shadow*, being shadowed itself by Christ, who spreads his wing over it. Now, what is the use of a shadow?

1. It is for a retiring place to rest in.

2. It is for defence against the extremity of heat.

3. It is for delight, if the shades be good and wholesome.

For, as philosophers express the nature of trees, there be some trees which yield noisome shadows, some trees have a heavy, noxious, dangerous shadow, because there comes a scent from the tree, as naturalists observe, which annoys the brains. But he speaks here of good trees. Israel is a tree that yields a shadow unto all; that is, all that are under Israel shall rest quietly, and not be annoyed with the heat of God's wrath, and the like. They shall be delighted, having a sweet refreshing under the church.

God, in Scripture, is often said to be a shadow, and his people to be under ' the shadow of his wings,' Ps. xxxvi. 7. But God and the church are all one in this, for they that are under the church's shadow are under God's shadow; for the church is Christ's, and Christ God's. Therefore to be under the church is to be under God, and to be in the church is to be under God's protection. They both agree, as we see, Mic. v. 7. The church is said to be dew, because God bedews the church, and the church bedews others; and here the promise is, ' I will be as the dew unto Israel,' where the same name is attributed unto God. Christ is a vine, and the church is a vine, John xv. 1. Christ is a dew and a shadow. So is the church, because Christ communicates his excellencies to her, and she hers unto others. Therefore there can be no offence in applying this to the church, which is the proper meaning of the place; for the church is a shadow for rest and freedom from annoyance unto all that come under her.

Quest. To clear this a little. What solace and rest do men find under the shadow of the church?

Ans. There is a rest and a peace in the church, for all things are at peace with the church, even the very stones in the field, Job v. 23 ; nothing can hurt the children of the church, ' God will be and is a sun and shield unto them,' Ps. xxxiv. 11 : a shield to keep off all ill, and a sun to confer all good unto them. So his promise is to Abraham, ' I will be thy buckler, and thine exceeding great reward,' Gen. xv. 1. A buckler to keep ill from him, and ' an exceeding great reward' for good. Therefore it is a sweet shadow to be under the church, where God is all in all to them, who makes all things work for good unto them, even the greatest evil. Now, what a delightful thing is it to have a resting-place with them which either suffer no ill, or God turns all ill to their great good! where God is a ' sun and a shield,' a ' buckler,' and an ' exceeding great reward,' as he is to his church and children!

And then, again, God is about his church as a ' wall of fire,' Zech. ii. 5, to protect it, not only as a shadow to keep off storms, but as a wall of fire to keep off and consume enemies. God, in regard of protection of his church, is a compassing unto them, as it is in Job. Saith Satan, ' Hast thou not made a hedge about him, and all that he hath?' Job i. 10. There was a hedge about Job, his wife, children, and goods, which the devil durst not enter, nor make a gap in, until God gave him leave. Therefore those that are under the shadow of the church, they are safe, and may rest quietly.

But this is especially understood spiritually. The church is a shadow, and herself under a shadow spiritually, that is, in regard of spiritual evils, from the worst enemies. For out of the church, where is any fence for the greatest ill of all, the wrath of God? In the church of God there is set down a way of pacification, how the wrath of God is taken off and appeased in reconciliation by the death and sufferings of Jesus Christ, whereby the believing soul attaineth peace and joy unspeakable and glorious. Out of the church there is no means at all to pacify the greatest ill. Therefore there is no true rest out of the church, nothing but stings and torments of conscience. And as there is a shelter against the wrath of God, which burns to the bottom of hell, so here is a remedy against death and damnation. For now death is made a friend to the church, and the children of the church, for the sting of it is taken away, so that it doth them more good than anything in the world, ending all their misery and sinning, and opening a passage unto eternal happiness. All other petty ills that attend upon death are nothing. There is a rest from all these whatsoever, for all afflictions have a sanctified use to God's people for their good. There is therefore a rest and refreshing in the church for all that come under it.

And as this is true of the church in general, so it is true of particular families, that are little churches. There is rest and happiness in them. God blesseth all under the roof of a godly man. Whosoever comes under that shadow comes for a blessing, or for further hardening. We see in the current of Scripture ordinarily that when God converted any one man, he converted his whole family. 'Salvation is this day come to thy house,' saith Christ to Zaccheus, Luke xix. 9. When salvation came to his heart, it came to his house; all was the better for it. So the jailor, when he believed, he and his whole house were baptized, Acts xvi. 33. When God blesseth the governor once, then it is supposed all the house comes under the covenant of grace. Abraham and his house were blessed, Gen. xxii. 17. But this holds not always, for there was a Ham in good Noah's family. Still there will be the ravens and wild beasts among the tame beasts. There will be an Ishmael in Abraham's family, a Doeg in the church of Judah, a Judas in Christ's family, and a Demas among God's people. That is, let the family be never so good, you shall have some by God's judgment naught in the same. As it is said of Jeremiah's figs, the good figs were exceeding good, and the bad exceeding bad, Jer. xxiv. 3. There is none so good as those that are in a gracious family, and none so naught as such who are naught there. Because they are cursed and under a curse, being bad under such gracious means, being like the ground which receives the rain and showers from heaven, and yet is not the better for it, and so is accursed, Heb. vi. 7, 8. If a man who is untoward were in a gracious family, it is supposed he would be better, but those who are naught, where they should be good, under abundance of means, such are in danger to be sealed to eternal destruction. Such being bad, are very bad, who though they break not out to dangerous enormities, because of the place, yet to have a barren, untractable heart under abundance of means, is to be hardened to destruction, without a special mercy to make it work afterwards. For some who have lived in gracious families, though for the present the seed fructified not, yet have afterwards found that seed fructify after a long time, and have blessed God that ever they came under such a shadow. Therefore, though such barrenness be a dangerous sign, yet must we not suddenly either condemn ourselves or others in this case. Because in the things of God in the church it is as in nature. The seed springs not as

soon as it is sown.   So that grace at length which hath seemed to lie dead,
after many years may sprout out.   Monica, St Austin's mother, was a gracious woman whilst he was an untoward young man, as appeareth by his
own Confessions, yet his mother having prayed much for him, he was converted after her death, and became a glorious father and instrument of the
church's good (*l*).   It is ordinary amongst us.   Many, when they
have gone astray, reflect home upon themselves, consider under what
means they have been, calling to mind the gracious instructions they have
had, and so, by God's assistance, are new men.   Therefore let none despair
in regard of time or place, because God may have further aims than we can
reach to.   But unless God give a special blessing after such watering, it is
for the increase of condemnation not to profit under such abounding
means, but still to be like Pharaoh's lean kine, full fed and lean still, Gen.
xli. 17, *seq.*   For the promise is, ' Those that are under his shadow shall
return.'

There is here a fit occasion offered to spend much time in pressing care
upon those that are governors, that even out of love unto those that are
under them, they would labour to be gracious; because if they be gracious,
God will give them those that are in their family.   The whole family was
baptized when the master was baptized; and when any man was called,
the whole family came within the covenant.   When Shechem and Hamor
were circumcised, all the city was circumcised also, Gen. xxxiv. 24.   It is
true especially of governors.   There is no man hath grace for himself alone.
God gives special graces to special persons, to be a means to draw on many
others.   Wheresoever grace is, it is of a spreading nature.   It is said here
of such, ' their branches shall spread.'   It is communicative, and of a
piercing nature, a little whereof will work strangely.   As we know, a little
short speech of a poor maid to Naaman the Assyrian,* how it wrought, and
was the occasion of his conversion, 2 Kings v. 3.   So a little savoury speech
will often minister occasion of many heavenly thoughts.   God so assists it
with his Spirit, that it often doth a great deal of good.

Quest. But why are all in the family the better for the governor that is
good ?

Ans. Because God gives them grace and wisdom to walk holy before
them, and to shine as lights, expressing and shewing forth the virtues of
God which they have felt ; as we see David professeth, Ps. ci. 2, to walk
singularly and exactly in all things in the perfect way, that so he might
please God and men, shining out before them in an holy, glorious conversation in the midst of his family.   And as by their example, so by their
authority, they use to bring all under them to outward obedience at the
least, which bringeth a blessing to the family.   Because, when grace is once
kindled in the master, he will see all at least come to outward conformity.
They cannot work grace in them ; but as the prophet speaks, they may
compel them to use the means, or else not to suffer a wicked and untoward person to dwell under their shadow.   We know why God said that he
would not conceal his secrets from Abraham, because he knew he would
instruct and teach his family in the fear of God, Gen. xviii. 19.   So this
may be said of every one that is an Abraham, a governor of a family.
They labour to tell them all things that have done good to themselves.
Therefore they are the better for living under their shadow.   Nay, further,
not only the governor of the family, but if there be any graciously good in
the family, they do much good.   Laban's family was the better for Jacob,

* Syrian.—ED.

Gen. xxx. 27 ; and Potiphar, he and the jailor both, prospered the better for Joseph's sake, Gen. xxxix. 5, 23; so Naaman, that great captain, fared the better for his poor maid, 2 Kings v. 3, *seq.* It is a true position. God stablisheth grace in none who are gracious for themselves merely, but for the good of others also that converse with them. Whether it be governor or servants, no man liveth to himself, and for himself only, but for the good of all within their reach.

Use 1. For use therefore, first, this shall be for encouragement to all governors of families, *to be good, if not for themselves, yet in love to those that are theirs.* It may be, some have no care of their own souls or good. But hast thou no care of thy children, of thy wife that lieth in thy bosom, or of thy servants ? If thou hast not a heart of stone or marble, surely thou wouldst desire that for them, that thou dost not for thyself. Think of this, at least thou wouldst have thy children good and prosper. Labour then, if we would have all prosper who come under our roof, that our families may be little churches of God, that all who come under our shadow may revive and return. Therefore, out of love to those that belong to us, let us labour to be good. Is it not a pitiful thing, that some who are governors of others, they look to them as to beasts, and use their service as a man would use the service of his beast ? They feed their bodies, and think they have no charge of their souls. Now this is one reason why all that come under the shadow of a good governor are the better ; because they take care for their instruction and best good; that they live in obedience to God's ordinances, and not like wild creatures, ruffians, vagabonds, Cains, and the like. What a strange thing is this, to have a care of the body, the worser part, and neglect the more excellent part, their souls !

Use 2. Make we also this use, of trial. Art thou a good and a gracious governor indeed ? *Then grace in thy heart is communicative.* It will spread over thy family. Thou wilt labour to make thy children and thy servants good ; to make all good that come under thy roof. Other things are not always communicative. Gold is a dead thing, and other goods thou mayest keep by thee, which do not spread. But if thou hast the best good, faith and love, with a gracious heart, this is like oil, or like fire, which will not be held in, but out; and shew themselves they will, and shine in their kind. So grace is a spreading, communicative thing. All that comes therefore under the shadow of a gracious family, are said to return and be the better for it. Make this therefore an use of trial, whether thou be a gracious governor or not. If thou canst say with Joshua (when he called the people together, saith he, Do what you will, I know what I will do, ' I and my house will serve the Lord.' If you will be, idolaters, or so and so; ' but I and my house will serve the Lord,' Josh. xxiv. 15). So certainly there is no man who in truth of heart fears the Lord, but he is able to say, ' I and my house will serve the Lord.'

Use 3. Lastly, for terror, *let us behold the dangerous and cursed estate of those that dwell out of Christ's shadow,* the church, and good means ; who lie open to the indignation of God and storm of his wrath; who howsoever they may bless themselves in a thing of naught, yet it is a fearful thing to lie under a curse ; and that soul must needs be barren where the dew of grace falls not, for God usually derives* spiritual and heavenly things by outward means. ' They that dwell under his shadow shall return.' They shall return to God ; and by returning to him, return as it were and revive ; as when in a swoon, a man's spirits return again, he is said to revive. But the ground

* That is, ' communicates.—G.

of returning is, that they shall return to God, and come under his roof in the church. But more immediately this is true, ' they shall return,' and shall quicken and revive in returning ; which we spake of in the beginning of the chapter. Only this shall be added to that, that a wicked man, out of judgment of the danger of his estate, may make a stop ; but turning is more than so. In this case a man turns his face to God and heavenwards ; to good things formerly neglected, on which he turned his back formerly. What is turning, but a change of posture, when the face is turned towards that the back was to before ? So it is in this spiritual turning to God. When heavenly things are in our face, when God and Jerusalem, the church, are in our eyes, still minding heavenly things and not earthly, then we are said to return. And therefore these converts mentioned in Jeremiah are thus described in their conversion, ' asking the way to Zion, with their faces thitherward,' Jer. l. 5. Whereas before in the days of our corruption, we turned our backs to God ; now when we return, ' we set the Lord always before us,' Ps. xvi. 8, in everything. This is properly to return, to revive and flourish also in returning. Thus we have heard how all who live under the shadow of Christ do return, and what use we should make of it.

THE NINTH SERMON.

They that dwell under his shadow shall return ; they shall revive as the corn, and grow as the vine : the scent thereof shall be as the vine of Lebanon.
—Hos. XIV. 7.

OUR desire of good things is not so large as God is bountiful in satisfying our desires, and going beyond them, as we see in this chapter. Their hearts were too narrow to receive all that good which God intended them. ' Receive us graciously.' This was their petition : whereunto God answers, ' That he would be as the dew unto them ; that they should grow as the lily, and cast forth their root as Lebanon, and their branches shall spread :' that they should grow in all dimensions, upwards and downwards, and spread in beauty and smell. ' Their beauty shall be like the olive, and their smell like Lebanon.' And because he would be God-like, like himself, that is, thoroughly and abundantly gracious and merciful, he doth not only, as we have heard, promise a blessing to Israel himself, but unto all near unto him, and belonging to him. ' Those that dwell under his shadow shall return ; they shall revive as the corn.'

We are all too shallow to conceive either the infinite vastness of God's justice to impenitent sinners, or his boundless mercy and goodness to his poor church and children. Therefore God, to help our weak conceit in this kind, borroweth all the excellencies of nature, and makes use of them in grace. He takes out of the book of nature, into his book, what may instruct our souls ; and therefore sets down the growing estate of a Christian, by all excellent comparisons that nature will afford ; many whereof we have gone over. The last we spake of was, that mercy which God superabundantly shews unto the friends and servants of the church, ' Those that dwell under his shadow shall return.' Now, those that shall thus return, they revive in returning ; for they turn to the fountain of life, to the Sun of righteousness. They come under God's grace. Therefore they must needs return and revive in vigour, as they return to God : which vigour is especially meant here, when he saith, ' Those that dwell under his shadow shall return.'

' They shall revive as the corn.'

Now, how doth the corn revive? Not to speak of that comparison that the godly are corn, and not chaff, as the wicked are, who are driven to and fro, Ps. i. 4, without any solidity, which, though true, is not here especially aimed at. For it is supposed that they who are good and gracious, have a substance, solidity, usefulness, and goodness in them, like corn, not being empty chaff which the wind blows away. This is useful to mention; but to come to the scope indeed* by the prophet.

1. ' They shall revive as the corn.' In this, first, that as the corn when unsown, it lies dead in the granary, fructifieth not, but when it is sown springs up to an hundredfold, as we read of in Isaac's time, who received so much increase, Gen. xxvi. 12. So it is with converted Christians. Before they were under any gracious means, or in a good place, they lay as it were dead, and did not spring forth. But afterwards, being planted and sown under gracious means, in good company, in a good family, then they increase and grow up and multiply. ' They revive like the corn.'

2. And then again, as it is with the corn, though it seem to die, and doth indeed die in some sort, covered with winter storms, ere it spring out from the oppressions of frost and snow, and hard weather, as if it were altogether perished; yet, notwithstanding, it is all the while a-preparing for springing up again more gloriously. So it is with the church, which seems to die often in regard of spiritual mortification by afflictions, whereby it is dead to the world; yet all this while there is a blessed life in the spirit, preparing the soul, under the hard pressures of all weathers, to a glorious springing up again. Therefore the church hath no hurt by afflictions, no more than the corn hath by the winter, which is as necessary for it as the spring-time or summer. For else, how should the earth be ripened and prepared? How should the worms and weeds be killed, if it were not for hard weather? So it is with a Christian: those afflictions that he suffers, and under which he seems to be buried, they are as useful to him as all his comforts. Nay, a Christian is more beholden to afflictions for his graces and comforts than he is to outward blessings. One would think that the goldsmith were a-spoiling his plate when he is a-burning of it, when all that while the dross is but a-consuming out of it; and the vessel so hammered and beaten out, is but a-preparing to be a vessel of honour, to stand before some great man. So it is with a Christian: an ignorant person looking but one way, thinks God neglects such a one; and that if God cared for such a one, or such a one, would or could such and such things befall them? they conclude hence, as the Psalmist saith, ' God hath forsaken him,' Ps. lxxi. 11, and forgotten him. And as Christ the head of the church was thought to be forgotten and neglected, even when he was most dear and precious unto God, so even they all this while. The Spirit of God is working an excellent work in them, preparing and fitting them for grace and glory. Therefore, in that respect also, ' They shall revive as the corn.'

3. Thirdly, ' They shall revive as the corn' in regard of fructification. It is true both of the church and of particular graces. We see one grain of corn, when it is almost perished and turned to froth, nothing in a manner; presently out of it springs a stalk, and thence an ear, and in that many ears, God giving it a body sixty or a hundredfold, as he pleaseth. So it is with a Christian: when he is planted, he will leaven others, and

* Qu. ' intended?'—ED.

those, others and others. A few apostles leavened the whole world, scattering the gospel like lightning all over the same. So it is true of grace in God's children; it is like a grain of mustard-seed at the first, yet it grows up and fructifies, Mat. xiii. 31, from knowledge to knowledge, faith to faith, and grace to grace; from virtue to virtue, from strength to strength, from one degree to another; nothing less at first, and nothing more great or glorious in this world in progress of time; nothing so admired of God, and pleasing unto man, as this which makes one all glorious and without spot.

Oh, what can be said more to encourage us to come under gracious means, to love God and his ordinances, good company, and the communion of saints—considering they are such happy people! 'Those that are under their shadow shall return,' revive, and be vigorous. 'They shall revive as the corn,' which doth, when it seemeth to be dead, notwithstanding all weathers, grow up and multiply. And whereas it seemed dead before and lay hid, being sown it grows. So being planted in the church, we shall grow. For there is a hidden virtue in the least grace, in the least of God's ordinances, more than we are aware of. Saith Christ, 'Where two or three are gathered together in my name, there am I in the midst of them,' Mat. xviii. 20. Much more is this made good in great congregations and families. But this is not all; he saith,

'They shall grow as the vine.'

Howsoever, the church which is the mother church grows before in the former words: the new church that comes under her shadow, shall grow in the same manner. 'They shall grow as the lily; their branches shall spread;' and more, it is said here, 'They shall grow as the vine.' It is a comparison delightful to the Holy Ghost, to compare Christ to a vine; the church to a vineyard, and Christians unto vines, but such as draw all their moisture and fatness in them from Christ the true vine, their sweetness being a derivative sweetness,

'They shall grow as the vine.'

1. The vine we know is a fruitful plant, as we read in the Judges, ix. 9, 13. The olive and the vine would not forsake their sweetness to be a king; for it is said by them, that they revive God and man, being pleasing to them. So every true Christian is like a vine for fruitfulness. He is a tree of righteousness; a plant of God's own planting; a vine that spends himself in bearing fruit.

2. Again, as it is fruitful, so it is exceedingly fruitful, abounding in fruit, So Christians are vines, not only for a little fruit that they bear, but because they are abundantly fruitful, which is premised, that if they do as they should do, they shall be vines abundant in the work of the Lord.

3. And further, the vine as we know is never a whit the worse for pruning; but is pruned and cut, as our Saviour speaks, 'that it may bring forth the more fruit,' John xv. 2. So the church and people of God are never a whit the worse for afflictions; for as the best vines need dressing and pruning, the best ground ploughing, the best linen washing, the best metal the fire, to consume away the dross, the best things we use having something amiss, so the best Christians need dressing and purging from the great Husbandman, whereby they are not the worse, but the better; having thereby much corruption purged away from them. As the pruning of the vine makes it not the worse, but draws wild things from it, which would draw away the strength of the vine, a Christian is the better for his afflictions, wherein the glory of the church especially consists. For the church never thrived better than in Egypt, where they laboured to crush

and to cut the vine. God brought his vine out of Egypt for all .this, maugre all the malice of the enemies. The church was never more glorious in its own seat than it was in Babylon under the captivity. How glorious then was the church in Daniel and others !

4. Again, to the outward appearance, the vine is a rugged, unseemly plant, being not sightly and beautiful to look on; yet it is abundantly fruitful under that unsightliness. So if we look to the outward state and face of the church, it is nothing else to look to but a deformed company, defaced by affliction, lifeless here, as it were, ' having their life hid up with God in Christ,' Col. iii. 3, as the apostle speaks. Their life here is covered over with many afflictions, crosses, infirmities, and disgraces, whereunto they are subject, like unto other men. Therefore as it was the state of the Head to have no outward form or beauty, though inwardly he was all glorious, so the beauty of the church is inward ; for outward show, it being unsightly like the vine, crooked and uneven, there being nothing delightful in it, unless it be in regard of the fruit that comes from it. So it is with the church of God and particular Christians; who, though in outward government they have not that policy and outward glory other governments have, yet there is an inward secret work of God's government of the church by contraries which exceeds all other policies, wherein he brings glory from shame, life by death. He brings down and lifts up. When he is about his excellent work he humbleth first. This is an ordinary way. Therefore we must not take offence at any outward deformity that we see in the church, and in God's children, when they seem to be trampled upon. They are but as vines, unsightly to the eye ; they have a life, though it be a hidden one.

It is excellently set down by Ezekiel, Ezek. xv. 3, what the vine is of itself. It is serviceable for nothing. We cannot make a pin of it. It is such a brittle wood, as is good for nothing but to bear fruit. So, take a Christian that professeth religion, if he be not fruitful in his place, of all men he is the worst; of all men he is either the best or the worst. As the vine, if it bear fruit, it is the best, though it be an unsightly tree ; but otherwise it is fit for nothing but the fire. Therefore let no man glory in his profession, that he is baptized, hears sermons, and reads. But where is thy fruit ? Wherefore serves the dressing and pruning of the vine but for fruit ? If there be no fruit, a Christian is the worst man that lives ; worst, in regard that he is bad under good means ; and in condition, he is the worst of all men, his torment is the greater. Those that are barren and unfruitful under means, the time will come that they will wish they had never enjoyed such a testimony against themselves.

5. And further, a vine is so weak that it must be propped and supported along, or else it will lie on the ground. Such is the estate of the church, which must have something to fence it and underprop it. God is the strength of the church. It is a wondrous weak plant. The children of God are wondrous weak, and exposed to a wonderful deal of misery. In regard whereof, and of the injuries and weaknesses they are exposed to, they must have support. A Christian is compared to the shiftless things, sheep, lambs, and doves ; and in the plants they are compared to the vine, which needs a strong support. And, as Solomon saith of the conies, though ' they are a weak people of themselves,' Prov. xxx. 26, yet notwithstanding they have a strong rock over their heads, where they are safe ; though they be as weak as the vine. So God's people, though they be weak of themselves, yet they have a strong support to uphold them. God, by the

ordinances of magistracy and ministry, especially by his Spirit, keeps them up and supports them, that they spread in largenes and in fruitfulness.

Use 1. Is this so? Then let us examine ourselves, what our fruit is. If we be vines, what is our fruit? what comes from us? Certainly if we do not shew forth that fruit we should, in our lives and conversations, in our speech, carriage, and actions, when we are called to it, it is an argument that as yet the dew of God's grace hath never fallen upon us, so as it must before we come to heaven. As was said before, a man may endure a dead plant in his ground, but in his orchard he will not. He may endure weeds in pastures, in neglected grounds, but not in his garden. If we be lilies in God's garden, and vines in his orchard, we must be fruitful and grow, or else God will not endure us. Of all woes, the greatest woe lies upon them who enjoy plentiful and abundant means, and yet are not fruitful, Mat. xi. 21.

Use 2. That we are vines, and God's vines, it is in the next place an use of comfort, that God therefore will have a care of us if we be fruitful. He will have a special care of that place where his vines are planted. If we see many gracious persons and families, who are conscionable in their practice and conversation, we may rest assured that God the great husbandman will have a special care of those choice vines, and the places they live in. They carry the blessing of God with them wheresoever they go, with a shadow and protection, making every place the better for them. For God will care for those vines which bring forth much fruit; as it is in Isaiah, 'Spoil it not, for there is a blessing in it,' Isa. lxv. 8. If a Christian be fruitful, and labours to be more fruitful, God gives a prohibition—' He is my vine, do him no harm.' ' Touch not mine anointed, nor do my prophets no harm,' Ps. cv. 15. Satan himself, and all creatures in heaven and in earth, have a prohibition to touch his vines no further than shall be for their good. Will a man suffer men to come into his orchard to break down his vines? He will not. Surely though the sins of this nation be very great, yet one thing ministereth hope; God hath a great many vines under his shadow and protection, many conscionable magistrates, ministers, and people of other professions, governors of families and the like, which walk holily. God will spare the vineyard, even for the vines that bear fruit. A notable place amongst others we have, Cant. ii. 15, ' Take us the foxes and the little foxes that spoil the vine; for our vines have tender grapes.' There is in every church not only gross papists, and foreign enemies, that would root out all, if it were in their power, but subtle foxes also; men that pride themselves in devilish policy, to undermine the church and children of God; who wheresoever they see vine or grapes, they malice that. Both the means, and grace wrought by the means, is the object of their cruelty. Subtle foxes they are; who account it a great deal of glory to be accounted politic men; to do mischief secretly and closely in the church. Will God suffer these foxes? No; he will not. ' Take us the foxes, the little foxes that destroy the vines,' Cant. ii. 15. God hath young growing vines, so as he will not only care for the great vines, but for the tender vines also. Christ hath a care of his lambs; as he said to Peter, ' Lovest thou me,' &c., ' Then feed my lambs,' my little ones, John xxi. 15. So Christ speaks in the gospel of these little ones. ' I tell you (of a truth) that the angels of these little ones behold the face of my Father,' &c., Mat. xviii. 10. And so he speaks in another place. ' A bruised reed will he not break, and smoking flax will he not quench, until he bring forth judgment unto victory,' Isa. xlii. 1, 2. So likewise he promiseth, ' that he will carry the lambs in his bosom, and gently lead them that are with young,' Isa. xl. 11.

Use 3. The next use shall be for encouragement unto weak ones. Should tender and weak Christians then be discouraged, for whom God is so careful? Surely no. Put case they bring forth but little fruit ; yet, O destroy it not, for a blessing is in it. Therefore let us not be discouraged, if we be God's vines ; which is known and discovered, not by the abundance of fruit only, but by the kind of our fruit also. If it come from the Spirit of God, and relish of the Spirit, though it be not in such plenty, yet a vine is not a thorn. A Christian is not to be discouraged, though he bring not forth abundance of fruit at the first. There are different degrees and tempers of soil, and of ages in Christianity; which is spoken to encourage those that are good ; and yet are discouraged, because it is not with them, as with some other Christians of their acquaintance. Know, that there is no set measure of grace necessary to salvation, but truth. God doth assign us a measure of grace according to his good pleasure, and according as he hath purposed to make us profitable to others in the use of means. Those whom he means to use for suffering or doing of great matters in the church, those he fits suitably for that he means to call them to ; others have not that abundance of grace, out of God's wisdom, who knows best how to dispense his own graces to his own glory. If we allow not ourselves in our weaknesses, but groan under them, hate them, and strive against them, reaching towards perfection; in this case our weaknesses shall not hurt our salvation, but God will perfect his power in our weakness, 2 Cor. xii. 9.

So we see it is not the multitude of fruit, but the sincerity of it. If it be true, that makes a Christian. If there be truth of grace, it will out and spread the branches ; it shall not always be so with us. Sincerity and endeavour to grow, with a desire and thirst after growth, makes a man a Christian. Therefore, as was said, we must not be discouraged, though our growth and spreading be not like others. Every Christian hath his measure. Though every one be bound to go further and further, from faith to faith, and grace to grace ; yet there is a blessing in a little, and a promise also to him that useth it well. ' To him that hath, it shall be given,' Mat. xiii. 12. Christ hath a care that the foxes do not hurt the little tender grapes. Let none therefore be discouraged for their non-proficiency in the ways of God, so as to go back and leave off. He knows best, when and how to take away the baits, snares, and temptations that are set to catch them and discourage them. Let God alone with his own work, who is the great vine-dresser. Do thou thine own work ; attend upon good means ; wait upon God ; and then let the malice of the world and the devil be what they will, he will have a care of his vines ; and the more care, the more young and tender they are, &c.

These considerations may affect us, not only to take good by the vine for our bodies, but for our souls also, and so the same thing may cherish both body and soul. A Christian by grace hath an extracting virtue to draw holy uses out of everything ; as the Holy Ghost here compares us to a vine, to teach us these and the like things now unfolded. The last thing promised is,

' The scent thereof shall be as the vine of Lebanon.'

This Lebanon was a mountainous place, on the north side of Judea, wondrous fruitful in all kind of trees, in cedars, and goodly vines ; so it did abound in spice, and all goodly things. Therefore, to shew that a Christian should be the best of his rank, he fetches comparisons from the best things in nature.

'The scent thereof shall be as the vine of Lebanon.'

Now the vine of Lebanon had a sweet scent in it, both to draw to the liking, and then to delight in the taste and taking thereof. So it is with the graces of God in his children, they carry, as it were, a sweet scent with them, both to draw others to delight in, and taste of the same things.

Quest. But how comes it to pass that Christians send forth so sweet as cent?

Ans. Because they are in Christ, in whom the ointment and all sweetness is in fulness. From him the Head, first, and from thence it is derived unto the members ; all who* must partake of this ointment. As it is said of the head of Aaron, that that ointment which was poured on his head ran down to his skirts, and all his rich attire about, Ps. cxxxiii. 2. So that sweetness in Christ is poured on the skirts, all along upon his members ; even the meanest Christian receiveth 'grace for grace,' John i. 16, sweetness from Christ. The virgins, that is, such as defile not themselves with idolatry, and such other lewd courses, they follow after Christ in the smell of his sweet ointments, Cant. i. 3. It is spoken of Christ, who carrieth such a sweet smell with him, as 'all his garments smell of myrrh, aloes, and cassia,' &c., Ps. xlv. 8. So sweet is the smell of Christ, when he is unfolded in his benefits and offices, that the pure and holy virgin souls of the saints follow after it. 'His name is as an ointment poured out,' Cant. i. 3 ; that is, himself is his name, and his name is himself, as the Hebrew proverb is: Christ made known in the unfolding of the word, that is, his name. When the box is opened, all in Christ is like ointment. In the preaching of the word, all is sweet, and nothing but sweet in Jesus. Now a Christian, being a member of Christ, and a virgin soul following Christ, must needs draw sweetness from him, casting out that scent unto others, drawn from him, because they partake of Christ's anointing. What is the name of a Christian, but a man anointed with Christ's ointment, one anointed to be a king and a priest in some sort? Rev. i. 6. Therefore they carry the favour of him wheresoever they go. Aaron the high priest had sweet garments, Exod. xxxix. 26, which made a savour where he went, having bells and sweet pomegranates at the bottom of his garment. He had not only bells to discover him, but sweet pomegranates also. So it is with every Christian. Not only the minister, but every Christian, is a priest under the New Testament, and carrieth a savour with him ; graces that spread and cast a sweet scent in all places wheresoever, which they exercise upon all good occasions. As St Paul expresseth it, 'They savour the things of the Spirit,' Rom. viii. 5. Those who are in Christ, they have the Spirit of Christ, or they are none of his. And having the Spirit of Christ, they savour of the things of the Spirit ; that is, their thoughts, speeches, actions, and conversation are savoury. Those 'that are in the flesh,' saith the apostle, 'cannot please God,' Rom. viii. 8, they are unsavoury. A carnal man hath no savour in his speeches. They are either worldly or civil, without spiritual savour; because he hath nothing of the Spirit of Christ to savour of. 'His heart,' saith Solomon, 'is little worth,' Prov. x. 20. The like we may say of his thoughts, actions, and affections ; they are unsavoury and little worth. He hath a dead heart to goodness ; and thence whatsoever goodness cometh from him is forced, and against the hair, as we say. But a Christian having the Spirit of Christ, and therewith communion with Christ, all his discourses and actions are for the most part savoury; those he acteth

* That is, 'all of whom.'—ED.

as a Christian. Therefore from his communion with Christ, it is said here, 'His smell shall be as Lebanon.'

'The scent thereof shall be as the vine of Lebanon.'

Delightful both to God and holy, blessed spirits, likewise to the church and to the angels which are about us, and pleasing to our own spirits; for there issueth a wondrous contentment even to the conscience of a person, which is fruitful and abundant in goodness. That soul receiveth an answerable proportion of comfort. As it is with heat, that accompanieth fire alway, so there is a kind of heat of comfort which naturally accompanieth the heat of any good action. There remaineth a sweet relish to the conscience of the performer, reflecting, with humility upon himself, with thankfulness to God, from whose dew, as we have heard before, cometh whatsoever is good. Reflecting on this with an eye to the principal cause, it breeds a great deal of comfort to the soul. As it was said of Josiah, the memory of Josiah was like the ointment of the apothecary; whereas, on the contrary, it is said, 'The remembrance of the wicked shall rot,' Prov. x. 7. God threateneth the Jews that they should be a hissing to all nations, and that they should be abominable to all kind of people, Deut. xxviii. 37 (for what is so odious now as the name of a Jew?), yet certainly this whole promise shall be verified even of them, this whole chapter having an eye unto the calling of the Jews. The time will come that the scent of these odious people, who are now the object of hatred unto all people, 'shall be as the vine of Lebanon.'

Use 1. If this be so, it cuts off a carnal exception of senseless persons, that think they can stop men's mouths with this, I cannot make so much show as you, but I hope I have as good a heart to God as you or as the best. But a Christian is a vine that brings forth grapes and much fruit, and casts a scent from him, as 'the scent of Lebanon,' upon all fit occasions; for his words should be 'as the apples of gold set with pictures of silver,' Prov. xxv. 11. He is seasonable in his actions of consolation, and bringeth forth his fruit in due season, as the promise is, Ps. i. 3; for Solomon sheweth that everything is made beautiful in his season, Eccles. iii. 11. Those, therefore, that have not a good word to speak, but rather express the contrary, rotten, unsavoury discourse, vain in their conversation, savouring nothing that is good, how have they as good a heart to God as the best? No; this is not to be a Christian, who should savour like Aaron's garments, or like these graces coming from his Head to him; who should spread abroad his sweetness unto others, 'shining out as a light,' Philip. ii. 15, amongst others. Therefore, away with this base plea. A rotten speech argueth a rotten heart. What can come out of a vessel but such as is within it? If the issues be naught, what is the vessel but naught? If all be unsavoury outward, what is there but a rotten heart within?

Use 2. Again, if Christians should cast a scent and savour, this should move and stir them up, if they will answer their title to be Christians, sweet, anointed persons, priests to God, to labour more and more to be spiritual, and savour the things of the Spirit, and to labour for more and more communion with Christ in the use of all sanctified means, that they may have the Spirit of Christ in their conversation, shewing forth the humility, patience, love, and obedience of Christ. As Peter speaks and exhorteth us, 'to shew forth the virtues of him who hath called us from darkness into his marvellous light,' 1 Pet. ii. 9. Then we answer our title, and 'cast forth a scent like Lebanon,' when inwardly and outwardly all things join to make us fruitful and savoury before God and man.

Quest. What will come of it if we be fruitful and savoury?

Ans. 1. God will be more pleased in all our actions, and will ' smell a sweet savour of rest,' as it is said of Noah, Gen. viii. 21, after his coming out of the ark; for God delights in his own graces, which he admireth in us. As he said to the woman of Canaan, ' O woman, great is thy faith, be it unto thee as thou wilt,' Mat. xv. 28. God, as it were, stands admiring his own graces, he is so delighted with the faith, love, prayers, and patience of his children, which is further excellently expressed in the Canticles, ' Who is this that cometh up out of the wilderness like pillars of smoke, perfumed with myrrh and frankincense, and all the spices of the merchant?' Cant. iii. 6. Christ there is brought in admiring* at his church and children, conflicting through all the miseries and incumbrances of this world, which hinder and oppose their journey to heavenwards, wherein they thrust forth all the practice of their holy graces, which smell like spices. Then let us not envy God, the saints, and holy people the sweetness of our graces, but let our scent smell abroad to the content and comfort of all, that they may delight in these graces that come from us, in our humility, patience, faith, love, sincerity, and all these graces wherein we resemble Christ and shew forth his holy virtues. Therefore, for our own comfort and delight of all, and to assure ourselves of heaven and of the love of God whilst we live here, let us labour to be fruitful in our conversation, and to cast forth a scent in regard of others, which hath an attractive, drawing force. For when they see a holy, fruitful, and gracious conversation, it casts forth a scent, and makes others like religion. So God is glorified, and religion is adorned. What greater ornament to religion than to see a fruitful, gracious Christian, who hath ability and a heart to do good upon all occasions, with an humble, meek, peaceable spirit, taught of God to be so for the good and love of others?

There must be pomegranates with bells, a sweet conversation with words, a little whereof will do more good to others than a great many words. A good conversation is sweet, and hath a kind of oratory joined with it. Therefore, if neither for God, or Christ, or others, yet for our own sakes, and the reflection of that good scent upon ourselves, let us be fruitful. A man cannot grow in fruitfulness but he must needs grow in comfort, peace, and joy. Nothing cheereth and solaceth the heart of a Christian more than this, the conscience† that God honoureth him to be fruitful, to do good, and cast a sweet savour, to draw others to good things. This will comfort us upon our deathbeds more than all other things. Therefore, in all these respects, for love of God, others, and ourselves, which are delighted with the expressions of our graces, let us labour to be fruitful trees in God's garden, and to bring forth much fruit, that we may send forth ' a scent like Lebanon.'

Now, who would not be in such an estate and condition as this, as to have title to all these gracious promises, for ' the dew ' of grace to fall upon him, ' to grow as lilies ' in height, and to spread as other plants do, to grow upwards and downwards, to be ' rooted as cedars ' and ' fruitful as vines ' ? The Spirit of God sets himself here to shew spiritual things by earthly comparisons, to make us the more capable of them. The misery of the contrary condition may well stir us up to seek after the forementioned. For what a misery is it to have the curse of God upon one's soul, to have it like the barren wilderness, void of all grace and comfort that may delight others, or is spiritual, savoury, or savingly good. So all these promises tend

---

* That is, ' wondering.'—G.　　　　　† That is, ' consciousness.'—ED.

to encourage us to be in the condition of God's children, that when we are in that estate we may comfort ourselves, and be able to claim our part, portion, and interest in these excellent promises.

Thus, by God's blessing, we have passed over the particulars of God's gracious promises to his church and all that shall come under the church, all which should encourage us to go to God, and do as the church doth here, ' take words to ourselves,' and desire God ' to take away all iniquity, and heal all our backslidings,' and that we may renounce all vain confidence, as the church doth here, who is taught to trust horses no longer, ' Asshur shall not save us.' And then let us, as was said, cleave unto the blessed promises, that we may improve them and make them our own every day more and more. Therefore, let us have in the eye of our soul the excellency of growth, or else we shall not value these promises. Let us consider what an excellent condition it is to grow, flourish, and be fruitful, having a due esteem of all these promises beforehand. Do but consider how excellent a Christian is that groweth above others, what a majesty he hath in his carriage, how undauntedly he walks in all oppositions whatsoever, as a lion in his courses, Prov. xxviii. 1 ; how he overlooks hell, wrath, death, damnation, and all ; what a sweet communion he enjoyeth with God in all the disconsolations that the world puts upon him. He carrieth his heaven in his heart and a paradise within him, which is planted with all graces ; whereas another man carrieth his hell about him.

Wherefore, let us take such courses to help ourselves as the church doth here, trust in God, and not in man or in the arm of flesh, and be encouraged, from all that hath been said, to have a good conceit* of God, to be fruitful, and draw on others to goodness, that God, his saints, and angels may be delighted with the scent of our graces, and ourselves comforted ; that we may rejoice in our portion and lot that God hath dealt so graciously to us, and glory more that he hath made us members of Christ and heirs of heaven than in any condition of this world. O the incomparable, excellent state of a Christian, above all the glory of this world! who not only groweth, but shall grow to heavenwards still ; and as he hath begun to hate sin, shall hate it more and more. God hath undertaken it shall be so. Ephraim, after all these sweet promises and dew of grace, shall say, ' What have I any more to do with idols ? ' &c., the prosecution whereof must be referred † until the next time.

THE TENTH SERMON.

Ephraim shall say, What have I any more to do with idols ? I have heard him and observed him : I am like a green fir-tree: from me is thy fruit found.
—Hos. XIV. 8.

WE have heard at several times heretofore, how God, out of the largeness of his goodness, goeth beyond those desires which he putteth into his people's hearts. They briefly entreat him to ' do good' to them, and to deal graciously with them ; and he answereth them largely, ' That he will be as the dew to them, that they shall grow as the lily, and cast forth their roots as Lebanon.' All set out by most excellent comparisons, helping grace by nature, our souls by our bodies, and our spirits by our senses. As we have

* ' That is, ' conception.'—G.   † That is, ' delayed.'—G.

souls and bodies, so God applieth himself to both : ' His branches shall spread ; his beauty shall be as the olive, and his smell as Lebanon.'

Then in the seventh verse, his gracious promise reacheth unto those who dwell under the church. ' Those that dwell under his shadow shall return, they shall revive as the corn, and grow as the vine,' &c. The new church that shall come under the shadow of the old, shall flourish as the ancient did. ' They that dwell under his shadow,' that is, under Ephraim's and Israel's shadow, ' shall return,' and be partakers of the same dew of grace.

Now this eighth verse containeth a further gracious promise to Ephraim, upon his repenting and former resolutions. Ephraim said, ' Asshur shall not save us, we will not ride upon horses: neither will we say any more to the work of our hands, Ye are our gods.' Now what saith God here, repeating the words of Ephraim ? Ephraim ' shall say' is not in the original ; but only set down to express what the meaning is ; whereas Ephraim said, ' What have I any more to do with idols ? ' Ephraim shall have this answer, ' I have heard him, and observed him, I am like a green fir-tree : from me is thy fruit found.'

As though the Lord had said, let not Ephraim think that when he hath forsook idols, he hath forsaken his comfort, as though there were no comfort in walking according to the rule of my word and laws. Let him know, that instead of these poor and base comforts, either in gross idolatry, or other more cunning idolatries whatsoever, which formerly took him up, that now he shall exchange them for more solid and substantial comforts. For ' I have heard him and observed him.' So that let him see what he loseth in parting with base corruptions, worldly lusts, pleasures, and the like, he shall find it more abundantly supplied in a far more excellent manner in me, and in the fruits and effects of my love unto him ; so as he shall find that there is nothing lost by entering strictly into my service. And whereas formerly he walked in a vain shadow, in relying on ' Egypt, Asshur, and the works of his own hands ; ' now he shall have a far more excellent shadow, which no storm, nor rain, nor injury of weather can pierce through. ' I am like a green fir-tree unto him.' Not such a shadow as those his idols were, who could not keep off the storm of God's wrath from him ; nor such a shadow as Jonah's gourd was, which flourished for one day, and was nipt the next, Jonah iv. 7. No ; I will be constant and permanent as myself, ' I will be as the green fir-tree ; ' a constant shadow to keep back all annoyance whatsoever ; not like the cursed noisome shadow of idols, under which Ephraim rested before. But ' I will observe and regard him, and be like a green fir-tree unto him.' I will not only be a shadow and shelter of defence unto him from injury and molestation, that he may rest quietly ; but he shall be also fruitful. Though the fir-tree be not so fruitful, yet ' from me is thy fruit found.' Whatsoever he is in himself, yet this shall not be matter of discouragement unto him. I am all-sufficient, there is enough in me to supply him with ; ' from me is thy fruit found.' But to take them in order.

' Ephraim shall say, What have I any more to do with idols,' &c.

Some think the words come upon Ephraim's observing and hearing of him ; so as when God is seen in his most excellent majesty and glory, and observed as he is just, merciful, and wonderful, terrible in himself, that this manner of hearing and observation causeth flesh and blood so to stoop and reform, as they yield themselves, and resign up all unto God ; seeing htat miserable condition they are in, and what an infinite distance there is betwixt their impurity and God's most excellent holiness. As we read of Isaiah, when he had seen God in his throne of majesty, ' Woe is me !' saith he, ' for I am undone ; because I am a man of unclean lips, and I dwell in the midst of a people of unclean lips : for mine eyes have seen the King, the Lord of hosts,' Isa. vi. 5. And so of Job, ' I have heard of thee by the hearing of the ear, but now mine eye seeth thee ; wherefore I abhor my-self, and repent in dust and ashes,' Job. xlii. 5, 6. Which, indeed, is true in the general, that a man then truly repenteth and turneth unto God, when he knoweth God and himself to purpose, and never effectually until then ; for Christ, who cannot lie, and is truth itself, calleth this kind of knowledge eternal life. ' This is life eternal, to know thee to be the only very God, and whom thou hast sent, Jesus Christ,' John xvii. 3. But, though this be a general truth, yet we take it here rather for an encouragement unto Ephraim, as before, that nothing is lost by cleaving unto God's ways, and forsaking of sin. Now whereas, ' Ephraim shall say, what have I any more to do with idols ? ' In the words we may consider.

1. *The manner of expression, with a great indignation of soul,* ' What have I any more to do,' &c.

2. *The matter so hated with indignation, is idolatry,* their former idols, ' Ephraim shall say, What have I any more to do with idols ? '

Ephraim, we see, renounceth idolatry. But in what manner is this done ? with an high indignation of zeal and hatred : ' What have I any more to do with idols ? ' He doth not say, Now that Ephraim hath left idolatry, I will supply all these comforts that they had by idols. But Ephraim loathes idolatry. Therefore he saith, ' What have I any more to do with idols ? ' It is a figurative question, implying a strong denial with a strong indigna-tion. ' What have I any more to do with idols ? ' I have had too much to do with them : I have now nothing to do with idols. It is a negation and denial, with as great aversation * and abomination as can be possibly expressed : for in such questions, the denial is set forth more strongly by a negation, and with a greater emphasis, than by any affirmation is possible to express. So elegant is the Spirit of God, in setting forth spiritual things in a heavenly and transcendent manner.

' Ephraim shall say, What have I any more to do with idols ?' &c.

Hence, in that Ephraim shall say thus, and say it with such vehemency of spirit and indignation, we may observe in general,

There is excellent use of the affections.

God hath planted the affections in us, to be as the wind, to carry the soul to and fro, forward or backward : for affections are planted in the soul, answerable to things aimed at by it. For, as in the nature of things, there be good and bad, delightful and hateful, hurting or pleasing ; so an-swerably God hath framed the soul to the nature of things. For good things, God hath planted affections in us to join, clasp, embrace them and welcome them ; as love, joy, delight, and such like. And for evil things, he hath planted affections to avoid them ; as indignation, hatred, and the like. Indeed, religion is mainly in the affections, whereof there is excellent use. Take away them, and take away all religion whatsoever. A man, were it not for his affections, is like *mare mortuum,* the dead sea that never stirreth. Therefore it is but a doting, idle conceit of these rigid men, that take away affections ; much like the folly of them, who, because they have been drunk with wine, do therefore cut up all the vines. But the way were, to moderate the excess, not to cut up the vines. So for the affections, we

* That is, ' aversion.'—G

must not root them up, or cut them down, but order them aright.   For what doth the first commandment require, Thou shalt have no other gods but me; but a right ordering of all the affections of the soul, joy, delight, trust, and fear, and the whole frame of them to be carried to God?   For the inward worship of God is nothing else but the excellent working of these affections suitably to the law, with the detestation of the contrary.   It is not knowledge that makes a man a good man, but the affections.   The devil and wicked spirits know much; but they have no love, joy, or delight in them.   Therefore we must value ourselves and things, as we are in our will and affections; for so God valueth us, and we should value others thereby.   This well done would bring us a wondrous deal of comfort, and stop our too much and rigid judging and censuring of others.

' Ephraim shall say, What have I any more to do with idols?'

Now in particular we see here, that Ephraim not only leaveth idols, but there is planted in him a sound indignation against them; whence we may learn,

That it is not enough to leave sin, but we must loathe sin also.

A notable place to this purpose, we have in the prophecy of Isaiah, what they should do after their conversion, in the case of hatred to idolatry. ' Ye shall defile also the covering of thy graven images of silver, and the ornament of thy molten images of gold: thou shalt cast them away as a menstruous cloth; thou shalt say unto it, Get thee hence,' Isa. xxx. 22. There is a hatred and a strong loathing indignation against sin, when it is discovered in the pollution and vileness thereof; which affection of hatred, God hath planted to draw the soul away from anything that is truly hurtful to it.   It is not enough to leave sin for some by-ends, as fear of punishment, shame, and the like; but we must loathe it also.   The prophet David, when he professeth his love to the law, how proveth he it?   ' I hate and abhor lying,' Ps. cxix. 163.   And so again, ' Do not I hate them, O Lord, that hate thee? and am not I grieved with those that rise up against thee? I hate them with perfect hatred, I account them mine enemies,' Ps. cxxxix. 21.   Here is hatred, and perfect hatred with abomination.

Reason 1. The reason is, because God is a Spirit, John iv. 24; *and looks to the bent of our spirits*, seeing what we love and what we hate.   Therefore the strength of this consideration draweth the soul to hate and love, with God, as he hates and loves; and as much as may be, to hate sin as he doth.

Reason 2. And then again, *he requireth our heart especially*.   ' My son, give me thy heart.'   Give me thy love in that which is good, and hate that which is ill.   What ill we leave, we must hate first; and what good we do, we must first love, or else we shall never do either of them acceptably to purpose.   What the heart doth not, is not done in religion.   If it hath no hand in the avoiding of ill, it is not avoided.   If it have no hand in the doing of good, it is not done before God.   Therefore in true conversion, there must be a loathing of sin.

Reason 3. Thirdly, because in all true conversion there *is a new nature put in us*.   Now the new creature, which partaketh of the divine nature, whereby we resemble God, it hath an antipathy to the greatest ill, which is sin, the cause of all other evils whatsoever; which maketh us opposite to God, defileth the soul, and hindereth our sweet communion with him.   A new creature, we know, hath a new disposition, and is opposite to the works of the flesh; they are contrary to one another.   So that we see it clear, that we must not only leave but loathe sin.

Quest. But how may we know, discern, and try this true hatred of sin ?

Ans. First, true hatred is *universal.* He who hates ill truly, hates in universally in the whole kind. As we see in wicked men and devils, who hate God and all goodness. So on the contrary, those that are good hate all ill whatsoever, whether it pleasure or displeasure them ; they stand not upon it, they hate the very nature of all ill. Those whose obedience and affections are partial, they hate some evils, but not others, which is not true hatred wrought by the Spirit of God, for that is universal to the whole kind.

2. Then also, wheresoever true hatred is, *it is unplacable and unappeasable.* There's no true end of sound hatred, but by the abolishing altogether of that thing it hates ; as we see the hatred of Satan to the church and people of God is unappeasable and unquenchable. Nothing in the world ean stay Satan's hatred, nor the hatred of his instruments, who hate the remembrance of God's people. Therefore the very name of Calvin and Luther must be put out of their books, to satisfy their hatred, not only when they are dead, burn their bones, but abolish their memory, if they can, (*m*). So there is the like disposition in God's people to that which is ill. A godly disposi-tion, it hateth sin even to the death, and is not quiet until all sin be abo-lished. Whereupon it is never quiet in this life, but desires heaven, not enduring patiently the least relics and rags of sin ; desiring that that which it so hateth, might have no being at all. Those who mince and cull things, who are so gentle and tender towards their sins and corruptions, in them-selves and others ; is this that hatred which is unappeasable, and never rests, till it see either a thorough reformation, or abolishing of what it so hateth ? Wherein it is a more rooted affection than anger. For hatred is a rooted offensive displeasure, against persons and things ; and so rooted, as that nothing in the world can root it out. Anger may be appeased. It is appeased in God, and it may and must be in men. But hatred is im-placable, aiming at the annihilation of the thing so hated.

3. Again, where true hatred and indignation is, there *the nearer the ill is to us, the more we hate it, &c.* As we hate it in itself, so we hate it the more, the nearer it is to us. As a‾toad or any venomous thing, the nearer it is to us, we loathe and abhor it the more, so certainly, whosoever hates and abhorreth sin as sin (as it is a hateful thing to a renewed soul), so he hateth sin more in himself than in others, because it is nearest in his own bosom. Every man hates a snake more in his bosom than afar off, because it is more likely to do him harm there. Therefore those that flatter their own corruptions, and are violent against others, as Judah against Tamar, ' She shall be burned, bring her forth and burn her,' when himself had gotten her with child, Gen. xxxviii. 24. So many are severe in punishing of others, as if they were wondrous zealous ; but what are they in their own breast ? Do they reform sin in their own hearts and lives ? He that truly hates sin, he hateth his own sin more than others, because it is near him.

4. And so, in proportion, he that hates sin truly *will hate it in his own family, children and servants, more than in others abroad.* It was a great fault in David, that he cockered* up Adonijah, and others in his own house, whilst he was more strict abroad. Can men think to redress and hate sin in the commonwealth, and yet suffer it in their families ? True hatred is most conversant in its strength near hand. Those who suffer deboistness† and profaneness in their families, and never check it in their children and servants, they hate not sin. Whatsoever countenance they may take upon

* That is, ' indulged.'— G.   † That is, ' debauchery.'—G.

them, of reformation abroad, it cometh out of by-respects, and not out of true hatred.

5. Again, he that hateth sin truly as sin, *will hate the greatest sin in the greatest measure*, because he hates it as it is hateful. Now in the nature of things, the greatest sin deserveth the greatest abomination, and aversation* from it. Therefore he who truly hateth sin, he hates the greatest sin most of all. Those therefore that are very nice in less matters, and loose in greater things, it is but hypocrisy. For he who truly hates sin as sin, where the greatest sin is, thither he directs the edge of his hatred, which is the strongliest carried against the strongest ill. And such a one will not respect persons in evil, but wheresoever he findeth it, if he have a calling, there will be an answerable hatred of it. Therefore if one be a minister of the word of God, he will do as good Micaiah did, and will not balk† Ahab for his greatness, 1 Kings xxii. 9, *seq.*; and like good John Baptist, he will tell Herod of his faults. Because he hates sin as sin, therefore, where he hath a calling to it, he will hate it proportionably in the greatest measure. Good Eli in this case was too indulgent over his sons, 1 Sam. ii. 27, *seq.*; but we must love no man so nearly, as to love the ill in them.

6. Again, a man may know that he truly hates sin, *if he can endure admonition and reproof for sin*. He that hates a venomous plant which troubleth the ground, will not be displeased if a man come and tell him that he hath such a plant in his ground, and will help him to dig it up: surely he cannot be displeased with the party. So here, if a man do truly hate sin, will he be angry with him that shall tell him that he is obnoxious to such an evil, which will hurt him dangerously, and damn his soul if it be not helped? Surely no. Therefore let men pretend what they will, those who swell against private reproof, they do not hate sin as sin. Only add we this caution: a reproof may be administered with such indiscretion, out of self-love, and with a high hand, as that a man may dislike the carnal manner of reproving; but if it be done in a good manner, he that hates reproof, because he loveth himself and his sin, pretend what he will, he hates not sin.

7. So, *if a man love to be flattered in his sin, it is a sign he hates not sin truly*. For there is naturally a great deal of self-love in man, which makes him that he loves to be flattered in his sins; whereupon he comes to be abused to his own destruction, especially great men. Now, it is a sign of an ill state of soul to be subject to be abused by flattery, and to hate instruction. Saith Paul, 'Am I your enemy, because I have told you the truth?' Gal. iv. 16.

8. Again, we may know what our hatred to sin is, *by our willingness or unwillingness to talk of it or mention it, or to venture upon the occasions thereof*. Where hatred is, there is outward aversation. We fly from what we hate, and shun to frequent places where we may receive offence. Whatsoever hath an antipathy to nature, that we hate and run away from. Therefore those that present themselves to the occasions of sin, upon no calling, say what they will, they feed sin, and live according to the flesh. Those that hate a thing will never come near it if they can choose. Therefore, those that present themselves willingly to places infected, where there is nothing religious, but scorning of religion, your common representations of abomination, pretend what they will, their intent is to strengthen their own corruption, against the good of their souls. This is the issue. Those that hate sin will hate all that which may lead to it, the representations of

---

* That is, ' aversion' = turning from.—G.   † That is, ' avoid.'—G.

sin also. Can a man hate sin and see it acted? Wickedness is learned when one seeth it acted, as one of the ancients saith well. Therefore let us by these and the like trials take notice what our hatred to sin is.

Only this our zeal and indignation to sin must have a mitigation and be regulated, lest, like an exorbitant river, it exceed the bounds. Therefore, not to follow the school niceties in the exactness of differences, we will touch the mark a little, how this zeal and hatred to sin, in reproof especially, must be qualified; wherein we must consider divers things.

1. First, *our calling must be respected*. For howsoever we must carry an universal hatred to sin thus far, that we must not do it, yet in the discovery of hatred and dislike to others, we must consider what calling we have, and how far we go.

2. And it must be done *with a sweet temper*, keeping our distance, and reserving the due respect unto those in whom we shew our dislike. As we see Nathan, when he came to tell David of his fault, how he doth it, what art he useth! It must so be done as that it may appear to be done out of pure zeal, that it is no wild-fire nor no heat of nature; but that it cometh merely from the Spirit, and in much love, with mildness and pity, in which case it carrieth a wondrous authority. The discovery of hatred to the faults either in a minister or in a magistrate, though they must be truly dealt with, and have their faults told them, yet there must be respect had to their place, by reason of the weakness of men. As it is with the body, great men have their physicians as well as meaner, only their physic must be more costly, because perhaps of the tenderness of their constitutions; but as for their bodies, they must not be suffered to perish, nor will not. So for their souls, they must have that which other men have to help them, but it must be done with reservation and respect; as Paul, speaking to Festus the governor, calleth him 'most noble Festus,' &c., Acts xxvi. 25. Pressing also goodness in some sort upon king Agrippa, 'O king Agrippa, believest thou the prophets? I know thou dost,' Acts xxvi. 26. So we see how we may examine whether our hatred to sin be true or not.

Let every one therefore make use of it in their calling. Those that are entrusted with God's message, let them know that God's ambassadors are to be faithful in their message, for they serve a greater Lord than is upon the earth; and let them shew their true hatred of ill, and the danger of sin, wheresoever they find it. And for those that are governors of others, let them not think that they hate sin in themselves except they hate sin also in all that belongs to them, and reform it. For we see here an evidence of conversion. When Ephraim was converted, 'What have I any more to do with idols?' and, 2 Cor. vii. 11, there is an excellent description of the nature of repentance, by many parcels. The Corinthians had repented: how is this evidenced? 'Oh, behold,' saith he, 'this selfsame thing, that ye sorrowed after a godly sort, what carefulness it wrought in you; yea, what clearing of yourselves; yea, what indignation; yea, what fear; yea, what vehement desire; yea, what zeal; yea, what revenge!' What revenge and indignation against sin! A kind of extremity of hatred, a hatred quickened and kindled, the height of hatred. What indignation! Insinuating that wheresoever there is the truth of conversion, there will be indignation against sin in ourselves. As David confesseth of himself, having sinned, 'So foolish was I, and ignorant: I was as a beast before thee,' Ps. lxxiii. 22. When he suffered such a thought to lodge in his breast, that it was better with the children of the world than with the church of God, he was troubled for it. But when he went into the church of God, and saw the end of wicked men, then he saw his own foolishness in being so deceived, and speaks against himself with indignation. So wheresoever there is true conversion, there is hatred with indignation against ourselves. As in that place before alleged, they shall say unto their idols, 'Get thee hence,' Isa. xxx. 22, what have I any more to do with you? Which is a phrase of speech shewing a disposition of hatred to the utmost extension, 'Get you hence.' So Christ to the devil, 'Get thee behind me, Satan.' This is the right temper of a truly converted Christian, expressed by divers phrases in Scripture: by a denial of our lusts, by killing and crucifying, by pulling out the eye, and cutting off the right hand. Which phrases, do they not imply a great strength of hatred and indignation, when we must, as it were, pull out our own eyes; that is, our beloved sins, which are as dear to us as our eyes, and as useful as our right hands unto us? Yet these must be cut off, mortified, crucified, and denied, Col. iii. 5. Therefore let us not deceive ourselves; but let us judge of the truth of our conversion by our true hatred to sin in ourselves and others, and in all who are committed to our charge.

If this be so, what shall we judge of a cold, lukewarm temper? It is the nature of cold, to gather heterogeneal bodies together. As we see in the ice, there are straws, and stones, and heterogeneal things incorporated, because the cold congeals them together; but where there is fire, there is a separating of the dross from the good metal. So where the Spirit of God is, it is not so cold as to jumble sin and sin, this and that together; but it purgeth away that which is ill, and that which is good it makes better. For in what proportion the fire of God's Spirit stirs up that which is good, in that proportion there is a hatred of that which is ill. They are unparalleled affections. Those that love God, they hate evil. Those that are alike to all things, do shew that they have not this active true hatred against sin. No! 'Ephraim shall say, What have I any more to do with idols?'

Quest. But now, How shall we come to get this hatred against sin, and holy revenge and indignation against ourselves for that which is amiss in us?

Ans. First, we must every day labour to get a *clearer sight of the excellency of that which is good, and a nearer communion with God by prayer and meditation.* And then, when we have been with God, it will work an abomination of whatsoever is contrary unto him. Thus Moses, when he had talked with God in the mountain, at his return, seeing them dancing and sacrificing to the calf of gold, Exod. xxxii. 19, what did Moses? He brake the tables asunder. So it is with those that have communion with God, who is 'light itself, and in whom is no darkness,' 1 John i. 5, who is holiness and purity itself. Those who have effectually conversed with God in his ordinances, meditation, prayer, and the like, when they look upon sin, which is contrary to God, they look upon it with a more perfect hatred. So Isaiah vi. 5. When God appeared to the prophet, and touched his tongue* with a coal from the altar, saith he, 'Woe is me, for I am undone, because I am a man of unclean lips,' &c., 'for mine eyes have seen the King, the Lord of Hosts.' Thus, when once he had communion with God, he began to loathe himself. So, if we would hate evil, let us labour more and more to be holy, and to increase in that divine affection of love. For in what measure we love that which is good, in that measure we hate the evil: as it is, Ps. xcvii. 10, 'Ye that love the Lord, hate evil;' insinua-

* Lips.—G.

ting, that all that love the Lord hate evil. All those that are near unto God, they hate all sin. The more they grow into communion with God, the more they grow in the hatred of all that is contrary. Let us therefore never talk of love to God, and of piety, and such like; for if there be any grace or communion with God, we hate all sin in that measure as God hateth. He who hath no zeal to reform that which God hateth, he hath no love at all.

2. Again, the way to stir us up to hate sin in ourselves and others, and out of that hatred to reform it, is to set before us, *what it is in itself;* that it is the loathsomest thing in the world, worse than the devil himself: for it is sin which makes him a devil. That corruption, pride, worldliness, and profaneness, which we cherish, is worse than the devil himself, because this made him a devil. Let us make sin therefore as loathsome as we can, and then we shall hate it: and let us present it to our souls, as the most dangerous thing of all, the ill of ills, which bringeth all other evils upon us. This may appear more ugly in our sight, in that the foulness thereof could not be expiated but by the death of the Son of God. And consider what great torments he hath prepared for that which we so cherish. This proud, sinful, and carnal disposition of ours, so opposite to all goodness, God hath appointed to punish it with eternal separation from his presence. It maketh God hate his own creatures. ' Go, ye cursed, into everlasting fire, prepared for the devil and his angels,' Matt. xxv. 41.

3. And to stir us up to reform sin in all that belong unto us, we must consider *the dangerous condition that they live and die in, in whom this is not reformed*. Eternal torments, and separation from God. These things may help to work in our hearts a hatred of sin: and from this hatred, a reformation of it, with a zeal and indignation. Therefore let us labour more and more for this temper of soul, that we may be like God, and carry the characters of the children of God in us. There is no affection will distinguish us from hypocrites more than hatred, which cometh of love, which is the first-born and breeding affection of all others. For why do we hate any thing, but because it is opposite to that we love? Why do we hate ill, but because it is opposite to God and to Christ, whom we love? Amongst others, take we along this consideration with us, that it is the spear which wounded our blessed Saviour; and that it is that he hates most which we love most. Consider the holiness of God, that he would punish it in his own Son, ere it should not be punished.

4. And consider that *it is the bane of all our comfort, this which we so cherish, and that it embitters all things to us*. We cannot rejoice, no, not in the good blessings of God, whilst we are guilty of sin; neither can we pray comfortably whilst our hearts regard it, Ps. lxvi. 18. In this case, that which should rejoice the heart, communion with God, is terrible to us. What have I to do to take his name in my mouth, when I embrace such sins? Ps. l. 16. The day of judgment is terrible also; for how can a man think comfortably thereof, if therewith he expect a heavy doom for his sins he liveth in? So we may say of the day of death. None of these can be thought upon without terror, when therewithal it cometh to one's mind, the cutting off from their sins, and the ' terror of the Lord' against all sin whatsoever, 2 Cor. v. 11. It should be the joy of our hearts to think of these happy times: therefore, there must needs be a great deal of sin and atheism in our hearts when we cannot think comfortably of them. For either we believe not these things, and so are plain atheists; or else, if we believe them, we are exceeding foolish to lose future joys for the poor ' pleasures of sin for a season.'

5. Let us labour to *grow in grace more and more;* for the more we grow in the love of God and good things, the more we shall hate sin. For, whatsoever may be said for the growth in love, and cherishing of it to good things, the same may be said for the hatred of ill, in a contrary sense.

6. The last place shall be, *to place and drive our affections a contrary way, to translate and place them on a contrary object, when they are stirred up to evil attempts.* As, when hatred is stirred up, direct it to its proper object, sin ; when love is irregular, think with ourselves, that God hath not planted this affection for this object, but to carry me another way ; I must love God above all, and all that he loveth, for his sake. Hath God put love and hatred into my heart, to hate my brother whom I should love, and to love the devil, and hate God ? Oh no ! I should love God above all, and my brother as myself ; and hate the devil and all his works, whom I have renounced in my baptism. Therefore, in distempers of the affections, make a diverson, and turn them the right way. As physicians use to do, when the distempered blood runs dangerously one way ; if they cannot stop that, they open a vein to drive the course of the blood another way. So it is Christian policy, when the affections run dangerously one way, then to reflect thus upon ourselves : Aye, But is this the end why God hath placed this affection in me ? Certainly no ! He hath planted this affection in me for another purpose. Therefore, I will hate that which I should hate ; sin in general, and my own sin most of all, which makes me hate my brother. This should be our daily task and study, to take off the affections where they should not be placed, and to fix them where they should be placed ; and there to let them go amain, the faster the better ; restraining them where they should not run out.

Thus we ought to temper ourselves, and to work in ourselves as much as may be, a sound hatred to all sin, not only of the second table, but of the first also. The church here saith, ' What have I any more to do with idols ? ' Now I hate all vain inventions. And think not, with Gallio, that this belongeth not to us ; if we be magistrates, and called to do it, to stand for the cause of the church and true religion.

' What have I any more to do with idols ? '

The last thing to be observed from Ephraim's manner of expressing his indignation is—

Obs. That where love is not well contracted and begun, it will not hold to the end, but will end in eternal hatred.

The serpent and Eve* had some poor acquaintance together, as the issue proved. What did it end in ? ' The seed of the woman shall break the serpent's head,' Gen. iii. 15. This association and acquaintance ended in everlasting war and breach. So all covenants, leagues, and associations with those we should not join with, can never soder† handsomely together, but will end in everlasting hatred. What a strict league was in former times betwixt Ephraim and idols ! But when Ephraim's eyes are opened to see his idols devils, he detests and loathes all abominations, and is of another mind. ' What have I any more to do with idols ? ' He abominates them, as the word importeth.

Let us therefore beware with whom we join in intimate league. For what makes miserable so much, as the renting‡ of the affections from that they were strongly placed on ? when love is rent from the thing beloved ? If we place our affections, for some by-respects, upon wicked persons, this

* Printed ' Hevah.'—G.   † That is, ' solder.'—G.   ‡ That is, ' rending.'—G.

will cause so much the more torment and indignation against ourselves,
that were so foolish to suffer our affections to enter so deeply where they
should not.   Those that glory in their league with antichrist, and wonder
at the beast, Rev. xvii. 8, *seq.*, thinking him a demi-god : will this be
alway so ?   Oh, no ; when God opens the eyes of any of his people, they
shall hate them for ever.   So wicked persons, that now are led on to this
and that wicked course : shall this be always so ?   Woe to thee, if it be !
But the time may come that thou shalt say, ' What have I any more to do
with idols,' or with such an one's acquaintance ?   I cannot endure to look
on him : he tainted me, and misled me, and tempted me.   Now we must
be two, part we must, and I would we had never met together.   Therefore,
before we place our affections on any, consider who they be, whether we
be likely to live with them for ever or not ; whether there be any evidence
of grace in them.   If not, let them be two to us.   For whatsoever vanity
is in the things or persons we love, if we belong to God, we must be
separate from them, unless we will be damned.   Therefore we must be
wise to prevent the danger betimes.   Ephraim might have known before
the danger of idolatry, had he been wise and prudent ; but it is well he
knows it now at length, which causeth him so to abominate idols.   ' What
have I any more to do with idols ? '   Thus much is spoken, because of the
lukewarmness and cold temper, neutrality and halting of a great many in
the world, having so many sinful combinations and associations one with
another, as if these things were not material.

Now, let men consider what a disposition this is, and how it stands
with that disposition which must be in those that are members of Christ,
and look for heaven.   Let a Christian always remember what he is, and
what he hopes for, and this will put him in a right temper.   1. What he
is : a king, and an heir of heaven, &c.   After which he should reason with
good Nehemiah, ' Shall such a man as I fly ? ' shall such a man as I do
this ?   I am redeemed from my sins, and advanced to be a king to rule
over my lusts, to be an heir of heaven and eternal happiness in the
world to come, to reign with Christ ; and shall I do thus and thus ?
Doth this stand with my new temper, this sin, this filthiness, this base
action and thoughts that I am tempted to and encumbered with ?   Shall
such a man as I follow these base actions, ways, and companions ?   Consider we this well, and then it will breed Ephraim's resolution, ' What
have I any more to do with this base lust ? '   What hath it to do with me,
or I with it ?   Is this and this action befitting a king, and an heir of
heaven, and a new creature ?   And if a man be in authority, then let him
consider what Mordecai said to Esther, ' What if thou be called to the
kingdom for such a purpose ? '   Esther iv. 14.   What if thou be called to
this place or dignity for this purpose, to reform such and such abuses ?
Think with thyself, not only in particular what thou art, but in thy place,
what if thou be called to reform such abuses ; such unsound doctrines ; to
stand for God and for the truth.   This will breed this resolute indignation
of Ephraim in us, ' What have I any more to do with idols ? '   All which
is for the manner of Ephraim's indignation : a strong negation of an
abominated thing.   ' What have I any more to do,' &c.   The next, which
is the substance and matter abominated—idolatry—must be reserved for
some other time.

THE ELEVENTH SERMON.

Ephraim shall say, What have I any more to do with idols?   I have heard him, and observed him: I am like a green fir-tree: from me is thy fruit found.—Hos. XIV. 8.

WE have heard at several times heretofore how graciously God deals with his people, alluring them by many free and gracious promises to his service ; the particulars whereof we heard heretofore at large.

This 8th verse hath reference unto that which went before, ver. 3. There Ephraim renounceth his former idols. ' Asshur shall not save us,' &c. ; and here, ' Ephraim shall say, What have I any more to do with idols ?' Unto which the answer is, ' I have heard him, and observed him : I am like a green fir-tree unto him : from me is thy fruit found.' Now, in that ' Ephraim shall say, What have I any more to do with idols ?' this in sum is only the first part of the third verse, repeated in another manner : That Ephraim shall and will go on in abominating idols, be constant in his former resolution.   Therefore, in that Ephraim shall, by the Spirit of grace, go on in renouncing all false confidence, God sheweth here that Ephraim shall lose nothing by it, for he intends here the continuance of time.   ' I have heard him,' and I do hear him, and I will hear him, and respect him, and be like a shady green fir-tree to shade him, causing him also to be abundant in fruit.   ' From me is thy fruit found.'

' Ephraim shall say, What have I any more to do with idols ?'   Here we considered the manner of expression, and then the matter itself.

' Ephraim shall say, What have I any more to do with idols ?'

To come, therefore, to the matter itself specified, idolatry, against which Ephraim's indignation is directed :

' What have I to do with idols ?'

In handling whereof we must take in all these four together, that is—

1. *False doctrine*, which is the foundation of *idolatry*.

2. *Idols themselves ;* or,

3. *Idolatry*, which they tend to (for he which hates idols, hates them because he hates idolatry) ; or,

4. *Idolaters ;* as if he had said,

What have I any more to do with idolatrous doctrines, opinions, or conceits, or with idols framed according to these conceits, or with idolatry or idolaters ?   For these go together.   No man worships idols, but because he is poisoned in his conceits ; and idols are forbidden, because idolatry is dangerous ; and communion with idolaters is forbidden, because of idolatry. So that the doctrine, idols, idolatry, and communion with them, all these are objects of Ephraim's abomination and indignation.

' Ephraim shall say, What have I any more to do with idols ?'

It were to misspend precious time, appointed for better uses, to tell you of the abominable distinctions of the papists, of *Latria* and *Dulia*, (*n*) or to insist upon a discourse of heathenish idolatry ; truths, but not so profitable for us to spend time in.   Therefore, we will rather come to shew the reasons why Ephraim so abhorreth idolatry, idols, and conceits of all.

1. To begin, in the first place, with idols.   When Ephraim is truly converted, he hates them, because idols *are abominable to God*, unto whom

Ephraim is now converted. Ephraim hates idols, for idolatry is spiritual adultery. Religion is, as it were, a conjugal act of marriage ; so that a breach in religious worship is a breach of spiritual marriage. Now, the worshipping of idols being a breach of the conjugal act of marriage betwixt God and the soul, spiritual adultery, it must needs be abominable. For adultery is an abominable, filthy thing ; much more spiritual adultery. Therefore, saith Ephraim, ' What have I now any more to do with idols ? '

2. And then again, idolatry *frameth base conceits of God*. Whereas, on the contrary, we should elevate and raise up our hearts unto him ; idolatry pulls him down, and conforms him to our base conceits. Were it not a wrong to man to make him like a swine, or an ape, or some such ridiculous creature ? Who, in this case, would think himself well used ? There is not such disproportion betwixt any creature and man as there is betwixt the great God of heaven and earth, and the best creature that can be made to resemble him. Therefore, it is an abominable abuse and dishonour to the great majesty of God to be represented any kind of way.

3. Again, *consider the opposition between any representation of God, and God*. They are corruptible things ; God is incorruptible. They are visible ; God is invisible. They are vain and nothing ; God a being of himself, who giveth being unto all things. God is the living God, and the cause of all life. To be brief : the Scripture, to shew God's hatred of them, calleth them dunghill-gods, and Abel, as it is in this book, vanity, nothing, a name to alienate the affections from them. (*o*)

4. Yea, further, because *God is a jealous God*, Exod. xxxiv. 14, and will not give his glory to another. Ephraim, therefore, as soon as he cometh to know God, he hateth idols ; because he knows God, being a jealous God, could not endure them, Isa. xlii. 8.

Now, idolatry is committed when either we set up false gods in place of the true God, or when we worship the true God in a false manner.

Quest. But now another question may be moved, Whether the papists be idolaters or not ? For we live amongst many of them ; therefore we cannot be too wary of them.

Ans. The answer is affirmative. They are idolaters, and worse in some sort than the heathen idolaters were. Only change the names of the popish saints which they in popery worship, and the names that the heathen worship, and they will be all one. Now, names be no realities.

How may this be cleared ?

First, *they give the honour due to God to others*, which is idolatry. The religious worship only due unto God, they give unto other things. Christ, when he said, ' Him only shalt thou serve,' Mat. iv. 10, excepted the least divine worship from the creature. The devil, we know, would have had him fall down before him ; but Christ's answer is, ' Him only shalt thou serve ;' that is, him only shalt thou religiously prostrate thyself unto. So that religious worship is proper to God only. Now, this they give to saints ; for they pray to them, which is religious worship.

Obj. But they object, that they pray not directly to them, but to them as mediators, that they may pray to Christ for them.

Ans. 1. First, *they raise them above their degree, to make them mediators*, and so dethrone Christ of his office of Mediator, at least join copartners with him.

2. But this is not all. *They pray directly to saints* to help them against several ills, as they have several saints for several evils. Whatsoever they

say, who are not ashamed of lying to further their designs, yet their books and writings do testify the contrary.

3. Then again, *they vow to saints*, as in the form of their vows is seen. I vow to the Virgin Mary, &c. Now, a vow is a religious act. They vow to saints, and burn incense unto them, erect temples, and set apart days for their worship, and so break all the four commandments of the first table. In a good fashion, it is not unfit to remember them, that their memorial may be kept; but we are not to worship them.

4. And, besides saints, *they have other false gods;* for their head of the church is an abominable idol, unto whom they ascribe that which is proper unto Christ, to be the head of the church, which hath no influence from him, but all from Christ, the spiritual head thereof. Therefore the apostle complaineth of such ' who hold not the head,' &c., Col. ii. 19. Those of the Romish Church ' hold not the head,' hold not Christ, because they attribute that to saints and men which is proper to Christ only. They make the pope judge of all controversies, who must give authority to the word, and determine Scripture to be Scripture. What a shameful thing is this, to make him judge of the Scriptures, which must judge him at the last day. A pitiful thing it is to see ' a man of sin' go about to judge the righteous law of God, and to determine of that which must ere long determine him unto eternal torments, without particular repentance. Yet, being spiritually drunk, this folly they are given to, that they will be judge of that which must be judge of them. Many ways they make him an idol, ascribing that to him which is proper to Christ.

5. So likewise, *they make their sacraments to be idols.*

For, 1, they ascribe to the *water in baptism* power of conferring grace.

Now, grace is God's creature only; for all the creatures in heaven and earth cannot confer the least dram of grace. It is a thing of God's making. Now, to raise an element to confer grace, and then to trust in it, *ex opere operato*, for the conferring of it, is to make an idol of it.

2. And for *the bread*. None of all the heathens ever had such an abominable idol as the mass, a breaden god, for they worshipped living creatures, and there is not the worst living creature but it is better than a piece of bread; and yet they worship that, for, by their own confession, if the intention of the priest be not to the action, there is nothing but bread. How may the minds, then, of men be tormented when they may or shall think perhaps the priest hath no such intention, and so are in danger of idolatry. For, saith the psalmist, ' their sorrows shall be multiplied that hasten after another god,' &c., Ps. xvi. 4. So certainly the sorrows and scruples of those that are idolaters shall be multiplied. They cannot but be much tormented in soul sometimes. Coster (*p*), himself a forward Jesuit, acknowledgeth ' that if, upon the words of consecration, the bread be not turned and transubstantiated into the body of Christ, we are the most abominable idolaters of the world.' But we make the minor and assumption, long since proved by the late worthies of our church * (*q*), but there is no such transubstantiating of the bread into the body of Christ. Therefore, by their own consent, they are the most abominable idolaters of the world, worse than the heathen.

8. And in their *equalising traditions*, which are but the inventions of man's brain, *with the Scriptures*, they commit idolatry, in that they make their very church an idol. But what should we speak of their church,

* B. Jewel, D. Rainolds, D. Fulk, D. Whitaker, D. Willet, Perkins, &c. See Note *q*.—G.

when they have the pope, who is their church virtually? for what is said of the one may be said of the other. When they come to the issue, the church is nothing but the pope. Whatsoever their church or councils say, he is the whole church. Many ways they are gross idolaters, especially the common people. For though they say they give not *Latria*, worship to the image, but *Dulia*, service, but can the common people distinguish, who give worship to all alike? To say we worship not the image, but God before the image, was the heathen's excuse, as we may see in Arnobius (*r*). Can the common people distinguish? No; for they are ignorant images themselves. In this they are worse than the heathens, because they have more light, and still the more light the more sin. For they have been foretold that the whore of Rome should be the mother of all fornications, the spiritual Babylon, Sodom, and Egypt in regard of idolatry, the mother of all these abominations, Rev. xvii. 5. Now, for them who have been forewarned hereof, and in so much light still, to continue idolaters, and persist in false worship, is to be worse than the heathens, who had not the like light and warning.

Ques. But what is the reason that they are so impudent and audacious?

Ans. 1. First, to answer with the Scriptures, *they are drunk with the whore's cup*, Rev. xvii. 2; and we know a drunken man dares do anything.

2. And then, again, as the psalmist speaks, because those who worship idols *become blockish and stupid like unto them*, for an idol is a blockish, dead thing, so idolaters are stupid, dead things in a sort, who are seldom converted, partly because they are drunk, and partly because they are stupid, like the idols they worship, Ps. cxv. 8.

Use 1. If this be so, as it is too true to the eye of the whole world, then *how ought we to bless God, who hath brought us out of this palpable Egyptian darkness, out of spiritual Sodom*, as Lot was out of that Sodom! Gen. xix. 17. Oh, we cannot be thankful enough, nor ought we to desire to return to Sodom again, or unto Egypt. Where, then, is place left for neutrality? Those neuters, that will be of neither religion! Is such a disposition from the Spirit of God, which maketh Ephraim say here, ' What have I any more to do with idols?' Ephraim would not be a neuter. Therefore, what shall we say unto them that present themselves to Masses, in their travels especially? Is this to say with Ephraim, ' What have I any more to do with idols?' We must ' believe with the heart, and confess with the mouth, to salvation,' Rom. x. 9. If a man might escape with having his heart to God-wards, and his body prostrate, where were confession? In Elias's time, God told him, that there were left seven thousand in Israel, who had not bowed the knee to Baal, that is, who made no bodily prostration, 1 Kings xix. 18. Therefore, as the papists do not join with us, so neither ought we with them, if we hold the contrary religion false. In this case we should not present ourselves with them in any service.

Use 2. Again, if this be true, *what do we think of reconcilers of religion?* A thing impossible, as the apostle sheweth. ' For what communion hath God with Belial? Christ with antichrist?' 2 Cor. vi. 14, 15. What communion? The question is a strong negation, as that of Ephraim here. ' What have I now any more to do with idols?'

Obj. But some may say, We differ from them only in circumstance.

Ans. We may ask any man who hath his brains in his head, *whether idolatry be a circumstance or not?* it being clear that they are as great idolaters as the heathens, in many instances. If any affirm that idolatry is a circumstance, there is no disputing with such a one. That which is the sin, which makes God abhor and desert his own people, is that a circumstance? Is that a circumstance, which is the chief sin against the first table? Granting that they are idolaters, that the pope is 'antichrist,' and Rome to be 'Babylon' (s), and Babylon to be the 'mother of all fornication,' this must needs follow, that there can be no reconciling of these two religions. We may come near them, and become papists, but they will never come near us, to be good Christians.

Use 3. Again, if this be so, that popery be idolatry, and that we must beware of all idolatry, let us take heed, therefore, *that we have nothing to do with them more than we must needs.* Converse with them in our callings, we may; because, as an ancient father saith, we be compossessors of the world, and not of religion. We must go out of the world, if we will not have to do with them sometimes in the places where we live; but amity is very dangerous with such. The Scripture runs much upon it. Should we love them whom God hates? It was Eve's fault, that without a calling she ventured to talk with the serpent. We should therefore shun conversing and parley with them as much as may be. As there were rails set about Mount Sinai, to keep off the people from touching the mountain; so God hath set hedges about the second commandment, to keep us off from offending in it, as it was usual with God in this kind. As, when he would keep them far from murder, he forbade them to kill the dam with the young, Deut. xxii. 6, and not to seethe a kid in his mother's milk, Exod. xxiii. 19; only to restrain them from murder, that abominable sin. Such precepts the Jews call 'the hedges of the commandments' (t). So for idolatry, the Scripture would have us 'hate the garment spotted with the flesh,' Jude, verse 23; 'to defile the coverings of the images, to account them as a menstruous cloth,' &c., Isa. xxx. 22; and 'to have nothing to do with the unfruitful works of darkness,' Eph. v. 11; [and] to hate all monuments of idolatry. As Augustine saith of monuments, 'Any monument moves and stirs up the mind;' so anything that may move or stir us to idolatry, we should abhor, and keep afar off from it.

And therefore the commandments are set down in the highest pitch of the sin, to shew that we should avoid all the degrees under that which leads to so great a breach, and that we should hate all those steps and leadings to the sin itself. We should therefore beware of popish writers, and do with them as was done with the magic books in the Acts, burn them all, lest they corrupt ourselves and others, Acts xix. 19. Learn we this of the papists, who hate our books, burn them, or lock them up safe; yea, hate the very names of Luther and Calvin, much more their books.

In this case it is with the soul of man as with water, that relisheth of that soil through which it runs, if it run through a hot soil, as baths through a sulphury soil, it tastes of that. So the spirit of a man tastes of those authors he runs through. Therefore such who converse much in popish writings, unless ministers who have a calling that way to confute them, are in danger to be ensnared by them.

Use 4. And then, again, if we must hate all idolatry, *we must take heed of occasions.* Not like some looser Christians, which make no matter of crucifixes. How doth the spirit of Ephraim here agree with such? A crucifix is but a teacher of lies, representing only the outside, and that falsely; for there is no expression in Scripture, what kind of man Christ was. And if there were, yet the apostle sheweth, 'that we must now no more know him any more after the flesh,' 2 Cor. v. 16. Not as such a man, as tall and fair, &c.; but know him as the Mediator, as king of

heaven and earth, avoiding all lewd, base conceits of him. People in this
kind are too bold, and run too near popery. A father saith well, ' No man
is safe that is near danger.' We are commanded to ' fly from idolatry,'
1 Cor. x. 14. We must not come near the pit's brink, lest we fall in.
Run and fly from it as from a serpent, dally not with the occasions.

But to leave this gross idolatry, to speak of something which more nearly
concerneth us, and which we are prone to. Though we hate the gross
idolatries, yet there be some we are more nearly addicted to; as,

First of all, there is a proneness in us, in our worship, *to conceive false
conceptions and ideas of God;* and so in place of worshipping God, we worship an idol of our own brain.

Quest. It may be said, How shall we conceive of God when we worship
him ?

Ans 1. First of all, negatively, do not dishonour God *in imagining any
character of an infinite incomprehensible God*, but conceive of him as an infinite essence.

2. And then, *conceive not absolutely of God*, but of God distinguished in
three persons, the Father, Son, and Holy Ghost; or else we conceive an
idol. For there are three persons in one common nature; and in our
prayers we must not conceive the nature without the persons.

3. In the third place, we must not in our prayers conceive of God, *without Christ the Mediator*. For even as God was only to be known and spoken
to towards the tabernacle; so Christ is the tabernacle now, where God manifests his gracious presence, and will be worshipped in him the Mediator.
For God, considered out of Christ, is a ' consuming fire;' without Christ,
no converse with God. Let us therefore take Christ along with us, when
we go to God. Go to him by God in our nature, our Immanuel; and so
we shall conceive of God aright, and not worship an idol of our own
brain.

4. Again, there is another thing which is a common abuse among Christians, wherein they come near to idolatry, *when they transform God to be
like themselves in their affections*, as it is the property of all unregenerate
men to do so. Idolatry is so natural, it cannot but transform God to be
like itself. As for instance, a man that is not a gracious man, in the pride
of his sinful course, thinks that God is like unto him. ' Thou thoughtest
that I was like unto thyself; therefore I will come against thee,' &c., Ps.
l. 21. As oppressors, and such who grow great by ill courses, they justify
thus much. Would God let me alone if he did not approve of my courses?
So they make God like themselves. And so the good fellows of the world,
they make God to allow all their dissoluteness, because he lets them alone.
So those that are fierce and cruel by nature, who delight in cruelty, vexation, and blood, they transform God, as though he delighted in such
things, and make him a God of blood. So others transform God to be all
mercy. This is to make God an idol, and as ill as if they transformed
him into this and that creature; worse than the heathens, in regard of
their light under the gospel; yet this is the disposition of many Christians
now-a-days.

Quest. What was the reason why the heathens worshipped Bacchus and
Venus, such abominable gods ?

Ans. They, to countenance their lusts and drunkenness, deify them : an
abominable sin of the heathen, for which God gave them up to other sins.
Doth not our sin come near theirs, when we make God to countenance our
sin, and cite Scripture for it, as if God can countenance sin in his word ?

This is to transform God into our own abominable conceits. Those, therefore, who bless themselves in any sinful course, they are guilty of idolatry in the worst kind that may be ; for it is as ill to transform God to allow of such courses, as to transform Christ to die for such who go on in their sins without remorse, or to transform him into the likeness of such and such vile creatures.

5. Further, there is another sort of idolatry Christians are subject unto— *to set up somewhat in their hearts higher than God.* There is no man without grace, but he doth so until his conversion. Nay, when a man is converted, he is prone to this, to idolize and set up something above that which should be in the heart. Hereupon Paul, Col. iii. 5, calleth covetousness, idolatry ; because a covetous man placeth those affections upon his own wealth, which should dwell in God : for, ' he saith to the wedge of gold, Thou art my confidence,' Job xxxi. 24, thinking his wealth shall bear him out in any ill cause whatsoever. And then, again, that time which he should spend in thinking of God and of a better life, he buried those thoughts in his muck and wealth, toiling and moiling in the world, when he should serve God. Thus the covetous man is an idolater.

6. And there are some guilty of idolatry, likewise, in another kind, *such as have men's persons too much in admiration,* that deify them, especially if they be in great place : such who will offend God before they will offend them ; and whereas for God's glory they should deny themselves, they deny themselves, and make themselves fools, for men ; and to please them by whom they hope to rise, deny both wit and honesty. This is abominable idolatry, and such are as far from heaven and salvation, as those that fall before an idol, if they repent not. Oh, if these men that study to please men, and deny themselves for them, would be as careful to please God, as they have been to please men, how happy, and what excellent Christians would they be ! As a great man-pleaser in his time said, ' If he had served God as well as he had served his master the king in that time, God had not left him so in his old years ' (*u*).* To set up any man so high in our affections, as for him to deny ourselves, crack our consciences, and do things unlawful, will be misery in the end. ' If I please men,' saith Paul, ' I am not the servant of Christ,' Gal. i. 10. He meaneth sinful pleasing, for there ought to be service and respect. Due honour must be given unto those who carry God's image, our governors, yea, great respect and honour, and nothing in this kind can be too much ; but to go beyond our bounds herein, is to commit idolatry. As the heathen did, when the government of Rome was turned into an empire, some of their emperors were made gods by them after Augustus's time, wherein they could not have devised to have done them greater wrong, for they came most of them to fearful ends (*v*). It is ill for any man to have God his co-rival ; for no greater misery can befall a man, than to be set up in God's room, so to rule a man's honesty, will, and conscience at his pleasure ; for God is a jealous God, and will not endure such idolatry.

7. And so, in the next place, they frame Christ an idol, *in taking him without his cross.* They will be of the true religion ; but when they come to suffer anything, if it be but a frown, a reproach or disgrace, they give out and fall back. Such, they frame to themselves an idol, a false Christ ; for the knowledge of Christ is never without the cross, some cross or other, some persecution or other in some kind. ' All who will live godly in Christ, shall suffer persecution,' 2 Tim. iii. 12. A man may live godly,

* A Scottish Regent before his execution. See Note *u*.—G.

and not suffer persecution ; but he that will live godly in Christ, so as he sheweth his nature to be altered, carrying an antipathy against all false courses, and so as the world may conceive that he is such an one, it is impossible that he should live in the world without persecution, because he shall meet with those that are of an opposite disposition. Therefore, to frame a smooth Christ, all comfort, is to frame a false Christ, and a false religion,—to frame an idol that hath no truth in it, that never was, nor never will be to the end of the world.

8. Again, unconverted persons especially are prone to another idolatry, *to set up their own wits and wills instead of God's.* So as there is not a greater enemy to religion than our own conceits and wills, which will have a model of religion of our own brain, which must stand, let what will come of it. This is the fault especially of great learned persons, who take upon them conceits and apprehensions of things, and then doat upon these brats of their own brain. And so for will, to have our own will in all things ; as the speech is, ' My mind to me a kingdom is.' I will have my will, whatsoever come of it. This is idolatry ; for whosoever will come to heaven must deny his will. The first lesson in Christ's school is self-denial, Mat. xix. 21, 24 : denial of wit and will, to have no more wit and wisdom, especially in divine things, than God will teach us ; and no more will, which is distinct and opposite to Christ's will, but to bring our wills to his in all things. When men will go about great affairs, and set upon things in their own wit and strength, never praying nor depending upon God for a blessing, this is a kind of idolising of parts to work out things by policy, strength, wits, and parts. As that heathen atheist could say, ' Let cowards pray, if they will ;' but his success was answerable. So is it not the common atheism of the world ? They go about things in confidence of their wit and parts, and so hope to attain a glorious issue ; whereas God, who overthrows Babels, takes delight to confound all their devices. It is his daily practice ' to send the rich empty away, and exalt the humble and meek,' Luke i. 52. Those who set upon things rashly without prayer, as though they were lords of all, and without dependence upon God, promising themselves good success, they make idols of themselves. As a proud man is an idol, ' he worships himself,' whilst he leans to his own wit, plots, and parts. Carnal men thus idolise themselves.

9. Again, you have some who are none of the worst who commit this great sin of idolatry, *by trusting to the outward performances and tasks of religion,* thinking that God must needs be bound unto them, when they have done so many tasks, read, and prayed, or heard so many sermons, or done a good deed. But here lieth the spiritual subtlety, in that they set up these things too high, when, if they find not that success they look for, then they inwardly murmur against God; when rather all these things should be done with a spirit of humility and subjection, using them only as means whereupon we expect God's blessing, craving his assistance and strength to do them in a holy and a self-denying manner. When we do otherwise, and trust to the outward tasks and performances we do, we make them idols. And you have many that go along with outward performances who never come to a dram of grace, because they trust to the outward performances, and look not to the life and soul of them, which is the Spirit of God assisting, quickening, strengthening, blessing them. The life of a Christian is a perpetual dependence upon God in the use of means, and not an idolising of them, to be careless when he hath done his task.

10. But a more subtle idolatry than this is of another kind, *when we trust too much to the work of grace, and rely not upon God in Christ*, in the matter of justification and acceptation to life everlasting, which is a fault, both,

1. Before conversion.

2. After conversion.

First, *before conversion*. When we think we have not done so much good, and been sufficiently humbled, and therefore that God will not be merciful to us, as if Christ must take us with dowry of good deeds, or else he cannot ; whereas all grace is promised upon our entry and coming into the covenant of grace, upon our believing, when we come with empty hearts and hands. ' The poor,' saith Christ, ' receive the gospel ; and those that are lost, Christ is sent to save them, and to call in the weary and heavy laden,' Mat. xi. 5, ix. 13, xi. 28.

2. And *after conversion*. Those that are in the state of grace oftentimes want that comfort in the main point of justification and acceptation to life everlasting, which they should have, because they look into their imperfections, seeing this and that want, and so are swallowed up of discomfort ; whereas, if we had all the graces in the world, yet we must live by faith, relying upon the merits of Christ. For our good works bring us not to heaven, as a cause, but only are helps and comforts to us in our walking to heaven. For if we had all the sins of all men, yet Christ's all-sufficient righteousness is sufficient for to do them all away, if we can go out of ourselves, and cleave to that. Therefore, in trouble of conscience we must not look either to our good or our ill, but to God's infinite mercy, and to the infinite satisfaction of our blessed Saviour the Lord Jesus Christ ; there, as it were, losing ourselves, seeing our sins as mountains drowned in the infinite sea of his mercy. The blood of Christ ! That will pacify and stay the conscience. Nothing else can give rest to our souls. If we look to our works and to the measure of our sanctification, what saith holy Paul in the like case ? ' Yea, doubtless, and I count all things but loss, for the excellency of the knowledge of Christ Jesus my Lord, for whom I have suffered the loss of all things, and do count them but dung, that I may win Christ,' Phil. iii. 8, even his righteousness and best works. Therefore there is no regard to be had of them in that case. Wherefore when we would speak comfort to a distressed conscience, we must not look to his ill or good, but to the command, ' This is his command, that we believe,' 1 John iii. 23. And look to the all-sufficiency of God in Christ, and the promises, whereby we honour God in giving him the glory of his truth, and depart with comfort. Therefore, though we hate gross idolatry, yet we see there are many ways wherein the soul may be seduced, whereby we may come very near that sin which our soul hateth, by trusting too much to something out of God.

Use 5. If then the case be thus, *how shall we come to reform it*, for a use of direction, so as to fly from all idolatry, and to say with Ephraim, ' What have I now any more to do with idols ?'

First of all, *do but consider God's hatred unto all sorts of idolaters ;* for he accounts such to hate him, and so accordingly punisheth them. In the second commandment, those that are given to idolatry in any kind, are such as hate God, which is a horrible thing ; and yet, notwithstanding, this is the disposition of all such as are idolaters. So far forth as they are idolaters, they hate God, for the more we know God, the more we shall hate all idols, ' What have I now any more to do with idols ?'

2. Labour *to grow in the sound knowledge of God and of Christ, and of their all-sufficiency.* Mark St Paul's method, Col. ii., and in other places, when he would draw us from all outward things, he speaks gloriously of the fulness of Christ, ' In him dwelleth all the fulness of the Godhead bodily,' Col. ii. 9 ; and, ' In him you are complete.' When he would draw them from ' touch not, taste not, handle not, worshipping of angels, and from counterfeit humility,' Col. ii. 21, &c., he labours to dispossess them of these idolatrous conceits, and to possess them of the fulness of Christ. If in him we have fulness, why should we look for any thing out of him ? If we be complete in him, if all fulness be in him, why do we seek any thing out of that fulness ? Thus the holy apostle shutteth up his first epistle, ' Babes, keep you from idols,' 1 John v. 21. What is promised there ? Christ is eternal life, all is in him ; whereupon presently comes this, ' Babes, keep you from idols ?' If life and happiness, and all be in Christ, if we be complete in him, and the fulness of all be in him, why should we go out of him for anything ? When God would persuade Abraham to leave all idolatry, Gen. xvii. 1, and all things else, to depend wholly upon him, what doth he first possess him with ? ' I am God all-sufficient,' &c. Know God in covenant all-sufficient, and Christ in the fulness of his high perfections as Mediator, in whom is all fulness and life eternal, in whom we are complete ; we shall then be so far from going out of him for any thing, as we shall be of the same mind with Ephraim, ' What have I now any more to do with other intercessors and mediators ?' what have I to do with will-worship ? what need I go to other cursed means, when God is all-sufficient ? It is the scope of the new covenant of grace, that we should glory in God only, who hath made Christ unto us ' wisdom, righteousness, sanctification, and redemption,' 1 Cor. i. 30. And all this, because that whosoever glorieth in him, should not go out of him for any thing. The more we know therefore the fulness of Christ, and God's mercy in him, the more we shall abhor all idolatry, with the kinds and degrees of it.

3. Another help and means to cure this disposition in us is, *to know that we are naturally wondrous prone to it in one degree or another.* It is reckoned up, Gal. v. 20, as a work of the flesh ; and, naturally, man hath a working fancy, to set up somewhat in his heart and understanding above, and besides God, imaginations to adulterate things. Men live by sense, and imagination is next to sense, so that naturally all men are idolaters before conversion, in one kind or other, and doat so upon their own, that they will not be driven out of themselves unto God in Christ, without a great deal of grace. As men naturally love the child of their own body, so men love the children of their own brain.

Quest. What is the reason that it is so hard to convert a papist ?

Ans. Because it is will-worship, a device of their own brain, suiting their natural will and appetite. And what makes them so furious, as all idolaters are cruel : though they be mild of their own nature, yet as idolaters, they are cruel. It is because it is a device of their own brain, a brat, a child of their own begetting, wherefore they strive to maintain it, because it is their own. Let us therefore conceive thus much, that it is no easy matter to free the soul from idolatry, and all the degrees of this cursed disposition. This will make us beg earnestly the Spirit of God, by which only we shall subdue this idolatrous proud conceit, Rom. viii. 5, and lay ourselves open to Christ, to be disposed of as he pleaseth. Beg the Spirit only, whereby we shall mortify the cursed deeds of the flesh, for nature will never subdue nature. The Spirit of God therefore is that which can, and must free us from all dregs and tainture of this cursed disposition, which the Jews were so scourged for, and hardly* driven from.

4. Again, consider *God's punishments in this kind*. As we see, Rev. ix. 20, where the Turk is said to be raised up against all these idolaters, that would not be kept from worshipping the devil and the image of the beast; yet for all this, it is said, 'they did not repent.' And so the Jewish church was still punished with enemies raised up against them for their idolatry. And it is to be expected that the idolatry of these western churches will at length pull down antichrist himself, which must be before the conversion of the Jews. For what hinders their conversion now? The world is full of idolaters, even Christians; and therefore there must be a confusion of antichrist's idolatrous worship before the conversion of the Jews, who will not return whilst that scandal is in their eye. Therefore, that we may help forward that glorious work, let us labour as much as we can to purge the church of this, in drawing others from idolatry, that we may help to make way for those glorious times a-coming; for this Scripture specially hath relation unto the calling of the Jews, not to be fulfilled till then, when 'Ephraim shall say, What have I now any more to do with idols?' with that for which we have been so plagued for in former times.

5. And withal let us consider this, that the end of all false worship, when it is left, *is grief and shame, befooling and shaming of ourselves for it.* 'Ephraim at length shall say, What have I any more to do with idols?' to cherish pride and self-conceit? which, if ever I come to heaven, I must renounce, hating myself for my own pride and folly.

6. And so for idolaters themselves, why *should we consort ourselves with these, of whom we shall say one day, What have we any more to do with them?* We must be separated from them here, or in hell live with them for ever. What will then be the hell of hell? Mutual cursing of one another. Thy familiarity and acquaintance, thy provocations and allurements, brought me into these torments! If we belong to God, late or soon, there must be these speeches, 'What have I now any more to do with such and such lying vanities?'

Therefore let us not think will-worship a slight matter; for, we see, popery is nothing else but a bundle of man's devices. We see in Scripture, when the dearest friends of Christ came unto him with devices of their own, and good intentions, Christ notwithstanding saw the devil in them. Peter made a great confession, 'Thou art the Son of the living God,' Mat. xvi. 16, and then he came 'Master, spare thyself,' ver. 22; whereunto Christ replied, 'Get thee behind me, Satan,' ver. 23. God is never more provoked than when men think to honour him with their own devices; stablishing a false, and neglecting his own true, worship. And there is usually little amendment of these kind of persons, because they carry with them a show of wisdom, as Paul saith, Col. ii. 23, and great humility; which things being so carried with a show of some grace and wisdom (though they be desperate folly in the conclusion), men hardly will part withal. As we see of corporal adultery, few of them are reclaimed, because it hath a bewitching, alluring power; which is most true of the spiritual adulterers. There are few of them reclaimed, until God, by some severe judgment, alter and bring down the proud imagination to serve him as he will be served; so as to say with Ephraim here, 'What have I now any more to do with idols?'

Well, that we may abhor idolatry the more, consider two or three direct

* That is, 'with difficulty.'—G.

places. 'Who required these things at your hands?' saith God, Isa. i. 12.
When we think to please him with voluntary devised things, this will strike
them dumb then. The things that God requires being so easy and so few,
yet we to omit them all, and to devise new things of our own, our reward
shall be, 'Who required these things at your hands?' And then again
saith God, 'In vain they worship me, teaching for my precepts the devices
of men,' Mat. xv. 9. See then the vanity of idolaters, who, though they
would do nothing in vain, yet do all their will-worship in vain. It is not
only idolatry, but obstinate idolatry, the Romish doctrine. 'We would
have cured Babel, but she would not be cured,' Jer. li. 9. Is this a
light cause of our coming out of Babylon? Do we leave them for trifles,
when they stand guilty of abominable idolatry? You may see here, if so
be Ephraim out of holy affection say, 'What have I now any more to do
with idols?' what to think and judge of those that would bring God and
idols together. If Ephraim had been of the temper that many men now
are, he might have said, 'Tush! what need we care for idols, crucifixes, and
the like? There is not such a distance betwixt them and us, why may not
both religions stand together? This new-fangled niceness is but the distempered devices of some few giddy-headed men, who know not what they
would have.' This is the wisdom of many men in our times, who reckon
that there is not an eternal, irreconcilable distance between light and darkness, the service of God and that of idols. 'We cannot serve two masters,'
saith Christ, Mat. vi. 24. Yes, they say, we may serve two masters, Antichrist and Christ, God and Belial. Oh! but what saith Ephraim? 'What
have I now any more to do with idols?' There can be no mixture, you
know, where there is abomination. That church, Rev. iii. 15, which was
neither hot nor cold, may parallel many now in our times, who are neither
hot nor cold, papists nor protestants, but politic atheists, who will be both
or neither, whatsoever may best serve and advance their worldly ends.
How doth God look upon such? Saith he, 'I will spue them out of my
mouth.' God hates such most of all: 'now I would thou wert either hot
or cold.' If this be the affection of God's people toward idols and
idolaters, an utter aversation; and shall we think to jumble and mingle
contrary things together, to serve God and the devil, Christ and antichrist?

Thus we see what to think of the temper of these men. In lighter
matters indeed we may enjoy our own private opinions in some things.
As St Paul saith in lesser things, 'If any man be otherwise minded, God
shall reveal it unto him,' Phil. iii. 15. But when he comes to the point of
justification by Christ in God's worship, what saith he? 'If any man be
otherwise minded, God shall reveal it?' No. But 'if I, or an angel from
heaven, teach otherwise, let him be accursed,' Gal. i. 8. Now, when men
teach another doctrine and worship, joining with gross idolaters in that worship, there we must be of Paul's spirit, 'If I, or an angel from heaven, teach
otherwise, let him be accursed.' The Holy Ghost at first appeared in the
form and shape of a dove, Mat. iii. 16, which is a meek and mild creature,
that hath no talons to hurt with. Yet notwithstanding, at another time,
he appeared in 'fiery tongues,' Acts ii. 3, to shew that the same Spirit
that in lesser things maintaineth peace and love, when it is set against any
sin, especially against that sin of sins, idolatry, which brings God's vengeance
upon kingdoms and states, and roots them out; there the Holy Ghost
must appear in fire. That element must be in the hearts of people against
sin. That, though to persons that have their slips, and in lesser matters,

there must be the spirit of a dove, yet there must be in men the spirit of courage, indignation, abomination, and hatred unto the idolatry of the times, that we may say from our hearts with Ephraim, 'What have I now any more to do with idols?'

Therefore, *let us join with those that we shall live for ever with in heaven*, and go in the best courses, and we shall never need to fear separation, nor want encouragements to well-doing. Thus shall we neither grieve nor be ashamed to say with Ephraim, 'What have I now any more to do with idols?' At the length the kings of the earth, who adore the whore, they shall come and eat her very flesh, Rev. xvii. 16. So it will be the end of those that reign in other men's consciences, and in a manner will be accounted gods, that all which is gotten with wrong to God, shall be renounced with grief, shame, and detestation of the persons of those that make idols of others, and will be made idols in the hearts of others; thinking themselves not enough respected, unless they command the conscience. The end of such cannot be good. All this must end in loathing, shame, and detestation. 'What have I now any more to do with idols?' said Ephraim; and what have I now any more to do with such and such profaneness, hypocrisy, double-dealing, and the like? shall such persons, thus sinful, say one day, with shame and horror of conscience. Wherefore, let us meet God betimes, and renounce our idols of all sorts, that God may come 'to hear us, observe us, and be as a green fir-tree unto us,' &c. Whereof, if God please, we shall hear more the next time.

THE TWELFTH SERMON.

Ephraim shall say, What have I any more to do with idols? I have heard him and observed him: I am like a green fir-tree: from me is thy fruit found.—Hos. XIV. 8.

THE words, as we heard heretofore, are a gracious answer unto the prayer which God himself, by his Spirit, had dictated to Ephraim: as likewise a reward of Ephraim's reformation. Aided by grace, Ephraim shall say, 'What have I now any more to do with idols?' 'God will hear him and observe him, and be like a green fir-tree unto him.' For, saith God, 'from me shall Ephraim's fruit be found.' Whereby we see, that whensoever God doth alter the soul by his grace, there he also breeds divorce and division between it and all idolatry; a disposition in some sort like himself, having those sympathies and antipathies he hath towards sin and goodness. Now, because God is a jealous God, and cannot abide idols; therefore Ephraim, being sanctified by the Spirit of God, is minded as God is, 'What have I any more to do with idols?'

1. God hath framed the soul, *that it may enjoy the chief good*, and avoid the chief ill especially; for petty goods and petty ills are not so behoveful. Yet notwithstanding, God will have us avoid all ill, and embrace all good, and he hath made the soul into an answerable condition. Therefore hath he planted affections therein tending to good; as love, and joy, and delight, especially made for the embracing of the main good, thereby to go out of itself, and close with that main chief good, in closing wherewith it may be happy.

2. And then, *to avoid the chief ill, sin and damnation,* he hath planted affections of aversation, abhorring, hatred, grief, and the like.   Thus hath he framed the soul for these main ends, without which affections the soul were as *mare mortuum,* that dead sea.   The affections are the wings and the wind of the soul, that carry it unto all which it is carried unto.   Especially, when the wind of God's Spirit blows upon it, then it is carried out of itself; for of itself it cannot love or hate as it should; but God must raise the affections, and lay them down again.   We have not the management of our hearts.   Grace teacheth us to do all.

The particular then here is, *indignation and hatred.*   ' What have I now any more to do with idols ?'   So that the proper affection in God's children, which should be conversant about that which is ill, and sinfully ill, is hatred and indignation.   Here is hatred with indignation, the extent of the affection.

Reas. 1. The reason whereof is, when God's children are once converted, *they have a new nature put into them,* like unto Christ, whose Spirit they have.   What he hates, they hate.   He hates all sin, and nothing but sin.   He hates the devil himself for sin, and no further.

2. Then, again, when once they are God's children, *they have a new life put into them,* which hath antipathy to all that is contrary to it.   Every life in any creature hath antipathy to every enemy thereof.   There is antipathy in doves to birds of prey ; and in the lamb to the wolf, because they are enemies to the life and being of them.   So in the soul of a Christian, so far as grace is renewed, there is an antipathy, aversation, and abhorring of that which is contrary.   What have I to do with sin in any kind ?   When grace hath altered the disposition of a man's heart, then sin and he are two ;   two indeed, in the most opposite terms that may be.   What have I any more to do with my former delightful sins ?   We are two now, for we were before nothing but sin.   And, indeed, where this hatred is not, there men may leave sin, because sin leaves them; but this is not enough, God would have us to hate it with indignation.   ' What have I now any more to do with it ?'

Quest. But how should we come to have this true hatred of sin, as Ephraim should have ?

Ans. 1. Amongst those helps formerly named, this is a main one, to represent to the soul (as the soul is quick and nimble in such apprehensions) *the odiousness of sin,* that it is a truly hateful thing; and therefore, that our affection of hatred cannot be better set nor employed upon any object than that of sin.   For let us consider that it is not only ill in itself, defiling the soul and hindering communion with God ; but it is also the cause of all ills, being the ill of ills, as God is the good of goods.   For our troubles and terrors of conscience, we may thank sin, and for all that we suffer every day in our conditions of life.   What is all, but the fruit of our own ways ? ' Wherefore suffereth living man ?' saith the prophet ; ' man suffereth for his sin,' Lam. iii. 39.   ' Thine own inventions have brought these things upon thee ; therefore they are bitter unto thee, they shall pierce thy bowels,' Jer. iv. 18.   Shall we not, therefore, hate that which is the cause of all mischief to us ?   If we had an enemy, especially if he were a soothing false enemy, that under pretence of love should seek our bane and ruin, and join with our worst enemies, would we not hate such an enemy ?   Sin is the greatest enemy which we have in the world, and doth us more harm than the devil himself ; for it betrays us to the devil, and, under pretence of favouring and pleasing our nature, betrays us.   It is a false, deceitful enemy, which cometh not in an ugly shape, but closes with the soul in a kind of conjugal love, Delilah-like enticing and alluring us, whereby it hath the more advantage and strength, in that it appears in a lovely, pleasing, and not in an imperious, commanding manner. Therefore, it should be the more hateful to us. Shall we not hate such an enemy as always dogs us, and hinders us? hinders us from doing anything well, and puts us on to all that is ill. It is such an enemy, that we cannot go about to pray, or do any good thing, but it hangs upon us, and clogs us in all our performances. If a man knew that such an one as made love to him and all his were his great grand enemy, aiming at his destruction, would a man ever love such a man? Thy base, false, revengeful, covetous, worldly heart, it joins with Satan, without which he could not hurt thee. Shall a man cherish that which betrays him to his worst enemy, the devil? and then, should he cherish that which makes a breach betwixt him and his best friend? If a man saw one so maliciously evil towards him, as to sow dissension by all means he could betwixt him and his best honourable friend, by whom he was maintained in all things, would not a man hate such a one? What doth sin else but breed division and enmity betwixt God and us? And further, when it hath moved us to do ill, it crieth for vengeance against us at God's hands. Conscience, soundly awakened, is always clamorous to pull somewhat from God against us. Are not sinners justly called fools? Either men must be atheists to deny all, or else, if they cherish sin, they must needs be fools, and stark mad, if they confess this, that they join with that which is their chief enemy. Therefore, learn to be wise to salvation; make not with Solomon's fool a sport of sin, Prov. x. 23, of swearing, of defiling ourselves and others, seeing God threateneth damnation unto such.

Ans. 2. And then again, *avoid all parley and intercourse with sin in the first suggestions*, or with wicked persons that may draw us away. Use sin ruggedly and harshly, as they do here. ' What have I to do with idols?' Do but entertain parley with it, and it is of such an insinuating nature, that it will encroach daily, and spread over the soul suddenly, betraying it to the devil. Therefore, use it hardly in the first beginnings, and avoid Satan in the first suggestions, if we love the peace of our souls; as Ephraim here, ' What have I any more to do with idols?' For as we say in case of honesty, they come too near that come to have the refusal. They should not have so much hope from a chaste person. There should be such a modest carriage as should not give any one the boldness to adventure in that kind. So if a man carry himself remotely from sinful courses, he shall have a great deal of peace from wicked men, who dare not so much as adventure to draw away such a one. They know he is resolved. Therefore, constant resolution against all sin and wicked men will breed a great deal of peace, so as to say with Ephraim, ' What have I any more to do with idols?'

Ans. 3. And *we must know that this hatred comes from the life of God in us*. Therefore we must by all means maintain spiritual life; and then, as we grow spiritual, we shall grow in the detestation of sin, a sense of joy in good things, with a hatred of all that is contrary. A man can never hate sin till he hath the Spirit of Christ in him. For there be three queries, whereof this is the last.

1. The first is set down, ' No man said, What have I done?' Jer. viii. 6. When conscience in a man is awakened once, he saith, Oh! what have I done? what case am I in?

2. The second query of a wakened conscience is, ' What shall I do?'

As that, 'Men and brethren, what shall we do to be saved?' Acts ii. 37.   He
that truly saith, ' What have I done ?' if conscience be awakened, will also
say, ' What shall I do ?'   You shall not need to drive him when the question is answered, ' What shall I do to be saved ?' that is, by casting myself
upon God in Christ.

3. We need not put the question, he will say of himself, ' What have I
any more to do with that which is contrary to that which saves me ?'
' What have I to do with idols ?'   This comes in in the last place.   1. A
man is awakened out of his natural condition.   2. Then he goes to God
in Christ.   And then, 3. There is a spiritual life wrought in him, which
stirs him up to hate all that is contrary unto it.   ' What have I now any
more to do with idols ?'

' For I have heard him and observed him.'

' I have seen and observed him,' some read the words, but very few (w) ;
which is thus a very good and pious construction of them. ' What have I
now any more to do with idols ?'   As if Ephraim should say these words,
' I have seen him and observed him ;' that is, because I have seen him and
observed ; therefore, ' What have I now any more to do with idols ?'   As
soon as a man comes to hear God speak, and to observe God, down goes
all idols ; for, indeed, the respect to idolatry, and anything that is naught,
it falls down in the soul, as the knowledge of the true God is lifted up, and
as affection to good things are raised up in the soul.   ' What have I to do
with idols any more ?'   ' I have seen and observed him.'   As Job said of
himself when he had seen God, ' I abhor myself, and repent in dust and
ashes,' Job xlii. 6 ; much more all false courses.   I abhor them all, now
that ' I have seen and observed him.'

This is a safe, pious, and good sense ; but the words, under correction,
are fitliest applied unto God himself, as if God rather than Ephraim said
thus, ' I will hear him and observe him ;' I will do thus and thus ; ' I will
be as a green fir-tree,' to shade him from danger, and to make him fruitful.

Obj. But you will say, Ephraim cannot cast away idols till God respect
him first.   Therefore, this is promised in the second place.   ' Ephraim
shall say, What have I to do with idols ?'   And God shall say, ' I have
seen him, heard him, and observed him,' when he hath cast away idols.

Ans. To this the answer is : Indeed, in the order of nature, God doth
first stir us up to pray to him, and promiseth us respect and hearing of our
prayers, after which we cast away idols ; but the experience of it is after
we have done the deed.   After that we have found God experimentally
gracious, protecting and hearing of us, then we cast away idols.   So this
experience a Christian finds when he abominates and rejects ill ways.   Then
he finds God all-sufficient, as indeed God is never fully felt and known till
we renounce all other helps.   So the general point is,

Obs. That nothing is lost by renouncing idolatry and carnal confidence in any
worldly thing.

For God makes a supply in himself. ' I will hear him and observe him.'
Nothing is lost, for God will be true of his promise. ' Seek ye first the
kingdom of God and his righteousness, and all other things shall be ministered unto you,' Mat. vi. 33. The truth of God, and then his mercy, makes
this good. Is not God merciful to his children when they renounce all
false confidence ?   In regard of the truth of his promise and mercy, he will
make good this, that nothing is lost by cleaving to him.   We read in the
story of our own times, in King Edward the Sixth's reign, the same day
that there was reformation of idolatry in London, purging of churches from

roods* and idols, the same day was that noble victory and conquest in the north parts over the enemies (*x*). So God answered their care in reforming things amiss with good success.

On the contrary, when we go on with favouring abuses and corruptions, yet expecting good success, it is in vain. Let Ephraim come to say, 'What have I to do with idols?' and see then whether God will respect him or not. Do nations or persons think that God will respect them or bless them, whilst they do that which is abominable to him? No; when Ephraim saith, 'What have I to do with idols?' then presently comes, God 'will hear and observe him, and look to him;' as you have it in that gracious promise, 'The eyes of the Lord are open unto all them that fear him, and his ears are open to their prayers,' Ps. xxxiv. 15. His eyes and his ears. Indeed, God is all eye and all ear. The best friend in the world cannot have his eye always upon us. The mother's eye cannot be always upon her child. She must have a time to sleep, when neither her eyes nor ears are open to her child's prayers. It may cry, and die in crying sometimes, before she can help it. But if we renounce sin, we have a gracious Father 'who will hear us, observe us, and see us,' and not only hear and see, but, as the Scripture phraise s, do that that follows all this. Where he sees, he will pity and relieve; and where he hears, he will pity and protect.

'I have heard him, I have observed him.' God will hear, when once we renounce sin. 'If I regard iniquity in my heart, God will not hear my prayers,' Ps. lxvi. 18, saith David. But when I do not regard iniquity, God will hear my prayers. Then a man may know that God will hear him, when once he hath renounced sin, and comes with clean hands and heart to God. As it is in Isaiah, they were corrupted in their course, and yet came to God, Isa. i. 11, *seq*, but he rejects all; so in the last of that prophecy, he accounts of their sacrifices as of the cutting off of a dog's neck, because their hands were full of blood, and they were full of sin, Isa. lxvi. 3. Reform abuses, let there be personal and national reformation; and then come and reason the matter with God, and see whether he will regard us or not. The Spirit, it is said, makes requests for the saints, and 'God knoweth the meaning of the Spirit, because it makes request according to the will of God,' Rom. viii. 27. The same Spirit that stirs us up to amend our lives, and fly idolatrous courses, the same Spirit stirs us up to pray to God, according to the will of God; and then God hears the desires of his own Spirit. Of all judgments in the world, this is the greatest, to pray and not to be heard; for when we are in misery, our remedy is prayer. Now when that which should be our remedy is not regarded, what a pitiful thing is that? Now, here is an excellent blessing set down, to pray, and for God to hear, 'I will hear him, and observe him.' Because then, God and Ephraim were of one mind, and join in one, therefore God cannot but hear and regard Ephraim, being of his mind, to love and to hate what he loves and hates. As soon as ever the prodigal began to hate his former courses, the father came out to meet him, Luke xv. 20, *seq.*; and so of David, 'I said I will confess my sins to God,' Ps. xxxii. 5. I said, that is, in my heart, I resolved to confess to God, and thou forgavest mine iniquity. God heard his resolution. We cannot else entertain a full purpose to go to God, unless there be a cessation from sin. The prodigal, for all his contrition, was afraid to be shaken off his father, for his dissolute life. Oh, but the father provides a banquet. So it is when we turn to God, and re-

* That is, 'crosses,' as in Scotland, Holyrood = holy cross.—G.

solve a new life, to cast away our idolatries, and former abominations ; presently, ' God hears us, and observes us,' and is ready to meet us.

There is an excellent place, even touching Ephraim himself. ' I have surely heard Ephraim bemoaning himself : Thou hast chastised me, and I was chastised, as a bullock unaccustomed to the yoke : turn me to thee, and I shall be turned ; thou art the Lord my God, &c. Is Ephraim a dear son ? is he a pleasant child ? for since I spake against him, I do earnestly remember him still ; therefore my bowels are troubled for him : I will have mercy upon him,' Jer. xxxi. 18. If Ephraim begin to bemoan himself for his folly, presently follows, that God's bowels are turned to him ; so it is said of Ephraim here. After he had renounced idols, God's bowels are turned towards him, ' I have heard him, and observed him.' Which yields us a sweet and comfortable consideration, *to turn to God from all our sinful courses*, because God is so ready to forgive, and to forgive great sins. What if our sin be idolatry, the grand sin of the first table ? Yet if Ephraim say, ' What have I do with idols ?' (though it be spiritual adultery), yet if Ephraim begin to renounce idolatry, God will say, ' I have heard him, and observed him.' If your sins were ' as red as crimson,' saith God, ' I will make them as white as wool,' &c., Isa. i. 18. Crimson sins, double-dyed sins, it is no matter what they are, if we come to God. There is more mercy in him than sin in us. If Ephraim say, What have I to do with my former evil courses, ' God will hear him, and observe him.'

It is never better with a Christian, than when he hath renounced all wicked courses, (though he thinks himself undone if he leaves his former Delilah delights). But there is no such matter, for we shall find an hundredfold more in God, as Christ speaks, ' Whosoever leaves father or mother, brother or sister, house or kindred for me, shall have a hundredfold in this world,' Mat. xix. 29 ; that is, they shall have it in contentment and grace, in peace of conscience, and perhaps in the things of this life in another kind. What lost Abraham when he obeyed God, and forsook his father's house ? God was all-sufficient for him. He grew a rich man. And what lost he by giving Isaac to God ? He received his son again, of whom there came an innumerable seed. And what lost holy David, in waiting for the time that he should come unto the kingdom, without making haste ? He came quietly to the possession of the crown ; whereas Jeroboam, who made more haste, after God had told him he should reign, he was cursed in his government, and none of his posterity came to good. There is nothing lost by depending and waiting upon God, and renouncing of carnal confidence. We think naturally we are undone. Oh, there is no such matter, as David speaks, ' When my father and mother forsaketh me, yet the Lord taketh me up,' Ps. xxvii. 10. As we know in the gospel, when the blind poor man was excommunicated and cast out, after he had spoke somewhat stoutly to the Pharisees, ' Will ye also be his disciples ?' John ix. 27, yet then Christ takes him presently into his company, being expelled by them. What lost he by this ? So when Israel had lost all their fleshpots in Egypt, they had no loss, for God provided them manna from heaven, and what lost they by that ? They had angels' food instead of their garlic and onions.

' I have observed him.'

That is, I will have a special eye to him ; I will look to him in all conditions and states whatsoever. God never slumbers nor sleeps. Like the master of the house in the parable, who, when the poor man came for bread, Luke xi. 5, all the rest being asleep, is awaked, and raised up by the importunity of the poor man. So the great master of the family of heaven and earth, that governs all, he wakes day and night, and never sleeps ; herein going beyond the care of the dearest friends we have in the world, for they must have a time to sleep. The mother, though she love the child as her own bowels, yet notwithstanding she must have a resting time, and perhaps in that time the child may miscarry ; but God always observes ; his eye is always upon his children, they are before him, written ' in the palms of his hands, he hath them in his eye,' Isa. xlix. 16 : as in Exodus, you have there God brought in observing the children of Israel. ' I have seen, I have seen the affliction of my people Israel,' Exod. iii. 7. They thought themselves neglected of God, but he tells Moses, ' I have seen, I have seen,' I know it very well ; he adds knowledge to sight. So there is no affliction in this world to God's children, but God in seeing sees. As before, he hears the groans and sighs ; so he sees the most intimate inward affliction whatsoever that afflicts the soul ; as they were grieved in very soul at the tyranny of Pharaoh. Oh, but God in seeing he sees, whose eyes are ten thousand times brighter than the sun ! This is a consolation, when one thinks that no man sees and regards ; alas, what shall become of me ! Why should any man say so, that hath God to go to, who is all eye, and all ear ! God hears and sees ; his ears are always open, as it is often shewed, especially, Ps. xxxiv. 15.

It is said, ' His ears are open to their prayers, and his eyes to see their afflictions.'

Quest. But with what kind of eye doth God see the afflictions of his children ?

Solution. He sees them with a tender, compassionate eye ; for he aboundeth in those affections which he hath put into a father and mother. There is no mother would suffer her child to miscarry, if she could help it. God sees surely* some afflictions are for our good, or he would relieve us ; for as he hath a compassionate eye, so he hath a tender heart, and a powerful hand. He sees wicked men also ; but his eyes in regard of them are ' like a flame of fire,' not only because he is quick-sighted, but because he sees with a revengeful† eye ; and as his eyes are like a flame of fire, so likewise he hath feet of brass to tread them to powder, Rev. i. 14, 15.

Use 1. And this likewise is no little part of our comfort ; for when we suffer anything in this world, it is from ill men for the most part, except it be in those afflictions wherein we more immediately deal with God, as in sickness, &c. But in persecution in the world, our trouble lies with men. Therefore it is our comfort, God sees our trouble, and their malice ; and as he is ready to help the one, so he is to revenge the other.

Use 2. And as it is a point of comfort, so of great encouragement to be bold in God's cause. What ! shall we be baser than the base creatures ? Take but a dog in his master's sight, you see how he will fight. Take the meanest and basest creature, when it hath a superior nature to itself, that it ‡ is wiser and greater, that encourageth and sets it on, that it knows will see it take no harm, these base creatures will be courageous ; which otherwise if it had none to set it on, had no courage at all, at least not so much. And shall we in the sight of God, and when we are set in his quarrel, and have his encouragement and his command, with promise of his presence and assistance, flinch and fly off then ? It argues a great deal of atheism and infidelity of heart. God sees me and looks on me while I fight, and while I stand for his cause. God's cause is true and just, God

* That is, ' assuredly.'—G.   † That is, ' avenging.'—G.   ‡ Qu. ' it knows ? '—ED.

sees me, and he sees who opposeth me. In regard of the eye of God therefore, let us be courageous in these things that are agreeable to the mind of God, whatsoever they be, whether matters of justice or piety.

Use 3. Again, if God have such an ear to hear us, let us have an ear to hear him, and an eye to look to him. Let us have Moses' eye to look on him who is invisible, Heb. xi. 26. His eye is upon us, and let our eye be to him ; both may be together. When these two eyes meet ; when my heart tells me that God seeth me, and that I see God looking upon me, this makes courageous. Therefore as God hears and sees us, so we must have an eye to see him that is invisible. And so we pass from these words, ' I have heard him and observed him ;' and what the prophet's meaning is. ' I have heard him, and will hear him ; I have observed him, and will observe him.' For they contain a perpetual action in God; not that he hath, and will not do it now, but what he hath done and will do. That he sets down here in borrowed speeches, for he saith also,

' I will be like a green fir-tree to him: from me is thy fruit found.'

God will be ' like a green fir-tree' in regard of shadow. A fir-tree is a high tree, a goodly, smooth tree, barren in regard of fruit, but it hath thick leaves, which hinders rain from falling upon those who rest under the shadow thereof, and likewise keeps the sun from annoying them. So it is a fit tree for shadow, and the fitter, because it hath no fruit. For usually those trees which spend not themselves this way, they spend themselves in leaves, and have a perpetual greenness, which is supplied with that which should be fruit in fruitful trees. Therefore he sets it down by this comparison of a fir-tree, that so God will keep back all showers, tempests, and storms, and all annoying heat, and he will do it perpetually, as the fir-tree hath a perpetual greenness ; and he will do it with pleasure and delight, as it is a delightful shadow. But because the fir-tree hath no fruit on it, God will not only be a shadow to his children to keep ill from them, but he will be a fruitful tree to them. 'From me,' saith God, ' shall thy fruit be found;' that is, whatsoever good thou doest, thou shalt have it from me. All fruitful comfort comes from me, and all grace. Whatsoever is good for thee, for prosperity of soul or body, all is from me. So we see how God conveyeth himself and his mercy here by sweet comparisons, dealing very familiarly with us, and speaking to us in our own language. We will take both in order as they lie.

God will be as a fir-tree in regard of shadow to the passenger, and keeping off of storms. The great God, and the good God, who is goodness itself, hath provided in this world not only good for us, but hath also promised defences against all annoyances. In the comparison itself, we will observe somewhat concerning the goodness of God ; for as in this life we are subject to many inconveniences, wants, and necessities ; so God hath supply for all, even outward necessities. We are subject to cold, for that we have the element of fire ; we are subject to storms, he hath provided garments, and skill to make them ; so in our travels, he hath provided some trees especially to shelter us. We cannot name any inconvenience of this life, but the rich God in his goodness hath provided a suitable supply. Doth God take care for this fading, perishing life, which is but as a vapour? and hath he good things for it, and fences from the ill and annoyances of it, till we have fulfilled our pilgrimage upon earth ? And will not that God have a care of our best life of grace that shall end in glory, that we shall have all things necessary for life and godliness, which hath the promise, not of this life only, but of a better, 1 Tim. iv. 8. He that is so good to this

natural life, will be much more in things concerning a better life, which he
would have us mind more. ' I will be as a green fir-tree unto him.'

God will be as a fir-tree, especially in regard of shadow, to keep from all
annoyance both of storm and of the sun ; for the sun in those hot countries
annoys them very much, as the spouse complains of her blackness, 'because
the sun had shined upon her, Cant. i. 5, ' to be black as the tents of Kedar,'
&c. Whence we may observe by the way,

*There is not the most comfortable refreshing creature in the world, but take
it in excess, it harms and annoys.*

What more comfortable than water ? yet if it prevail and abound, it is a
destroying creature, as we see in the deluge and divers inundations. What
more comfortable than fire ? and what more terrible if it exceed ? What
more cherishing, refreshing, and quickening than the sun ? Yet in the
excessive heat thereof, it scorcheth and parcheth things. So in the sun of
prosperity and all other good things in the world, it is best to have and
enjoy all things with moderation ; for if we have grace to qualify them, all
things are good ; otherwise the excess hurts us. Therefore beg of God
wisdom to temper and moderate the best good in this world, which otherwise hurts us. For even the excessive heat of the sun in those countries
makes them glad of the shadow of the fir-tree.

Thus God doth not only give a shadow, but a comfortable shadow and
defence to his people, which is therefore called ' the shadow of his wings.'
' How oft,' saith Christ to Jerusalem, ' would I have gathered thee, as the
hen gathereth her chickens under her wings ? ' Mat. xxiii. 37. It is not only
a shielding from hurts, and dangers, and storms, but a sweet defence, with
rest and quiet. As those that are weary compose themselves to rest under
a shadow, so in God is our rest ; ' Come unto me,' saith Christ, ' all ye that
are weary and heavy laden, and ye shall find rest to your souls,' Mat. xi. 28.
All rest is in Christ, and in God's mercy in Christ. We see, then, after
we have forsook idolatry, God is to us instead of all the good we had by
idols. We lose nothing by it. ' God will be as a green fir-tree.'

Whence the point is, *there is a protection, rest, and defence provided for
God's people, when once they have renounced their idolatry and sinful courses.*

Those who refuse the shelter of idols, God will be a shelter unto them,
' a green fir-tree unto them,' another manner of shelter than that which
idols or any other creature can give them. Every man will have some
shelter, shield, or other to cover him, this or that great man to shield or
shelter himself under. A rich man, he hath riches ; another, this or that
defence. Every man that hath any wit about him will have some shelter,
and not lie open to all storms when they come. But the only true shelter
is God himself to a Christian. All other refuges are but shadows, that is,
they are nothing, but like Jonah's gourd, which may shelter for a time, but
there is a worm of vanity that will eat them out. Riches and the favour of
men may shelter for a time, but there is a worm at the bottom which will
root them out. Death will consume them and those they depend upon.
But God is a true shelter to his people, an everlasting habitation, as it is
written, ' Thou art our habitation from generation to generation, Ps. xc. 1.
We dwell in him as in our rock and castle. He is an everlasting habitation, not only a shadow, but a tower and a castle to dwell in. Therefore
the only wise man is the Christian. For, as Noah, when the flood came
upon the old world, and swept them away, had an ark to save himself in,
so have all God's children a house to get over their heads in the worst
times, which is God's blessed protection, in whom they are safe. Let us

think often of these things. What a blessed thing it is to be in the state of a Christian, that hath alway a certain and sure protection, quiet, and rest in God! And what a fearful thing is it to be as the Ahithophels of this world! to be as Cain, Judas, or Saul! who are shrewd in counsel and policy, and yet, when conscience is awakened by the storm of God's wrath, want a shelter, whilst he who is above conscience, and should be a shelter to them, frowns upon them. What a pitiful state is this! The wickedest man in the world, though he have never so great dependence, parts, and strength from human helps, yet when the storm of God's wrath comes, he is as a naked man in the midst of a storm, and knows not whither to go. Therefore let us be wise to have God for our shelter, if we would not be like these miserable politicians and worldlings.

Now, from this, that the shadow is comfortable in those hot countries, where the sun is directly over their heads, comes these sweet phrases in the Psalms and other Scriptures : ' Thou shalt keep me under the shadow of thy wings. As the apple-tree amongst the trees of the forest, so is my beloved amongst the sons. I sat down under his shadow with great delight,' &c., Cant. ii. 3. The church speaks of Christ, ' I sat under his shadow with great delight, and his fruit was sweet to my taste.' The like you have in many places in the Psalms. I will name one or two, more pregnant than the rest, to help our memories, and to breed a deeper impression of so comfortable a point. Ps. lxiii. 7. There the psalmist speaks of resting under the shadow of God's wings. And so in that other sweet and excellent psalm, in the greatest extremities of God's people, ' He that dwelleth in the secret place of the Most High,' that is, God, ' shall abide under the shadow of the Almighty,' Ps. xci. 1. He says after, ' I will say of the Lord, He is my refuge and fortress ;' for where God tells a man that he is a hiding-place and a shadow, there faith adds the application presently ; and then he goes on, speaking of himself, ' He shall cover me with his feathers ; under his wings will I rest ; his truth shall be my buckler. Thou shalt not be afraid of the terror by night ; nor of the arrow by day ; nor of the pestilence that walketh in the dark. A thousand shall fall,' &c., vers. 4–7. So that we see how God doth that to our souls and conditions that the fir-tree, which is God's good creature, doth to the body in the time of storm and heat, that is, he doth refresh us under the shadow of his wings. He is a sweet, comfortable, and gracious God unto us. This, you see, is a clear truth ; yet, because it is so comfortable, we will enlarge it further. Look what God speaks, ' The Lord will create upon every dwelling-place of mount Zion, and upon her assembly, a cloud and smoke by day, and the shining of a flame of fire by night ; for upon all the glory shall be a defence,' Isa. iv. 45. See what a comfortable shadow God is! He saith, ' He will create.' If they want the comfort of the fir-tree, and such like shadows, he says, ' God will create,' that is, make them of nothing. He will ' create upon every dwelling-place of mount Zion,' where his children dwell, and upon their assemblies, ' a cloud and a smoke by day ;' that is, when they are annoyed by the sun, God will create a cloud to keep the rage and the scorching heat of the sun from them, and then a ' shining flame of fire by night,' because in the night we need light, for ' upon all the glory shall be a defence,' that is, upon all the glorious saints of God. They are glory, for there is a Spirit of glory put into them, 1 Pet. iv. 14. The people of God, in whom God will glorify himself, are glorious, and shall be further glorified, and they shall in the mean time have a defence by day and by night from all dangers whatsoever.

Thus it is clear that God will be a shadow to his people, as the fir-tree, which is an allusion to that grand passage of his providence in conducting the children of Israel out of Egypt, where God, to guide them, provided a 'cloud by day, and a pillar of fire by night,' Exod. xiv. 20. The same pillar which was lightsome to the Israelites, was dark to the Egyptians, which cloud and pillar of fire continued, God conducting them, till they came into the land of Canaan. He shadowed them by day with a cloud, and lighted and heated them by a pillar of fire at night, thus conducting them till they came to Canaan. So we, passing through the wilderness of this world till we come unto our celestial Canaan, heaven, God will be a 'cloud' by his gracious special providence, to keep all ill whatsoever from us, and a 'pillar of fire' to lighten and direct us till we come to our heavenly Canaan, where he will be all in all, when we shall need neither sun nor moon, nor have anything to annoy us, Rev. vii. 16. There the noonday shall not burn us with heat of the sun, nor the fire by night. When we are in heaven there shall be no annoyance of the creature. There shall be no more want of light, because we shall have all light and refreshing there for ever and ever. For, as it is written, then 'all tears,' all sorrow, and cause of sorrow, shall be for ever wiped away, an allusion whereunto we have comfortably set down, Ps. cxxi. 7. The more we shall enrich and refresh our memories with thinking of these things, the more comfort will sink into our hearts. The 121st psalm is all spent on comfort in this kind. 'I will lift up mine eyes to the hills, whence cometh my salvation. My help cometh from the Lord, who made heaven and earth,' all my help is from him. 'He will not suffer my foot to be moved; he that keeps Israel will neither slumber nor sleep.' 'He will not slumber;' that is, his eyes are always open to see, as his ears to hear. 'Behold, he that keepeth Israel doth neither slumber nor sleep. The Lord is thy keeper, thy shadow, so that the sun shall not smite thee by day, nor the moon by night. The Lord shall preserve thy going out and thy coming in, from this time for ever.' Thus we see this Scripture is a large gloss and commentary upon this truth, that God, with a special providence and protection, cares for his children, to keep them from all ill. He will be as the fir-tree to them in regard of shadow. Whence we observe in special,

That this life of ours, whilst* we come to heaven, is subject to scorchings and many annoyances, and those both outwardly and inwardly, from ourselves and from others.

First, for *outward annoyances,* how many of them is our poor life subject unto! and for inward terror and boiling heat of conscience, when God in anger discovers himself unto us, and sets our sins in order before us. Oh then, if we have not a shadow; if God in mercy through Jesus Christ be not a shadow to keep that boiling heat from us, what will become of the poor conscience? especially if Satan adds his poisoned fiery darts, poisoning, inflaming the conscience with temptations to despair, Ps. l. 21, as if God had forsaken and were angry; or when God seems angry, then he seems like a consuming fire. Oh, who can abide it, when all these fiery temptations are joined with God's anger! Yet the dearest of God's saints are subject to these inward boiling heats of God's anger. 'My God, my God, why hast thou forsaken me,' said the head of the church himself, Matt. xxvii. 46; and see how Job complains, 'Thou hast set me as a butt to shoot at,' Job xvi. 12. And, in regard of this spiritual desertion, David complains much throughout the Psalms. So this our life is subject to out-

* That is, '*until.*'—Ed.

ward and spiritual annoyances from God, from Satan, and from ourselves and the world ; every way annoyed with scorchings and heat, what need [of] a shadow, a protection, a defence else ? That supposeth this.

If this be so, then consider how fearful the condition of those people is, that are not under the shadow of the Almighty ; who have not God as a fir-tree to shadow and cover them ; that he is not a cloud by day to, and a pillar of fire by night ; that have not him for a hiding-place to spread the wings of his mercy over them. What is the state of such people ? surely howsoever God feed them, and fills their belly with good things in this world for a time ; yet their case will be fearful, when God lets loose conscience, and Satan's fiery darts against them. Judge then hereby what our state is by nature without God. The same sun which cherisheth and comforteth, also tortures and scorcheth us : so God is a sun, a quickening sun to his children, Mal. iv. 2, yea, a vigorous sun, who hath healing under his wings ; but to the wicked he is a scorching and consuming fire, Heb. xii. 29. ' It is a fearful thing to fall into the hands of the living God,' Heb. x. 31, who is so dreadful. He will not be a shadow to the wicked in an excellent manner. He indeed permits them to have many shadows in this world, many sweet comforts, and keeps them also from many dangers ; but they have not that worthy portion which Hannah had from her husband, 1 Sam. i. 5, love at the hour of death. And in time of temptation, when these comforts leave them, what shadow have they then ? none at all, but are as naked men in a storm, subject to the fury of God's eternal wrath. The things which are most comfortable to God's people are most terrible to them, as it is said in one of those plagues poured out upon antichrist (for all the vials there spoken of tend to the punishing of antichrist), there is a vial poured forth upon the sun, Rev. vi. ; which reflecting and lighting upon them, causeth them to blaspheme, they were so scorched with it. The sun, by probable interpreters, is said to be the word of God, which, when it is opened, is sweet and comfortable to God's people, but shining upon men that are naught, especially at the hour of death, in affliction and in distress, it speaks no comfort to them, but causeth them to despair, rage and storm. Nay, profane men, when they are at the best, they rage and storm at the direction of the sun, because it discovers to them that which they would not have known.

Use 1. Now, what use should we make of this ? Will God be a shadow to his people to keep them from all evil, as his promise was to Abraham in the covenant of grace : ' I will be thy buckler,' to keep ill from thee, and ' thy exceeding great reward,' Gen. xv. 1. And in the Psalms, God promiseth to be a sun for good, and a shield to keep off all ill, Ps. lxxxiv. 11. Will God bestow good, and keep off ill from us ? Then labour to come willingly under the shadow of the Almighty, to serve him, and to make God in covenant our God, that he may be a ' shield and a hiding-place ' unto us, and a shadow in all extremities whatsoever. Those that attend upon great persons, they do it upon this hope : Oh, if I belong to such a great person, he will shelter me, that every base person shall not wrong me ; I shall now have some prerogatives. Doth carnal policy teach poor creatures who are subject to abuse it, to get some shelter of great, noble men to be privileged? and shall not spiritual wisdom teach us to get under the great God, under the shadow of his wings ? None can come near to annoy us without his special will and leave, as in the story of Job. The devil durst not annoy him, Job i. 12, nor enter into the swine, Mat. viii 31, much less hurt God's children. Shall we not, therefore, get under the service of our God ? can any man shelter us better ? There is no service to that of a king ; but is there any service to the King of kings, and Lord of lords ? Will he suffer his children to be abused in his own sight, or his followers disgraced ? Surely no. Therefore make this use of it, to get into the service of the great God, which is a rich, secure, and safe service.

Use 2. Again, it yields us an use of resolution, for to obey God, and to go boldly on in a good course. What should we fear, when God is our master ? He will shield us, and keep us safe, and give his angels charge over us, to shew that he hath a care over us. Indeed, he hath many keepers under him, but he is the grand keeper, who sets all a-work. For angels, magistrates, ministers, and our friends keep us ; but God's Spirit within us, and his gracious good providence without us, are our chief keepers. Therefore let all our care be to serve God, and to be in his ways. He will keep us in his ways. What an encouragement is this to be in good courses, where we may look for the shadow of the Almighty God, without tempting of him ! If a man be in an ill way and course, he cannot look that the Almighty should shadow him. His heart will tell him, now God may withdraw his shelter and wing from me ; he may leave me naked to the devil and to the malice of men ; he may strip me of all comfort in my soul and conscience, and give me up to terrors of heart out of his way. If I trust him now, I tempt him, because he will be a defence only in his own ways. Therefore let us labour always to be in those ways, and then God will be as a green fir-tree unto us.

Use 3. And, last of all, let it be an use of comfort unto us, for all the time of our life to come. Whatsoever may come, we yet pass under a buckler. Let a whole shower and shot of arrows* fall upon us, we have a buckler. ' Thou, Lord, art my buckler ; thou, Lord, art my defence, my hiding-place, my castle,' Ps. xviii. 1, 2. We are subject to a world of dangers whilst we live here, but we have God instead of all, to keep off all. He is a buckler, a shield, a shadow, and a hiding-place. Let what ill soever be presented to our thoughts, there is in God some fence against it. For this purpose we have many excellent passages in Ps. xviii., which was made after a great deliverance. ' I love the Lord, my buckler, my shield, my defence,' as if he should say, I have in my lifetime been annoyed with many troubles, but I have found experience of God in all. ' He is my buckler, my shield, my fence,' everything to me. So let us comfort ourselves in this. Let come what will come, all shall come well to God's children. He will keep them, if not outwardly, yet in that they most desire to be kept in. He will preserve their spirits ' from every evil work,' 2 Tim. iv. 18, from doing ill, and from desperate falling from God ; and he will guard them inwardly, ' by the peace of God which passeth understanding,' Philip. iv. 7. It shall guard their hearts ; they shall have inward peace in the midst of all the troubles of this world : a great comfort ! What a rejoicing is it to a poor passenger, when he passeth by the highway side in a hot, burning day, or in a storm, to see a goodly high tree, with spreading boughs, that he may hide and repose himself under it from the storm or heat. This pleaseth him marvellously, as Jonah's gourd did him. Do these outward poor contentments so refresh us in this world ? and shall we not think that God, which provides such poor contentments for this sorry life in this world, will he not provide a shadow in regard of the main dangers ? Surely he will, if we trust him, and shew our trust by casting ourselves upon him in obedience suitable to our calling. Saith the apostle,

* Qu. ' a whole shower of shot and arrows ?'—G.

' I am persuaded that neither things present, nor to come, nor life, nor
death, nor anything, shall be able to separate us from the love of Christ
Jesus our Lord,' Rom. viii. 38, 39. Therefore let us be afraid of nothing
that can befall us. God will be a shield and a buckler, and all in all to
us in a good way. We have abundance of comfort everywhere in Scripture, and want nothing but faith to apply it home in practice. Therefore
we ought to beg of God so to enlarge our faith, that as his promises and
comforts are very large, so may our vessels be to retain all these excellent
comforts and sweet promises.

All other comforts in the world are but like Jonah's gourd; for all other
shadows yield only a shadow for a while, and then the sunshine or east
wind is like a worm to nip them asunder. Never trust, then, or lean to
such shadows as these be, of friends, riches, &c., which are shadows men
ordinarily rely upon. I have such and such a friend, a place, and the like,
my mountain is thus and thus strong. All these are Jonah's gourds.
There is a worm of vanity will be at the root of all, and consume all. All
other shadows are but mere shadows. What is more transient than a
shadow? But God's shadow is like a green fir-tree. It never fails nor
forsakes us, as all other shadows and contentments do whatsoever. But
God saith, ' He will be like a green fir-tree unto thee.' Yet this is not all,
nor enough, for after this he adds,

' From me is thy fruit found.'

God is not only to his children a fir-tree in regard of shadow, that tree
abounding in leaves very thick, whereby we are kept from annoyance of
scorching heats of troubles and terrors of conscience and persecution, &c.
This is not all, but he saith also,

' From me is thy fruit found.'

A fir-tree, though it be for thickness of the leaves a very good shade, yet
it is a barren, fruitless tree; but God is such a tree as hath both shadow
and fruit. In God there is a supply of all wants whatsoever. All the
scattered excellencies of all creatures being united in God, and eminent in
him, it is in him, and in him in a divine, gracious, eminent, and comfortable manner. All the creatures, as they come from God, are his creatures,
neither is there any creature but hath somewhat of God in it. Therefore,
God vouchsafes to take names from the creatures. To be a rock of salvation, he is as a rock to build on; to be a shadowing tree, because he is a
defence from ill; and to be a fruitful tree, because he yields good, and comfort, and grace, as he doth fruit. When we see anything that is useful, we
may say, this we have from God in an eminent manner, this preservation
and comfort. Do I in my passage to heaven find such comfort in the
creature? When I am passing through a wild place, have I such comfort
in the shadow of a tree? or when I am hungry, am I so refreshed by a
fruitful tree? What comfort, then, is there in God, in heaven, in glory,
when there are such comforts in the way of my pilgrimage in this world?
Therefore, God is said here, both to be a fir-tree and a fruitful tree. For
then the passenger travelling through a wild, barren place, thinks himself made
when he can retire from the scorching of the heat, and also therewithal find
fruitfulness. Shade and fruit concurring, he thinks himself marvellously
happy. This is the state of a Christian that hath God for his God, being in
covenant with him. He is not only a strong protection and defence from
all annoyance (as God shadows us, and is a buckler from all evils, both inward and outward, from Satan, and all kind of evils and wrath), but he is
also a fruitful tree too. ' From me is thy fruit found.'

THE THIRTEENTH SERMON.

I am like a green fir-tree ; from me is thy fruit found.—Hos. XIV. 8.

THIS holy prophet, as we heard heretofore, did prophesy more than sixty years among the ten tribes, even until the time immediately preceding their captivity and misery, in like manner as Jeremiah and Ezekiel did to the other Jews. Now, because in the worst times God always had a remnant, and yet hath, therefore it is the prophet's care, in this chapter which we have gone over, to instruct them in divers particulars of reformation, as we have heard at large, ' to return to the Lord,' ' to take words to themselves,' which words, as we have heard, are also taught them, backed with many sweet promises and encouragements in God's answer to their petitions : the last whereof insisted and stood upon was this, that God promiseth to be like a green fir-tree unto Ephraim, who personated all the ten tribes. Ephraim thought before to shadow and fence himself by idols, and league with other idolatrous nations, which were like Jonah's rotten gourd unto them, poor shadows and defences ; but saith God, ' I will be a fir-tree' for shadow to Ephraim, to defend him from all dangers whatsoever ; and then in the next place he adds,

' From me is thy fruit found.'

A fir-tree is a green tree, but it hath no fruit. The excellencies of the creatures are applied to God, but not the defects. Therefore, when comparisons are taken from the creatures and given to God, we must always except the defects, supplying the same by some other clearing comparison. So God is not only a fir-tree for shelter and defence, but he is a fruitful tree. So a fir-tree is not ; and therefore without comparison, God hath more in him than any creature hath. For all that excellency which is in all the creatures is in him, and that in a far more eminent manner ; therefore, he is both a shelter and fruit. If a passenger in distress have not only a fir-tree to shelter him and shadow him, but a fruit-tree also to feed him, he thinks he is made when God thus comforts him. So a Christian, he hath not only shelter from the wrath of God, but he hath also a place of rest and quiet, the mercy of God to keep him, and the word and sacraments to feed him. God is a fruit-tree as well as a fir-tree.

' From me is thy fruit found.'

That is, whatsoever is graciously or comfortably good to us, in us, or issues from us, is all from God. Hence first of all we observe for our instruction,

From a man's self comes nothing that is graciously good.

Whatsoever is savingly good is altogether from God. ' Without me,' saith Christ, ' you can do nothing,' John xv. 5. Saint Paul was wondrous chary * of this point. 1 Cor. xv. 10 he saith ' he laboured more abundantly than they all : yet not I ' (he recalls himself), ' but the grace of God in him that did all ;' and of myself, as of myself, I cannot so much ' as think a good thought.' It is from God that we have means to make us fruitful, and from the gracious working of his Spirit comes it that they are effectual. That we think a good thought, or open our mouths to speak a good word, it is from God's Spirit enabling us thereto. ' Open thou my mouth,' saith the psalmist, ' and my lips shall shew forth thy praise.' We are tongue-

* That is, ' wary ' = circumspect.—G.

tied and our lips sealed unless God open them. We cannot speak one
savoury, seasonable word to further our accompt. We may speak empty
words, but never a word comes from the heart that is gracious and good,
but it must be by the Spirit of God. It is he who works all our works in
us and for us. ' He begins the good work in us, and perfects it to the
day of the Lord,' Isa. xxvi. 12, Phil. i. 6. The truth of this is wondrous
clear.

If this be so, then undoubtedly the differences in the graces of men, it is
from another, merely from God and God's Spirit. There is indeed difference in men, but this is originally fetched from the grace of God's Spirit.
The good use of freedom, that we talk so much of, it is from God, as well
as the endowments of it. We have free will, but the use of it is not in our
power, to use this or that at our pleasure ; for ' it is God which gives the
will and the deed,' Phil. ii. 13, of his good pleasure. Not only the deed,
but the will too ; we should make the will an idol else. For so many wills,
so many idols, if we think one man in himself can difference himself by his
will.

Again, in that God saith, ' From me is thy fruit found,' we may learn
hence,

That fruit that is gracious comes from us and from God too.

It is our fruit and God's, so that there is a subordination of gracious
works under God. The fruit we have is from God, yet it is our fruit too.

Quest. How can this be ?

Sol. Yes, easily. We speak the words, but it is God that opens our lips.
We believe, but it is God that gives us grace to believe. We do the action,
but God gives us grace to do it. God opened the heart of Lydia to believe,
Acts xvi. 14, so that God and we meet together in the same action. We
have parts, understanding, will, affections, bodies and souls. Therefore
the actions are said to be ours, because God works in us as understanding
creatures ; but God sets the wheel a-going, so that the actions are originally
his, and ours subordinately under him, ' From me is thy fruit found.'

If so be that God and man join in one action (' From me is thy fruit
found ;' as though he should say, Whatsoever thou hast or sayest that is
good, it is from me ; here we see how, and why good works cannot merit,
though they come from God, as all goodness doth), yet in regard they come
from us too, we add some tainture thereunto from our corrupt nature.
What God and Christ himself doth, is absolute and perfect, as justification ;
but what fruit he works in us, there is somewhat of the old Adam in us,
which taints the beauty of the work. It is God's fruit, coming from him,
and yet our fruit also, coming from us ; which being so much tainted
should humble us, in that we add nothing to the truth of God's work in us,
but abasement and defilement by our corruptions. ' From me (saith God) is
thy fruit found,' so much as is supernaturally good ; but because our
nature is not altered on the sudden, but still tastes of the ' old leaven,'
1 Cor. v. 7, therefore there can be no meriting of salvation by any works we
do, because they are not perfectly good.

Use 1. The clearing of these points, in our judgment, *they serve to work
in us a deep humiliation*, seeing that we have nothing in ourselves but stains
and defilements, all that is good in us coming from God, ' From me is thy
fruit found.' What is from ourselves then, if all good in us comes from
God ? We are a barren and a cursed soil, nothing that is good can come
from us. Even as the earth was cursed after Adam's fall, and brought forth
nothing but briers and thorns, so our soul naturally is a cursed soil in

itself, and brings forth nothing but weeds and thorns. Our hearts are like the barren wilderness, full of evil, noisome lusts and affections. Therefore this serves to abase us, that we be not lifted up with any good in us ; for as that is altogether from God's Spirit, so likewise we of ourselves add nothing to it, but somewhat which may diminish the value thereof.

Use 2. Here, again, for matter of judgment, *you have a difference between the state of nature and the state of grace,* I mean of innocent nature, for in Adam we had a standing in ourselves, being trusted with our own good ; but now under the second covenant, under the second Adam, Christ Jesus, we have many graces to fit us for heaven, and many good works we do, but all the fruit we have and yield is from God. So that now this is a grand difference. Adam, as it were, had the keeping of his own happiness locked up in himself ; but we have our happiness, graces, and whatsoever is good for us, shut up in Christ as the spring and fountain, which is the reason of the perpetual stability and permanent condition of God's children, once his and ever his. And put the case, we want this or that help, yet this pre-judiceth not the perpetuity of the condition of God's children, because those graces which come immediately from God's Spirit, may be conveyed some-times without means, as well as with them. Therefore, whatsoever decay is in the branches that are grafted into this noble Vine, Christ Jesus, in whom we bear all the fruit we bear, yet notwithstanding there is life ever-lasting for us in the root, which is by little and little distilled into us. The leaves may fall, outward things may decay, but there is life alway in the root of a Christian, because he is in Christ, and hath his fruit from him ; he cannot want fruit, no more than Christ can want influence and vigour, John xv. 5. Which shews us the excellent state of a Christian under the new covenant of grace, that now we fetch all out of ourselves, and it is happy for us that we do so. For without Christ we can do nothing. As without the soul the body can do nothing, so without the Spirit of Christ we can do nothing ; from him is all. This is the reason why we must not trust to any grace in ourselves, that comes from us, because grace comes from God in Christ. Trust God, the spring whence it comes, whose the fruit is : God the Father in Christ, from whom all fulness comes, and is derived unto us, or else we make but an idol of grace, if we trust too much to grace. Look to the spring whence all comes to us. ' From me is thy fruit found.'

Quest. Again, for further instruction, What is the reason that some have more grace than others, and more comfort, some having grace and comfort in one degree, and some in another ?

Sol. Hence it is : ' From me is thy fruit found.' It comes from the freedom of God in Christ, who according to his good pleasure gives the will and the deed, whence we have grace sometimes in the vigour, sometimes in a weaker and lesser degree, the fault being in ourselves too. Yet, notwithstanding, there is a liberty in the Spirit of Christ, to give a more or less measure of grace, to shew that our good we do springs not from ourselves. Which also is the reason of the difference betwixt Christians, because God will shew that he is the disposer and the dispenser of his own graces and com-forts. And that is the reason also why we must perform this duty of wait-ing upon God in the use of means, though we find no sense of grace and comfort from him for the present, ' From him our fruit is found.' Wait his leisure. He suspends grace and comfort until a fit time, in regard of the degree ; but yet there is alway some grace left, though he suspends the increase thereof until a fit time, because he would have us know that it is of his giving. Christians who are acquainted herewith, they will not tie God to their time, but humbly go on in the use of means, who though they find not their spirits and their comforts enlarged so as at other times, nor so great, nor as other folks are ; yet can say, Lord, thou givest the will and the deed according to thy good pleasure, all comes from thee; therefore I will use the means and depend upon thee because I have all from thee freely. God gives a spirit of prayer, and then the thing we pray for, all is from him, ' From me is thy fruit found.' Do we find the ordinances fruitful, the preaching of the word to open our understandidgs, to kindle our affections, to enlighten our judgments ? It is the Spirit of God that joins with the means, that are dead of themselves, to make them fruitful. What are the ordinances without God, but empty conduit-pipes of them-selves ? Therefore, ' From me is thy fruit found.'

Use 3. This should teach and direct us also *in all things to look up to God in all use of means.* Lord, I may read, hear, and use helps and means long enough, to little or no purpose, unless thou give a blessing. Paul may plant and Apollos may water, but if thou give not fruit from heaven, all is to no purpose, 1 Cor. iii. 6. We forget this, and therefore prosper accordingly. We think we can work fruit out of the means, by our own wit. Oh ! it is not so ! Whatsoever is comfortable or gracious in the use of means, it is merely God's blessing. And therefore seeing all our fruit whatsoever, that is good, comes from God, let us stir us up to practise the spiritual worship of God, to adore God, to beg of his fulness in Christ Jesus, and likewise to resign ourselves in all conditions unto him. Lord, I put myself upon thee ; all my fruit is from thee ; thou canst sanc-tify any condition unto me. This adoration and resignation are parts of the spiritual worship of God. And likewise the service of the Lord in fear and reverence, that inward service of the Spirit ; all depends upon this, that all our fruit is from God. Therefore I must serve him, and serve him as he must be served, in spirit and truth, John iv. 24. What makes a man reverence another ? I depend upon him ; without him I sink. Will this make a man serve man ? And will it not make us serve God, and serve him with fear ? What breeds an awful fear ? This, that if he withdraw his influence, I fall into sin, despair, and discomfort. So that the ground of all fear of God, and service springing from this fear, it is from hence, that from him all my fruit, all my grace and comfort, is found; therefore I must have grace to serve him, as a God in fear. For if the soul be not possessed and seasoned with this heavenly doctrine, that all comes from him, then surely where is God's service ? What becomes of it ? . Where is that adoration and magnifying of God in our hearts ? Where's that putting off ourselves upon him in all conditions ?

Use 4. Again, this enforceth another part of God's spiritual and heavenly worship, *cleaving to God in our affections*, especially these two, in our faith and love ; that as all comes from and by Jesus Christ, so thereby we may draw from him the fruit of grace and comfort. So that this spiritual cleav-ing and uniting of our souls to Christ, it comes from this, that I have all from him, therefore I must cleave to him ; seeing whatsoever is spiritual, holy, and comfortable I must have from him. Therefore if we would wor-ship God in spirit and truth, as we should do, and set him up in his due place in the soul, let us labour to have our judgments sanctified in this, that all comes from God. If we were surely grounded in the goodness, mercy, and riches of God's grace, and knew that all our fruit comes and is from him, this would make us to conclude that therefore it is reason that we should worship him and depend upon him strictly. As the prophet speaks of idols, that they can neither do us good nor harm, Jer. x. 5, enforcing that they should not fear them, so we may say of all other things distinct from God, they can neither do good nor harm, except God enable them. Will you be slaves to men? They cannot do good nor harm, but as God uses them, whose creatures they are. Therefore the worship of God is also founded hence, that God does all good or harm. If men do it they do it from him, he gives them leave; as it is said of Shimei, God bid him rail on David, 2 Sam. xvi. 10. If they do us good, they are his conduits, whereby he deriveth good to us; therefore all is from him. We see then how all the true and hearty worship of God comes from this, 'From me is thy fruit found.'

Use 5. This should make us likewise, as to worship God in spirit and in truth, so *to be resolute in good causes*, whatsoever come of it. Look for a ground, and then be resolute; because all comes from God, who will stand by us in his own cause and quarrel.

But if I forsake this and that support, I shall lay open myself to injuries and wrongs.

Mark what the Spirit of God saith, 'Ye that love the Lord, hate that which is evil,' Ps. xcvii. 10. But if I hate that which is evil, idols, &c., as Ephraim here doth, I shall be despised and trampled upon. No! saith he, 'God preserves the souls of his; he will be a shield and a buckler; a sun and a shield; and no good thing shall be wanting to them that lead a godly life,' Ps. lxxxiv. 11. God will be a sun for all good, and a shield to keep off all ill; therefore let us be resolute in good causes. Whence comes all shifting, halting, imperfect walking, and inconstances in the ways of God, but from this, that men know not where to have men? They are not grounded on this, that whatsoever is fruitful and good comes from God, who will give whatsoever is fruitful and good in depending upon him. This made the three children in Daniel courageous. They knew they should have fruit from God; that is, grace, comfort, and peace, the best fruit of all. And therefore 'know, O king, that we will not worship thine idol, nor fall down before it,' Dan. iii. 18. So holy Esther, being well grounded, could say, 'If I perish, I perish,' Esth. iv. 16. I know the cause is good; and if all help in the creature be removed and taken away, yet I shall have fruit in God.

Let us therefore carry this about us, as a principle of holy life, to know that our good is hid up in God, and not in the creature; so that if all help were taken away, yet we have it immediately, purer and better in the fountain. What if there were not a creature in the world to help me? What if all were against me? Yet God may make all their powers and endeavours fruitful. There is such fruit from God, that he can make the worst things which befalleth us fruitful when he pleaseth. There is a blessing in curses and crosses, a good fruit in them! Who can do him harm that God turneth the bitterest things he suffers to his good? Let none be daunted in a good cause, but go on resolutely, seeing God hath all in himself. Was not Moses forty days without any earthly comfort on the mount? Exod. xxxiv. 28. And Christ also without natural sustentation so long? Mat. iv. 2. Did not God give light without a sun in the first creation? We are tied to means, but he is not. We think if such friends and helps be taken away, that then all is gone; but what were they? Were not they means which God used at his good pleasure, and cannot he give comfort without them? Yes, certainly! The greatest comfort and grace is oft-

times given immediately from God, when he salutes the soul by his own
Spirit, as he did Paul and Silas in the dungeon; who, in the midst of discomfort, had their spirits enlarged to sing hymns at midnight, Acts xvi. 25,
God reserving that comfort for that time.   Therefore seeing all comfort is
from God, and he is not tied to this or that means, nay, can bless all contrary means, is not this a ground of resolution?

Use 6. Therefore now make a use of comfort of it, seeing all fruit is from
God, who is in covenant with his children in Jesus Christ, and who will
improve all his attributes for their good, his wisdom, goodness, power, and
mercy.   Let them therefore *take comfort to themselves, that howsoever the
world may take their friends from them, riches, liberty, and what you will,
can they take God and fruit from them?*   No! 'From me is thy fruit
found.'   If they could take away the Spirit of God, grace, and comfort
from us, it were something; but can they do that?   No!   The worst they
can do is to send us to heaven, to the fountain of all grace and comfort;
so that in this world they cannot cast us into any condition wherein we
cannot have communion with God, in whom all the scattered excellencies
of the creature are gathered together, meeting as it were in a centre.   It is
he that comforts us in our friends, that shews bowels to us in our mothers,
wisdom and care towards us in our parents.   The bowels of a mother, the
care of a friend, the strength of wise assistance, hath he not all in himself,
if all be taken away?   He hath all.   Therefore let Christians comfort themselves, that they can never be in a condition wherein fruit shall be taken
from them.   The poor worldling labours all his life for fruit, riches, and
friends; and when he dies, then his fruit faileth him and falls, his leaf
withereth.   What becometh of his fruit then?   He laboured for that
which yields him nothing but vexation and death.   But a Christian doth
otherwise; he labours for grace and comfort to keep his communion and
peace with God; and when all is taken away, either by the injury and
wrongs of men, or by the extremity of the times, or as all will, in the hour
of death, his fruit is most after, in death, and after death, more than can
be by our narrow hearts conceived in the excellency thereof.   Oh! the
excellent estate of a Christian!   Imagine such a one to have a tree that
grows in heaven, and sends forth fruit and branches to him in whatsoever
state he is in.   And so indeed God reacheth fruit from heaven to the soul,
being in prison and misery.   He reacheth from thence the fruit of grace,
of spiritual strength and comfort: a blessed estate!   Therefore let Christians comfort themselves in their condition, 'that all their fruit is from
him;' and that God especially will then shew himself abundant when they
stand most in need of him.   Other trees bear no fruit in winter and in
storms, but God giveth fruit most in the worst times.   He is a God that
comforteth the abject.   As it is 2 Cor. vii. 6; and here is said, that 'in
him the fatherless findeth mercy.'   We have most fruit from him in the
worst times.   Then especially he delighteth to shew himself a God, when
no comfort can be had from the creature.

Therefore do not despair, but lay up this against evil times; never fear
for the time to come.   Let the mountains be cast into the midst of the
sea, and let the earth and all rage, as the psalmist says, and let things run
upon a head; come what can come, God is where he was, and God's children
are where they were, in regard of the main comfort, Ps. xlvi. 2.   They
cannot be in such a condition, as that they can be deprived of their God,
and of his assistance: 'From me is thy fruit found.'   Therefore care not
for any condition that thou art in, this or that, thou shalt have that condi-

tion which shall be comfortable to thee, though many like beasts go on, and look for no fruit from God.

Use 7. And let this also be an encouragement, *to walk with God sincerely and uprightly in all times*, not fearing any creature, or danger from the creature, because our fruit is from God. What if we lose this or that? We know what was said to Amaziah by the prophet. But what shall become of the hundred talents? saith he. God is able to give thee much more, 2 Chron. xxv. 9. So in the loss of friends, having this and that took* from us, let us comfort ourselves. Aye, but God is not taken from us. He who derives † comfort by this or that friend, can supply it better by his own Spirit. And whatsoever we part with in a good cause, let us remember what Christ saith. ' He that parts with father or mother, with house or land for my sake, shall have a hundredfold in this world, and afterwards life everlasting, Mat. xix. 29. He shall have all made up in grace, which is a hundred times better than anything that is here. He shall have contentment, which is better than the things themselves. Sometimes he shall, missing one worldly comfort, have more friends stirred up; but howsoever, in want of one, he shall be supplied in another comfort that he never dreamt of in this world. So that God is abundant to them that stick close to him in sincerity; he shall find him abundant in the things of this life, in one comfort or other.

Therefore, by these mercies of God here mentioned, let us be entreated to be in love with the condition of a Christian life, and say, as Ephraim here, ' What have I any more to do with my former corrupt courses, or idols ?' Give a peremptory answer to all sinful courses and suggestions, either from others or from our own corrupt nature. ' What have I any more to do with you ?' No; God shall be my God : for if I can resign myself wholly to God, and renounce the creature and all things else, God will be as a ' green fir-tree,' and hear me. I shall lose nothing by it. Be then in love with a Christian course; for it is the sweetest and the safest course, and never wants comforts from heaven : and it is the most honourable course that can be, for it will hold our communion and peace with the great God of heaven and earth; for though we break with others, we shall be sure of him. In which case take heed of that base suggestion which the devil himself was ashamed to own, ' that we serve God for nought,' Job i. 9. What! shall we renounce idolatry and wicked courses, and think that God will not have fruit for us? Shall I think, if I leave my sinful gain, that I or my posterity shall beg or starve for it? Do we serve a God that hath no fruit, that is a dead tree, or a barren wilderness? No; we serve a God that had all in himself before he made the world, and hath all the excellency in himself contained in the creatures. It is not in vain to serve him. ' Doth Job serve God for nothing ?' said the devil. Therefore it is a suggestion worse than Satanical, to think we serve God for nothing, or to think, like those hypocrites mentioned by the prophet, that God regards not our fasting or our devotion, Isa. lviii. 3. No; we shall not lose a good word for God. Not a tear, but he hath a bottle for it, Ps. lvi. 8 ; not a sigh, or a groan, or a farthing, not a minute's time well spent shall be lost. He will pay us for every ill word we endure for his sake, for every disgrace, loss, or cross. Do we serve that God there is no fruit in? 'From me is thy fruit found.'

Whatsoever our condition be in the world, let us comfort ourselves with these things, and think that it is not in vain to serve the Lord; for we cannot serve a richer, nor a more kind master and Lord. First of all, he gives us opportunity and means whereby fruit may be wrought in us, and then he works the fruit of grace and comfort in us, and afterwards rewards and crowns his own fruit. But we add imperfections and inventions of our own, and so mar or stain all. But we deal with a gracious God in covenant, who pities us as a father doth his children, accepts and rewards what is his, and pardons what is our own. Therefore let thus much be effectual for the guiding of our lives, and comforting of us in a good course. If we take ill courses, we must look for no fruit from God, but fruits of his displeasure ; if we eat of the forbidden tree, we shall eat and reap ' the fruits of our own ways,' bitter fruits. For in this case, Jesus Christ, who is a sweet Saviour, will be a judge to us ; and he who is ' the Lamb of God,' will be angry, so as we shall reap the fruit of his indignation. In the Revelation, divers are brought in desiring ' the hills and mountains to fall upon them, to cover them from the presence of the Lamb,' Rev. vi. 16. Let us not, therefore, turn a sweet Saviour to a rigorous Judge, by adventuring upon courses wherein we cannot look for fruit ; but let us commend ' our souls in well-doing unto him, as unto a faithful Creator and Redeemer,' 1 Pet. iv. 19. And as it is, ' Let us acknowledge him in all our ways,' Prov. iii. 6 ; for it is good to acknowledge and look to him, that is, look to him for strength, quickening, success, grace, and light to direct us : acknowledge him in all our ways, and treasure up this comfort, that ' all fruit is found from God.' If we take good courses, we shall ever be fruitful, and have fruit from him, ' out of his fulness ; for, saith he, ' From me is thy fruit found.'

THE FOURTEENTH SERMON.

Who is wise, and he shall understand these things? prudent, and he shall know them? for the ways of the Lord are equal, the just shall walk in them: but the transgressors shall fall therein.—HOS. XIV. 9.

THESE words seal up the whole prophecy ; for the prophet, immediately before prophesying of the captivity, discovers to them at length their sins, as we heard, their idolatry, adding new idols to their former idols, Baal to the calves. The princes removed the bounds, old orders and laws ; the prophets they were fools, and did not see the judgments of God hanging over their heads ; and none of them all could see their ' grey hairs,' Hosea vii. 9, that is, the signs of their own ruin. After which, out of a Christian love, care, and conscience of his duty, by direction of the Spirit of God, he prescribes an excellent way how they should carry themselves, by returning to the Lord. ' Take words unto yourselves,' renounce all false confidence in Asshur, and all domestic helps at home, horses and the like, and fly to God as your best sanctuary. Then he shews what God will do to them, answer all the desires he had put into their hearts. ' I will heal their backslidings, and love them freely,' &c.

Now, because these were great matters of great consequence, to make them either happy in the observing them, or miserable in neglecting them, you see how he shuts up all in a most weighty close. ' Who is wise, and he shall understand these things ? prudent, and he shall know them ? for the ways of the Lord are equal,' &c.

Wherein the scope of the prophet is to stir up a holy regard of what hath been spoken. He would not have all lost for want of attention or application ; and therefore he here stirs them up to a holy use of all, which stirring up is excellently and figuratively clothed with an *epiphonemy*, or acclamation, ' Who is wise, and he shall understand these things ?' &c. He doth not say, Let men understand these things, but ' Who is wise, and who is prudent ?' let them consider of these things ; and then the exhortation is backed with many reasons.

1. *It is wisdom and prudence* to regard these things I have spoken. ' Who is *wise?* and who is *prudent?*'

2. And then again, *they are the ways of God* that are spoken of, and they are straight and equal in themselves. ' For the *ways*,' &c.

3. And they lead *to happiness directly, without winding and turning.* A man is sure to attain his journey's end in them ; and if they will take example of those who only are exemplary to them, he tells them, ' the just shall walk in them.' They shall not walk alone ; they shall have the company of ' a cloud of witnesses,' who prosper and walk on cheerfully in this way, and attain happiness in the end.

4. Then the last argument is taken from the *contrary end of all them who cavil and snarl at God's ways and truth,* that think themselves witty to pick quarrels with somewhat in God's book, as it is a common fashion now-a-days to have a divinity of men's own. ' Transgressors,' such as are opposite to God's ways, ' they shall fall in these ways ;' that is, they take offence at these ways, and so fall into sin, and by falling into sin, fall into misery, till at last they fall into hell, which is the end of all quarrellers with divine truths. They fall and dash themselves upon them, and so eternally perish.

Now, these are strong and forcible reasons to enforce care and attention of what hath been spoken. It is ' wisdom and prudence ;'. and ' the ways of the Lord' here ' are straight,' and then ' all godly people walk in them,' ' and those that stumble at them are sure to perish,' and do perish in them ; not that they are a cause of their perishing, but by reason of the malice of men, finding fault and picking quarrels with them, they fall first into sin, and then into misery. Thus we have the scope of the words.

' Who is wise, and he shall understand these things.'

First of all, we must know that the prophet here in this figurative speech makes a kind of exclamation, ' Who is wise !' He doth, as it were, secretly mourn at the apostasy and fewness of those that be truly wise ; as if he had said, I have given you many directions, and shewed you what sins lead to destruction ; I have shewed what course ye are to take, and the bounty of God to those that return ; but ' who is wise and prudent to regard these things ?'

In the words, therefore, in regard of the speaker, the prophet, we may observe this ere we come particularly to them, *the character of a holy, mer-ciful, gracious, and wise man ;* that when he hath spoken things to excellent purpose, he would not have those things lost, but out of mercy and compassion, mingled with a great deal of heavenly wisdom, would have the best fruit of all he hath spoken. Which was the custom of the men of God in the Scriptures, the Spirit of God leading them to strike the nail home ; when they taught truths, to lay the word close upon the conscience, as much as they could. What is the whole book of Deuteronomy, as the word signifieth,* but a repeating of the former laws ? Moses thought all to

* Deuteronomy, *i.e.*, Δευτερονόμιον = the Law again or repeated.—G.

no purpose, unless he repeated laws, and fastened them upon the soul. So our Saviour Christ still when he had spoken excellent things, saith, ' Let him that hath ears to hear, hear,' Mat. xi. 15. So saith Jeremiah, ' Who is wise to consider these things ?' Jer. ix. 12 ; and the conclusion of that excellent psalm is just thus, ' Who is wise to consider these things ?' Ps. cvii. 43. And saith Moses, ' O that they were wise, that they would think of these things,' &c., Deut. xxxii. 29. So everywhere in Scripture you have such fastening of things, where truths have been spoken, in application of them ; which doth justify the course of God's messengers in bringing the word home unto men's consciences, because that which is spoken loosely in general, no man applieth in particular to himself. We who are messengers of God must therefore bring things home to the conscience. ' Who is wise, and he shall understand these things,' &c.

But that which more nearly concerneth us is, whereas first of all he propounds this exhortation, to regard these things under this holy acclamation, ' Who is wise, and who is prudent ?' we see, first of all,

Obs. That there are but few who are truly wise and prudent.

Few that enter the right way ; for our Saviour sheweth that ' narrow is this way, and few there be that find it,' Mat. vii. 14. The point needs not much proof, it is so plain and well known ; wherefore it is now touched only, making way to other things. The reason hereof is clear.

Reason. Most men, we see, live by sense, will, and passion, and not by faith, whereby they enthral the wisdom they have, and make it prisoner to sinful passions and affections, rejecting thoughts of their own future happiness ; and though it behove them in this world to be broken of their will, yet they will have it here, though they perish and be damned for it hereafter. This is the state of the unbroken heart of man, till he have grace in him. Yea, it is the state of all men, especially those that are puffed up, either by their own place, humour, or the flattery of others. They will have their will. *Mens mihi pro regno,* as one said. Now, this being the proud, poisonful nature of man, we must not think it a strange thing that there are so few wise and prudent ; for a man cannot be wise and passionate ; for his passion transforms him to be a beast, a devil. Now, because most men live by sense and by humour, which is a life they are nuzzled * in (especially those that are subject to flatterers), therefore few come to be truly wise and prudent, to have so much steadiness and sobriety of spirit as to deliberate what is to be done. They will not in cold blood give leisure to their humours (but feed them), to consider what is best. This being the humour of the world, no wonder that there be so few prudent and wise.

Use 1. Since things are thus, learn this of it. If there be so few prudent and wise, as the prophets complain in all times, ' To whom is the arm of the Lord revealed ? and who hath believed our report ?' &c., Isa. liii. 1, then *take heed of living by example,* that we be not led away with the sway and error of the times ; for seeing there are few ' wise and prudent,' it is better and safer to follow one man reformed by judgment than a thousand others. One man is worth a thousand, who is led with judgment and by the Spirit of God.

Use 2. And likewise *take no scandal† if you see men run upon heaps in the broad and worst way,* for that men have always done. It is the complaint of all the prophets in all times, calling the better sort few. ' As the grapes after the vintage, like a few scattered ears of corn after harvest,' Isa. xvii.

* That is, ' nursed.'—G.   † That is, ' let it not be a stumbling-block.'—G.

5, 6. ' One of a city, and two of a tribe, a few of all,' Jer. iii. 14. Therefore now let us seal this truth with this exhortation.

Use 3. That we labour *to be of that few that are truly wise and prudent.* Examine, are we of those few or not, and what have we in us that may secure us to be of this small number ? for if we be not, we shall never be saved. For Christ's flock ' is a little flock,' Luke xii. 32 ; and few there be that shall enter in at that strait gate. What hast thou, then, which may discover unto thine own soul that thou art of that number, and not of the common multitude that shall be damned ? It is a thing worth the inquiring of our souls. What have we in us that may characterise us to be God's true servants, Christ's true children, and members of the church ? and never rest in a common persuasion of common grace, which castaways may have as well as we. We must strive for some distinct grace, that reprobates cannot attain unto.

' Who is wise, and he shall understand these things ? prudent,' &c.

But to come more particularly to the words, ' Who is wise, and he shall understand these things ? ' The holy man of God here in his exhortation, naming wisdom, singling out ' wise and prudent ' men, ' Who is wise, and who is prudent ?' he toucheth men upon the quick, right vein ; for who is there that would not be thought wise and prudent ? A corrupt man naturally rather desires to be thought sinful than weak; judge him as you will, so you judge him not to be an unwise, an unprudent man. A proud man, till he be subdued and humbled, had rather be thought dishonest than simple, because if he be dishonest, he thinks it is out of choice; but to be simple, this argueth imperfection, and not freedom and bravery of spirit. Therefore, it being the natural desire and instinct of all men to be thought wise and to be so, he endeavours to work upon that affection in them, ' Who is wise ? ' &c. Well, saith he, I know you all desire to be thought ' wise and prudent men.' Would you make it good that you are so indeed ? Believe my sayings ! This is the way ; whosoever is wise, let him understand these things ; and he that is prudent let him hearken to these things that I have spoken.

Man at first, when he had communion with wisdom itself, was a wise creature till he hearkened to Satan, and so lost all, ' becoming as the beasts which perish,' Ps. xlix. 12. Yet in that glorious building, since the corruption of nature, this amongst that rubbish is reserved, that above all things there is a desire to be happy and wise, which two desires are naturally the leading desires in men, to desire to do well, and to be wise. Therefore, the prophet here, upon that which is left in man's nature, takes advantage to build true wisdom and knowledge indeed.

To come, then, in brief, to shew what this wisdom and prudence is ; for there is some distinction between wisdom and prudence. *Wisdom* is a heavenly light set up in the soul by the Spirit of God, whereby it discerneth the general truths concerning God, ourselves, the state of the church, the privileges of Christianity, and such like. In sum, it is a right, divine apprehension of spiritual truths.

And *prudence:* this is a kind of sharpness of spirit, whereby the Spirit of God directs the soul, knowing the right general principles, to particular cases. Prudence is an application of the general knowledge of general things to particulars, and is an ordering of the life in particular exigencies and cases in a right order, according to the direction of the Spirit, as we have it, Prov. viii. 12, ' I wisdom dwell with prudence.' Divine wisdom, wheresoever it is, dwells with prudence ; that is, where God doth enlighten the understanding to conceive aright of the mysteries of salvation, there it dwells with prudence; that is, it directs the soul to an orderly carriage of life towards God and man, and in regard of itself, every way as it should do, in all estates, times, and conditions. That is meant here by prudence, a particular gift whereby a man is fit to consult and deliberate of things in particular to be done, in particular cases of conscience, and the like. Now, wisdom and prudence, they are both together in God's people, howsoever perhaps one is more excellent than another. Some are wiser, who have a deeper search of truths in general; and some are more prudent in their ways, that are weaker Christians for the main general truths. Yet there is not a good Christian but he hath so much prudence as will bring him to heaven. But God giveth extraordinary wisdom to some, because they are leaders of others. Yet though in God's dispensation there be a difference, yet in every Christian they are joined together. There is no Christian but he is wise for himself, which is prudence. This is, as it were, the salt which seasoneth all other graces and knowledge whatsoever; for what is knowledge without discretion but a foolish humour? what is patience but blockishness if a man do not discern how, why, and upon what ground to be patient? what is religiousness without this but superstition? and what is zeal but an indiscreet heat, if it be not seasoned with this prudence? yea, and what is constancy itself but an indiscreet rigour and stiffness without wit? So that it is the seasoning of all other graces whatsoever, that which puts bounds and measure unto all. Therefore, he joins it with wisdom, ' Who is wise? and who is prudent?' Good, as we say, consists of a whole, entire cause, unto which must be occurrence* of all circumstances together. One defect may make it to be sinful. So this is prudence, to observe a due order, clothed with circumstances of the manner and season of every good action and duty. Therefore, he joins here prudence, ' Who is wise, and he shall understand these things? prudent, and he shall know them?'

Now, these be the two graces that lead and guide a man's life. There must be first a general understanding and light of the soul, and then there must be a particular light to apply this general to particulars. Prudence is, as it were, the steward of the soul, which dispenseth the light thereof, according to particular occasions.

Now, for wisdom and prudence, we will not insist long on them, only we will draw towards a right discerning of them, squared and proportioned to our understandings by resemblances of other things. For a man may know what they are in divine things by some proportion to human things, what they are there as to give a little light to it.

1. He is a wise, prudent man in the world that will be sure to make *the greatest his friend*. So God, being the greatest of all and most able to do us good, he is a wise and prudent man that makes him his friend, and cares not who he break with, so he break not with God.

2. And we account him also a wise and prudent man in the world, that, like the wise steward in the gospel, *provides for the worst times*. What course did he take for himself herein? He provides for, as he foresees, danger, Mat. xvi. 3. So spiritual wisdom and prudence will direct a man what is best for his latter end, his eternal rest and happiness in another world. Heavenly wisdom prefixeth to† a man a full view of his latter end, and that which followeth thereupon in another world, and so makes him provide beforehand and direct all things to that end. A wise man will not have things to seek when he comes to make use of them, like the foolish virgins, who had their oil to seek when they should have had it ready,

---

* That is, 'concurrence.'—G.　　　　　† That is, 'sets before.'—ED.

Mat. xxv. 8.   He is truly spiritually wise towards his latter end, that, as he knows there is a state to come, so is truly prudent to have all things ready against that time, that, considering the uncertainty of this life, he may not be surprised unawares, like those glorious* virgins who had a lamp without oil.

3.   And amongst men he is also counted a wise and prudent man *that makes a right choice;* for this is wisdom when a man discerneth a difference, and answerably makes his choice.   *Simile mater erroris,* saith one, Likeness is the mother of error (*y*).   There is a likeness between good and bad in the world, and between truth and error.   Now, he is a wise man who is not catched with these resemblances, but discerneth a difference between temporal and eternal things, shadows and substances, realities and appearances of things, and suitably chooseth eternals before temporals, the favour of God before the favour of men, and, in a word, those things which concern everlasting happiness before those that are perishing.   Wisdom is seen in choice.   By these few instances named, we may see what heavenly wisdom and prudence is, by proportion of wisdom and prudence in earthly things.   Now, considering that there is a better state in another world than in this, he must needs be a wise man that orders things so as that he may not lose eternity.   Most men in the world are penny-wise and pound-foolish, as we say, wise to a particular end, to get particular favours and riches, so to satisfy their intentions ; but for the main, which is wisdom indeed, to look to their last estate and happiness, and to fit their actions and courses that way, how few are wise to purpose !   How few provide for eternity ! Therefore, no marvel the prophet saith, ' Who is wise ? and who is prudent ?' because men live by sense, and not by faith.

' Who is wise, and he shall understand these things ? prudent, and he shall know them ?'

Obs.   Now, the next thing to be observed hence is this, *that the wise and prudent only know these things.*   There must be wisdom and prudence before we can know divine truths, and make use of them.

Obs.   And then observe further, *that true wisdom and prudence carries men to God's word.*   ' Who is wise to understand these things ?'   By divine truth we grow wise and prudent, the Spirit joining with the same, and then we come to make a right use of them.   There must be first a spiritual wisdom and prudence, enlightened by the Spirit, ere we can make use of the word aright, to taste and relish it.   Because, though the word be light, yet light alone is not sufficient to cause sight, but there must concur unto the outward light an inward sight.   Grace must illuminate the understanding, and put a heavenly light into the soul.   As by the light within meeting with the light without, the eye being the instrument of sight, applying itself to the thing, thence comes sight.   So there be divine truths out of us, wherewith, when the Holy Ghost puts an inward light into the soul, sanctified wisdom and prudence, then the inward light meeting with the light without, we see and apprehend.   The Spirit, therefore, must join to work wisdom and prudence.   Naturally we are all dead, and have lost our spiritual senses.   Therefore the Spirit of God must work in us spiritual senses, sight, and taste, that we may see, discern, and relish heavenly things, which, ere we can do, there must be an harmony betwixt the soul and the things ; that is, the soul must be made spiritual, answerable to the heavenly things pitched upon, or else, if the soul be not set in a suitable frame, it can never make a right use of them.

* That is, ' over-confident.'—ED.

Now, when the understanding of a man is made wise by the Spirit of God, it will relish wisdom and prudence. For the Spirit of God, together with the Scripture, takes the scales off the eyes of the soul, subdues rebellious passions in the affections, especially that rebellion of the will, putting a new relish in all, so as they come to love, affect,* and joy in heavenly things. Now, when these scales of spiritual blindness are fallen off the eyes of the soul, and when rebellion is removed from the will and affections, then it is fit to join and approve of heavenly things, else there is a contrariety and antipathy betwixt the soul and these things. As the body, when the tongue is affected with some aguish humour, cannot relish things, though they be never so good, but affecteth and relisheth all things suiting that distemper ; so it is with the soul. When it is not enlightened it judgeth all things carnally, there being an antipathy between the soul and divine truths brought home unto it. Perhaps a soul not enlightened or sanctified will apprehend the generalities of truth very well, but when they are pressed home to practice, then, unless the soul be changed, it will rise up and swell against divine truths, and reject the practice of them. Without subduing grace, to alter and change the soul, the affections thereof are like the March suns,'which stir up a great many humours, but not spending them, they breed aguish humours and distempers. So the light of the word in a carnal heart, it meets with the humours of the soul, and stirs them ; but if there be not grace in the soul to subdue these affections, it stirs them up to be the more malicious, especially if they be pressed to particular duties in leaving of sinful courses. So that the Spirit of God must alter the understanding, and subdue the will and affections, ere there can be a conceiving of divine truths savingly. Therefore, before these acts, he joins these graces. ' Who is wise ? and who is prudent ?' &c.

Use. The use hereof is thus much : Not to come to the divine truth of God with human affections and spirits, but to lift up our hearts to God. Why, Lord, as things themselves are spiritual, so make me spiritual, that there may be a harmony between my soul and the things ; that as there is a sweet relish in divine truths, so there may be a sweet taste in me, to answer that relish which is in divine truths ; that the wisdom of thy word and my wisdom may be one ! Then a man is wise. There is not the commonest truth, or practical point in divinity, but it is a mystery, and must be divinely understood, and must have prudence to go about it as we should do. Repentance and the knowledge of sin, it is a mystery till a man be sanctified in his understanding. He can never know what spiritual misery is till the inward man be enlightened and sanctified, to know what a contrariety there is between sin and the Spirit of God. As no man can know thoroughly what sickness is but he that hath been sick ; for the physician doth not know sickness so well as the patient who feels it ; so it is with a holy man, sanctified with the Holy Ghost. Tell him of sin, he feels it, and the noisomeness of it, the opposition of it to his comfort and communion with God. Only the spiritual enlightened man can tell what repentance, sin, sorrow for sin, and the spiritual health of the soul is. Therefore it is said here, ' Who is wise ? and who is prudent? and he shall understand these things.'

* That is, ' choose ' = cherish.—G.

THE FIFTEENTH SERMON.

Who is wise, and he shall understand these things? prudent, and he shall know them? for the ways of the Lord are right, the just shall walk in them: but the transgressors shall fall therein.—Hos. XIV. 9.

AT length, by divine assistance, we are come unto the conclusion of this short chapter, wherein the Holy Ghost, from God, hath shewed such bowels of mercy and tender compassion unto miserable sinners, encouraging them to return unto the Lord by many and several arguments, being formerly insisted upon. Our last work was to shew you what wisdom and prudence was, the difference of them, and how that none, without these endowments, are able to know and make use of divine truths and mysteries of religion. ' Who is wise, and he shall understand these things? prudent, and he shall know them?' &c.

We came then to shew, that there must be prudence and wisdom, before we can understand divine truths; there must be an illumination within. It is not sufficient to have the light of the Scripture outwardly, but there must be a light of the eye to see; there must be wisdom and prudence gathered from the Scriptures. Now, wisdom and prudence, if they be divine, as here is meant, it is not a discreet managing of outward affairs of our personal condition, but an ordering of our course to heavenward. Wherefore a man may know whether he be wise and prudent by his relishing of divine truths, for otherwise he is not wise and prudent in these things which are the main.

Now, having shewed that only the wise and prudent can conceive and make a right use of these great things delivered, he comes to shew and defend the equity of God's ways, how crooked soever they seem to flesh and blood. These things ought to be hearkened unto, because they are the ways of God.

' The ways of the Lord are right.'

By *ways* here, he understandeth the whole law and gospel, the whole word of God; which he calleth *right*, not only because,

1. They are righteous in themselves; but,
2. Because they reform whatsoever is amiss in us, and rectify us; and
3. Work whatsoever is needful for our good and salvation.

Now more particularly, God's ways are,

1. Those ways wherein he walks to us; or,
2. The ways that he prescribes us to walk in; and,
3. Our ways, as they are conformable to his.

Any of these are the ways of God; of all which more hereafter.

1. *The ways wherein he walks to us,* because many of them are untraceable, as unsearchable to us, are not here meant; as those of election, predestination and reprobation; the reasons whereof, if we take them comparatively, cannot be searched out. Why God should take one and not another, it is an unsearchable way. But take a man single, out of comparison, the ways of God will appear to be right, even in that harsh decree which many men stumble so much at. For none are ever brought in the execution of that decree to be damned, but you shall see ' the ways of the Lord right,' who a long time together offers them a great deal of mercy, which they refusing, and resisting the Holy Ghost, taking wilfully contrary courses, work out their own damnation. So that at length the issue of those unsearch-

able ways will appear to be right in every particular ; howsoever the comparative reason at the first, why God singles out one man and not another, will not appear.

2. As for the *ways of his providence*, in governing the world, and ruling of his church, this is the way of God which is right ; all which ways, though we cannot in all particulars see in this world, yet in heaven, in the light of glory, we shall see what cannot now be seen in the light of grace and nature. For there be mysteries in providence. Who can tell the reason why, of men equally good, one should be sorely afflicted, and the other should go to heaven without any affliction in a smooth way ? None can give a reason of it ; but we must subscribe to the hidden wisdom of God, whose ways are unsearchable in his providence. Yet are they most right, though they be above our conceit. If we could conceive all God's ways, then they were not God's ways ; for in his ways to us, he will so carry them, as he will shew himself to be above and beyond our shallow conceits.

But the ways especially here meant, are the ways which he prescribes us to walk in ; and they are,

1. What we must believe ; and then,

2. What we must do. There is,

First, obedience of faith, and then obedience of life.

These are God's ways prescribed in the word, and only in the word.

3. Now *our ways*, when they join with *God's ways*, that is, when our life, purposes and desires of the inner-man, in our speeches, carriage, and conversation, agree with God's ways, then in some sort they are God's ways, ' the just shall walk in them.' They shall walk in these ways, that is, in those ways which God prescribeth. As for those ways wherein God walks to us, we have not so much to do here to consider them. But by walking in the ways which he prescribes, we shall feel that his ways to us will be nothing but mercy and truth. ' The ways of the Lord are right,' Ps. cxlv. 17. Those ways that he prescribes to men to be believed and done, they are right and straight, that is, they are agreeable to the first rule of all. Right is the judgment and will of God. He is the first truth and the first good ; the prime truth and good, which must rule all others, *mensura mensurans*, as they use to speak in schools ; the measure that measures all other things. For all other things are only so far right, as they agree to the highest measure of all, which is God's appointment and will. So the ways of God are said to be right ; because they agree to his word and will. They are holy and pure, as himself is just, pure, and holy.

' The ways of the Lord are right.'

Right, as they agree to that which is right and straight ; and right likewise, because they lead directly to a right end. We know a right line is that which is the shortest between two terms. That which leads from point to point, is the shortest of all other lines. *So God's ways are right and straight.* There are no other ways which tend directly to happiness, without error, but God's ways ; all other ways are crooked ways. So God's ways are right, as they look to God, and as they look unto all other inferior courses. They are right to examine all our ways by, being the rule of them. And they are right, as they look to God's will, and are ruled by him.

' The ways of the Lord are right.'

Hence observe we in the first place, that the first thing we should look to in our conversation, must be to know this for a ground.

Obs. That man is not a prescriber of his own way, and that no creature's will is a rule.

We must embrace, therefore, no opinion of any man, or any course enjoined or prescribed by any man, further than it agrees with the first truth and the first right. God's ways are right ; right as a standard, that is, a measure to measure all other measures by. So God's will and truth revealed is a right rule, and the measure of all other rules whatsoever. Directions therefore, which we have of things to be believed and done from men, must be no further regarded than as they agree with the first standard. Therefore they are mistaken, and desperately mistaken, that make any man's will a rule, unless it be subordinate to that which is higher, at which time it becometh all one with the higher rule. When a man subordinates his directions to God's, then God's and his are all one. Otherwise without, this subordination, we make men gods, when we make their will a rule of our obedience. ' The ways of the Lord are right.' But of this only a touch by the way ; the main point hence is.

Obs. The word of the Lord is every way perfect, and brings us to perfection.

As we may see at large proved, Ps. xix. 7, &c., where whatsoever is good, comfortable, profitable or delightful, either for this life or the life to come, is all to be had from thence. And the wise man saith, ' Every word of God is pure,' &c., Prov. xxx. 5 : a similitude taken from gold, which is fined till it be pure, as it is expressed in another place, ' The words of the Lord are pure words, as silver tried in a furnace of earth, and purified seven times,' Ps. xii. 6. And so the apostle to Timothy. ' All Scripture is given by inspiration of God, and is profitable for doctrine, for correction, for reproof, for instruction in righteousness, that the man of God may be perfect, throughly furnished unto all good works,' 2 Tim. iii. 16.

Use 1. Since then the ways of God are so right, just, pure, and perfect, *this is first for reproof of them that add hereunto ;* as our Romish adversaries, who do herein, by their traditions and additions, condemn God either of want of wisdom, love, and goodness, or of all. So as all defects charged upon the word, are charged upon God himself, who did not better provide and foresee for his church what was good for it. But the wise man condemneth this their audacious boldness, where he saith, ' Add thou not unto his words, lest he reprove thee, and thou be found a liar,' Prov. xxx. 6. They bar reading of the Scriptures, or to read them in English especially, lest the people become heretics. They think it safe to read their own books and idle dreams, but reject the word of God, and then, as Jeremiah speaks, ' What wisdom is in them ?' Jer. viii. 9. Surely none at all ; for the only wisdom is, to be governed by God's most holy word.

Use 2. Again, *it is for instruction unto us, to rest and rely upon this so holy, right, pure, and perfect word.* Since it is so sure and firm, we are to rest upon the promises, and tremble at the threatenings, though we see not present performance of them, because not one of them shall fail. For, saith Christ, ' Heaven and earth shall pass away, but one jot and tittle of the law shall not fail,' Matt. v. 28. What maketh so many judgments to overtake men, but their unbelief? what made their carcases to fall in the wilderness, so as they could not enter into the land of Canaan, but their unbelief? for, saith the text of them, ' They could not enter, because of unbelief,' Heb. iii. 19. Infidelity, and not believing God, is the root and cause of all our woe. It began with our first parents, and it cleaveth too close unto us, even unto this day. This cometh from our atheism and self-love ; that if a mortal man promise or swear unto us, we believe him, and rest upon his word ; but all that the great God can do unto us by promises, commandments, threatenings, allurements, and gracious examples, will not make us give credit to his word, but rather believe Satan, and our own false and deceitful hearts. As, for instance, God hath promised, that ' if our sins were as red as scarlet, yet he will make them whiter than the snow,' Isa. i. 18 ; though they be never so strong for us, yet he hath promised ' to subdue them,' Micah vii. 19. If our wants be never so great, yet if we will trust in God, he hath promised to relieve us, and hath said, ' that he will not fail us nor forsake us,' Isa. l. 10 ; Heb. xiii. 5, if we cast our care upon him. So, for the threatenings, we must believe that there is never a one of them but they shall come to pass, as sure as the promises shall be made good. If these thoughts were firmly settled in us, that ' the ways of the Lord are right,' and therefore must be all accomplished in their time, it would make us restless to fly from sin, and the punishments threatened, which all ' lie at the door,' Gen. iv. 7, and will quickly be upon us, if they be not avoided by sound and hearty repentance.

Use 3. Lastly, if every commandment be right, sure, and just, then when God commandeth do it, though the apparent danger be never so great, and though it be never so contrary to flesh and blood, pleasure, profit, or preferment, yet *know it is firm and sure, and that our happiness stands in doing it, our misery in disobeying it,*—as we know it was with Adam. What a sudden change did his disobedience work in himself, all the world since being leavened with that miserable contagious fall of his ! And for the whole world this is a general, we never want any good, but for want of love and obedience unto it. ' Great prosperity shall they have,' saith David, ' who love thy law, and no evil shall come unto them,' Ps. cxix. 165. And we never had nor shall have any hurt, but from our unbelief and disobedience to the holy, pure, and perfect word of God, which is attended with comfort and prosperity here, and endless glory hereafter.

' The ways of the Lord are right.'

In the next place, if the ways of the Lord be right and straight, so straight that they lead directly to the right end, then it is clear,

Obs. That the best way to come to a good and right end, is to take God's ways. For it is a right way, and the right way is always the shortest way. Therefore, when men take not God's ways, prescriptions, and courses, they go wide about, and seldom or never come to their intended end. God's way is the right way, and therefore brings a man to his right end. Sometimes men will have their turnings, their *diverticula*, and vagaries, but they find by experience that God's ways they are the right ways, so as they never attain to comfort and peace until they come again into those ways. God until then suffereth them to be snared and hampered, and to eat the fruit of their own ways, and then they see the difference of God's ways and theirs, and that God's ways are the best, and the straightest ways unto true happiness.

Indeed, God suffers sometimes men that will have their own ways to come quickly to them, as some men hasten to be rich, and God suffers them to be rich hastily : yet they are none of God's ways which they take, but climb up by fraud and deceit. Aye, but that is only a particular end which God suffereth them to attain by byeways ; but what will be the upshot ? Where will all these ways end at length ? Surely in hell. For when a man goes out of the right, and straight, and direct way, to be great in the world, he is like a man who goes out of his way, which is further about ; who yet, when he is in that way, goes on through thick and thin, because he will gain some way. He goes on through thickets and hedges, fair and foul, where he gets many scratches, brushes and knocks. Doth any think in the world to attain his particular ends without* the direct ways of God ? God may suffer him to attain his particular end, but with many flaws, knocks, and brushes upon his conscience, which many times he carrieth with him unto his grave ; and finds it a great deal better, both to attain unto his particular ends by God's ways, and to have no more of anything in the world than he can have with a good conscience. For, though they be good men, ofttimes God suffers such men to have bruises in their conscience all their days, that they and others may know that the best way is the straight and right way, which at last will bring us best to our end.

Having thus made it good, ' that the ways of the Lord are right,' now, for conclusion of all, the prophet begins to shew the divers effects these right ways of God have in two sorts of people, the godly and wicked.

I. The just shall walk in them :

II. That the transgressors shall fall therein.

I. *The just shall walk in them.* Who be the just men here spoken of? Such are just men who give to every one their due ; that give God his due in the first place, and man in the second place, whereby it is framed. ' The just shall walk in them ;' that is, they shall proceed and go on in them till they be come to the end of their race, the salvation of their souls. And, more particularly,

(1.) Just men first, are such, *who have respect unto all God's commandments*, Ps. cxix. 6. Though in their disposition they find some more hard to them than others, yet they do not allow themselves to break any, but strive so much the more earnestly and constantly to observe them, as they find their natures opposite to them. Now hypocrites, howsoever they do many things in show, yet, like Herod and Judas, their hearts run in a wrong channel ; they allow themselves to live in, and like of some sin. The young man in the gospel had not a respect unto all God's commandments, though Christ loved his amiable parts, Mat. x. 21. To this purpose James saith, ' Whosoever shall keep the whole law, and yet offend in one point, he is guilty of all,' James ii. 10. That is, he who alloweth himself in any one sin, he is guilty of all. Ask Judas, Is murder good ? He would have said, no : but he was covetous, and allowed himself in it, and so drew upon him the guilt of all the rest. God is he who forbids sinning against them all. He who forbids one, forbids all ; and being rightly turned to God, the same authority makes us leave all. It is not sin, but the allowance of it, that makes an hypocrite.

(2.) Again, *they do things to a good end*, the glory of God, and the good of man. For want hereof, the alms, prayers, and fasting of the scribes and Pharisees (because they did nothing out of love to God or man, but for vainglory and carnal respects), are condemned of Christ. So some are brought in at the last day, saying, ' Lord, Lord, have we not in thy name prophesied, and in thy name cast out devils, and in thy name done many wonderful works,' Mat. vii. 22 ; and yet Christ professeth not to know them, but calleth them ' workers of iniquity.' They had gifts and calling, and delivered true doctrine, &c. But here was their failing, ' They prophesied *in* his name, but not *for* his name.' Their actions were good in themselves, and for others, but the end of them was naught, and therefore both they and their works are condemned. Yet this is not so to be understood, but that God's children have some thoughts of vainglory, which accompanieth and creepeth into their best actions ; but they do acknowledge this

* That is, ' outside of.'—ED.

for a sin, confess it, and desire the Lord to pardon and subdue it, and then it shall never be laid to their charge. Because having of infirmities is not contrary to sincerity, but allowing of them, and living in them; in which case the Lord is more pleased with our humiliation for our sin, than the motions to vainglory did offend him.

(3.) Thirdly, *a desire to grow in grace, and to become better and better*, is a sign of uprightness. Christian righteousness, as it sees still need, so it still desires more grace and less sin; because he who hath a true heart, seeth both the want and worth of grace, and feeleth his want. A man feels not the want of faith, humility, and love, till he have it in some sort, as it is said, Philip. iii. 15, ' As many as are perfect are thus minded,' to wit, so many as are upright: all is one.

(4.) Lastly, this just uprightness is known *by love of the brethren*. ' By this we know we are translated from death to life, because we love the brethren,' 1 John iii. 14. Contrary to which is that disposition which envieth at all things which suits not with their humours: as James speaketh of those who prefer men, and have their persons in admiration, in regard of outward things, despising inferiors, James ii. 2.

Use 1. If therefore we will ever be counted righteous persons, let us keep these rules set down here, have a respect to all God's commandments, do all things to the glory of God, desire to grow in grace, and love the brethren.

2. And so it is also for consolation unto such who are thus qualified; for unto them belongeth all the promises of this life, and of that to come. They are in a blessed estate, for ' all things are theirs,' 1 Cor. iii. 21, because they are Christ's. Therefore it is their bounden duty, having an upright heart, to rejoice in God, as the prophet speaks: ' Rejoice in the Lord, ye righteous, for praise is comely for the upright,' Ps. xxxiii. 1; lii. 9. None have cause to rejoice but upright men.

1. Because they of all others have title and right to joy. 2. Because they have command to do it, seeing heaven is theirs. All the promises are theirs, and they are heirs of all things. It is a comely service, and the work of heaven.

Obj. Against this some object. Oh, but I find many sins, passions, and infirmities in myself; how then can I joy in God?

Ans. To this we answer briefly, that the passions and infirmities of God's servants are not contrary to Christian uprightness and righteousness; for St James saith, that ' Elias was a man subject to like passions and infirmities as we are,' James v. 17, yet he was a righteous man, though a man subject to the like passions as we are. Therefore the passions of Christians are not contrary to Christian, but to legal, righteousness. But ' we are not under the law, but under grace,' Rom. vi. 15. The first covenant of works bids us have no sin; the other covenant bids us allow no sin. Thus much is for that question, What is meant by *just men?* It remains now that we should further inquire into that mystery, how it is that just men walk in the ways of God, and prosper therein, when yet wicked men, called ' transgressors,' fall therein. But this being a mystery, by your patience we will take time to unfold what we have to speak hereof the next time, if God be so pleased.

THE SIXTEENTH SERMON.

*The ways of the Lord are right: the just shall walk in them; but the trans-
gressors shall fall therein.*—Hos. XIV. 9.

GOD's children have their times of deadness and desertion, and again their
times of quickening and rejoicing. Weeping doth not always remain unto
them for their portion, ' but joy cometh in the morning,' Ps. xxx. 5. In
the worst times the saints have always some comforts afforded them, which
supporteth them against all the storms and tempests they endure. They
have always a Goshen, Exod. ix. 22, to fly to. Others shall perish in
that way, wherein they shall walk and escape.

' The just shall walk in them, but the transgressors shall fall therein.'

Thus far we are now come in the unfolding of this chapter, having shewed
God's rich and incomparable mercies to miserable and penitent sinners ;
how ready God is to embrace such, as this rebellious people named were,
with all the arguments used to make them return unto the Lord. We are
now come at last unto the upshot of all, a discovery of the several effects
and works God's word hath upon both sorts of people here named and
aimed at.

' The just shall walk in them, but the transgressors shall fall therein.'

These were very bad times ; yet there were just men, who walked in the
ways of God : so that we see—

In the worst times, God will have always a people that shall justify wisdom.
God will have it thus, even in the worst times, that ' the just shall walk
in them.' Though before he saith, ' Who is wise ? and who is prudent ? '
yet here he shews that there shall be a number who shall ' walk in God's
ways,' who though they go to heaven alone, yet to heaven they will.
Though they have but a few that walk in God's ways with them, they will
rather go with a few that way, than with the wicked on the broad way to
hell. Alway God hath some who shall walk in his way ; for if there were
not some alway who were good, the earth would not stand ; for good men
they are the pillars of the world, who uphold it. It is not for wicked men's
sake that God upholds the frame of the creatures, and that orderly government. We see all is to gather together the number of his elect, of whom
in some ages there are more, and in some less, of them born, thereafter as
God breathes and blows with his Spirit. For according to the abundant
working of the Spirit, is the number of the elect. Yet in all ages there are
some, because it is an article of our faith, to believe ' a holy catholic
church.'* Now it cannot be an article of faith, unless there were alway some
that made this catholic church ; for else there should be an act of faith,
without an object. Therefore we may always say, I believe that there are
a number of elect people that walk in the ways of God to heaven-wards.

And what is the disposition of these some ? To have a counter motion
to those of the times and places they live in. Some are foolish, not caring
for the ways of God, cavilling at them. But the ' just shall walk in them,'
that is, they take a contrary course to the world, that slights wisdom.
Thus in all times it is the disposition of God's children to go contrary to
the world in the greatest matters of all. They indeed hold correspondency,
in outward things, but for the main they have a contrary motion. As we
say of the planets, that they have a motion contrary to the wrapt motion.

* Creed, Article IX. Cf. Pearson and Smith, *in loc.*—G.

Being carried and hurried about every twenty-four hours with the motion of the heavens, they have another motion and circuit of their own, which they pass also. So it is with God's people : though in their common carriage they be carried with the common customs and fashions of the times, yet they have a contrary motion of their own, whereby being carried by the help of God's Spirit, they go on in a way to heaven, though the world discern it not. They have a secret contrary motion, opposite to the sins and corruptions of the age and times they live in. Therefore, in all ages it is observed for a commendation to go on in a contrary course to the present times. Noah in his time, Lot in his time, and Paul in his time, who complains, ' All men seek their own,' Philip. ii. 21. It is a strange thing that Paul should complain of all men seeking their own, even then when the blood of Christ was so warm, being so lately shed, and the gospel so spread ; yet ' all men seek their own.' And he speaks it with tears ; but what became of Paul, and Timothy, and the rest ? ' But our conversation is in heaven, from whence we look for the Saviour, the Lord Jesus Christ,' &c., Philip. iii. 20. Let all men seek their own here below, as they will, we have our conversation contrary to the world. ' Our conversation is in heaven,' &c. So that they hold out God's truth in the midst of a crooked and perverse generation, that is, when every man takes crooked ways and courses in carnal policy ; yet there are a company that notwithstanding walk in the right ways of God, clean contrary to others. The just will walk in the right ways of God. As holy Joshua said, ' Choose you what you will do, but howsoever, I and my father's house will serve the Lord,' Josh. xxiv. 15. So when many fell from Christ for a fit, because his doctrine seemed harsh, Peter justified that way. When Christ asked him, Will ye also leave me with the rest who are offended ? ' Lord,' saith he, ' whither shall we go ?' We have tasted the sweetness of the word, and felt the power thereof : ' Whither shall we go, Lord ? thou hast the words of eternal life,' John vi. 68. So God's people have an affection, carriage, and course, contrary to the world.

Reason. The reason is taken from their own disposition; they are partakers of the divine nature, 2 Pet. i. 4, which carrieth them up to Godwards against the stream and current of the time.

Use. The use hereof, shall be only a trial of ourselves in evil times, whether or not then, *we justify God's ways and the best things.* If we do, it is a sign we are of the number of God's elect, to defend and maintain good causes and right opinions, especially in divine truths, which is the best character of a Christian. Others in their own sphere have their degree of goodness, but we speak of supernatural divine goodness. A man may know he belongs to God, if he justify wisdom in the worst times, if he stand for the truth to the utmost, thinking it of more price than his life. It is the first degree to religion, ' to hate father and mother, wife and children, and all for the gospel,' Luke xiv. 26. Now when a man will justify the truth, with the loss of anything in the world, it is a sign that man is a good man in ill times.

Therefore, in ill times let us labour to justify truth, both the truth of things to be believed, and all just religious courses, not only in case of opposition being opposed, but in example, though we say nothing. Noah condemned the world, though he spake not a word, by making an ark, Heb. xi. 7 ; so Lot, Sodom, though he told not all Sodom of their faults. So a man may justify good things, though he speak not a word to any man, for such a one's life is a confutation and sufficient witness for God against the world. Therefore it is good, though a man do not confront the world in his speeches, yet notwithstanding, at least to hold a course contrary to the world in his conversation. We have need of a great deal of courage to do this ; but there is no heavenly wise man, but he is a courageous man. Though in his own spirit he may be a weak man, yet in case of opposition, grace will be above nature, he will shew then his heavenly wisdom and prudence, and of what metal he is made, by justifying wisdom in all times, ' The just shall walk therein.' But to come more directly to the words,

' The just shall walk in them.'

A just and righteous man that is made just by them, shall walk in them. Hence we may observe,

Obs. That first men must have spiritual life, and be just, before they can walk. Walking is an action of life. There must be life before there can be walking. A man must first have a spiritual life, whereby he may be just, and then he will walk as a just man. For, as we say of a bowl,* it is Austin's comparison, it is first made round, and then it runs round ; so a man is first just, and then he doth justly. It is a conceit of the papists, that good works do justify a man. Luther says well, that ' a good man doth good works.' Good works make not the man. Fruit makes not the tree, but the tree the fruit. So we are just first, and then we walk as just men. We must labour to be changed and to have a principle of spiritual life ; then we shall walk and have new feet, eyes, taste, ears, and senses ; all shall then be new.

Again, in the second place, the necessity of it appears hence, that there must be first spiritual life in the inward man, ere a man can walk, because there will not else be a harmony and correspondency betwixt a man and his ways. A man will not hold in those ways that he hath an antipathy to ; therefore, his nature must be altered by a higher principle, before he can like and delight in the ways of God. This is that which God's children desire first of God, that he would alter their natures, enlighten, change and quicken them, work strongly and powerfully in them, that they may have a sympathy and liking unto all that is good ; first they are just, and then they walk in God's ways.

' The just shall walk in them.'

Obs. In the next place, we may observe hence, *that a just man, he being the prudent and wise man, he walks in God's ways.* That is, spiritual wisdom and prudence, together with grace, righteousness, and justice, they lead to walking in obedience. Let no man therefore talk of grace and wisdom or prudence altering him, further than he makes it good by his walking. He that is just, walks as a just man ; he that is wise, walks wisely ; he that is prudent, walks prudently. Which is spoken to discover hypocrisy in men, that would be thought to be good Christians and wise men, because they have a great deal of speculative knowledge. Aye, but look we to our ways, let them shew whether we be wise or foolish, just or unjust. ' If a man be wise, he is wise for himself,' Prov. ix. 12, as Solomon saith, to direct his own ways ; ' The wisdom of the wise, is to understand his own way that he is to walk in,' Prov. xiv. 8. If a man have not wisdom to direct his way in particular, to walk to heavenward, he is but a fool. For a man to know so much as shall condemn him, and be a witness against him, and yet not know so much as to save him, what a miserable thing is this ? Now all other men that know much, and walk not answerable, they know so much as to condemn them, and not to save them. Our Saviour

* That is, a ' ball' for bowling.—G

Christ he calleth such ' foolish builders,' Matt. vii. 27, that know and will not do; so unless there be a walking answerable to the wisdom and prudence prescribed, a man is but a foolish man.

Therefore let it be a rule of trial, would we be thought to be wise and prudent, just and good? Let us look to our ways. Are they God's ways? Do we delight in these ways, and make them our ways? Then we are wise, prudent, and just.

' The just shall walk in them.'

As the just shall walk in them, so whosoever walks in them are just, wise, and prudent; for is not he prudent, who walks in those ways that lead directly to eternal happiness? Is not he a wise man, that walks by rule in those ways where he hath God over him, to be his protector, ruler, and defender? Is not he a wise man, who walks in those ways that fits him for all conditions whatsoever, prosperity or adversity, life or death, for all estates? He that walks therefore in God's ways, must be the only wise man.

Now, what things doth this walking in the ways of God imply?

1. First, *perspicuity*. Those who walk in the ways of God, they discern those ways to be God's ways, and discern them aright.

2. Then when they discern them to be God's good ways, answerably *they proceed in them from step to step;* for every action is a step to heaven or to hell. So a just man, when he hath discovered a good way, he goes on still.

3. And then *he keeps an uniform course*, for so he doth who walks on in a way. He makes not indentures* as he walks, but goes on steadily in an uniform course to a right end. So a just man, when he hath singled out the right way, he goes on in that steadily and uniformly.

4. And likewise where it is said, the just walks in them, it implies *resolution to go on in those ways* till he come to the end, though there be never so much opposition.

But how shall we know whether we go on in this way or not?

First, he that goes on in a way, the further he hath proceeded therein, looking back, *that which he leaves behind seems lesser and lesser in his eye;* and that which he goes to greater and greater. So a man may know his progress in the ways of God, when earthly profits and pleasures seem little, his former courses and pleasures seeming now base unto him. When heaven and heavenly things seem near unto him, it is a sign he is near heaven, near in time, and nearer in disposition and in wisdom to discern, because the best things are greatest in his eye and esteem. In this case, it is a sign that such a one is removed from the world, and is near unto heaven, having made a good progress in the ways of God.

It implies likewise in the *second* place, *an uniform course of life*. Such a one doth not duties by starts now and then, but constantly. Therefore we must judge of men by a tenure of life, what their constant ways are. Sometimes though they be good men, they may step away into an ill way, and yet come in again. Sometimes an ill man may cross a good way, as a thief when he crosseth the highway, or a good man steps out of the way; but this is not their way, they are both out, and to seek, of their way. A wicked man when he speaks of good things, he is out of his way; he acts a part and assumes a person he is unskilful to act; therefore he doth it untowardly. But a man's way is his course. A good man's way is good, though his startings be ill; and an ill man's way is naught, though for passion, or for by-ends, he may now and then do good things. Therefore, considering

* That is, ' zig-zags.'—ED.

that the walking in the ways of God is uniform and orderly ; let us judge of ourselves by the tenure of our life, and course thereof. And let those poor souls who think they are out of the way, because they run into some infirmities now and then, comfort themselves in this, that God judgeth not by single actions, but according to the tenure of a man's life, what he is. For oftentimes God's children gain by their slips, which makes them look the more warily to their ways for ever after that. He that walks in the way to heaven, if he be a good man, he looks to make surer footing in the ways of God after his slips and falls. He labours also to make so much the more haste home, being a gainer by all his slips and falls. Let none therefore be discouraged, but let them labour that their ways and courses may be good, and not only so, but to be uniform, orderly, and constant, and then they may speak peace to their own souls, being such as are here described, ' The just shall walk in them.'

Third, again, he that will walk aright in God's ways, he must be *resolute against all opposition whatsoever*, for we meet with many lets, hindrances, and scandals,* to drive us out of the way. Sometimes the ill lives of those who walk in these ways, sometimes their slips and falls, sometimes persecution, and our own natures, are full of scandals, subject to take this and that offence, and then we are ready to be snared on the right hand, or feared and scared on the left. And our nature, so far as it is unsanctified, is prone to catch, and ready to join with the world ; therefore we have need of resolution of spirit and determination. As David, ' I have determined, O Lord, and I will keep thy laws ; I have sworn that I will keep thy righteous judgments,' Ps. cxix. 106. This is a resolute determination.

Fourth, and then again, pray to God with David that he *would direct our ways*. ' Oh, that my ways were so directed to keep thy laws !' Ps. cxix. 3. I see that my nature is ready to draw me away to evil, and perverse crooked courses. I see, though I determine to take a good course, that there is much opposition ; therefore, good Lord, direct me in my course, direct thou my thoughts, words, and carriage. Therefore, that we may walk stedfastly, let us resolve with settled determination, praying to God for strength ; otherwise resolution, with dependence on our own power, may be a work of the flesh. But resolve thus, these are right ways and straight, they lead to heaven, happiness, and glory ; therefore I will walk in them, whatsoever come of it. We have all the discouragement which may hinder us in the ways of God. For as we are travellers, so we are soldiers, warfaring men that meet with many rubs, thorns. Therefore to walk amidst such dangerous ways we must be well shod with the preparation of the gospel of peace, that is, patience, and reasons taken from thence. God hath provided spiritual armour in the word against all oppositions that meet with us, so that by resolution and prayer to him, using his means, we may go through all.

Now for a further help for us to walk constantly and resolutely in the ways of God.

1. Take first *the help of good company*. If we see any man to walk in a good way, let him not walk alone, but let us join ourselves with those that walk in God's ways ; for why doth God leave us not only his word to direct us which way to go, but likewise examples in all times, but that we should follow those examples ? which are like the pillar of fire which went before Israel unto Canaan. We have a cloud and a pillar of examples before us, (unto which he alludes, Heb. xii. 1), to lead us unto heaven, not only the word, but examples in all times. ' Walk, as you have us, for an example, Philip.

* That is, 'stumbling-blocks.'—G.

iii. 17, saith Paul.   Therefore it is a character of a gracious disposition to join with the just, and those who walk in the ways of God.   We see there is in all the creatures an instinct to keep company with their own kind ; as we see in doves, sheep, geese, and the like.   So it comes from a supernatural gracious instinct of grace, for the good to walk and company with the good, helping them on in the way to heaven.   It is therefore a point of special wisdom to single out those for our company, who are able to help us thither, as it is for travellers to choose their company to travel with.

2.   Again, if we would walk aright in the ways of God, *let us have our end in our eye, like unto the traveller.*   Look on heaven, the day of judgment, those times either of eternal happiness or misery, which we must all come to.   The having of these in our eye, will stern* the whole course of our life ; for the end infuseth vigour in our carriages, and puts a great deal of life in the use of the means, breeding a love of them, though they be harsh. Therefore we must pray and labour for patience, to conflict with our own corruptions, and those of the times we live in.   This is unpleasant to do ; but when a man hath his aim and end in his eye, this inspires such vigour and strength in a man, that it makes him use means and courses contrary to his own natural disposition, offering a holy violence unto himself.   As thus, it is not absolutely necessary that I should have this or that, or have them all, or in such and such a measure ; but it is absolutely necessary that I should be saved, and not damned ; therefore this course I will take, in these ways I will and must walk which lead to salvation.   Let us therefore with Moses have in our eye, ' the recompence of the reward,' Heb. xi. 26 ; and with our blessed Saviour, the head of the faithful, have before our eyes ' the joy that was set before him,' which will make us pass by all those heavy things that he passed through.   Let us with the holy men of ancient time, have ' the prize of that high calling' in our eye, to make us, notwithstanding all opposition, press forward towards the mark.

3.   And then again, because it is said indefinitely here, ' They shall walk in these ways,' remember always *to take wisdom and prudence along with you in all your walkings.*   It is put indefinitely, because we should leave out none.   For, as we say in things that are to be believed, Faith chooseth not this object, and not another; so obedience chooseth not this object ; I will obey God in this, and not in this, but it goes on in all God's ways. Therefore, if we would walk on aright in God's ways, there must be consideration of all the relations as we stand to God.   *First, what duties we owe to God in heavenly things,* to please him above all, whomsoever we displease, and to seek the kingdom of heaven and his righteousness before all, that all things may follow which are needful for us, Mat. vi. 33.   So, in the *next* place, when we look to ourselves, to know *those ways which are required of us in regard of ourselves ;* for every Christian is a temple wherein God dwells ; therefore we are to carry ourselves holily, to be much in prayer and communion with God in secret.   A man is best distinguished to be a good walker by those secret ways betwixt God and his soul, those walks of meditation and prayer wherein there is much sweet intercourse betwixt God and the soul.   Therefore, in this case a man makes conscience of his communion with God in his thoughts, desires, affections, using all good means appointed of God to maintain this communion.

4.   Then we should look to our own carriage in the use of the creatures, *to carry ourselves in all things indifferently,* because wisdom and prudence is seen in those things especially, to use things indifferent, indifferently ;

* That is, ' steer, guide, regulate.'—G.

not to be much in the use of the world, in joy or sorrow, but in moderation to use these things, being sure to set our affections upon the main.

5. And so in things indifferent, not to do them *with offence and excess;* but to see and observe the rule in all things of indifferency.

6. And for our carriage to others in those ways, let us consider what we owe *to those above us,* what respect is due to governors, and what to others; what to those who are without; what to those who are weak.   We owe an example of holy life unto them, that we give no occasion of scandal; and also to walk wisely towards them that are without, that we give no occasion for the ways of God to be ill spoken of.

7. And for all conditions which God shall cast us into, remember *that those be ways which we should walk seemly in.*   If prosperity, let us take heed of the sins of prosperity, pride, insolency, security, hardness of heart, and the like.   If adversity, then let us practise the graces thereof, take heed of murmuring and repining, dejection of spirit, despair, and the like.   This is to walk like a wise man in all conditions, in those relations he stands in.

8. *For our words likewise and expressions to others,* in that kind of our walking, that they may be savoury and to purpose, that we labour to speak by rule, seeing we must give an account of every ' idle word' at the day of judgment, Mat. xii. 36.   So that in all our labours, carriage, and speech, we must labour to do all wisely and justly.   These are the ways of God, and ' the just shall walk in them.'

Negatively, what we must avoid in all our walking.

Remember in general, we must never do anything against religion, against conscience, against a man's particular place and calling, or against justice.   Let us not touch upon the breach of any good thing, especially of religion and conscience.   Thus a man shall walk in the ways of God, if with wisdom and prudence he consider what ways are before him to God, to himself, to others; in all conditions and states of life, to see what he must, and what he must not do, and then to walk in them answerably.

For our encouragement to walk in God's ways in our general and particular callings.

1. Know first, *they are the most safe ways of all.*   Whatsoever trouble or affliction we meet withal, it is no matter, it will prove the safest way in the end.   For as it was with the cloud which went before God's people, it was both for direction and protection ; so the Spirit of God, and the ways of God, as they serve for direction, so they serve for protection.   God will direct and protect us if we walk in his ways.   Let him be our director, and he will be our preserver and protector in all times.

2. Again, they are *the most pleasant ways of all.*   All wisdom's ways are paved with prosperity and pleasure ; for when God doth enlarge and sanctify the soul to walk in them, he giveth withal a royal gift, inward peace of conscience, and joy unspeakable and glorious, with an enlarged spirit. God meets his children in his own ways ; they are therefore to walk there. Let a man start out of God's ways, he meets with the devil, with the devil's instruments, and many snares.   But in God's ways he shall be sure to meet with God, if he walk in them with humility and respect to God, looking up for direction and strength, and denying his own wisdom.   In this case a man shall be sure to have God go along with him in all his ways. In God's ways expect God's company.   Therefore they are the safest and the most pleasant ways.

3. And they are the *cleanest and holiest ways of all;* having this excellent property in them, that as they lead to comfort, so they end in comfort ;

they all end in heaven, Ps. xix. 9. Therefore let us not be weary of God's ways, of Christianity and our particular callings ; wherein what we do, let us do as God's ways, having sanctified them by prayer, and do it in obedience to God. They are God's ways when they are sanctified. God hath set me in this standing, I expect his blessing therein, and what blessing I find, I will give him the praise. God hath appointed that in serving man I serve him ; therefore we must go on in our particular ways, as the ways of God, doing everything as the work of God, and we shall find them the comfortablest and pleasantest ways which end in joy, happiness, and glory.

Use 1. The use hereof may be first reprehension unto those *who can talk but not walk*, that have tongues but not feet, to wit, affections; that come by starts into the narrow way ; but yet be never well till they turn back again into the world, that broad way which leads unto destruction.

Use 2. Secondly, it is for instruction, *to stir us up to walk in God's ways ;* as Ps. i. 1, 2, ' Blessed is the man that walketh not in the counsel of the ungodly, &c. But his delight is in the law of the Lord, and in that law doth he meditate day and night.'

Use 3. Thirdly, this is for consolation ; if this be our walk, *then God will walk with us, and the angels of God shall have charge of us to keep us in all our ways*, Ps. xxxiv. 7; and though, like David, we slip out of the way, yet this not being our walk, we come to the way again. Though God's children miss of their way, yet their resolution, choice, and endeavour was to walk in the way ; therefore such are still in a blessed estate, and keep their communion with God. A man is not said to alter his way till he alter his choice and resolution. The best man may have an ill passion, and miss the way, but he will not turn from it willingly. And the worst man may have a good passion, and come into the way, but never continue in it to make this walk.* From all which it appeareth that they are only righteous persons who continue to walk in the ways of God. It is therefore consolation unto them who take that course. Though all the world go another way, yet they must imitate just men. And for us, we must imitate these just men, though they be never so few in the world and despised. If we would be counted the servants of God, we must imitate those that walk in those paths.

II. Now it is said that the other sort, wicked men, the ways of God shall have quite a contrary course in them.

' But the transgressors shall fall therein.'

As one and the selfsame cloud was both light to the Israelites and darkness unto the Egyptians, Exod. xiv. 20 ; so the same ways of God prove both light and darkness, life and death, to the godly and wicked. As the apostle speaks, unto ' the one they are the savour of life unto life, and unto the other the savour of death unto death,' 2 Cor. ii. 16. Therefore now here is the conclusion of all. If no warning will serve the turn of all what hath been given and said, yet the word of God shall not return empty, it shall effect that for which it was sent, Isa. lv. 11; one work or other it will do, even upon the most perverse.

' The transgressors shall fall therein.'

Obs. Whence we see and may observe, *that the same word which is a word of life and salvation to the godly, is an occasion of sin and perdition unto the wicked.* The same sun which makes flowers and herbs to smell sweet, makes carrions to smell worse. The same word which made the apostles believe and confess Christ, did also make many others of his disciples go

* Qu. 'to make it his walk?'—G.

back from him, saying, 'This is a hard saying, who can bear it?' John xiii. 60.
So, Acts xiii. 48, the same word which made the unbelieving Jews blaspheme, did make 'as many as did belong unto eternal life believe.' And
when Christ preached, many blasphemed, and said he had a devil; others
trusted and defended him. So saith Paul, the same word to some is, 'the
savour of death unto death, and to some the savour of life unto life,' 2 Cor.
ii. 16; and so in another place he speaks of the same word, 'But we preach
Christ crucified, unto the Jews a stumblingblock, and unto the Greeks
foolishness; but unto them which are called, both Jews and Greeks, Christ
the power of God, and the wisdom of God,' 1 Cor. i. 23, 24. To this
purpose, Peter speaks of Christ, ' Unto you therefore who believe, he is precious; but unto them which are disobedient, &c., a stone of stumbling, and a
rock of offence, even unto them who stumble at the word, being disobedient,
whereunto also they were appointed,' 1 Pet. ii. 7, 8. The reasons are,

Reason 1. Because ' The natural man perceiveth not the things of the
Spirit of God: for they are foolishness unto him; neither can he know
them, because they are spiritually discerned; but he that is spiritual judgeth
all things,' &c., 1 Cor. ii. 14.

Secondly, ' Because they who do evil hate the light,' John iii. 19, and
therefore, cannot love what they hate. ' This,' Christ saith, ' is the condemnation, that light is come into the world, and men loved darkness better
than light, because their deeds were evil.'

Thirdly, Because they are blinded, 2 Cor. iv. 4; therefore they are led
away by the god of this world, Satan, so that they cannot perceive anything
that is spiritual, for God hath not given them a heart to perceive, &c.,
Deut. xxix. 4.

Fourthly, Because they want faith, which is called ' the faith of God's
elect,' Tit. i. 1; and we know, ' without faith it is impossible to please
God,' Heb. xi. 6; for it is said that ' the word profited not those unbelieving Jews, because it was not mingled with faith in those who heard it,'
Heb. iv. 2.

Fifthly, Because the word is like the sun, which causeth plants to smell
sweet, and a dunghill to smell stinking. So it works grace in some, and
extracts the sin and foul vapours out of others.

Use 1. The use is, first, reproof unto them who *stumble at the wholesome doctrines of the word;* of election, reprobation, predestination, and the
like. Such indeed stumble at Christ himself. He is a stumblingblock unto
them, as Peter speaketh, 1 Pet. ii. 8. They stumble at Christ who stumble
at his word.

Use 2. Secondly, *not to love the word the worse, because evil men be made
the worse by it;* which shews rather the mighty power of the word which
discovereth them, and will not let them be hid, unmasking hypocrites to
themselves and others. As we must not like the sun the worse, because it
makes carrion smell; nor the fan, because it winnoweth away the chaff;
so must we not fall out with the word, because it hath these effects upon
wicked men.

Use 3. Lastly, it is for consolation unto them that, when their sin is
reproved, *fall not out with the word, but with their sin.* When they are
excited to duty, they hate their corruption, and do endeavour to walk
honestly without reproof. This shews the word is not the savour of death
unto death to them, but the savour of life unto life; which St Paul makes
a sign of election, ' When they receive the word of God, as the word of
God, with thanksgiving,' 1 Thes. ii. 13. This indeed is a matter of praise,

to give God thanks for his good word, which saves our souls, and comforts us here in the way of all our pilgrimage, till we arrive at heavenly glory.

For conclusion of all, what then remaineth on our part to be done? Surely, to hearken no more to flesh and blood, to the world or the devil; but to hear what God saith in his most holy word, Ps. xxxii. 10, and to frame our hearts with a strong resolution to this ' returning,' here exhorted to. Oh, if we knew the many miseries and sorrows which attendeth wretched and miserable sinners, and sinful courses here and hereafter, it would be our first work to follow God's counsel to his people; to return from our sinful ways; to meet so gracious and merciful a God; that he may, as his promise is, ' heal our backslidings,' and be ' as the dew unto us,' to make us fruitful and abundant in every good and perfect work.

What can be said more for our encouragement than that which hath been delivered in this chapter? God, the party offended, who is Jehovah, God all-sufficient, exhorts us to return unto him, who is able and willing to help. And he also, out of his rich goodness, forewarneth us of the dangerous estate a sinner is in; who, being ' fallen by his iniquity,' ought therefore to pity himself. Return and not run on in a further course of disobedience and backsliding. And words are put in our mouths, dictated by God himself, which needs must be very prevailing with him. What an encouragement is this! Yea further, as we have heard, these petitions are all answered graciously and abundantly, above all they did ask; wherein God surmounteth our desires and thoughts, as we heard at large. Whereby we also may be confident to have our petitions and suits in like sort granted; if we go unto God with his own words and form prescribed. If we ' take with us words' of prayer, we shall be sure to vanquish all our spiritual enemies; for faithful prayer works wonders in heaven and earth, James v. 17. And that God doth not bid us be religious to our loss, he sheweth that we shall lose nothing by following his counsel, and walking in a religious course of life; having abominated our idols, ' He will observe us, and see us,' and be a shelter unto us, having a derivation of fruitfulness from his fulness. ' In me is thy fruit found.'

Lastly, we have heard who can make right use of these things delivered. Only ' the wise and prudent;' such only can understand heavenly things to purpose. ' His secret is with them that fear him,' Psa. xxv. 14; and ' wisdom is only justified of her children,' Mat. xi. 19. When others have no heart given them to perceive God's ways aright, as Moses speaketh, ' transgressors' fall in God's ' right ways,' whilst the just walk comfortably in them. O then let us hate sin every day more and more, and be in love with religion and the ways of God; for that is the true good, which is the everlasting good, that better Mary's part, which shall never be taken away, Luke x. 42. ' Whosoever drinks of this living water shall never thirst again,' John iv. 14. The best things of this world have but a shadow, not the substance of goodness. Let us then be wise for ourselves, and pity ourselves in time, ' whilst it is called to-day,' because, as our Saviour speaks, ' the night approacheth, wherein no man can work,' John ix. 4. O then let us often examine our hearts and covenant with them, let us see our sins as they are, and God's goodness as it is; that our ' scarlet sins' may be done away as a mist from before him, Isa. i. 18. O banish away our atheism, which, by our sinful conversation, proclaimeth us to be of the number of those fools, who have said in their heart that there is no God, Psa. xiv. 1. This serious consideration always makes first a stop, and then a returning; to believe indeed that there is a God who made the world, and a judgment to come.   This, God by Moses, calleth true wisdom indeed, ' To remember our latter end.'   ' Oh,' saith he, ' that they were wise, that they would think of these things,' Deut. xxxii. 29.   Of which things ? The miseries which attend sin here and hereafter ; and the blessings and comforts which follow a godly life both here and hereafter, ' That they would remember their latter end,' the neglect whereof, Jeremiah sheweth, was the cause ' that they came down wonderfully, and had no comforter, because they remembered not their latter end.'*

Therefore, let us study this point well, that there is a God, and a judgment to come ; and this will compel us, even out of self-love, to return from our sinful courses, and make a stop.   By this means, we shall not need a Philip's boy (z) to cry to us every day, we are mortal and must die ; if our meditations once a day be both in heaven and hell.   These strong considerations (aided with strong rational reflectings on ourselves) will keep us within compass, overawe us, and make us quake and tremble to go on in sin ; which is worse than the devil in this, that thereby he became a devil. This will drive us to fly unto God, that he may ' heal our backslidings,' who is described ' with healing under his wings,' Mal. iv. 2 ; who, in the days of his flesh, healed all miserable and ' returning backsliders,' who ever came unto him.   Therefore, let us lay to heart these things, that so we may be kept in soul and body, pure and unspotted, holy and without blame in his sight, until the day of redemption, ' When our mortality shall put on immortality, and our corruptible incorruption, to reign with God for ever and ever,' 1 Cor. xv. 54, seq.

* Qu. Isaiah ? and the reference, xlvii. 7.—G.

NOTES.

(a) P. 256.—' Return,' &c.   It is very emphatical and significant in the original. Cf. Ackerman (*Prophetæ Minores*. . . . . Vienna, 1830) ; and Henderson (8vo, 1845), the latter especially, confirmatory of Sibbes.

(b) P. 286.—' It was well done by Luther, who, in a Catechism,' &c.   See his ' *Catechesis*' in Opera, *in loc.*

(c) P. 287.—' We have some bitter spirits (Lutherans they call them . . . . therefore to be in the sacrament).'   The reference is to the well-known dogma of *consubstantiation* as contrasted with, and even opposed to, the papists' *transubstantiation*. Both are explained in the following sentence from Barrow (Serm. 31, Vol. II.) : ' It may serve to guard us from divers errours, such as are that of the Lutheran *consubstantialists*, and of the Roman *transubstantiators*, who affirm that the body of our Lord is here upon earth at once present in many places (namely), in every place where the host is kept, or the eucharist is celebrated.'   Cf. Richardson, *sub voce.*

(d) P. 296.—' It was well spoken by Lactantius,' &c.   The thought is found several times in his *De Divino Præmio* and *De Opificio Dei* and *De Falsa Religione.*   Cf. Edition by Aldus, 1515, pp.240, 304, and 1, *seq.*

(e) P. 297.—' As the Jews call them, he hath hedges of the commandments.' Consult Kalisch (' Historical and Critical Commentary on the Old Testament . . . Exodus [8vo, 1855]) ; on Exodus xxiii. 19 ; and Maurer there ; and on Deuteronomy xxii. 6.'   For Rabbinical and other lore on the subject, Works of John Gregory, 4to, 1665, pp. 90–98.

(f) P. 303.—' And so we might go on in other resemblances.'   To all wishing to see the analogy carried out with wealth of quaint thought and illustration, we would. commend the ' Soul's Sickness' of Thomas Adams (Works, Vol. I., pp. 471–506) ; also, as not at all inferior, and indeed abounding in even more recondite lore and unexpected flashes of wit, Bishop Gr. Williams, ' Of the Misery of Man,' in his ' Seven Golden Candlesticks.'   (Folio, 1635, pp. 565–661.)

(g) P. 337.—' As we see now in these wars of Germany.'   Cf. Memoir, Vol. I., pp. lvii.–viii.   The ' now' from 1620–21, onwards.

(*h*) P. 347.—' Man is, as it were, a sum of all the excellencies of the creatures ; a little world indeed.' This idea will be found worked out in quaint fashion by Bishop Earle, in his ' Micro-cosmography,' and by Capt. T. Butler, in his ' Little Bible of Man.' 1649.

(*i*) P. 349.—' The word in the original is a " standard-bearer,"' Titus iii. 8. . . . Cf. Ellicott, *in loc.*, together with extracts and illustrations·given in Kypke, Observ. ii. 381 ; Loesner, Obs. p. 430. The word is προιστημι. The noun, προστάτης = a leader, champion. Wycliffe renders it ' Be bisie to be abouen other in good werkis ' (Hexapla . . . . Bagster) ; and, perhaps, ' standard-bearer' catches the idea, if it departs from the exact wording.

(*j*) P. 350.—' The fragrancy of the smell is smelt of passengers as they sail along the coast.' One of Richard Sibbes's hearers, John Milton (see our Memoir, Vol. I., p. liii.), has finely put this :—

> ' . . . . As when to them who sail
> Beyond the Cape of Hope, and now are past
> Mozambique, off at sea north-east winds blow
> *Sabean odours from the spicy shore*
> *Of Araby the blest.'*—*Paradise Lost*, B. IV., 159–163.

(*k*) P. 351.—' The church of God riseth out of the ashes of the martyrs, which hitherto smells sweet, and puts life in those who come after, so precious are they both dead and alive.' The sentiment is preserved by the poet, concerning the ' actions of the just,' in the familiar lines :—

> ' . . . . The actions of the just
> Smell sweet and blossom in. the dust.'
> *(James Shirley*, ' Death's Final Conquest ').

Shirley was a ' student' of Catharine College, Cambridge.

(*l*) P. 355.—' Monica, St Austin's mother, ... he was converted *after* her death.' &c. This is a somewhat singular blunder on the part of Sibbes. Augustine was ' converted' *before* his mother's death, as the touching narrative in the ' Confessions ' has made immortal. Cf. B. VIII., 30 ; B. IX., 17, *et alibi.*

(*m*) P. 370.—' Calvin and Luther . . . . burn their bones,' &c. If this does not apply literally to Calvin and Luther, it yet holds good of many like-minded. Every one remembers what was done to Wycliffe's ' bones,' and also Fuller's characteristic conceits upon the scattered ashes, to which none will refuse Dr Vaughan's approving ' Well-spoken—Honest one !' Cf. Vaughan's John de Wycliffe, D.D., a monograph (4to. 1853), pp. 521, *seq.* To Wycliffe may be added Bucer, concerning the ' burning of whose bones I take the following verses from Faithful Teat's rare ' Ter Tria ' (18mo. 1669, 2d edition, pp. 142, 143).

> ' What though revengeful papists burne
> Dear Bucer's bones? still hope's his urne,
> Till's ashes to a phœnix turne.
> And live afresh.' (From ' Hope.')

(*n*) P. 377.—' The abominable distinctions of the papists of *Latria* and *Dulia*.' That is, λατρεία and δουλεία, commonplaces in the popish controversy. Cf. Faber, ' Difficulties of Romanism,' and almost any of the standard treatises *pro* and *con.*

(*o*) P. 378.—' Calleth them dunghill-gods, and Abel, as it is in this book, vanity,' &c. The allusion of Sibbes in the former is perhaps to Beelzebub, worshipped by the Philistines of Ekron = the fly-god, *i. e.*, dunghill-bred fly. ' Abel ' means ' vanity,' and the reference is not to Abel—the proper name of Adam's second-born son—but to Hosea xii. 11.

(*p*) P. 379.—' Coster himself, a forward Jesuit.' That is, John Costerus or Costerius in his ' Comment . . . . pro Catholicæ Fidei Antiquitate et Veritate,' (Paris, 1569).

(*q*) P. 379.—' Late worthies of our church.' The following are the principal works on the popish controversy, by the eminent writers enumerated :—

1. Bishop Jewel.—(1.) ' Apologia Ecclesiæ Anglicanæ,' 1562. (2.) 'An Apology for Private Mass ; with a learned answsere to it by Bishop Jewell,' 1562. (3.) Various ' Answers ' to Hardinge and others.

2. John Rainolds, D.D.—' The summe of the Conference betweene John Rainoldes and John Hart, touching the Head and Faith of the Church,' &c., &c., 1584, and various editions.

3. William Fulke.—Very many works. For list, consult Watt's Bibl. Brit. *sub nomine.*

4. Dr William Whitaker.—Cf. our Memoir of Sibbes, pp. lxxxi–ii.

5. Andrew Willet.—His great work is his ' Synopsis Papismi,' 1600 ; but he is author of other masterly, if somewhat vehement, treatises on the controversy. Consult Watt *sub nomine.*

6. William Perkins.—His ' Works ' abound in confutations of popish errors, written with great intensity. He has one special treatise of rare merit, ' The Reformed Catholike ; or a Declaration shewing how neere we may come to the present Church of Rome in sundrie points of Religion ; and wherein we must for ever depart from them.' (Cambridge, 1597.)

(*r*) P. 380.—' To say we worship not the image but God . . . so we may see in Arnobius.' Arnobius here referred to was one of the apologists of Christianity in the African church during the third century. His ' Disputationum Adversus Gentes Libri ' (ex Editione Fausti Sabæi, Rome, 1542), remains a still vital book. It has passed through many editions. Again and again the question of image-worship comes up in it.

(*s*) P. 381.—' Rome to be Babylon.' Cf. Canon Wordsworth's conclusive little work, ' Babylon ; or the question considered, " Is the Church of Rome the Babylon of the Apocalypse ?" ' 12mo.

(*t*) P. 381.—' Hedges of the commandments.' Cf. note *e.*

(*u*) P. 383. ' As a great man-pleaser,' &c. Sibbes places in his margin, ' A Scottish Regent, before his execution.' This must refer to the Earl of Morton, Regent of Scotland, beheaded in 1581, on a very doubtful charge of treason. It is difficult to explain Sibbes's use of ' man-pleaser,' in relation to Knox's illustrious friend. But ' man-pleaser ' was a favourite term of reproach with the Puritans, which John Squier, in his extraordinary introduction to his sermon from Luke xviii. 13, thus sarcastically notices, ' If my text should lead me to avouch the dignity and authority of the superiours in our clergy, I should not escape that brand, behold a time-servant and a *man-pleaser* ' (4to, 1637, page 2). Better example far he might have taken from his contemporary, Shakespeare. I refer to the famous saying of Wolsey, (Henry VIII. iii. 2)—

> ' . . . . O Cromwell, Cromwell !
> Had I but serv'd my God with half the zeal
> I serv'd my king, he would not, in mine age,
> Have left me naked to mine enemies.'

(*v*) P. 383.—' Were made gods . . . came . . . to fearful ends.' This holds of nearly all the Cæsars. For ample proof, consult Smith's Dictionary of Greek and Roman Biography and Mythology, under the respective emperors, especially Caligula and Nero.

(*w*) P. 392.—' " I have seen and observed him," some read the words, but very few.' Cf. authorities cited in note *a.*

(*x*) P. 393.—' The same day was that noble victory and conquest in the north parts over the enemies.' The allusion is to the Battle of Pinkie, on September 10. 1547, between the English, under the Earl of Hertford, Protector. and the Scotch, when the latter were totally defeated. It was one of the most decisive victories, with least loss to the conquerors, of any in history. There fell scarcely two hundred of the English ; while, according to the lowest computation, above ten thousand Scots perished, besides fifteen hundred taken prisoners. 1547 (and according to Sibbes, 10th September) is usually reckoned as the ' completion ' of the English Reforma-tion, although the reformed religion was not established until the accession of Elizabeth, in 1558.

(*y*) P. 415.—' Simile mater erroris.' This is a principle which is very often stated, in various forms, in the writings of Bacon.

(*z*) P. 433.—' We shall not need a Philip's boy.' The allusion is to the (I suppose), apocryphal story of Philippus II., father of Alexander the Great, having a boy appointed for the purpose of reminding him, by a daily repetition of it, of his ' mortality.' So sensual and volatile a nature was very unlikely to do so wise a thing.

G.

THE GLORIOUS FEAST OF THE GOSPEL.

THE GLORIOUS FEAST OF THE GOSPEL.

NOTE.

'The Glorious Feast' was published in a thin quarto in 1650. The title-page is given below.* For various mistakes in the pagination of the original edition, consult bibliographical 'List' in our last volume. **G.**

* Title-page :—

THE
GLORIOVS FEAST
OF THE
GOSPEL.
OR,

Christ's gracious Invitation and royall
Entertainment of Believers.
Wherein amongst other things these comfortable
Doctrines are spiritually handled :

Viz
1. *The Marriage Feast between Christ and his Church.*
2. *The vaile of Ignorance and Vnbeliefe removed.*
3. *Christ's Conquest over death.*
4. *The wiping away of teares from the faces of God's people.*
5. *The taking away of their Reproaches.*
6. *The precious Promises of God, and their certaine performance.*
7. *The Divine Authority of the Holy Scriptures.*
8. *The Duty and comfort of waiting upon God.*

Delivered in divers Sermons upon *Isai.* 25 Chap. 6, 7, 8, 9 Verses,
BY
The late Reverend, Learned and faithfull Minister of the Gospell,
RICHARD SIBBS, D.D. Master of *Katharine-*
Hall in *Cambridge,* and Preacher at Grayes-Inne, *London.*
Prov. 9. 1, 2, 3, 4, 5.

Wisdome hath builded her house ; she hath hewen out her seven Pillars.
She hath killed her beasts ; she hath mingled her wine ; she hath also furnished her
Table.
She hath sent forth her Maidens ; she cries, &c.
who so is simple let him turne in hither, &c.
Come eate of my bread, and drink of my wine that I have mingled, &c.

Perused by those that were intrusted to revise his Writings.
London, Printed for *John Rothwell* at the Sun and Fountaine in *Pauls*
Church yard, neare the little North-doore. 1650.

TO THE READER.

So much of late hath been written about the times, that spiritual discourses are now almost out of season. Men's minds are so hurried up and down, that it is to be feared they are much discomposed to think seriously as they ought, of their eternal concernments. Alas! Christians have lost much of their communion with Christ and his saints—the heaven upon earth—whilst they have wofully disputed away and dispirited the life of religion and the power of godliness, into dry and sapless controversies about government of church and state. To recover therefore thy spiritual relish of savoury practical truths, these sermons of that excellent man of God, of precious memory, are published. Wherein thou art presented.

I. *With an invitation to a great and wonderful feast, the marriage feast of the Lamb.* An admirable feast indeed; wherein Jesus Christ, the eternal Son of God, is the bridegroom, where every believer that hath 'put on' the Lord Jesus, Rom. xiii. 14, 'the wedding garment,' Mat. xxii. 11, is not only the guest, but the spouse of Christ, and the bride at this wedding supper. Here Jesus Christ is the master of the feast, and the cheer and provision too. He is the 'Lamb of God,' John i. 29, the 'ram caught in the thicket,' Gen. xxii. 13. He is the 'fatted calf,' Luke. xv. 23. When he was sacrificed, 'wisdom killed her beasts,' Prov. ix. 2. At his death, 'the oxen andf atlings were killed,' Mat. xxii. 4. 'Αληθῶς βρῶσις καὶ ἀληθῶς πόσις. His 'flesh is meat indeed, and his blood is drink indeed,' John vi. 55. And that thou mayest be fully delighted at this feast, Christ is the 'rose of Sharon,' the 'lily of the valley,' Cant. ii. 1. He is a 'bundle of myrrh,' Cant. i. 13, a 'cluster of camphire,' Cant. i. 14; his name is 'an ointment poured out,' Cant. i. 3, and 'his love is better than wine,' Cant. i. 2. In Christ are 'all things ready,' Mat. xxii. 4, for 'Christ is all in all,' Col. iii. 11. And great is the feast that Christ makes for believers, for it is the marriage feast which the great King 'makes for his Son,' Mat. xxii. 2; the great design and aim of the gospel being to exalt the Lord Jesus Christ, and give 'him a name above every name,' Philip. ii. 10. Great is the company that are bid, Luke xiv. 16, Jews and Gentiles. God keeps open house, 'Ho, every one that thirsteth, come,' Isa lv. 1, and 'whosoever will, let him come, and freely take of the water of life,' Rev. xxii. 17. Great is the cheer that is provided. Every guest here hath Asher's portion, 'royal dainties and bread of fatness,' Gen. xlix 20. Here is all excellent best wine, 'wine upon the lees well refined,' Isa. xxv. 6. Here is 'fat things,' yea, 'fat things full of marrow,' Rev. ii. 17, the 'water of life,' Rev. xxii. 17, and the fruit of 'the tree of life which is in the midst of the paradise of God,' Gen. ii. 9. All that is at this feast is of the best, yea, the best of the best.

Here is variety and plenty too. Here is ' bread enough and to spare.'
Caligula and Heliogabalus their feasts, who ransacked the earth, air, and
sea to furnish their tables, were nothing to this. And above all, here is
welcome for every hungry, thirsty soul. *Super omnia vultus accessere boni.*
He that bids thee come, will bid thee welcome. He will not say eat when
his heart is not with thee. The invitation is free, the preparation great,
and the entertainment at this feast—suiting the magnificence of the great
King—is full and bountiful. All which is at large treated of in these excellent sermons, which are therefore deservedly entitled, ' The marriage
Feast between Christ and his Church.' We read of a philosopher that,
having prepared an excellent treatise of happiness, and presenting it unto
a great king, the king answered him, ' Keep your book to yourself, I am
not now at leisure,' (a). Here is an excellent treasure put into thy hand ;
do not answer us, I am not now at leisure. Oh, do not let Christ stand
' knocking at thy heart, who will come and sup with thee,' Rev. iii. 20, and
bring his cheer with him. Oh, let not a ' deceived heart turn thee any
longer aside to feed upon ashes,' Isa. xliv. 20 ; feed no longer with swine
' upon husks,' Luke xv. 16, while thou mayest be filled and satisfied ' with
bread in thy father's house,' Luke xv. 17.

But this is not all ; if thou wilt be pleased to peruse this book, thou wilt
find there are many other useful, seasonable, and excellent subjects handled
besides the marriage-feast.

II. Jesus Christ hath not only provided a feast, but because he is desirous
that all those for whom it is provided should come to it (which only they
do that believe), *he takes away the veil of ignorance and unbelief from off
their hearts ;* and here you shall find this skilful preacher hath excellently
discoursed what this veil is, how it naturally lies upon all, and is only
removed by the Spirit of Christ. And if the Lord hath ' destroyed this
covering from off thy heart,' we doubt not, but the truth of this heavenly
doctrine will shine comfortably into thy soul.

III. Jesus Christ, to make his bounty and mercy further appear in this
feast, *he hath given his guests the ' bread of life,' and hath secured them from
the fear of death.* They need not fear. There is no *mors in ollâ* at this
feast. We may feast without fear. Jesus Christ by his ' tasting of death
hath swallowed it up in victory,' 1 Cor. xv. 54. Christ doth not make his
people such a feast as it is reported Dionysius the tyrant once made
for his flatterer Damocles, who set him at a princely table, but hanged a
drawn sword in a small thread over his head.* But Christ would have us
triumph over the king of fears, who was slain by the death of Christ, and
we thereby delivered from the bondage of the fear of death, Heb. ii. 14, 15.

At other feasts they were wont of old to have a death's head served in
amongst other dishes, to mind them in the midst of all their mirth of their
mortality (which practice of the heathens condemns the ranting jollity of
some loose professors in these times). Κατῆλθεν εἰς θάνατον ἀθάνατος, καὶ τῶ
θανάτῳ καθεῖλε θάνατον. But here, Christ serves in death's head, as David
' the head of Goliah,' 1 Sam. xxxi. 9, the head of a slain and conquered
death. Our Sampson by his own death ' hath destroyed death, and hath
thereby ransomed us from the hand of the grave, and hath redeemed us
from death,' Hos. xiii. 14, and the slavish fear of it. All which is at large
handled in these following sermons for thy comfort and joy, that thou
mayest triumph in his love, through whom thou art more than conqueror.

* For this well-known anecdote, consult Cicero (*Tusc.* v. 21.), and Horace (*Carm.*
iii., l. 17).—G.

IV. Because ' it is a merry heart that makes a continual feast,' Prov. xv. 15, and that this feast might be a gaudy-day* indeed unto thy soul, Christ doth here promise, ' to wipe away all tears from off the faces of his people,' Isa. xxv. 8. The gospel hath comforts enough to make glad the hearts of the saints and people of God. The ' light of God's countenance' will refresh them with ' joy unspeakable and glorious,' 1 Pet. i. 8, in the midst ' of the valley of the shadow of death,' Psa. xxiii. 4. A truly godly person can weep for his sins, though the world smile never so much upon him ; and 'though he be never so much afflicted in the world, yet he can and will ' rejoice in the God of his salvation,' Hab. iii. 18. In these ser-mons thou hast this gospel-promise sweetly opened and applied ; wherein thou shalt find directions when, and for what, to mourn and weep, and the blessedness of all true mourners, ' whose sorrow shall be turned into joy,' John xvi. 20.

V. In these sermons you shall further find, *that though Jesus Christ respect his people highly, and entertain them bountifully, yet they have but coarse usage in the world, who* are wont to revile them as ' fools' and ' mad-men,' as ' seditious rebels,' ' troublers of Israel,' ' proud and hypocritical persons.' But blessed are they that do not ' stumble at this stone of offence,' Rom. ix. 32, that wear the ' reproaches of Christ as their crown,' and by ' well-doing put to silence the ignorance of foolish men,' 1 Pet. ii. 15 ; for let the world load them with all their revilings, yet ' the spirit of glory rests upon them,' 2 Cor. xii. 9, and in due time he will roll away their reproach, ' and bring forth their judgment as the light, and their righteous-ness as the noon-day,' Ps. xxxvii. 6.

VI. And because a Christian here hath more in hope than in hand, more in reversion than in possession, ' walks by faith' rather than sense, and ' lives by the word of God, and not by bread alone,' Mat. iv. 4, thou shalt have here, Christian reader, a sweet discourse *of the precious promises of Christ* which he hath left us here to stay the stomach of the soul, till we come to that feast of feasts in heaven ; that by this glimpse we might in part know the ' greatness of that glory which shall be revealed,' 1 Peter v. 1 ; that the first fruits might be a pawn of the harvest, and the ' earnest of the Spirit,' Ephes. i. 14, a pledge of that full reward we shall have in heaven, where we shall be brimful of those ' pleasures that are at God's right hand for ever,' Ps. xvi. 11. Christ hath given us promises to uphold our faith and hope, till faith be perfected in fruition, and hope end in vision, till Jesus Christ, who is here the object of our faith, be the reward of our faith for ever.

VII. Now because the comfort of the promises is grounded in the faith-fulness of him that hath promised, this godly and learned man, hath strongly asserted *the divine authority of the holy Scriptures*, proving that they are θεόπνευστοι, that they are the very word of God, that they are ἀυτόπιστοι and ἀξόπιστοι, worthy of all acceptation, and belief, for their own sakes ; a truth very seasonable for these times, to antidote thee against the poison-full errors of blasphemous anti-scripturists.

VIII. Lastly, because that God often takes a long day for performance of the promise, thou shalt find herein the doctrine *of waiting upon God*, ex-cellently handled ; a duty which we earnestly commend unto thy practice, as suitable to these sad times. Say, O say with the church, ' In the way of thy judgments, O Lord, we have waited for thee,' Isa. xxvi. 8 ; and with the prophet, ' I will wait upon the Lord that hideth his face from the

---

* That is, = a ' day of rejoicing.'—G.

house of Jacob, and I will look for him,' Isa. viii. 17. And rest assured, that ' none of the seed of Jacob shall seek him in vain,' Isa. xlv. 19 ; he will not ' disappoint their hope, nor make their faces ashamed that wait for him,' Isa. xlix. 23.

Thus we have given you a short prospect of the whole, a brief sum of that treasure which these sermons contain. We need say nothing of the author ; his former labours ' sufficiently speak for him in the gates,' Prov. xxxi. 23 ; his memory is highly honoured amongst the godly-learned. He that enjoys the glory of heaven, needs not the praises of men upon earth. If any should doubt of these sermons, as if they should not be truly his, whose name they bear, let him but observe the style, and the excellent and spiritual matter herein contained, and he will, we hope, be fully satisfied. Besides, there are many ear-witnesses yet living, who can clear them from any shadow of imposture. They come forth without any alteration, save only some repetitions (which the pulpit did well bear), are here omitted.

The Lord make these, and all other the labours of his servants, profitable to his church. And the Lord so ' destroy the veil ' from off thy heart, that thou mayest believe, and by faith come to this feast, the joy and comfort whereof may swallow up all the slavish fear of death, dry up thy tears, and roll away all reproach. And the Lord give thee a waiting heart, to stay thy soul upon the name of the Lord, to believe his word, and his faithful promises, that in due time thou mayest ' rejoice in the God of thy salvation.' This is the earnest prayer of

ARTHUR JACKSON.*
JAMES NALTON.†
WILL. TAYLOR.‡

LONDON, *April* 19. 1650.

---

* Jackson, like Sibbes, was a native of Suffolk, having been born at Little Waldingfield, in 1593. He won the respect of even Laud. It is told that when the ' Book of Sports ' was commanded to be publicly read, he refused compliance, and was complained of for his contumacy to the Archbishop, but that prelate would not suffer him to be molested. ' Mr Jackson,' said he, ' is a quiet and peaceable man, and therefore I will not have him meddled with.' Sheldon manifested like esteem for him. At the Restoration, when Charles II. made his entrance into the city, Jackson was appointed by his brethren to present to him a Bible, as he passed through St Paul's Churchyard, which was in his parish ; when he addressed the king in a congratulatory speech, which was graciously received. He was also one of the Commissioners of the Savoy. He died, Aug. 5. 1666, one of the most venerable of the ' ejected ' two thousand. Consult ' Nonconformist's Memorial,' vol. i. pp. 120–124 ; also ' Memoir ' prefixed to his ' Annotations,' vol. iv.

† This ' man of God,' beloved by Richard Baxter, and all his like-minded contemporaries, was called ' The Weeping Prophet,' because of his peculiarly tender and tearful nature. He also was one of the ' two thousand,' but died shortly afterwards in 1663. In a copy of Sedgwick's ' Bowels of Tender Mercy Sealed in the Everlasting Covenant' (folio 1661), in our possession, is the following inscription, Mary Nalton, her book, given by her dear husband, Ja. Nalton, Sept. 14. 1661.' Consult ' Noncf. Mem.,' vol. i. pp. 142–144.

‡ This ' William Taylor,' was probably the author of a sermon in the ' Morning Exercises,' and the same for whom Dr Spurstowe preached a remarkable funeral sermon. He died in 1661.   G.

THE MARRIAGE FEAST BETWEEN CHRIST AND HIS CHURCH.

In this mountain shall the Lord of hosts make unto all people a feast of fat things, a feast of wines on the lees; of fat things full of marrow, of wine on the lees well refined.—ISAIAH XXV. 6.

IN the former chapter the holy prophet having spoken of the miseries and desolation of the church, in many heavy, sad, and doleful expressions; as ' the vine languisheth, the earth is defiled under the inhabitants thereof, because they have transgressed the laws, changed the ordinance, and broken the everlasting covenant; therefore the earth shall be accursed, and they that dwell therein shall not drink wine with a song,' &c. Here you see all sweetness and rejoicing of heart is departed from them; yet even in the midst of all these miseries, God, the God of comforts, makes sweet and gracious promises to his church, to raise it out of its mournful estate and condition. And therefore the prophet, in the former part of this chapter, speaks of blessing God for the destruction of his enemies, and for his great love to his church. And when he had spoken of the ruin of the enemy, he presently breaks out with thanksgiving, breathing forth abundant praises to his God; as it is the custom of holy men, guided by the motion of the blessed Spirit of God, upon all occasions, but especially for benefits to his church, to praise his name, not out of ill affection at the destruction of the adversaries, but at the execution of divine justice, for the fulfilling of the truth of his promise; as in the first verse of this chapter, ' O Lord, thou art my God; I will exalt thee, I will praise thy name; for thou hast done wonderful things; thy counsels of old are faithfulness and truth.' When the things that were promised of old were brought to pass, the church was ever ready to give God the glory of his truth. Therefore, rejoice not when thine enemies fall; but when the enemies of the Lord are brought to desolation, then we may, nay, we ought to sing, ' Hallelujah' to him that liveth for ever and ever.

I will now fall upon the very words of my text. ' In this mountain shall the Lord of hosts make unto all people a feast of fat things,' &c. These words they are prophetical, and cannot have a perfect performance all at once, but they shall be performed gradually. The promise of ' a new heaven and a new earth,' 2 Pet. iii. 13, shall be performed. The conversion of

the Jews, and the bringing in of the fulness of the Gentiles, shall gradually
be brought to pass. All the promises that ever God hath made, before the
second coming of Christ to judgment, shall be accomplished. God hath
made his peace with us in the gospel of peace ; and when all these promises
shall be fulfilled, then all imperfection shall be done away, and we shall
never be removed from our Rock ; but our joy shall then be full. Nay,
even in this life we have some degrees of perfection. We have grace, and
the means of grace ; the ordinances of Christ, and a testimony of everlasting glory.

' In this mountain will the Lord of hosts make a feast.'

In these words ye have set down a glorious and a royal feast ; and the
place where this feast is to be kept is ' Mount Zion ;' the *feast-maker* is ' the
Lord of Hosts ;' the *parties invited*, are ' all people ;' *the issues of it, and the
provision* for the feast, are ' fat things,' and ' wine' of the best ; a feast of
the best of the best, a feast of the fat and of the marrow, a feast of ' wine
on the lees well refined.'

Here you may see that God doth veil heavenly things under earthly
things, and condescends so low as to enter into the inward man by the
outward man. For our apprehensions are so weak and narrow, that we
cannot be acquainted with spiritual things, but by the inward working of
the Spirit of the Almighty.

This ' mountain' is *the place* where this feast is made, even ' mount
Zion ;' which is a type and figure of the church, called in Scripture, ' the
holy mountain.' For as mountains are raised high above the earth, so the
church of God is raised in excellency and dignity above all the sorts of
mankind.

Obs. 1. *As much as men above beasts, so much is the church raised above all
men.* This mountain is above all mountains. The ' mountain of the Lord'
is above all mountains whatsoever. ' Thou, O mountain, shalt stand immoveable,' when all other mountains shall smoke, if they are but touched.
This is the mountain of mountains. The church of God is most excellent
in glory and dignity, as ye may see in the latter end of the former chapter,
how the glory of the church puts down all other glories whatsoever. ' The
moon,' saith the prophet, ' shall be confounded, and the sun ashamed, when
the Lord of Hosts shall reign in Mount Zion, and in Jerusalem, and before
his ancients gloriously.' So that the brightness of the church shall put
down the glory of the sun and of the moon. Thus you see the church of
God is a mountain.

Reason. First, *Because God hath established it upon a stronger foundation
than all the world besides*. It is founded upon the goodness and power and
truth of God. Mountains of brass and iron are not so firm as this mountain. For what sustains the church but the word of God ? And being built
upon his word and truth, it may very well be called a mountain, for it shall
be as mount Zion, which shall never be removed, Ps. cxxv. i. It may be
moved, but never removed. Thus, in regard to the firmness and stability
thereof, it may rightly be termed a mountain.

Obs. 2. Again, *we may here speak in some sort of the visibility of the
church*. But here will arise a quarrel for the papists, who when they hear
of this mount, they presently allude* it to their church, Their church, say
they, is a mount ; so saith the Scripture.

I answer, *Firstly*, We confess in some sort their church to be a mount
(though not this mount), for Babylon is built on seven hills ; but if this

* That is, = ' make it refer to.'—G.

prove her a church, it is an antichristian church. *Secondly*, That the
Catholic Protestantial* church had always a being, though sometimes invisible. The apostle, writing to the Romans, exhorts them ' not to be high-
minded, but fear;' for, saith he, ' if God hath broken off the natural
branches, perhaps he will break off you also,' Rom. xi. 21, 24. And, indeed,
for their pride and haughtiness of mind, they are at this day broken off.
Christ, that ' walks between the seven golden candlesticks,' Rev. i. 12, did
never say that the church of Smyrna or Ephesus should always remain a
visible church to the eyes of the world, neither were they; for to this very
day they lie under bondage and slavery to the Turk. The mount hath
been always visible, though not always alike gloriously visible. For there
will be a time when the church shall fly into the wilderness, Rev. xii. 6.
Where, then, shall be the glorious visibility of the church? There is a
time when all shall follow the beast. The papists themselves confess that
in antichrist's time the church shall scarce be visible. The essence of a
thing and the quality of a thing may differ. The church is a church, and
visible, but not always equally, and alike gloriously visible; yet those that
had spiritual eyes, and did look upon things with the spectacles of the
Scripture, they could always declare the church was visible; for, from the
beginning of the world, the church had always lustre enough sufficient to
delight, and draw the elect, and so shall have to the end of the world,
though sometimes the church may have a mist before it, as Austin speaks:
' It is no wonder that thou canst not see a mountain, for thou hast no eyes.'
But the papists have seen this mountain. As they have always been bloody
persecutors of the church, they have seen enough to confound them. For
we have nothing in our church, but they have the same; only ours is
refined, and freed from idolatry. We have two sacraments, they have
seven. We have Scripture, they have traditions, which they equal with it.
We have Scriptures pure, they, corrupt. So that our church was in the
midst of theirs, as a sound and more uncorrupt part in a corrupt body.

This mountain is the church. ' The Lamb standeth upon mount Zion,
and with him a hundred forty and four thousand, having his Father's name
written in their foreheads,' Rev. xiv. 1. Christ standeth in the church,
and standing in mount Zion he is accompanied with those that his Father
hath given to him before the world was. Therefore those that belong to
this holy mountain, they are Christ's. ' And in this mountain shall the
Lord of hosts make a feast for all people.' And this feast is a royal feast,
a marriage feast, wherein the joy and comfort of God's people are set down
by that which is most comfortable among men. *The founder of the feast* is
' the Lord of hosts.' It is only he that is able to prepare a table in the
wilderness, that is mighty and of ability to feast his church with a spiritual
and holy banquet. We all live at his table for the feeding of our bodies,
but much more in regard of our souls. He can make a feast for the whole
man, for he is Lord of the conscience; and he is to spread a table for the
whole world. Nay, more, if there were so many, he can furnish a table for
ten thousand worlds. He is the God of all spiritual comforts, and the
' God of all consolation.' He is infinite, and can never be drawn dry, for he
is the fountain of eternal life. All graces and comforts in the Scripture are
called the comforts and graces of the Holy Spirit, because God is the giver
of them by his Spirit. Who can take away the wound of a guilty conscience, but he that hath set the conscience in the hearts of men? He, if
he pleaseth, can take away the burden of a grieved conscience, and supply

* That is, ' Protestant.'—G.

it, instead thereof, with new and solid comforts. He knoweth all the windings and turnings of the soul, where all the pain and grief lieth; and he cannot but know it, because he only is above the soul. He is therefore the fittest to make the soul a feast. He only can do it, and he will do it.

' In this mountain shall the Lord of Hosts make a feast.'

Why is he called the ' Lord of Hosts?'

It is an usual term to set forth the glory of God, to make his power and the greatness of his majesty known amongst the children of men.

' He shall make a feast for all people.'

Those that are invited to this glorious feast are 'all people.' None excepted, none excluded, that will come to Christ! Some of all sorts, of all nations, of all languages! This hath relation to the time of the gospel. The church at first had its being in particular families, but afterwards more enlarged. The church at the first was of the daughters of men, and the sons of God. The children of the church mingled with a generation of corrupt persons, that would keep in no bounds; but after Abraham's time there was another generation of the church, that so it was a little more enlarged. Then there was a third generation, a divided generation, consisting of Jews and Gentiles. So that, when Christ came into the world, the bounds of the church began to enlarge themselves more and more, so that now it is in this happy condition, ' Come ye all unto me, all that are heavy laden,' Mat. xi. 28. Both Jews and Gentiles, all are invited, whosoever they are, ' nothing is now unclean,' Acts x. 15. Christ is come, and hath made ' to all people a feast of fat things.' It must be a feast, and of fat things, for all the world shall be the better for it. The Jews shall be converted, and the fulness of the Gentiles shall come in. And yet it is no prejudice to any particular man, because the things ye are to taste of are spiritual. Go to all the good things in the world : the more one hath of them the less another must have, because they are earthly, and so are finite. But in spiritual things all may have the whole, and every man in particular. Every man enjoyeth the light of the sun in particular, and all enjoy it too. So the whole church, and only the church, enjoys the benefit and comfort of this feast; but under the name of this church come all the elect, both ·Jews and Gentles, and therefore it must be the Lord of Hosts that can make such a feast as this is, a feast for all people. No other is able to do it.

This feast is ' a feast of fat things, full of marrow and of wine on the lees well refined,' *the best that can be imagined, the best of the best.* A feast is promised, a spiritual feast. The special graces and favours of God are compared to a feast made up of the best things, full of all varieties and excellencies, and the chief dish that is all in all, is Christ, and all the gracious benefits we by promise can in any wise expect from him. All other favours and blessings, whatsoever they are, are but Christ dished out, as I may speak, in several offices and attributes. He is the original of comfort, the principle of grace and holiness. All is included in Christ. Ask of him and ye shall obtain, even the forgiveness of your sins, peace of conscience, and communion of saints. Ask of Christ, as of one invested with all privileges for the good of others. But yet this is by his death. He is the feast itself. He is dished out into promises. Have you a promise of the pardon of sins? It is from Christ. Wouldst thou have peace of conscience? It is from Christ. Justification and redemption? It is from Christ. The love of God is derived to us by Christ, yea, and all that we have that is good is but Christ parcelled out.

Now, I will shew why Christ, with his benefits, prerogatives, graces, and comforts, is compared to a feast.

First. In regard *of the choice of the things.* In a feast all things are of the best ; so are the things we have in Christ. Whatsoever favours we have by Christ, they are choice ones. They are the best of every thing. Pardon for sin is a pardon of pardon. The title we have for heaven, through him, is a sure title. The joy we have by him is the joy of all joys. The liberty and freedom from sin, which he purchased for us by his death, is perfect freedom. The riches of grace we have by him are the only lasting and durable riches. Take anything that you can, if we have it by Christ, it is of the best. All worldly excellencies and honours are but mere shadows to the high excellencies and honour we have in Christ. No joy, no comfort, no peace, no riches, no inheritance to be compared with the joy, peace, and inheritance which we have in Christ. Whatsoever we have by him, we have it in a glorious manner. And therefore he is compared to fat, to ' fat things full of marrow,' ' to wine, to wine on the lees,' that preserveth the freshness of it ; the best wine of all, that is not changed from vessel to vessel, but keepeth its strength. And, indeed, the strength and vigour of all floweth from Jesus Christ in covenant with us.

The love of Christ is the best love, and he himself incomparably the best, and hath favours and blessings of the choicest.

Second. Again, as in a feast, besides choice, *there is variety,* so in Christ there is variety answerable to all our wants. Are we foolish ? He is wisdom. Have we guilt in our consciences ? He is righteousness, and this righteousness is imputed unto us. Are we defiled ? He is sanctification. Are we in misery ? He is our redemption. If there be a thousand kinds of evils in us, there is a thousand ways to remedy them by Jesus Christ. Therefore, the good things we have by Christ are compared to all the benefits we have in this world. In Christ is choice and variety. Are we weak ? He is meat to feed us, that we may be strong. He will refresh us. He is the best of meats. He is marrow. So, are our spirits faint ? He is wine. Thus we have in Christ to supply all our wants. He is variety.

There is a plant among the Indians called by the name of *coquus ;* * the fruit thereof serveth for meat and drink, to comfort and refresh the body. It yieldeth that whereof the people make apparel to clothe themselves withal, and also that which is physical,† very good against the distempers of the body. And if God will infuse so much virtue into a poor plant, what virtue may we expect to be in Christ himself? He feedeth our souls to all eternity, puts upon us the robes of righteousness, heals the distempers of our souls. There is variety in him for all our wants whatsoever. He is food, physic, and apparel to clothe us ; and when we are clothed with him, we may with boldness stand before the majesty of God. He is all in all. He is variety, and all. There is something in Christ answerable to all the necessities of God's people, and not only so, but to their full content in everything.

Third. Again, as there is variety in a feast, so there is *sufficiency, full sufficiency.* ' We beheld the only begotten Son of God, full of grace and truth,' John i. 14. And being full of grace, he is wise, and able to furnish this heavenly banquet with enough of all sorts of provisions fit for the soul to feed upon. There is abundance of grace, and excellency, and sufficiency in Christ. And it must needs be, because he is a Saviour of God's own sending. . ' Labour not therefore for the meat that perisheth, but for the

That is, ' cocoa.'—G.   † That is, ' medicinal.'—G.

meat that the Son of God shall give you; for him hath God the Father sealed,' John vi. 27; that is, sent forth for this purpose, to ' feed the church of God,' 1 Pet. v. 2. As there is an all-sufficiency in God, so in Christ, who by the sacrificing of himself was able to give satisfaction to divine justice. Therefore saith he, ' My flesh is meat indeed, and my blood is drink indeed,' John vi. 55; that is, spiritually to the soul he is food indeed, and can satisfy God's justice. If we consider him as God alone, he is a ' consuming fire,' Heb. xii. 29; or as a man alone, he can do nothing; but considered as God-man, he is meat indeed, and drink indeed. And now the soul is content with that which divine justice is contented withal. Though our conscience be large, yet God is larger and above our consciences. Therefore, as there is variety of excellency, so is there sufficiency and fulness in Christ. What he did, he did to the full. He is a Saviour, and he filleth up that name to the full. His pardon for sin is a full pardon; his merits for us are full merits; his satisfaction to divine justice a full satisfaction; his redemption of our souls and bodies a full redemption. Thus all he did was full.

Fourth. A feast is for *company*. It is *convivium*. There is converse at it. So Cicero prefers the name of *convivium* among the Latins before the Greek name συμπόσιον (b). And this feast is not for one. We are all invited to it. The excellency of Christ's feast consisteth in the communion of saints; for whosoever takes part of it, their spirits must agree one with another. Love is the best and chiefest dish in this feast. The more we partake of the sweetness of Christ, the more we love one another. Christ by his Spirit so works in the hearts of the children of men, that, bring a thousand together of a thousand several nations, and within a little while you shall have them all acquainted one with another. If they be good, there is agreement of the spirit and sympathy between them. There is a kindred in Christ. He is the true Isaac. The death of Christ and the blood of Christ is the ground of all union and joy and comfort whatsoever. The blood of Christ sprinkled upon the conscience will procure that peace of conscience that shall be a continual feast unto the soul. This feast must needs be wonderful comfortable, for we do not feast with those that are like ourselves, but we feast with God the Father, and the Holy Spirit, sent by Christ, procured by the death of Christ. The angels at this feast attend us; therefore, it must needs be joyful. No joy comparable to the joy of a feast. This is not every feast. This is a marriage feast, at which we are contracted to Christ. Now, of all feasts, marriage feasts are most sumptuous. This is a marriage feast for the King's Son, for Christ himself; and therefore of necessity it must be full of all choice varieties, and of the sweetest of things, of the most excellentest of things, and of the quintessence of things. Here is all joy that belongeth to a feast. Here it is to be had with Christ. What acquaintance can be more glorious than that which is to be had between Jesus Christ and a Christian soul? when we have hope of better things to come, then we find the sweetness of this communion. No harmony in the world can be so sweet as the harmony maintained between Christ and the soul. When we have this, and are made one with God in Christ, our joy must needs then be unspeakable. When the contract is once made between the soul and Christ, there cannot but be abundant joy. When the soul is joined with Christ by faith, it cannot but solace itself in a perpetual jubilee and a perpetual feast in some degrees.

Fifth. Again, for a feast ye have *the choicest garments*, as at the marriage of the Lamb, ' white and fine linen,' Rev. xix. 8, which is the righteousness of the saints. When God seeth these robes upon us and the Spirit of Christ in us, then there is a robe of righteousness imputed, and a garment of sanctity, whereby our souls are clothed. So this is a feast that must have wonderful glorious attire ; and when this marriage shall be consummated, we are sure to have a garment of glory put upon us.

Sixth. This was signified in old time by the Jews.

1. In the feast of the passover (not to name all resemblances, but only one or two). *The lamb for the passover,* you know, was chosen out of the flock from amongst the rest four days before the time appointed for that feast. So Christ is the true Paschal Lamb, chosen of God before the foundation of the world was laid, to be slain for us.

2. Again, *manna* was a type of Christ. It came from heaven to feed the hungry bodies of the Israelites in the wilderness. Even so came Christ, sent from God the Father, to be the eternal food and upholder of the souls and bodies of every one of us. Manna was white and sweet ; so was Christ, white in righteousness and holiness, and also sweet to delight the soul. Manna fell upon the tents in the night ; and Christ came when darkness was spread over all the world. God gave manna freely from heaven ; so Christ was a free gift, and he freely gave himself to death, even to the cursed death of the cross, for us. All, both poor and rich, they gathered manna. Christ is a common food for king and subject. All take part of Christ. Neither Jew nor Gentile are exempted, but all may come and buy freely without money. Of this manna he that had least had enough. So here he that hath least of Christ, though he take him with a trembling hand, yet he shall have enough, for Christ is his. Whosoever hath the least grace, if it be true and sound, hath grace enough to bring him to eternal life. The Jews wondered at the manna, saying, What thing is this ? (*c*). So it is one of Christ's names to be called ' Wonderful,' Isa. ix. 6. Grace and favour from Christ is true spiritual manna to the soul. Manna fell in the wilderness : even so must we remain in the wilderness of this wretched world until we come to heaven. Christ is manna to us, and very sweet in the conveyance of his word and sacraments. When the Israelites came into the land of Canaan the manna ceased, not before. So when we come to heaven, the elect's purchased possession, we shall have another kind of manna for our souls. We shall not there feed on Christ, as in the sacrament ; no, but we shall see him ' face to face, and know as we are known,' 1 Cor. xiii. 12. In the wilderness of this world it is fit God should convey this heavenly manna to the soul whatsoever way he pleaseth. Manna could not fall until the Israelites had spent all the provision they brought with them out of Egypt ; and we cannot taste of that heavenly manna of our Father until our souls are drawn away from all worldly dependences and carnal delights. Then, indeed, manna will be sweet and precious.

What is this heavenly manna, what is Christ and his Father, what is the word and sacraments, to a depraved, vicious heart, stuffed full with earthly vanities ? Alas ! it loatheth all these. As none tasted of manna but those that came out of Egypt, so none shall taste of Christ but those that are not of the world, that are come out of Egypt, out of sin and darkness. Manna fell only about the tents of Israel, and in no other part of the world, but only there, that none might have the privilege to eat of it but God's peculiar, chosen ones. Christ falls upon the tents of the righteous, and none shall taste of this blessed, spiritual food but such as are the Israel of God, such as are of the church, such as feel the burden of sin and groan under it. Oh ! the very taste of this heavenly manna is sweet to their souls,

and to none but them.   Thus ye see the feast that Christ maketh for us
in mount Zion, and that this manna doth typify Christ with all his benefits.

3.   Again, *the hard rock in the wilderness*, when it was strucken* with the
rod of Moses, presently water gushed out in abundance, which preserved
life to the Israelites ; so Christ, the rock of our salvation, the strength of
his church, the rock and fortress of all his saints, when his precious side
was gored with the bloody lance upon the cross, the blood gushed out, and
in such a manner and such abundance, that by the shedding thereof our
souls are preserved alive.   He is both manna and the rock of water.   Manna
had all in it, so had the rock ; and all necessities are plentifully supplied by
Christ.   The church of God hath always had bread to satisfy spiritual
hunger.   It never wanted necessary comforts.   It is said, Rev. xii. 6,
' When the church fled into the wilderness, God fed her there,' alluding
to the children of Israel fed by manna.   The Jews did not want in the
wilderness, nor the church of God never wanted comfort, though in the
midst of the persecution and oppression of all her enemies.   When Elias
was in the wilderness, he was fed,' 1 Kings xvii. 4, 6.   The church of God
shall not only be fed in her body, but in her soul, for Christ hath hidden
manna for his elect.   This doth typify the exceeding joy of the church, the
hidden manna, ' that neither eye hath seen, nor ear heard of, neither
can it enter into the heart of man to conceive of those joys,' 1 Cor. ii. 9,
that the church of God shall have when the marriage shall be consummated.
Joy in the Holy Ghost, and peace of conscience, they are hid from the world,
and sometimes from God's people themselves, though they shall enjoy them
hereafter.

4.   *All the former feasts* in times past were but types of this.   The feast
of tabernacles, the feast of the passover, the spiritual manna, and all other
holy feasts, were but to signify and to shew forth this feast by Christ.   But
there is this difference between the type and the thing signified.   By the
type, the passover lamb was quite eaten up ; but this passover, Christ, that
was slain for sin, can never be eaten up.   We feed upon him with our souls.
He cannot be consumed as the passover lamb, nor as manna, which was
gone when the sun arose.   Yea, that manna that was laid up for a remembrance before the ark, became nothing, but Christ is in heaven for evermore for the soul to feed upon.   Though these were resemblances, yet these
failed, as it is fit resemblances should fail, that is, come short of the body
of the thing itself.   Thus you see the spiritual comforts of a Christian may
well and fitly be compared to a feast.

5.   Thus you see God provideth a feast, and inviteth all.   *In the sacrament you have a feast*, a feast of varieties, not only bread, but wine—to shew
the variety and fulness of comfort in Christ.   He intendeth full comfort.
As for our adversaries the papists, they have dry feasts.   They give the
people the bread, but the wine they keep for themselves.   But God in Christ
intendeth us full comfort.   Whatsoever Christ did, it was full.   His merits
are complete, and his joy was full.   He is fulness itself ; and, therefore,
whatsoever comes from him must needs be, as he himself is, both full and
sweet.   He intendeth us full consolation.

Use. Therefore, we ought to be prepared to partake of this feast, in such
a manner as that we may have full joy, and full comfort ; for there is in
Christ enough to satisfy all the hungry souls in the world, he himself being
present at this heavenly banquet.   ' All fulness dwells in him,' Col. i. 19,
from which ' we have all received, and grace for grace.'   Therefore,

* That is, ' struck.'—G.

1. *Let us labour to have large hearts:* for as our faith groweth more and more, so we shall carry more comfort and more strength from this holy feast. As the poor widow, if her vessels had not failed, the oil had not ceased; if there had been more vessels, there had been more oil, 2 Kings iv. 6. Our souls are as these vessels. Let us therefore labour, and make it our great business to have large souls, souls capable to drink in this spiritual oil of gladness; for as much faith as we bring to Christ, so much comfort we shall carry from him. The favours of God in Christ being infinite, the more we fetch from him, the more glory we give unto him. But if they were finite, we should offend his bounty, he might soon be drawn dry, and so send us away with an uncomfortable answer, that he was not able to relieve us. But Christ is infinite, and the more we have from him, the more we may have. 'To him that hath shall be given,' Mat. xiii. 12. The oftener we go to Christ, the more honour and glory we bring unto him. This is a banquet to the full.

We are now come to the banquet, and Christ is the founder of it; nay, he is the feast itself. He is the author of it, and he it is that we feed upon.

Use 2. Let us labour not to be straight* receivers of the sacrament, but suck in abundance from Christ with a great deal of delight, that we may come together not for the worse but the better, considering what a great deal of strength and grace is required as very necessary for the maintaining of spiritual life.

THE SECOND SERMON.

In this mountain shall the Lord of hosts make unto all people a feast of fat things, a feast of wines on the lees; of fat things full of marrow, of wines on the lees well refined.—ISAIAH XXV. 6.

I HAVE shewed that Christ and his benefits are compared to a feast, and in what respects they are fitly resembled by a feast, and have pressed that we should prepare for it, first by getting large hearts. Now, in the second place, that we may have comfort at this feast, *we must labour for spiritual appetite;* for to what end and purpose is that man at a feast that hath no stomach? I shall therefore shew what means we are to use to get eager stomachs and holy appetites after this feast.

(1.) *The appetite is raised with sour things,* as anguish of spirit and mournfulness of heart for sin. If we will ever relish Christ aright, we must labour to have a quick apprehension of our sins. We must do as the Jews did at the passover. They ate it with sour herbs, that they might thereby have the sharper stomachs. So must we. We must cast our eyes into our own hearts, and consider what vile wretches we are, how full of sin and vanity; and this will be as sour herbs to the Paschal Lamb. We must join the sweet benefits and privileges that we have in Christ with the consideration of our own wretched and miserable condition, and then this heavenly ordinance cannot but be sweet and comfortable to our souls. I beseech you, enter into your own souls, and consider seriously under what guilt you lie, and this will whet your appetite. 'A full stomach despiseth the honeycomb,' Prov. xxvii. 7; but in this appetite there is sense of emptiness, and from that sense of emptiness pain, and from pain an earnest desire of satisfaction. Thus it is in spiritual things. We want Christ, and all the spiritual comforts that flow from him. There is an emptiness in us, and we

* Qu. 'strait?'—ED.

see a need every day to feed upon the mercies of God in Christ. There is an emptiness in our souls, and there must be a sense of that emptiness, and pain from that sense, which must stir up a strong endeavour to follow after that that we do desire. Then Christ indeed is sweet, when we find our souls hungering and thirsting after him.

(2.) Again, if so be we would have that appetite of spirit that is fit for this feast, *we must purge our souls from the corruptions of flesh and spirit,* ' perfecting holiness in the fear of God,' 2 Cor. vii. 1. We must cleanse our souls from those lusts and passions that daily cleave unto them. All crudities must be taken away, that the edge of the stomach may not be flatted :* for while these earthly carnal corruptions lie upon the soul, we can expect no spiritual appetite to heavenly things. Let us therefore examine ourselves, what filth lies upon our souls, and what corrupt inclinations are there, that so they may be purged, and our desires be carried fully after Christ in the sacrament.

(3.) Another means to get appetite is *to consider thoroughly what is required of a Christian, well to maintain the trade of Christianity.* It is another manner of thing than we take it for, to entertain communion with God, to perform holy duties in an holy manner, to bear the yoke as a Christian should do. Here is a great deal of strength required ; and because corruptions will mix themselves amongst our best performances, there must be a great deal of mercy from God to pardon them. And whence is all this but by the death of our blessed Saviour Jesus Christ ? For his sake, God hath a forbearing eye. Now, if we consider what a degree of spiritual strength and vigour we should have to go through with these duties, this would sharpen our stomachs and spiritual appetites, to furnish ourselves with grace from Christ to go through with these holy services. There must be an exercising of all the duties of Christianity, which is an estate that must be maintained with a great deal of charge and labour. A man can do no service acceptable to God but by grace ; and grace must feed the soul with fruitful knowledge in the power of faith. And when the soul feeleth a necessity of grace, Oh ! then, beloved, it hungers and earnestly thirsteth after the love of God in Christ. We need to every trade a great deal of knowledge. Then surely the calling of Christianity needeth a great deal. A Christian must expect much both in prosperity and adversity, as the apostle saith, ' I have learned to want and to abound, to be in honour and to be in disgrace, and I can do all things through Christ that strengthens me,' Philip. iv. 12. Now, because there is so much goings so, out for the maintenance of Christianity, we must also bring in much grace, and faith, and love, and holiness, or else we shall never be able to uphold this condition. Where there is an exercise of Christianity, there will be an appetite to heaven ; that is our best calling. For when that we have done all that we can, that, that we must have comfort from, is Christianity. Therefore, labour with all labour to be holy and able Christians. All other callings are but for this present life ; but that that is for eternity is this calling of Christianity. And this is only to fit us here in this world for an everlasting condition of glory in the world to come.

(4.) Again, if we would have a desire and appetite to heavenly things, *we must labour to get acquaintance, and constantly converse with those that are good.* The old proverb is, ' Company will make a man fall to,' especially the company of those that are better than ourselves. For very emulation, men will be doing as others do. When men live amongst those whose

* That is ' flattened,' = appetite destroyed.—G.

hearts are framed this way, they must be equal. Conversation with those that have good relish of spiritual things, and shew forth grace in their lives, setteth an appetite upon our desires, to desire the same things that they do. Thus St Paul writeth to the Gentiles to stir up the emulation of the Jews. Therefore receive this likewise for the procuring of a spiritual appetite. To go on.

(5.) The next thing that may stir up our desires to get an appetite to the best things, is seriously to consider, *that we cannot tell how long we have to live, or may enjoy the benefit of the means of grace.* Those that sit at table and discourse away the greatest part of dinner time in talk, had need at last to fall to so much the faster, by how much the more negligent they had been before in eating. We cannot tell how long we may enjoy this spiritual feast that God makes for us. Therefore, be stirred up to get spiritual appetites ; for we know not how long God will spread a table for us. We know not how long we shall enjoy our lives ; and if we be surprised on the sudden, we may suffer a spiritual famine, a famine of the soul, if we have nothing to comfort us beforehand ; and of all famines, a spiritual famine is most grievous, most fearful. Therefore do as Joseph did, and be wise. He in the seven years of plenty gathered for seven years of famine that was to come upon the land of Egypt, Gen. xli. 36, *seq.* Alas ! if we have nothing laid up beforehand, what will be our end ? We shall lie open to God's wrath and anger. Nothing can support our souls in the evil time. Wherefore, as you desire at that day to have comfort of those things ye shall stand most in need of, labour to get a good appetite. For to perish and starve at a feast is a shame ; to famish in the liberty of the gospel and plenty of spiritual meat, is shameful and dishonourable. Thus you see, beloved, not to be large in the point, how you may procure such an appetite as is fit for such an holy feast. First, by getting a sense of sin ; secondly, by seeing a necessity of Christ ; thirdly, by purging out those lusts that lie upon the soul ; fourthly, by conversing with those that are spiritually minded ; and lastly, by considering the time to come.

Use 3. It is not enough to have a stomach, but we must have *a spiritual disposition of soul to heavenly things, as we have to outward things.* Labour to have a taste of good things, and a distinguishing taste of heavenly things from other things. God is the God of nature, and hath furnished us with five senses ; and as he hath given us sense to apprehend, so he hath furnished the creature with varieties of excellences, suitable to all our several senses. He will not have objects in the creature without sense, nor sense in man without objects. He hath furnished man with senses, and variety of senses, and given fit and proportionable objects for those senses. The soul also hath her sense. Wheresoever there is life, there is sense. God having given spiritual life to the soul, he doth maintain that life with spiritual food. As in a feast there is sight, and the eye is not only fed there with rich furniture, but with variety of dainties ; the ear likewise and the smell is satisfied, the one with music, the other with sweet savours. So in this feast there is to delight both the ear and the smell of the soul, the one with hearing the gracious promises of Jesus Christ, and the other in receiving the sweet savour of that sacrifice that was offered up once for all. Nothing so sweet to the soul as the blessings of Christ. He is sweet in the word, as the vessel that conveyeth him into our souls. Thus you see in this feast all the senses, the sight, the smell, the taste, and hearing, all are satisfied, and a great care had, in the provision for the feast, that our outward man may be pleased. And shall the Lord of Hosts make a feast, and not content the whole man ?　He is for our sight, if we have spiritual eyes to see ; the ear, if we have ears to hear.　All the senses are exercised here.　What is the reason why carnal men cannot relish a pardon for sin, and justification, and sanctification, and holiness, nor go boldly to God ? It may be they have good, sweet notions of these, but they have no spiritual taste or relish of them, and all because they want spiritual life.　None but a Christian can have spiritual taste answerable to a spiritual life.　Taste is a kind of feeling, one of the most necessary senses ; and a Christian cannot be without relish and feeling.　Yea, it is the very being of a Christian to have a taste of spiritual things.　Of all other senses, there is a stronger application in taste.　The other senses fetch their objects afar off ; but as for taste, there is a near application in it, and therefore most necessary. Every life is maintained by taste.　' Taste and see how good the Lord is,' Ps. xxxiv. 8.

Now, taste doth two things ; it doth relish that that is good, and disrelish the contrary.　There must be a spiritual taste to discern of differences. There can be no spiritual taste but it must know what is good and profitable for the soul, and what is not.　Because God will not have our tastes to be wronged, ye see what course he takes.　First, the eye seeth what things we taste on, and if the eye be displeased, so also is the smell.　Thus God layeth before us spiritual things, knowledge of good and bad, and giveth us many *caveats*, and all because he would not have us to taste things hurtful for the soul, nor poison instead of meat.　Now, when we have tasted that which is good, let us take heed it be not a taste only, lest we fall into the sin against the Holy Ghost.

Use 4.　Again, beside taste, *there must be a digesting of what we taste, and that thoroughly, in our understandings.*　When we apprehend a thing to be true and good, it must be digested thoroughly into the affections.　Love to the best things must be above all other love whatsoever ; yet this must be digested.　Men oftentimes have sweet notions, but, alas ! they are but notions ; they do not digest them into their affections.　It is the last digestion that nourisheth ; and when any spiritual truths are understood thoroughly, then comes in spiritual strength ; and hereupon the soul comes and sucks in that virtue which is for the nourishment of it.　Thus it is in the soul ; upon digestion there is nourishment.

Again, there must be a faculty to retain what we have received, that it may be digested.　Ye have many that love to hear, but they do not digest. If there be nothing in the soul, nothing can be extracted ; and therefore we must learn to retain necessary truths, that so upon occasion they may come from the memory into the heart.　Though, indeed, they are not in their proper place when they are in the memory only, yet notwithstanding, if they are there, they may with ease be brought down into the soul.

Use 5.　Then *we must labour to walk in the strength of spiritual things.*　For what is the use of this feast but to cherish both soul and spirit ?　The use of spiritual things which we have through Christ is to cherish and enliven. It conveyeth strength to us, that we may walk in the strength of Christ, as Elias did forty days in the strength of his food, 1 Kings xix. 8.　And consider, though in our consciences and conditions we have variety of changes, yet in Christ we have several comforts suitable to all our several conditions. If so be our sins trouble us, we should watch over ourselves, that we be not over much cast down, but feed upon spiritual things in consideration of pardon for sin in the blood of Christ.　This is the grand issue of all that Christ hath traced out in the forgiveness of sins.　He is not, he cannot be

divided. Where he pardons sins, he sanctifieth ; where he sanctifieth, he
writes his law in their hearts. So that there is a chain of spiritual favours.
Where the first link is, all the rest follow. Where forgiveness of sin is,
there is the Spirit, and that Spirit sanctifieth, and comforts, and is an earnest of everlasting life. Therefore, feed especially upon the favours of
God, and get forgiveness of sins, and then all the rest of the chain of grace
and spiritual life will follow.

Sometimes we stand in need of present grace and comfort, and we are
undone if comforts and grace are not at hand, never considering the promises that are to- come ; as that promise of Christ, ' I will be with thee to
the end of the world, fear not,' Mat. xxviii. 20. No temptation shall befall
us, but we shall have an issue out of it, and it shall work together for the
good of all those that fear God. This is *aqua vitæ* to the soul of man.
Therefore the gracious promises of Christ and his Holy Spirit we should
ever remember to get into our souls ; for when all other comforts fail, then
cometh in the comforts of the Spirit, who will be with us and uphold us in
all extremities. If we had nothing in this world to comfort our spirits, yet
let us rejoice in hope of glory to come. ' Our life is hid with Christ,' Col.
iii. 3. We have ' the hidden manna,' Rev. ii. 17. ' In him we rejoice in
hope of glory,' Rom. v. 2. And the way to maintain a Christian, holy life,
is to make use of all the privileges of Christianity, and of those promises
that convey these privileges to our souls.

Now that we may the better do this, observe continually what it is that
hinders us, that we cannot feed upon spiritual things as we should do.
Whatsoever it is, we must labour constantly to remove it.

Now, what must follow after this feast ? (1.) *Why! spiritual cheerfulness!*
If we find this in our duties of Christianity, it is a sign we have fed upon
spiritual things. The nature of a spiritual feast is to empty the soul of
sin, and to fill it full of gracious thoughts and actions. Instead thereof it
moderates all things. It makes us use the world as if we used it not.
When we can do this, we may certainly know that our souls have tasted of
abundance of benefit by this feast.

A man that hath no spiritual joy is drowned for the most part in the
contentments of the world, drowned in riches and honours ; and these are
like to strong waters immoderately taken, instead of cheering the spirits,
[they] exhaust and kill them. He that hath the joy of heaven here by
faith, is mortified to all other base delights, ' he only mindeth the things
above, where Christ is,' Col. iii. 1. And therefore the exhortation, or rather
command, ' Seek the things that are above,' hath this promise in fit
method annexed to it, ' and then all other things shall be cast in upon you,'
Mat. vi. 33. Riches and honours in the world ; and if not them, yet so
much as is necessary, and mortification of our sins, and the lusts of the flesh.

Again, if we have fed upon spiritual things for our souls, (2.) we shall *be
thankful*. That man that hath tasted how good and gracious the Lord
hath been to him in this world, and how full of joy and comfort he will be
to him in another world, in consideration of this, his soul cannot choose
but be thankful to God.

Here we see how to make this spiritual food fit for our souls, that Christ
provideth for us. And if there be such joy as we have said there is in
spiritual things, what use should we make further of them, but labour from
hence (3.) *to justify the ways of godliness against our own false and carnal
hearts, and against the slanderous imputations of the world.* When our
hearts are ready to be false to us, and hanker after the contentments of

the world, and are ready to say the best contentments that they can enjoy is in the things below; let us answer our base and false disputing hearts, that the ways of wisdom, the ways that God directs us to, they only are the ways of pleasure. And religion is that that makes the hearts of the children of men joyful; and 'a good conscience only makes a continual feast,' Prov. xv. 15, so long as man liveth. But especially at the hour of death, when all the comforts of the world cease, then conscience standeth our friend.

Obj. But the world's objection is, that of all kind of men in the world, those that profess religion are the most melancholy.

Ans. But if it be so, it is because they are not religious enough. Their sins are continually before their eyes. They have pardon for sin, and freedom from the guilt of sin, but know it not. They have good things, and do not know them. And so in regard of spiritual comforts, God's people may have spiritual joy, and inward consolation, and yet not know of it. There may be such a time when they may be sad and droop, and that is when they apprehend God doth not look pleasantly upon them. But the true character of a Christian is to be cheerful, and none else can be truly cheerful and joyous. Joy is usurped by others. There is no comfort in them that can be said to be real. All the joy of a man that is a carnal man is but as it were the joy of a traitor. He may come to the sacraments, and feast with the rest of God's people, but what mirth or joy can he have so long as the Master of the feast frowns upon him? Where Christ is not, there God is not reconciled. No joy like that joy of him that is assured of the love of God in Christ. A man may sometime through ignorance want that joy that belongeth to him. 'Rejoice, ye righteous, and be glad,' Ps. xxxiii. 1. It belongeth to those that are in Christ and to the righteous to rejoice, for joy is all their portion. They only can justify the ways of God against all reproaches whatsoever. But the eyes of carnal men are so held in blindness, that they can see no joy, no comfort in this course. As it is said of Austin before his conversion, he was afraid to turn Christian indeed, lest he should want all those joys and pleasures that the world did then afford him; but after he was converted, then he could cry, 'Lord, I have stayed too long from thee,' and too long delayed from coming in to taste of the sweetness of Jesus Christ.*

Take a Christian at the worst, and he is better than another man, take him at the best. The worst condition of God's children far surpasseth the very best condition of graceless persons. The issue of things shall turn to his good that is a member of Christ, a child of God, an heir of heaven. The evil of evils is taken away from him. Take him at the worst, he is an heir of heaven; but take the wicked at the best, he is not a child of God, he is a stranger to God, he is as a branch cut off, and as miserable a wretch as ever Belshazzar in the midst of his cups, trembling and quaking with fear and astonishment, when he saw the writing on the wall, Dan. v. 24, *seq.* When a man apprehends the wrath of God hanging over his head, though he were in the greatest feast in the world, and amongst those that make mirth and jollity, yet seeing vengeance ready to seize upon him, it cannot but damp all his joy and all his carnal pleasures; and therefore only a Christian hath a true title to this feast.

I beseech you, let us labour earnestly to have our part and portion in the things above. But what shall they do, that as yet apprehend no interest in Jesus Christ? Why! let them not be discouraged, for all are compelled

* See footnote p. 89.—G.

to come into this feast, both blind and lame.   The servants are sent to bring
them in.   The most wretched people of all, God doth invite them.   All
are called to come in to this feast that are sensible of their sins ; and that,
God requires at our hands, or else we can have no appetite to taste of this
feast.   God saith, ' Come all,' Isa. lv. 1.   Aye, but, saith the poor, sinful
soul, I have no grace at all !   Why ! but yet come, ' buy without money ;'
the feast is free.   ' God's thoughts are not as thy thoughts are ;' ' but as
heaven is high above the earth, even so are his thoughts above thy thoughts,'
Isa. lv. 8, 9.   Poor wretch ! thou thinkest thou hast led a wicked life, and
so thou hast !   Aye, but now come in, God hath invited thee, and he will
not always be inviting thee.   Therefore come in, and study the excellencies
of Christ.   When such persons as these see they need mercy, and grace,
and reconciliation, and must either have it or else be damned for ever,
now they are earnest to study the favour and love of God in Christ ; now
they bestir themselves to get peace of conscience and joy in the Holy
Ghost ; now they see salvation to be founded only on Christ, and all other
excellencies belonging to Christianity ; and therefore he goeth constantly
provided with grace and holiness, so in this life that he may not lose his
part in glory in the life to come.   Think of this and pray for it, as they
in the gospel. ' Lord, evermore give me of that bread,' John vii. 34.   Here
is hope that thou mayest be saved, because thou art invited to come in.   To
what end is the ministry of the gospel, but to entreat thee to be reconciled ?
Oh ! let this work upon our souls when we hear of the excellencies of these
things !   And together with them, consider of the necessity that is cast
upon us to obtain them, and that we must have them or else be damned
eternally.   We must do as the lepers did, who said one to another, ' Why
sit we here till we die ?   If we say, We will enter into the city, why, the
famine is in the city, and we shall die there : and if we sit still here, we
shall also die.'   Now, what course took they ?   ' They said one to another,
Let us enter into the camp of the Syrians, there is meat to feed us,' 2 Kings
vii. 3, 4.   So saith the soul, If I go into the city of the world, there I shall
be starved ; if I sit still, I shall also perish.   What shall I now do ?   I
will venture upon Jesus Christ ; he hath food that endures to eternal life,
and if I perish there, I perish.   If I have not Christ I must die, the wrath
of God hangeth over my head, and I cannot escape.   Alas ! poor soul,
now thou seest thy wretchedness, cast thyself upon him, and come in.   If
thou venturest, thou canst but die !   Adventure therefore, put thyself upon
God's mercy, for he is gracious and full of compassion.

Those that have given up themselves to Christ, let them study to honour
God and Christ, by taking those comforts that are allotted to them.   When
any man inviteth us to a feast, he knoweth if we respect him we will fall
to.   God hath bestowed his Son upon us, and will he not with him give
us all things ?   Let us not therefore dishonour the bounty of our good God, but
come in, and labour to have our hearts more and more enlarged with the
consideration of the excellency of these eternal comforts.   The fulness of
Christ is able to satisfy the soul, though it were a thousand times larger
than it is.   If it were possible that we could get the capacity of angels, it
could not be sufficient to shew forth the fulness of pleasures that are provided for a Christian.   Let us therefore labour with all labour to open our
hearts to entertain these joys, for we cannot honour God more than of his
bounty to receive thankfully what he freely offers.   To taste plentifully in
the covenant of grace, of these riches, and joy, and hope of things to come,
glorious above all that we are able to think of ; I say, this is the way to

honour God under the gospel of hope. Of things that are infinite, the more we take, the more we may take, and the more we honour him that giveth. Let us therefore enter deeply into our special sins, there is no fear of despair. Think of all thy wants, and of all thy sins; let them be never so many, yet there is more to be had in Christ than there can be wanting in thee. The soul that thinks itself full of wants is the richest soul, and that that apprehendeth no want at all, no need of grace or Christ, is always sent empty away. Grieve therefore for thy sins, and then joy that thou hast grieved, and go to God for the supply of all thy wants. The seeds of joy and of comfort are sown in tears and grief in this world; but yet we know we shall reap in joy in the world to come.

Remember this, we have we know not what to go through withal in this valley of tears. That speech of Barzillai was good and excellent, who being by David himself invited to the court, answered, 'I am now grown old, I am not fit for the court, for my senses are decayed and gone,' 2 Sam. xix. 32, *seq*. Even so the time will come when our sense of relishing earthly pleasures will utterly be lost. We are sure to go to our graves, and we know not what particular trouble we may meet with in this world and go through, if we live to a full age. Alas! what are all comforts here to the comforts of eternity? When our days are spent on earth, then comes in the eternity of pleasure or everlasting sorrow. Oh then if, when we shall leave all behind us, we have the joy of the Holy Ghost in our hearts, it will advance us above all the suggestions of sin or Satan, and bring us cheerfully above to the tribunal seat of Christ. Labour therefore to have a spiritual relish of soul, to grow in grace and comforts of the Holy Ghost; for the time will come when we shall wish that we had had more than we have. Every one will repent of looseness and slackness in the ways of holiness. Therefore let us labour earnestly to be good husbands for our souls for the time to come.

THE THIRD SERMON.

And in this mountain shall the Lord of hosts make unto all people a feast, &c. And he will destroy in this mountain the face of the covering cast over all people, and the veil that is spread over all nations.—ISAIAH XXV. 6, 7.

I HAVE heretofore spoken of the feast that God makes to his church, specially in the latter times, which was specially performed at the first coming of Christ, when the Gentiles came in; but the consummation and perfection of all will be at the day of judgment. Then God will spread a table for his to all eternity.

We have spoken heretofore at large of the resemblance of spiritual good things, by this comparison of a feast. God sets out spiritual things by outward, because we cannot otherwise conceive of them; the best things in grace, by the best and sweetest things in nature. And thus God enters into our souls by our senses, as we see in the sacrament.

But we have spoken at large of this. Our care must be to have a special taste, a spiritual appetite to relish this feast that God provides. Naturally we are distasteful. We relish not spiritual and heavenly things; we savour not the things of God. And the Spirit of God must alter our savour and taste, as he doth. Wheresoever there is spiritual life, there is spiritual relish of heavenly truths.

Now let me add this further, *that though it be made by God, yet we must*

bring something to this feast.   Christ feasteth with us, as ye have, Rev. iii.
20.   He sups with us, not that we have grace from ourselves, or can bring
anything; he bringeth his own provision with him when he suppeth with
us; but yet by the covenant of grace whereby he enters into terms of friendship with us, we must sup with him, we must have grace to entertain him,
though it is at his own cost; yet we must have something.   He doth not
require us to pay our debts, but he giveth us wherewith.   Secretly he bids
us come, but giveth a secret messenger to draw us; he sends his Spirit
certainly.   Certainly he will have us bring something when we come to
feast, but it is of his own giving.   And that we are to bring is humble and
empty souls, wherein we are to delight ourselves in sense of our unworthiness; and the spirit of faith to believe his promises.   That pleaseth him,
when we can honour him with a spirit of faith, and then a spirit of love,
and new obedience springing from a spirit of faith and love.   These be the
things Christ requires we should have.   Our souls must be thus furnished
that Christ may delight to dwell with us; and therefore it is a good importuning of God, ' Lord, I desire thou shouldst dwell in me, and prepare
my soul as a fit temple;' vouchsafe me the graces thou delightest in,
and delightest to dwell in.   So we may beg of God his Holy Spirit to
furnish our souls, so as he may dwell and delight in us.

But we have spoken largely of the former verse.   I will now speak of the
next that followeth.

' And I will destroy in this mountain the face of covering cast over all
people, and the veil spread over all nations, to swallow up death in victory;
the Lord will wipe away tears from all faces; and the rebukes of his people
shall be taken from the earth, for the Lord hath spoken it.'

These depend one upon another, being the several services of the feast.
He promiseth a feast in the sixth verse.   And what be the several services?
He will destroy in this mountain, this church, the face of covering cast over
all people, &c.   He will take away the veil of ignorance and unbelief, that
they may have special sight of heavenly things, without which they cannot
relish heavenly things; they can take no joy at this feast.

And then, because there can be no feast, where there is the greatest
enemy in force and power, he swallows up death in victory.   Death keeps
us in fear all our lifetime.   That that swalloweth up all kings and
monarchs, the terror of the world, death, shall be and is swallowed up by
our head, Christ, and shall be swallowed up by us in victory.   In the mean
time we are subject to many sorrows which cause tears; for tears are but
drops that issue from that cloud of sorrow; and sorrow we have always in
this world, either from sins or miseries, or sympathy in tears of that kind.
Well, the time will come that tears shall be wiped away, and the cause of
tears; all sorrow for our own sins, for our own misery, and for sympathizing
with the times wherein we live.   Our time shall be hereafter at the day of
resurrection, when all tears shall be wiped from our eyes.   God will perform that office of a mother to wipe the children's eyes, or of a nurse to
take away all cause of grief whatsoever, else it cannot be a perfect feast.

Aye, but there are* reproaches cast upon religion and religious persons!
It goeth under a veil of reproach, and the best things are not seen in their
own colours; nor the worst things; they go under vizards here.

But the time will come that the rebukes of his people shall be taken away.
The good things, as they are best, so shall they be known to be so; and
sin, and base courses, as they are bad, and as they are from hell, so they

* Misprinted ' is.'—G

shall be known to be. Everything shall appear in its own colours ; things shall not go masked any longer. And what is the seal of all this ? The seal of it is, ' The mouth of the Lord hath spoken it.' Truth itself hath spoken it, and therefore it must needs be. Jehovah, that can give a being to all things, he hath said it.

We have heard why the church is called a mountain. He will destroy, or swallow up,* as the word may signify, the face of covering, or the covering of the face ; the veil which is the covering of the face, and particularly expressed in that term always; the veil that is spread over all nations.

God will take away the spiritual veil that covers the souls of his people, that is between them and divine truths. It hath allusion to that of Exod. xxxiv. 34, 35, about Moses when he came from the mount. He had a veil, for the people could not behold him. He had a glory put upon his face, that they could not look upon him with a direct eye, and therefore he was fain to put a veil upon his face, to shew that the Jews could not see, as Paul interprets it, 2 Cor. iii. 15, ' To this day,' saith he, ' when Moses is read, there is a veil put upon their hearts.' They could not see that ' the law was a schoolmaster to bring to Christ,' Gal. iii. 24, the ceremonial law and the moral law. God had a blessed end, by the curse of it, to bring them to Christ. They rested in the veil, their sight was terminated in the veil, they could not see through to the end and scope of it. Nevertheless, when they shall turn to the Lord, the veil shall be taken away.

1. From the words, consider first of all, *that naturally there is a veil of ignorance upon the soul.*

2. Secondly, *God doth take away his† veil;* and God by his Spirit only can do it.

3. Thirdly, *that this is only in his church.* And where this veil of ignorance is taken off, there is feasting with God and spiritual joy, and delight in the best order ; and where it is‡ taken off there is none of it.

First of all, by nature, *there is a veil of covering over all men's spirits.* To understand this better, let us unfold the terms of veil a little. There is a veil either upon the things themselves that are to be seen, or upon the soul which should behold them.

(1.) The veil *of things themselves* is when they be hidden altogether, or in part ; when we know part, and are ignorant of part. And this veil upon the things ariseth from the weak apprehension of them ; when they are not represented in clear expressions, but in obscurity of words or types ; when we see them only in types or obscure phrases, which hideth sometime the sight of the thing itself. The manner of speech sometimes casteth a veil on things ; for our Saviour Christ spake in parables, which were like the cloud, dark on the one side, light on the other, dark towards the Egyptians, light towards the Israelites. So some expressions of Scripture have a light side, that only the godly see, and a dark side, that other men, good wits, as natural men, see not.

(2.) Again, there is a veil *upon the soul and upon the sight.* If the things be veiled, or the sight veiled, there is no sight. Now the soul is veiled when we be ignorant and unbelieving; when we are ignorant of what is spoken and revealed, or when we know the terms of it, and yet believe it not.

(3.) Now, this veil of ignorance and unbelief continueth in all unregenerate men *until grace takes away the veil.* Besides, before a thing can be seen, the object must not only be made clear, and the eyesight too, but

* ' Swallow.'—Dr J. A. Alexander in his ' Commentary' adopts the rendering of Sibbes here.—G.   † Qu. ' this ?'—ED.   ‡ Qu. ' is not ?'—ED.

there must be *lumen deferens*, a light to carry the object to the eye. If that be not, we cannot see. As the Egyptians, in the three days of darkness, had their eyes, but there wanted light to represent the object, and therefore they could not go near one to another. It is the light, and not sight. If there be sight and no light to carry and convey the object, we cannot say there is sight.

That which answereth to this veil is the veil of Scripture, whereby heavenly things are set out by a mystery. A mystery is, when something is openly shewed and something hidden.

When something is concealed, as in the sacrament, they be mysteries. We see the bread, we see the wine, but under the bread and wine other things are intended, the breaking of the body of Christ, and the shedding of his blood, and in that the love and mercy of God in Christ, in giving him to death for us, and Christ's love to give himself to satisfy divine justice. These be the things intended, which only the soul sees and apprehendeth. And so all things in the church, indeed, are mysteries, the incarnation of Christ, the union of both natures, that Christ should save the world by such a way as he did, that he should bring us to glory by shame, to life by death, to blessing and happiness by being a curse for us. It is a mystery to bring contrary out of contrary : that so glorious a person as God should be covered with our weak and sinful nature. It was a mystery, the Jews stumbled at it. Light came, and the darkness could not comprehend the light. And, as Christ was a mystery himself, so the church is a mystery. That God should so much delight in a company of poor men, the off-scouring of the world, to make them temples of his Holy Spirit, and heirs of heaven, men that were under the scorn of the world, this is a mystery. So all is mystical, the head, the members, the body, the church, and every particular point of religion. There is a mystery in repentance. No man knoweth what sorrow for sin is but the true gracious person. No man knows what it is to believe but he that hath an heart to believe. No man knoweth what peace of conscience and joy of the Holy Ghost is but those that feel it. So that is a mystery. And therefore ' great is the mystery of godliness,' saith the apostle, 1 Tim. iii. 16. Not only in the points themselves, but even the practice of religion is a mystery too. Repentance and faith, and new obedience and love, and the comforts of religion, are all mysteries. There is a veil upon them in all these points, that a carnal man cannot see them.

You see, then, in what sense there is a veil of the things, and in what sense there is a veil on men's hearts ; that is, either the things themselves are hid, or if the things be open, they want sight and light of knowledge, and they want faith to believe. Beloved, we live in times that the object is clear to us, the things themselves are made clear ; as who knoweth not what Christ is, and the notion of the incarnation, and of the union with him. We know them notionally. They be opened and revealed to us very clearly, all the articles of faith, and mysteries of religion, so that there is no obscurity in the object. The things are clear, specially in these places of knowledge. But yet, notwithstanding, there is a veil upon the soul. The soul of every man that is not graciously wrought upon by the Spirit of God hath a veil of ignorance and unbelief.

First of all, *of ignorance.* There is a vale * of ignorance in many, and in all men naturally a veil of ignorance of spiritual things. For, unless they be revealed, they can never be known to angels themselves. The angels

* Qu. ' veil?'—ED.

themselves know not the gospel till it be opened, and therefore they be students in it continually, and the best men in the world know nothing in the gospel further than it is revealed. But there is a veil of ignorance upon them that know these things notionally, because they do not know them as they should know them; they do not know them in *propria specie*, spiritual and heavenly things as spiritual and heavenly things. They do not know spiritual things as spiritual things, they have a human knowledge of spiritual things. Those that want grace, they know the grammar of the Scripture and divinity, and they know how to discourse as schoolmen do, from one thing to another, and to argue. They know the logic and rhetoric of the Scripture, but they stick in the stile. There is something they are ignorant of; that is, they have not an eye of knowledge, as we call it. They do not see the things themselves, but only they see things by another body's spirit, and they have no light of their own. And so no man knoweth naturally but the children of God what original sin is, what corruption of nature is, nor knows sin in its own odious colours, to be filthy, and to be dangerous as it is. To draw the curse and vengeance of God upon it, this is not known, but by the Spirit revealing the odiousness of sin, that the soul may apprehend it, as Christ did when he suffered for it, and as God doth. A gracious man seeth it as God seeth it, because by the Spirit of God he seeth the filthiness and odiousness of it, and the danger it draweth after it.

Second. And so in any points of religion naturally, *a man sees not them spiritually, as they are, and as God sees them, but he seeth them by a human light.* He seeth heavenly things by a human light, notionally, and merely to discourse of them. He seeth not intritively * into the things themselves. He seeth them *sub aliena specie*, under another representation than their own. Only a godly man seeth spiritual things as the Spirit of God, and seeth them as they are, knows sin as it is, knoweth grace to be as it is, and knoweth faith. What it is to believe, what it is to have peace of conscience, and the pardon of sins. He knoweth these things in some sense intritively, though not so as he shall do when he shall see these things in heaven, when he shall see face to face. There is a great difference in it. He sees them intritively in respect of the knowledge of other men, though he sees but in a glass in regard of the knowledge he shall have in heaven. As St Paul saith, ' For we see but as in a glass.' But he that sees in a glass seeth more life than he that sees the dead picture of a man. So, though we see but in a glass heavenly things, yet we see them better than those that see them in a dead notion. Though it be nothing to the knowledge we shall have in heaven, yet it is incomparable above the knowledge of any carnal natural man upon the earth.

Third. Again, naturally men have veils of ignorance *upon the most divine things.* Of spiritual things, such as is union, and as is the communion between Christ and us, and the mystery of regeneration in the new creature, such as is the joy in the Holy Ghost, the inward peace of conscience. I will not name the particulars to insist on them, but give you only an instance. Though they know the notion of these things, yet they are altogether ignorant of them. Their knowledge is a mere outward light. It is a light radicated† in the soul. It is not as the light of the moon, which

---

* Qu. ' intuitively,' or ' interiorly ?'—G.; or, ' introitively ?'—ED.

† There seems to be a confusion here, as if a sentence had been left out. It must be the knowledge, not of ' natural,' but of ' gracious,' men, that is as a light radicated or rooted in the soul.—ED.

receiveth light from the sun, but it is a light radicated and incorporated into the soul, as the light of the sun is, by the Spirit. It is in the soul. It is not only upon the soul, but in the soul. The heart sees and feeleth, and knoweth divine truths. There is a power and virtue in the sight and knowledge of a gracious man. There is none in the knowledge of a carnal man. The light of a candle hath a light in it, but no virtue at all goeth with it; but the light of the sun, and the light of the stars, they have a special virtue, they have heat with them, and they have an influence in a special kind on inferior bodies working together with the light. So it is with heavenly apprehension and knowledge. It actually conveyeth light. But with the light there is a blessed and gracious influence, there is heat and efficacy with that light. But though a carnal man know all the body of divinity, yet it is a mere light without heat, a light without influence. It is not experimental. As a blind man can talk of colours, if he be a scholar, and describe them better than he that hath his eyes, he being not a scholar. But he that hath his eyes can judge of colours a great deal better. Oftentimes, by book, a scholar can tell you foreign countries better than he that hath travelled, yet the traveller that hath been there can tell them the more distinctly. So he that is experienced in that kind, though a stranger, can measure another man's ground better than himself. He can tell you here is so many acres. But he that possesseth them knows the goodness of them, the worth of them, and improveth them to his own good. And so it is with many. They can measure the points of religion, and define and divide them. Aye, but the poor Christian can taste, can feel them, can relish and improve them. His knowledge is a knowledge with interest, but other men's knowledge is a knowledge with no interest or experience at all. So that there is naturally a veil of ignorance on the heart of every natural man.

Christianity is a mystery. Till conversion there is a mystery in every point of religion. None know what repentance is but a repentant sinner. All the books in the world cannot inform the heart what sin is or what sorrow is. A sick man knoweth what a disease is better than all physicians, for he feeleth it. No man knoweth what faith is but the true believer. There is a mystery also in love. Godliness is called a mystery, not only for the notional, but the practical part of it. Why do not men more solace themselves in the transcendent things of religion, which may ravish angels? Alas! there is a veil over their soul, that they do not know them, or not experimentally. They have no taste or feeling of them.

And so there is a veil of unbelief. There is no man without grace that believeth truly what he knoweth; but he believeth in the general only, he believeth things so far forth as they cross not his lusts. But when particular truths are enforced on a carnal man, his lusts do overbear all his knowledge, and he hath a secret scorn arising in his heart, whereby he derideth those truths and goeth against them, and makes him think certainly these be not true, and therefore he believeth them not. If a man by nature believed the truths he saith he knoweth, he would not go directly against them. But the ground of this is, there is a mist of sinful lusts that are raised out of the soul, that darkens the soul, that at the present time the soul is atheistical and full of unbelief. For there is no sin but ignorance and unbelief breatheth it into the soul, and maketh way for it; for if a man knew what he were about, and apprehended that God saw him, and the danger of it, he would never sin. There is no sin without an error in judgment, there is a veil of ignorance and unbelief. What creature will run into a pit when he seeth it open? What creature will run into the fire, the most dull creature? Man will not run into that danger that is open to the eye of the soul, if there were not a veil of ignorance, at least unbelief, at that time upon the soul. All sin supposeth error.

And this should make us hate sin the more. Whensoever we sin, specially against our conscience, there is atheism in the soul at that time, and there is unbelief. We believe not the truth itself. No sinner but calleth truth into question. When he sinneth, he denieth it or questioneth it; and therefore there is a veil on every man naturally over his heart by ignorance and unbelief. The truths themselves are clear. God is clear, and the gospel is light, *mens, lux;* you know they know things in the object, but in us there is darkness in our understandings; and therefore the Scripture saith not we are dark only, but ' darkness itself,' 2 Cor. vi. 14. The clouds that arise are like the mists that do interpose between our souls and divine things, arising from our own hearts; and the love of sinful things raise such a cloud, that we know not, or else believe not, what is spoken. To proceed.

Obs. 2. *God only can reveal and take away the veil of ignorance and unbelief from off the soul.* I will speak specially of this veil.

Reason 1. The reason is, there is such a natural unsuitableness between the soul and heavenly light and heavenly truths, that unless God opens the eye of the soul, and puts a new eye into the soul, it can never know or discern of heavenly things. There must be an eye suitable to the light, else there will never be sight of it. Now, God can create a new spiritual eye to discern of spiritual things, which a natural eye cannot. Who can see things invisible? Divine things are invisible to natural eyes. There is no suitableness. He that must reveal these and take away the veil must create new light within as well as a light without. Now, God, and only God, that created light out of darkness, can create light in the soul. ' Let there be light.' He only can create a spiritual eye, to see the things that to nature are visible.*

There be four things in sight. 1. The object to be beheld. 2. The light that conveyeth it. 3. The organ that receiveth it. 4. And the light of the eye to meet the light without. So it is in the soul. Together with divine truths, there must be light to discover them; for light is the first visible thing that discovers itself and all things else. And then there must be a light in the soul to judge of them, and this light must be suitable. A carnal, base spirit judgeth of spiritual things carnally like himself, because he hath not light in his own spirit. The things are spiritual, his eye is carnal. He hath not a light in his eye suitable to the object, and therefore he cannot judge of them, for the Scripture saith plainly 'they are spiritually discerned,' 1 Cor. ii. 14. Therefore, a carnal person hath carnal conceptions of spiritual things, as a holy man doth spiritualise things by a spiritual conception of them.

There be degrees of discerning things. The highest degree is to see things ' face to face ' as they be in heaven; the next to that is to see them in a glass, for there I see the motion and true species of a man, though not so clearly, as when I see him face to face; therefore we soon forget the species of it in a glass. We have more fixedness of the other, because there is more reality. We see things put into water, and that is less; but then there is a sight of man in pictures which is less than the rest, because we see not the motion. It is even so; a carnal man scarce sees the dead resemblance of things. In Moses's time they saw things in water, as it were blindly, though true; but we see things in a glass of truth as clearly as

* Qu. ' invisible?'—ED.

possibly we can in this world.   In heaven we shall see face to face, snall see him as he is.   And then will be the joy of this excellent feast, and the consummation of all sweet promises, which here we can but have a taste of.

Reason 2.   So that is the first reason of it, that God is only * the taker away of the veil, which ariseth from the unsuitableness between the soul and divine truths.

There is nothing in the heart of man but a contrariety to divine light.   The very natural knowledge, that is contrary.   Natural conscience, that only checketh for gross sins, but not for spiritual sins.   Obedience and civil life, that makes a man full of pride, and armeth him against self-denial and against the righteousness of Christ and justification.   There is nothing in the soul but, without grace, riseth against the soul in divine things.

Reason 3.   Again, *there is such disproportion between the soul, being full of sin and guiltiness, and heavenly things, that are so great, that the heart of man will not believe unless God convinceth the soul, that God is so good and gracious, though they be great and excellent, yet God will bestow them upon our souls ;* and therefore he sendeth the Spirit, that overpowers the soul, though it be full of fear and guilt that sin contracts.

Though we be never so unworthy, he will magnify his grace to poor sinners ; and without that the soul will never believe there is such an infinite disproportion between the soul and the things, between the sinful soul and the Spirit, so that God must overpower the soul to make it believe.

The Scripture is full of this.   As we are naturally ignorant and full of unbelief, so God only can overpower the soul and take away the veil of ignorance.

Reason 4.   *All the angels in heaven, and all the creatures in the world, the most skilful men in the world, cannot bring light into the soul, they cannot bring light into the heart.*   They can speak of divine things, but they understand them little.   But to bring light into the heart, that the heart may taste of them and yield obedience to believe, that they cannot do.   And therefore, all God's children, they be *theodidactoi*,† taught of God.   God only hath the privilege to teach the heart, to bend and bow the heart to believe.

So that God only by his Spirit takes away the veil of ignorance and unbelief.

Obs. 3.   Now, the third thing is, *that this is peculiar to the church and to the children of God*, to have the veil taken off.   ' *In this mountain*,' saith the Scripture, ' the veil of all faces shall be swallowed up or taken away.'

I partly shewed in the former point, that it is peculiar to God's children to have the veil taken off.   There is a veil in all things.   Either the things be hid from them, as amongst the Gentiles, or if the things be revealed, there is a veil upon the heart ; their lusts raise up a cloud, which, until God subdue by the Holy Spirit, they be dark, yea, darkness itself.   Goshen was only light when all Egypt was in darkness ; so there is light only in the church, and all other parts in the world are in darkness.   And amongst men in the church there is a darkness upon the soul of unregenerate men, that be not sanctified and subdued by the Spirit of God.   And all godly men are lightsome, nay, they be ' lights in the world,' Phil. ii. 15.   As wicked men are darkness, so gracious men, by the Spirit of God, are made lights of the world from him that is the true light, Christ himself.

It is peculiar to the church to know the greatest good, and the greatest evil.   It is nowhere but in the church, who are the people of God.   None

---

* That is, ' God only is.'—G.

† That is, Θεοδίδαχτοί.   Cf. John vi. 45 ; 1 Thess. iv. 9.—G.

but God's elect can know the greatest evil, that is, sin, which the Spirit of God revealeth; and the greatest good, that is, God's mercy in Christ, and sanctifying grace. The same Spirit doth both. As light doth discover foul things as well as fair; so the same Spirit of God discovers the loath-someness of sin, and the sweetness of grace. Where the one is,* there is never the other; where there is not truly a deep discerning of sin, there is never knowledge of grace; there is none but in the church. Those that have the spirit of illumination, they have sanctification likewise.

We shall make use of all together. You see, then, what naturally we are, and that God's grace must take away the veil; and this is from all them within the church, and in the church those whom God is pleased to sanctify.

Obs. In the fourth place. *Where this veil is taken off from any, there is with it spiritual joy and feasting,* as here he joineth them both together. ' I will make a feast of fat things, and will take away the veil,' ver. 7.

Reason. The reason of the connection of this, is, that same Spirit that is a Spirit of revelations, is a Spirit of comfort; and the same Spirit that is the Spirit of comfort, is a Spirit of revelation. All sweetness that the soul relisheth cometh from light, and all light that is spiritual conveyeth sweet-ness, both together. Beloved, there is a marvellous sweetness in divine truths. In Christ is all marrow, and in religion forgiveness of sins, and inward peace, and joy, and grace, fitting us to be like to Christ, and for heaven. They be incredibly sweet, they be all marrow. Aye, but they are only so to them that know them. Now God's Spirit, that revealeth these things to us, doth breed a taste in the soul. The Spirit of illumina-tion to God's children, is a Spirit of sanctification likewise; and that sanctification alters the taste and relish of the will and affections, that with discovery of these things, there is a taste and relish of them. It is *sapida scientia,* a savoury knowledge they have. And therefore where he maketh a feast, he taketh away the veil; and where he takes away the veil, he makes a feast. What a wonderful satisfaction hath the soul, when the veil is taken off, to see God in Christ reconciled! to see sin pardoned! to see the beginnings of grace, which shall be finished and accomplished in glory! to discern that ' peace which passeth understanding,' &c., Philip. iv. 7. What a marvellous sweetness is in these things!

They cannot be revealed to the knowledge spiritually, but there is a feast in the soul, wherein the soul doth solace itself; so both these go together.

And therefore we should not rest in that revealing that doth not bring a savour with it to the soul. Undoubtedly, that knowledge hath no solace and comfort for the soul, that is not by divine revelation of heavenly truths.

We see the dependence of these one upon another. Then let us make this use of all:

Use 1. Since there is a veil over all men by nature, the work of ignorance and unbelief, and since God only taketh it away by his Holy Spirit, and since that only those that be godly and sanctified have this taken off: while this is, there is a spiritual feast, joy, and comfort, and strength; then *let us labour to have this veil taken off; let us labour to have the eyes of our understandings enlightened, to have our hearts subdued to believe; let us take notice of our natural condition.* We are drowned and enwrapt in darkness, the best of all. It is not having knowledge what we are by nature; it is not any knowledge that can bring us to heaven; there must be a revelation,

* Qu. ' is not ?'—ED.

a taking away of the veil. How many content themselves with common light of education, and traditionary knowledge! So they were bred and catechised, and under such a ministry! But for spiritual knowledge of spiritual things, how little is it cared for! And yet this is necessary to salvation. There is great occasion to press this, that we rest not in common knowledge. If religion be not known to purpose, it is like lightning, which directs not a man in his way, but dazzles him, and puts him quite out of his way. Many have flashes of knowledge that affect them a little ; but this affection is soon gone, and directs them not a whit in the ways of life. And therefore labour that the will and affections may be subject. Beg of God a 'fleshy heart,' 2 Cor. iii. 3, an heart yielding to the truth. We know ear-truths will harden, as none is harder than a common formal Christian. A man had better fall into the hands of papists, than into the hands of a formal hypocritical Christian. Why? They pride themselves in their profession. No persecutors worse than the Scribes and Pharisees, that stood in their own light. They were more cruel than Pilate. And therefore if we be informed, but not truly transformed, to love the truth we know, and hate the evil we know, it maketh us worse.

And then it enrageth men the more. The more they know, the more they be enraged. Men when truths be pressed, which they purpose not to obey, they fret against the ordinance, and cast stones, as it were, in the face of truth. When physic doth raise humours, but is not strong enough to carry them away, they endanger the body ; and where light is not strong enough to dispel corruption when it raiseth corruption, it enrageth it. When men know truth, and are not moulded into it, they first rage against it, and then by little and little fall from it, and grow extreme enemies to it. It is a dangerous thing, therefore, to rest in naked knowledge. Beg then of God that he would take away the veil of ignorance and unbelief, that light and life may go together, and so we shall be fit to feast with the Lord.

Means. Now that we may have true saving knowledge, first, we *must attend meekly upon God's ordinances*, which be sanctified to this end to let in light to the soul.

1. Will we know sin and our state by nature, and how to come out of it ; then together with this revelation *must come an heavenly strength into the soul, a heavenly taste and relish;* and therefore attend upon the ordinances, and labour for an humble soul, empty of ourselves ; and do not think to break into heavenly things with strength of parts. God must reveal, God must take away the veil only by his Holy Spirit in the ordinance. The veil is taken away from the object, in opening of truths ; but the veil must be taken away from the object, and from the heart too. There must be knowledge of the object, as well as an object. The object must be sanctified and fitted to the persons, else divine truths will never be understood divinely, nor spiritual truths spiritually. Labour to be emptied of yourselves. In what measure we are emptied of our self-conceitedness and understanding, we be filled in divine things. In what measure we are emptied of ourselves, we are filled with the Spirit of God, and knowledge, and grace. As a vessel, in what measure it is emptied, in that measure it is fit to be filled with more supervenient liquor ; so in what measure we grow in self-denial and humility, in that measure we are filled likewise with knowledge. He will teach an humble soul that stands not in its own light, what it is to repent, to believe, to love ; what it is to be patient under the cross ; what it is to live holily, and die comfortably. The Spirit of God will teach an humble, self-denying soul all these things ; and therefore

labour for an humble, empty soul, and not to cast ourselves too much into the sins and fashions of the times, as the apostle, ' Be not conformed to this world, but be ye transformed by the renewing of your mind,' &c., Rom. xii. 2.

2. *When a man casteth himself into the mould of the times, and will live as the rest do, he shall never understand the secrets of God, and the good pleasure of God;* for the world must be condemned. The world goeth the broad way. And therefore we must not consider what others do, but what God teacheth us to do.

3. And add to this, *what we know, let us labour to practise.* ' But he that doth the will of my Father, shall know of every doctrine, whether it be of God or no,' John vii. 17. We must do, and we shall know.

Quest. But can we do before we know ?

Ans. The meaning is this, that we have, first, breeding and education, and some light of the Spirit* turneth it presently to practice, by obedience to that knowledge. And then you shall know more. He that doth these things, he shall know all. They shall know that do practice what they know already. ' To him that hath shall be given,' Mat. xiii. 12 ; that is, to him that hath some knowledge, and putteth in practice what he hath, God will increase the talent of his knowledge ; he shall know more and more, till God revealeth himself fully in the world to come.

4. And therefore *be faithful to ourselves, and true to the knowledge we have, love it,* and put it into practice. When divine truths are discovered, let the heart affect them, lest God giveth us up to believe lies. We have many given up to this sin. Because when truths are revealed, they give way to their own proud scornful hearts, they know not the love of the truth. God knoweth what a jewel the truth is ; and since they despise it, God giveth them up to believe lies. And take heed, practise what we know, and love what we know, entertain it with a loving affection.

A loving affection is the casket of this jewel. If we entertain it not in love, it removes from us its station, and being gone, God will remove us into darkness.

And remember it is God that taketh away the veil of ignorance and un-belief. And therefore make this use of it.

2. *To make our studies and closets, oratories,*† not to come to divine truths, to out-wrestle the excellency of them with our own wits; but to pray to God, as you have Ps. cxix. 18, ' Open mine eyes, and reveal thy truth.' And St Paul prayeth for the 'spirit of revelation,' Eph. i. 17. And so desire God to reveal and take away the veil from us, that he will open divine truths to our souls; that since he hath the key of David, that ' opens, and no man shutteth,' Rev. iii. 7, that he would open our understandings to conceive things, and our hearts to believe. He hath the only key of the soul. We can shut our souls, but cannot open them again. So we can shut our hearts to divine truths, we can naturally do this ; but open them without the help of the Spirit we cannot. He can open our understandings, as he did the disciples'. He can open our hearts to believe ; he can do it, and will do it. If we seek to him, he will not put back the humble desires of them that fear him. And therefore for heavenly light and heavenly revelation, all the teaching of the men of the world cannot do it. If we know no more than we can have by books, and men that teach us, we shall never come to heaven ; but we must have God teach the heart, as well as the brain. He must teach not only the truths themselves, as they be discovered, but the love of them,

* Qu. 'of the spirit ; turn, &c. ?'—ED.   † That is, 'places of prayer.'—G.

the faith in them, the practice of them; and he only can do this, he only can teach the heart, he only can discover the bent of the heart, and Satan's wiles that cast a cloud upon the understanding. The Spirit only can do it; and therefore in all our endeavours, labour to get knowledge, and join holiness and divine grace, and pray to God that he would reveal the mystery of salvation to us.

Quest. But how shall we know whether we have this heavenly light and revelation or no? whether the veil be yet upon our hearts or no? I will not be long in the point.

Ans. 1. We may know it by this. The apostle Peter saith to express the virtue of God's power, 'He hath called us out of darkness to his *marvellous* light,' 1 Pet. ii. 9. The soul that hath the veil taken from it, *there is a marvelling at the goodness of God, a wondering at the things of faith.* And the soul sets such a price upon divine things, that all is ' dung and dross' in comparison of the excellent knowledge of Jesus Christ, Philip. iii. 8. Wherefore is it that thou wilt reveal thyself to us, and not unto the world? as admiring the goodness of God. What are we? What am I, that God should reveal these things to me, and not to the world? that many perish in darkness and shadow of death, though they hear of divine things, yet they, teaching rebellion and unbelief, are not moulded to them, and so perish eternally? There is a secret admiration of the goodness of God to the poor soul, and a wonderment at spiritual things. 'O! how sweet is thy law,' saith David, Ps. cxix. 103. And teach me the wonders of thy law, and joy unspeakable and glorious, and peace that passeth understanding, Philip. iv. 7. These things be high to the soul.

Ans. 2. By the taste of what they have, they wonder at that little, and at that they look for, *and are carried with desire still further and further, which is a farther evidence.* They that have any spiritual knowledge, they be carried to grow more and more, and to enter further and further into the kingdom. Where there is not a desire still, till they come to the full measure that is to be had in Jesus Christ, there is no knowledge at all. Certainly a gracious soul, when once it sees, it desires still to feel the power and virtue of Christ in it, as Paul counted all dung in comparison of this knowledge, to know myself in Christ, and feel the power of his death in dying to sin, and virtue of his resurrection in raising me to newness of life. It was Saint Paul's study to walk still to the high price* of God's calling, and where that is not, no grace is begun.

Ans. 3. And again, where divine light is, and the veil taken away, *it is the sanctified means;* for God works by his own instruments and means, and they be able to justify all courses of wisdom. ' Wisdom is justified of her children,' Mat. xi. 19. By experience they be able to say the word is the word. I have found it casting me down, and raising me up, and searching the hidden corners of my heart. I have found God's ordinances powerful, the word and sacrament. I have found my hope, faith, strength, and spiritual comfort, and therefore I can justify them; for I have found, tasted, and relished of these things, which worketh that upon the soul which Christ did on the body. I find mine eyes, I find my deaf ears opened. I can hear with another relish than before. I find a life and quickening to good things, though it be weak. I had no life at all to them before. I find a relish which I knew not before. So that there be spiritual senses whereby I am able to justify that these things be the things of God. So that they that have divine truths can justify all the ordinances of God by their own

* The old way of spelling ' prize.'—G.

experience. As Peter answered when Christ asked him, Will you be also gone ? Be gone ! said Peter ; ' Whither should we go ? thou hast the words of eternal life,' John vi. 68. I have found thy words efficacious to comfort and strengthen and raise, and shall I depart from thee, who hast the words of eternal life ? And so take a soul that the Spirit of God hath wrought upon. Ask whether they will be careless of means of salvation, not to pray, or hear, or receive the sacrament. By these have I eternal life conveyed. God hath let in by these comfort, and strength, and joy, and shall I leave these things ? No ; I will not. ' Whither shall I go ? thou hast the words of eternal life.' Are we able to justify these things by the sweetness we have found in them ? Then certainly God hath shined upon the soul, and, together with strength and light, conveyed sweetness to the soul.

Ans. 4. A godly man *seeth things with life, his sight worketh upon him.* It is a transforming sight. As the apostle saith, ' We all behold the glory of God, and are changed,' 2 Cor. iii. 18. Sight of light and life goeth together with a Christian ; as Christ saith, ' he is the light of the world,' John ix. 5, and ' the life of the world,' John i. 4. First light, for life cometh with light, and light conveyeth life. All grace is dropped into the will through the understanding ; and wheresoever Christ is life, he is light, because true knowledge is a transforming knowledge. But if religion be not known to purpose, it hardens and makes worse.

We are now by God's good providence come to farther business, to partake of these mysteries ;* yet it should be the desire of our souls that our eyes may be opened, that in these divine and precious mysteries he would discover hidden love, which is not seen with the eyes of the body. They may see and taste and relish his love and goodness in Jesus Christ ; that as the outward man is refreshed with the elements, so the inward man may be refreshed with his Spirit, that they may be effectual to us ; that we may justify the course God takes, so far as to come charitably and joyfully to them.

THE FOURTH SERMON.

I will destroy in this mountain the face of the covering cast over all people, and the veil that is spread over all nations. He will swallow up death in victory, &c.—ISA. XXV. 7, 8.

WE have heretofore at large spoken of the spiritual and eternal favours of God, set out in the former verse, ' In this mountain will the Lord of Hosts make a feast of fat things.' While our soul is in the body, it is much guided by our fancy. Spiritual things are therefore presented by outward, and conveyed to the soul that way ; only we must remember that there is a far greater excellency in the things themselves than in their representation. For what is all banquets, fatness with marrow, wine on the lees, to the joy and sweetness of religion, begun here, and accomplished in the world to come ?

In Christ there is nothing but all marrow and sweetness in religion, that may refresh a man in the lowest condition, if he can but have a taste of it.

Now because the spiritual things of Christ do us no good, as long as they are hid, therefore the Holy Ghost setteth down a promise, ' that God will

* In the margin, ' Application of this to the sacrament.'—G.

take away the covering cast on all people, and the veil spread over all nations.'

But there be some things that will damp all mirth. Now here is security against them, that our joy may be complete ; and this in the next verse, to which I now come, ' He will swallow up death in victory, he will wipe away tears from all faces.' The prophet having spoken of a great feast before, an excellent feast, sets forth here the services of that feast. What is it that accompanies it ?

First of all, there shall be light to discover the excellency of the feast; the veil is taken away, and a knowledge given to know divine things in a spiritual manner.

Then, which will damp all feasts, the fear of death is taken away. ' He will swallow up death in victory, and wipe away all tears,' that is, all sorrow. The effect is put for the cause. This is an excellent promise, an excellent service in this spiritual banquet. Suppose a man were set at a feast furnished with all delicates, royally attended, clothes suitable, and had a sword hung over his head ready to fall upon him, it would cast such a damp on his spirit, as would spoil the joy of this feast. So to hear of spiritual excellencies, and yet death, and hell, and damnation coming along, alas! where is the comfort you speak of. And therefore to make the feast more perfect, there is not only light and knowledge, but removal of it ever may damp the feast. So this must needs come in to comfort all the rest. ' He shall swallow up death in victory, and wipe away tears from all faces.' Death is here represented to us under the word victory, as a combatant, as one that we are to fight withal, a captain.

And then here is the victory of him, Christ overcomes him, and overcomes him gloriously. It is not only a conquest, but a swallowing of him up. Usually God useth all sorts of enemies in their own kind. He causeth them that spoil to be spoiled, them that swallow up to be swallowed up. So death the great swallower shall be swallowed up.

Beloved, death is the great king of kings, and the emperor of emperors, the great captain and ruling king of the world ; for no king hath such dominion as death hath. It spreads its government and victory over all nations. He is equal, though a tyrant. As a tyrant spares none, he is equal in this. He subdueth young and old, poor and rich. He levels sceptres and spades together. He levels all. There is no difference between the dust of an emperor and the meanest man. He is a tyrant that governeth over all. And so there is this equity in him, he spares none.

He hath continued from the beginning of the world to this time ; but he is a tyrant brought in by ourselves, Rom. v. 19, *seq.* Sin let in death. It opened the door. Death is no creature of God's making. Satan brought in sin, and sin brought in death. So that we be accessory ourselves to the powerful stroke of this prevailing tyrant. And therefore sin is called the cause of death. Sin brought in death, and armeth death. The weapon that death fights with, and causeth great terror, it is sin. The cause is armed with the power of the wrath of God for sin, the fear of hell, and damnation. So that wrath, and hell, and damnation, arming sin, it bringeth a sting of itself, and puts a venom into death. All cares, and fears, and sorrows, and sicknesses, are less and petty deaths, harbingers to death itself; but the attendants that follow this great king are worst of all, as Rev. vi. 8, ' I saw a pale horse, and death upon it, and after him comes hell.' What were death, if it were not for the pit, and dungeon that followeth it ? So that death is attended with hell, and hell with eternity. Therefore here is a strange kind of prevailing. There is no victory where there is no enemy, and therefore death must needs be an enemy, yea, it is the worst enemy, and the last enemy. Death is not planted in the forlorn hope, but it is planted at last for the greatest advantage, and is a great enemy. What doth death ? It depriveth us of all comfort, pleasure, communion with one another in this life, callings or whatsoever else is comfortable. The grave is the house of oblivion. Death is terrible of itself, even to nature, as Augustine saith, where it is not swallowed up of Christ ; for it is an evil in itself, and as I said, armed with a sting of sin, after which follows hell.

Now this death is swallowed up. When the Scripture puts a person upon death,* it is not uncomely for us to speak as the Scripture doth. The Scripture puts a person upon death, and a kind of triumphing spirit in God's children over death. ' O death, where is thy sting ? O grave, where is thy victory ?' 1 Cor. xv. 55. Death is the greatest swallower, and yet it is swallowed up by Christ. Death hath swallowed up all, and when it hath swallowed up, it keepeth them. It keeps the dust of kings, subjects, great and small, to the general day of judgment, when death shall be swallowed up of itself. It is therefore of the nature of those that Solomon speaks of, that cry, ' Give, give,' Prov. xxx. 15, and yet is never satisfied, like the grave, yet this death is swallowed up in victory.

But how cometh death to be swallowed up ? Christ will swallow up death in victory, for himself and his.

Reason. First of all, because sin brought in death, our Saviour Christ became sin, a sacrifice to his father's justice for sin. He was made sin for us, he was made a curse for us, to take away the curse due to us ; and sin being taken away, what hath death to do with us, and hell, and damnation, the attendants on death ? Nothing at all. Therefore, Col. ii. 10, upon the cross Christ did nail the law, and sin, and the devil. There he reigned over principalities and powers, which were but executioners let loose by reason of our sins. And God being satisfied for sin, the devil hath nothing to do with us, but to exercise us, except it be for our good. So that he hath swallowed up death, because by his death he hath taken away sin, and so the power of Satan, whose power is by sin. And therefore it is excellently set down, Heb. ii. 14, ' He also took part of flesh and blood, that through death he might destroy him that had the power of death, that is, the devil.' So Christ by death overthrew Satan, that had the power of death, because by death he took away sin, the sins of all, and bore our sins upon the cross, and was made sin for us, that knew no sin. He is ours, if we believe. For then Christ is given to a particular man when he believes. Beloved, Christ upon the cross did triumph over all our spiritual enemies, sin, and death, and all. It was a kingdom of patience. You know there is a double kingdom of Christ ; a kingdom of patience, and a kingdom of power.

1. Christ on the cross suffering punishment due to sin, overcame the law, and the devil, and sin, which is the kingdom of patience.

2. The kingdom of power he hath in heaven. If Christ were so able in his kingdom of patience to conquer our greatest enemies, what will he do in his kingdom of power? As Paul reasoneth, ' If by his death we are saved, much more now he triumphs in heaven, and appears for us, is he able to convey greater matters to us,' Rom. v. 21.

If Christ in the days of his flesh did conquer, how glorious will his conquest be at the day of judgment ! *Now*, Christ hath conquered all in his own person, as our head ; *then* he will conquer for us in his mystical body.

---

* That is, 'personifies.'—ED.

What is now done in his person, shall be done in his members. In the mean time, faith is our victory, his conquest over death our victory; his victory over all our spiritual enemies is our victory. Every one that believeth is a conqueror of death, though he die, because he sees it conquered in Christ his head ; and as it is truly conquered in him, so Christ will conquer it in all his members. For as Christ in his natural body is gone to heaven, there to appear in our behalf, so shall mystical Christ be wholly in glory. He will not leave a finger. We shall all triumph over all our spiritual enemies. As Christ's natural body is glorious in heaven as our head, so shall also his mystical body be.

You see then how death is swallowed up by Christ as our surety, as the second Adam upon the cross ; and truly swallowed up in him. And by faith this victory is ours, and time will come when in our own persons it shall be swallowed up in victory.

This might be enlarged, but I haste to make use of it.

Mark, I beseech you, how death is swallowed up by Christ in his own person for our good. He gave a great way to death, for death seized on him upon the cross. Death severeth soul from body. Death had him in his own cabinet, his grave, for three days. Nay, this great king and tyrant death, had a great conquest over Christ himself. But here was the glory of this victory ! When death, this great conqueror of the world, had Christ upon the cross, and in his own dominion, in the grave, where he rules and reigns, consuming and swallowing up all, death was fain to give up all ; and Satan thought to have had a great morsel when he devoured Christ, but there was an hook in his divine power that catched him, that when he thought to have swallowed up Christ, was swallowed up himself. His head was then broken. He never had such a blow, as by Christ on the cross, when he was overcome, being a scorn of the world visibly, yet invisibly in God's acceptation of that sacrifice, and in a spirit of faith. Christ triumpheth over Satan. Death was subdued even in his own kingdom, and that makes the victory great.

Death by seizing on Christ without right, Christ hath freed us from the evil of death when it had right to us. Death hath lost all its right by fastening on Christ, and so is become as a drone* without a sting. So the great swallower of all is swallowed up itself at last by Christ.

Use 1. Now for comfortable use of it. First, let us consider *that God oftentimes giveth a great deal of way to his greatest enemies.* God useth a stratagem of retiring ; he seems to retire and give liberty to his enemies, but it is to triumph and trample upon them with greater shame. He will tread them to dust afterward. Christ gave death a great deal of liberty. He was crucified and tormented, then had† to the grave, and there he lay. And this was to raise a greater triumph over this great prevailer, over the world and death itself.

It is continued so in the church. Doth not he give way to the enemies of the church ? They may come to say, Aha, aha, so would we have it. Now the poor children of God are where we would have them, but then comes sudden destruction. God, to make his victory more glorious, and more to discover their cruelty, comes upon them when they be in the top of pleasure, and the church in the bottom of abasement. Then God swalloweth up all in victory, as Christ did death when it seemed to have been itself victorious.

This is a very comfortable consideration, for if death be overcome when

* That is, the 'drone' bee.—G.   † That is, 'taken.'—G.

it seemed to overcome Christ, what need we fear any other enemy ? Christ hath broken the net, as an eagle or great bird, and the rest escape by him.

You may enlarge this in your own meditations. He will swallow up death in victory. This is said for the time to come, he *will* swallow up death. But Paul saith it is also past, and swallowed up already. Faith saith it is done ; and so it is in our head. Were it not comfortable now to all true-hearted Christians, to hear that the church fareth better, and that the enemies were swallowed up, for they be but the instruments of this inferior death? Let us get the spirit of faith, and see them all conquered, for certainly they shall have the worst at last. He that hath swallowed up death in victory, will swallow up all that be the cause of death. And therefore the Scripture speaks of these things as past, ' Babylon is fallen, as a millstone cast into the bottom of the sea,' Rev. xviii. 21.

Get a spirit of faith, and we shall never be much troubled with Babylon ; for all the enemies of Christ, and adherents to that man of sin, must down, and partake of the judgments threatened in the Revelations. Heaven hath concluded it, and all the policy of Rome and hell cannot disannul it. They be already swallowed up to faith, and Christ will rule till he hath put them all under his feet, Ps. cx. 1 ; which shall be done, not only to destroy them, but to raise himself higher, in giving them up to their confusion.

Use 2. Again, if death be swallowed up in victory, labour *to be one with Christ crucified, for union with him.* Begin with union with Christ crucified. The first union is with Christ abased, and then with Christ glorified. And therefore labour to see sin, that brought in death, subdued by the power of Christ's death in some measure, and then we shall have comfort in his death glorified. For in my ' holy mount' death is swallowed up, that is, the true church of Christ. Labour to be members of Christ, otherwise death will come as a tyrant indeed, armed with a terrible sting, in his full force to assail you. It is the most terrible thing to see death come armed with the wrath and anger of God, and attended with hell and damnation. Labour, therefore, to be one with Christ crucified, to get our sins crucified, and ourselves partakers of his death ; and then no damnation, no fear of death to them that are in Christ. They may die, but they are freed from eternal death, and they shall rise again, even as Christ's body rose, to glory.

Get, therefore, into Christ, and desire the power of his death subduing sin. In what measure we grow in that, we grow in boldness and joy, and whatsoever privileges follow Christ.

Use 3. Again, when we be in Christ, true members of him, then *let us be thankful to God for this victory, thankful to Jesus Christ that hath given us victory*. When we think of death, of sin, of judgment, of hell, of damnation, let us be framed as a Christian should. Now let him that hath the most terrible and fearful things in the world as conquered enemies, say, Oh, blessed be God for Christ, and blessed be Christ for dying for us, and by death disarming death of his sting ! That now we can think of it in our judgments quietly ; now we can think of all these as conquered enemies : this is the fruit of Christ's death. They are not only enemies, but friends in Christ. Sin, the remainder of it—(the guilt of it, that bindeth over to damnation, is taken away)—the remainders of it serve to humble us, make us feel the power of pardon, and to desire another world, where we shall be all spiritual. So that death is a part of our jointure. ' All things are yours, life and death,' 1 Cor. iii. 22. Death doth us many excellent services. It is a door and passage to life. Death is the death of itself, destroyeth itself. We never truly live till we die, and when we die, we are past fear of death. So that sin dieth, misery dieth, death dieth. Though it takes us from comforts, and employments, and friends here, yet it is a change to a better place, and better company, and better employments, and better condition, to be in a glorious condition to eternity ; and therefore we have cause to bless God in Christ, that took our nature, and in our nature disarmed our greatest enemy, sin, and so disarmed death, and freed us from the wrath of God, and hell, and damnation. Oh, we can never be thankful enough for this !

Use 4. Again, if death be swallowed up in victory, *let us be ashamed of the fear of death*, because Christ saith he will swallow him up, as he hath already in his own person. Shall we be afraid of an enemy that is swallowed up in our head, and shall be swallowed up in every one of us ? If we cherish fear, we shew we look not for an interest in this promise ; for it is a promise, that ' in this holy mountain death shall be swallowed up in victory,' and why should we fear a conquered enemy ? None will fear an enemy that is conquered.

Obj. But how came Christ to fear death, and we not to fear ?

Ans. Christ had to deal with death armed with a terrible sting, with sin, and the wrath of God for sin. And, therefore, when he was to die, ' Father, let this cup pass from me,' Matt. xxvi. 39. But death is disarmed to us. He had to encounter with sin and the wrath of God, and death in all its strength. But we are not so. We are to deal with death like the brazen serpent, that hath the shape of death, but no sting at all. It has become a drone ever since it lost its sting in Christ. Life took death, that death might take life, as he said. The meaning is, Christ's life itself took death, that we that were so subject to death, that we were death itself, might take life. Oh blessed consideration ! Nothing comparable to the consideration of the death of Christ ! It is the death of death.

And then again we are sure of victory. It is conquered in our head, and shall be in us. But you say we are to conflict with the pangs of death, and many troubles meet in death. It is true, but it is conquered to faith, and in Christ our head. We must fight. Christ traineth us to overcome death ourselves by faith, and then we are sure of victory. Join these two together. It is conquered in Christ our head, and shall be conquered of us. Death keeps our dust, and must give them all again.

Obj. But in the mean time we die.

Ans. 'Tis so, but we are sure of victory. He will protect us in our combat, that hath conquered for us. We fight against death and the terror of it, in the strength and faith of his victory. Join these three together.

He that hath been our Saviour in life, will be so to death, and not exclusively, then to leave us, but to death, and in death, for ever ; yea, most ready to help us in our last conflict. Indeed, to wicked men death is terrible, for he sendeth the devil to fetch them out of the world ; but for those that be his, he sendeth his angels to fetch them, and he helps them in their combat. We must not therefore fear over much. There is a natural fear of death. Death wrought upon Christ himself, God-man ; not only death, but such a death. He was to be left of his Father, and lie under the sense of the wrath of God ; the separation of that soul from the body he took upon him was terrible ; and therefore he saith, ' If it be possible, let this cup pass from me :' that was nature, and without it he had not been true man. But that I say is, that grace may be above nature. Death is a time of darkness. It strips us of earthly comforts, friends, callings, employments ; but then comes the eye of faith to lay hold of the victory on Christ in time to come, when death shall be only swallowed up in victory; and then the glorious state to come, to which death bringeth us. So that here faith must be above sense, and grace above nature, and therefore I beseech you, let us labour for it.

There be two sorts of men to whom I would speak a little.

First. Those that in a kind of bravery seem to slight death; men of base spirits, as we call them; fools, vain-glorious spirits, empty spirits. Is there any creature, unless in Christ, able groundedly* to slight so great an enemy as death, armed with a sting of sin, and attended with hell and damnation? The Romish and devilish spirits are terrible; but if thy sins be not pardoned, it is the most terrible thing in the world to die, for there is a gulf afterwards. What shall we say, then, of single combatants, that for vainglory are prodigal of their lives, that for a foul word, a little disgrace, will venture on this enemy, that is armed with sin, and if they die, they die in sin.† And which is the miserable condition of him that dies in sin: his death opens the gate to another death, which is eternal. They say they have repented, but there is no repentance of a sin to be committed. Canst thou repent of a sin before it be committed? that is but a mockery of God. And what saith the Scripture? Is it not the most terrible judgment under heaven to die in our sins? A man that dies in sin dies in hell: he goeth from death to hell, and that eternal.

I wonder, therefore, that the wisdom of flesh and blood should take away men's wit, and faith, and grace, and all, so much as to slight death, and repentance, as if it were so easy. Now, beloved, death is a terrible thing. It hath a sting, and thou shalt know it. If thou hast not grace to feel the sting of it whilst thou livest, when thou diest the sting will revive; then thy conscience shall awake in hell. Drunkenness and jollity take away sense of sin; but sin will revive, and conscience will revive. God hath not put it into us for nought. Death is terrible, if not disarmed beforehand. And if thou go about to die without disarming it before, it will not be outfaced. It is not an enemy to be scorned and slighted. And, therefore, be Christians in good earnest, else leave profession, and perish eternally. For we must all die; and it is a greater matter than we take it. But if we be true Christians, it is the sweetest thing in the world, an end of all misery, a beginning of true happiness, an inlet to whatsoever is comfortable. Blessed are they that are in the Lord by faith, and them that die in the Lord. Their death is better than the day of life. Our birthday brings us into misery; and therefore let me speak to true Christians, and bid them be ashamed of fearing death too much, which, of an enemy is become a reconciled friend.

Second. This may in the next place *yield great consolation to those that are in Christ Jesus,* that death by Christ is swallowed up in victory; and the rather, because the Holy Ghost meaneth more than a bare victory over death. Death is not only subdued, but is made a friend to us, as Ps. cx. 1, it is said ' his enemies shall be his footstool.' Now a footstool is not only trampled upon, but an help to rise. And so death is not only subdued, but it advanceth God's children, and raiseth them higher. It is not only an enemy, but a reconciled friend; for he doth that which no friend in the world can do. It ends all our misery, and is the inlet into all happiness for eternity. And whatsoever it strips us of here, it giveth us advantage of better in another world. It cuts off our pleasures, and profits, and com-

* That is, ' on good grounds.'—G.
† In the margin, ' of [the] duellist.'—G.

pany, and callings here ; but what is that to our blessed change afterward, to our praying of God for ever, to the company of blessed souls, and the profits, and pleasures at the right hand of God for evermore ?   And therefore it is not only conquered, but to shew the excellency of his power, he hath made it a friend of an enemy, and the best friend in the world.   It indeed separates soul from body, but it joineth the soul to Christ ; so that the conjunction we have by it is better than the separation, if the conjunction makes us partake of our desire.   ' I desire to be dissolved,' saith St Paul, Philip. i. 23, but that is not well translated.   ' I desire to *depart*, and to be with Christ, which is best of all.'   So that it is not only not an enemy, but a friend.   And therefore the apostle makes it our jointure, part of our portion, all things are yours.   Why ? ' You are Christ's, and Christ is God's,' 1 Cor. iii. 22.   What are ours ? ' Things present, things to come, life, death,' 1 Cor. iii. 22, 23.   And well may death be ours, because sin is our enemy ; that remainder, that is kept in our nature to exercise us, and humble us, and fit us for grace.   As Austin saith, I dare be bold to say, it is profitable for some to fall, to make them more careful and watchful, and to prize mercy more.   So that not only death, but sin and the devil himself is ours; for his plots are for our good.   God over-shooteth him in his own bow.   ' He will give them over to Satan,' saith the apostle, ' that they may learn not to blaspheme,' 1 Tim. i. 20.   Yet though they have a spirit of blasphemy by the humbling of their bodies, they be taught not to blaspheme ; so that not only death, but sin, and he that brought sin into the world, the devil, are become our friends.

This being so, it may be for special comfort that we fear not the king of fears.   The devil hath great advantage by this affection of fear, when it is set upon this object death.   Overcome death, and all troubles are overcome. Who will fear anything that hath given up himself to God?   ' Skin for skin, and all that a man hath, will he give for his life,' Job ii. 4.   The devil knoweth that well enough.   Therefore ' fear not,' saith Christ, ' them that can kill the body,' Mat. x. 28.   Fear causeth snares, saith Solomon, Prov. xxix. 25, snares of conscience.   But if a man hath overcome the fear of death once, what more is to be done ?   What if they take away life, they cannot take away that that is better than life, the favour of God.   If we die in the Lord, we die in the favour of God, which is better than life; and we shall be found in the Lord at the day of judgment, and shall be for ever with the Lord in heaven; and therefore this is a ground of resolution in good causes, notwithstanding all threats whatsoever, because death itself is swallowed up in victory.

The worst the world can do is to take away this nature of ours.   When they have done that, they have done all they can; and when they have done that, they have done a pleasure.   That is not to be feared, saith Tertullian, that frees us from all that is to be feared (*d*).   What is to be feared in the world?   Every sickness, every disgrace?   Why, death frees us from all.   We do see every day takes away a piece of one's life, and when death cometh it overthroweth itself; for the soul goeth presently to the place of happiness.   The body sleepeth a while, and death hath no more power.

' He that believeth in me,' saith Christ, ' he shall not see death, but is passed from death to life,' John v. 24.   He shall not see spiritual death; but as he lives in Christ, shall die in Christ, and rise again in Christ.   He that hath the life of grace begun, shall have it consummate without interruption. It is a point of wonderful comfort, that death is so overcome that we be in heaven already.   And it is no hard speech, but stands with the truth of

other points ; for are not Christ and we all one ?   His body is there, and
is not he the head of his mystical body?   He that carried his natural body,
will not he carry his mystical body thither too ? will he be in piecemeal in
heaven ?   Therefore we are in heaven already the best part of us.   We are
represented in heaven, for Christ represents us there as the husband doth
the wife.   He hath taken up heaven for us.

Christ cannot be divided, as Austin saith.   'We sit in heavenly places
already with Christ,' Eph. i. 3.   And what a comfort is this, that while we
live we are in heaven, and that death cannot hinder us from our resurrection, which is the restoring of all things.   And therefore, as the apostle
saith, 'Comfort one another with these things,' 1 Thess. iv. 18.   These things
indeed have much comfort in them.

Let us labour then to be comfortable: this use the apostle makes of it ;
and fruitful in our places, upon consideration of the victory we have by
Christ.   1 Cor. xv.   It is an excellent chapter that largely proveth Christ's
victory, as the cause of our victory, because he is the first fruit that sanctifieth all the rest.   'Finally, my brethren, be constant, immoveable, always
abounding in the works of the Lord, knowing that your labour is not in vain
in the Lord.'   He raiseth that exhortation of fruitfulness and constancy
from this very ground of the victory Christ hath gotten by death.   'O death,
where is thy sting?   O grave, where is thy victory? Thanks be to God
through Jesus Christ.'   'And therefore be constant, immoveable, always
abounding in the work of the Lord, knowing that your labour shall not be
in vain in the Lord,' 1 Cor. xv. 58.   Make that use the apostle doth of
fruitfulness to God for Christ, that we can think of death, and sin, the
devil, and all his malice, and not be afraid ; yea, think of them all with
comfort, that we be not only freed from their tyranny, but they be our friends.

Christ hath the key of hell and death ; a saying taken from the custom
of governors that carried the key.   He hath the government and command
of hell and death.   Now if Christ hath command of death, he will not suffer
death to hurt his members, or triumph always over them.   He will keep
them in the grave.   Our bodies are safe in the grave.   The dust is fitted
for a heavenly, for another manner of body than we have now ; and Christ
that hath the key will let them out again.   Therefore trust a while till
times of restoring come, and then we shall have a glorious soul, and glorious
body, as the apostle saith, 1 Cor. xv. 43.   I beseech you, think of these
things, and get comfort against the evil day.   And to that end, be sure to
get into Christ, that we may be in Christ, living, and dying, and be found
in Christ.   For what saith the Scripture ? 'Blessed are they that die in the
Lord,' Rev. xiv. 13.   It is an argument of blessedness to die for the Lord,
but if it be not in the Lord, it is to no purpose.   If there is granted this happiness of dying for the Lord, it is well ; 'but blessed are they that die in the
Lord.'   Why ? 'They rest from their labour.'   Death takes them off from
their labours.   All their good works go to heaven with them.   So saith
the Spirit, whatsoever the flesh saith.   And there is no resting till that
time.   Their life is full of troubles and combers,* and therefore labour to
get assurance that we are in Christ, that we be in Christ, and die in Christ,
and then 'there is no condemnation to them that are in Christ.'

How besotted are we to put away preparation of death till it comes !
He that forgets Christ and getting into Christ, all his lifetime, it is God's
just judgment that he should forget himself in death.   We see how a villain
that hath no care of his own life, may have power of another man's life.

* That is, 'cumbers,' cares.—G.

And therefore labour to be engrafted into Christ by faith; and that we may know it by the Spirit of Christ prevailing in us over our natural corruptions more and more. As the apostle saith, ' There is no condemnation to them that are in Christ;' for the spirit of life, ' the law of the spirit of life which is in Christ, hath freed me from the law of sin and death,' Rom. vi. 7, seq., the condemning law of sin. If the law of the spirit of life which is in Christ the head, be in us in any measure, it frees us from the condemning law of sin, that it carrieth us not whither it would. Then we may say with comfort, ' There is no condemnation to them that are in Christ;' for the law of the spirit of life in Christ hath freed us from the condemning, tyrannizing law of sin and death,

Sin hath no law. It is in us as a subdued rebel, but it sets not up a throne. Some hope to be saved by Christ, and yet they set up sin a throne in the soul. Sin biddeth them defile themselves, and they must obey it. This is a woeful estate! How can they expect to die in the Lord, but such as are freed by the law of the spirit of life? New lords, new laws. When kings conquer, they bring fundamental laws; and when we are taken from Satan's kingdom into the kingdom of Christ, the fundamental laws are then altered. Christ by his Spirit sets up a law of believing, and praying, and doing good, and abstaining from evil. The law of the spirit of life frees us from the law of sin and death.

I beseech you, enlarge these things in your thoughts. They be things we must all have use of beforehand, against the evil day. It should be comfortable and useful to us all, to hear that our enemy, our greatest enemy, death, is swallowed up in victory. And yet there is more comfort in the text.

THE FIFTH SERMON.

And all tears shall be wiped away from all faces.—Isa. XXV. 8.

Not only death shall be swallowed up in victory, but God ' will wipe away all tears from all eyes.' Religion shall be religion; good things shall be good things. Nothing shall go under false notions. All tears shall be wiped away. We have now many causes of tears. In the world there is continual raising of clouds, that distil into drops of tears. Had we nothing without us to raise a vapour to be distilled in tears, we are able to raise up mists from our own mists, from our own doubts and conflicts within.

As we should weep for our own sins, so for the sins of others. As we may see in Jeremiah, where the prophet saith, ' O that my head were a fountain of tears, that I might weep continually for the sins of my people,' Jer. ix. 1. And indeed good men are easy to weep, as the heathen man observeth (e). They are easy to lament, not only for their own sins, but the sins and misery of another.

Our blessed Saviour himself, we never read that he laughed. We have heard that he wept, and for his very enemies, ' O Jerusalem, Jerusalem,' Mat. xxiii. 37. He shed tears for them that shed his blood. Tears were main evidences of Christ's sweetness of disposition; as that he would become man, and a curse, and die for us, and that he would make so much of little children, and call all to him that were weary and heavy laden, that he never refused any that came to him. He that wept specially for the

miseries and afflictions, this shewed his gracious and sweet disposition.
And that in heaven, he is so full of sympathies in glory, that when Paul
persecuted the church, ' Why dost thou persecute me ? ' Acts x. 4 ; so,
though he is free from passion in heaven, he is not free from compassion,
from sympathy with his church.   And so every child of God is ready, not
only to grieve for his own sins, and the misery that followeth them, but the
sins and miseries of others.   ' Mine eyes gush out with rivers of tears,'
saith the prophet David, Ps. cxix. 136, when he saw that men brake the
law of God, whom he loved.

A true natural child takes to heart the disgrace of his father.   If we be
not grieved to see our father disgraced, we are bastards, not sons.   They
that make sport of sin, what are they ?   Alas ! they have not one spark of
the spirit of adoption.   They are not children, who rejoice at that at which
they should grieve.

So St Paul, ' I have told you often, and now tell you weeping, there be
many enemies of the cross of Christ,' Philip. iii. 18.   When he saw some
men preach against, and others enemies of the cross of Christ, whose end
is damnation, he telleth them of it weeping.

We have cause, therefore, to mourn for the sins of others, and for the
miseries of others, whether we respect God, or the church, or ourselves.

First, the love of God moveth us to weep when we see him dishonoured.

*Second, if we love the church, we should mourn for any sins that may
prejudice their salvation.*

Doth it not pity any*man to see an ox go to slaughter ? to see a man of
parts otherwise, by sinning against conscience, going to slaughter ? to see
an ordinary swearer, an unclean person, a profane wretch, covering himself
with pride as a garment, scorning God, and the world, and all ?   Can a
Christian look upon this, see flesh and blood, like himself, under the gospel,
under a cursed condition unavoidable, without serious repentance, and
not be affected with it ?   Can a man see a poor ass fall under a burden,
and not help to take it up, and yet see man falling to hell, and not be
affected with it ?   Thus we see we have cause enough of tears.   And as
there is cause, so we should be sensible.   We ought to take to heart the
afflictions of Joseph.   He is a dead man that hath not sense in this kind.
If we go to the body and state, or anything about a man, there is cause of
grief.   Hath not every member many diseases ? and is not our lives a kind
of hospital, some sick of one thing, some of another ?   But as there is cause
we should be sensible of it, we are flesh and not stones, therefore it is a
sottish opinion, to be stockish and brutish, as if to outface sorrow and grief
were a glory.

Use 1. When our Saviour was sent into the world, *Christi dolor, dolor
maximus, there were no patience without sensibleness.*   Away, then, with that
iron, that flinty philosophy, that thinks it a virtue to be stupid ; † and as
the apostle saith, ' without natural affections,' Rom. i. 31.   He counteth
it the greatest judgment of God upon the soul, yet they would have it a
virtue.   Why should I smite them any more ? saith God ; they have no
sense, no feeling, Isa. i. 5.

The proud philosopher thought it was not philosophical to weep, a proud
stoical humour,‡ but Christians desire it.

And therefore we ought to labour to be more sensible, that we might
make our peace, and reverence the justice of God, and be more sensible of

---

* That is, ' draw pity from any man.'—G.   † That is, ' insensible.'—G.
‡ One of the commonplaces of *Stoicism.*—G.

him afterwards. It is most true, that *Sapiens miser, plus miser;* the more wise any man is, the more sensible of misery. And therefore of all men, the best men have most grief, because they have most quick senses. They be not stupified with insensibility and resoluteness, to bear it bravely, as the world ; but they apprehend with grief, the cause of grief And as they have a more sanctified judgment than other men, so they have a more wise affection of love, and a quicker life of grace. Where life is, there is sense ; and where there is a clear sight or cause of grief, there is most grief. Therefore the best men have most grief, because they be most judicious, most loving.

Then they have most grace to bear it out of all others. Therefore, considering there is cause in ourselves and in others of grief continually, we ought to labour to be sensible of it, else it were no favour to have tears wiped away.

So that there is cause of tears, and tears is a duty of Christians, sensible of the cause both of sin and misery upon one and another.

Use 2. And as it is an unavoidable grief, *so it is good we should grieve.* We must stoop to God's course, we must bring our hearts to it, and pray (that since our necessities and sins do call for this dispensation, that we must under correction, he will make us sensible of his rod), that he would make good his covenant of grace, ' to take away our stony hearts, and give us hearts of flesh,' Ezek. xi. 19, that we may be sensible.

Most of graces are founded upon affection, and all graces are but affections sanctified. What would become of grace, if we had not affections ? Therefore, as there is cause of grief, and tears from grief, we ought to grieve. It is a condition, and a duty : a condition following misery, and a duty following our condition.

Take heed of that which hinders sensibleness of troubles and judgment, that is, hardness of heart, forgetfulness, studying to put away sorrow with sin. For we ought to be sensible, and ought to labour to be sensible, to know the meaning of every cross in ourselves and others.

But suppose we have crosses, and we must be sensible of them, then it followeth, ' God will wipe away all tears from our eyes.' Is there nothing for the present, no ground of comfort ? Yes. As we ought to be sensible of grief, so we ought to be sensible of matter of joy for the present, specially if we consider the time to come. The life of a Christian is a strange kind of life. He ought to grieve, and he ought to joy. He hath occasion of both, and he ought to entertain both ; for that that we ought to aim at specially is joy, and if we grieve, it is that afterwards we might joy. We must be sensible of any affliction, that we might joy afterwards, and we ought to labour for it. For is not the joy of the Lord our strength ? Are not we fit to do service, when our spirits are most enlarged ? And is it not a credit to religion, when we walk in comfort of the Holy Ghost ? Is it not a scandal, when we droop under the cross ? We ought to be sensible, yet not so as to forget matter of joy and comfort. And therefore, as we ought to grieve, so we ought, when we have grieved, to keep up the soul with consideration of joy for the present as much as we can, yea, to pick out matter of comfort from the very cross. That is the heart of a Christian, not only to joy in other matters, but to pick comfort out of grief. God suffers me to fall into this or that condition. It is a fruit of his fatherly love. He might suffer me to run the broad way, to be given up to a reprobate sense and hard heart, but he doth not do so. Pick out matter of comfort from grief.

Then consider the presence of God in it. Indeed, I have matter of grief, but I find God moderating it. It might be far worse, it is his mercy I am not consumed ; I find God by it doing me good, I find myself better by it, I cannot well be without it. Who would not labour to be sensible of a cross, when he looketh up to God's cross, and justice, and mercy ? He hath rather cause to joy, than to grieve in the very cross itself.

But specially mark what the Holy Ghost saith here. We ought not to be cast down overmuch with any cross, considering God ' will wipe away all tears from our eyes,' that is, all natural tears, and the miseries of this life. There shall be no more misery, no more sickness, no more trouble.

And then all tears that arise from consideration of sin, and misery following sin. Death is the accomplishment of all mortification. It is a comfort we shall not always lead this conflicting life, but the war between the flesh and spirit will be taken up ; the sense will be removed. We shall be out of Satan's reach, and the world's reach one day, which is a great comfort to consider. Whatsoever the cause is, the cause shall be removed ere long. If the cause be desertion, for that God leaveth us comfortless, we shall be for ever hereafter with the Lord. If the cause be separation from friends, why we shall all meet together ere long, and be for ever in heaven. If the cause be our own sins, we shall cease hereafter to offend God, and Christ will be all in all. Now sin is almost all in all. Sin and corruption bear a great sway in us. If the matter of our grief be the sins of others, and the afflictions of others, there is no sin in heaven, ' no unclean thing shall enter there,' Rev. xxi. 27. The souls of perfect men are there, and all are of one mind. There is no opposition to goodness, there all shall go one way ; there, howsoever they cannot agree here, all shall have mutual solace and contentment in one another : they in us and we in them, and that for ever. You cannot name them, or imagine a cause of tears, but it shall be removed there. Nay, the more tears we have shed here, the more comfort we shall have. As our troubles are increased here, our consolation shall increase. That we suffer here, if for a good cause, will work our ' eternal and exceeding weight of glory,' 2 Cor. iv. 17. We say April showers bring forth May flowers. It is a common speech, from experience of common life. It is true in religion. The more tears we shed in the April of our lives, the more sweet comfort we shall have hereafter, If no tears are to be shed here, no flowers are to be gathered there. And, therefore, besides deliverance from trouble, here is comfort, God will take away all cause of grief, and all kinds of grief whatsoever.

And therefore thus think of it.

The next thing to be considered is the order. First, we must shed tears, and then they must be wiped away. After a storm, a calm ; after sowing in tears, comes reaping in joy. What is the reason of that order ?

Reason 1. The reason is *our own necessity.* We are in such a frame and condition since the fall, that we cannot be put into a good frame of grace without much pain. The truths of God must cross us, and afflictions must join with them. For the sins contracted by pleasure, must be dissolved by pain. Repentance must cost us tears. We may thank ourselves if we have brought ourselves to a sinful course. For the necessity of this order, a diseased person must not be cured till he feel some smart of the wounds.

Reason 2. Again, consider it is *for our increase of comfort afterwards,* that God will have us shed tears ; and then to have our tears wiped away, because we be more sensible of joy and comfort after sorrow. We cannot be sensible of the joys of heaven, unless we feel the contrary here. And therefore of all men, heaven will be the most heaven to them that have had their portion of crosses and afflictions here. First, therefore, shed tears, and then they must be wiped away, because joy is most sensible. As it is with the wickedest of all men, they be most miserable that have been happiest, because their soul is enlarged by their happiness, to apprehend sorrow more quickly and sensibly. So they that have been most miserable here, shall have most joy hereafter.

Use 1. Now for use. Here is not only the mercies of God in Christ, but the tender mercy; that whereas our life is full of tears, which we have brought upon ourselves, yet God stoops so low as to wipe our eyes, like a father or mother. His mercy is a sweet and tender mercy. And, as the psalmist saith, when we are sick ' he maketh our beds in our sickness,' Ps. xli. 3. Christ will come and serve them that watch and serve him; nay, he will attend them, and ' sup with them,' Rev. iii. 20. He is not only mercy and goodness, but there be in him bowels of mercy. He not only giveth matter of joy and comfort, but he will do like a tender-hearted mother, wiping away all tears from our eyes. We cannot apprehend the bowels in God's love, the pity and mercy of God towards them that be his, and afflicted in the world, specially in a good cause. Though they be never so many, if they be penitent tears, he will wipe them all away.

And whereas we must shed tears here, that we may be comforted hereafter, take heed that we do not in this life judge by sight, but by faith. ' If we live by sight, we are of all men most wretched,' 1 Cor. xv. 19. In the world the children of God are most miserable, and of the children of God, the best saints. Who hath more cause of tears than the best saints? It is but seed-time here. While seed-time continues, there be tears. The husbandman, while it is seed-time, cannot do his office but with trouble. The minister cannot do his office, but he is forced to take to heart the sins of the times, to see his work go backward. Governors of families and such, they carry their seed weeping. Yea, the best men cannot do good sometimes, but they do it with trouble in themselves, and with conflict of corruptions. There is no good sown here, but it is sown in tears; yet take no scandal at this, ' God will wipe away all tears.'

The Head of the church, our blessed Saviour, and all his gracious apostles, what a life did they live! The glorious martyrs that sealed the truth with their blood! And therefore, as the apostle saith, ' If our happiness were here only, we were of all men most miserable,' 1 Cor. xv. 19. If we judge by sight, we shall condemn the generation of the righteous. We live by sight, when we see any cast down with sight of sin, sense of temptation, distress of conscience, [and] we think him forlorn. Oh, take heed of that! For those that shed tears here, God will wipe them all away. ' Woe to them that laugh now, for they shall mourn hereafter,' Luke vi. 25. Though we weep here, yet matter of joy enough shall spring up hereafter. ' Afflictions will yield a quiet fruit of righteousness to them that are exercised thereby,' Heb. xii. 11. We may not see their fruits presently, but afterwards. And therefore be not discouraged for anything we can suffer here, or for the church, if we see her under pressure. As darkness is sown for the wicked, the foundation of their eternal torment is laid in their joy; so the ground and foundation of all a godly man's joy is laid in tears. ' Blessed are they that mourn, for they shall be comforted,' Mat. v. 4. Yet for the present there is more matter of joy than grief, if we look with both eyes; as we ought to have double eyes, one to be sensible of our grief, as we must be, the other of our comfort, that we may not be surprised with grief. There

is a sorrow to death, an overmuch sorrow. It is unthankfulness to God to
forget our comforts, as it is stupidity to forget our sorrow. Take us at the
worst, have not we more cause of joy than sorrow? Mark Rom. v. 1, *seq.*:
' Being justified by faith, we have peace with God, and rejoice under hope
of glory.' Nay, afterwards, saith he, ' we rejoice in tribulations.' And
why? upon what ground? ' Knowing that tribulations bring experience,
and experience hope, and hope maketh not ashamed.' Now we rejoice in
God reconciled in Christ. So that as we ought to look with one eye upon
the grief, that we may have ground to exercise grace, which we are not
capable of without sensibleness, so we must look to grounds of joy. Our
life is woven of matter of sorrow and joy ; and as it is woven of both, affections should be sensible of both, that they may be more apprehensive of the
grounds of comforts.

When the day of persecution approacheth, this will make us comfortable,
for our life is a valley of tears; and shall not we go through this valley of
tears, to this mount where all tears shall be wiped away from all eyes?
When we be dejected with the loss of any friend, they say as Christ said to
the women, ' Weep not for me,' Luke xxiii. 28. They be happy, ' and all
tears are wiped away from their eyes.' And therefore as it is matter of
comfort while we live, so ground of comfort when we die. For there is
occasion of sorrow in death, parting with friends and comforts of this world.
Then tears are shed in more abundance, and then we bethink ourselves of
former sins, and there is renewing of repentance more than at other times ;
yet then are we near the time of joy, and nearest the accomplishment of
the promise that ' all tears shall be wiped away.'

And so you have the whole state of a Christian life, an afflicted condition. Aye, but it is a comfortable condition. The more afflictions here, the
more comfort here, but specially hereafter. The life of a carnal man is all
in misery. If he falls to joy, he is all joy ; if to sorrow, he is all sorrow.
He hath nothing to support him. He is like a Nabal, he sinketh like a
piece of lead to the bottom of the sea, 1 Sam. xxv. 37, 38; like Ahithophel,
down he goeth, 2 Sam. xvii. 23. When he is upon the merry pin, he is
nothing but joy. But a Christian's state and disposition are both mixed.
He hath ground of sorrow for his own sins, and for the sins and miseries
of the times. So he hath matter of comfort for the present, in the favour
of God, in the pardoning of sins, in the presence of God, in delivering him
from trouble. He hath special ground of joy in hope of glory in time to
come. Therefore, as we have a mixed state, labour for a mixed disposition,
and labour to be in a joyful frame, so to grieve, as out of it to raise matter
of joy. And when we would joy, grieve before, for joy is sown in grief.
The best method of joy is for to take away all that disturbeth our joy.
Search the bottom of the heart ! see what sin is unconfessed, unrepented
of ! Spread it before God, desire God to pardon it, to seal the pardon !
When our souls are searched to the bottom, then out of that sorrow springeth
joy ; and out of these sighs and groans that cannot be expressed, cometh
joy unspeakable and full of glory. If a man will be joyful, let him labour
to weep first, that the matter that interrupteth his joy may be taken away.
Those that will be joyful, and not search to the bottom, must needs with
shame be brought back to sorrow. When we will joy to purpose, let us
judge ourselves, that we may not be judged of the Lord ; mourn for our
sins, and then lay hold upon the promise, that ' all they that mourn for
sin shall be comforted,' Mat. v. 4. And blessed are they that shed tears
here, for all tears shall be wiped away.

We are subject to wrong ourselves, both good and bad : for the good think, if they be in misery, they shall be ever so ; the bad, if they be in prosperity, they shall always be so, and they bless themselves in it. Now the joy of the hypocrites is as the ' crackling of thorns,' Eccl. vii. 6, and the grief of the godly is but short. And therefore let not the wicked fool themselves with groundless hopes, nor the godly vex themselves with needless fears ; but put off conceitedness of the long continuance of troubles. Time is but short, and ere long God ' will wipe away all tears from our eyes.' No mists, no clouds, shall be extended to heaven. The state in heaven shall be like the state of heaven, and there is no cloud there, but all pure, all serene. Therefore in Christianity consider not their beginning but their ends. ' Mark the end of the upright, for the end of the upright is peace,' Ps. xxxvii. 37. Ways have their commendation from the term in which they end. 'If by any means I may attain the resurrection of the dead,' saith Paul, Philip. iii. 11. Through thick and thin, fair and foul, rugged winds, dry or bloody death ; if by any means I may come to the resurrection of the dead, the first degree of glory, all is well. It is a good way that ends well. *Non quâ, sed quò.* Consider not what way he brings us to heaven, but whither he brings us. If he bring us to heaven through a valley of tears, it is no matter ; for in heaven ' all tears shall be wiped from our eyes.' And therefore Christianity is called wisdom. ' And this wisdom is justified of her children,' Mat. xi. 19. What is the chiefest point of wisdom ? To look home to the end, and to direct all means to that end. He is wise that is wise for eternity. The wicked will have their payment here. ' But woe to them that laugh, for they shall mourn,' saith Christ, Luke vi. 25. They will not stay for ground of joy hereafter, but will have present payment. But though the ways of Christians be foul, and wet with tears, yet blessed are they ; for God ' will wipe away all tears from their eyes.' ' Comfort one another with these words,' 1 Thess. iv. 18.

THE SIXTH SERMON.

And he shall swallow up death in victory; and God will wipe away tears from all faces; that the rebukes of his people may be taken away from off the earth: for the Lord hath spoken it.—Isa. XXV. 8.

You have heard heretofore of a *feast* provided for God's people, the *founder* of it being God himself, who only can indeed comfort (that which is specially to be comforted) the soul and the conscience, he being above the conscience. The *place* where the feast is kept is ' mount Zion,' the church of God. The delicacies are described by ' fat things, wine refined on the lees,' &c. The best of the best that can be thought of, which is Christ with all his benefits ; who is bread indeed, and drink indeed, that cherisheth and nourisheth the soul to life everlasting. And because there should be nothing to disturb the solemnity of the feast, he promises to ' destroy the face of covering,' ' to take away the veil spread over all nations,' the veil of ignorance and infidelity, to shine upon the soul, and fill it full of knowledge and heavenly comfort. And because there can be no comfort where death is feared, being the greatest enemy in this life, therefore he will ' swallow up death in victory,' and all that makes way for death, or attends death. And when this is taken away, all the attendants vanish with it, ' God will wipe away all tears from all faces.' Because the best things have not the best entertainment in the world, nor the best persons, God promiseth that the rebukes of his people shall be taken away from off the earth; what they are they shall be known to be. These be very great matters, and therefore there is a great confirmation, they have a seal, and what is that ? ' The Lord hath spoken it.'

The last day I shewed that God's children shall shed tears, and that they have cause to do it. I will now enlarge it a little.

It is the condition of men since the fall. In paradise before there was no cause of tears, nothing was out of joint, all in frame. There was no sin, therefore no sorrow, therefore no apprehension of sorrow. And so in heaven there shall be no tears, because no cause of it; they shall be as far from heaven as the cause. This life is a valley of tears, a life of misery, and therefore we shed tears here. And we want no cause of it as long as sin is in the world, and sorrow, and misery that followeth sin; our own sins and the sins of others, our own miseries and the miseries of others. And surely a child of God finds this the greatest cause of mourning in this world, that he hath a principle in him always molesting him in the service of God. He cannot serve God with that cheerfulness. His unfeelingness, that he cannot be so sensible of God, dishonoured by himself and others, is his burden. He is grieved that he cannot grieve enough. He can find tears for other things, matter of this enough, as the heathen man could say (f). A man loseth his estate, and hath tears for them ; but forceth tears for other things which are the true ground of grief. A child of God hath a remainder of corruptions, which puts him on to offend against God, and hinders him in his service, in the liberty and cheerfulness of it. And this he complains of with Paul and others, ' Miserable man that I am,' not for his affliction, though that was much, but ' who shall deliver me from this body of death ?' Rom. vii. 24.

Case 1. I will here add a case. *Some say they cannot weep, but they can grieve; whether then is it necessary or no to weep?* Tears are taken for the spring of tears ; grief, all grief, shall be taken away. Tears are but the messengers of grief; and oftentimes the deepest apprehension, that takes things deeply, cannot express it in tears. In some the passages fetching the conceit to the heart are made more tender that they can weep. Now, the grief of a Christian is a judicial * grief; a rational grief, not only sensible tears must have sensible grief, but a Christian's grief is a sensible, judicial grief. He hath a right judgment of things that cause sorrow, willeth it, and tears are only an expression of it.

But how shall I know whether grief be right or no ? There be tears God hath no bottle for. ' Thou puttest my tears into thy bottle,' Ps. lvi. 8. He makes much of them. They be *vinum angelicum*, as he saith. God is an angel to his people, to wipe away their tears. But some tears God hath no bottle for, hypocritical tears, Delilah's tears, tears of revenge and anger, Esau's tears. And therefore the true tears that God will wipe away, are such as first of all follow our condition here, our misery. God will wipe them away. If we speak of tears from a judicial ground,

1. The spring of true tears *is the love of God, and of Christ, and of his church, and the love of the state of Christianity.* Tears spring from love, these tears specially.

Oh ! a Christian takes to heart that God should be so ill used in the world ; that Christ, the Saviour of the world, should find such entertainment, that he should have anything in him that should offend such a

* That is, 'judicious.'—ED.

Saviour! This unkindness stingeth him to the heart. He takes it griev-ously that God should be abused. *Lætitia habet suas lachrymas*, there is not only grief that is the immediate cause of tears, but another cause beforehand; that is, love. Joy likewise hath its tears, though they be not here meant specially.

2. Again, tears are good and sound when we weep *for our own sins as well as the sins and miseries of others.* And I will add more, we must weep for the sins of others as well as for our own. For it is a greater sign of the truth of grace to take to heart the sins of others more than our own. You will say this is a kind of paradox, for often a man may take to heart his own sins as matter of terror of conscience; not his sins, as contrary to God, having antipathy to him, being opposite to the state of the soul, not as sin is properly sin, but to be grieved and vexed for sin as it hath vexation and terror of conscience. When a man can take to heart the sins of another, and that truly as it is an offence of his good God, and a crucify-ing again of his sweet Saviour, these be true tears indeed. It is more sign of grace than to weep for a man's own sins.

Some are taken up with terrors of conscience, that let their children, family, and friends alone. Their heart is eaten up with self-love, and they be near eaten up with their own terrors of conscience. But here is true grief and an hatred of sin in a right respect, when it exerciseth itself upon others as well as upon ourselves.

3. Again, tears arise from the right spring, from true grief, *when we can weep in secret.* Oh! saith Jeremiah, if you do so and so, ' My soul shall weep in secret for your pride,' Jer. xiii. 17. Here was a good soul indeed. Many will have tears of comfort in public, &c. Aye, but when they can weep in secret for their own sins and the sins of others, it is an evidence of a right spring of grief.

4. Again, when tears tend *to reformation of what they grieve for;* for else they be *steriles lachrymæ*, barren tears. Do they tend to reform what we weep for? Do they tend to action? Affections are then good when they carry to action; as grief, love, joy, they are all for action. When we weep and grieve, and reform withal, it is a good sign. I will name no more. You see then that grief is sound when it springeth from the love of God, and is for the sins of others as well as our own, and our own as well as others; when it stirs up to reformation; when it is in secret; and there-fore let us examine our grief by these and the like evidences. It will be a good character of a gracious soul. Then God will carry himself as a sweet nurse, or loving mother to her child, that sheddeth tears. God will ' wipe away all these tears.' Oh! the transcending love of God! His love is a tender love. The love of a mother, the love of a nurse! It is not love, but the bowels of love, the bowels of mercy and compassion. How low doth he stoop to wipe away the tears of his children! ' God will wipe away all tears.'

I will propound one question more, and then proceed. But we are bid to rejoice always. Why then is it required that we weep and mourn? Can two contraries stand together?

Case 2. I answer, very well. For we may grieve, as we have matter of grief, and are in a condition of grief; and we may rejoice, and ought to rejoice, as we look to the promise that God ' will wipe away all tears.' When we think of the present cause, we cannot but grieve; but when we look beyond all troubles, we cannot but joy; it hath influence of joy into our heart. Nay, for the present we may joy and grieve, without looking to eternity sometimes. If we consider that we have offended God, done that that grieveth his Spirit, that is matter of grief. But when we consider we have Christ at his right hand, that speaketh peace for us, and makes our peace by virtue of his mediation, that giveth comfort. So that we have cause of joy, and cause of grief, about the same things at the same time.

We are never in such a state of grief here, but if we look about us, look forward, look upward . . . . .* A Christian, that is, a good Christian, is a person that hath many things to look after, that he may manage his estate of Christianity wisely. He is to look to himself and his sins, to the mercies of God in Christ, to the constancy of it, that it is answerable to the fruit of it in peace and joy here, and happiness hereafter, which are constant too. His grace, as himself, is constant, the fruits of it constant. Therefore ' rejoice evermore.' And, saith the apostle, ' I know what I say, I am well advised, ' evermore rejoice,' Philip. iv. 4. So that the life of a Christian is a mixed life, nay, the ground of our joy is our sorrow and grief, and joy is sown in grief. If we will rejoice indeed, let us mourn indeed. True joy ariseth and springs out of sorrow.

I proceed to the next. ' And the rebukes of his people shall be taken away from off the face of the earth.' Another benefit that makes the feast sweet and comfortable is this : ' He will take away the rebukes of his people.' And here is the same method to be used, *that God's children, his church, and people, are under rebukes, and under reproach.*

We need not stand to prove the truth of it. It is true, *first, the head of the church, and the church itself, and every particular member, they go under rebukes.* For the head of the church, we should spend the time to no purpose to prove it. What was Christ's life ? It was under a veil. He appeared not to be what he was. You know he was esteemed the chief of devils, an enemy to his prince, to Cæsar. I will not spend time in clear truths.

For the church itself, you see in the book of Esther, iii. 8, ' There is a strange people that acknowledge no law, they be against the laws of the prince.' They pass under the imputation of rebels. The poor church, that had thoughts of peace, the meek church of God, they counted as enemies of the state, as Christ, the head, was. And so the church in Babylon, under what rebukes was it ? They reproached them, ' By the waters of Babylon we sat down and wept, when they said, Sing us one of the songs of Zion,' Ps. cxxxvii. 1. The church sitteth by the waters of Babylon all this life. The world is a kind of Babylon to God's people, and then sing us one of your songs. Where is now your God ? say the hearts of wretched people, when they saw the people of God in disgrace. Tully could say of the nation of the Jews, ' It sheweth how God regardeth it ; it hath been so often overcome.' † Thus the heathen man could scorn the state of God's people. You see how the psalmist complains in the name of particular Christians, ' Where is his God ? he trusted in him, let him save him,' Ps. xxii. 8. Oh, this was daggers to David's heart. ' It pierced to my heart when they said, Where is thy God ?' Ps. xlii. 10. To touch a Christian in his God, as if God had no care of him, it is more than his own grief and affliction. So when a child of God is rebuked and affronted, when religion must suffer by it, so that the head of the church, the members of the church, are under rebukes, as it may be proved, if I carry you through all stories.

At this day, the church of the Jews, you see what it is come to : the nation of the Jews, under what reproach it is. And surely this prophecy

---

* This sentence is left thus unfinished.—G.

† Cicero Orat. Pro Flacco, c. 28. See footnote, vol. I., p. 303.—G.

aimeth partly at the conversion of the Jews. It shall be accomplished at the resurrection, when all tears shall be perfectly wiped away. But it hath relation to the conversion of the Jews. In what state are they now? Are they not a word of reproach? Moses's speech is verified of them, 'They shall be a hissing to all nations,' 2 Chron. xxix. 8. And is not it a proverb, Hated as a Jew?

Reason. But what is the reason of it? Not to stand long upon the point, you know there be two seeds in the world, the seed of the serpent and the seed of the woman; and the enmity between them is the true ground, and the antipathy in the hearts of carnal men to goodness. There is a light shineth in the life of them that be good, and them that be ill hate the light, as discovering themselves to themselves, and to the world, not to be that they seem to be. There is a saltness in the truth. It is savoury, but it is tart, whether in the word preached, or howsoever truth layeth open what is cross to corruption. And hereupon pride and self-love in carnal men studieth how to overcast all they can the names of those that be better than themselves with a cloud of disgrace. It is the property of vile men to make all others vile, that they may be alike. Men cannot abide distinctions of one from another. The Scripture distinguisheth the 'righteous man, more excellent than his neighbour,' Prov. xii. 26; but they will not have that. The hatred of distinction is the cause they make all as bad as they can. And hereupon it is that good things were never clothed in the right habit, nor ill things neither, but do pass under a veil. Take away the true garment of grace and holiness and goodness, and put a false veil upon it, it passeth not under that that it is in this world, because wicked men will not suffer it, but will raise up the credit of other things, of empty learning, or empty things, or vain courses, and cry up the credit of worldly things, that they may seem to be wise, and not fools, that are carried to those things. The best things had never the happiness to pass under their own names; but they had other coverings. Truth goeth always with a torn and scratched face; it is a stranger in the world, and hath strange entertainment.

Use 1. If this be so, we ought to take heed *of laying a scandal or reproach upon religion.* Salvian complains in his time that wickedness had gotten that head, that those that were good and honourable, *mali esse volunt, ne a malis abhorreantur (g)*, they that were good studied to be vile, that they might not be vilified of others. 'Oh,' saith he, 'how much is Christ beholden to the world, that those that own him, and own goodness, and own his cause, should be therefore base, because they be his friends.' Take heed of taking scandals.

Use 2. We had need be wise, that we be not taken in this snare of Satan, *to mistake error for truth, and good for evil.* Satan and his agents make things pass under contrary representations. Superstition goeth for religion, and religion for superstition, schism, and heresy. It hath always been so. Therefore seek wisdom to discern aright. The devil hath two properties, he is a liar and a murderer; the one makes way for the other, for he could not murder unless he did lie. The devil himself will not be an open murderer if he can help it. The fraudulent persecution is worse than the violent. If he can bring to hell by fraud and lying, he will never do it by violence. He is a liar, that he may be a murderer; for when he can raise an imputation upon the church and children of God, that they be rebels, enemies of state, then he may *cum privilegio* be a murderer. When he hath tainted God's people in the conceit of the world, then they find that entertainment not which they deserve, but which they be apprehended to deserve, when the conceit of other men towards them is poisoned. ' Oh, this sect is spoken against everywhere,' say they to Paul, Acts xxviii. 22. Therefore we had need be wise ; for if the instruments of Satan, led with his spirit, had not hoped that slanders should take, they would never have been so skilful in that trade. But they know they shall find some shallow fools that will believe them, without searching into the depths of them, and take up persons and things under prejudice. It is enough for them that this is said of them. They have neither wit nor judgment, nor so much patience, from following their lusts, as to examine them ; and that makes them so mad as they are. *Calumniare audacter, aliquid hærebit*, slander stoutly, something will stick, they are sure of it. That which hath raised and ruined many a man, is that of Haman's casting of jealousy upon those that are better than themselves. That was Haman's trick, and so will be the practice of the wicked, as it hath been from the beginning, so to the end of the world. ' Thou art not Cæsar's friend,' say they, and it is enough to Pilate, John xix. 12. Thus it has been, and will be to the end of the world. Therefore we had need to be wise, that we be not misled. Men will never leave to speak ill till they have learned to speak better, till the Spirit of God hath taught them.

Now, it is said that Christ will take away the rebukes of his people. That is the promise. As they are, they shall be known to be. He will set all in joint again. Harmony is a sweet thing, and order is a sweet thing. Time will come when things that are now out of order to appearance, shall be all set in their due order again. Those that are basest shall be lowest, and those that be excellent shall be highest. This is a-working and framing now. In this confusion we must look to the catastrophe, the conclusion of all. He will ' take away the rebukes of all.' God is the father of truth, and truth is the daughter of time. Time will bring forth truth at last. And those that be honourable indeed shall be honourable. It is as true as God is just ; for goodness and holiness are beams of God ; and will he suffer it always to pass under a false veil ? There is not an attribute of God but shall shine forth gloriously, even all his excellency and dignity. There is nothing shall be above him and his excellency. No ; though he seems for a while not to rule in the world, or have power, but suffers them to go away with it that are his enemies, he is working another thing by suffering them, he is working the glory of his children, and confusion of his enemies. There is nothing in God but shall gloriously shine, and nothing in his children, no beams of God, but shall gloriously shine, to the confusion of the world. They that are good shall be known to be good, God will bring their righteousness to light. The witnesses that vexed the world, and had base entertainment, they were slain and disgraced, but they rose again, and were carried to heaven, Rev. xi. 12, *seq.*, as Elias. So there will be a resurrection of name, a resurrection of reputation. That that is good shall be good, and that that is bad shall be bad. It shall be known to be as it is. This is for comfort.

Use 1. You hear, therefore, what course to take under disgrace. What shall we do when the church passeth under disgrace, as it is now ? A protestant is worse than a Turk or a Jew amongst the railing papists. Among ourselves we see under what reputation the best things go. It is too well known to speak of. And the scandal taken from hence doth extremely harden. It keeps men from religion, it draweth many from religion that have entered into it, because they have not learned so much self-denial as to venture upon disgrace. And surely where no self-denial is, there is no religion. Christ knew what doctrine he taught when he taught self-denial in this respect.

What shall we do, therefore? 1. Labour first of all for *innocency*, that if men will reproach, they may reproach without a cause.

2. Then labour for a *spirit of patience* to serve Christ with. 'Great is your reward when men speak evil of you,' Mat. v. 12, for a good cause. It is the portion of a Christian in this life to do well and suffer ill. Of all, certainly they are best, that, out of love to goodness, are carried to goodness, without looking to rewards or disgrace; that follow with a single eye. Labour, therefore, for patience, and not only so, but,

3. For *courage*. For the moon goeth its course, and lets the dog bark. We have a course to run, let us keep our course constantly; pass through good reports and bad reports; be at a point what the world thinks. We seek applause at another theatre than the world.

4. Again, then, labour for *sincerity under rebukes*, that we have a good aim, such an aim as Paul had, 'If I be mad and out of my wits,' 1 Cor. v. 13, 14. He being earnest for his master, Christ, they count him out of his wits. If I be out of my wits it is for Christ. 'If I be sober, it is for you, the love of Christ constraineth me to be so,' 2 Cor. v. 14. Get the love of Christ, and that will make a man care for nothing. If I go beyond myself, it is to God. As David said, when he was mocked by Michal, 'It is to the Lord,' when he danced before the ark,' 2 Sam. vi. 20, 21. *Bonus ludus*, a good dance, where Michal scoffeth, and David danceth. Where gracious men magnify God, and have Michals to scoff at them, it is *bonus ludus*. God will look upon them, for it is to the Lord. Labour that our aims be good, and it is no matter what the world judgeth of them.

5. And when all will not do, *commend our credits to God by prayer*. As we commend our souls and conditions, so our reputations, that he would take care of them, that he would bring our righteousness to light, that it should shine out as the noonday. So David doth, he complains to God, and commendeth all to him, prayeth him to take part against his enemies, to right his cause. And when we have done that, we have done our duty. Yet withal hope for better things, be content to pass under the world as unknown men, and to be inwardly worthy, and pass as unknown men. Rich men, if truly rich, they will applaud themselves in their bosoms, though the world disgrace them, yet at home I am thus furnished. And so a Christian that knoweth his worth, that he is a child of God, heir of heaven, that he is attended upon by angels, that he is a jewel to God in his esteem, [he thinks this] to be absolutely the best thing in the world. He knoweth the worth of a Christian, and his own worth as being a Christian. He applauseth* and comforteth himself, in that he knoweth he hath a hidden life, a state of glory hidden in Christ. Now it is covered with disgrace and disrespect in the world, scorned and reproached, but what is that to him? It is an hidden life, and for the present he knoweth his own excellency, and, therefore, can pass through good report and bad report. 'I care not for man's day,' saith Paul, 'there is another day to which I must stand,' 1 Cor. iv. 3.

And thus if we do, as Peter saith, 'There is a spirit of glory shall rest upon us,' 1 Pet. iv. 14. The ground we have of comfort under rebuke and disgrace, there is a spirit of glory. What is that? A large spirit enlarging our hearts with inward comfort, inward joy, inward love of God. 'A

* That is, 'applaudeth.'—G.

spirit of glory shall rest upon you,' and shall continue with you as long as disgrace shall continue.   He opposeth this to all disgrace he meeteth with in the world.

God putteth sometimes a glory and excellency upon his children under disgrace and ill usage in the world, that he will daunt the world, as Stephen's face did shine as the face of an angel, which came from a spirit of glory that rested upon him, and expressed himself to be the servant of God. He that takes away from our good report, if we be good, he addeth to our reward.   Our Saviour Christ saith as much, ' Blessed are you when you be ill spoken of, for great is your reward,' Mat. v. 11, 12.

THE SEVENTH SERMON.

And the rebukes of his people shall he take away from all the earth: for the mouth of the Lord hath spoken it.—ISA. XXV. 8.

Use 3. This is a great promise, *and I pray you be comforted with it.* For of all grief that God's people suffer in the world, there is none greater than reproach, disgrace, and contumely. *Movemur contumeliis plus quam injuriis,* we are more moved with reproaches than injuries.   Injuries come from several causes, but disgrace from abundance of slighting.   No man but thinks himself worthy of respect from some or other.   Now, slanders come from abundance of malice, or else abundance of contempt; and therefore nothing sticks so much as reproaches, specially by reason of opinion and fancy, that raiseth them over high.

Our Saviour, Christ, ' endured the cross and despised the shame,' Heb. xii. 2.   That shame that vain people cast upon religion and the best things, they despise that and make that a matter of patience.   They knew the cross would not be shaken off, persecution and troubles must be endured, and therefore they ' endured the cross, and despised the shame.'   Now, to bear crosses, take the counsel of the holy apostles, look up to him, consider Christ ; and whatsoever disgrace in words or carriage we shall endure, we are sure, though we shall never know it till we feel it by experience, ' the spirit of glory shall rest upon us,' and rebuke shall be taken away.

Ere long there will be no glory in heaven and earth but the glory of Christ and of his spouse, for all the rest shall be in their own place, as it was said of Judas, that ' he went to his place,' Acts i. 25.   Their proper place is not to domineer, but to be in hell, and ere long they shall be there.   Heaven is the proper element of the saints ; that is the place of Christ, the head, and where should the body be but with the head ? where the spouse but with the husband ?   I say this shall come to pass, that all the wicked shall be in their place, and all the godly in theirs with Christ, and then shall the rebukes of God's people be taken away.   A great matter, and therefore it is sealed with a great confirmation, ' The Lord Jehovah hath spoken it.'   Therefore it must and will be so.   ' The mouth of the Lord hath spoken it.'   This is not in vain added, for the Lord knoweth well enough we need it to believe so great things, that there is such a feast provided, and that there is such a victory over death, our last enemy, and that there will be such glory, that all the glory shall be Christ's and his spouse's, that the wicked that are now so insolent shall be cast into their proper place with the devil, by whose spirit they are led.   They be great matters, and there is great disproportion between the present condition and that condition in heaven ;

and infidelity being in the soul, it is hard to fasten such things on the soul, that so great things should be done. But they are no greater than God hath said, and he is able to make good his word. ' The Lord hath said it,' and when God hath said it, heaven and earth cannot unsay it. When heaven hath concluded it, earth and hell cannot disannul it. ' The mouth of the Lord hath spoken it ;' that is, truth itself hath spoken it that cannot lie. A man may lie and be a man, and an honest man too. He may sometimes speak an untruth ; it taketh not away his nature. But God, who is pure truth, unchangeable truth, truth itself, cannot lie.

When we hear of great matters, as matters of Christianity be great matters, they be as large as the capacity of the soul, and larger too, and yet the soul is large in the understanding and affection too; when we hear of such large matters, *we need a great faith to believe them*. Great faith needeth great grounds, and therefore it is good to have all the helps we can. When we hear of great things promised, great deliverances, great glory, to strengthen our faith, remember God hath spoken them. He knoweth our weakness, our infirmity, and therefore helps us with this prop, ' The mouth of the Lord hath spoken it.' Let us therefore remember those great things are promised in the word of God, in the word of Jehovah, that can make them all good, that gives a being to all his promises. He is being itself, and gives being to whatsoever he saith. He is able to do it. Set God and his power against all opposition whatsoever from the creature, and all doubts that may arise from our own unbelieving hearts, ' The mouth of the Lord hath spoken it.'

Quest. But ye will say, the prophet Isaiah saith it, whose words they were.

Ans. I answer, Isaiah was the penman, God the mouth. The head dictateth, the hand writeth. Christ the head dictates, and his servant writeth. So that holy men write as they were inspired by the Holy Ghost, a better spirit than their own. ' Why do ye look on me ?' saith Isaiah. Think not it is I that say it ; I am but a man like yourselves ; but ' the mouth of the Lord hath spoken it.'

We should not regard men, nor the ministry of men, but consider who speaks by men, who sendeth them, with what commission do they come. Ambassadors are not regarded for themselves, but for them that send them. And therefore Cornelius said well, ' We are here in the presence of God to hear what thou wilt speak in the name of God,' Acts x. 33. And so people should come with that reverend* expression, We are come in the presence of God the Father, Son, and Holy Ghost, in the presence of the blessed angels, to hear what thou shalt say in the name of God, by the Spirit of God. We are not to deal with men, but with God. And therefore he saith, ' The mouth of the Lord hath spoken it.'

Quest. 2. Hence may this question be easily answered, Whence hath the Scripture authority ?

Ans. Why, from itself. It is the word ; it carrieth its own letters testimonial with it. Shall God borrow authority from men ? No ; the authority the word hath is from itself. It hath a supreme authority from itself. And we may answer that question about the judge of all controversies, What is the supreme Judge ? The word, the Spirit of God in the Scriptures. And who is above God ? It is a shameless, ridiculous impudency of men that will take upon them to be judges of Scripture, as if man would get upon the throne, and as a judge there judge. The Scriptures must judge all ere long, yea, that great antichrist. Now an ignorant man, a

* That is, ' reverent.'—G.

simple man, that perhaps never read Scriptures, must judge of all controversies, yea, that that is judge of all and of himself, the word, which is from
the very mouth of God,

Quest. 3. You will ask me, How shall I know it is the word of God if the
church tells us not?

Ans. A carrier sheweth us these be ¦letters from such a man, but when
we open the letter, and see the hand and seal, we know them to be his.
The church knows the word, and explaineth it; and when we see and feel
the efficacy of the word in itself, then we believe it to be the word, for there
is that in the word that sheweth it to be the word:

1. *The majesty that is in it.*

2. The matter that is *mysterious*, forgiveness of sins through a mystery,
forgiveness of sin,* victory over death, life everlasting in the world to come,
great matters, 'which eye hath not seen, nor ear heard, nor entered into the
heart of man,' 1 Cor. ii. 9. If it had not been revealed, it could not have
entered into the heart of angels, it containeth such glorious, transcending
mysteries. And then again,

3. The word to all them that belong to God *hath the Spirit of God,*
by which it passeth, rightly accompanying it, witnessing to the soul of
man that it is so; and, 4, *by a divine efficacy* it is mighty in operation.
What doth it in the heart? (1.) It *warmeth the heart* upon the hearing, and speaking, and discoursing of it, as when the disciples went
to Emmaus, Luke xxiv. 32. (2.) It hath a heat of Spirit going with it to
affect the heart *with heavenly joy and delight;* it hath power going with it
by the Spirit to raise joy unspeakable and glorious; it hath a power to
pacify the soul amidst all troubles. When nothing will still the soul, the
Spirit of God in the word will do it by its divine power. (3.) Yea,
it will *change a man* from a beastly or devilish temper to a higher
and happier estate, as you have it, Isaiah xi. 6–9. It makes lions lambs,
leopards kids. And what is the ground of all? In that very place
'the earth shall be full of the knowledge of the Lord.' The knowledge of
God reconciled is such a powerful knowledge that it hath a transforming
virtue to alter men's dispositions. What was Paul before conversion? and
Zaccheus? Therefore, it is the word, because it hath divine operation to
heat the soul, and raise the soul, and change the soul, and (4.) *cast down the
soul,* as low in a manner as hell, in sense of its own misery. It will make
a Felix to tremble, a man that it doth not effectually work upon. The
truths of it are so moving that it will make a carnal man to quake. When
Paul spake of judgment to come, of giving account of all that is done in the
flesh, when a possibility of it was apprehended, it made Felix to quake.
It makes mountains level, and it fills up the valleys. The word can raise
up the soul; when man is as low as hell, and looketh for nothing but
damnation, the Spirit with the word will fetch him from thence; as the
jailor, Acts xvi. 31, there was little between him and hell, 'What shall I
do to be saved? Why, believe in the Lord Jesus.' And with these words
there went out an efficacy. He believed, and he afterward was full of joy.

The first gospel ever preached in pardon was by God himself. Never
was any creature so near damnation as our first father Adam, cast from the
greatest happiness, *miserrimum est fuisse felicem;* for he that enjoyed before
communion with God and his angels, having sinned, and having conscience
of his sin, considering his great parts, and apprehension of the state he had
been in, this must needs affect him deeply; and being in this condition,

* Probably a misprinted repetition.—G.

the promise of the 'seed of the woman to break the serpent's head,' revived him.

There is a strange efficacy in the gospel. The Roman empire was the greatest enemy that the church ever had The ten persecutions you see what they were ;* and yet notwithstanding the word grew upon them and never rested, the spreading of the gospel, and the Spirit with it, till the cross got above the crown, as it did in the time of Constantine, and so it continueth.

5. And must not this be a divine word which hath this efficacy, to revive, comfort, change, cast down, raise up again, *search secrets, search the heart to the bottom?* A poor idiot† that comes to hear the word of God, when he hears the secrets of his heart laid open by the word, he concludes certainly, ' God is in you, and you are God's ministers,' 1 Cor. iv. 25. The word ' divideth between the marrow and the bone,' Heb. xv. 12 ; it arraigneth the heart before God's tribunal seat. Those that are saved, it hath these effects in them that I have named. And if you ask how they know whether the word be the word ? A man may answer, I have found it to be so, raising me up, comforting me, and strengthening me. I had perished in my affliction if the word had not raised me. *Principles are proved, you know, from experience,* for they have nothing above them. There is no other principle to prove the word, but experience from the working of it. How know you the light to be the light, but by itself, and that fire is hot, but by itself? Principles prove themselves only by experience ; and this principle is so proved by itself, that there is no child of God but can say by experience, that the word is the word.

6. *If a man might go to reason, one might bring that which could not be easily answered for the satisfaction of an atheist.* Let him but grant there is a God, he will grant one thing in religion or another. But let him grant there is a God and a reasonable creature, then there must be a service, a religion ; and this service must be according to some rules prescribed ; for the superior will not be served as the inferior pleaseth. He must discover what good the superior intendeth, and what duties he expects. This must be revealed in some word. God and the reasonable creature, and religion, make a necessity of a word, and that must be the word we have, or another ; and what word in the world is probable to be the word but this ?

Obj. You will say it may be corrupt.

Ans. The Jews looked to the Old Testament, that it should not be corrupted ; for they knew every syllable in it, and preserved every letter. It is one part of their superstition, and God blesseth that superstition to take away all such cavils. For the New Testament the Jews cared not for ; but heretics on their side watch over it that there should be no corruption ; they will so observe one another. But what are these reasons to those which the soul of a gracious Christian knoweth by the operation of the word upon the heart ?

Use 1. And, therefore, *let us regard it as the word of God;* hear it as the word of God ; read it as the word of God. A company of profane wretches you shall have, the scums and basest of the people, that will discourse, and to grace their discourse, they must have Scripture phrases ; but whose word is it ? It is the word of the great God. Eglon was a heathen king, and yet when a message came from God, he arose up and made obeyance,‡

---

* See Note *b*, vol. I. p. 384.—G.   † See Note *e*, vol. I. p. 290.—G.

‡ This interpretation of the ' rising up' of Eglon anticipates Bishop Patrick *in loc.*—G.

Judges iii. 20. We should never read the word but with reverence, considering whose book it is, and that we must be judged by it another day.

Use 2. If it be the word, I beseech you consider what we say, and *know that God will make every part of it good.* There shall not a jot of it fail, nothing of it shall miscarry. God speaketh all these words. And, therefore, if you be blasphemers, you shall not carry it away guiltless. God hath said it. If you continue not to obey, you are under God's curse. Unless you repent you shall perish. Every threat God will make good. You must repent and get into Christ, else perish eternally. God hath said it, and we may confirm it in the unfolding and reading of it. The time is coming for the execution of it, and then God is peremptory. Now God waiteth our leisure, and entreateth us, but if we will not repent, we shall have that arrow in our sides that will never be gotten out till we die in hell. Whose sins are condemned in Scripture, they are condemned by God; and whom we shut heaven to, by opening the Scriptures, God will shut heaven to. The opening of the Scriptures is the opening of heaven. If the Scripture saith, a man that liveth in such a sin shall not be saved, heaven shall be shut to him; he is in a state of death, he is strucken, and remaineth in danger till he repenteth. How many live in sins against conscience, that are under the guilt and danger of their sins. They be wounded, they be struck by the word. There is a threat against their sins, although it be not executed; and they be as much in danger of eternal death as a condemned traitor, only God suffers them to live, that they may make their peace. They have blessed times of visitation. Oh, make use of it! It is the word of God; and know that God will make every part of his word good in threats as well as in promises.

Use 3. Take occasion from hence likewise to shame ourselves for our infidelity* in the promises. When we are in any disconsolate estate, we are in Job's case. Being in trouble, the consolation of the Almighty seemed light to him, Job. xv. 11. These be the comforts of God. When we come to comfort some, though the sweet promises of the gospel be opened, yet they do not consider them as being the word, the consolations of the Almighty, and therefore they seem light to them. But it should not be so. Consider they be the comforts of the word, and therefore we should hear them with faith, labour to affect† them, and shame ourselves. Is this God's word that giveth this direction, that giveth this comfort, and shall I not regard it? Is it the consolation of the Almighty, and shall not I embrace it? Therefore we should be ashamed, not to be more affected with the heavenly sweet things promised of God than we are.

A man that refuseth heavenly comforts to embrace comforts below, how should he reflect upon himself with shame? Hath God promised such things, God that cannot lie? and shall I lose my hope of all these glorious things, for the enjoying of the pleasures of sin for a season? I profess myself to be a Christian, where is my faith? where is my hope? A man must acknowledge either I have no faith; for if I had faith believing God speaking these excellent things, I would not venture my loss of them to get the enjoyment of poor temporary things here, for the good things promised in another world. Labour, therefore, to bring men's hearts to believe the word, and desire God to seal to our souls that it is so.

Means. I will give one direction. *Labour for the Spirit of God, that writ the word, that indited the word.* Beg of God to seal to our souls that it is the word, and that he would sanctify our hearts to be suitable to the

* That is, 'disbelief,' or 'unbelief.'—G.   † That is, to 'love' them.—G.

word, and never rest till we can find God by his Spirit seasoning our hearts, so that the relish of our souls may suit to the relish of divine truths, that when we hear them we may relish the truth in them, and may so feel the work of God's Spirit, that we may be able to say, he is our God. And when we hear of any threatening, we may tremble at it, and any sin discovered, we may hate it. For unless we, by the Spirit of God, have something wrought in us suitable to the word, we shall never believe the word to be the word. And therefore pray the Lord, by his Spirit to frame our hearts to be suitable to divine truths, and so frame them in our affections, that we may find the word in our joy, in our love, in our patience, that all may be seasoned with the word of God. When there is a relish in the word, and in the soul suitable to it, then a man is a Christian indeed to purpose. Till then men will apostatize, turn papist, turn atheist, or any thing, because there is a distance between the soul and the word. The word is not engrafted into the soul. They do not know the word to be the word by arguments fetched from the word, and therefore they fall from the power of the word. But if we will not fall from divine truths, get truth written in the heart, and our hearts so seasoned by it, and made so harmonious and suitable to it, that we may embrace it to death, that we may live and die in it.

To go on :

' In that day shall it be said, Lo, this is our God; we have waited for him.'

Here is a gracious promise, that shutteth up all spoken before. He spake of great things before. And now here is a promise of a day, wherein he will make all things promised, good to the soul of every believing Christian.

' In that day it shall be said, This is our God; we have waited for him; he will save us.'

It is an excellent portion of Scripture to shew the gracious disposition that the Spirit of God will work in all those that embrace the gracious promises of God. The time shall come when they shall say, ' Lo, this is our God; we have waited for him, and now we enjoy him.'

The points considerable are these :

1. First of all by supposition that there be *glorious excellent things promised to the people of God ;* rich and precious promises of feasting, of taking away the veil, of conquest over death by victory, of wiping away tears and removing rebukes. Great things, if we go no farther than my text.

2. Secondly, *these have a day when they shall be performed*, which is not presently ; for the end of a promise is to support the soul till the performance. God doth not only reserve great things for us in another world, but to comfort us in the way, doth reach out to us promises to comfort us till we come thither. There is a time when he will perform them, and not only a time, but there are likewise promises of performance. At that time the promises of these great things shall be performed.

3. The next thing is, *that God will stir up in his children a disposition suitable*. That is, the grace of waiting. As great things were promised before, so the soul hath a grace fit for it. ' We have waited for thee.'

4. And as they wait for them, while they are in performing, *so they shall enjoy them*. ' We have waited for thee, and we will be glad in thy salvation.' We shall so enjoy them, that we shall joy in them. Good things, when they be enjoyed, they be joyed in.

5. Again, ' we shall rejoice in our salvation, we shall glory in our God.'

After they be a while exercised in waiting, then cometh performance, then they be enjoyed, *and they be enjoyed with joy, in glorying in God.* For that is the issue of a Christian, when he hath what he would enjoy, when he enjoyeth it with joy, when the fruit of it is that God hath his glory, and therefore the heart can rejoice in his salvation.

Then there is a day, as for the exercising of his people here by waiting, so there is a day of performing promises. 'In that day.' That is, a day of all days. When that day cometh, then all prophecies and promises shall be accomplished to the uttermost.

But before that great day, there is an intermediate performance of promises assisted by waiting, to drop comfort to us by degrees. He reserveth not all to that day. There is lesser days before that great day. As at the first coming of Christ, so at the overthrow of antichrist, the conversion of the Jews, there will be much joy. But that is not that day. These days make way for that day. Whensoever prophecies shall end in performances, then shall be a day of joying and glorying in the God of our salvation for ever. And therefore in the Revelations where this Scripture is cited, Rev. xxi. 4, is meant the conversion of the Jews, and the glorious estate they shall enjoy before the end of the world. 'We have waited for our God,' and now we enjoy him. Aye, but what saith the church there? 'Come, Lord Jesus, come quickly.' There is yet another, 'Come, Lord,' till we be in heaven. So that though intermediate promises be performed here, yet there is another great day of the Lord to be performed, which is specially meant here.

6. The last thing considerable in the words is the manner of expression. They are expressed full of life, and with repetition, to make them sure and more certain, 'In that day it shall be said, This is our God; we have waited for him; he shall save us.' He bringeth them in speaking these words of affection.

Indeed, when we come to enjoy the performance of God's gracious promises, if we should live to see the fulness of the Gentiles come, and Jews called, we should speak of it again and again. Affections are large, and few expressions will not serve for large affections. It will be no tautology to say, 'This is our God; we have waited for him.'

Beloved, times are yet to come which may much affect the hearts of the children of God. Howsoever we may not live to see the performance of these things, yet we shall all live to see that day of judgment, and then we shall say, 'This is our God; we have waited for him.' We now see God in the promises, and then we shall see him 'face to face,' whom we have waited for in the promises, and we shall see him in heaven for ever.

'Lo, this is our God; we have waited for him.' While we live here we are in state of waiting, we are under promises, and a condition under promises is a waiting condition; a condition of performance is an enjoying condition. We are in a waiting condition till our bodies be raised out of the grave; for when we die we wait for the resurrection of our bodies. We may say as Jacob when he was dying, 'I have waited for thy salvation.' We are in a waiting condition till body and soul be joined together at the day of judgment for ever.

And there we should labour to have those graces that are suitable for this condition. The things we wait for are of so transcending excellency, as glory to come, that they cannot be waited for, but* the Spirit, by the things waited for, fitteth us to wait for them. A man cannot wait for glory of soul

---

* That is, ' unless.'—ED.

and body, but the Spirit that raiseth up faith to believe, and hope to wait, will purge, and fit, and prepare him for that glorious condition. ' He that hath this hope purifieth himself, as he is pure,' 1 John iii. 3. Oh, it is a quickening waiting, and a purging waiting. It is efficacious by the Spirit to fit and purify his soul suitable to that glorious condition he waits for. Where that is not, it is but a conceit. A very slender apprehension of the glory to come will make men better. He that hath hope of heaven and happiness under glory, it will make him suitable to the place he looketh for.

THE EIGHTH SERMON.

He shall swallow up death in victory; and the Lord God will wipe away tears from off all faces; and the rebukes of his people shall he take away from off all the earth: for the Lord hath spoken it. And it shall be said in that day, Lo, this is our God; we have waited for him, and he will save us: this is the Lord; we have waited for him, we will be glad and rejoice in his salvation.—Isa. XXV. 8, 9.

To come closer to the particulars. ' It shall be said in that day, Lo, this is our God.' The mouth of the Lord hath spoken gracious things before, hath promised a feast, and an excellent feast. God's manner is first of all to give promises to his church. Why? His goodness cometh from his goodness, his goodness of grace cometh from his goodness of nature. ' He is good and doth good.' Now the same goodness of disposition which we call bounty, that reserveth heaven and happiness for us in another world, the same goodness will not suffer us to be without all comfort in this world, because the knowledge and revelation of the glory to come hath much comfort in it. Therefore in mercy he not only intendeth performance of glory, but out of the same fountain of goodness he intendeth to reveal whatsoever is good for his church in the way to glory. So that promises of good come from the same goodness of God by which he intendeth heaven. For what moved God to come out of that hidden light, that no man can come into, and discover himself in his Son? The word in his promises to reveal his mind to mankind, and make known what he will have us to do, and what he will do to us. But only his goodness is the cause of all. And therefore the end of promises in God's intention is to comfort us in the way to heaven, that we may have something to support us. They are *promissa, quasi præmissa.* They are promises and premises, and sent before the thing itself.

Now here it cometh that the glory to come is termed the joy of heaven and the glorious estate to come. ' You have need of patience, that you may get the promises.' Heaven and happiness is called the promises, because we have them assured in promises. The blessings of the New Testament are called promises; as the children of the promise, yea, the heirs of glory; because all is conveyed by a promise, therefore all happiness is conveyed by a promise.

Now the promises are of good things. They are for the spring of them, *free,* from God's free goodness; for the measure of them, *full;* for the truth of them, *constant,* even as God himself that promiseth. And therefore we may well build upon them.

Use. Before I go any farther, I beseech you let us account the promises of the good we have *to be our best treasure, our best portion, our best riches,* for they be called precious promises, 2 Pet. i. 4 ; not only because they be precious in themselves, but because they are from the precious love of God in Christ to us. They are likewise for precious things. They are laid hold of by precious faith, as the Scripture calleth them, and therefore they are precious promises. Let us not only account of our riches that we have ; for what is that we have, to what we speak of, to that we have in promise ? A Christian is rich in reversion, rich in bills and obligations. Christ hath bound himself to him, and he can sue him out when he pleaseth. In all kinds of necessity, he can sue God for good. He can go to God and say, ' Remember thy promise, Lord, wherein thou hast caused me thy servant to trust,' Ps. cxix. 49 ; and can bind God with his own word.

But I take this only in passage as the foundation of what I am to speak.

From the mouth of God you see the great promises delivered ; and now we have waited for them. That which answereth promises is expectation and waiting.

The second thing, therefore, between the promises, wherein God is a debtor, and the performance, is, that *there is a long time, a long day.* Oftentimes God takes a long day for performing of his promise, as four hundred years Abraham's posterity went to be in Egypt. And it was four thousand years from the beginning of the world till the coming of Christ, which was the promise of promises, the promise of the seed, a great long day. And therefore Christ is said to come in ' the latter end of the world.' Abraham had promise of a son, but it was not performed till he was an old man. Simeon had a promise to see Christ in the flesh, but he was an old man, ready to yield up the ghost, before it was performed. God taketh a long day for his promises ; long to us, not to him, ' for to him a thousand years are but as one day,'

Reason 1. The promises of God are long in performing ; for *to exercise our faith and our dependence to the full ;*

Reason 2. *To take us off from the creature ;* and

Reason 3. *To endear the things promised to us,* to set the greater price upon them when we have them. Many other reasons may be given, if I intended to enlarge myself in that point. A Christian hath a title to heaven. As soon as he is a Christian, he is an heir to heaven. Perhaps he may live here twenty or forty years more before God takes him up to glory. Why doth he defer it so long ?

Reason 4. The reason is, *God will fit us for heaven by little and little,* and will perfume us as Esther was perfumed before she must come to Ahasuerus, Esth. ii. 12. There were many weeks and months of perfuming. So God will sweeten and fit us for heaven and happiness. It is a holy place ; God a holy God. Christ is that holy one ; and for us to have everlasting communion with God and Christ in so holy a place, requireth a great preparation. And God, by deferring it so long, will mortify our affections by little and little, and will have us die to all base things here in affection before we die indeed. David had title to the kingdom as soon as ever he was anointed ; but David was fitted to be an excellent king, indeed, by deferring the performance of the promise till afterward. So in our right and title and possession of heaven, there is a long time between.

Our Saviour Christ was thirty-four years before he was taken up to heaven, because he was to work our salvation. And he was willing to suspend his glory for such a time, that he might do it ; to suspend his glory due to him from the first moment of his conception. For by virtue of the union, glory was due to him at the first ; but because he had taken upon him to be a Mediator, out of love he would suspend his glory due to him, that he might suffer. And so God, by way of conformity, will suspend the glory due to us, that we may be conformed to Christ. Though we have right to heaven as soon as we are born,* yet God will suspend the full performance of it ; because he will by correction and by length of time subdue by little and little that which maketh us unconformable to our head.

And can we complain for any deferring of heaven when we are but conformed to our glorious head, who was content to be without heaven so long ?

But to go on. As there be gracious and rich promises, and they have long time of performance to us, and ' hope deferred makes the soul languish,' Prov. xiii. 12 ; so God vouchsafeth a spirit to fit that expectation of his, a spirit of hope and waiting. And this waiting hath something perfect in it, and something imperfect. It is a mixed condition. There is good, because there is a promise ; for a promise is the declaration of God's will concerning good. But because it is a promise of a thing not performed, there is an imperfection. So there is a mixture in the promise, and a mixture in the grace. Hope and expectation and waiting is an imperfect grace. That there be glorious things, it is perfection of good ; that we have them not in possession, that is the imperfection. So that hope is something, but it is not possessed ; a promise is something, but it is not the performance ; a seed is something, but it is not the plant.

Thus God mixeth our condition here of perfection and imperfection. He will have us in state of imperfection, that we may not think ourselves at home in our country, when we are but in our way. Therefore he will have us in a state of imperfection, that we may long homeward ; yet he will have it a state of good, that we may not sink in the way.

And not only promises ; for in the way to heaven God keeps not all for heaven. He lets in drops of comfort oftentimes in the midst of misery. He doth reveal himself more glorious and sweet than at other times. There is nothing reserved for us in another world, but we have a beginning, a taste, an earnest of it here, to support us till we come to the full possession of what remaineth. We shall have full communion of saints there ; we have it here, in the taste of it. We know what it is to be acquainted with them that be gracious spirits. We have praising of God for ever there. We know the sweetness of it here in the house of God, which made David desire this one thing, ' that he might dwell in the house of God, to visit the beauty of God,' &c., Ps. xxvii. 4. There we shall have perfect peace ; here we have inward peace, unspeakable and glorious, ' a peace that passeth understanding,' Philip. iv. 7, in the beginning of it. There we shall have joy without all mixture of contrariety ; here we have joy, ' and joy unspeakable and full of glory,' 1 Peter i. 8. There is nothing in heaven that is perfect, that is sweet, and good, and comfortable, but we have a taste and earnest of it here. The Spirit will be all in all there ; there is something of it in us now. More light in our understandings, more obedience in our wills, more and more love in our affections, and it is growing more and more.

And therefore all is not kept for time to come ; we have something beginning here besides promises. There is some little degrees of performance. So that the state between us and heaven is a state mixed of good and imperfection.

Now God hath fitted graces suitable to that condition, and that is ex-

* That is, ' born again.'—G.

pectation or waiting, a fit grace and a fit disposition of soul from* imperfect condition, that is afterwards to be perfected ; for fruition is the condition of perfect happiness, not of waiting ; for waiting implieth imperfection.

This waiting carrieth with it almost all graces. Waiting for better times in glory to come, it hath to support it. It is a carriage of soul that is supported with many graces. For, first, we wait for that we believe. We have a spirit of faith to lead to it. And then we hope before we wait, and hope is the anchor of the soul, that stayeth the soul in all the waves and miseries of the world. It is the helmet that keeps off all the blows. This hope issues from faith ; for what we believe, we hope for the accomplishment of it.

So that all graces make way for waiting, or accompany it. The graces that accompany the waiting for good things in time to come are *patience*, to endure all griefs between us and the full possession of heaven ; then *longsuffering*, which is nothing else but patience lengthened, because troubles are lengthened, and the time is lengthened. So there is patience, and patience lengthened, which we call long-suffering ; and then, together with patience and long-suffering, there is *contentment*, without murmuring at the dispensation of God ; something in the soul that he would have it to be so. He that hath a heart to rise, because he hath not what he would have, he doth not wait with that grace of waiting that issueth from a right spring.

God reserveth joy for the time to come, for our home. We should be content to have communion with God and the souls of perfect men ; and not murmur though God exerciseth us with many crosses here. And therefore the Scripture calleth it a *silence*, ' In silence and in hope shall be your strength,' Isa. xxx. 15. The soul keepeth silence to God in this waiting condition, and this silence quells all risings in the soul presently ; as David, ' My soul kept silence unto the Lord,' Ps. xxxix. 2. It will still all risings of the heart, issuing from a resignation of the soul to God, to do as he will have us to do. So it implieth patience and longsuffering, contentment, holy silence, without murmuring and repining.

And then it implies *watchfulness* over ourselves, till we come to the full accomplishment of the promises, that we carry not ourselves unworthily in the mean time ; that we should not spend the time of our waiting in wickedness, to fetch sorrow from the devil, and the world to comfort us, or to be beholden to Satan. This is no waiting, but murmuring and rebellion, when in crosses and discomforts we cannot be content, but must be beholden to the devil, so there must be watchfulness ; and not only so, but *fruitfulness* in waiting. For he waits that waiteth in doing good, that waiteth in observance. He waiteth for his master's coming, that is doing his duty all the time in a fruitful course of observance and obedience ; else it is no waiting. Waiting is not merely a distance of time, but a filling up of that time with all gracious carriage, with obedience, and with silence, with longsuffering and contentment, and watchfulness [that] we take not any ill course, and observance, and with fruitfulness, that we may fill up times of waiting till performance, with all the graces, that we may have communion with God.

It is another manner of grace than the world thinks. What is the reason of all the wickedness of the world, and barrenness, and voluptuousness, but because they have not learned to wait ? They hear of good things, and precious things promised ; but they would have present payment, they will have something in hand. As Dives, ' Son, son, thou hast had thy good

* Qu. ' for ? '—ED.

things here,' Luke xvi. 25, they will have their goods things here. And what is the reason of wickedness, but because they will have present pleasures of sins ?   We must prefer the afflictions of Christ before the pleasures of sin, Heb. xi. 25.   Now that shortness of spirit to have reward here is the cause of all sin.   They have no hope, nor obedience, nor expectation to endure the continuance of diuturnity.*   Where then is patience, and hope, and contentment ?

The character of a Christian is, that he is in a waiting condition, and hath the grace of waiting.   Others will have the pleasures of sin, their profits and contentments, else they will crack their consciences, and sell Christ, God, heaven, and all.

A Christian, as he hath excellent things above the world, so he hath the grace of expectation, and all the graces that store up and maintain that expectation till the performance come.

And therefore it is an hard thing to be a good Christian, another thing than the world taketh it to be.   For mark, I beseech you, what is between us and heaven, that we must go through, if ever we will come there.   Between us and heaven, the thing promised, there be many crosses to be met withal, and they must be borne, and borne as a Christian should do. 'Through many afflictions we must enter into the kingdom of heaven,' Acts xiv. 22. Besides crosses, there be scandalous offences, that be enough to drive us from profession of religion, without grace.   Sometimes good men by their failings, and fallings out, they fall into sin, and fall out ; and that is a scandal to wicked men.   Oh, say they, who would be of this religion, when they cannot agree among themselves ?   This is a great hindrance and stop. It is a scandal and rub in the way, not so much in themselves.   We are full of scandal ourselves, catch at anything that we may except against the best ways.   There is a root of scandal in the hearts of all, because men will not go to hell without reason.

Now because we are easy to take offence, rather than we will be damned without reason, it is not easy to hold out.   Besides this, Satan plies it with his temptations from affliction, and from scandal ; he amplifies these things in the fancy.   Who would be a Christian ?   You see what their profession is.   And so he maketh the way the more difficult.

And then again, look at our own disposition to suffer, to hold out, to fix. There is an unsettledness, which is a proper† infirmity in our natures since the fall.   We love variety, we are inconstant, and cannot fix ourselves upon the best things, and we are impatient of suffering anything.   We are not only indisposed to do good, but more indisposed to suffer any ill. The Spirit must help us over all this, which must continue all our life long.   Till we be in heaven, something or other will be in our way.   Now the Spirit of God must help us over all these afflictions.   We shall never come to heaven to overcome afflictions, and scandals, and temptation, which Satan plies us here withal.   And then to overcome the tediousness of time, this needeth a great deal of strength.   Now this grace of expectance doth all.   And therefore it is so oftentimes stood upon in Scripture.   In Isaiah, and in the Psalms, how often is it repeated ; Ps. xxxvii. 7.   ' Wait on the Lord; if he tarry, wait thou.'   The Lord will wait for them that wait for him ; and it is the character in Scripture of a Christian.   Moses, he saith, such as waited for the consolation of Israel, Gen. xlix. 18, before Christ came in the flesh, such a one is one that ' waiteth for the consolation of Israel,' Luke ii. 25. To have a gracious disposition, and a grace of waiting was the character of

* That is, ' long continuance.'—G.   † That is, ' natural.'—G.

good people. Now since the coming of Christ, the character of the New Testament is, to wait for Christ's appearance. 'There is a crown of glory for me, and not only for me, but for all them that love his appearance,' 2 Tim. iv. 8. That is an ingredient in waiting, when we love the thing we wait for. And so Titus ii. 12, 'The grace of God that teacheth to deny ungodliness and worldly lusts, and to live holily, and justly, and soberly in this present evil world, looking for and waiting for this glorious appearing of Jesus Christ.'

So that looking with the eye of the soul partly on the first coming of Christ, which was to redeem our souls, and partly upon the second, which is to redeem our bodies from corruption, and to make both soul and body happy, it makes a man a good Christian. For the grace of God on the first, teacheth us to deny ungodliness; and looking for Christ's appearing, maketh us zealous of good works. You have scarce any epistle, but you have time described for looking for the coming of Christ, as Jude, 'Preserve youselves in the love of God, and wait for the coming of Christ.' So that as there be gracious promises, and a long day for them, God vouchsafeth grace to wait for the accomplishment of them.

Now as God giveth grace to wait, so he will perform what we wait for; as they say here, 'We have waited.' That is the speech of enjoying. God will at length make good what he hath promised; and what his truth hath promised, his power will perform. Goodness inclineth to make a promise, truth speaks it, and power performeth it, as you shall see here.

'We have waited,' &c.

In God there is a mouth of truth, a heart of pity, and an hand of power. These three meeting together, make good whatsoever is promised. 'He will fulfil the desires of them that fear him,' Ps. cxlv. 19. The desires that God hath put into his children, they be kindled from heaven; and he will satisfy them all out of his bowels of pity and compassion. He will not suffer the creature to be always under the rack of desire, under the rack of expectation, but he will fulfil the desire of them that fear him. And therefore learn this for the time to come.

Though we wait, God will perform whatsoever we wait for. And therefore, 'Lo, we have waited for him.' As there is a time of promising, so there is a time of performing; as there is a seedtime, so there is a time of harvest. There is a succession in nature, and a succession in grace; as the day followeth the night, and the Sabbath the week, and the jubilee such a term of years; and as the triumph followeth the war; and as the consummation of marriage followeth contract; so it is a happy and glorious condition, above all conditions here on earth. Therefore in this text you have not only the seedtime of the Christian (we may sow in tears, and in expectation, as in sowing), but here is likewise the harvest of a Christian. As there is time of sowing, so there is time of reaping; as time of waiting, so of enjoying. We have waited, and now, lo, we have what we waited for.

But why doth not the Holy Ghost set down a certain time, but leaveth it indefinite, 'In that day.' God keeps times and seasons in his own power; the point of time in general he leaveth it. There is a day; but the point and moment of time he keepeth in his own power. It is enough to know there is a day, and a day that will come in the best season. God's time is the best time. When judgments were threatened upon the wicked, they say, 'Let us eat, and drink, for to morrow we shall die,' 1 Cor. xv. 32. So Saul, 'To-morrow thou shalt die,' 1 Sam. xxviii. 19, and was he the better? So where there is a certain time of God's coming in judgment, godly men would not be the worse, and wicked men never the better.   Therefore God reserveth it indefinite, ' In that day.'

There is a day, and it is a glorious day, a day of all days, a day that never will have night, a day that we should think of every day, ' That day,' by way of excellency.   And before that day there be particular days in this world, wherein God sheweth himself, and fulfils the expectation of his children, to cherish the grand expectation of life everlasting.   As in times of trouble they expect of God, and wait for deliverance in God's time, and they must be able to say, ' Lo, we have waited.'   Because it is a beginning and pledge of the great performance that shall be consummate at that great day, and of all the miseries that shall then be removed ; so there is a day when the Jews' shall be converted, and the fulness of the Gentiles brought in, and the man of sin discovered, and consumed by the breath of Christ.   And when the church of God seeth them, they may say, ' Lo, we have waited for the Lord,' and lo, he is come ; that we looked for is now fulfilled.   So that God reserveth not the fulfilling of all the promises to the great day of all days, but even in this life he will have a ' that day.'

And it were very good for Christians in the passages of their lives to see how God answereth their prayers, and delivereth them.   Let them do as the saints in the Old Testament, that gave names to places where they saw God, as Peniel, Gen. xxxii. 30, he shall see God, and Abraham, ' God will be seen in the mount,' Gen. xxii. 14.   So Samson and others they gave names to places where they had deliverance, that they might be moved to be thankful.   A Christian taketh in all the comforts of this life to believe the things of the last great day.   ' Lo, we have waited for him.'

That shall be a time of sight and fruition, of full power and full joy, which is reserved for heaven ; then we shall say, ' Lo ! behold, this is the Lord.'   The more we see God here, the more we shall see him hereafter.   There be many ways of seeing, so as to say, ' Lo, this is the Lord ! '   We may say, from the poorest creature, ' Lo, this is the Lord ! '   Here are beams of his majesty in the works of his justice and mercy, ' Lo, here is the Lord ! '   The Lord hath brought mighty things to pass, the Lord is marvellous loving to his children.   ' Behold and see the salvation of the Lord ! '   We may say, ' Lo, here,' and see something of God in every creature.   No creature but hath something of God.   The things that have but mere being have something of God ; but the things that have life have more of God.   And so in some there is more, in some less of God.

But in the church of God specially, we may see his going in the sanctuary.   Lo, this God hath done for his church.   And in the sacraments, we may say, I have seen the Lord, and felt the Lord in his ordinance by his Holy Spirit.   We do all this before we come to see him in heaven.   But that is not meant specially.

We shall say, ' Lo, this is the Lord ! ' when we shall see him in heaven. All sight here leadeth to that sight.   Faith hath a sight here, but it is in the word and sacrament, and so imperfect ; but the sight in heaven is immediate and perfect, and therefore opposed to faith.   We live by faith, and not by sight.   In heaven we shall live by sight ; not that we live not by sight here in some degree, for the lesser sight leadeth to the greater sight. But in comparison of sight in heaven, there is no sight.   The Scripture speaketh of sight of God comparatively.   Moses ' saw God,' that is, more than any other ; and Jacob ' saw God,' that is, comparatively more than before, but not fully and wholly.   We can apprehend him, but not comprehend him, as they say.   We may see something of him, but not wholly.

But in heaven we shall have another sight of God, and then we shall say, 'Lo, this is the God we have waited for!' We shall see Christ face to face.

Beloved, that is the sight indeed. And if ye will ask me whether we shall see God then or no, consider what I said before. This is the God we have waited for in obedience, and fruitfully.

If we shall be ravished with the sight of God, surely if we see him here, we may see him there. We see him with the eye of faith, we see him in the ordinance, we have some sight of God that the world hath not. God discovereth himself to his children, more than to the world; and therefore they say, 'Thou revealest thyself to us, not unto the world,' John xiv. 22. A Christian wonders that God should reveal his love, and mercy, and goodness to him, more than to others. And therefore, if we belong to God, and shall see him hereafter, we must see him now. As we may see him, we must have some knowledge of him. And if we see God any way, all things in the world will be thought of no request, in comparison of the communion of God in Christ, as, 'We have seen the Lord, and what have we to do with idols?' Hosea xiv. 8. The soul that hath seen Christ, grows in detestation of sin, and loatheth all things in comparison.

And then, again, if we shall ever see God in glory, in this glorious and triumphing manner, 'This is the Lord,' this sight is a changing sight. There is no sight of God, but it changeth, and alters to the likeness of God, when he calls to look up to him, and he looks on us in favour and mercy. The best fruit of his favour is grace, of peace, and joy, for these be beams that issue from him, grace, as beams from the sun. But wherever God looks with any favour, there is a conformity to Christ, a gracious, humble, pitiful, merciful, obedient disposition, which is an earnest of the Spirit of Christ.

And there is a study of purity, of a refined disposition from the pollutions of the world. 'The pure in heart shall see God,' Mat. v. 8. They that hope to see God for ever in heaven, will study that purity that may dispose and fit them for heaven. And there is such a gracious influence in it, that they that hope for heaven, the very hope must needs help to purify them.

As there is grace suitable to waiting, so there is an influence from the things hoped for, to give vigour to all grace. As all the graces of a Christian fit and enable him for heaven, so hope of heaven yields life to all grace. There is a mutual influence into these things. God vouchsafeth discovery of these glorious things, to help us to wait, to be patient, and fruitful, and abundant in the work of the Lord. And the more we wait fruitfully, and patiently, and silently, the more we see of heaven. So that as in nature, the seed bringeth the tree, and the tree the seed; so in the things of God, one thing breeds another, and that breeds that again. So that waiting and grace fit us for heaven, and the thought of heaven puts life and vigour into all the graces that fit us for heaven. What is our faith to those glorious things we shall see hereafter? What is patience, but for consideration of that? What is hope, but for the excellency of the object of hope? And what were enduring of troubles, if something were not in heaven to make amends for all? They help us to come to glory, and the lively, hopeful thoughts of those things, animate and enliven all the graces that fit for heaven. If ever we shall hereafter possess heaven, and say, 'Lo, this is he we have waited for,' we must see him here, so as to undervalue all things, to see him with a changing sight; for the object of glory

bringeth them to heaven. He will perfume his spouse, and make her fit for an everlasting communion with him in heaven.

The third thing is, that as there be promises, and these promises are not presently fulfilled, which put us in a state of waiting, *so God giveth grace to uphold in waiting.* Waiting is not an empty time, to wait so long, and no grace in the mean time ; but waiting is a fitting time for that we are to receive afterwards.

We see in nature, in the winter, which is a dull time to the spring and harvest, and the times are very cold ; yet it ripens and mellows the soil, and fits it for the spring. There is a great promotion of harvest in winter. It is not a mere distance of time. So between the promise and heaven itself, it is not a mere waiting time, and there is an end ; but it is a time which is taken up by the Spirit of God in preparing the heart, in subduing all base lusts, and in taking us off from ourselves, and whatsoever is contrary to heaven. The time is filled up with a great deal of that which fits us for glory in heaven. The gracious God that fits us for heaven, and heaven for us, fits us with all graces necessary for that condition. As faith to believe, patience to wait for, and to depend on that which he seeth not, to be above sense ; a grace of hope to wait for that which he believeth, to be an anchor to his soul in all conditions whatsoever. And then a grace of patience to wait meekly all the while. And then long-suffering, patience lengthened out. As the tediousness is long between us and heaven, so there be lengthening graces. We would have all presently, ' How long, Lord, how long ?' Rev. vi. 10. We are so short, even David and others ; and therefore God giveth grace to hold out and lengthen our spiritual faith, and hope, and perseverance, and constant courage to encounter with all difficulties in the way. When the spirit of a man beholds heaven, and happiness, and God, it makes him constant, in some sort as the things he beholdeth, for the Spirit transformeth him to the object. Now, he beholds a constant covenant ; and as faith looks upon a constant God, constant happiness, and constant promises, it frameth the soul suitable to the excellency of the object it layeth hold upon.

And then the Spirit of God in the way to heaven subdueth all evil murmurings and exceptions, in suffering us not to put forth our hands to any iniquity. Though we have not what we would have, he keeps us in a good and fruitful way ; for to wait is not only to endure, but to endure in a good course, fitting us for happiness, till grace end in glory.

In the fourth place, *God will perform all his promises in time.* As the church saith here, ' This is the Lord ; we have waited for him.' Now, he hath made good whatsoever he hath said.

To enlarge this point a little. As there is a time of waiting, so there will be a time when God's people shall say, ' Lo, this is the Lord, we have waited for him.' Why ?

Reason 1. *God is Jehovah.* A full and pregnant word ! A word of comfort and stay for the soul is this word Jehovah ! He is a God that giveth a being to all things, and a being to his word, and therefore what he saith he will make good. He is Lord of his word. Every man's word is, as his nature, and power, and ability is, the word of a man, or the word of an honest man, but being the word of a God, he will make all good.

Reason 2. And then he will make all good, because *he is faithful.* God, he saith it, and he will do it.

Reason 3. You need no more reason *than pity to his people,* his bowels of compassion. The hearts of people would fail if he should stay too long,

And therefore out of his bowels in his time, which is the best time, not only because he is faithful, but because he is loving and pitiful, he will make good all his promises. And then he will do it.

Reason 4. *For what is grace, but an earnest of that fulness we shall have in heaven?* What is peace here but an earnest of that peace in heaven? And what is joy here but an earnest of fulness of joy for evermore? And will God lose his earnest? Therefore we shall enjoy what God hath promised, and we expect, because we have the earnest. It is not a pledge only, for a pledge may be taken away, but an earnest, which is never taken away, but is made up in the full bargain. Grace is made up in glory, as beginnings are made up with perfection. Where God layeth a foundation, he will perfect it. Where God giveth the first-fruits, he will give the harvest.

But it will be a long time before, because he will exercise all grace to the uttermost. You see how Abraham was brought to the last. In the mountain God provideth for a sacrifice, when the knife was ready to seize on Isaac's throat, Gen. xxii. 12, 13.

We should answer with our faith God's dealing; that is, if God defer, let us wait, yea, wait to the uttermost, wait to death. He is our God to death, and in death, and for ever. If God perform his promise at the worst, then, till we are at the lowest, we must wait.

And, therefore, one character of a child of God from others is this. Give me the present, saith the carnal, beastly man, the world; but God's people are content to wait. He knoweth what he hath in promise is better than what he hath in possession. The gleanings of God's people are better than the others' harvest. The other cannot wait, but must have present payment. God's child can wait, for he liveth by faith. And therefore we should learn patiently to wait for the performance of all God's promises.

And to direct a little in that, remember some rules, which every man may gather to himself, as,

1. *God's time is the best time. Deus est optimus arbiter opportunitatis,* the best discerner of opportunities. And ' in the mountain will God be seen.' Though he tarry long, he will come, and not tarry over long; and then all the strength of the enemy is with God. *Robur hostium apud Deum.* The strength of the enemy is in his hand; he can suspend it when he pleaseth.

2. ·Then, though God seems *to carry things by contrary ways to that he promiseth,* which makes waiting so difficult, yet he will bring things about at last. He promiseth happiness, and there is nothing but misery. He promiseth forgiveness, and opens the conscience to cry out of sin. Aye, but Luther's rule is exceeding good in this case. *Summa ars,* the greatest art of a Christian is, *credere credibilia,* &c., and *sperare dilata,* to hope for things a long time, and to believe God when he seemeth contrary to himself in his promise.

But though God doth defer, yet *in that day* he doth perform. It is set down indefinitely, for it is not fit we should be acquainted with the particular time. And therefore he saith, ' in that day.' He sets not down a particular time, but ' in that day,' wherein he meaneth to be glorious in the performance of his promise. There is a time, and a set time, and there is a short time, too, in regard of God, and a fit time. If the time were shorter than God hath appointed, then it were too short; if longer, too long. ' My times,' saith David, ' are in thy hands,' Ps. xxxi. 15. If they were in the enemy's hands, we should never be out ; if in our own, we would never enter ; if in our friends', their goodwill would be more than their ability. ' But my *times ;*'—he saith not, ' my time,' but—'my times are in thy hands ;' that is, my times of trouble and times of waiting. And it is well that they be in God's hands, for he hath a day, and a certain day, and a fit day to answer the waiting of all his people.

And when that day is come, you see how their hearts are enlarged, they will say, ' This is the Lord, we have waited for him.'

When God meaneth to perform his promise, either in this world or in the world to come, the world to come specially, when there shall be consummation of all promises, God shall enlarge the hearts of his people. ' This is the Lord; we have waited for him.' ' This is the Lord.' He repeats it again and again.

Our soul is very capable, being a spiritual substance ; and then God shall fill the soul, and make it comprehend misery, or comprehend happiness, when every corner of the soul shall be filled ; and then having bodies too, it is fit they should have a part ; so the whole man shall express forth the justice or mercy of God.

For the nature of the thing, it cannot be otherwise. Every member of the body shall be fit to glorify God. What the psalmist saith of his tongue, ' Awake, my glory,' he may say of every member, Do thy office in glorifying the Lord, and rejoicing in the Lord. *Pectus facit disertos.* The heart makes a man eloquent and full. So the performance of any promise fills the heart so full of affections, the affections are so enlarged ; and therefore we must not have affections to a court-kind of expressions, as they in old time, and the like court-eloquence, when men might not speak fully. But when joy possesseth the heart to the full, there be full expressions. ' This is the Lord, this is the Lord ; let us rejoice in him.' And therefore there seemeth so many tautologies in the Psalms, though they be no tautologies, but mere exuberances of a sanctified affection.

Oh ! beloved, what a blessed time will that be when this large heart of ours shall have that that will fill it ; when the best parts of us, our understanding, will, and affections, shall be carried to that which is better and larger than itself, and shall be, as it were, swallowed up in the fulness of God. And that is the reason of the repetition of the word, ' This is the Lord, this is the Lord.'

And it followeth, ' We will rejoice and be glad in his salvation.' When a gracious heart is full of joy, how doth he express that joy ? A wicked heart, when it is full of joy, is like a dirty river that runs over the banks, and carrieth a deal of filth with it, dirty expressions. But when a gracious heart expresseth itself, being full of joy, it expresseth itself in thanks and praises, in stirring up of others. ' Lo, this is our God ; we will rejoice and be glad in his salvation.' ' Is any merry ?' saith the apostle Saint James, ' let him sing,' James v. 13. God hath affections for any condition. ' Is a man in misery ? let him pray.' This is a time of mourning. Doth God perform any promise, and so give cause of joy ? let him sing. There is action for every affection, affection for every condition. And this may stir us up to begin the employment in heaven on earth here. We shall say so in heaven, ' Lo, this is the Lord; we have waited for him.'

For every performance of promises, be much in thankfulness. ' Our conversation is in heaven,' saith the apostle, Philip. iii. 10. And what is the greatest part of a Christian's conversation, but in all things to give thanks. Here the holy church saith, their matter of praise was too big for their soul,

and therefore they brake out in this manner. And so oftentimes a child of
God. His heart is so full, that it is too big for his body in the expression
of matter of praise. But it is his comfort that in heaven he shall have a
large heart, answerable to the large occasion of praise. I will not enlarge
myself in the common-place of thanksgiving.

In this condition we can never be miserable ; for it springs from joy,
and joy disposeth a man to thankfulness, and upon thankfulness there is
peace, and can we be miserable in peace of conscience ? Therefore, saith
the apostle, ' In all things give thanks, and let your requests be made
known to God,' Philip. iv. 6 ; and what will follow upon that, when I have
made known my requests, and paid my tribute of thanks ? ' Then the
peace of God which passeth understanding shall guide your mind,' Philip.
iv. 7. When we have paid to God the tribute we can pay him, then the
soul, as having discharged a debt, is at peace. I have prayed to God, I
have laid my petition in his bosom, I am not in arrearages for former
favours, ' therefore the peace of God which passeth all understanding shall
keep your hearts and minds.' Hannah had prayed once, went not away,
but prayed again, 1 Sam. ii. 1, seq. The happiness of heaven followeth
the actions of heaven. Praisings being the main employment of heaven,
the happiness and comfort of heaven followeth.

And howsoever these promises be fulfilled in heaven, yet they have a
gradual performance on earth. For he speaks certainly of the state of the
Jews yet to come, wherein there shall be accomplishment of all these
promises.

' We have waited for him ; he will save us.' Experience of God's performance stirs them up still to wait for him, and rejoice in his salvation.
Experience stirs up hope. The beginning of a Christian, and midst, is to
hope for the end ; and surely our beginning should help the latter end !
All a Christian's life should help the end. All former things should come
in and help his latter.

Beloved, we are too backward that way to treasure up the benefit of experience. There be few of years but might make stories of God's gracious
dealings with them, if all were kept ; the comforts past, and for time to
come, and all little enough. It was David's course, ' Thou art my God
from my mother's womb, and upon thee have I hanged ever since I was
born ; fail me not when I am old,' Ps. xxii. 10. Go along with God's
favours, and use them as arguments of future blessings. As former victories
are helps to get the second victory, every former favour helpeth to strengthen
our faith.

In the next, God is an inexhausted fountain, and when we have to deal
with an infinite God, the more we take of him the more we offer him.
It is no good plea to say, you have done courtesies, therefore do them still.
But we cannot honour God more than from former experience to look for
great things from the great God.

' We have waited for him, he will save us ; we have waited for him, and
we will rejoice in his salvation.' That which a child of God gives thanks
for and rejoices in, and labours for, is more and more experience of his
salvation. ' We will rejoice in his salvation.' There is not a stronger
word in all the Scripture, not in nature. He doth not say rejoicing in this
or that benefit, but in his salvation, that is, in deliverance from all evil.
We will rejoice in his preservation, when he hath delivered us, we will rejoice in his advancement of us, and we will rejoice in his salvation. And
therefore, when the wisdom of heaven would include all in one word, he

useth the word Jesus, all happiness in that word, that pregnant, full word, a Saviour.

So that God's carriage towards his children is salvation. He is the God of salvation, or a saving God. And God sent his name from heaven, and the angels brought it, the name of JESUS. Therefore look to the full sense of it. We have a Saviour that will answer his name; as he is Jesus, so he will save his people from their sins, Mat. i. 21. And therefore we will rejoice in his salvation. God dealt with us like a God, when he delivered us from all misery, from all sins, and advanced us to all happiness that nature is capable of. As he said before, he will wipe away all tears from all faces, and take away the rebukes of all people. He will punish the wicked with eternal destruction. And if he advanceth a people he will be salvation, than which he can say no more.

And this sheweth that the children of God rejoice, more than in anything else, in salvation, because it is the salvation of God, and because God is salvation itself. Heaven were not heaven, if Jesus and God in our nature were not there. And therefore the apostle saith, ' I desire to depart,' not to be dissolved, ' and to be with Christ, for that is better.' The sight of God, specially in our nature, God the second person taking our nature, that we might be happy, will make us happy for ever. In loving God, and joying in God, and enjoying God, makes full happiness; but that is not the cause of joy in heaven, but the cause of all is God's influence into us. Here in the world happiness is mediate, in God's revealing of himself to us by his Holy Spirit, in the use of means, in his dealings and deliverances, letting us see him by his grace, to see him, and joy and delight in him for ever. It is no good love that resteth in any blessings of God for themselves. It is an harlotry affection to love the gift more than the giver. So the saints of God they do all desire to see him as they may, and to joy in God, and enjoy God himself, and to see God in our nature, and to be with him for ever. Before he spake of a feast, and if the feast-maker be not there, what is all? In a funeral feast there is much cheer, but the feast-maker is gone. In heaven there is joy, but where is God, where is Christ, he that hath done so much, suffered so much for us, that hath taken possession of heaven, and keepeth a place for us there? What is heaven without him? Salvation, severed from him, is nothing.

We shall say when we are there, Lo, here is David, Abraham, St John, here the martyrs! Aye, but here is Christ, here is God, here is our Saviour, the cause of all, and the seeing of him in them, that he will be glorious in his saints, that maketh us rejoice. We shall see all our friends in heaven. There we shall see the excellency of the happiness of Christ, his love, his grace, his mercy.

The words are expressed with a kind of glorying, ' Lo, this is our God.' So that the joy of a Christian endeth in glory, and in the highest degree of glory, as you have it, Rom. v. 3, ' We glory also in tribulation, we glory in hope of glory,' nay, we glory in God as ours reconciled. And if we glory in him now as a God reconciled, what shall we do in heaven? Can a worldling glory in his riches, his greatness, his favour from such a man, as Haman did? And shall not a Christian glory in his God? and make his boast in his God? And therefore in this world we should learn to glory, before we come to that glory in heaven, specially when we be set upon by anything that is apt to discourage us. Glory then in our Head. Perhaps a Christian hath no wealth, no great rents to glory in, aye, but he hath a God to glory in, let him glory in him. The world may take all else from him, but not his God. As the church, in Cant. v. The virgins put the church to describe her beloved, 'What is thy beloved more than another beloved? My beloved is white and ruddy, the chiefest of ten thousand.' Then she goeth on in particulars, 'my beloved is thus and thus;' and if you would know what my beloved is, 'this is my beloved.' So a Christian that hath a spirit of faith should glory in God here, for heaven is begun here, and he should glory in Christ his Saviour, and should set Christ against all discouragements and oppositions. If you will know what is my beloved, 'this is my beloved, the chief among ten thousands.' Ps. cxv. 3. 'Our God is in heaven, and doth whatsoever he pleaseth, in heaven, and earth, and the deeps,' yea, we make our boast of God, saith the psalmist, when there is occasion. 'This is the Lord, this is our God; we have waited for him,' specially in times of afflictions; and what is the reason? This will hold out to eternity. 'This is our God.' As in the Revelations, it is a plea, and a glory for ever; for God is our happiness. As the schoolmen say, he is our *objective* happiness, and our *formal* happiness; he is our happiness, as he is ours, and he is ours in life and death, and for ever. So there is always ground of glory, only God doth discover himself to be ours by little and little, as we are able to bear him. He is ours in our worst times. 'My God, my God, why hast thou forsaken me?' Yet *my* God still, Mat. xxvii. 46.

He is our God to death, and he is ours in heaven. 'This is our God; we will rejoice in him.' And therefore well may we boast of God, because in God is everlasting salvation. If we boasted in anything else, our boasting would determine with the thing itself; but if we rejoice in God, we rejoice in that which is of equal continuance with our souls, and goeth along with the soul to all eternity.

And therefore we should learn to rejoice in God, and then we shall never be ashamed. It is spoken here with a kind of exalting, a kind of triumphing over all oppositions, 'Lo, this is our God.' Beloved, this, that God is our God, and Christ is ours, is the ground of rejoicing, and of all happiness. All joy, all comfort is founded upon this our interest in God; and therefore,

1. We must make this good *while we live here, that God is our God*, and that we may do so, observe this. Christ is called *Emmanuel*, God with us. God, in the second person, is God-man, and so God with us, and the Father in Emmanuel is God with us too. So we are God the Father's, because we are his. 'All things are yours,' saith the apostle, 'whether Paul or Apollos, things present, things to come. 'Why?' Because you are Christ's,' 1 Cor. iii. 22. Aye, but what if I be Christ's, Christ is God's? So we must be Christ's, and then we shall be God's. If Christ be ours, God is ours, for God is Emmanuel, in Christ, Emmanuel, God is with us in Christ, who is with us. God is reconciled to us in God and man, in our nature. And therefore get by faith into Christ, and get union, and get communion; by prayer open our souls to him, entertain his speeches to us by his word and Spirit and blessed motions, and open our spirits to him, and so maintain a blessed intercourse.

2. Make it good that God is our God *by daily acquaintance*. These speeches at the latter end are founded upon acquaintance before. 'This is our God.' Grace and glory are knit together indissolubly. If God be our God here, he will be ours also in glory; if not here, not in glory. There is a communion with God here, before communion with him in glory, and therefore make it good that God be our God here first, by union with

him. And then maintain daily acquaintance with him, by seeing him with the eye of faith, by speaking to him, and hearing him speak to us by his Spirit, joining in his ordinances, and then he will own us, and be acquainted with us. In heaven we shall say, 'Lo, this is our God.' We have had sweet acquaintance one with another : he by his Spirit with me, and I by my prayers with him. Our Saviour Christ will not be without us in heaven. We are part of his mystical body, and heaven were not heaven to Christ without us. With reverence be it spoken, we are the fulness of Christ, as he is the fulness of his church. And if he should want us, in some sort he were miserable, he having fixed upon us as objects of his eternal love. In what case were he if he should lose that object ? And therefore, as we glory in him, he glorieth in us. 'Who is this that cometh out of the wilderness ?' Who ? 'His beloved,' Cant. iii. 6. And, 'Woman, is this thy faith ?' Mat. xv. 28. He admires the graces of the church, as the church admires him. 'This is the Lord.' The church cannot be without him, nor he without the church. These words are spoken with a kind of admiration. 'Lo, this is the Lord, we will rejoice in him.' So I say, as there is thanks and joy, so there is admiration, 'Lo, behold !' This is a God worthy beholding, and so he wonders at the graces of his children. Beloved, there is nothing in the world worthy admiration. *Sapientis non est admirari.* It was a speech of the proud philosopher, a wise man will not admire, for he knoweth the ground (h). But in heaven the parts are lifted up so high that there is nothing but matter of admiration, things ' that eye hath not seen, nor ear heard, nor hath entered into the heart of man to conceive of,' 1 Cor. ii. 9. They be things beyond expression, and nothing is fit for them but admiration at the great things vouchsafed to the church.

And as with admiration, so with invitation. That is the nature of true thankfulness. There is no envy in spiritual things. No man envieth another the light of the Scriptures, but lo, behold with admiration and invitation of all others, 'This is the Lord.'

Let us therefore rejoice beforehand, at the glorious times to come, both to ourselves and to others ; be stirring and exciting one another to glory, and rejoice in God our salvation.

1. And, therefore, learn all to be stirred up from hence, *not to be offended with Christ, or with religion.* Be not offended, saith Austin, with the parvity* of religion. Every thing to the eyes of the world is little in religion. A Christian is a despised person, and the church, the meanest part of the world, in regard to outward glory. But,

2. Consider with the littleness, and baseness, and despisedness of the church, *the glory to come.* Time will come when we shall rejoice, and not only see, but boast with admiration, to the stirring up of others, 'Lo, this is the Lord.' And, therefore, say with our Saviour Christ, 'happy is he that is not offended with me,' Mat. xi. 6, nor with religion. There is a time coming, that will make amends for all. Who in the world can say at the hour of death, and day of judgment, Lo, this is my riches, this my honours ! Alas ! the greatest persons must stand naked to give account; all must stand on even ground to hold up their hands at the great bar. We may say to the carnal presumptuous man, Lo, this is the man that put his confidence in his riches. And none but reconciled Christians can say, ' Lo, this is our God.' Therefore take heed of being offended with anything in religion.

3. Again, if time to come be so transcendently glorious, *let us not be afraid to die,* let us not be overmuch cast down, for it shall end in glory. And

* That is, 'insignificance, smallness.'—G.

let us be in expectation still of good times, wait for this blessed time to come, and never be content with any condition, so as to set up our rest here. We may write upon every thing, *hic non est requies vestra*. Our rest is behind; these things are in passage. And therefore rest content with nothing here. Heaven is our centre, our element, our happiness; and every thing is contentedly happy, and thriveth in its element. The birds in the air, the fish in the sea, beasts on the earth, they rest there as in their centre. And that that is our place for ever, it is heaven, it is God. The immediate enjoying of God in heaven, that is our rest, our element, and we shall never rest till we be there. And therefore he is befooled for it, in the gospel, that setteth up his rest here. Whosoever saith I have enough, and will now take contentment in them, he is a fool. 'There is a rest for God's people,' Heb. iv. 9, but it is not here.

4. Neither *rest in any measure of grace, or comfort*. What is faith to sight? We have hope, an anchor, and helmet, that keepeth up many a soul, as the cork keepeth from sinking. What is this hope to the fruition of what we hope for? Here we have love, many love tokens from God. Aye, but what is love to union? Ours is but a love of desire. We are but in motion here, we lie in motion only; and our desires are not accomplished. What is this love to the accomplishing of the union with the thing beloved for ever? Here we have communion of saints. But what is this communion of saints to communion with God for ever? We have infirmities here, as others, which breedeth jealousies and suspicion. Aye, but we shall have communion in heaven, and there shall be nothing in us to distaste others, but everlasting friendship. Yea, our communion shall be with perfect souls. Our communion of saints here is our heaven upon earth, but it is communion with unperfect souls. Peace we have, aye, but it is peace intermixed, it is peace in the midst of enemies. There we shall have peace without enemies. Christ doth now rule in the midst of enemies. In heaven he shall rule in the midst of his friends. So that we can imagine no condition here, though never so good, but it is imperfect. And therefore rest not in anything in the world, no not in any measure of grace, any measure of comfort, till we be in heaven, but wait for the time to come, 'and rejoice in hope by which we are saved,' Rom. xii. 12. Wait still, and though we have not content here, yet this is not our home, this is a good refreshment by the way. As when the children of Israel came from Babylon, they had wells by the way, as in *Michae*,* they digged up wells. So from Babylon to Jerusalem we have many sweet refreshments; but they be refreshments far off the way. God digs many wells; we have breasts of consolation to comfort us, aye, but they are but for the way. And therefore let us answer all temptations, and not take contentment with anything here. It is good, but it is not our home. *Cui dulcis peregrinatio, non amat patriam.* If we have† eternity, love heaven, we cannot be overmuch taken with anything in the way.

5. And so for the church, *let us not be overmuch dejected for the desolation of the church*, but pray for a spirit of faith, which doth realise things to the soul and presents them as present to the soul, seeth Babylon fallen, presents things in the Scripture phrase, and in the words, 'Babylon is fallen,' forasmuch as all the enemies of the church fall. Mighty is the Lord that hath spoken, and will perform it, and, as the angel saith, 'it is done,' Rev. xix. 17.

---

* *Sic* . . . But qu. 'Micah' and the reference, Micah i. 4?—G. Or 'Baca?' Ps. lxxxiv. 6.—ED.

† Qu. 'love?'—ED.

So time will come ere long when it shall be said, ' It is done.' The church shall be gathered, and then, ' Lo, this is our God.'

It was the comfort of the believing Jews that the Gentiles should come. And why should it not be the comfort of the Gentiles that there be blessed times for the ancient people of God, when they shall all cry and say, ' Lo, this is our God ; we have waited for him long, and he will save us.' Therefore, be not overmuch discouraged for whatsoever present desolation the church lieth under. If it were not for this, ' we were of all men most miserable,' as Paul saith, 1 Cor. xv. 19. But there be times to come when we shall rejoice, and rejoice for ever, and make boast of the Lord. If it were not, ' we were of all men most miserable.' Howsoever happiness is to come, yet of all persons he is most happy that hath Christ and heaven. The very foretaste of happiness is worth all the world. The inward peace of conscience, joy in the Holy Ghost, the beginnings of the image of God and of happiness here, is worth all the enjoyments of the world. Ask of any Christian whether he will hang with the greatest worldling, and be in his condition ; he would not change his place in grace for all his glory. And therefore, set heaven aside, the very first fruits is better than all the harvest of the world. Let us therefore get the soul raised by faith to see her happiness. We need it all, for till the soul get a frame raised up to see its happiness here, specially in the world to come, it is not in a frame fit for any service, it will not stoop to any base sin. Where the affections are so possessed, they look upon all base courses as unworthy of their hope. What ! I that hope to rejoice for ever with God in heaven, that am heir of heaven, that have the image of God upon me, that am in covenant with God, to take any bestial course, to place my happiness in things meaner than myself, that have God to delight in, a God in covenant, that hath taken me into covenant with himself. So I say in all solicitations to sin, get ourselves into a frame that may stand firm and immoveable.

In all troubles let us know we have a God in covenant, that we may joy in him here, and rejoice with him in heaven for ever hereafter.

NOTES.

(*a*) P. 440.—' Keep your book to yourself.' Thomas Brooks in his ' Epistle Dedicatory ' to his ' Apples of Gold,' thus introduces the anecdote. ' I hope none of you, into whose hands it may fall, will say as once Antipater, King of Macedonia, did, when one presented him with a book teaching of happiness. His answer was (*ou scholazo*), οὐ σχολάζω, ' I have no leisure.'

(*b*) P. 448.—' Cicero prefers the name of *convivium*.' The allusion is to Cicero de Sen, 13 *fin*, which may be here quoted :—' Bene majores nostri accubitionem epularem amicorum, quia vitæ conjunctionem haberet, convivium nominarunt, melius quam Græci, qui hoc idem tum compotationem, tum concœnationem, vocant.'

(*c*) P. 449.—' The Jews wondered at the *manna*, saying, What thing is this ? ' ' Manna,' meaning ' What's this ? ' itself expresses and records their wonder.

(*d*) P. 477.—' That is not to be feared,' saith Tertullian, ' that frees us from all that is to be feared.' This is taken from Tertullian de Testimonio animæ ₰ iv., Non est timendum, quod nos liberat ab omni timendo.'

(*e*) P. 479.—' Good men are easy to weep, as the heathen man observeth.' Cf. Juvenal, xv. 133.

(*f*) P. 486.—'He can find tears,' &c.   Cf. Seneca de Consolatione ad Polybium, 4, § 2, larga flendi et adsidua materia est.'

(*g*) P. 489.—'Salvian complains in his time,' &c.   The thought is found in Salvianus de Gubernat. Dei., lib. 4, p. 74 (edition 1669), ... 'mali esse coguntur, ne viles habeantur.'

(*h*) P. 515.—'A wise man will not admire,' *i.e.*, wonder.   Cf. Horace, Epist. lib. i. p. 6, v. 1 ;—'Nil admirari,' &c.   The maxim is ascribed to Democritus.

G.

END OF VOL. II.